PRACTITIONER'S GUIDE TO CIVIL APPEALS IN TEXAS

PRACTITIONER'S GUIDE TO CIVIL APPEALS IN TEXAS

Editor-in-Chief

Robert Dubose

Contributing Authors

Douglas W. Alexander
Anna Baker
Kevin Dubose
Robert Dubose
Charles T. Frazier, Jr.
Marcy Hogan Greer
Wallace Jefferson
Jennifer Josephson
Dana Livingston
LaDawn H. Nandrasy
Melanie Plowman
Roger D. Townsend
Amy Warr

fastcase FULL COURT PRESS

Printed in the United States of America.

1 2 3 4 5 6 7 8 9 0

ISBN 978-1-949884-06-7

Summary of Contents

Table of Contents

Preface

I began my legal career shortly after the inauguration of board certification in civil appellate law. That was a watershed moment. Lawyers who enjoyed appellate work now had an incentive to develop an expertise in the nuances of appellate procedure and in the art of appellate advocacy. This innovation produced lawyers demonstrably qualified to assist the courts in formulating rules of law.

More than 25 years later, Texas appellate practice is among the most robust in the nation. Certification requires continued practice in the field and diligent study of new appellate trends—expertise that is reflected in the masterful way the authors have synthesized the sometimes arcane rules of advocacy involved in this specialty. This is the highest utility of the *Practitioner's Guide to Civil Appeals in Texas*, and not just for certified appellate advocates. As a former Justice and Chief Justice of the Supreme Court, I have witnessed too many instances in which a lawyer's seemingly minor mistake—in the preservation of error, in the formulation of issues for review, and even in oral argument—makes the difference between victory and defeat. These chapters work to minimize those unfortunate episodes, and to maximize the lawyer's most effective oral and written presentation. I am confident that it will become the go-to resource for specialists and novices alike.

Wallace B. Jefferson

December 2013

About This Book

Why this book?

At a time when most law firm libraries are shrinking, why would we write another practice book? There are several reasons.

First, appellate practice deserves a focused examination because it is different from other practice areas. On appeal, the standards and techniques of advocacy change. The standard of review requires some trial-court arguments be made differently on appeal. And because of the rules of preservation, some arguments cannot be made at all on appeal. Also, the most effective tools of written and oral advocacy vary from the trial court because of the unique mindset of appellate judges. Even the standards of ethics in interacting with opposing counsel change in some respects on appeal. So we highlight practical and strategic concerns unique to an appellate practice.

Second, although a handful of guides address practice in Texas appellate courts, most focus more on rules and procedure and less on strategy and advocacy. Some of those books are invaluable, and we often consult them. But we saw a need for a new volume that focuses on the unique strategic concerns that arise throughout the appellate process in Texas courts.

Third, this book is unique in that it is a collaborative effort of thirteen experienced appellate advocates. The authors are current and former members of a firm of only appellate counsel—Alexander Dubose & Jefferson LLP. We limit our practice to matters related to appeals, although that often includes handling the "law" side of litigation in trial courts. Because appeals are what we do, we care about issues of appellate strategy. This book addresses the types of issues that we commonly face and discuss within our firm. And we have not held back from frank opinions about appellate strategy, even if those opinions are at times not always the accepted wisdom of the community.

We hope that this book will be useful to a range of lawyers, from experienced appellate practitioners to those handling their first appeal in a Texas appellate court. We take a broad view of what constitutes appellate practice from conception of an appellate argument in the trial court to its grave on appeal—the mandate. We start with preserving arguments for appeal. We address not only the procedures for filing and arguing an appeal, but also issues that frequently face appellate lawyers, such as ensuring an adequate record and superseding a judgment during the appeal. We focus on written and oral argument strategies that are unique to the courts of appeals, as well as different strategies for advocacy in the Texas Supreme Court. And we address the often-neglected issue of how to wind up an appeal. We conclude the book by outlining strategies for developing an appellate practice.

Thanks

The authors are grateful for the assistance of others. Blake Hawthorne, Clerk of the Supreme Court of Texas, provided extensive assistance with the chapter on filing procedures. We appreciate editing and substantive assistance from Scott Sharp and our legal assistants Georgiana Holland, Janis Strother, and Kennon Welch, as well as cite-checking assistance from Megan Ceder, Timothy Dyer, and Johali Muzaliwa.

Robert Dubose

January 2019

About the Editor

Robert Dubose is a partner in the Houston office of Alexander Dubose & Jefferson LLP. He handles appeals with an emphasis on commercial and contract disputes, oil and gas, insurance coverage, and catastrophic injuries. He also works with trial lawyers on legal strategy before and during trial, frequently arguing the jury charge and preserving arguments for appeal.

Dubose authored the book, *Legal Writing for the Rewired Brain: Persuading Readers in a Paperless World* (ALM 2010). He is a co-author of the Texas chapter of the American Bar Association's *Appellate Practice Compendium* (2012). From 1998 to 2010 Dubose taught courses at the University of Houston Law Center, including Appellate Advocacy and Insurance Appeals.

Dubose graduated *magna cum laude* from Rice University and *cum laude* from Harvard Law School. He is Board Certified by the Texas Board of Legal Specialization in Civil Appellate Law. He is past-chair of the Appellate Section of the Houston Bar Association. He has been listed in *The Best Lawyers in America* since 2010.

About the Contributing Authors

The contributing authors for this volume are all current or former members of the appellate boutique firm Alexander Dubose & Jefferson LLP.

Douglas W. Alexander (*Texas Supreme Court* chapters) concentrates his appellate practice on proceedings before the Supreme Court of Texas. He has served as President of the Texas Supreme Court Historical Society, Chair of the Appellate Section of the State Bar of Texas, Adjunct Professor of Appellate Advocacy at the University of Texas School of Law, and Law Clerk to the Hon. John R. Brown, former Chief Judge of the United States Court of Appeals for the Fifth Circuit. Alexander is the 2013 recipient of the Texas Bar Foundation's Gregory S. Coleman Outstanding Appellate Lawyer Award, was named *The Best Lawyers in America*'s 2013 Austin Appellate Lawyer of the Year, and is listed in Chambers USA in Appellate Litigation. He is a Fellow of the American Academy of Appellate Lawyers, and has been board certified in civil appellate law by the Texas Board of Legal Specialization since 1990.

Anna Baker (*Briefs of Amicus Curiae*) is an attorney with the Austin office, where she concentrates on researching and briefing a wide range of appellate and litigation matters. Baker received her MBA and undergraduate degree from the McCombs School of Business at the University of Texas. After working as an investment systems analyst at Exxon, Baker attended the University of Texas School of Law, where she served on the Texas Law Review and was a member of the Order of the Coif.

Kevin Dubose (*Preserving Issues for Appeal, Appellate Ethics*) is a founding partner in the Houston office. He graduated from the University of Texas School of Law in 1979, and after an active civil litigation practice he began limiting his practice to appellate matters in 1985. He is a former Chair of the Appellate Sections of the State Bar of Texas and the Houston Bar Association, and has taught Legal Research and Writing and Appellate Advocacy at the University of Houston Law Center. He is a Fellow of the American Academy of Appellate Lawyers, and has been recognized for excellence in Appellate Law in Chambers, *The Best Lawyers in America*, and *Texas Super Lawyers*. He received the Chief Justice Jack Pope Professionalism Award from the Texas Center for Legal Ethics. He is a frequent author and speaker on Post-Trial Motions, Oral and Written Appellate Advocacy, and Appellate Ethics.

Robert Dubose (*Court of Appeals Briefs, Building an Appellate Practice*). *See* About the Editor.

Charles T. Frazier, Jr. (*Staying Execution and Superseding the Judgment, Appellate Motions*) is a partner in the Dallas office. A graduate of Baylor University School of Law, Frazier is an appellate specialist who has successfully argued before the Supreme Court of the United States, the Fifth Circuit Court of Appeals, and the Supreme Court of Texas. He also has appeared in all 14 intermediate Texas courts of appeals. Frazier authored the chapter on Texas supersedeas law in the treatise *Superseding and Staying Judgments: A National Compendium* (ABA TIPS 2007). He also authored the chapter "The Effect of Bankruptcy on the Appellate Process" in *A Defense Lawyer's Guide to Appellate Practice* (DRI 2004). Board certified in civil appellate law by the Texas

Board of Legal Specialization since 1994, Frazier has been listed in *The Best Lawyers in America* in appellate law as a specialty since 2009.

Marcy Hogan Greer (*Wrapping Up the Appeal*) is a partner in the Austin office. Greer is recognized for her work in federal and state trial and appellate courts throughout the country. Her practice consistently includes class action and mass tort cases, including federal and state multidistrict litigation. This experience contributed to her recognition in Chambers USA in Litigation: Appellate—Texas, *The Best Lawyers in America*, and *Texas Super Lawyers*. Greer is the National Editor of the first and second editions of *A Practitioner's Guide to Class Actions* (ABA 2010, 2017) and a frequent speaker and author on a wide variety of substantive and procedural strategies in trial and appellate litigation. Before joining the firm, she was a partner at Norton Rose Fulbright US LLP and a law clerk for the Hon. Carolyn Dineen King, the former Chief Judge of the U.S. Court of Appeals for the Fifth Circuit.

Wallace Jefferson (*Preface*) is a partner in the Austin office and the former Chief Justice of the Supreme Court of Texas. Serving on the Supreme Court from 2002 to 2013, and as Chief Justice from 2004 to 2013, he was the first African-American justice and the first African-American chief justice of the Texas Supreme Court. Jefferson served as president of the Conference of Chief Justices, an association of chief justices from the 50 states and U.S. territories. Before joining the Supreme Court, Jefferson was a partner in San Antonio-based appellate-specialty firm Crofts, Callaway & Jefferson, where he successfully argued two cases before the United States Supreme Court. He is a member of the American Law Institute and is certified in civil appellate law by the Texas Board of Legal Specialization. A graduate of the James Madison College at Michigan State University and the University of Texas School of Law, Jefferson is the namesake for Wallace B. Jefferson Middle School in San Antonio. He has just been honored with the 2013 Texas Exes' Distinguished Alumnus Award.

Jennifer Josephson (*Standards of Review and Scope of Review*) is a former partner with the firm and currently is of counsel with Reynolds Frizzell LLP. She graduated cum laude from Harvard Law School, where she served as a technical editor on the Environmental Law Review. Before joining a law firm, Josephson was a law clerk for the Hon. John R. Brown of the Fifth Circuit Court of Appeals.

Dana Livingston (*Petitions for Writ of Mandamus*) is a former partner of the firm and is currently a partner with Cokinos I Young in its Austin office. She is a former law clerk for the United States Court of Appeals for the Fifth Circuit and a former staff attorney for the Supreme Court of Texas. Livingston is board certified in civil appellate law by the Texas Board of Legal Specialization and served for six years as a member of the board's Civil Appellate Law Examination Commission. Livingston also taught appellate advocacy as an adjunct professor of law at the University of Texas School of Law for many years. Livingston has been selected by her peers for inclusions in *The Best Lawyers in America*® (Copyright by Woodward/White, Inc. of Aiken, S.C.) in the field of appellate law and in *Texas Super Lawyers*, and regularly speaks and authors articles on appellate practice. Livingston is the Editor of the *Appellate Practice Compendium* (ABA 2012), which is a two-volume practice guide covering appellate practice in all 50 states, all federal appellate courts, and the United States Supreme Court. She is also the author of the Fifth Circuit chapter in that book.

LaDawn H. Nandrasy (*Interlocutory Appeals*) is the firm's Managing Partner. A 1991 graduate of Southern Methodist University Dedman School of Law, Nandrasy has focused her practice on trial strategy and appeals involving complex business disputes. She began her practice with a national firm's appellate group, and joined Alexander Dubose & Jefferson LLP in 2008. She served on the State Bar Pattern Jury Charge Committee for the *Business, Consumer and Employment Law* volume from 2006 to 2018 (Chair 2015–2018), and currently serves on the State Bar Pattern Jury Charge Oversight Committee. Nandrasy has been listed in *Texas Super Lawyers* since 2003 (including Top 50 Women Texas Super Lawyers in 2011 and 2012), *The Best Lawyers in America* since 2013, and *Best Lawyers, D Magazine* in 2010–2014, 2016–2017, 2019 (including Best Women Lawyers in Dallas in 2010). She is a Fellow of the Texas and Dallas Bar Foundations, and is board certified in civil appellate law by the Texas Board of Legal Specialization.

Melanie Plowman (*The Record*) handles an appellate briefing and motions practice in a variety of areas of commercial litigation. Plowman received her undergraduate degree from Brown University and her J.D. degree from the University of Michigan Law School. She subsequently served as a clerk to Judge Robert M. Parker of the U.S. Court of Appeals for the Fifth Circuit and then to Judge R. Guy Cole of the U.S. Court of Appeals for the Sixth Circuit. After her clerkships, Plowman handled appeals in the Texas and federal appellate courts as an Assistant Solicitor General for the State of Texas, and also practiced with a national firm's appellate group, where she briefed appeals and dispositive motions in complex commercial litigation in state and federal courts around the country.

Roger D. Townsend (*Reversible Error, Oral Argument*) is a former partner with the firm and is currently a partner with Cokinos I Young in its Houston office. A Fellow in the American Academy of Appellate Lawyers, he served as its President during 2013. Townsend also is a past Chair of the Appellate Practice Section of the State Bar of Texas. He is board certified in civil appellate law by the Texas Board of Legal Specialization. Townsend served as Editor-in-Chief for the *Texas Appellate Practice Manual* (State Bar of Texas 1993), following which he was awarded a Certificate of Merit by the State Bar of Texas for his "outstanding contribution to the legal profession of Texas." More recently he served as National Editor for the treatise *Superseding and Staying Judgments: A National Compendium* (ABA TIPS 2007). He is a graduate of Harvard Law School.

Amy Warr (*Appealability and Notice of Appeal, Filing Procedures*) has been an appellate practitioner since 1997. She joined the firm in 2007 after serving five years as an Assistant Solicitor General for the State of Texas. Warr has been listed in *Texas Super Lawyers* since 2008 and was selected for inclusion in *The Best Lawyers in America* for 2013. She is board certified in civil appellate law by the Texas Board of Legal Specialization. Warr received her undergraduate degree from Brown University and graduated from the University of Texas School of Law, with honors, in 1995. She then served as a Briefing Attorney for Justice Craig Enoch on the Supreme Court of Texas. Currently, she is Chair of the Third Court of Appeals Pro Bono Program.

CHAPTER 1

Preserving Issues for Appeal

1-1 Introduction

The best way to think about preservation in the trial court is *not* to memorize a long list of technical requirements for every situation that can arise before, during, and after trial. That list will be covered in this chapter, and you can use this or other materials as a reference. But the best way to prepare for preservation decisions in the heat of battle is to understand the philosophical underpinnings of preservation practice, as well as the basic contours for preservation procedure. Those alone will provide the information you need in the great majority of situations.

The rules regarding preservation are not designed to weed out the unwary and unprepared so that only the smartest and most prepared lawyers qualify for the privilege of arguing a point on appeal. Rather, they reflect an understanding that appeals are expensive and time-consuming for litigants and for the court system, and second trials after remand are even more so. The time and expense of a retrial can be saved by rules that require lawyers to call problems to the attention of the trial court that can be taken care of in a first trial, in a manner and at a time when the court can correct the problem before it is too late for there to be a meaningful remedy.

1-2 Requirements of Preservation

In order to accomplish that goal, lawyers are required to do four things to preserve a point for appellate review:

(1) Make a complaint to the trial court by request, objection, or motion, on the record;

(2) Make the complaint in a timely fashion, so that the trial court can correct any error before it is too late;

(3) State the grounds for the complaint with sufficient specificity to make the trial court aware of the exact complaint; and

(4) Obtain a ruling from the trial court, on the record, so that it is clear that the trial court was made aware of the complaint and responded.[1]

Each of these requirements merits further discussion.

1-2:1 Complaint Made to Trial Court by Request, Objection, or Motion

A lawyer must do something to bring to the trial court's attention that an error has, or is about to, occur. The vehicle for raising that complaint depends on the circumstances, and courts are becoming increasingly lenient about which vehicle is used, as long as counsel does something to put the trial court on notice of a complaint.

Generally, a *request* is appropriate when a party wants to do or ask for something, such as requesting a change of venue, requesting a jury, requesting a jury shuffle, or requesting that their version of a jury question be submitted. An *objection* is a complaint about something that is going on before or during a trial, such as an objection to a summary-judgment affidavit, an objection to a biased venire member being seated on the jury, an objection to an improper question asked of a witness, an objection to a piece of evidence being offered, or an objection to a proposed judgment. A *motion* asks for legal relief, such as a motion for sanctions, a motion for summary judgment, a motion to strike a witness, a motion for directed verdict, or a motion for entry of judgment.

Additionally, the request, objection, or motion must appear in the record. If it can be filed in writing, and requested to be included in the Clerk's Record on appeal, that is usually sufficient. If it is an oral request, objection, or motion, the lawyer should make sure that a court reporter is present, that the proceedings are being recorded, and that the transcription of that part of the proceedings is included in the Reporter's Record on appeal. As far as the appellate court is concerned, if it does not appear in the Clerk's Record or the Reporter's Record, it did not happen, and the argument or error is not preserved.

1-2:2 Timely Complaint

Although the "timeliness" requirement is somewhat obscured in Texas Rule of Appellate Procedure 33.1(a), appearing simply as the one-word adjective "timely" preceding the series "request, objection, or motion," it is important enough to merit recognition as a separate element of preservation. In most situations, a complaint must be made before the objectionable event occurs, or at least immediately after it has happened, but certainly before the trial train has moved inexorably past the station. If not, even an otherwise proper objection will be considered waived.

This principle is best illustrated through examples, each of which is addressed in greater detail and supported by citations to case law later in this chapter:

- In voir dire an objection to the failure to strike a venire member for cause must occur before the jury is seated and the remainder of the venire is dismissed. At that point it becomes impossible for the court to correct the mistake by striking the juror and seating another member of the venire.
- A *Daubert*[2] objection to an expert witness must be made before the witness testifies, or, at the latest, immediately after the witness provides testimony that is objectionable. Waiting to object until after the witness has testified means that the jury already has heard the witness's full testimony and cannot realistically be expected to disregard that testimony.
- Proffering excluded testimony for the record must take place before the evidence has closed and the jury has retired to deliberate; otherwise if the judge,

upon hearing the proffer, decides that it should have been admitted rather than excluded, it is too late to right that wrong.

- Charge objections must be made before the charge is read to the jury, for similar reasons.

1-2:3 Complaint Must State Grounds With Sufficient Specificity

The complaint must be stated in such a way that the trial court is made aware of the precise complaint that will be made on appeal and has the chance to correct it. Error preservation is not an activity where "lying behind the log" is an effective trial strategy.

For example, vague evidentiary objections like "objection," or "hearsay," or "prejudicial" are not likely to preserve anything without a more specific description of why the evidence or question is objectionable. Similarly, a broad statement like "That violates the motion in limine" is not likely to preserve anything without more of an explanation.

The requirement of specificity does not mean that lawyers need to cite specific subsection numbers of statutes or evidentiary rules or pleadings. The specificity required is simply an explanation of the substantive nature of the complaint.

1-2:4 Obtain Trial Court Ruling on the Record

The requirement of a ruling is to make sure that the court was made aware of the complaint and responded to it in some way. Saying something under your breath that was not heard by the judge does not preserve anything, and the only way for the record to reflect that the court was aware of the complaint and consciously addressed it is to require a ruling.

This requirement is a little looser than the previous requirements. First, Rule 33.1 provides that the court must have ruled on the complaint "either expressly or implicitly."[3] Any lawyer should strongly prefer an express ruling rather than an implicit ruling, but courts have recognized circumstances in which subsequent events allow no other possibility but that the court intended to overrule the complaint.[4]

Second, if a trial court simply refuses to rule, a lawyer can preserve error by objecting to the refusal to rule on the record.[5]

As previously mentioned, an understanding of these four requirements will provide lawyers attempting to preserve error with what they need to know in most circumstances.

1-3 Pre-Trial Preservation of Error

1-3:1 Personal Jurisdiction

Unlike subject-matter jurisdiction—which can be raised at any point in the trial court or the appellate court, even if not previously preserved—objections to personal jurisdiction must be preserved by compliance with a rigid set of rules. An objection to personal jurisdiction must be raised in a sworn Special Appearance, which must be filed prior to any other pleading—except that other pleadings can be filed contemporaneously with the special appearance if they are contained in the same document.[6] A party can file other pleadings after the special appearance without waiving it, but only if they expressly state that they are filed "subject to" the special appearance.[7] (Other pleadings filed in the same instrument as the special appearance need not contain the "subject to" language.)[8] But the party filing a special appearance must obtain a ruling on the special appearance before requesting any other ruling or relief from the trial court.[9] Filing other pleadings before the Special Appearance, filing other pleadings when a Special Appearance is pending without saying "subject to," or obtaining a ruling from the trial court on something else before the Special Appearance has been ruled upon all constitute a general appearance, which waives all complaints about personal jurisdiction.[10]

A Rule 11 Agreement between the parties is *not* a plea, pleading or motion, or a request for affirmative relief from the trial court that waives a special appearance.[11] Similarly, seeking a trial court's resolution of discovery matters related to the special appearance does not waive the special appearance.[12]

1-3:2 Venue

Like personal jurisdiction, an objection to venue must be raised before, or concurrently with, an answer or any other pleading—*except a* special appearance, which must precede a motion to transfer venue.[13] Again, subsequent pleadings filed while the motion to transfer venue is pending should be made "subject to" the motion to transfer venue. A failure to challenge venue in a timely fashion waives an objection to venue, even if the objection to venue is based on a mandatory venue statute.[14]

1-3:3 Pleadings

Objections to pleadings, whether of form or substance, must be made through written special exceptions brought to the attention of the court before the charge is read to the jury in a jury trial, or before the judgment is signed in a non-jury case.[15] The objection must not only point out the particular pleading objected to, but must also point out "intelligibly and with particularity the defect, omission, obscurity, duplicity, or other insufficiency in the allegations in the pleading excepted to."[16]

After special exceptions are granted, a party who does not request an opportunity to amend or re-plead waives the right to argue on appeal that the defect could have been cured.[17] But if a party requests an opportunity to amend or re-plead, the court must allow it to do so.[18]

In the absence of special exceptions, pleadings are liberally construed.[19] If a pleading defect is not objected to, then the claim may be tried by consent if both parties present evidence, and the issue is developed at trial without objection.[20]

Pleadings can be freely amended until seven days before trial, unless a scheduling order provides otherwise.[21] Pleadings can even be amended after a trial, unless the opposing party presents evidence of surprise or prejudice.[22]

Certain matters must be pleaded in certain ways to be preserved. Certain types of pleas must be asserted in verified pleadings.[23] Matters constituting an avoidance or affirmative defense must be specifically pleaded.[24]

1-3:4 Discovery Sanctions

The important thing to remember here is that if a discovery dispute exists before trial, the party seeking sanctions must bring the problem to the court's attention and obtain a ruling prior to trial, or else the right to obtain sanctions is waived.[25] In *Remington Arms*, the party seeking sanctions did not move for sanctions or in any way apprise the trial court of any allegation of discovery abuse, but after an adverse verdict that party moved for and obtained a large sanction award. The sanctions award was reversed by the Supreme Court because sanctions for pre-trial conduct had been waived.[26] But in *Chevron Phillips Chemical Co. v. Kingwood Crossroads*,[27] one party moved for sanctions, and obtained an evidentiary hearing. At the end of the hearing, the trial court ruled that sanctions were warranted, that death penalty sanctions would not be assessed, that sanctions would be in the form of attorney fees, and the court would wait to decide the amount to award.[28] Although waiver is not expressly addressed in the opinion, the court affirmed the sanctions in the face of a waiver challenge when all rulings except the amount of the sanction were made prior to trial.

1-3:5 Summary-Judgment Motions

There are particular preservation issues to be aware of in summary-judgment practice.

1-3:5.1 Preserving Summary-Judgment Grounds

Summary judgment can only be granted on the grounds expressly stated in the summary-judgment motion itself.[29] Stating grounds in a supporting brief or in summary-judgment evidence is not enough, and will result in waiver.[30] Raising a ground for the first time in a reply brief will meet a similar fate.[31]

Similarly, to adequately preserve an argument against the granting of a summary judgment, the non-movant must expressly present that argument to the trial court in its response to the motion for summary judgment.[32]

1-3:5.2 Preserving Summary-Judgment Grounds in Pleadings

The grounds upon which a summary judgment is based also must be supported by pleadings on file at the time of the hearing.[33] A party may amend pleadings after filing a summary-judgment motion or response, but amended pleadings must be filed no later than seven days before the summary-judgment hearing or submission.[34] Pleadings filed within seven days of the hearing or submission must be filed with leave of court.[35] Leave of court to file an amended pleading within seven days may be presumed if (1) the summary judgment states that all pleadings were considered, (2) there is no indication on the record that the amended pleading was not considered, and (3) the opposing party does not show surprise.[36] To properly preserve a complaint that an amended pleading is not timely filed for a summary-judgment hearing, the opposing party must demonstrate surprise and move for a continuance.[37]

However, unpleaded claims or defenses raised in a motion for summary judgment may provide the basis for summary-judgment rulings if the opposing party does not object.[38] So, to preserve arguments about grounds for summary judgment not supported by pleadings, counsel should include objections to that effect in the non-movant's response or movant's reply.

A summary judgment should not be based on a pleading deficiency that can be cured by an amendment (a defect that should be raised by special exceptions).[39] But to preserve an argument that a summary judgment was granted without an opportunity to amend, the non-movant must raise that argument by timely objection.[40]

1-3:5.3 Preserving Complaints Concerning Opportunity for Discovery

A non-movant responding to a no-evidence motion for summary judgment who contends that it has not had an adequate opportunity for discovery must file either an affidavit explaining the need for further discovery or a verified motion for continuance.[41] The failure to do so waives any argument that the non-movant did not have an adequate opportunity for discovery.[42]

1-3:5.4 Preserving Objections to Summary-Judgment Evidence

Traditional motions for summary judgment and summary-judgment defenses must be supported by evidence, which must be filed by the same deadline as the motion or response it supports.[43] Late-filed evidence can only be filed with leave of court, and, absent leave, it cannot be considered.[44] The summary-judgment rule does not require that evidence be attached to the summary-judgment motion or response, just that it be on file at the time of submission.[45] But given uncertainties about whether discovery is filed, and the certainty that a judge reading the motion is unlikely to go to the files to retrieve filed discovery, the better practice is to attach all evidence to be relied upon.

Objections to summary-judgment evidence based on form (which includes hearsay, lack of personal knowledge, speculation, and competence) must be asserted, in writing, in a response or a reply, and must be ruled upon, or they are waived.[46] Texas courts are split on whether that ruling may be implied from the circumstances of a summary judgment.[47] An oral objection to summary-judgment evidence made at the hearing, but not preserved in written summary-judgment pleadings, cannot be considered.[48]

1-3:5.5 Preserving Objections to Timing of Summary-Judgment Motions, Responses, and Hearings

A motion for summary judgment must be filed 21 days before hearing or submission.[49] A motion may be filed late, but only upon leave of court.[50] Leave of court for late filing must be reflected in a written order.[51] But even if the motion is filed late and leave is not granted, objections to late filing are waived if the non-movant receives notice, appears at the hearing, and does not request a continuance.[52]

The summary-judgment response must be filed no later than seven days before submission,[53] but, again, late filing is permitted by leave of court.[54] Leave must be reflected by some affirmative act on the record, but that may include a separate order, recitation in the summary judgment, or an oral ruling contained in the Reporter's Record.[55]

There is no deadline provided in the rules for a movant's reply to a non-movant's response. The principal importance of a movant's reply for preservation purposes is to file written objections to the non-movant's summary-judgment evidence, and objections to summary-judgment evidence filed on the day of the hearing are not untimely and may be considered and ruled upon by the court.[56]

1-3:5.6 Preserving Objections to Ambiguous, Vague, or Unclear Summary-Judgment Motions

A complaint that a summary-judgment pleading is ambiguous or otherwise vague or unclear must be preserved by written special exceptions to that pleading raising the specific complaint.[57] The non-movant must file and serve the special exceptions at least seven days before the hearing, and therefore may include them in its summary-judgment response.[58] The movant must file and serve special exceptions at least three days before the hearing.[59] The party filing the special exceptions will need to secure a ruling, preferably an express, written one, to preserve the complaint.

1-3:6 Disqualifying, Recusing, or Objecting to a Judge

An objection that a judge is constitutionally disqualified from hearing a case cannot be waived; it can be raised at any point in the proceedings, including on appeal or in an attack on the judgment in a collateral proceeding.[60]

In contrast, a motion to recuse must be filed 10 days before a trial setting or hearing for which recusal is sought.[61] The motion must be verified, and must state with particularity the grounds for recusal.[62]

If a visiting or retired judge is assigned to hear a case, a party who objects to that judge must file an objection within seven days of the notice of assignment, or before the date of the first hearing or trial over which the appointed judge presides, whichever comes first.[63] If an assigned judge hears any matter in the case prior to objection, any objection to the assignment is waived.[64]

1-3:7 Requesting a Jury

In order to preserve the right to a jury trial in a civil case, a party must make a written request for a jury trial *and* pay the jury fee within a reasonable time before the trial setting, but in no event less than 30 days before the trial setting.[65]

1-4 Preservation of Error During Trial

1-4:1 Voir Dire

1-4:1.1 Right to Ask Particular Questions

If a lawyer is barred from asking particular questions of the venire in voir dire, the best practice is to dictate or submit specific questions into the record.[66] In the *Babcock* case from the 1980s, the Texas Supreme Court held that there is "no requirement to place specific questions in the record if the nature of the questions is apparent from the context."[67] In *Babcock*, the court held that context was provided by discussions regarding the motions in limine and an examination of one juror concerning the subject in question before the judge prohibited further questioning on that subject.[68] The court also noted that the party seeking to ask questions about the forbidden subject later asked to dictate specific questions into the record, but was denied the opportunity. *Babcock* might turn out differently if decided today.

More recently, the Supreme Court acknowledged the holding in *Babcock,* but nevertheless made clear that "[a] timely, specific presentation to the trial court of the manner of an inquiry is important because it is difficult to evaluate after a trial whether the trial court's denial of an inquiry caused a biased juror to be seated on the jury or to evaluate what additional information a party could have adduced for the exercise of peremptory strikes."[69] In *Babcock,* no specific questions were included in the appellate record, yet the court held that error was preserved;[70] in *Hyundai,* a specific question was included, but the court held that error was not preserved because it would be possible to rule a single question inappropriate without foreclosing an entire area of inquiry.[71]

1-4:1.2 Challenges for Cause

Another area of voir dire practice where preservation sometimes becomes an issue is an objection to the overruling of a motion to strike for cause. Most lawyers know to object to the overruling of the motion to strike, but there is a rigid three-part procedure necessary to preserve the objection, which is rarely complied with properly. In addition to moving to strike the juror for cause and being overruled, the complaining party also must:

(1) use a peremptory challenge to strike the objectionable juror;

(2) exhaust the remaining peremptory challenges; and

(3) advise the court that because of having to use a peremptory challenge against the venire person who should have been struck for cause, a specific objectionable venire person will remain on the jury list and be subject to being seated as a juror in the case.[72]

These steps must be complied with, on the record, and before the strikes are turned in.[73]

1-4:1.3 Jury Shuffle

If a party wishes to request a jury shuffle, that request must be made after the venire is presented, but before any voir dire examination begins.[74] Otherwise, the right to request a shuffle is waived.

1-4:1.4 Number of Jurors

Although a litigant in a civil trial is entitled to a 12-person jury,[75] parties can agree to try a case with fewer than 12 jurors.[76] Any complaint about the numerical composition of a jury must be made by objection before the verdict is returned or it is waived.[77]

1-4:2 Admitting and Excluding Evidence

1-4:2.1 Motions in Limine

Rulings on a motion in limine—whether good or bad—preserve nothing. If a motion in limine is overruled on a point, the party opposing the admission of that evidence still must object when offered at trial in order to preserve the objection.[78] If a motion in limine is granted and evidence is excluded, the party seeking to introduce the evidence still must offer the evidence on the record to preserve error in its exclusion.[79] The appellate complaint is directed at the ruling at trial, not the pre-trial ruling on the motion in limine.

So as far as preservation is concerned, a motion in limine conference is a non-event. Its principal value is to alert the court and counsel to issues that are controversial so that when they arise at trial they can be addressed outside the presence of the jury, preventing counsel or a witness from blurting out inadmissible material before there can be an objection and ruling. At least that's the theory.

1-4:2.2 Improperly Admitted Evidence

1-4:2.2a Requirement of Specific Ground Stated on the Record

To preserve objections to improperly admitted evidence, a party must make a timely objection, on the record, "stating the specific ground of objection, if the specific ground was not apparent from the context."[80] Lawyers should be reluctant to rely on the "apparent from the context" clause, and explain the specific ground for the objection whenever possible. Ideally, the objection should not only identify what specific evidence is objectionable, but also why it is objectionable.[81]

1-4:2.2b Requirement of Substantial Right Affected

Rule 103 states that reversible error cannot be predicated on an evidentiary ruling "unless a substantial right of the party is affected."[82] So, when possible, it helps explain how the admission affects the objecting party's substantial right.

1-4:2.2c Ruling on Record Outside of Jury's Presence Sufficient

Unlike a motion in limine conference, an evidentiary ruling made by the court during the trial that is on the record but outside the presence of the jury need not be repeated for the jury to preserve error.[83]

1-4:2.2d Re-assert Objection When Similar Evidence Offered

If similar evidence is offered subsequently, the objecting party should re-assert its objection to avoid waiver.[84] There is a line of cases holding that a party making a proper objection to the introduction of testimony that is overruled is entitled to assume that the judge will make the same ruling on other offers of similar evidence, and is not required to repeat the objection.[85] One court of appeals has acknowledged both of these lines of cases, characterized them as "seemingly contradictory," and concluded that, in these circumstances, waiver should be determined on a case-by-case basis.[86] The safer course is to continue to make the objection if there is any doubt.

1-4:2.2e Running Objections

One way to balance the risk of waiver through subsequently admitted evidence with the desire to avoid annoying the jury with excessive objections is the "running objection."[87]

But running objections are undertaken with some peril. The test for whether running objections preserve error weighs (1) the similarity of the subsequent testimony to the prior testimony, (2) the proximity of the running objection to the subsequent testimony, (3) whether the subsequent testimony is from a different witness, (4) whether the running objection was requested and granted, and (5) any other circumstances suggesting that the objection should be re-urged.[88] So, unless the subsequent evidence is very similar to the previously offered testimony, offered through the same witness, and in close proximity of time, reliance on a running objection may be misplaced, and may result in waiver.

1-4:2.2f Other Parties' Objections

Reliance on the objections of other parties (even co-defendants or co-plaintiffs) also is risky. It can preserve error in cases where the parties and the trial court expressly agree that an objection by one party will preserve error for all similarly situated parties.[89] But outside of that situation, reliance may be subject to parties being dismissed or making deals during trial that shift loyalties.

1-4:2.3 Exclusion of Favorable Evidence

To preserve error in the exclusion of evidence, the offering party must make an offer of proof of the substance of the evidence, unless it is "apparent from the context"—and, again, that phrase should rarely be trusted.[90] The offer should be made "as soon as practicable, but before the court's charge is read to the jury," and "outside the presence of the jury."[91] In the case of documentary evidence, the document itself should be offered and marked, and counsel should be sure to include those documents in the appellate record. For testimonial evidence, an offer should be made, on the record, in narrative form with counsel describing what the witness would testify to if allowed.[92] However, the court or a party may demand that the offer be made in question-and-answer form.[93]

1-4:3 Jury Charge

1-4:3.1 Preserving Error Under the Rules

Preserving error in the jury charge traditionally has been a complex and confusing enterprise, governed by Rules 274–79 of the Texas Rules of Civil Procedure. Under these rules, requirements for when to object or when to submit written requests in substantially correct form depend on which party has the burden of proof, whether the objection pertains to a question, instruction, or definition, and possibly other variables.

1-4:3.2 Simplified Judicial Alternative

In the landmark 1992 opinion, *State Department of Highways & Public Transportation v. Payne*,[94] Justice Hecht offered this assessment of the current situation, and a proposal for simplification:

> The preparation of the jury charge, coming as it ordinarily does at that very difficult point of the trial between the close of the evidence and summation, ought to be simpler. To complicate this process with complex, intricate, sometimes contradictory, unpredictable rules, just when counsel is contemplating the last

> words he or she will say to the jury, hardly subserves the fair and just presentation of the case. Yet that is our procedure. . . . Rather than attempt to decide under the pressure of the courtroom and in peril of losing appellate rights, whether an objection or a request is called for, cautious counsel might choose to do both in all cases—request and object. But if they are not kept separate, or if an appellate court later decides that the duplication obscured the real complaint, counsel's precaution may still result in a decision that the complaint was waived. . . .
>
> The flaws in our charge procedures stem partly from the rules governing those procedures and partly from caselaw applying those rules. Last year we asked a special task force to recommend changes in the rules to simplify charge procedures, and amendments are under consideration. Rules changes must await the completion of that process; we do not revise our rules by opinion.[95] We can, however, begin to reduce the complexity that caselaw has contributed to charge procedures. The procedure for preparing and objecting to the jury charge has lost its philosophical moorings. *There should be but one test for determining if a party has preserved error in the jury charge, and that is whether the party made the trial court aware of the complaint, timely and plainly, and obtained a ruling.* The more specific requirements of the rules should be applied, while they remain, to serve rather than defeat this principle.[96]

Even though the rule changes referred to by Justice Hecht never happened, the standard articulated by Justice Hecht that was premised on those expected changes has been widely cited as the new standard.[97] That seems to leave a potential conflict between Rules 274–79 of the Texas Rules of Civil Procedure as written,[98] and the more forgiving standard suggested by Justice Hecht in *Payne*. Cautious counsel should follow the rules strictly when they can, and fall back on Justice Hecht's opinion when they have to.

1-4:3.3 Minimal Requirements for Preserving Error

This much is clear: a party objecting to something included in the charge must "point out distinctly the objectionable matter and the grounds of the objection."[99] A party objecting to the failure to include a question, definition, or instruction should: (1) tender the requested question, definition, or instruction to the court, in writing and in substantially correct wording; (2) have the tender marked refused by the trial court; and (3) make sure that the refused tender is filed with the court and included in the appellate record.[100]

1-4:3.4 Format and Timing of Objections

Objections and requests must be made, either in writing or on the record, before the charge is read to the jury; objections made after the charge is read to the jury are waived.[101] Additionally, the trial court has discretion to set an earlier deadline for charge objections than the reading of the charge to the jury, as long as the deadline set by the court provides a reasonable amount of time for counsel to examine and object to the charge.[102]

1-4:3.5 Voluminous Objections

If an objection or request is "obscured or concealed by voluminous unfounded objections, minute differentiations or numerous unnecessary requests, such objection or request shall be untenable."[103] Presumably, an "untenable" objection or request fails to preserve error.

1-4:3.6 Adopting Objections by Reference

Another possible preservation pitfall is a prohibition against adopting objections or requests "by reference only."[104] Although the rule seems to envision one party adopting its own objections or requests to one part of the charge and applying them to another part of the charge by reference, it also has been applied to one party adopting the objections of another party by reference.[105]

1-4:3.7 Deemed Findings

If an element of a claim or defense (1) is omitted from the charge, (2) is supported by the evidence, (3) its omission is not objected to, and (4) no contrary findings are made by the court, it shall be deemed found in support of the judgment.[106] Accordingly, to avoid deemed findings lawyers should object to any elements omitted from the charge.

1-4:3.8 Invited Error

A party cannot request that an issue or instruction be submitted in the jury charge, and then complain on appeal that the part of the charge it requested was erroneous and should not have been submitted.[107] This has been described as a form of estoppel rather than a waiver.[108] One case has expressed the threshold requirement for invoking the invited-error doctrine as "persuading," the trial court to submit the charge later complained of on appeal, rather than merely requesting submission.[109] But that heightened standard does not seem to be supported by the cited case law or practical in application.

1-4:4 Opening and Closing Argument

When it comes to preservation, error during jury argument is divided into two categories: incurable jury argument and curable jury argument.

1-4:4.1 Incurable Jury Argument

Incurable jury argument has been defined as argument that "by its nature, degree, and extent constituted such error that an instruction from the court or retraction of the argument could not remove its effects."[110] Examples of incurable argument include:

- appeals to racial prejudice;[111]
- unsupported, extreme, and personal attacks on opposing parties and witnesses;[112]
- accusing the opposing party of manipulating a witness, without evidence of witness tampering;[113] and
- a personal expression of gratitude to the jury, in Spanish, to an all-Hispanic jury.[114]

Incurable arguments are "rare."[115] An incurable argument need not when the remark is made; in fact, error can be preserved by raising the complaint for the first time in a motion for new trial.[116] But if not raised during trial, incurable jury argument must be raised in a motion for new trial to be preserved.[117] That partly reflects the reality that an objection and instruction to disregard cannot cure the error anyway, and also an awareness that an objection only calls attention to the remark and accentuates it in the mind of the jury.

1-4:4.2 Curable Jury Argument

Curable jury argument is defined by process of elimination. Any allegedly improper jury argument that does not rise to the level of being an incurable jury argument is considered curable. A complaint about an improper but curable argument must be preserved by a timely and specific objection, coupled with a request for an instruction to the jury to disregard the improper remark.[118]

1-4:5 Strategic Decisions Concerning Preservation During Trial

1-4:5.1 Minimize Objections

The purpose of preserving error is to make it possible to raise arguments on appeal that will enhance the chance of winning on appeal. But the best way to enhance the chance of winning on appeal is to win in the trial court so that you are the appellee on appeal. Only a small fraction of appeals are successful, so statistically the party defending the appeal is much more likely to prevail than the party prosecuting the appeal. So what that means is that a higher priority should be placed on winning in the trial court than on preserving error in the event of an appeal.

Accordingly, be aware that an excessive amount of objections and other preservation techniques prolong the trial and may be annoying and/or boring to the jury, or even the trial judge. They also put you in a defensive posture because you look like you're trying to hide things and avoid the whole truth. That means that you should resist the temptation to view error preservation as a test to see if you can lodge an objection to every single objectionable event that takes place at trial. Instead, you should be selective, and choose your battles. Decide before trial which issues and which evidence are going to be important enough to justify imposing upon the jury's time and patience. Trust yourself to make hard choices and be willing to live with the results. In the long run, judicious restraint will serve you much better than proving that your opponent is not going to slip a single objectionable question or document by you.

1-4:5.2 Objecting on the Record When You Don't Want the Error Cured

Most objections and motions that are made at trial are lodged with the earnest intention of altering the way that the trial proceeds or the evidence the jury hears. Other objections and motions are made with the expectation that nothing will change, but for the sole purpose of preserving error. In fact, sometimes attorneys make objections to preserve error with no intention of the objection being granted because they think reversible error has been committed, but want to take their chances of trying the case with the knowledge that they can fall back on that reversible error if they have to.

In this situation, the challenge becomes doing and saying enough to preserve error, without running the risk of persuading the judge to sustain the objection. This can largely be accomplished by vocal tone, body language, and attitude. When you really want a judge to act, you should look the judge in the eye, speak slowly but firmly, and act as if this is something really important to you. When you don't want the judge to grant an objection, you can look down or away, speak without conviction, and state the bare minimum to express the grounds for the objection without elaborating. In other words, be enough of an actor to make the judge think that this is something you do not care greatly about, and may not even believe is correct, but someone has insisted that you go through the motions of making an objection on the record. The judge will probably appreciate a lawyer who does not treat every issue as life or death, and who seems to concede that they are not completely right and the other side completely wrong about every single issue. In all likelihood the judge will pick up on this cue and rule against you, thus preserving error, but not correcting the error that you do not want corrected.

1-4:5.3 Who Should Preserve Error?

Many cases are tried by a single lawyer, who must bear responsibility for managing all aspects of the trial, from marshalling evidence to managing motions and other filings to maintaining good relationships with the judge and jury. There are lawyers who have the skill set to wear all those hats and wear them well, and they deserve high praise.

But in cases where there is enough at stake to justify assembling a team of lawyers to handle the multiple tasks of modern trial litigation, consideration should be given to including an appellate specialist on that team. Especially if there is a likelihood that the case will be appealed regardless of outcome, it makes sense to get appellate lawyers involved early to let them help frame the issues for appeal, to familiarize them with the case so the learning curve is not as steep later, and to send a message to the other side that you are gearing up for the long haul. But there are particular advantages to having an appellate lawyer on the team related to the preservation of error:

- Assigning preservation of error to an appellate lawyer frees up the lead trial counsel to concentrate on persuading the jury by presenting evidence, examining witnesses, and making jury arguments.
- Appellate lawyers making objections can deflect the wrath of judges and juries who dislike the interruption of preserving error during trial so that it is not directed at the lead trial lawyer.
- An appellate lawyer is generally more familiar with the substantive law and with current trends in the appellate courts.
- An appellate lawyer, as a fresh player off the bench, has an advantage in arguing legal issues against an opposing trial lawyer worn down by the rigors of trial.

1-5 Post-Trial Preservation of Error

There are a variety of post-trial motions that can be filed for different purposes. Here we will focus solely on post-trial motions required to preserve different types of error that might be complained of on appeal.

1-5:1 Complaints of No Evidence or Legally Insufficient Evidence

This complaint must be raised in one of the following ways:

- motion for directed verdict or instructed verdict at the close of either side's evidence;
- objection to the submission of a jury question on "no evidence" grounds;
- motion for judgment non obstante veredicto (JNOV);
- motion to disregard the jury's answer to a vital fact question; or
- motion for new trial.[119]

Accordingly, if a "no evidence" complaint was not preserved at trial, it should be raised post-trial in a motion for JNOV, a motion to disregard a particular finding, or a motion for new trial.

If a "no evidence" argument is preserved in one of the first four methods listed above, and the party prevails on the point on appeal, the court of appeals can reverse and render a judgment in that party's favor. However, if a "no evidence" point is preserved *only* in a motion for new trial, the only relief that can be granted by the appellate court is a reversal and remand for a new trial.[120]

1-5:2 Complaints of Factually Insufficient Evidence

Complaints that jury findings are supported by factually insufficient evidence, or are so against the great weight and preponderance of the evidence as to be manifestly unjust, must be raised in a motion for new trial.[121]

1-5:3 Complaints of Inadequate or Excessive Damages

An attack on the amount of damages found by the jury is a form of a factual-sufficiency challenge, and also must be raised in a motion for new trial to be preserved.[122]

1-5:4 Complaints of Incurable Jury Argument Not Ruled On by the Trial Court

If no objection was made or ruling obtained concerning an incurable jury argument during trial, it must be raised in a motion for new trial to be preserved.[123]

1-5:5 Complaints on Which Evidence Must Be Heard

Rule 324 has a broad provision that any complaint that requires, and allows, the presentation of evidence must be raised in a motion for new trial.[124] The rule provides a non-exclusive list of examples of the types of complaints that might require additional evidence:

- jury misconduct;
- newly discovered evidence; and
- failure to set aside a default judgment.

1-5:6 Complaints in a Non-Jury Trial

1-5:6.1 Whether to File a Request for Findings and Conclusions

If a party anticipates appealing from a bench trial, its attorney would be well-advised to file a request for finding of fact and conclusions of law.[125] Although not listed as a requirement to preserve error like the previous categories, if no findings of fact or conclusions of law are filed, the reviewing court must imply all necessary fact findings in favor of the judgment.[126] Because that creates an almost insurmountable burden to reversal in most cases, findings of fact and conclusions of law should always be requested in a bench trial by any party that plans on appealing any part of the judgment. A party who prevailed and does not plan on appealing should not request findings and conclusions, but instead hope that the opposing party will fail to do so, and the benefits of the presumptions will flow to the prevailing party. But if the losing party does request findings and conclusions, the prevailing party should be prepared to tender its version of findings and conclusions to assist the trial court.

1-5:6.2 Initial Request and Notice of Past Due Findings

Requesting findings and conclusions can be a complex multi-step process, and Rules 296–99 should be carefully studied and strictly adhered to. If the court fails to file the requested findings and conclusions within 20 days, the requesting party must file a notice of past due findings within 30 days of the original request.[127] The failure to do so waives any complaint on appeal that the trial court did not file requested findings.[128] If a judge leaves the bench during this process of requesting findings and conclusions, the findings and conclusions must be signed by the judge who tried the case, even though that judge has left the bench, rather than the current sitting judge who did not hear the case.[129]

1-5:6.3 Requesting Additional Findings

If the Court files findings and conclusions, either party may make a request for additional findings or conclusions within 10 days.[130] Additional findings should be requested if the court omitted findings on a material element; amended findings should be requested if the court made an error in its findings or conclusions. The failure to request additional findings waives the right to challenge the lack of findings on appeal.[131]

Complaints that findings of a trial court are not supported by legally or factually sufficient evidence do *not* need to be raised in a post-trial motion in the trial court, but may be raised for the first time on appeal.[132]

1-5:7 Complaints on Matters Not Otherwise Appearing in the Record

If a matter does not appear in the record, for whatever reason, its absence can be remedied by a formal bill of exception filed in the trial court.[133] This may apply to excluded evidence for which the proponent did not make an offer of proof, or exhibits that were lost, or testimony that was transcribed incompletely or improperly.

Formal bills of exception also have been used to correct the trial court's failure to mark a tendered jury question or instruction as refused,[134] and are mentioned as a way to preserve error in the failure to accommodate a visually impaired litigant.[135] If the formal bill of exception conflicts with the Reporter's Record, the bill controls.[136] The formal bill of exceptions must be filed no more than 30 days after filing the notice of appeal in civil cases.[137]

Notes

1 *See* Tex. R. App. P. 33.1(a); Tex. R. Evid. 103.

2 *Daubert v. Merrell Dow Pharmaceuticals*, 509 U.S. 579 (1993).

3 Tex. R. App. P. 33.1(a)(2)(A).

4 *See, e.g., Dryzer v. Bundren*, No. 07-12-00167-CV, 2014 WL 1856849, at *2 (Tex. App.—Amarillo May 16, 2014, pet. denied) (mem. op.); *State v. Colonia Tepeyac, Ltd.*, 391 S.W.3d 563, 568 (Tex. App.—Dallas 2012, no pet.).

5 Tex. R. App. P. 33.1(a)(2)(B).

6 *See* Tex. R. Civ. P. 120a(1).

7 Tex. R. Civ. P. 120a(1).

8 *Dawson-Austin v. Austin*, 968 S.W.2d 319, 322–23 (Tex. 1998).

9 Tex. R. Civ. P. 120a(2).

10 *Exito Elecs. Co. v. Trejo*, 142 S.W.3d 302, 304 (Tex. 2004).

11 *Exito Elecs. Co. v. Trejo*, 142 S.W.3d 302, 305 (Tex. 2004).

12 *Exito Elecs. Co. v. Trejo*, 142 S.W.3d 302, 306–07 (Tex. 2004).

13 *See* Tex. R. Civ. P. 86, 120a.

14 *See Scott v. Wichita Cty.*, 248 S.W.3d 324, 326 (Tex. App.—Houston [1st. Dist.] 2007, no pet.).

15 Tex. R. Civ. P. 90.

16 Tex. R. Civ. P. 90.

17 *Parker v. Barefield*, 206 S.W.3d 119, 120 (Tex. 2006) (per curiam) (citing Tex. R. Civ. P. 33.1(a)).

18 *Friesenhahn v. Ryan*, 960 S.W.2d 656, 658 (Tex. 1998).

19 *Horizon/CMS Healthcare Corp. v. Auld*, 34 S.W.3d 887, 897 (Tex. 2000); *Kaldis v. Crest Finance*, 463 S.W.3d 588 (Tex. App.—Houston [1st. Dist.] 2015, no pet.).

20 *Ingram v. Deere*, 288 S.W.3d 886, 893 (Tex. 2009).

21 *See* Tex. R. Civ. P. 63, 166.

22 *Chapin & Chapin, Inc. v. Tex. Sand & Gravel Co.*, 844 S.W.2d 664, 665 (Tex. 1992); *Greenhalgh v. Service lloyd's Ins. Co.*, 787 S.W.2d 938 (Tex. 1990).

23 *See* Tex. R. Civ. P. 93.

24 *See* Tex. R. Civ. P. 94.

25 *See Remington Arms Co., Inc. v. Caldwell*, 850 S.W.2d 167, 170 (Tex.1993) ("[T]he failure to obtain a pre-trial ruling on discovery disputes that exist before commencement of trial constitutes a waiver of any claim for sanctions based on that conduct.").

26 *Remington Arms Co., Inc. v. Caldwell*, 850 S.W.2d 167, 170 (Tex. 1993).

27 *Chevron Phillips Chemical Co. v. Kingwood Crossroads*, 346 S.W.3d 37 (Tex. App.—Houston [14th. Dist.] 2012, pet. denied).

28 *Chevron Phillips Chemical Co. v. Kingwood Crossroads*, 346 S.W.3d 37, 73 (Tex. App.—Houston [14th. Dist.] 2012, pet. denied).

29 *Johnson v. Brewer & Pritchard, P.C.*, 73 S.W.3d 193, 204 (Tex. 2002); *McConnell v. Southside Indep. Sch. Dist.*, 858 S.W.2d 337, 339 (Tex. 1993).

30 *McConnell v. Southside Indep. Sch. Dist.*, 858 S.W.2d 337, 340–41 (Tex. 1993).

31 *See ADT Sec. Servs., Inc. v. Van Peterson Fine Jewelers*, 390 S.W.3d 603, 606 (Tex. App—Dallas 2012, no pet.).

32 *Priddy v. Rawson*, 282 S.W.3d 588, 597 (Tex. App—Houston [14th Dist.] 2009, pet. denied).

33 Tex. R. Civ. P. 166a(c).

34 Tex. R. Civ P. 63 (requiring amendment seven days before trial); *Goswami v. Metroplotian Sav. & Loan Ass'n.*, 751 S.W.2d 487, 490 (Tex. 1988) (a summary-judgment hearing is a trial for purposes of Rule 63); *Sosa v. Cent. Power & Light*, 909 S.W.2d 893, 895 (Tex. 1995) (per curiam) (applying Rule 63 to summary-judgment hearing).

35 *Sosa v. Cent. Power & Light*, 909 S.W.2d 893, 895 (Tex. 1995) (per curiam).

36 *Continental Airlines, Inc. v. Kiefer*, 920 S.W.2d 274, 276 (Tex. 1996); *Mensa-Wilmot v. Smith Intern., Inc.*, 312 S.W.3d 771, 778 (Tex. App.—Houston [1st Dist.] 2009, no pet.).

37 *Fletcher v. Edwards*, 26 S.W.3d 66, 74 ((Tex. App—Waco 2000, pet. denied).

38 *Roark v. Stallworth Oil & Gas, Inc.*, 813 S.W.2d 492, 495 (Tex. 1991).

39 *In re B.I.V.*, 870 S.W.2d 12, 13 (Tex. 1994).

40 *See San Jacinto River Auth. v. Duke*, 783 S.W.2d 209, 209–10 (Tex. 1990).

41 Tex. R. Civ. P. 166a(g); *Tenneco, Inc. v. Enter. Prods. Co.*, 925 S.W.2d 640, 647 (Tex. 1996).

42 *Jaimes v. Fiesta Mkt., Inc.*, 21 S.W.3d 301, 304 (Tex. App—Houston [1st Dist.] 1999, pet. denied).

43 Tex. R. Civ. P. 166a(c).

44 *Benchmark Bank v. Crowder*, 919 S.W.2d 657, 663 (Tex. 1996).

45 *See* Tex. R. Civ. P. 166a(c).

46 *Rockwall Commons Assoc., Ltd. v. MRC Mortg. Grantor Trust I*, 331 S.W.3d 500 (Tex. App—El Paso 2010, no pet.).

47 *Compare Parkway Dental Assocs., P.A. v. Ho & Huang Props., L.P.*, 391 S.W.3d 596, 603–04 (Tex. App.—Houston [14th Dist.] 2012, no pet.) (holding that trial court implicitly sustained movant's objections by grant of summary-judgment motion and by language used in the order); *with Bastida v. Aznaran*, 444 S.W.3d 98, 104 (Tex. App.—Dallas 2014, no pet.) ("The granting of a summary judgment motion 'does not necessarily provide an implicit ruling that either sustains or overrules the objections to the summary-judgment evidence.' . . . Objections to the form of summary judgment evidence are preserved for appellate review only if such objections are made and ruled on in the trial court.").

48 *Aguilar v. LVDVD, L.C.*, 70 S.W.3d 915, 917 (Tex. App—El Paso 2002, no pet.).

49 Tex. R. Civ. P. 166a(c).

50 *See Benchmark Bank v. Crowder*, 919 S.W.2d 657, 663 (Tex. 1996).

51 *Benchmark Bank v. Crowder*, 919 S.W.2d 657, 663 (Tex. 1996).

52 *Fertic v. Spencer*, 247 S.W.3d 242 (Tex. App.—El Paso 2007, pet. denied); *Negrini v. Beale*, 822 S.W.2d 822, 823 (Tex. App.—Houston [14th Dist.] 1992, no writ).

53 Tex. R. Civ. P. 166a(c).

54 *PNP Petroleum I, LP v. Taylor*, 438 S.W.3d 723, 730 (Tex. App—San Antonio 2014, pet. denied).

55 *Neimes v. Ta*, 985 S.W.2d 132, 138 (Tex. App—San Antonio 1998, pet. dism'd by agr.).

56 *Reynolds v. Murphy*, 188 S.W.3d 252, 259 (Tex. App—Fort Worth 2006, pet. denied).

57 *McConnell v. Southside Indep. Sch. Dist.*, 858 S.W.2d 337, 343 n.7 (Tex. 1993).

58 *McConnell v. Southside Indep. Sch. Dist.*, 858 S.W.2d 337, 343 n.7 (Tex. 1993).

[59] *McConnell v. Southside Indep. Sch. Dist.*, 858 S.W.2d 337, 343 n.7 (Tex. 1993).

[60] *See Buckholts Indep. Sch. Dist. v. Glaser*, 632 S.W.2d 146, 148 (Tex. 1982); *Kennedy v. Staples*, 336 S.W.3d 745, 750 (Tex. App.—Texarkana 2011, no pet.); *Zurita v. Lombana*, 322 S.W.3d 463, 470 (Tex. App.—Houston [1st Dist.] 2010, pet. denied).

[61] Tex. R. Civ. P. 18a.

[62] Tex. R. Civ. P. 18a.

[63] Tex. Gov't Code § 74.053(a).

[64] *In re Canales*, 52 S.W.3d 698, 704 (Tex. 2001) (orig. proceeding).

[65] Tex. R. Civ. P. 216(a).

[66] *See Hyundai Motor Co. v. Vasquez*, 189 S.W.3d 743, 758 (Tex. 2006) ("[T]o preserve a complaint that a trial court improperly restricted voir dire, a party must timely alert the trial court as to the specific manner in which it intends to pursue the inquiry").

[67] *Babcock v. Nw. Mem'l Hosp.* 767 S.W.2d 705, 708 (Tex. 1989).

[68] *Babcock v. Nw. Mem'l Hosp.* 767 S.W.2d 705, 708 (Tex. 1989).

[69] *Hyundai Motor Co. v. Vasquez*, 189 S.W.3d 743, 758–59 (Tex. 2006).

[70] *Babcock v. Nw. Mem'l Hosp.* 767 S.W.2d 705, 708 (Tex. 1989).

[71] *Hyundai Motor Co. v. Vasquez*, 189 S.W.3d 743, 759–60 (Tex. 2006).

[72] *Cortez v. HCCI-San Antonio, Inc.*, 159 S.W.3d 87, 90–91 (Tex. 2005).

[73] *Cortez v. HCCI-San Antonio, Inc.*, 159 S.W.3d 87, 91 (Tex. 2005); *Hallett v. Houston Nw. Med. Ctr.*, 689 S.W.2d 888, 890 (Tex. 1985).

[74] Tex. R. Civ. P. 223.

[75] Tex. Const., art. V, § 13.

[76] Tex. Gov't Code § 62.201.

[77] *Audia v. Hannold*, 328 S.W.3d 661, 663 (Tex App.—Dallas 2010, no pet.).

[78] *Blount v. Bordens, Inc.*, 892 S.W.2d 932, 944 (Tex. App.—Houston [1st Dist.] 1994), *rev'd on other grounds*, 910 S.W.2d 931 (Tex. 1995).

[79] *See Roberts v. Tatum*, 575 S.W.2d 138, 144 (Tex. Civ. App.—Corpus Christi 1978, writ ref'd n.r.e.).

[80] Tex. R. Evid. 103(a)(1).

[81] *Haney v. Purcell Co.*, 796 S.W.2d 782, 789 (Tex. App.—Houston [1st Dist.] 1990, writ denied).

[82] Tex. R. Evid. 103(a).

[83] Tex. R. Evid. 103(a)(1).

[84] *Richardson v. Green*, 677 S.W.2d 497, 501 (Tex. 1984).

[85] *Commerce, Crowdus & Canton, Ltd. v. DKS Constr., Inc.*, 776 S.W.2d 615, 620 (Tex. Civ. App.—Dallas 1989, no writ); *Bunnett/Smallwood & Co. v. Helton Oil Co.*, 577 S.W.2d 291, 295 (Tex. Civ. App.—Amarillo 1978, no writ); *Crispi v. Emmott*, 337 S.W.2d 314, 318 (Tex. Civ. App.—Houston 1960, no writ).

[86] *Sauceda v. Kerlin*, 164 S.W.3d 892, 919–20 (Tex. App.—Corpus Christi 2005), *rev'd on other grounds*, 263 S.W.3d 920 (Tex. 2008); *Atkinson Gas Co. v. Albrecht*, 878 S.W.2d 236, 242–43 (Tex. App.—Corpus Christi 1994, writ denied).

[87] *Volkswagen, Inc. v. Ramirez*, 159 S.W.3d 897, 907 (Tex. 2004).

[88] *In re A.P.*, 42 S.W.3d 248, 261 (Tex. App.—Waco 2001, orig. proceeding), *overruled on other grounds, In re A.M.*, 385 S.W.3d 74, 82 (Tex. App.—Waco 2012, pet. denied).

[89] *See Celotex Corp. v. Tate*, 797 S.W.2d 197, 201 (Tex. App.—Corpus Christi 1990, writ dism'd).

[90] *See* Tex. R. Evid. 103(a)(2).

[91] *See* Tex. R. Evid. 103(b).

92 *See* Tex. R. Evid. 103(b).

93 Tex. R. Evid. 103(b).

94 *State Dept. of Highways & Pub. Transp. v. Payne*, 838 S.W.2d 235 (Tex. 1992).

95 *Alvarado v. Farah Mfg. Co.*, 830 S.W.2d 911, 915 (Tex. 1992).

96 *State Dept. of Highways & Pub. Transp. v. Payne*, 838 S.W.2d 235, 240–41 (Tex. 1992) (emphasis added).

97 *See USAA Texas Lloyd's v Menchaca*, 545 S.W.3d 479, 487 (Tex. 2018); *Wackenhut Corp. v. Gutierrez*, 453 S.W.3d 917, 920 (Tex. 2015); *King Fisher Marine Serv., L.P. v. Tamez*, 443 S.W.3d 838, 842–47 (Tex. 2014); *Cruz v. Andrews Restoration, Inc.*, 364 S.W.3d 817, 829 (Tex. 2013).

98 *But see Alaniz v. Jones & Neuse, Inc.*, 907 S.W.2d 450, 451–52 (Tex. 1995) (per curiam) ("While *Payne* does not revise the requirements of the rules *452 of procedure regarding the jury charge, it does mandate that those requirements be applied in a common sense manner to serve the purposes of the rules, rather than in a technical manner which defeats them.").

99 Tex. R. Civ. P. 274.

100 *See* Tex. R. Civ. P. 276, 278. (Although Rule 276 requires the court to mark the tenders "refused" and sign them, some cases have held that a statement on the record that the request is refused will suffice. *See Dallas Mkt. Ctr. Dev. Co. v. Liedeker*, 958 S.W.2d 382, 386–87 (Tex. 1997), *overruled on other grounds, Torrington Co. v. Stutzman*, 46 S.W.3d 829 (Tex. 2000)).

101 Tex. R. Civ. P. 272.

102 *King Fisher Marine Serv., L.P. v. Tamez*, 443 S.W.3d 838, 843–46 (Tex. 2014).

103 Tex. R. Civ. P. 274.

104 Tex. R. Civ. P. 274.

105 *See C.M. Asfahl Agency v. Tensor, Inc.*, 135 S.W.3d 768, 795 (Tex. App.—Houston [1st Dist.] 2004, no pet.).

106 *See* Tex. R. Civ. P. 279.

107 *Gen. Chem. Corp. v. De La Lastra*, 852 S.W.2d 916, 920 (Tex. 1993).

108 *W&T Offshore, Inc. v. Meyers*, No. 14-16-00378, 2018 WL 6318404, at *3 (Tex. App.—Houston [14th Dist.] 2018, n.pet.h.).

109 *W&T Offshore, Inc. v. Meyers*, No. 14-16-00378, 2018 WL 6318404, at *3–4 (Tex. App.—Houston [14th Dist.] 2018, n.pet.h.) (citing *United Scaffolding, Inc. v. Levine*, 537 S.W.3d 463, 482 (Tex. 2017)); *Del Lago Partners, Inc. v. Smith*, 307 S.W.3d 762, 775 (Tex. 2010).

110 *Living Ctrs. of Tex., Inc. v. Penalver*, 256 S.W.3d 678, 680–81 (Tex. 2008); *see also Standard Fire Ins. Co. v. Reese*, 584 S.W.2d 835, 839 (1979).

111 *See Texas Employers' Ins. Ass'n v. Haywood*, 266 S.W.2d 856, 858 (Tex. 1954); *see also Moss v. Sanger et al.*, 12 S.W. 616, 619 (Tex. 1889).

112 *See Howsley & Jacobs v. Kendall*, 376 S.W.2d 562 (Tex.1964); *Southwestern Greyhound Lines, Inc. v. Dickson*, 236 S.W.2d 115 (Tex. 1951).

113 *See Howsley & Jacobs v. Kendall*, 376 S.W.2d 562, 565–66 (Tex. 1964).

114 *General Motors v. Iracheta*, 161 S.W.3d 462, 472 (Tex. 2005).

115 *Living Ctrs. of Tex., Inc. v. Penalver*, 256 S.W.3d 678, 681 (Tex. 2008).

116 *Phillips v. Bramblett*, 288 S.W.3d 876, 883 (Tex. 2009).

117 *See* Tex. R. Civ. P. 324(b)(5).

118 *Phillips v. Bramblett*, 288 S.W.3d 876, 883 (Tex. 2009).

119 *Cecil v. Smith*, 804 S.W.2d 509, 510–11 (Tex. 1991).

[120] *See Werner v. Colwell*, 909 S.W.2d 866, 870 n.1 (Tex. 1995); *Horrocks v. Texas Dept. of Transportation*, 852 S.W.2d 498, 499 (Tex. 1993) (per curiam).

[121] *See* Tex. R. Civ. P. 324(b)(2), (3); *Cecil v. Smith*, 804 S.W.2d 509, 510 (Tex. 1991).

[122] *See* Tex. R. Civ. P. 324(b)(4).

[123] *See* Tex. R. Civ. P. 324(b)(5).

[124] *See* Tex. R. Civ. P. 324(b)(1).

[125] *See generally* Tex. R. Civ. P. 296–99.

[126] *Torrington Co. v. Stutzman*, 46 S.W.3d 829, 842 (Tex. 2000).

[127] Tex. R. Civ. P. 297.

[128] *Las Vegas Pecan & Cattle Co. v. Zavala County*, 682 S.W.2d 254, 255–56 (Tex. 1984); *Guillory v. Boykins*, 442 S.W.3d 682, 693 (Tex. App.—Houston [1st Dist.], no pet.).

[129] *Ad Villari, L.L.C. v. Pak*, 519 S.W.3d 132, 136–43 (Tex. 2017).

[130] Tex. R. Civ. P. 298.

[131] *Pagare v. Pagare*, 344 S.W.3d 575, 581 (Tex. App.—Dallas 2011, pet. denied); *Smith v. Smith*, 22 S.W.3d 140, 149 (Tex. App.—Houston [14th Dist.] 2000, no pet.).

[132] Tex. R. App. P. 33.1(d).

[133] Tex. R. App. P. 33.2.

[134] *Wright Way Construction v. Harlingen Mall*, 799 S.W.2d 415, 421–22 (Tex. App.—Corpus Christi 1990, no writ).

[135] *Amerson v. Amerson*, No. 14-01-00625-CV, 2002 WL 1438672, at *1 (Tex. App.—Houston [14th Dist.] 2002, no pet.).

[136] Tex. R. App. P. 33.2(d).

[137] Tex. R. App. P. 33.2(e)(1).

CHAPTER 2

Standards of Review and Scope of Review

2-1 Introduction

"[A] standard of review is more than just words; rather, it embodies principles regarding the amount of deference a reviewing tribunal accords the original tribunal's decision."[1]

Knowing the appropriate standard of review is critical to deciding whether to appeal and to crafting a persuasive appellate argument. For example, a de novo standard of review is often better for appellants because the court of appeals will take a completely fresh look at the issue. Conversely, appellees benefit from the abuse-of-discretion standard of review, which requires substantial deference to the opinion of the lower court.

Courts also appreciate parties framing their arguments within the appropriate standard of review because it helps them decide the appeal correctly. Even when the standard of review makes winning the appeal difficult, it is more persuasive to frame the argument within the standard of review rather than to ignore the limits on the appellate court's authority to review a matter.

The scope of review is often part of the same discussion and is sometimes confused with the standard of review, though it is important to distinguish them. While the standard of review provides the framework for the decision, the scope of review determines which parts of the appellate record the reviewing court is to consider when applying the standard of review.[2]

This chapter will define standards of review that arise in appellate practice in the Texas state courts, and when they are most commonly applicable. It will also discuss the scope of review when the case law has addressed those parameters.

2-2 De Novo Standard of Review

The de novo standard of review is perhaps the easiest to understand and apply. "When conducting a de novo review, the reviewing tribunal exercises its own judgment and redetermines each issue of fact and law. In such a review, the reviewing tribunal accords the original tribunal's decision absolutely no deference."[3] Generally, appellate courts use a de novo standard to review a lower court's decision on a matter of law and the application of law to facts.

2-2:1 Substantive Matters Always Reviewed De Novo

The de novo standard of review applies to the following substantive determinations:

2-2:1.1 Determination of an Ambiguous Contract

The question of whether a contract is ambiguous is a matter of law for the court and is subject to de novo review.[4] An ambiguity exists when there are two or more reasonable interpretations of a contract, such that determining the intent of the parties becomes a fact issue.[5] "A contract is not ambiguous if the contract's language can be given a certain or definite meaning."[6]

The scope of review encompasses the entire contract and the surrounding circumstances: an appellate court determines whether a contract is ambiguous "by looking at the contract as a whole in light of the circumstances present when the contract was entered."[7] While the surrounding circumstances are relevant, parol evidence is outside the scope of review and may not be considered to create an ambiguity.[8] The parole evidence rule prohibits even surrounding circumstances evidence when the contract "by its terms, plainly and clearly discloses the intention of the parties or is so worded that it is not fairly susceptible of more than one legal meaning or construction."[9] If one party's interpretation is not reasonable under these rules, then the contract is not ambiguous and its interpretation is a question of law.

2-2:1.2 Construction of an Unambiguous Contract

If a court determines that a contract is unambiguous, then it will determine the meaning of the contract as a matter of law.[10] Because the construction of an unambiguous contract is a question of law for the court, it is reviewed de novo by an appellate court.[11] The reviewing court will examine the entire contract, with the goal of harmonizing and giving effect to each provision so that none is rendered meaningless and none is given controlling effect.[12] Words are given their "plain and ordinary meaning unless the instrument indicates the parties intended a different meaning."[13] The contract must be construed "from a utilitarian standpoint, bearing in mind the particular business activity sought to be served."[14]

The scope of review is limited to the language of the contract itself whenever possible.[15] But evidence of the facts and circumstances surrounding the execution of a contract may also be considered as an aid in the construction of the contract's language.[16]

All types of contracts are interpreted de novo on appeal, but specific kinds of documents have been singled out and specifically held to present questions of law subject to de novo review, including:

- arbitration agreements;[17]
- oil and gas leases;[18]
- property deeds;[19] and
- settlement agreements.[20]

The interpretation of an insurance policy is also a question of law, reviewed de novo,[21] but special rules apply in the insurance context. When the dispute involves a standard-form policy whose terms have been dictated by a state regulatory agency, then the court's goal is not to determine the intent of the parties to the contract, but the "ordinary, everyday meaning of the words to the general public."[22] But when a non-standard policy is at issue, or a provision that was individually negotiated, then the court must "determine and enforce the mutual intent of the parties to the contract."[23]

2-2:1.3 Application of Statute of Frauds

"Whether an agreement falls within the statute of frauds is a question of law."[24] That determination is therefore reviewed de novo.[25]

2-2:1.4 Interpretation of a Statute

Statutory construction is a question of law that is reviewed de novo on appeal.[26] The court explains the standard of review this way:

> When interpreting a statute, our primary objective is to ascertain and give effect to the Legislature's intent without unduly restricting or expanding the Act's scope. We seek that intent first and foremost in the plain meaning of the text. Undefined terms in a statute are typically given their ordinary meaning, but if a different or more precise definition is apparent from the term's use in the context of the statute, we apply that meaning. However, we will not give an undefined term a meaning that is out of harmony or inconsistent with other terms in the statute. Therefore, even if an undefined terms has multiple meanings, we recognize and apply only the meanings that are consistent with the statutory scheme as a whole.[27]

The court will depart from the "plain and common" meaning of the statute's words if that construction "leads to absurd or nonsensical results."[28] The court must read all words and phrases "in context" and construe them "according to the rules of grammar and common usage."[29] The court will also apply well-recognized rules of construction, such as the doctrine of *ejusdem generis,* which teaches that where specific items are followed by a generic catchall, like "other," "the latter must be limited to things like the former."[30]

Unlike ambiguous contracts, ambiguous statutes are also interpreted as a matter of law and subject to de novo review.[31] If a statute is ambiguous, the court will defer to agency interpretations of the statute, "provided that the agency's interpretation is reasonable and does not conflict with the plain language of the statute."[32]

In determining the legislative intent behind a statute, the court must consider the entire Act, not just isolated provisions.[33] An appellate court's scope of review may also include evidence of the following matters:

- the object sought to be attained;
- the circumstances under which it was enacted;
- the legislative history;
- the common law and prior statutes;
- the consequences of a particular construction;

- the construction of the statute by administrative agencies; and
- the title or preamble of the statute, plus any emergency provisions.[34]

The scope of review also includes the additional aids to construction that the legislature has included in the Code Construction Act. Thus, the appellate court may consider the legislature's definition of words like "shall," "person," and "property," even though those words are not defined in the statute at issue in the appeal.[35]

2-2:1.4a Tax-exemption Statutes

A party claiming a tax exemption must "clearly show" he or she falls within the exemption.[36] While the usual, de novo statutory standard of review applies, any doubts must be resolved in favor of the taxing authority and against the claimant.[37]

2-2:1.5 Constitutional Concerns

The Supreme Court applies a de novo standard of review to question of whether a statute is constitutional.[38] In conducting that analysis, the court indulges a presumption that statutes are constitutional and places a high burden on parties claiming otherwise.[39]

A party making an as-applied, substantive due course challenge to the constitutionality of an economic-regulation statute has the burden to demonstrate either: "(1) the statute's purpose could not arguably be rationally related to a legitimate governmental interest; or (2) when considered as a whole, the statute's actual, real-world effect as applied to the challenging party could not arguably be rationally related to, or is so burdensome as to be oppressive in light of, the governmental interest."[40] The standard of review for such a challenge must consider "whether the statute's effect as a whole is so unreasonably burdensome that it becomes oppressive in relation to the underlying governmental interest."[41]

2-2:2 Litigation Issues Reviewed De Novo

Many of the determinations a trial court makes during litigation present questions of law subject to a de novo standard of review. Several examples follow.

2-2:2.1 Existence of Subject-Matter Jurisdiction

The ruling on any plea that questions the trial court's subject-matter jurisdiction raises a question of law that is reviewed de novo.[42] There may be factual determinations relevant to subject-matter jurisdiction. Where disputed evidence implicates the court's subject-matter jurisdiction, the standard of review takes evidence favorable to the nonmovant as true, and indulges all inferences and resolves all doubts in favor of the non-movant.[43] If a fact issue exists, the plea must be denied pending resolution by the fact-finder.[44] If the non-movant fails to raise a fact-issue, the plea must be granted as a matter of law.[45]

The burden falls on the plaintiff to affirmatively establish that the trial court has subject-matter jurisdiction. Accordingly, the scope of the appellate court's review begins with the plaintiff's pleadings, which are construed liberally, taking the factual allegations as true.[46] If evidence has been tendered to negate jurisdiction, the appellate court may consider that, and must do so if it is necessary to resolving the issue.[47] If either the plaintiff's pleadings or the defendant's undisputed evidence negates subject-matter jurisdiction, the challenge must be granted.[48]

Subject-matter jurisdiction may be challenged under a variety of theories. The following grounds are reviewed de novo:

- *Ripeness.* As an element of subject-matter jurisdiction, ripeness is a legal question subject to de novo review. The issue may be raised by the court sua sponte.[49]
- *Sovereign immunity.* A plea to the jurisdiction based on sovereign-immunity challenges a trial court's jurisdiction, so an order granting such a plea is ordinarily reviewed de novo.[50] But when a plea to the jurisdiction challenges a plaintiff's factual allegations with supporting evidence, the court determines whether a material fact exists based on a summary-judgment-like standard: taking as true all evidence favorable to the plaintiff and indulging every reasonable inference and resolving any doubts in the plaintiff's favor.[51]
- *Appellate jurisdiction.* The Texas Supreme Court reviews the court of appeals' determination of its jurisdiction de novo.[52]
- *Pleading subject-matter jurisdiction.* Whether a plaintiff has pleaded sufficient facts to establish subject-matter jurisdiction is a question of law reviewed de novo.[53]
- *Pleas to the jurisdiction.* A plea to the jurisdiction challenges a trial court's subject-matter jurisdiction. The existence of subject-matter jurisdiction is a question of law.[54] Accordingly, a trial court's ruling on such a motion is reviewed de novo.[55]
- *Standing.* Because standing is a constitutional prerequisite to subject-matter jurisdiction, it is reviewed de novo.[56]
- *Mootness.* The appellate courts review de novo the issue whether a claim is moot.[57]

2-2:2.2 Existence of Personal Jurisdiction

Whether a court has personal jurisdiction over a defendant is a question of law. Thus, the trial court's decision to grant or deny a special appearance is reviewed de novo.[58] However, while the legal conclusion that personal jurisdiction exists is reviewed de novo, the trial court's factual findings supporting that conclusion, and all necessary implied findings, are reviewed under a legal or factual-sufficiency standard of review.[59]

The appellate court must determine whether the Texas long-arm statute applies and whether the non-resident defendant has established minimum contacts with the forum so the assertion of jurisdiction will comport with "traditional notions of fair play and substantial justice."[60] Because this is a fact-based inquiry, the scope of review encompasses all evidence that was before the trial court when it ruled.[61]

2-2:2.3 Exclusive Jurisdiction of an Agency

Determining if an agency has exclusive jurisdiction over an issue or subject matter requires statutory construction and raises jurisdictional issues. Thus, whether an agency has exclusive jurisdiction is a question of law that is reviewed de novo.[62]

2-2:2.4 Venue Determinations

A court may find that it has both subject-matter and personal jurisdiction and yet still be the wrong place for trial under the state's comprehensive venue statutes. A court of appeals conducts a de novo review of the entire record to determine whether a trial court's determination of joinder or intervention was proper under the venue statutes.[63]

2-2:2.5 Unconscionability and Public Policy

Typically, the trial court's decision whether to grant or deny a motion to compel arbitration is reviewed for abuse of discretion. *See* section 2-3:2.9. However, when the basis for denying a motion to compel arbitration is public policy or unconscionability, and there are no factual disputes, the appeal presents a question of law for the court and the standard of review is de novo.[64]

2-2:2.6 Grant of Dispositive Motions

Dismissals for want of jurisdiction, for failure to plead a cause of action or on summary judgment are reviewed de novo.

- *Dismissal for failure to cure on repleading after special exceptions.* A case may be dismissed when, after having been given the opportunity to re-plead in response to special exceptions, a plaintiff's petition still fails to state a cognizable cause of action. The standard of review on the legal question whether the pleading stated a cause of action is de novo.[65]

- *The grant of a motion for summary judgment.* A trial court's grant of summary judgment is reviewed de novo.[66] The appellate court's task is to determine whether there is more than a scintilla of probative evidence raising genuine issues of material fact. A traditional motion for summary judgment is properly granted where a defendant conclusively negates at least one essential element of a cause of action or conclusively proves all elements of an affirmative defense.[67] Similarly, a no-evidence motion for summary judgment is improperly granted when the non-movant presents more than a scintilla of evidence to create a genuine issue of material fact.[68]

  The scope of review includes the entire summary-judgment record, which is reviewed for legal sufficiency.[69] It will "'review the evidence presented by the motion and response in the light most favorable to the party against whom the summary judgment was rendered, crediting evidence favorable to that party if reasonable jurors could, and disregarding contrary evidence unless reasonable jurors could not.'"[70]

  Reviewing courts do not disregard the evidence supporting the motion; if they did, all summary judgments would be reversed.[71]

  If summary judgment is granted in response to both a no-evidence and a traditional motion for summary judgment, the court of appeals reviews the order in two steps. First, the court reviews the order under the no-evidence standard of review,[72] to determine whether the non-movant presented a scintilla of evidence to raise a fact issue on each challenged element.[73] If the non-movant survives review under that standard, then the reviewing court reviews the order based on the traditional motion under the de novo standard of review.[74] One court has explained that when both parties have presented evidence in the context of a hybrid motion, the differing burdens of proof are immaterial to appellate review, because the only issue is whether a fact issue exists—that is, whether there is more than a scintilla of probative evidence.[75]

Likewise, when the parties have filed cross-motions for summary judgment, and the trial court grants one motion and denies the other, an appellate court will review all the evidence and decide all the questions, granting the judgment the trial court should have rendered.[76]

An appellate court's review is generally limited to the grounds raised in the motion filed in the trial court; it is reversible error to affirm a summary judgment on a ground not expressly raised in the motion.[77] However, a trial court's error in ruling on an unspecified ground may be harmless, and thus not warrant reversal, if the omitted ground it precluded as a matter of law by other grounds raised in the case.[78] This situation may arise, for example, when conclusive evidence that was presented to the trial court negates a cause of action that was not challenged by the summary-judgment motion.[79]

One aspect of a summary-judgment ruling not reviewed de novo is the trial court's decision to exclude or admit summary-judgment evidence, which is reviewed like other evidentiary rulings for an abuse of discretion.[80]

2-2:2.7 Determination of Whether Expert Testimony Is Required to Establish Standard of Care in a Negligence Case

One of the questions a trial court must determine is the quality and quantum of evidence necessary to establish the standard of care in a negligence case. The question whether the standard of care requires expert testimony is a question of law that is reviewed de novo.[81]

2-2:2.8 Conflicts of Law/Choice of Law

The trial court's determination of which state's law applies to the resolution of a dispute is a question of law, which is reviewed de novo on appeal.[82] The scope of review includes the entire record, which is reviewed in light of the principles stated in the Restatement (Second) of Conflict of Laws to determine which state has the most significant relationship to the transaction at issue or the controversy to be resolved.[83]

2-2:2.9 Collateral Estoppel and Res Judicata

Whether retrial of an entire lawsuit or an issue is precluded under the collateral estoppel or res judicata doctrines is a question of law that is reviewed de novo on appeal.[84]

2-2:2.10 Jury-Charge Issues

Some jury charge issues are reviewed de novo, while others are reviewed for abuse of discretion. The following are examples of legal rulings related to a jury charge, which are reviewed de novo.

- *Definitions.* When the content of a trial court's definition in a jury charge is challenged as legally incorrect, the standard of review is de novo.[85]
- *Submission of controlling issues.* Whether the charge submits the proper controlling issues in the case, in terms of theories of recovery or defense, is a question of law, which is reviewed de novo on appeal.[86]
- *Challenges to jury findings.* When determining whether jury findings irreconcilably conflict, appellate courts apply a de novo standard of review.[87] Determining whether jury findings may be reconciled so that they do not conflict is also a question of law subject to de novo review.[88] A trial court's decision to disregard a jury finding because a legal principle prevents a party from prevailing on its claim or defense is reviewed de novo by the appellate court, as well.[89]

2-2:2.11 Review of a Directed Verdict or Judgment Notwithstanding the Verdict (JNOV)

JNOVs and directed verdicts may be based on evidentiary grounds, and in that case are reviewed under sufficiency-of-the-evidence standards of review.[90] But a JNOV or directed verdict also may be granted because a legal principle precludes recovery. When those orders are based on a question of law, they are reviewed de novo on appeal.[91]

2-2:2.12 Conclusions of Law Issued After a Bench Trial

An appellate court reviews a trial court's conclusions of law issued after a bench trial de novo and upholds them if the judgment can be sustained on any legal theory supported by the evidence.[92] Because conclusions of law resolve legal issues, they may not be challenged for factual sufficiency, but the appellate court's de novo review encompasses the trial court's legal conclusions drawn from the facts.[93]

2-2:2-13 Determining Whether a Claim Is a Health Care Liability Claim

A court must construe the Texas Medical Liability Act[94] to determine whether a claim is a health care liability claim subject to the Act.[95] Accordingly, the standard of review is de novo.[96] It has been held that "[t]he breadth of the statute's text essentially creates a presumption that a claim is [a health care liability claim] if it is against a physician or health care provider and is based on facts implicating the defendant's conduct during the course of a patient's care, treatment, or confinement. But the presumption is necessarily rebuttable."[97]

The standard of review in determining whether a claim based on the violation of safety standards constitutes a health care liability claim is slightly different. While still a matter of statutory interpretation subject to de novo review, the court must determine whether the safety standards at issue "have a substantive relationship with the providing of medical or health care."[98] "The pivotal issue in a safety standards-based claim is whether the standards on which the claim is based implicate the defendant's duties as a health care provider, including its duties to provide for patient safety."[99] Because the line between safety standards–based claims that are health care liability claims and those that are not is not always clear, the Court created a non-exclusive set of considerations for making that decision:

1. Did the alleged negligence of the defendant occur in the course of the defendant's performing tasks with the purpose of protecting patients from harm;
2. Did the injuries occur in a place where patients might be during the time they were receiving care, so that the obligation of the provider to protect persons who require special, medical care was implicated;
3. At the time of the injury was the claimant in the process of seeking or receiving health care;
4. At the time of the injury was the claimant providing or assisting in providing health care;
5. Is the alleged negligence based on safety standards arising from professional duties owed by the health care provider;
6. If an instrumentality was involved in the defendant's alleged negligence, was it a type used in providing health care; or
7. Did the alleged negligence occur in the course of the defendant's taking action or failing to take action necessary to comply with safety-related requirements set for health care providers by governmental or accrediting agencies?[100]

2-3 Abuse-of-Discretion Standard of Review

2-3:1 Scope and Standards

At the opposite end of the spectrum from the de novo standard of review is the abuse-of-discretion standard of review. This standard is difficult to apply because it is amorphous. Generally speaking, the abuse-of-discretion standard applies when the trial judge or jury was better suited to make the decision being challenged. One example is judging the credibility of a witness; because the jury and trial judge observed the witnesses first-hand, their credibility determinations are not second-guessed by an appellate court.

The abuse-of-discretion standard also applies in situations that require the flexibility of the trial court, such as matters of pre-trial and trial administration, the scope of examination of a witness, and submission of the charge to a jury.

Neither the scope nor the standard of abuse-of-discretion review can be simply stated. "Every abuse-of-discretion review is not identical because 'a trial judge's discretion may be applied to scores of situations and in many different ways.'"[101] The trial court's discretion is generally reviewed under a totality of the circumstances test which "presumes a multitude of potential factors and a balancing of evidence on either side."[102]

The test for abuse of discretion is whether the trial court acted without reference to guiding rules and principles or its action was arbitrary or unreasonable.[103] The question on appeal is not whether the court of appeals would have reached the same result or whether it agrees with the trial court's ruling.[104] Nor is a reasonable error in judgment by the trial court an abuse of discretion.[105]

A trial court has no discretion in determining the applicable law or applying the law to the facts.[106] "[A] clear failure by the trial court to analyze or apply the law correctly will constitute an abuse of discretion."[107] In other words, an abuse of discretion may be established as a matter of law in this situation.

The abuse-of-discretion standard of review is complicated by the fact that it may overlap with other standards. As noted above, there are times when a trial court's ruling will depend on both fact findings and the application of law to the found facts. A trial court abuses its discretion when its ultimate determination turns on findings of fact that were not supported by legally or factually sufficient evidence.[108]

When evidence of a substantive and probative character supports the decision, there is no abuse of discretion.[109] "[I]t is only when the evidence is such that the trial court could have made but one decision, yet made another, that . . . the trial court abused its discretion."[110] Likewise, "[w]here there are two permissible views of the evidence, the factfinder's choice between them cannot be clearly erroneous."[111] Put another way, "to find an abuse of discretion when factual matters are in dispute, the reviewing court must conclude that the facts and circumstances of the case extinguish any discretion in the matter."[112]

2-3:1.1 When Does the Standard Apply?

Conceptually, the abuse-of-discretion standard of review applies in the following circumstances:

(1) when a trial court attempts to exercise power that it does not legally possess;

(2) when a trial court declines to exercise power vested in it by law when the circumstances require that it be exercised;

(3) when a trial court exercises discretion without sufficient information upon which a rational decision may be based; and

(4) when a trial court makes an error of law by:

  (i) making a choice that is not within the range of choices the law permits;

  (ii) arriving at a choice in violation of an applicable legal rule or principle; or

  (iii) making a choice that is unreasonable under the law given the factual context.[113]

If a case falls into one of these categories, the abuse-of-discretion standard of review will apply on appeal.

A final consideration to keep in mind is that a trial court's clear abuse of discretion may be reviewed by mandamus if there is "no adequate remedy at law," meaning that the error cannot be adequately corrected by direct appeal. That general proposition applies to many of the rulings discussed below.[114]

2-3:2 Pre-Trial Rulings Reviewed for Abuse of Discretion

The abuse-of-discretion standard of review applies to many matters that arise before trial. The following are some examples.

2-3:2.1 Venue

A trial court's decision whether to enforce a mandatory venue statute is reviewed for abuse of discretion.[115]

2-3:2.2 Scheduling the Docket

A trial court has wide latitude in establishing a schedule for its docket and enforcing that schedule through orders, including orders of dismissal. Orders in those contexts are reviewed for abuse of discretion.[116] An appellate court may not arbitrarily interfere with that schedule.[117]

2-3:2.3 Pleading Matters

Various rulings regarding pleading issues are reviewed for abuse of discretion.

- *Forum non conveniens.* A trial court has discretion in ruling on a motion to dismiss for forum non conveniens, but must take guiding principles into account.[118]
- *Special exceptions.* A trial court may dismiss a case if the challenged party fails to amend his pleading to cure a defect pointed out in special exceptions.[119] Dismissal on these grounds is reviewed for abuse of discretion.[120] In conducting its review, the appellate court construes the challenged pleading liberally, accepting all of its allegations as true.[121] However, if a case is dismissed on special exceptions because it fails to state a cause of action, that legal conclusion is reviewed de novo.[122]
- *Severance.* Under Rule 41, a trial court may sever claims so that they are tried separately.[123] A trial court's order of severance is reviewed for abuse of discretion.[124] That exercise of discretion will be reviewed in light of three judicial considerations: (1) the controversy includes more than one cause of action, (2) the severed claim could be asserted in an independent lawsuit, and (3) the claims are not so interwoven as to involve the same facts and issues.[125]
- *Consolidation.* A trial court has broad discretion to consolidate cases that involve common issues of law or fact.[126] An order to consolidate is reviewed for abuse of discretion within the confines of several relevant principles: (1) the actions relate to substantially the same transaction, occurrence, subject matter, or question, (2) the same evidence will be material, relevant, and admissible in each case, and (3) no party will be prejudiced, or at least the prejudice is balanced by considerations of judicial economy and convenience.[127]
- *Joinder.* Trial courts have broad discretion under regarding the joinder of parties because there is no standard of formula for determining whether a person falls under Texas Rule of Civil Procedure 39.[128] Appellate courts do not disturb joinder rulings except for an abuse of discretion.[129]
- *Intervention.* Although a party has a right to intervene in a case,[130] the trial court has broad discretion to strike the intervention.[131] On review, the appellate court will determine whether that discretion was abused by considering whether (1) the intervenor meets the requirements of Rule 60, (2) the intervention will not excessively complicate the case with new issues, and (3) the intervention is essential to protecting the intervenor's interests.[132]
- *Interpleader.* When an innocent party has genuine doubts as to which of two parties is entitled to property in his possession, it may file an interpleader.[133] The trial court's decision to allow the interpleader is reviewed for abuse of discretion with the caveat that every reasonable doubt is to be resolved in favor of the stakeholder's right to interplead.[134]

- *Jury demand.* Because the right to a trial by jury is constitutionally protected, trial courts have limited discretion to remove a case from the jury docket.[135] A court has no discretion to refuse a jury trial when a party has timely requested it and paid the jury fee.[136] That denial is harmful error if the case requires the resolution of a material fact issue.[137] Even when a party has not timely requested a jury and paid the fee, trial courts are warned that a jury trial should be permitted if it will not interfere with the court's docket, delay trial, or prejudice the opposing party.[138]

2-3:2.4 Official-Immunity Defense

Official immunity may be asserted by a governmental employee as an affirmative defense against personal liability.[139] The defense helps preserve the sovereign-immunity defense of the governmental employer.[140] The defense is available for the employee's "good-faith performance of discretionary duties within the scope of the employee's authority."[141] The good-faith standard is analogous to an abuse-of-discretion standard: It protects "all but the plainly incompetent or those who knowingly violate the law."[142] The test is whether evidence establishes that "a reasonably prudent officer, under the same or similar circumstances, could have believed the need for the officer's actions outweighed a clear risk of harm to the public from those actions."[143]

2-3:2.5 Discovery Rulings

Evidence is presumed discoverable under Texas law to further the policy that cases be resolved "by what the facts reveal, not by what facts are concealed."[144] A trial court's rulings on discovery disputes are reviewed for abuse of discretion.[145] Discovery rulings subject to this standard of review include the following:

- *Protective orders.* A trial court's ruling on protective orders, which balance the public's interest in open court proceedings against a litigant's desire for privacy, is reviewed for abuse of discretion.[146]

- *Admissions.* A trial court's decision to allow a party to withdraw or amend answers to a request for admissions is reviewed for abuse of discretion.[147] The appellate court will review the trial court's exercise of discretion in light of the following requirements: (1) proof of good cause for the change, (2) lack of undue prejudice to the opponent, and (3) serving legitimate discovery purposes.[148]

- *Late filing.* A trial court's finding of good cause for the late filing of discovery responses is reviewed for abuse of discretion.[149] But as a matter of law, inadvertence of counsel alone is not sufficient to support that finding.[150]

- *Supplementing discovery.* Even though a party timely and completely responds to discovery requests, it remains under an obligation to amend or supplement responses when new information becomes available.[151] When a party fails to supplement in a reasonably prompt manner, the trial court may exclude the evidence unless the supplementing party shows good cause for failing to timely supplement or that the opposing party will not be unduly surprised or prejudiced.[152] These determinations by the trial court are reviewed for abuse of discretion.[153] If evidence that was not timely produced is admitted over objection, the objecting party must prove both that its admission was erroneous under the above-stated standard and that it was harmful.[154] The court of appeals must consider the entire record to decide that issue.[155]

- *Orders compelling production or other discovery.* A trial court's order compelling discovery is reviewed for abuse of discretion.[156] Compelling overly broad discovery, or discovery not permitted by the Rules, is an abuse of discretion as a matter of law.[157] Mandamus relief may be available to remedy that kind of order, when a direct appeal would be inadequate.[158]

- *Privilege.* A trial court's ruling that a privilege has been waived is reviewed for abuse of discretion.[159] Similarly, a trial court's ruling on the production of trade secrets is reviewed for abuse of discretion.[160] A trial court's refusal to review documents in camera, when such a review is needed to decide a privilege question, is an abuse of discretion as a matter of law.[161]

2-3:2.6 Sanctions Rulings

Sanctions may be awarded under several sources of law, including Rules 13 and 215 of the Texas Rules of Civil Procedure, Chapters 9 and 10 of the Texas Civil Practice and Remedies Code, and the court's inherent power to sanction bad-faith conduct that interferes with a core function of the court. Generally, sanctions awards are reviewed for abuse of discretion in light of the purposes for which sanctions are permitted: (1) to secure compliance with discovery rules and orders, (2) to deter violations of the discovery rules, and (3) to punish parties that violate the rules.[162] A trial court abuses its discretion if its sanctions order is arbitrary or unreasonable because it was made without reference to guiding rules and principles, but not when some evidence supports its decision.[163]

However, a sanctions award that violates constitutional due-process requirements will never withstand appellate scrutiny because trial courts lack discretion to determine what the law is or to apply the law to the facts.[164] To comply with due process, a sanctions order must be just and may not be excessive.[165] "[A] trial court may not impose a sanction that is more severe than necessary to satisfy its legitimate purpose."[166]

Because the standards for imposing sanctions differ slightly depending upon the source of law, so does the scope of review.

- *Pre-trial discovery sanctions under Civil Procedure Rule 215.* The appellate court reviews pre-trial discovery sanctions to determine whether its ruling was arbitrary and capricious, in light of all the facts before the trial court at the time it ruled.[167] All but the most severe discovery sanctions under Rule 215 are not appealable until the trial court renders final judgment, and the usual preservation rules apply.[168]

- *Sanctions under Civil Procedure Rule 13.* Sanctions under Rule 13 are appropriate when filed papers were (a) groundless and (b) either brought in bad faith or brought to harass.[169] The trial court must issue an order stating the particulars of the good cause it found to impose sanctions.[170] Rule 13 sanctions are reviewed for abuse of discretion.[171] The appellate court will consider the record before the trial court at the time it ruled to determine whether the sanction is just because it was imposed against the true offender, tailored to cure any prejudice resulting from the improper conduct, and no more severe than necessary.[172] The trial court's findings and its good-cause basis for sanctions must have been made after notice and hearing,[173] and must reflect that the challenged party consciously committed a wrong for a dishonest, malicious, or discriminatory purpose.[174] Sanctions may be reversed on appeal for failure to comply with either the procedural or the substantive requirements.[175] The scope of review of Rule 13 sanctions is limited by the presumption that pleadings and papers are filed in good faith, which the movant has the burden of overcoming.[176]

- *Sanctions under Chapters 9 and 10 of the Texas Civil Practice and Remedies Code.* Sanctions can be imposed under Chapters 9 and 10 when the challenged filing lacks a reasonable basis in fact or law, or was filed for an improper purpose. These sanctions are reviewed for abuse of discretion.[177] The appellate court will review the entire record to determine whether the sanction is just because there is a direct nexus between the improper conduct and the sanction imposed.[178] Because all papers are presumed to be filed in good faith, the sufficiency of the movant's evidence to overcome that presumption factors into this abuse-of-discretion review.[179] The trial court must issue an order describing the conduct it found to have violated the requirements of the chapter and the bases for imposing sanctions.[180] A trial court abuses its discretion when it fails to comply with these requirements.[181]

- *Death-penalty sanctions.* A trial court's discretion to enter death penalty sanctions is restricted by the requirement that the sanction must be just: (1) there must be a direct connection between the offensive conduct and the sanction, and (2) the sanction may not be excessive.[182] The appellate court will review the trial court's order, and the existing facts and circumstances, for compliance with those standards.[183]

- *Disqualification of counsel.* An order disqualifying counsel is reviewed for abuse of discretion,[184] usually under the mandamus standard.[185] Because disqualification is such a severe remedy, the trial court must adhere to an exacting standard to ensure that a motion to disqualify is not a dilatory tactic.[186] Logically, this requires the court to consider the motion to disqualify, within the context of the larger proceeding, more stringently than most abuse-of-discretion reviews.

  Disqualification may be sought when an attorney acquires access to an opponent's privileged materials outside the normal course of discovery. In such a case, the trial court must consider all the facts and circumstances, by application of a multi-factor test, to determine whether disqualification is required to ensure fairness.[187] As with all misapplications of law, a trial court that orders disqualification based on an erroneous legal standard abuses its discretion.[188]

- *Inherent-power sanctions.* A trial court may impose sanctions under its inherent power when a party acts in bad faith and abuses the judicial process by interfering with a core function of the court.[189] A trial court should revert to its inherent power to sanction only when the applicable rules do not cover the conduct at issue.[190] And, the trial court is required to consider evidence and make factual findings in support of sanctions issued under its inherent power.[191] These sanctions are reviewed for abuse of discretion, and the failure to make the required findings automatically renders the sanction an abuse of discretion.[192]

2-3:2.7 Grant or Denial of Temporary Injunction

An appellate court's review of a trial court's denial of a temporary injunction "is strictly limited to a determination of whether there has been a clear abuse of discretion by the trial court in determining whether the applicant is entitled to a preservation of the status quo pending trial on the merits."[193] A trial court's grant of a temporary injunction is also reviewed for abuse of discretion.[194] The appellate court will review the temporary injunction record created in the trial court.[195] The scope of review does not permit a review of the merits of the underlying case.[196] The trial court's judgment may not be reversed unless it was "so arbitrary that it exceeded the bounds of reasonable discretion."[197]

2-3:2.8 Plea in Abatement

A trial court's ruling granting or denying a plea in abatement is reviewed for abuse of discretion.[198] Under certain circumstances, such as proof that a sister court has dominant jurisdiction, the trial court's duty to grant an abatement becomes mandatory and it lacks discretion to deny that relief.[199]

2-3:2.9 Grant or Denial of Motion to Compel Arbitration

A trial court's denial of a motion to compel arbitration is reviewed for abuse of discretion.[200] Similarly, a trial court's order compelling arbitration is reviewed for an abuse of discretion.[201] The appellate court will defer to the trial court's fact-findings if supported by evidence, but will review legal conclusions de novo.[202]

The underlying question of whether a valid agreement to arbitrate exists between the parties is reviewed de novo.[203] Similarly, the question of to whether an arbitration agreement is enforceable is subject to de novo review.[204] Mandamus will issue to correct a trial court's abuse of discretion in failing to stay litigation and compel arbitration.[205]

2-3:2.10 Class Certification and Related Rulings

A trial court's ruling on class action certification is reviewed for abuse of discretion, but not all presumptions are indulged in favor of its order.[206] Instead, the record must reflect that the trial court conducted a rigorous analysis and actual conformance with the applicable rules is indispensable.[207]

The trial court's ruling on opt-out requests is reviewed for abuse of discretion.[208]

A trial court's approval of a class-action settlement agreement is also reviewed under the abuse-of-discretion standard.[209] The trial court's exercise of discretion will be viewed from the context of the many substantive and procedural considerations that establish the settlement to be in the best interests of the class.[210]

2-3:2.11 Adequacy of Expert Report in Health Care Liability Case

The expert report required to support a health care liability claim must meet specific requirements, or it is subject to being stricken.[211] Determining the adequacy of that report and whether it should be stricken are matters within the trial court's discretion.[212] It will defer to the trial court's factual determinations if they are supported by evidence, but the trial court's legal determinations are reviewed de novo.[213] The appellate court's scope of review is limited by the statutory requirements and purposes of the Texas Medical Liability Act, which mandate sustaining an objection if the report does not reflect an objective, good faith effort to comply with the statutory requirements.[214] A bare conclusion is not sufficient—the expert must set out the applicable facts and explain how and why a breach of duty caused the claimed injury.[215] The reviewing court looks no further than the report itself to make this determination.[216]

2-3:2.12 Leave to Cure Deficient Expert Report in Health Care Liability Case

When an expert report is submitted to prove a health care liability claim, but it is deficient, the trial court may grant an extension to cure the deficiency.[217] An extension should be granted when the report can be cured to serve the purpose of eliminating frivolous claims and preserving meritorious ones.[218] An appellate court will consider the adequacy of any report filed by the plaintiff with its motion for leave to cure in reviewing the trial court's exercise of discretion.[219]

2-3:2.13 Dismissal of Lawsuit for Want of Prosecution

When a trial court dismisses a case for want of prosecution, the appellate court reviews that ruling for abuse of discretion.[220] In addition to the grounds stated in Texas Rule of Civil Procedure 165a, a trial court may also exercise its inherent power to dismiss a case that has not been prosecuted with reasonable diligence.[221] In those cases, the court may review the entire history of the case, as well as the sufficiency of any stated reasons for the delay.[222] The appellate court may also consider whether the trial court complied with the rules, including providing clear notice before entering an order of dismissal.[223]

2-3:2.14 Default Judgments

When a trial court has granted a default judgment, appellate review determines whether the failure to grant a motion for new trial (the necessary preservation step) was an abuse of discretion.[224]

The trial court's discretion to deny a motion for new trial following a default judgment is bound by the factors set forth in *Craddock v. Sunshine Bus Lines, Inc.*[225] Failure to grant a new trial is an abuse of discretion if the defendant shows: (1) the failure to answer was not intentional or the result of conscious indifference, (2) the defendant has a meritorious defense which is demonstrated in the new trial motion, and (3) granting the motion will not cause delay or otherwise prejudice the plaintiff.[226] The scope of review is two-fold. The first element is satisfied if the defendant's factual assertions negate conscious indifference and are not controverted.[227] Determining whether the defendant established the second factor requires a review of the entire record without regard to whether the facts are controverted—in other words, assuming the truth of defendants' allegations.[228]

2-3:2.15 Rulings Incident to a Summary-Judgment Motion

A trial court's rulings preceding a grant of summary judgment, such as whether to grant leave to file a late response or whether to grant a continuance of the motion, are reviewed for abuse of discretion.[229] The scope of review requires the appellate court to consider the entire record to ensure that the movant presented evidence of good cause to the trial court.[230]

A trial court's rulings on objections to summary-judgment evidence are also reviewed for abuse of discretion.[231] This includes a trial court's ruling whether an affidavit supporting or opposing a motion for summary judgment complies with Texas Rule of Civil Procedure 166a(f).[232]

2-3:2.16 Ruling on a Motion for a Trial Continuance

A trial court's ruling on a motion for continuance is reviewed for abuse of discretion.[233] When the motion is based on the unavailability of a witness, a trial court does not abuse its discretion if it denies the motion for continuance because it does not meet the requirements of Rule 252.[234] Continuances may also be granted, within the trial court's discretion, when counsel is unavailable or serving in the legislature.[235]

2-3:2.17 Recusal or Disqualification of the Judge

Texas Rule of Civil Procedure 18a(j) specifies the appellate standard of review for recusal orders. An order denying a motion to recuse is reviewable only for abuse of discretion following a final judgment.[236] An order granting a motion to recuse is not reviewable.[237]

An order granting or denying a motion to disqualify may be reviewed by mandamus and on appeal.[238] The 2011 amendments to the Rule do not provide a standard of review for disqualification orders. The limited authority applying this rule has used the abuse of discretion standard.[239]

2-3:2.18 Sealing Orders

Because court records are presumptively open and public, an order sealing the record must strictly comply with the Rules.[240] Sealing orders are subject to immediate interlocutory appeal for abuse-of-discretion review, cabined by the Rule's requirements.[241]

2-3:3 Trial Rulings Reviewed for Abuse of Discretion

Many of the trial court's rulings during trial are reviewed for abuse of discretion. Examples of these orders are described below.

2-3:3.1 Motion in Limine

A motion in limine alerts the court to evidentiary objections which may be asserted during trial, and seeks a preliminary ruling to avoid the risk that the jury will hear inadmissible evidence.[242] Obtaining a ruling on a motion in limine does not usually preserve error for appeal.[243] But the violation of a limine order may entitle the opposing party to relief ranging from an instruction to disregard, sanctions, and even mistrial. On appeal, the trial remedy is reviewed under an abuse-of-discretion standard because each of the available remedies falls within a trial court's discretion.

2-3:3.2 Judicial Notice

A trial court may take judicial notice of a variety of matters upon proper request and supported by the relevant information.[244] The decision to take judicial notice is largely, but not entirely, left to the discretion of the trial court.[245] A trial court's exercise of discretion to take judicial notice of an adjudicative fact is reviewed for proof that the fact was "verifiably certain."[246] But when a party has properly requested that the trial court take judicial notice of the law of another state, and provided that law, the trial court has no discretion to refuse to do so.[247] If a party fails to provide sufficient evidence, a trial court's decision not to take judicial notice is reviewed for abuse of discretion.[248]

This issue often arises in connection with attorney fees. When a breach-of-contract case is tried to the bench, the trial court may take judicial notice of (1) the content of the case file, to determine how much work was involved, and (2) the customary fee charged for similar work.[249] However, a trial court may not rely on judicial notice to award fees in a declaratory judgment case.[250]

2-3:3.3 Seating the Jury

A trial court's rulings regarding jury strikes are typically reviewed for abuse of discretion.

- *Peremptory challenges.* The abuse-of-discretion standard applies to challenges asserting that peremptory strikes were used for racially discriminatory purposes.[251] Orders re-aligning the parties for the allocation of peremptory strikes are also reviewed for abuse of discretion.[252]
- *Voir Dire.* The trial court's exclusion of questions during voir dire is reviewed for abuse of discretion.[253] The reviewing court will determine whether the court precluded questions needed to determine whether proper grounds existed for a for-cause challenge or whether intelligent grounds for a peremptory strike existed.[254]
- *Rulings on for-cause challenges.* A trial court's decision to allow a for-cause challenge on the ground that a venire member is partial is reviewed for abuse of discretion. "Because trial judges are present in the courtroom and are in the best position to evaluate the sincerity and attitude of individual panel members, they are given wide latitude in both conducting voir dire proceedings and in determining whether a panel member is impermissibly partial."[255]

2-3:3.4 Invoking the Rule

Invoking "the Rule" sequesters fact witnesses during trial.[256] The Rule is mandatory once invoked, except that a trial court has broad discretion to determine what persons' presence is "essential to the presentation of the cause."[257] Likewise, the trial court has discretion to exclude or admit the testimony of a witness who has violated the Rule.[258]

2-3:3.5 Opening Statements

Trial courts have wide latitude in allowing or limiting opening statements, and their orders in that regard are reviewed for abuse of discretion.[259]

2-3:3.6 Admission of Evidence

The admission of evidence is a matter committed to the trial court's discretion.[260] An appellate court may not reverse an evidentiary ruling if there is any legitimate basis for it.[261] Several categories of evidence are discussed below.

- *Expert testimony.* A ruling that expert testimony satisfies, or does not satisfy, the reliability standards for its admission is reviewed for abuse of discretion.[262] The trial court's discretion is limited by the requirements that it rigorously examine (1) the validity of the facts and assumptions underlying the opinion, (2) the principles, research, and methodology supporting the expert's conclusions, and (3) the manner in which the principles and methodologies are applied to the facts and assumptions.[263] The trial court must also determine that each part of an expert's opinion is reliable before exercising its discretion to admit it.[264] The admission of expert testimony may also be challenged on no-evidence grounds, in which case the ruling is subject to the legal-sufficiency standard of review.[265]
- *Hearsay and other rulings governed by the Rules of Evidence.* A trial court's admission of testimony that is claimed to be hearsay or to be otherwise excluded by the Rules of Evidence is reviewed for abuse of discretion.[266]
- *Orders regarding evidence not produced in discovery.* Under Texas Rule of Civil Procedure 193.6, the sanction of excluding evidence at trial that was not produced in discovery is automatic. However, the evidence need not be excluded if the proponent shows (1) good cause for the failure to produce it, (2) lack of unfair surprise to the opponent, or (3) lack of prejudice to the opponent.[267] Determining whether the exception to automatic exclusion has been proved is within the trial court's discretion and reviewed for abuse.[268]

2-3:3.7 Mistrial

The trial court has discretion to grant a mistrial for trial misconduct, the admission of prejudicial evidence, or other reasons.[269] Its exercise of discretion is reviewed for abuse.

2-3:3.8 Jury Charge

Some aspects of jury charge practice are reviewed for abuse of discretion; others are reviewed de novo.[270] The following are examples of when the abuse-of-discretion standard applies:

- *The decision to submit or refuse an instruction.* The decision to submit or refuse an instruction on an issue is reviewed for abuse of discretion.[271] "A trial court abuses its discretion when it submits a jury question that is neither supported by the pleadings nor tried by consent."[272] The considerations relevant to appellate review of this exercise of discretion are whether the instruction (1) assists the jury, (2) accurately states the law, and (3) is supported by pleadings and evidence.[273] Although the latter two facts are law-based, the ultimate question with regard to an issue supported by law, pleading, and evidence is "whether the request was reasonably necessary to enable the jury to render a proper verdict."[274] The refusal to submit an instruction is error only if the omission "probably caused the rendition of an improper judgment."[275]

- *Broad-form submission.* Generally speaking, a trial court's decision to submit the jury charge in broad form under Rule 277 of the Texas Rules of Civil Procedure is reviewed for abuse of discretion.[276] But the submission of separate issues may be required as a matter of law under the presumed harm analysis of the *Casteel*[277] line of cases.[278]

- *Jury deliberation.* Matters including scheduling and sequestering of a jury during its deliberations are committed to the trial court's discretion and reviewed for abuse.[279] The trial court has discretion in answering questions the jury asks during deliberations.[280] Trial court decisions to submit a supplemental charge or a "dynamite charge" urging the jury to reach a verdict are reviewed for abuse of discretion.[281]

- *Jury misconduct.* Determining whether jury misconduct occurred is usually a question of fact that is binding on reviewing courts and reviewed only for clear abuse of discretion.[282] If the appellate issue is not whether the challenged conduct occurred, but instead, whether conduct that admittedly occurred was misconduct, then the question is likely a legal issue reviewed de novo.[283] To prevail on this theory on appeal, a party must overcome the presumption that no misconduct occurred with proof that (1) the misconduct occurred (generally in the form of a juror affidavit), (2) it was material, and (3) based on the entire record, it probably resulted in harm.[284]

2-3:4 Miscellaneous Trial Court Determinations

2-3:4.1 Attorney Fees Awarded Under the Declaratory Judgments Act

A trial court has discretion to award attorney fees under the Declaratory Judgments Act when the fees are both reasonable and necessary and equitable or just.[285] Whether such fees are reasonable and necessary is a factual matter governed by both the sufficiency standards of review[286] and the abuse-of-discretion standard because a trial court may abuse its discretion by awarding fees when there is insufficient evidence that they were reasonable or necessary.[287] The equity and justness of these awards is reviewed for abuse of discretion.[288]

2-3:4.2 Family Law Orders and Judgments

Several trial court determinations in the family law context are reviewed for abuse of discretion. In the family-law context, legal- and factual-sufficiency challenges[289] are not independent grounds of error, but are relevant to the review of a trial court's exercise of discretion.[290] "To determine whether the trial court abused its discretion because the evidence is legally or factually insufficient to support the trial court's decision, [the appellate court] consider[s] whether he trial court (1) had sufficient evidence upon which to exercise its discretion and (2) erred in its application of that discretion."[291] The first prong is tested under the relevant sufficiency standard and the second prong is tested under a reasonableness standard.[292]

- *Order of child support.* A trial court's order setting the amount of child support cannot be reversed on appeal unless the complaining party demonstrates a clear abuse of discretion.[293]

- *Appointment of conservator of a child.* A trial court judgment or order appointing the conservator of a child is reviewed for abuse of discretion.[294] But the related issue of terminating parental rights is reviewed under the much more stringent clear-and-convincing evidence standard.[295]
- *Grant of an adoption.* Granting an adoption is a matter committed to the sound discretion of the trial court, which will only be overturned for abuse.[296]
- *Division of the marital estate.* A trial court is afforded broad discretion in dividing the marital property upon divorce and its division will not be disturbed absent an abuse of discretion.[297] The legal sufficiency of the evidence weighs into this determination, but is not an independent ground for reversal.[298]
- *Amount of child support.* "The determination of the amount of child support to be paid is left to the discretion of the trial court and will not be disturbed on appeal absent a clear showing of abuse of discretion."[299]

2-3:4.3 Rulings Granting a Motion for New Trial

For mandamus review of a trial court order granting a motion for new trial, the standard of review is abuse of discretion.[300]. A trial court always abuses its discretion in granting a motion for new trial if it fails to set forth a "cogent and reasonably specific explanation of the reasoning that led the court to conclude that a new trial was warranted."[301] That explanation must state a reason for new trial that is legally appropriate and that is tied to the specific facts and circumstances of the case, rather than stating merely pro forma language.[302] The reasons articulated by the trial court in a new-trial order are subject to merits-based mandamus review.[303]

New trial based on jury misconduct. A determination of whether jury misconduct occurred is often a fact-intensive inquiry committed to the sound discretion of the trial court as long as it is supported by some evidence.[304]

2-3:4.4 Re-opening the Evidence After Trial

A trial court's ruling on a motion to re-open the evidence after trial is reviewed for abuse of discretion.[305]

2-3:4.5 Petitions for Expunction

Trial court rulings on petitions for expunction, which are civil proceedings, are reviewed for abuse of discretion, unless they turn on a question of law, in which case they are reviewed de novo.[306] It is an abuse of discretion to order expunction unless the petitioner satisfies all of the requirements of Article 55.01 of the Texas Code of Criminal Procedure. "The trial court has no equitable discretion to permit expunction where it is not allowed [by statute]."[307]

2-3:4.6 Bills of Review

The standard of review of a trial court's grant of an equitable or statutory bill of review is abuse of discretion.[308]

2-3:5 "Clear" Abuse of Discretion

2-3:5.1 Mandamus

Mandamus may be available to reverse a trial court ruling that constitutes a "clear abuse of discretion," assuming that there is also no adequate remedy by direct appeal.[309] A clear abuse of discretion exists when a trial court "'reaches a decision so arbitrary and unreasonable as to amount to a clear and prejudicial error of law.'"[310] Under this standard, factual or other matters committed to the trial court's discretion cannot be disturbed unless the relator establishes that the trial court could reasonably have reached only one decision.[311] The trial court's legal determinations and application of the facts to the law are reviewed with little or no discretion.[312] There has been little analysis of the distinction between an abuse of discretion and a *clear* abuse of discretion, but the language suggests that a clear abuse of discretion is a quantitatively higher standard. A "normal" abuse of discretion may be established by showing the trial judge acted arbitrarily; a "clear" abuse of discretion requires a showing that the trial judge's act was so arbitrary as to amount to a prejudicial error of law. A clear abuse of discretion may also exist when a trial court "clearly fails to analyze the law correctly or apply the law correctly to the facts."[313]

Types of rulings that are reviewed by mandamus include discovery rulings, sanctions, disqualification of counsel,[314] and the grant of a motion for new trial. However, mandamus is an extraordinary remedy that is denied far more often than it is granted.[315]

2-3:5.2 Permanent Injunction

Permanent injunctions are also reviewed for clear abuse of discretion.[316] Fact findings in support of the permanent injunction are reviewed under the same sufficiency standards that apply to other factual determinations, which are discussed in the next section of this chapter.[317]

2-4 Sufficiency of the Evidence Standard of Review

There are three different standards for reviewing fact findings. They apply when facts are found by a jury in its verdict or by a trial court in formal Findings of Fact.[318] They also apply to implied findings of fact when the appellate record contains the clerk's and reporter's records.[319]

- The legal-sufficiency standard applies to a challenge asserting that no evidence supports a finding or that the finding was conclusively established.
- The factual-sufficiency standard applies to a challenge asserting that a finding is against the great weight and preponderance of the evidence.
- The clear-and-convincing evidence standard of review applies in limited circumstances, primarily when required by statute.

2-4:1 Legal-Sufficiency Standard of Review

The same legal-sufficiency standard of review applies to any ruling that takes an issue away from the trier of fact and decides it as a matter of law, including summary judgments, directed verdicts, JNOVs, and appellate no-evidence challenges.[320] Although the standard is the same, the evidence is sometimes viewed in the light most favorable to the winner (i.e., to the verdict or fact-finding), and sometimes in the light most favorable to the loser (i.e., the party who lost a motion for summary-judgment, directed verdict, or JNOV).[321]

2-4:1.1 Rationale

The most-cited law review article in Texas legal history explained the rationale behind the legal-sufficiency standard more than 50 years ago:

> "No evidence" points must, and may only, be sustained when the record discloses one of the following situations: (a) a complete absence of evidence of a vital fact; (b) the court is barred by rules of law or of evidence from giving weight to the only evidence offered to prove a vital fact; (c) the evidence offered to prove a vital fact is no more than a mere scintilla; (d) the evidence establishes conclusively the opposite of the vital fact.[322]

The effect of these standards is this:

> When the evidence offered to prove a vital fact is so weak as to do no more than create a mere surmise or suspicion of its existence, the evidence is no more than a scintilla and, in legal effect, is no evidence.[323]

By contrast, the "scintilla" standard is satisfied when the evidence "rises to a level that would enable reasonable and fair-minded people to differ in their conclusions."[324]

If the appellant bore the burden of proof at trial, it must show on appeal that the fact it is advocating was conclusively established in its favor; conversely, if the appellant did not have the burden of proof at trial, it must establish on appeal that no evidence supports the jury's finding against it.[325] The same standards apply to the legal-sufficiency review of findings of fact by the trial court.[326] The complaint in that case must challenge specific findings; otherwise, it is not justiciable and the fact findings are binding on appeal.[327]

2-4:1.2 Scope of Legal-Sufficiency Review

The Texas Supreme Court's opinion in *City of Keller v. Wilson*[328] defines the legal-sufficiency standard and scope of review. The Court was asked to determine whether a court conducting a legal-sufficiency review was to review all the evidence or only that portion supporting the judgment, since previous authorities were split on that issue. The Court concluded that both scopes of review ultimately arrive at the same conclusion because of exceptions requiring the consideration of certain evidence under the exclusive approach, and the disregard of certain evidence under the inclusive approach. The Court's conclusion bears repeating in full:

> Whether a court begins by reviewing all the evidence or disregarding part in a legal-sufficiency review, there can be no disagreement about where that review should end. If the evidence at trial would enable reasonable and fair-minded people to differ in their conclusions, then jurors must be allowed to do so. A

> reviewing court cannot substitute its judgment for that of the trier-of-fact, so long as the evidence falls within this zone of reasonable disagreement.
>
> Similarly, there is no disagreement about how a reviewing court should view evidence in the process of that review. Whether a reviewing court starts with all or only part of the record, the court must consider evidence in the light most favorable to the verdict, and indulge every reasonable inference that would support it. But if the evidence allows of only one inference, neither jurors nor the reviewing court may disregard it.
>
> Given these premises, it is no coincidence that the two standards should reach the same result—indeed they must. Any scope of appellate review smaller than what reasonable jurors could believe will reverse some verdicts that are perfectly reasonable; any scope of review larger than what reasonable jurors could believe will affirm some verdicts that are not.
>
> . . .
>
> The final test for legal sufficiency must always be whether the evidence at trial would enable reasonable and fair-minded people to reach the verdict under review. Whether a reviewing court begins by considering all the evidence or only the evidence supporting the verdict, legal-sufficiency review in the proper light must credit favorable evidence if reasonable jurors could, and disregard contrary evidence unless reasonable jurors could not.[329]

2-4:1.3 Evidence That May Not Be Disregarded

But the *Keller* Court provided much more detailed advice along the way. The Court's analysis was multi-faceted and focused on the various categories of evidence that a reviewing court may or may not disregard in determining whether a finding is supported by no evidence. Evidence contrary to the judgment cannot be disregarded by a reviewing court when there is no favorable evidence, the contrary evidence renders the favorable evidence incompetent, or the evidence conclusively establishes the contrary.[330] Categories of contrary evidence that may not be disregarded include:

2-4:1.3a Contextual Evidence

There are many circumstances in which the context must be considered to determine whether there is any evidence supporting a finding.

For example:

(i) an entire publication must be considered before determining whether a statement within it is defamatory;[331]

(ii) an entire contract must be considered before determining its meaning;[332]

(iii) the context, individual characteristics, and relationship must be considered in determining whether any evidence supports an intentional infliction of emotional distress finding; [333] and

(iv) evidence may not be misconstrued as supporting a verdict when it did not do so in fact.[334]

2-4:1.3b Competency Evidence

Incompetent evidence does not support a judgment, even if it was admitted without objection.[335] Thus, evidence bearing on the competency of the evidence on which a finding is based cannot be disregarded.[336] The following considerations apply to determining what evidence must be considered to determine the competency of the evidence on which a finding is based.

(i) If expert testimony is required, a reviewing court may not disregard evidence showing that a witness is not qualified to render an opinion.[337]

(ii) If an expert opinion is based on factual assumptions, evidence showing those assumptions to be false may not be disregarded by the reviewing court.[338]

(iii) Expert testimony that fails to meet reliability standards is no evidence, so a reviewing court may not disregard evidence showing that the opinion lacks a scientific basis or is otherwise unreliable.[339] As previously noted, a trial court's decision that expert testimony is reliable and thus admissible is reviewed under the abuse-of-discretion standard. However, an appellant may also argue on appeal that the unreliability of the evidence makes it legally insufficient to support a verdict.[340] It is this latter type of challenge that is subject to the legal-sufficiency standard of review. Under this standard, the appellate court will "independently consider whether the evidence at trial would enable reasonable and fair-minded jurors to reach the verdict."[341] The scope of review includes the entire record, including evidence that might tend to show the opinion is incompetent or unreliable.[342]

2-4:1.3c Circumstantial Evidence

When a claim or defense is supported only by meager circumstantial evidence, it does not rise above a scintilla; if the fact-finder has to guess whether a vital fact exists, it is supported by no evidence.[343] Accordingly, a reviewing court must consider whether the evidence supports inferences at odds with the finding as well as it supports the finding itself.[344]

2-4:1.3d Conclusive Evidence

A reviewing court may not disregard evidence that conclusively establishes the opposite of a finding or conclusively negates the finding.[345]

(i) Jurors are not free to reach a verdict at odds with undisputed evidence that allows only one logical inference.[346] But if jurors can disbelieve the evidence, it is not undisputed.[347]

(ii) Evidence often becomes conclusive when it concerns a physical fact that cannot be denied. For example, no evidence supports a jury's verdict of paternity when a blood test conclusively disproves it.[348] This determination is very fact-specific.[349] It essentially means that "proper review prevents jurors from substituting their opinions for undisputed truth."[350]

2-4:1.3e Standards Higher Than a Preponderance

If the plaintiff is required to prove its case by more than a preponderance of the evidence, as in parental-termination, defamation, and punitive damages cases, evidence contrary to the verdict may not be disregarded by the reviewing court.[351]

2-4:1.3f Consciousness Evidence

Evidence contrary to a finding may not be disregarded by a reviewing court when the finding involves a party's knowledge, intent, or motive.[352] This consideration applies in at least the following circumstances:

(i) gross-negligence findings, where the review must encompass all the surrounding facts and circumstances;[353]

(ii) insurance bad-faith cases, where the review must consider evidence that coverage was unclear as well as evidence that it was clear;[354]

(iii) discrimination cases, where discharged employees must affirmatively show that termination was a pretext;[355]

(iv) sovereign-immunity cases, where courts must consider evidence that the government employee acted appropriately along with evidence that she should have acted differently;[356] and

(v) discovery-rule cases where a party's knowledge must be considered in determining whether the statute of limitations is tolled.[357]

2-4:1.4 Evidence That Must Be Disregarded

On the other hand, evidence contrary to a finding must be disregarded by a reviewing court in a variety of contexts. The overarching rule is this: "whenever reasonable jurors could decide what testimony to discard, a reviewing court must assume they did so in favor of their verdict, and disregard it in the course of legal sufficiency review."[358] Examples of situations in which the reviewing court must disregard evidence are also detailed in the Supreme Court's *City of Keller* opinion:

2-4:1.4a Credibility Evidence

The fact-finder is the sole judge of the credibility of a witness and the weight given to a witness's testimony. Courts may not consider evidence that would lead them to reach a credibility determination different from that of the fact-finder.[359] Because credibility determinations are usually not express findings, the reviewing court must conclude that they were made in favor of the actual findings.[360] Jurors may disregard even uncontradicted testimony from lay or expert witnesses in many cases, and the reviewing court must assume they did so if necessary to support the finding. But the fact-finders' credibility determinations must also be reasonable—they may not disregard undisputed evidence that is "clear, positive, direct, otherwise credible, free from contradictions and inconsistencies, and could have been readily controverted."[361] So a reviewing court may consider evidence establishing or disproving those factors in determining whether the jury's credibility determinations are binding.[362]

2-4:1.4b Conflicting Evidence

The general rule is that a reviewing court must assume that the fact-finder resolved any conflicting evidence in favor of the finding and may not reach a contrary result on the basis of conflicting evidence.[363] However, it may well be up to the reviewing court to determine whether the evidence at issue actually conflicts or instead pertains to different issues.[364]

2-4:1.4c Conflicting Inferences

In general, it is the fact-finder's province to determine what inferences may be drawn from the evidence, provided that the inference is supported by evidence and not a guess.[365] Thus the reviewing court will assume inferences were made in support of the verdict unless such an inference could not have been made by a reasonable fact-finder.[366] Nonetheless, "'a jury may not reasonably infer an ultimate fact from meager circumstantial evidence which could give rise to any number of inferences, none more probable than another.'"[367]

2-4:1.5 Recent Pronouncements

Since *City of Keller*,[368] the standard and scope of review for legal sufficiency has often been stated as follows:

> In reviewing for legal sufficiency of the evidence, we consider the evidence in the light most favorable to the verdict, disregarding all contrary evidence that a reasonable jury could have disbelieved. Even though the evidence is viewed in the light most favorable to the verdict, it cannot be considered in isolated bits and pieces divorced from its surroundings; it must be viewed in its proper context with other evidence.[369]

If the appellate court reaches a conclusion contrary to a fact finding after conducting a legal-sufficiency review, it must do more than merely recite that it has reached a contrary conclusion.[370] Instead, the appellate court "should explain, with specificity, why it has substituted its judgment for that of the trial court."[371]

2-4:2 Factual-Sufficiency Standard of Review

When a party claims on appeal that the evidence is factually insufficient to support a finding, the reviewing court must weigh *all* the evidence in the record.[372] The appellate court reverses when it is "so against the great weight and preponderance of the evidence as to be clearly wrong and unjust."[373] The evidence is reviewed in a neutral light, rather than in favor of the finding.[374] Although the appellate court reviews all the evidence, it does not reweigh the evidence and may not reverse merely because it feels that a different result would be more reasonable.[375]

Although the above description states the general standard, some courts and commentators distinguish factual-sufficiency review challenges brought by parties with the burden of proof or those without the burden of proof.

- "When the party without the burden of proof at trial brings a factual sufficiency attack to reverse a finding favoring the party with the burden of proof by a preponderance of the evidence, the appealing party must establish that all the evidence, considering evidence both for and against the failure to find, is so contrary to the great weight and preponderance of the evidence as to be clearly wrong and manifestly unjust."[376]
- "When the party having the burden of proof by a preponderance of the evidence seeks to reverse, on factual-sufficiency grounds, his or her failure to secure a favorable finding, that party must show that, on consideration of all the evidence, the failure of the jury or court to find in favor of the issue is against the

great weight and preponderance of the evidence. Reversal should occur only when the great weight and preponderance of the evidence supports an affirmative answer."[377]

A court of appeals that reverses a trial court judgment on factual-sufficiency grounds must clearly recite in its opinion why the evidence was factually insufficient to support the jury's finding.[378] Even a memorandum opinion should focus on "the basic reasons why the law applied to the facts leads to the court's decision."[379] An opinion overruling a factual-sufficiency challenge need not provide such an explanation.[380]

Factual-sufficiency review is the sole domain of the intermediate appellate courts. The Texas Supreme Court may not review the factual sufficiency of the evidence to support a finding.[381] However, the Supreme Court does have the "'responsibility to ensure that the intermediate appellate courts follow applicable legal standards in making their review of the evidence.'"[382] Thus, it is not powerless to correct "a clearly erroneous review of the evidence."[383] In this context, that review is limited to ensuring that the intermediate appellate court "detailed all of the relevant evidence and clearly stated why that evidence was factually insufficient."[384] If the court of appeals did not meet that standard, the Texas Supreme Court may reverse and remand to the court of appeals for reconsideration under the correct standard.[385]

2-4:3 Clear-and-Convincing Standard of Review

Certain matters are required by statute to be proved by clear-and-convincing evidence. In response to this heightened burden of proof, a reviewing court applies an "elevated" standard of review to determine whether the fact-finder "could have formed a firm belief or conviction that its finding was true."[386] In this context, the reviewing court considers all the evidence, and looks at it in the light most favorable to the finding.[387]

The clear-and-convincing standard of review requires the appellate court:

- to assume the fact-finder resolved disputed facts in favor of the finding if it could reasonably do so;
- to disregard all evidence that a reasonable fact-finder could have disbelieved or found incredible but;
- not to disregard all evidence that does not support the finding as that could skew the analysis.[388]

The clear-and-convincing burden of proof and associated elevated standard of review apply to findings of:

2-4:3.1 Exemplary Damages

"[E]xemplary damages may be awarded only if the claimant proves by clear and convincing evidence that the harm with respect to which the claimant seeks recovery of exemplary damages results from: (1) fraud; (2) malice; or (3) gross negligence."[389] Plaintiff's burden of proving these elements by clear-and-convincing evidence may not be shifted to the defendant or satisfied by evidence of ordinary negligence, bad faith, or deceptive practices.[390] If exemplary damages are allowed by statute only when specific circumstances or a certain culpable mental state exist, the jury must find those matters by clear-and-convincing evidence.[391] The jury must be unanimous in these findings.[392]

To determine whether these requirements have been met, the reviewing court will review the entire record, much like it does in an evidentiary sufficiency review, except that "a higher quality of evidence is necessary to tip the scales."[393] The reviewing court must also ensure that the conduct supporting the award of exemplary damages is "independent and qualitatively different from" the harms compensable by actual damages.[394]

To make this determination, the court of appeals will "look at all the evidence in the light most favorable to the finding to determine whether a reasonable trier of fact could have formed a firm belief or conviction that its finding was true."[395] This requires the assumption that the fact-finder resolved all disputed facts in favor of its finding if a reasonable fact-finder could do so and disregarded all contrary evidence that the fact-finder could have disbelieved.[396] The appellate court may not, however, disregard ***undisputed*** findings that do not support the finding.[397] In light of this evidence, the court of appeals must determine whether the fact-finder could have formed a firm belief or conviction regarding the malice, fraud, or gross-negligence predicate.[398]

2-4:3.2 Gross Negligence

Gross negligence must be proven by clear-and-convincing evidence.[399] Accordingly, the heightened standard of review applies to gross-negligence findings.[400]

2-4:3.3 Temporary Civil Commitment

When the State seeks to have a person committed for temporary mental-health services, it must prove by clear-and-convincing evidence that the individual is mentally ill and that as a result he or she is likely to cause serious harm to himself or herself or to others.[401] The statute defines this burden of proof as requiring expert testimony and recent evidence of overt acts or continuing patterns of behavior tending to establish the standards for commitment.[402] This statutory requirement is reviewed for adherence to the elevated standard or review that applies when the burden of proof is clear-and-convincing evidence; a bit more than a scintilla of evidence is not sufficient.[403]

2-4:3.4 Termination of Parental Rights

A court may involuntarily terminate a parent–child relationship only if it finds by clear-and-convincing evidence that the parent has committed one of the acts specified by statute and that termination is in the best interest of the child.[404] The Family Code defines "[c]lear and convincing evidence as 'the measure or degree of proof that will produce in the mind of the trier of fact a firm belief or conviction as to the truth of the allegations sought to be established.' "[405] "This heightened burden of proof results in a heightened standard of review."[406] The standard of review "must take into consideration whether the evidence is such that a factfinder could reasonably form a firm belief or conviction about the truth of the matter," which protects the rights of a parent more than a traditional legal-sufficiency standard would do.[407]

2-4:3.5 Defamation

Some defamation claims must be proved by clear-and-convincing evidence. The First Amendment protects critics of public officials from defamation claims by requiring proof of actual malice, which must be made by clear-and-convincing evidence.[408] In this context as well, that standard requires evidence that will support "a firm conviction that the fact to be proved is true."[409]

2-4:4 Special Considerations in Bench Trials

As noted previously, Findings of Fact filed by the court after a bench trial are reviewed in the same manner as a jury verdict.[410] But what happens when the trial court does not file Findings of Fact after a bench trial?

If Findings were not properly requested, all findings on any reasonable theory and consistent with the evidence and the law will be deemed in support of the judgment.[411] If no reporter's record was filed, the reviewing court will presume that the trial court heard sufficient evidence to make the deemed findings.[412] But if a complete reporter's record appears in the appellate record, then the sufficiency of the evidence is not presumed and the deemed findings are subject to review for legal and factual sufficiency.[413]

If Findings were properly requested but not filed, harm is presumed.[414] However, if a complete reporter's record is in the record on appeal, and it "affirmatively shows that the complaining party suffered no injury," then the failure to make findings is not harmful.[415] Harm occurs when an appellant is "forced to guess the reason(s) why the trial court ruled against him."[416] If there is only a single ground of recovery, there is no need to guess, but when there are multiple theories of recovery or defense, an appellant must guess at the trial court's rationale, contrary to the purpose of Rules 296 and 297.[417]

2-5 Special Standards of Review

2-5:1 Rational Relationship Standard of Review

The rational relationship standard of review applies when a party makes a substantive due-process challenge to the action of a governmental entity, such as a city. A municipality's exercise of its police power to create and enforce ordinances may not be arbitrary or unreasonable.[418] The standard of review considers whether "the [city's] actions rationally could have been related to a proper exercise of its police power."[419] To conduct that review, the appellate court will consider the evidence in the record to determine whether it is "at least fairly debatable that the decisions were rationally related to a legitimate governmental interest."[420] The ultimate issue whether the ordinance or regulation complies with due process is a question of law, reviewed de novo.[421]

This standard of review also applies when a party claims that he or she has been denied equal protection of the law under the Texas Constitution, but no fundamental right or suspect classification is at issue. Petitioners must show they were treated differently than others who are similarly situated and that their different treatment "is not rationally related to a legitimate governmental purpose."[422] The appellate court must "consider whether the challenged action has a rational basis and whether use of the challenged classification would reasonably promote that purpose."[423] The scope of review is not limited to "courtroom fact-finding" and may include "rational speculation unsupported by evidence or empirical data."[424]

2-5:2 Appellate Review of Decision Not to Dismiss Claims of Certain Constitutional Rights

A specific set of statutes applies when a person is sued in connection with his or her exercise of certain constitutional rights, including the rights of free speech, petition, and association.[425] Those actions are subject to summary dismissal proceedings, except in the circumstance where the party asserting the claims "establishes by clear and specific evidence a prima facie case for each essential element of the claim in question."[426] In this context, clear-and-specific evidence has been defined as evidence "unaided by presumptions, inferences, or intendments."[427]

Prima facie evidence is defined as that which "until its effect is overcome by other evidence, will suffice as proof of a fact in issue."[428] Whether a prima facie case has been established is a question of law reviewed de novo.[429]

Accordingly, the standard of review under Section 27.005(c) is as follows: the appellate court "determine[s] de novo whether the record contains a minimum quantum of clear and specific evidence that, unaided by inferences, would establish each essential element of the claim in question if no contrary evidence is offered."[430]

2-5:3 Review of Trial Court's Order Confirming or Vacating Arbitration Award

A trial court's decision to vacate an arbitration award may be based only on specified statutory grounds and certain narrowly defined common-law grounds.[431]

An appellate court's review of that decision is de novo and the scope of review includes the entire record.[432] What makes the standard of review unique is that the court's review is constrained by a "strong presumption in favor of enforcing arbitration awards," and the limited role of the courts in reviewing such awards.[433] Under these standards, even clear errors of fact and law do not justify vacating an award.[434]

2-5:3.1 Statutory Grounds

The statutory grounds for vacating an arbitration award are:

(a) On application of a party, the court shall vacate an award if:

(1) the award was obtained by corruption, fraud, or other undue means;

(2) the rights of a party were prejudiced by:

(A) evident partiality by an arbitrator appointed as a neutral arbitrator;

(B) corruption in an arbitrator; or

(C) misconduct or willful misbehavior of an arbitrator;

(3) the arbitrators:

(A) exceeded their powers;

(B) refused to postpone the hearing after a showing of sufficient cause for the postponement;

(C) refused to hear evidence material to the controversy; or

(D) conducted the hearing, contrary to Section 171.043, 171.044, 171.045, 171.046, or 171.047, in a manner that substantially prejudiced the rights of a party; or

(4) there was no agreement to arbitrate, the issue was not adversely determined in a proceeding under Subchapter B, and the party did not participate in the arbitration hearing without raising the objection.[435]

If the party moving for vacatur does not prove one of these grounds, or a common-law ground, the appellate court must affirm a judgment confirming the award.

2-5:3.2 Common-Law Grounds

There are only a few common-law grounds for vacating an arbitration award. They are:

- *Gross mistake.* Gross mistake is something of a misnomer as a common-law ground for vacating an arbitration award. It exists only when an award is so egregious that it implies bad faith and the failure to exercise honest judgment on the part of the arbitration panel.[436]
- *Manifest disregard of the law.* To prove that vacatur is warranted under this theory, the movant must show that the arbitrators knew and understood well-established law, but simply chose to ignore it.[437]
- *Violating a clearly articulated and fundamental public policy.* Texas law permits a court to vacate an arbitration award "in an extraordinary case in which the award clearly violates carefully articulated, fundamental policy" such as a constitutional provision, rule or statute.[438]

All of these vacatur grounds are reviewed de novo, and in light of the entire record, but very narrowly.

2-5:4 Review of Exemplary Damages Award for Due-Process Compliance

An award of exemplary damages must comply with the Due Process Clause of the United States Constitution, because a "'grossly excessive'" award "'furthers no legitimate purpose and constitutes an arbitrary deprivation of property.'"[439] When exemplary damages are challenged as violating due process, the appellate court reviews them in light of the evidence relevant to three "guideposts" that determine their constitutionality.

2-5:4.1 Degree of Reprehensibility of Defendant's Conduct

The degree of reprehensibility is determined by considering, among other things, (a) whether the harm was physical rather than economic, (b) whether the tortious conduct recklessly disregarded the health or safety of others, (c) whether the target of the conduct was financially vulnerable, (d) whether the conduct was an isolated incident or repetitive, and (e) whether the harm resulted from intentional trickery or malice as opposed to an accident.[440] The reviewing court balances these factors, bearing in mind that the award of *actual* damages is presumed to have fully compensated the plaintiff, so that exemplary damages are warranted only if something more is required to achieve punishment or deterrence.[441] Some of the acts demonstrating reprehensibility include bribing a witness, threatening a witness, and tampering with evidence.[442]

2-5:4.2 Disparity Between Actual or Potential Harm Suffered by Plaintiff and Punitive Damages Award

This factor looks at the ratio of actual to punitive damages.[443] A reviewing court looks at exemplary damages knowing that few awards greater than a single-digit ratio will satisfy due process and that awards over a 4:1 ratio are constitutionally suspect.[444] Larger ratios are generally sanctioned only when a "particularly egregious act has resulted in only a small amount of economic damage."[445] Conversely, when the actual damages award is substantial, only a smaller ratio—as small as 1:1—may be constitutionally permissible.[446]

2-5:4.3 Difference Between Punitive Damages Awarded by Jury and Civil Penalties Authorized or Imposed in Comparable Cases

When applying this standard to the review of an award of exemplary damages, the appellate court remains mindful that the legislature establishes policy, so that a legislative judgment regarding the appropriate sanction for specific conduct should be heeded.[447]

2-5:5 Review of Agency Decision

In some cases, the Texas Legislature has granted jurisdiction to agencies to decide a contested case. The Texas Administrative Procedure Act establishes the proper standards of review in such cases.[448] The scope of judicial review is provided by the law under which review is sought: trial de novo or substantial evidence review.[449]

2-5:5.1 Trial De Novo Review

When the governing statute specifies that judicial review is by trial de novo, "the reviewing court shall try each issue of fact and law in the manner that applies to other civil suits in this state as though there had not been an intervening agency action or decision. . . ."[450]

2-5:5.2 Substantial-Evidence Review

When the governing statue specifies that judicial review is for substantial evidence, and when the governing statute fails to define the scope of review, then the reviewing court "may not substitute its judgment for the judgment of the state agency on the weight of the evidence on questions committed to agency discretion."[451] Instead, the reviewing court:

(1) may affirm; and

(2) shall reverse if the appellant's substantial rights have been prejudiced by administration findings or conclusions that:

  (A) violate the Texas Constitution or a statute;

  (B) exceed the agency's authority;

(C) were reached through an unlawful procedure;

(D) are affected by an error of law;

(E) are not reasonably supported by "substantial evidence considering the reliable and probative evidence in the record as a whole;" or

(F) was arbitrary and capricious or an abuse of discretion.[452]

"At its core, the substantial evidence rule is a reasonableness test or a rational basis test. . . . The reviewing court, then, concerns itself with the ***reasonableness*** of the administrative order, not the *correctness* of the order. The rule prevents the court from 'usurping the agency's adjudicative authority even though the court would have struck a different balance.'"[453]

The record of proceedings before the agency is filed with the court, which reviews the agency rulings without a jury.[454] A party may tender additional evidence if there was good reason to not present it to the agency, but in that case the agency may change its ruling based on the new evidence and submit any change to the reviewing court.[455]

2-5:5.3 Who Is an "Affected Person"?

The right to request a contested-case hearing before an agency may involve the determination of who is an "affected person." This determination is left to the discretion of the agency.[456] The test for abuse of discretion in this context is whether the agency "'(1) fails to consider a factor the Legislature directs it to consider; (2) considers an irrelevant factor; or (3) weighs only relevant factors that the Legislature directs it to consider, but still reaches a completely unreasonable result.'"[457]

2-6 Recommended Resource

W. Wendell Hall, *Standards of Review in Texas*, 38 St. Mary's L.J. 47 (2006). This is a comprehensive, thoroughly researched summary of the standards of review applicable to more than 100 trial court rulings arising during the pre-trial, trial, and post-trial stages of litigation.

Notes

1 *Quick v. City of Austin*, 7 S.W.3d 109, 116 (Tex. 1998).

2 W. Wendell Hall, *Standards of Review in Texas*, 38 St. Mary's L.J. 47, 58 (2006).

3 *Quick v. City of Austin*, 7 S.W.3d 109, 116 (Tex. 1998) (citations omitted).

4 *Kachina Pipeline Co. v. Lillis*, 471 S.W.3d 445, 449 (Tex. 2015) ("Whether a contract is ambiguous is itself a legal question for the court."); *Anglo-Dutch Petroleum Int'l, Inc. v. Greenberg Peden, P.C.*, 352 S.W.3d 445, 449–50 (Tex. 2011); *Nat'l Union Fire Ins. Co. of Pittsburgh, PA v. CBI Indus., Inc.*, 907 S.W.2d 517, 520 (Tex. 1995).

5 *Kachina Pipeline Co. v. Lillis*, 471 S.W.3d 445, 449 (Tex. 2015) ("A contract is not ambiguous simply because the parties disagree over its meaning. Rather, if a written contract is so worded that it can be given a definite or certain legal meaning, then it is not ambiguous.") (internal quotation marks and citations omitted); *Columbia Gas Transmission Corp. v. New Ulm Gas, Ltd.*, 940 S.W.2d 587, 589 (Tex. 1996).

6 *Plains Exploration & Production Co. v. Torch Energy Advisors Inc.*, 473 S.W.3d 296, 305 (Tex. 2015).

[7] *Anglo-Dutch Petroleum Int'l, Inc. v. Greenberg Peden, P.C.*, 352 S.W.3d 445, 449–50 (Tex. 2011) (noting that the existence of an attorney–client relationship is a circumstance to be considered in determining whether a contract is ambiguous); *National Union Fire Ins. Co. of Pittsburgh, PA v. CBI Indus., Inc.*, 907 S.W.2d 517, 520 (Tex. 1995).

[8] *See Anglo-Dutch Petroleum Int'l, Inc. v. Greenberg Peden, P.C.*, 352 S.W.3d 445, 451 (Tex. 2011) ("Extrinsic evidence cannot be used to show that the parties probably meant, or could have meant, something other than what their agreement stated.").

[9] *Plains Exploration & Production Co. v. Torch Energy Advisors Inc.*, 473 S.W.3d 296, 305 (Tex. 2015).

[10] *Plains Exploration & Production Co. v. Torch Energy Advisors Inc.*, 473 S.W.3d 296, 305 (Tex. 2015) ("Absent ambiguity, contracts are construed as a matter of law.").

[11] *Kachina Pipeline Co. v. Lillis*, 471 S.W.3d 445, 449 (Tex. 2015) ("The construction of an unambiguous contract is a question of law, also reviewed de novo."); *see also Chrysler Ins. Co. v. Greenspoint Dodge of Houston, Inc.*, 297 S.W.3d 248, 252 (Tex. 2009) ("Our review of an unambiguous contract, like any other legal question, is de novo."); *Coker v. Coker*, 650 S.W.2d 391, 393 (Tex. 1983).

[12] *Plains Exploration & Production Co. v. Torch Energy Advisors Inc.*, 473 S.W.3d 296, 305 (Tex. 2015); *Kachina Pipeline Co. v. Lillis*, 471 S.W.3d 445, 449 (Tex. 2015); *see also Seagull Energy E&P, Inc. v. Eland Energy, Inc.*, 207 S.W.3d 342, 345 (Tex. 2006) ("We examine and consider the entire writing in an effort to harmonize and give effect to all the provisions of the contract so that none will be rendered meaningless.").

[13] *Kachina Pipeline Co. v. Lillis*, 471 S.W.3d 445, 449 (Tex. 2015) (internal quotation marks and citation omitted).

[14] *Plains Exploration & Production Co. v. Torch Energy Advisors Inc.*, 473 S.W.3d 296, 305 (Tex. 2015); *Kachina Pipeline Co. v. Lillis*, 471 S.W.3d 445, 449 (Tex. 2015) (internal quotation marks and citation omitted).

[15] *Plains Exploration & Production Co. v. Torch Energy Advisors Inc.*, 473 S.W.3d 296, 305 (Tex. 2015) ("In construing a written contract, our primary goal is to ascertain the parties' true intentions as expressed in the language they chose."); *Kachina Pipeline Co. v. Lillis*, 471 S.W.3d 445, 449 (Tex. 2015) ("In construing a contract, a court must ascertain the true intentions of the parties as expressed in the writing itself.") (internal quotation marks and citation omitted); *Seagull Energy E&P, Inc. v. Eland Energy, Inc.*, 207 S.W.3d 342, 345 (Tex. 2006) ("Our primary concern when interpreting a contract is to ascertain and give effect to the intent of the parties as that intent is expressed in the contract.").

[16] *Kachina Pipeline Co. v. Lillis*, 471 S.W.3d 445, 449 (Tex. 2015) ("We may consider the facts and circumstances surrounding a contract, including the commercial or other setting in which the contract was negotiated and other objectively determinable factors that give context to the parties' transaction.") (internal quotation marks and citation omitted); *see Sun Oil Co. (Delaware) v. Madeley*, 626 S.W.2d 726, 731 (Tex. 1981) ("Evidence of surrounding circumstances may be consulted.").

[17] *Rachal v. Reitz*, 403 S.W.3d 840, 843 (Tex. 2013); *see also In re Labatt Food Serv., L.P.*, 279 S.W.3d 640, 643 (Tex. 2009) ("Whether an arbitration agreement is enforceable is subject to de novo review."); *J.M. Davidson, Inc. v. Webster*, 128 S.W.3d 223, 227 (Tex. 2003).

[18] *Tittizer v. Union Gas Corp.*, 171 S.W.3d 857, 860 (Tex. 2005) ("An oil and gas lease is a contract, and its terms are interpreted as such.").

[19] *Cooke v. Morrison*, 404 S.W.3d 100, 111 (Tex. App.—Houston [1st Dist.] 2013, no. pet.) ("A deed is subject to the same rules of interpretation and construction as a contract.").

[20] *McCoy v. Rogers*, 240 S.W.3d 267, 276 (Tex. App.—Houston [1st Dist.] 2007, pet. denied) (agreed judgment reviewed under rules of contract interpretation); *McWhinney v. Ameriquest Mortg. Secs., Inc.*, No. 01-13-00761-CV, 2014 WL 6853602, at *3 (Tex. App.—Houston [1st Dist.] Dec. 4, 2014, no pet.) (mem. op.) (settlement agreement); *Eastman Gas Co.*,

L.L.C. v. Goodrich Petroleum Co., L.L.C., 456 S.W.3d 319, 325 (Tex. App.—Texarkana 2015, pet. denied) ("The enforceability of a [Rule 11] settlement agreement is a question of law.").

21 *Chrysler Ins. Co. v. Greenspoint Dodge of Houston, Inc.*, 297 S.W.3d 248, 252 (Tex. 2009) ("The interpretation of an insurance contract is generally subject to the same rules of construction as other contracts.").

22 *RSUI Indem. Co. v. The Lynd Co.*, 466 S.W.3d 113, 139 (Tex. 2015).

23 *RSUI Indem. Co. v. The Lynd Co.*, 466 S.W.3d 113, 139 (Tex. 2015).

24 *Petrohawk Props., L.P. v. Jones*, 455 S.W.3d 753, 763 (Tex. App.—Texarkana 2015, pet. dism'd).

25 *Petrohawk Props., L.P. v. Jones*, 455 S.W.3d 753, 763 (Tex. App.—Texarkana 2015, pet. dism'd).

26 *Greater Hous. P'ship v. Paxton*, 468 S.W.3d 51, 58 (Tex. 2015); *Thompson v. Tex. Dept. of Licensing & Regulation*, 455 S.W.3d 569, 571 (Tex. 2014) ("The construction of a statute is a question of law we review de novo.").

27 *Greater Hous. P'ship v. Paxton*, 468 S.W.3d 51, 58 (Tex. 2015) (internal quotation marks and citations omitted); *see also Ross v. St. Luke's Episcopal Hosp.*, 462 S.W.3d 596, 501 (Tex. 2015); *Thompson v. Tex. Dept. of Licensing & Regulation*, 455 S.W.3d 569, 571 (Tex. 2014); *Atmos Energy Corp. v. Cities of Allen*, 353 S.W.3d 156, 160 (Tex. 2011) (court's task is to give effect to legislature's "expressed intent").

28 *Ross v. St. Luke's Episcopal Hosp.*, 462 S.W.3d 596, 501 (Tex. 2015).

29 *Ross v. St. Luke's Episcopal Hosp.*, 462 S.W.3d 596, 501 (Tex. 2015); *Thompson v. Tex. Dept. of Licensing & Regulation*, 455 S.W.3d 569, 571 (Tex. 2014) (quoting Tex. Gov't Code § 311.011(a)).

30 *Ross v. St. Luke's Episcopal Hosp.*, 462 S.W.3d 596, 504 (Tex. 2015).

31 *Atmos Energy Corp. v. Cities of Allen*, 353 S.W.3d 156, 160 (Tex. 2011) ("A court may consider the object sought to be obtained, circumstances under which the statute was enacted, and the consequences of a particular construction when construing statutes, whether or not the statute is ambiguous."); *see Galbraith Eng'g Consultants, Inc. v. Pochuca*, 290 S.W.3d 863, 867–68 (Tex. 2009) (reviewing de novo an ambiguity in a statutory term).

32 *Thompson v. Tex. Dept. of Licensing & Regulation*, 455 S.W.3d 569, 571 (Tex. 2014) (noting that deference is afforded "only if" the statute is ambiguous).

33 *Cascos v. Tarrant Cnty. Democratic Party*, 473 S.W.3d 780, 786 (Tex. 2015) (noting that lower court erred by taking "a snippet of language out of its statutory context" and by reading agency discretion out of the statute); *Ross v. St. Luke's Episcopal Hosp.*, 462 S.W.3d 596, 501 (Tex. 2015); *Rachal v. Reitz*, 403 S.W.3d 840, 844 (Tex. 2013).

34 Tex. Gov't Code § 311.023; *see Atmos Energy Corp. v. Cities of Allen*, 353 S.W.3d 156, 160 (Tex. 2011) (referencing object sought to be obtained, circumstances under which statute was enacted, and consequences of construction); *Ojo v. Farmers Group, Inc.*, 356 S.W.3d 421, 430 (Tex. 2011) (considering legislative history); *Galbraith Eng'g Consultants, Inc. v. Pochuca*, 290 S.W.3d 863, 867–68 (Tex. 2009) (focusing on the consequences of a particular construction).

35 *See* Tex. Gov't Code §§ 311.005, 311.016.

36 *Tex. Student Housing Auth. v. Brazos Cnty. Appraisal Dist.*, 460 S.W.3d 137, 140–41 (Tex. 2015).

37 *Tex. Student Housing Auth. v. Brazos Cnty. Appraisal Dist.*, 460 S.W.3d 137, 140–41 (Tex. 2015).

38 *Patel v. Tex. Dept. of Licensing & Reg.*, 469 S.W.3d 69, 87 (Tex. 2015); *Harris County Hosp. Dist. v. Tomball Reg'l Hosp.*, 283 S.W.3d 838, 842 (Tex. 2009); *Perry v. Del Rio*, 67 S.W.3d 85, 91 (Tex. 2001).

39 *Patel v. Tex. Dept. of Licensing & Reg.*, 469 S.W.3d 69, 87 (Tex. 2015) (noting that the same presumption and high burden apply to constitutional challenges to agency regulations).

40 *Patel v. Tex. Dept. of Licensing & Reg.*, 469 S.W.3d 69, 87 (Tex. 2015).

41 *Patel v. Tex. Dept. of Licensing & Reg.*, 469 S.W.3d 69, 87 (Tex. 2015).

42 *Suarez v. City of Texas City*, 465 S.W.3d 623, 632 (Tex. 2015); *Hearts Bluff Game Ranch, Inc. v. State*, 381 S.W.3d 468, 476 (Tex. 2012); *City of Elsa v. Gonzalez*, 325 S.W.3d 622, 625 (Tex. 2010); *State v. Holland*, 221 S.W.3d 639, 642 (Tex. 2007).

43 *Suarez v. City of Texas City*, 465 S.W.3d 623, 632 (Tex. 2015).

44 *Suarez v. City of Texas City*, 465 S.W.3d 623, 632 (Tex. 2015).

45 *Suarez v. City of Texas City*, 465 S.W.3d 623, 632 (Tex. 2015).

46 *Heckman v. Williamson County*, 369 S.W.3d 137, 150 (Tex. 2012); *see also Texas Dep't of Parks & Wildlife v. Miranda*, 133 S.W.3d 217, 226 (Tex. 2004) ("We construe the pleadings liberally in favor of the plaintiffs and look to the pleaders' intent.").

47 *Heckman v. Williamson County*, 369 S.W.3d 137, 150 (Tex. 2012) ("[W]e must grant the plea if the defendant presents undisputed evidence that negates the existence of the court's jurisdiction. . . ."); *see also Bland Indep. Sch. Dist. v. Blue*, 34 S.W.3d 547, 555 (Tex. 2000) (noting the court should confine itself to the evidence relevant to the jurisdictional issue).

48 *See Heckman v. Williamson County*, 369 S.W.3d 137, 150 (Tex. 2012).

49 *Mayhew v. Town of Sunnyvale*, 964 S.W.2d 922, 928 (Tex. 1998).

50 *See Hearts Bluff Game Ranch, Inc. v. State*, 381 S.W.3d 468, 476 (Tex. 2012) (noting in the absence of a properly pled takings claim, sovereign immunity shields the state from a trial court's subject-matter jurisdiction); *Texas Dep't of Parks & Wildlife v. Miranda*, 133 S.W.3d 217, 225–26 (Tex. 2004).

51 *Alamo Heights Indep. Sch. Dist. v. Clark*, 544 S.W.3d 755, 771 (Tex. 2018).

52 *CMH Homes v. Perez*, 340 S.W.3d 444, 447 (Tex. 2011); *Villafani v. Trejo*, 251 S.W.3d 466, 467 (Tex. 2008).

53 *St. Agnes Acad. v. Texas Alcoholic Beverage Comm'n*, 391 S.W.3d 277, 279 (Tex. App.—Austin 2012, no pet.).

54 *Tex. Dept. of Parks & Wildlife v. Miranda*, 133 S.W.3d 217, 226 (Tex. 2004) (sovereign-immunity claim at issue).

55 *Tex. Dept. of Parks & Wildlife v. Miranda*, 133 S.W.3d 217, 226 (Tex. 2004).

56 *State v. Naylor*, 466 S.W.3d 783, 787 (Tex. 2015) (holding that an appellate court always has jurisdiction to determine standing, may do so sua sponte, and applies a de novo standard of review); *Texas Dep't of Transp. v. City of Sunset Valley*, 146 S.W.3d 637, 646 (Tex. 2004); *see also Texas Ass'n of Bus. v. Texas Air Control Bd.*, 852 S.W.2d 440, 444 (Tex. 1993) ("Because standing is a component of subject matter jurisdiction, we consider . . . standing under the same standard by which we review subject matter jurisdiction generally."); *see also JPMorgan Chase Bank, N.A. v. Prof'l Pharmacy II*, __ S.W.3d __, No. 02-11-00373-CV, 2014 WL 7473779, at *4 (Tex. App.—Fort Worth Dec. 31, 2014, no pet. h.) (scope of review includes entire record).

57 *Heckman v. Williamson County*, 369 S.W.3d 137, 149–50 (Tex. 2012).

58 *See Moncrief Oil Int'l, Inc. v. OAO Gazprom*, 414 S.W.3d 142, 150 (Tex. 2013); *Retamco Operating, Inc. v. Republic Drilling Co.*, 278 S.W.3d 333, 337 (Tex. 2009) (reviewing of a trial court's denial of defendant's special appearance is a question of personal jurisdiction, which is reviewed de novo); *Moki Mac River Expeditions v. Drugg*, 221 S.W.3d 659, 574 (Tex. 2007); *American Type Culture Collection, Inc. v. Coleman*, 83 S.W.3d 801, 805–06 (Tex. 2002).

59 *See BMC Software v. Marchand*, 83 S.W.3d 789, 793–95 (Tex. 2002) (discussing the standard of review for appellate courts reviewing trial courts' finding of facts and conclusions of law). The legal-sufficiency standard is discussed in § 2-4:1; factual-sufficiency standard in § 2-4:2.

60 *Retamco Operating, Inc. v. Republic Drilling Co.*, 278 S.W.3d 333, 338 (Tex. 2009).

61 *See BMC Software v. Marchand*, 83 S.W.3d 789, 795 (Tex. 2002) (noting that implied findings are not conclusive when the record on appeal includes full Clerk's and Reporter's Records).

62 *Subaru of Am., Inc. v. David McDavid Nissan, Inc.*, 84 S.W.3d 212, 222 (Tex. 2002).

63 *Surgitek, Bristol-Myers Corp. v. Abel*, 997 S.W.2d 598, 603 (Tex. 1999) (citing Tex. Civ. Prac. & Rem. Code § 15.003(c)(1)).

64 *Royston, Rayzor, Vickery, & Williams, LLP v. Lopez*, 467 S.W.3d 494, 499 (Tex. 2015) ("The ultimate issue of whether an arbitration agreement is against public policy or unconscionable is a question of law for the court.").

65 *See Martin v. Clinical Pathology Laboratories, Inc.*, 343 S.W.3d 885, 891 (Tex. App.—Dallas 2011, pet. denied) ("When a trial court dismisses a case on special exceptions for failure to state a cause of action, we review that determination of law de novo."); *Sanchez v. Huntsville Indep. Sch. Dist.*, 844 S.W.2d 286, 288 (Tex. App.—Houston [1st Dist.] 1992, no writ) (noting that the factual allegations of the petition are taken as true for purposes of this review).

66 *Shell Oil Co. v. Writt*, 464 S.W.3d 650, 654 (Tex. 2015); *Kachina Pipeline Co. v. Lillis*, 471 S.W.3d 445, 449 (Tex. 2015) ("A declaratory judgment granted on a traditional motion for summary judgment is reviewed de novo."); *State v. Ninety Thousand Two Hundred Thirty-Five Dollars & No Cents in U.S. Currency ($90,235)*, 390 S.W.3d 289, 292 (Tex. 2013); *see also Frost Nat'l Bank v. Fernandez*, 315 S.W.3d 494, 508 (Tex. 2010).

67 *KCM Fin. L.L.C. v. Bradshaw*, 457 S.W.3d 70, 79 (Tex. 2015); *Cantey Hanger, LLP v. Byrd*, 467 S.W.3d 477, 481 (Tex. 2015) (noting that a party moving for traditional summary judgment on an affirmative defense must conclusively prove that defense); *Hankel v. Norman*, 441 S.W.3d 249, 251 (Tex. 2004) (citing *Frost Nat'l Bank v. Fernandez*, 315 S.W.3d 494, 508 (Tex. 2010)).

68 *KCM Fin. L.L.C. v. Bradshaw*, 457 S.W.3d 70, 79 (Tex. 2015) (noting trial court mut grant a no-evidence motion "unless the nonmovant raises a genuine issue of material fact on each challenged element"); *Boerjan v. Rodriguez*, 436 S.W.3d 307, 312 (Tex. 2014); *see also Smith v. O'Donnell*, 288 S.W.3d 417, 424 (Tex. 2009).

69 *See* § 2-4:1.

70 *Boerjan v. Rodriguez*, 436 S.W.3d 307, 311–12 (Tex. 2014) (quoting *Timpte Indus., Inc. v. Gish*, 286 S.W.3d 306, 310 (Tex. 2009), in turn citing *Mack Trucks, Inc. v. Tamez*, 206 S.W.3d 572, 582 (Tex. 2006)); *see also Buck v. Palmer*, 381 S.W.3d 525, 527 (Tex. 2012) appellate court reviews record "'in the light most favorable to the nonmovant, indulging every reasonable inference and resolving any doubts against the motion'" (quoting *City of Keller v. Wilson*, 168 S.W.3d 802, 824 (Tex. 2009)).

71 *City of Keller v. Wilson*, 168 S.W.3d 802, 824–25 (Tex. 2005).

72 *See* § 2-4:1.

73 *Merriman v. XTO Energy, Inc.*, 407 S.W.3d 244, 248 (Tex. 2013); *Ford Motor Co. v. Ridgway*, 135 S.W.3d 598, 600 (Tex. 2004).

74 *Merriman v. XTO Energy, Inc.*, 407 S.W.3d 244, 248 (Tex. 2013) (citing *Ford Motor Co. v. Ridgway*, 135 S.W.3d 598, 600 (Tex. 2004)); *see also Diez v. Alaska Structures, Inc.*, 455 S.W.3d 737, 740 (Tex. App.—El Paso 2015, no pet.) (noting that the traditional motion for summary-judgment burden is "less stringent").

75 *Neely v. Wilson*, 418 S.W.3d 52, 59 (Tex. 2013).

76 *Sw. Bell Tel., L.P. v. Emmett*, 459 S.W.3d 578, 583 (Tex. 2015); *Mann Frankfort Stein & Lipp Advisors, Inc. v. Fielding*, 289 S.W.3d 844, 848 (Tex. 2009).

77 *G&H Towing Co. v. Magee*, 347 S.W.3d 293, 297 (Tex. 2011).

78 *G&H Towing Co. v. Magee*, 347 S.W.3d 293, 297–98 (Tex. 2011).

[79] *G&H Towing Co. v. Magee*, 347 S.W.3d 293, 297–98 (Tex. 2011).

[80] *Lujan v. Navistar, Inc.*, 555 S.W.3d 79, 85 (Tex. 2018); *Starwood Mgmt., L.L.C. v. Swaim*, 530 S.W.3d 673, 678 (Tex. 2017) ("We review the rendition of summary judgments de novo. But we review a trial court's decision to exclude evidence for an abuse of discretion.").

[81] *FFE Transp. Services, Inc. v. Fulgham*, 154 S.W.3d 84, 89–90 (Tex. 2004).

[82] *See Compaq Computer Corp. v. Lapray*, 135 S.W.3d 657, 672 (Tex. 2004) ("Generally, the issue of which state's law applies is a question of law we resolve by reviewing the record de novo.").

[83] *Minnesota Mining & Mfg. Co. v. Nishika Ltd.*, 955 S.W.2d 853, 856 (Tex. 1996) (per curiam).

[84] *Andrew Shebay & Co., P.L.L.C. v. Bishop*, No. 01-12-00118-CV, 2013 WL 1844213, at *2 (Tex. App.—Houston [1st Dist.] May 2, 2013, no. pet. h.) (mem. op.) ("Questions of collateral estoppel are matters of law that we review de novo."); *Ex parte Doan*, No. 03-08-00704-CR, 2012 WL 6698987, at *2 (Tex. App.—Austin Dec. 21, 2012, no pet.) (mem. op.) (applying the doctrine of res judicata is the application of law to the facts, which is a question of law reviewed de novo on appeal).

[85] *Transcontinental Ins. Co. v. Crump*, 330 S.W.3d 211, 221 (Tex. 2010).

[86] *United Scaffolding, Inc. v. Levine*, 537 S.W.3d 463, 469 (Tex. 2017); *Gutierrez v. People's Mgmt. of Tex. I, Ltd.*, 277 S.W.3d 72, 77 (Tex. App.—El Paso 2009, pet. denied).

[87] *Beltran v. Brookshire Grocery Co.*, 358 S.W.3d 263, 267 (Tex. App.—Dallas 2011, pet. denied) (citing *Bender v. S. Pac. Transp. Co.*, 600 S.W.2d 257, 260 (Tex.1980)); *see also Man Indus. (India), Ltd. v. Midcontinent Express Pipeline, L.L.C.*, 407 S.W.3d 342, 365–66 (Tex. App.—Houston [14th Dist.] 2013, pet. filed) (applying de novo review to conflict between express and implied findings).

[88] *Adams v. Allstate County Mut. Ins. Co.*, 199 S.W.3d 509, 512 (Tex. App.—Houston [1st Dist.] 2006, pet. denied).

[89] *See Houston Lighting & Power Co. v. City of Wharton*, 101 S.W.3d 633, 638 (Tex. App.—Houston [1st Dist.] 2003, pet. denied) ("Because the court's ruling was based upon a legal conclusion, we review the court's ruling de novo.").

[90] *See* § 2-4:1.

[91] *JSC Neftegas-Impex v. Citibank, N.A.*, 365 S.W.3d 387, 396 (Tex. App.—Houston [1st Dist.] 2011, pet. denied); *NETCO, Inc. v. Montemayor*, 352 S.W.3d 733, 738 (Tex. App.—Houston [1st Dist.] 2011, no pet.).

[92] *See BMC Software v. Marchand*, 83 S.W.3d 789, 794 (Tex. 2002) ("Appellate courts review a trial court's conclusions of law as a legal question."); *see also Cooke v. Morrison*, 404 S.W.3d 100, 107 (Tex. App.—Houston [1st Dist.] 2013, no pet.) ("We review a trial court's conclusions of law de novo, and we will uphold the conclusions if the judgment can be sustained on any legal theory supported by the evidence.").

[93] *Cooke v. Morrison*, 404 S.W.3d 100, 107 (Tex. App.—Houston [1st Dist.] 2013, no pet.).

[94] Tex. Civ. Prac. & Rem. Code §§ 74.001–507.

[95] *Ross v. St. Luke's Episcopal hosp.*, 462 S.W.3d 496, 501, 504 (Tex. 2015); *Loaisiga v. Cerida*, 379 S.W.3d 248, 254–55 (Tex. 2012).

[96] *Ross v. St. Luke's Episcopal hosp.*, 462 S.W.3d 496, 501, 504 (Tex. 2015); *Loaisiga v. Cerida*, 379 S.W.3d 248, 254–55 (Tex. 2012).

[97] *Loaisiga v. Cerida*, 379 S.W.3d 248, 256 (Tex. 2012).

[98] *Ross v. St. Luke's Episcopal hosp.*, 462 S.W.3d 496, 501, 504 (Tex. 2015); *see also Galvan v. Mem'l Hermann Hosp. Sys.*, 476 S.W.3d 429, 429 (Tex. 2015) (per curiam).

[99] *Ross v. St. Luke's Episcopal hosp.*, 462 S.W.3d 496, 505 (Tex. 2015); *followed in Reddic v. E. Tex. Med. Ctr. Reg. Health Care Sys.*, 474 S.W.3d 672 (Tex. 2015).

[100] *Ross v. St. Luke's Episcopal hosp.*, 462 S.W.3d 496, 505 (Tex. 2015).

[101] *Perry Homes v. Cull*, 258 S.W.3d 580, 597–98 (Tex. 2008) (quoting W. Wendell Hall, *Standards of Review in Texas*, 38 St. Mary's L.J. 43, 67 (2006)).

[102] *Perry Homes v. Cull*, 258 S.W.3d 580, 598 (Tex. 2008).

[103] *Downer v. Aquamarine Operators, Inc.*, 701 S.W.2d 238, 241–42 (Tex. 1985); *Perry Homes v. Cull*, 258 S.W.3d 580, 602 (Tex. 2008) (O'Neill, J., concurring).

[104] *Perry Homes v. Cull*, 258 S.W.3d 580, 602 (Tex. 2008) (O'Neill, J., concurring).

[105] *Smalowski v. Wooten*, 332 S.W.3d 404, 411 (Tex. 2011); *see also E.I. du Pont de Nemours & Co. v. Robinson*, 923 S.W.2d 549, 558 (Tex. 1995) ("A reviewing court cannot conclude that a trial court abused its discretion if, in the same circumstances, it would have ruled differently or if the trial court committed a mere error in judgment.").

[106] *Walker v. Packer*, 827 S.W.2d 833, 840 (Tex. 1992).

[107] *Walker v. Packer*, 827 S.W.2d 833, 840 (Tex. 1992); *see also In re RSR Corp.*, 475 S.W.3d 775 (Tex. 2015) (orig. proceeding) ("A trial court abuses its discretion if it incorrectly analyzes or applies the law.").

[108] *Bocquet v. Herring*, 972 S.W.2d 19, 21 (Tex. 1998) ("It is an abuse of discretion for a trial court to rule . . . without supporting evidence."); *see also General Tire, Inc. v. Kepple*, 970 S.W.2d 520, 525–26 (Tex. 1998); *In re A.B.P.*, 291 S.W.3d 91, 95 (Tex. App.—Dallas 2009, no pet.) (reviewing court conducts sufficiency review to determine whether trial court had enough evidence upon which to exercise its discretion).

[109] *In re C.H.C.*, 392 S.W.3d 347, 349 (Tex. App.—Dallas 2013, no pet. h.).

[110] *Perry Homes v. Cull*, 258 S.W.3d 580, 602 (Tex. 2008) (O'Neill, J., concurring).

[111] *Goode v. Shoukfeh*, 943 S.W.2d 441, 446 (Tex. 1997); *see also General Tire, Inc. v. Kepple*, 970 S.W.2d 520, 526 (Tex. 1998) ("An abuse of discretion does not exist where the trial court bases its decisions on conflicting evidence.") (internal quotation marks and citation omitted).

[112] *Samlowski v. Wooten*, 332 S.W.3d 404, 410 (Tex. 2011) (internal quotation marks and citation omitted).

[113] W. Wendell Hall, *Standards of Review*, 38 St. Mary's L.J. 47, 62–63 (2006).

[114] The quirks in the abuse-of-discretion standard in the mandamus context are discussed in § 2-3:5.

[115] *In re Cont'l Airlines, Inc.*, 988 S.W.2d 733, 735 (Tex. 1998).

[116] *Ho v. Univ. of Tex. at Arlington*, 984 S.W.2d 672, 693–94 (Tex. App.—Amarillo 1998, pet. denied) (citing *Clanton v. Clark*, 639 S.W.2d 929, 931 (Tex. 1982)); Tex. R. Civ. P. 245.

[117] *In re Elliott*, No. 06-10-00101-CR, 2010 WL 2683150, at *2 (Tex. App.—Texarkana Jul 7, 2010, orig. proceeding) (mem. op.).

[118] *See In re Pirelli Tire, L.L.C.*, 247 S.W.3d 670, 673 (Tex. 2007) ("[A] trial court abuses its discretion if its forum-non-conveniens ruling is arbitrary, unreasonable, and without reference to guiding principles.").

[119] *Gatten v. McCarley*, 391 S.W.3d 669, 673 (Tex. App.—Dallas 2013, no pet.); Tex. R. Civ. P. 91.

[120] *See Baylor Univ. v. Sonnichsen*, 221 S.W.3d 632, 635 (Tex. 2007) (holding the trial court did not abuse its discretion in dismissing breach of contract claims); *Holt v. Reproductive Servs., Inc.*, 946 S.W.2d 602, 604 (Tex. App.—Corpus Christi 1997, writ denied).

[121] *Gatten v. McCarley*, 391 S.W.3d 669, 674 (Tex. App.—Dallas 2013, no pet.); *Holt v. Reproductive Servs., Inc.*, 946 S.W.2d 602, 604 (Tex. App.—Corpus Christi 1997, writ denied).

[122] *Gatten v. McCarley*, 391 S.W.3d 669, 673–74 (Tex. App.—Dallas 2013, no pet.).

[123] Tex. R. Civ. P. 41.

[124] *F.F.P. Oper. Partners, L.P. v. Duenez*, 237 S.W.3d 680, 693 (Tex. 2007).

[125] *F.F.P. Oper. Partners, L.P. v. Duenez*, 237 S.W.3d 680, 693 (Tex. 2007) (quoting *Guaranty Fed. Sav. Bank v. Horseshoe Oper. Co.*, 793 S.W.2d 652, 58 (Tex. 1990)).

[126] Tex. R. Civ. P. 174(a).

[127] *In re Gulf Coast Bus. Dev. Corp.*, 247 S.W.3d 787, 794 (Tex. App.—Dallas 2008, orig. proceeding); *Crestway Care Ctr. Inc. v. Berchelmann*, 945 S.W.2d 872, 873–74 (Tex. App.—San Antonio 1997, orig. proceeding).

[128] *Ablon v. Campbell*, 457 S.W.3d 604, 610 (Tex. App.—Dallas 2015, pet. denied).

[129] *Ablon v. Campbell*, 457 S.W.3d 604, 610 (Tex. App.—Dallas 2015, pet. denied).

[130] Tex. R. Civ. P. 60.

[131] *Guaranty Fed. Sav. Bank v. Horseshoe Oper. Co.*, 793 S.W.2d 652, 657 (Tex. 1990).

[132] *Guaranty Fed. Sav. Bank v. Horseshoe Oper. Co.*, 793 S.W.2d 652, 657 (Tex. 1990).

[133] Tex. R. Civ. P. 43.

[134] *Bryant v. United Shortline Inc. Assur. Servs., N.A.*, 972 S.W.2d 26, 31 (Tex. 1998).

[135] Tex. R. Civ. P. 216, 220.

[136] *Caldwell v. Barnes*, 154 S.W.3d 93, 98 (Tex. 2004) (per curiam).

[137] *Mercedes-Benz Credit Corp. v. Rhyne*, 925 S.W.2d 664, 667 (Tex. 1996).

[138] *General Motors Corp. v. Gayle*, 951 S.W.2d 469, 476 (Tex. 1997).

[139] *Texas Dept. of Pub. Safety v. Bonilla*, 481 S.W.3d 640, 642 (Tex. 2015) (per curiam).

[140] *Texas Dept. of Pub. Safety v. Bonilla*, 481 S.W.3d 640, 642 (Tex. 2015) (per curiam).

[141] *Texas Dept. of Pub. Safety v. Bonilla*, 481 S.W.3d 640, 642–43 (Tex. 2015) (per curiam).

[142] *Texas Dept. of Pub. Safety v. Bonilla*, 481 S.W.3d 640, 643 (Tex. 2015) (per curiam).

[143] *Texas Dept. of Pub. Safety v. Bonilla*, 481 S.W.3d 640, 643 (Tex. Dec. 4, 2015) (per curiam).

[144] *Jampole v. Touchy*, 673 S.W.2d 569, 573 (Tex. 1984); *In re Univar USA, Inc.*, 311 S.W.3d 175, 181 (Tex. App.—Beaumont 2010, no pet.).

[145] *General Tire, Inc. v. Kepple*, 970 S.W.2d 520, 525–26 (Tex. 1998) (internal quotation marks and citations omitted).

[146] *General Tire, Inc. v. Kepple*, 970 S.W.2d 520, 526 (Tex. 1998).

[147] *Stelly v. Papina*, 927 S.W.2d 620, 621 (Tex. 1996) (per curiam).

[148] *Stelly v. Papina*, 927 S.W.2d 620, 621 (Tex. 1996) (per curiam).

[149] *Remington Arms Co. v. Canales*, 837 S.W.2d 624, 625 (Tex. 1992).

[150] *Remington Arms Co. v. Canales*, 837 S.W.2d 624, 625 (Tex. 1992) (citing *Alvarado v. Farah Mfg. Co.*, 830 S.W.2d 911, 915 (Tex. 1992)).

[151] Tex. R. Civ. P. 193.5.

[152] Tex. R. Civ. P. 193.6(a).

[153] *See Fort Brown Villas III Condo. Ass'n, Inc. v. Gillenwater*, 285 S.W.3d 879, 881–82 (Tex. 2009) (finding that the trial court did not abuse its discretion in striking an untimely affidavit).

[154] *Boothe v. Hausler*, 766 S.W.2d 788, 789 (Tex. 1989) (per curiam).

[155] *Boothe v. Hausler*, 766 S.W.2d 788, 789 (Tex. 1989) (per curiam).

[156] *In re Does*, 337 S.W.3d 862, 864–65 (Tex. 2011) (per curiam).

[157] *In re Deere & Co.*, 299 S.W.3d 819, 820 (Tex. 2009) (per curiam).

[158] *In re Deere & Co.*, 299 S.W.3d 819, 820 (Tex. 2009) (per curiam); *In re Weekley Homes, L.P.*, 295 S.W.3d 309, 322 (Tex. 2009).

[159] *Transamerican Natural Gas Corp. v. Flores*, 870 S.W.2d 10, 12 (Tex. 1994).

[160] *See In re Bass*, 113 S.W.3d 735, 738 (Tex. 2003) (where a party seeking production has not shown a necessity for the requested trade secret materials, the trial court's action is an abuse of discretion).

[161] *In re E.I. DuPont de Nemours & Co.*, 136 S.W.3d 218, 223 (Tex. 2004).

[162] *Bodnow Corp. v. City of Hondo*, 721 S.W.2d 839, 840 (Tex. 1986) (per curiam).

[163] *Nath v. Tex. Children's Hosp.*, 446 S.W.3d 355, 361 (Tex. 2014) ("We review the imposition of sanctions under an abuse of discretion standard." (citing *Low v. Henry*, 221 S.W.3d 609, 614 (Tex. 2007))); *see also Bodnow Corp. v. City of Hondo*, 721 S.W.2d 839, 840 (Tex. 1986) (per curiam).

[164] *Nath v. Tex. Children's Hosp.*, 446 S.W.3d 355, 361 (Tex. 2014).

[165] *Nath v. Tex. Children's Hosp.*, 446 S.W.3d 355, 361 (Tex. 2014); *see also Bodnow Corp. v. City of Hondo*, 721 S.W.2d 839, 840 (Tex. 1986) (per curiam).

[166] *Cire v. Cummings*, 134 S.W.3d 835, 839 (Tex. 2004).

[167] *Downer v. Aquamarine Operators, Inc.*, 701 S.W.2d 238, 242–43 (Tex. 1985).

[168] *Bodnow Corp. v. City of Hondo*, 721 S.W.2d 839, 840 (Tex. 1986) (per curiam); *see also Braden v. Downey*, 811 S.W.2d 922, 929 (Tex. 1991) (finding that a district court abused its discretion by levying monetary sanctions to be paid before final judgment).

[169] Tex. R. Civ. P. 13.

[170] Tex. R. Civ. P. 13.

[171] *American Flood Research, Inc. v. Jones*, 192 S.W.3d 581, 583 (Tex. 2006).

[172] *American Flood Research, Inc. v. Jones*, 192 S.W.3d 581, 583 (Tex. 2006).

[173] Tex. R. Civ. P. 13.

[174] *Parker v. Walker*, 233 S.W.3d 535, 539–40 (Tex. App.—Houston [14th Dist.] 2007, no pet.).

[175] *Keever v. Finlan*, 988 S.W.2d 300, 312 (Tex. App.—Dallas 1999, pet. dism'd) (holding that a trial court abuses its discretion when it fails to make the required findings).

[176] *Nath v. Tex. Children's Hosp.*, 446 S.W.3d 355, 361 (Tex. 2014).

[177] *Low v. Henry*, 221 S.W.3d 609, 614 (Tex. 2007).

[178] *Nath v. Tex. Children's Hosp.*, 446 S.W.3d 355, 361 (Tex. 2014); *see also Low v. Henry*, 221 S.W.3d 609, 614 (Tex. 2007) (noting that the trial court must ensure that a direct nexus exists).

[179] *Low v. Henry*, 221 S.W.3d 609, 614 (Tex. 2007).

[180] Tex. Civ. Prac. & Rem. Code § 10.005.

[181] *Rudisell v. Paquette*, 89 S.W.3d 233, 238 (Tex. App.—Corpus Christi 2002, no pet.).

[182] *Chrysler Corp. v. Blackmon*, 841 S.W.2d 844, 849 (Tex. 1992); *Transamerican Natural Gas Corp. v. Powell*, 811 S.W.2d 913, 917 (Tex. 1991).

[183] *Transamerican Natural Gas Corp. v. Powell*, 811 S.W.2d 913, 917 (Tex. 1991) (reviewing trial court's exercise of discretion).

[184] *In re RSR Corp.*, 475 S.W.3d 775 (Tex. 2015) (orig. proceeding); *In re Cerberus Cap. Mgmt., L.P.*, 164 S.W.3d 379, 382 (Tex. 2005) (per curiam).

[185] *See* § 2-3:5.1.

[186] *In re Nitla S.A. de C.V.*, 92 S.W.3d 419, 422 (Tex. 2002).

[187] *In re RSR Corp.*, 475 S.W.3d 775 (Tex. 2015) (orig. proceeding) (citing *In re Meador*, 968 S.W.2d 346, 351–52 (Tex. 1998) (orig. proceeding)).

[188] *In re RSR Corp.*, 475 S.W.3d 775 (Tex. 2015) (orig. proceeding).

[189] *Union Carbide Corp. v. Martin*, 349 S.W.3d 137, 147 (Tex. App.—Dallas 2011, no pet.).

[190] *Union Carbide Corp. v. Martin*, 349 S.W.3d 137, 147 (Tex. App.—Dallas 2011, no pet.).

[191] *Union Carbide Corp. v. Martin*, 349 S.W.3d 137, 147 (Tex. App.—Dallas 2011, no pet.).

[192] *Union Carbide Corp. v. Martin*, 349 S.W.3d 137, 147 (Tex. App.—Dallas 2011, no pet.); *Polansky v. Berenji*, 393 S.W.3d 362, 367 (Tex. App.—Austin 2012, no pet.).

[193] *Brooks v. Expo Chem. Co.*, 576 S.W.2d 369, 370 (Tex. 1979) (citing *Davis et ux. v. Huey*, 571 S.W.2d 859 (Tex. 1978)).

[194] *Butnaru v. Ford Motor Co.*, 84 S.W.3d 198, 204 (Tex. 2002).

[195] *Brooks v. Expo Chem. Co.*, 576 S.W.2d 369, 371 (Tex. 1979).

[196] *Navarro Auto-Park, Inc. v. San Antonio*, 580 S.W.2d 339, 340 (Tex. 1979) (per curiam).

[197] *Butnaru v. Ford Motor Co.*, 84 S.W.3d 198, 204 (Tex. 2002).

[198] *Wyatt v. Shaw Plumbing*, 760 S.W.2d 245, 248 (Tex. 1988).

[199] *Wyatt v. Shaw Plumbing*, 760 S.W.2d 245, 248 (Tex. 1988).

[200] *In re Labatt Food Serv., L.P.*, 279 S.W.3d 640, 642–43 (Tex. 2009).

[201] *In re Am. Homestar of Lancaster, Inc.*, 50 S.W.3d 480, 483 (Tex. 2001).

[202] *In re Labatt Food Serv., L.P.*, 279 S.W.3d 640, 643 (Tex. 2009).

[203] *Jody James Farms, JV v. Altman Group, Inc.*, 547 S.W.3d 624, 633 (Tex. 2018).

[204] *In re Labbatt Food Serv., L.P.*, 279 S.W.3d 640, 643 (Tex. 2009).

[205] *In re Merrill Lynch & Co.*, 315 S.W.3d 888, 891 (Tex. 2010) (construing Federal Arbitration Act); *see also In re Labbatt Food Serv., L.P.*, 279 S.W.3d 640, 642–43 (Tex. 2009).

[206] *Southwestern Bell Tel. Co. v. Mktg. on Hold Inc.*, 308 S.W.3d 909, 915 (Tex. 2010); *Henry Schein, Inc. v. Stromboe*, 102 S.W.3d 675, 691 (Tex. 2003).

[207] *Henry Schein, Inc. v. Stromboe*, 102 S.W.3d 675, 690 (Tex. 2003) (quoting *Sw. Refining Co. v. Bernal*, 22 S.W.3d 425, 434–35 (Tex. 2000)).

[208] *San Benito v. Rio Grande Valley Gas Co.*, 109 S.W.3d 750, 757 (Tex. 2003).

[209] *General Motors Corp. v. Bloyed*, 916 S.W.2d 949, 955 (Tex. 1996).

[210] *General Motors Corp. v. Bloyed*, 916 S.W.2d 949, 955 (Tex. 1996).

[211] Tex. Civ. Prac. & Rem. Code § 74.351(r)(6).

[212] *Van Ness v. ETMC First Physicians*, 461 S.W.3d 140, 142 (Tex. 2015); *TTHR Ltd. P'ship v. Moreno*, 401 S.W.3d 41, 44 (Tex. 2013); *Jelinek v. Casas*, 328 S.W.3d 526, 539 (Tex. 2010); *American Transitional Care Centers of Tex., Inc. v. Palacios*, 46 S.W.3d 873, 877–78 (Tex. 2001).

[213] *Van Ness v. ETMC First Physicians*, 461 S.W.3d 140, 142 (Tex. 2015).

[214] *Van Ness v. ETMC First Physicians*, 461 S.W.3d 140, 141 (Tex. 2015) (noting that a good-faith effort is shown where the report informs the plaintiff of the conduct called into question, provides a basis for the trial court to conclude the claim has merit, and contains no material deficiency); *TTHR Ltd. P'ship v. Moreno*, 401 S.W.3d 41, 44 (Tex. 2013).

[215] *Van Ness v. ETMC First Physicians*, 461 S.W.3d 140, 142 (Tex. 2015).

[216] *American Transitional Care Centers of Tex., Inc. v. Palacios*, 46 S.W.3d 873, 878 (Tex. 2001).

[217] Tex. Civ. Prac. & Rem. Code § 74.351(c).

[218] *Samlowski v. Wooten*, 332 S.W.3d 404, 411 (Tex. 2011).

[219] *Samlowski v. Wooten*, 332 S.W.3d 404, 411 (Tex. 2011).

[220] *MacGregor v. Rich*, 941 S.W.2d 74, 75 (Tex. 1997) (per curiam).

[221] *Veterans' Land Bd. v. Williams*, 543 S.W.2d 89, 90 (Tex. 1976) (per curiam).

[222] *Veterans' Land Bd. v. Williams*, 543 S.W.2d 89, 90 (Tex. 1976) (per curiam).

[223] *See Alexander v. Lynda's Boutique*, 134 S.W.3d 845, 850–52 (Tex. 2004) (reviewing the record for clear notice).

[224] *Utz v. McKenzie*, 397 S.W.3d 273, 278 (Tex. App.—Dallas 2013, no pet.) (citing *Dolgencorp of Tex., Inc. v. Lerma*, 288 S.W.3d 922, 925 (Tex. 2009)).

[225] *Craddock v. Sunshine Bus Lines, Inc.*, 133 S.W.2d 124, 126 (Tex. 1939).

[226] *In re R.R.*, 209 S.W.3d 112, 114–15 (Tex. 2006) (per curiam) (citing *Craddock v. Sunshine Bus Lines, Inc.*, 133 S.W.2d 124, 126 (Tex. 1939)).

[227] *In re R.R.*, 209 S.W.3d 112, 114–15 (Tex. 2006) (per curiam) (citing *Craddock v. Sunshine Bus Lines, Inc.*, 133 S.W.2d 124, 126 (Tex. 1939)); *Utz v. McKenzie*, 397 S.W.3d 273, 278 (Tex. App.—Dallas 2013, no pet.) (conscious indifference is proven by evidence that defendant knew it was sued but did not care; generally, a decent excuse will negate that finding).

[228] *In re R.R.*, 209 S.W.3d 112, 115–16 (Tex. 2006) (per curiam).

[229] *Carpenter v. Cimarron Hydrocarbons Corp.*, 98 S.W.3d 682, 685 (Tex. 2002).

[230] *Carpenter v. Cimarron Hydrocarbons Corp.*, 98 S.W.3d 682, 687–88 (Tex. 2002).

[231] *Smith v. DeLooze*, No. 13-14-00092-CV, 2015 WL 124447, at *2 (Tex. App.—Corpus Christi-Edinburg Jan. 8, 2015, no pet. h.) (mem. op.).

[232] *Smith v. DeLooze*, No. 13-14-00092-CV, 2015 WL 124447, at *2 (Tex. App.—Corpus Christi-Edinburg Jan. 8, 2015, no pet. h.) (mem. op.).

[233] *Commercial Standard Ins. Co. v. Merit Clothing Co.*, 377 S.W.2d 179, 181 (Tex. 1964); *New York Party Shuttle, L.L.C. v. Bilello*, 414 S.W.3d 206, 217 (Tex. App.—Houston [1st Dist.] 2013, no pet.).

[234] *New York Party Shuttle, L.L.C. v. Bilello*, 414 S.W.3d 206, 217 (Tex. App.—Houston [1st Dist.] 2013, no pet.); Tex. R. Civ. P. 252.

[235] Tex. R. Civ. P. 253 (absence of counsel), 254 (attendance on legislature) (A continuance based upon a counsel's or party's membership in the legislature is mandatory in most instances).

[236] Tex. R. Civ. P. 18a(j)(1)(A).

[237] Tex. R. Civ. P. 18a(j)(1)(B).

[238] Tex. R. Civ. P. 18a(j)(2).

[239] *See In re Garcia*, No. 13-12-00440-CV, 2012 WL 3792112, at *3 (Tex. App.—Corpus Christi Aug. 31, 2012, orig. proceeding [mand. denied]) (mem. op.).

[240] *See* Tex. R. Civ. P. 76a.

[241] *In re Samsung Telecommc'ns of Am., Inc.*, Nos. 05-99-01949-CV & 05-99-01960-CV, 1999 WL 1081387, at *1 (Tex. App.—Dallas Dec. 2, 1999, orig. proceeding) (not designated for publication).

[242] *In re R.N.*, 356 S.W.3d 568, 574–75 (Tex. App.—Texarkana 2011, no pet.).

[243] *Kaufman v. Comm'n for Lawyer Discipline*, 197 S.W.3d 867, 873 (Tex. App.—Corpus Christi 2006, pet. denied).

[244] Tex. R. Evid. 201–04.

[245] *Guyton v. Monteau*, 332 S.W.3d 687, 692–93 (Tex. App.—Houston [14th Dist.] 2011, no pet.) (taking judicial notice is not appropriate simply because a fact is known to the judge personally).

[246] *Guyton v. Monteau*, 332 S.W.3d 687, 693 (Tex. App.—Houston [14th Dist.] 2011, no pet.); *see also Tranter v. Duemling*, 129 S.W.3d 257, 262 (Tex. App.—El Paso 2004, no pet.) (facts described by Tex. R. Evid. 201(b)(2) are known as "verifiably certain facts").

[247] Tex. R. Evid. 202; *see also Cutler v. Cutler*, 543 S.W.2d 1, 3 (Tex. Civ. App.—Dallas 1976, writ ref'd n.r.e.).

[248] *Holden v. Capri Lighting, Inc.*, 960 S.W.2d 831, 833 (Tex. App.—Amarillo 1997, no pet.).

[249] *Hartis v. Cent. Furniture Indus., Inc.*, 230 S.W.3d 723, 737 (Tex. App.—Houston [14th Dist.] 2007, no pet.) (citing authorities).

[250] *Gorman v. Gorman*, 966 S.W.2d 858, 867 (Tex. App.—Houston [1st Dist.] 1998, pet. denied).

[251] *Goode v. Shoukfeh*, 943 S.W.2d 441, 446 (Tex. 1997).

[252] *Amis v. Ashworth*, 802 S.W.2d 379, 382–83 (Tex. App.—Tyler 1990, orig. proceeding).

[253] *In re Commitment of Hill*, 334 S.W.3d 226, 229 (Tex. 2011).

[254] *In re Commitment of Hill*, 334 S.W.3d 226, 229 (Tex. 2011) (citing *Babcock v. Nw. Mem'l Hosp.*, 767 S.W.2d 705, 709 (Tex. 1989)).

[255] *Murff v. Pass*, 249 S.W.3d 407, 411 (Tex. 2008) (internal citations omitted).

[256] *See* Tex. R. Evid. 614 ("witnesses are excluded so that they cannot hear the testimony of other witnesses"); Tex. R. Civ. P. 267.

[257] Tex. R. Civ. P. 267(b)(3); *see also Drilex Sys., Inc. v. Flores*, 1 S.W.3d 112, 116–17 (Tex. 1999) (finding that excluding cumulative testimony was not abuse of discretion).

[258] *Drilex Sys., Inc. v. Flores*, 1 S.W.3d 112, 117–18 (Tex. 1999).

[259] *Guerrero v. Smith*, 864 S.W.2d 797, 800 (Tex. App.—Houston [14th Dist.] 1993, no writ); *Ranger Ins. Co. v. Rogers*, 530 S.W.2d 162, 170 (Tex. Civ. App.—Austin 1975, writ ref'd n.r.e.).

[260] *Gharda USA, Inc. v. Control Sol'ns, Inc.*, 464 S.W.3d 338, 347 (Tex. 2015); *National Liab. & Fire Ins. Co. v. Allen*, 15 S.W.3d 525, 527–28 (Tex. 2000); *E.I. du Pont de Nemours & Co. v. Robinson*, 923 S.W.2d 549, 558 (Tex. 1995).

[261] *Owens-Corning Fiberglas Corp. v. Malone*, 972 S.W.2d 35, 43 (Tex. 1998).

[262] *Gharda USA, Inc. v. Control Sol'ns, Inc.*, 464 S.W.3d 338, 347 (Tex. 2015); *E.I. du Pont de Nemours & Co. v. Robinson*, 923 S.W.2d 549, 558 (Tex. 1995); *United Blood Servs. v. Longoria*, 938 S.W.2d 29, 30 (Tex. 1997) (per curiam).

[263] *Whirlpool Corp. v. Camacho*, 298 S.W.3d 631, 637 (Tex. 2009).

[264] *Whirlpool Corp. v. Camacho*, 298 S.W.3d 631, 637 (Tex. 2009).

[265] *Whirlpool Corp. v. Camacho*, 298 S.W.3d 631, 638 (Tex. 2009).

[266] *Perry Homes v. Cull*, 258 S.W.3d 580, 598 (Tex. 2008); *National Liab. & Fire Ins. Co. v. Allen*, 15 S.W.3d 525, 529 (Tex. 2000).

[267] Tex. R. Civ. P. 193.6(a), (b).

[268] *F&H Invs. Inc. v. State*, 55 S.W.3d 663, 669 (Tex. App.—Waco 2001, no pet.) (quoting *Alvarado v. Farah Mfg. Co.*, 830 S.W.2d 911, 914 (Tex. 1992)); *but see Oscar Luis Lopez v. La Madeleine of Tex., Inc.*, 200 S.W.3d 854, 864 (Tex. App.—Dallas 2006, no pet.) (conducting legal-sufficiency review).

[269] *In re R.N.*, 356 S.W.3d 568, 575 (Tex. App.—Texarkana 2011, no pet.).

[270] *See* § 2-2:2.10 for the discussion of de novo review of jury-charge issues.

[271] *Shupe v. Lingafelter*, 192 S.W.3d 577, 579 (Tex. 2006) (per curiam).

[272] *JPMorgan Chase Bank, N.A. v. Prof'l Pharmacy II*, __ S.W.3d __, No. 02-11-00373-CV, 2014 WL 7473779, at *5 (Tex. App.—Fort Worth Dec. 31, 2014, no pet. h.).

[273] *Thota v. Young*, 366 S.W.3d 678, 687 (Tex. 2012) (quoting *Columbia Rio Grande Healthcare, L.P. v. Hawley*, 284 S.W.3d 851, 855–56 (Tex. 2009)).

[274] *Shupe v. Lingafelter*, 192 S.W.3d 577, 579 (Tex. 2006) (per curiam) (citations omitted).

[275] This reversible-error standard is discussed in Chapter 3.

[276] *Texas Dep't of Human Servs. v. E.B.*, 802 S.W.2d 647, 649 (Tex. 1990); Tex. R. Civ. P. 277.

[277] *Crown Life Ins. Co. v. Casteel*, 22 S.W.3d 378, 381 (Tex. 2000).

[278] This reversible-error standard is discussed in Chapter 3.

[279] Tex. R. Civ. P. 282.

[280] *Watts v. Watts*, 396 S.W.3d 19, 21–22 (Tex. App.—San Antonio 2012, no pet.) (citing Tex. R. Civ. P. 286).

[281] *Lochnivar Corp. v. Meyers*, 930 S.W.2d 182, 187 (Tex. App.—Dallas 1996, no writ) (citing *Stevens v. Travelers Ins. Co.*, 563 S.W.2d 223, 229 (Tex. 1978) (noting dynamite charges are described as such due to blasting a jury from a deadlock to a verdict)).

[282] *Golden Eagle Archery, Inc. v. Jackson*, 24 S.W.3d 362, 372 (Tex. 2000) (interpreting Tex. R. Civ. P. 327(b), 606); *Pharo v. Chambers Cnty.*, 922 S.W.2d 945, 948 (Tex. 1996).

[283] *Pharo v. Chambers Cnty.*, 922 S.W.2d 945, 948 (Tex. 1996).

[284] *Golden Eagle Archery, Inc. v. Jackson*, 24 S.W.3d 362, 372 (Tex. 2000).

[285] Tex. Civ. Prac. & Rem. Code § 37.009.

[286] The legal-sufficiency standard is discussed in § 2-4:1; factual-sufficiency standard in § 2-4:2.

[287] *Bocquet v. Herring*, 972 S.W.2d 19, 21 (Tex. 1998).

[288] *Bocquet v. Herring*, 972 S.W.2d 19, 21 (Tex. 1998).

[289] The legal-sufficiency standard is discussed in § 2-4:1; factual sufficiency in § 2-4:2.

[290] *Grotewold v. Meyer*, 457 S.W.3d 531, 533 (Tex. App.—Houston [1st Dist.] 2015, no pet.); *see also Moore v. Moore*, 383 S.W.3d 190, 198 (Tex. App.—Dallas 2012, pet. denied).

[291] *Bradshaw v. Bradshaw*, 555 S.W.3d 539, 549 (Tex. 2018); *Grotewold v. Meyer*, 457 S.W.3d 531, 533 (Tex. App.—Houston [1st Dist.] 2015, no pet.).

[292] *Grotewold v. Meyer*, 457 S.W.3d 531, 533 (Tex. App.—Houston [1st Dist.] 2015, no pet.).

[293] *Worford v. Stamper*, 801 S.W.2d 108, 109 (Tex. 1990); *see also Ilff v. Ilff*, 339 S.W.3d 74, 78 (Tex. 2011) (noting that this grant of discretion to the trial court is limited by Texas Family Code sections 154.121—154.123).

[294] *In re J.A.J.*, 243 S.W.3d 611, 616 (Tex. 2007).

[295] *In re J.A.J.*, 243 S.W.3d 611, 616 (Tex. 2007).

[296] *In re W.E.R.*, 669 S.W.2d 716, 716–17 (Tex. 1984) (per curiam).

[297] *Roberts v. Roberts*, 402 S.W.3d 833, 838 (Tex. App.—San Antonio 2013, no pet.).

[298] *Roberts v. Roberts*, 402 S.W.3d 833, 838 (Tex. App.—San Antonio 2013, no pet.).

[299] *Grotewold v. Meyer*, 457 S.W.3d 531, 533–34 (Tex. App.—Houston [1st Dist.] 2015, no pet.).

[300] *In re Bent*, 487 S.W.3d 170, 178 (Tex. 2016) (noting "the abuse-of-discretion standard applies to merits review" of an order granting a new trial "just as it does in all mandamus proceedings").

[301] *In re United Scaffolding, Inc.*, 377 S.W.3d 685, 688–89 (Tex. 2012).

[302] *In re United Scaffolding, Inc.*, 377 S.W.3d 685, 688 (Tex. 2012).

[303] *In re Toyota Motor Sales, U.S.A., Inc.*, 407 S.W.3d 746, 758 (Tex. 2013); *see In re Wyatt Field Serv. Co.*, 454 S.W.3d 145, 150 (Tex. App.—Houston [1st Dist.] 2014, orig. proceeding) (determining proper process for merits-based factual-sufficiency review of a new trial order).

[304] *Pharo v. Chambers Cnty.*, 922 S.W.2d 945, 949 (Tex. 1996).

[305] *Greater Fort Worth & Tarrant Cnty. Cmty. Action Agency v. Mims*, 627 S.W.2d 149, 151 (Tex. 1982); *In re Estate of Johnson*, No. 06-11-00034-CV, 2011 WL 3503188, at *3 (Tex. App.—Texarkana Aug. 11, 2011, no pet.) (mem. op.).

[306] *Ex parte S.D.*, 457 S.W.3d 168, 170 (Tex. App.—Amarillo 2015, no pet.).

[307] *Ex parte S.D.*, 457 S.W.3d 168, 171 (Tex. App.—Amarillo 2015, no pet.).

[308] *Ablon v. Campbell*, 457 S.W.3d 604, 608–09 (Tex. App.—Dallas 2015, pet. denied) (statutory bill of review under Probate Code § 867) (citing *Valdez v. Hollenbeck*, 410 S.W.3d 1, 9 (Tex. App.—San Antonio 2013, pet. granted) (equitable bill of review)).

[309] *Walker v. Packer*, 827 S.W.2d 833, 839 (Tex. 1992) (citations omitted).

[310] *Walker v. Packer*, 827 S.W.2d 833, 839 (Tex. 1992) (quoting *Johnson v. Fourth Court of Appeals*, 700 S.W.2d 916, 917 (Tex. 1985)); *see also In re Cerberus Cap. Mgmt., L.P.*, 164 S.W.3d 379, 382 (Tex. 2005) (per curiam).

[311] *Walker v. Packer*, 827 S.W.2d 833, 839–40 (Tex. 1992); *see also In re RSR Corp.*, 475 S.W.3d 774 (Tex. 2015) (orig. proceeding) ("[W]e may not make factual determinations in

mandamus proceedings."); *in re Mem'l Hermann Hosp. Sys.*, 464 S.W.3d 686, 698 (Tex. 2015) (orig. proceeding) ("A reviewing court may not substitute its judgment for that of the trial court regarding the resolution of fact issues or matters committed to the trial court's discretion.").

312 *Walker v. Packer*, 827 S.W.2d 833, 840 (Tex. 1992); *see also In re RSR Corp.*, 475 S.W.3d 775 (Tex. 2015) (orig. proceeding) ("A trial court abuses its discretion if it incorrectly analyzes or applies the law.").

313 *In re Wyatt Field Servs. Co.*, 454 S.W.3d 145, 149 (Tex. App.—Houston [1st Dist.] 2014, orig. proceeding) (citing *In re Cerebus Cap. Mgmt., L.P.*, 164 S.W.3d 379, 382 (Tex. 2005) (orig. proceeding) (per curiam)).

314 *In re RSR Corp.*, 475 S.W.3d 775 (Tex. 2015) (orig. proceeding) (holding that a party whose counsel is improperly disqualified has no adequate remedy by appeal, so mandamus will be granted if the trial court abused its discretion).

315 Mandamus practice and standards are discussed further in Chapter 6.

316 *Triantaphyllis v. Gamble*, 93 S.W.3d 398, 402 (Tex. App.—Houston [14th Dist.] 2002, pet. denied); *Priest v. Tex. Animal Health Comm'n*, 780 S.W.2d 874, 875–76 (Tex. App.—Dallas 1989, no writ).

317 *Triantaphyllis v. Gamble*, 93 S.W.3d 398, 402 (Tex. App.—Houston [14th Dist.] 2002, pet. denied).

318 *Ortiz v. Jones*, 917 S.W.2d 770, 772 (Tex. 1996) ("A trial court's findings of fact are reviewed for factual sufficiency of the evidence under the same legal standards as applied to review jury verdicts for factual sufficiency of the evidence."); *Catalina v. Blasdel*, 881 S.W.2d 295, 297 (Tex. 1994).

319 *BMC Software v. Marchand*, 83 S.W.3d 789, 795 (Tex. 2002) (when findings are implied in favor of trial court ruling, but the clerk's and reporter's records are included on appeal, then "these implied findings are not conclusive and may be challenged for legal and factual sufficiency in the appropriate appellate court").

320 *City of Keller v. Wilson*, 168 S.W.3d 802 (Tex. 2005); *see also Bank of Am., N.A. v. Eisenhauer*, 474 S.W.3d 264, 265 (Tex. 2015) (per curiam) (holding that a JNOV is reviewed de novo); *Gharda USA, Inc. v Control Sol'ns, Inc.*, 464 S.W.3d 338, 347 (Tex. 2015); *In re Estate of Hamner*, No. 09-13-00218-CV, 2015 WL 474274, at *2 (Tex. App.—Beaumont Feb. 5, 2015, no pet. h.) (mem. op.) (directed verdict); *JPMorgan Chase Bank, N.A. v. Prof'l Pharmacy II*, __ S.W.3d __, No. 02-11-00373-CV, 2014 WL 7473779, at *11 (Tex. App.—Fort Worth Dec. 31, 2014, no pet. h.) ("An appeal from the denial of a motion for directed verdict is a challenge to the legal sufficiency of the evidence."); *Aon Risk Servs. Sw., Inc. v. C.L. Thomas, Inc.*, No. 13-13-00205-CV, 2014 WL 7233379, at *2 (Tex. App.—Corpus Christi-Edinburg Dec. 19, 2014, no pet.) (mem. op.) (a JNOV is reviewed for legal sufficiency unless it was based on the ground that a legal principle precludes recovery, when it is reviewed de novo); *Shanklin v. Bassoe Offshore (USA) Inc.*, 415 S.W.3d 311, 316 (Tex. App.—Houston [1st Dist.] 2013, pet. denied).

321 *See Boerjan v. Rodriguez*, 436 S.W.3d 307, 311–12 (Tex. 2014) (evidence is reviewed in the light most favorable to the party against whom summary judgment was granted); *Ford Motor Co. v. Castillo*, 444 S.W.3d 616, 620 (Tex. 2014) ("[W]e must view the evidence in the light most favorable to the verdict."); *Merriman v. XTO Energy, Inc.*, 407 S.W.3d 244, 248 (Tex. 2013) (evidence is reviewed in the light most favorable to the party against whom a directed verdict was granted).

322 Robert W. Calvert, *"No Evidence" & "Insufficient Evidence" Points of Error*, 38 Tex. L. Rev. 361 (1960); *Gharda USA, Inc. v. Control Sol'ns, Inc.*, 464 S.W.3d 338, 347 (Tex. 2015) (citing cases relying on Calvert article).

323 *Jelinek v. Casas*, 328 S.W.3d 526, 532 (Tex. 2010) (quoting *Kindred v. Con/Chem, Inc.*, 650 S.W.2d 61, 63 (Tex. 1983)).

[324] *Merrell Dow Pharms., Inc. v. Havner*, 953 S.W.2d 706, 711 (Tex. 1997) (quoting *Burroughs Wllcome Co. v. Crye*, 907 S.W.2d 497, 499 (Tex. 1995)).

[325] *Dow Chem. Co. v. Francis*, 46 S.W.3d 237, 241–42 (Tex. 2001).

[326] *Compass Bank v. Nacim*, 459 S.W.3d 95, 101–02 (Tex. App.—El Paso 2015, no pet.).

[327] *Compass Bank v. Nacim*, 459 S.W.3d 95, 101–02 (Tex. App.—El Paso 2015, no pet.).

[328] *City of Keller v. Wilson*, 168 S.W.3d 802 (Tex. 2005).

[329] *City of Keller v. Wilson*, 168 S.W.3d 802, 827 (Tex. 2005) (footnotes omitted); *see also Kingsaire, Inc. v. Memendez*, 477 S.W.3d 309, 313 (Tex. 2015) ("In conducting a legal-sufficiency review, we consider the evidence and reasonable inferences tending to support the finding and disregard contrary evidence and inferences.").

[330] *City of Keller v. Wilson*, 168 S.W.3d 802, 810–11 (Tex. 2005).

[331] *City of Keller v. Wilson*, 168 S.W.3d 802, 811 (Tex. 2005) (citing cases).

[332] *City of Keller v. Wilson*, 168 S.W.3d 802, 811 (Tex. 2005) (citing cases).

[333] *City of Keller v. Wilson*, 168 S.W.3d 802, 811–12 (Tex. 2005) (citing cases).

[334] *City of Keller v. Wilson*, 168 S.W.3d 802, 812 (Tex. 2005).

[335] *City of Keller v. Wilson*, 168 S.W.3d 802, 812 (Tex. 2005).

[336] *City of Keller v. Wilson*, 168 S.W.3d 802, 812 (Tex. 2005).

[337] *City of Keller v. Wilson*, 168 S.W.3d 802, 812–13 (Tex. 2005); *see also Jelinek v. Casas*, 328 S.W.3d 526, 533 (Tex. 2010) (when expert testimony of causation is required, lay evidence is legally insufficient and constitutes no evidence as a matter of law).

[338] *City of Keller v. Wilson*, 168 S.W.3d 802, 813 (Tex. 2005).

[339] *City of Keller v. Wilson*, 168 S.W.3d 802, 813 (Tex. 2005).

[340] *Whirlpool Corp. v. Camacho*, 298 S.W.3d 631, 638 (Tex. 2009).

[341] *Whirlpool Corp. v. Camacho*, 298 S.W.3d 631, 638 (Tex. 2009).

[342] *Gharda USA, Inc. v. Control Sol'ns, Inc.*, 464 S.W.3d 338, 347 (Tex. 2015); *Whirlpool Corp. v. Camacho*, 298 S.W.3d 631, 638 (Tex. 2009).

[343] *City of Keller v. Wilson*, 168 S.W.3d 802, 813 (Tex. 2005).

[344] *City of Keller v. Wilson*, 168 S.W.3d 802, 814 (Tex. 2005).

[345] *City of Keller v. Wilson*, 168 S.W.3d 802, 814–15 (Tex. 2005).

[346] *City of Keller v. Wilson*, 168 S.W.3d 802, 814–15 (Tex. 2005).

[347] *City of Keller v. Wilson*, 168 S.W.3d 802, 815 (Tex. 2005).

[348] *City of Keller v. Wilson*, 168 S.W.3d 802, 816 (Tex. 2005).

[349] *City of Keller v. Wilson*, 168 S.W.3d 802, 815–16 (Tex. 2005).

[350] *City of Keller v. Wilson*, 168 S.W.3d 802, 817 (Tex. 2005).

[351] *City of Keller v. Wilson*, 168 S.W.3d 802, 817 (Tex. 2005).

[352] *City of Keller v. Wilson*, 168 S.W.3d 802, 817 (Tex. 2005).

[353] *City of Keller v. Wilson*, 168 S.W.3d 802, 817 (Tex. 2005).

[354] *City of Keller v. Wilson*, 168 S.W.3d 802, 817–18 (Tex. 2005).

[355] *City of Keller v. Wilson*, 168 S.W.3d 802, 818 (Tex. 2005).

[356] *City of Keller v. Wilson*, 168 S.W.3d 802, 818 (Tex. 2005).

[357] *City of Keller v. Wilson*, 168 S.W.3d 802, 818 (Tex. 2005).

[358] *City of Keller v. Wilson*, 168 S.W.3d 802, 820 (Tex. 2005).

[359] *City of Keller v. Wilson*, 168 S.W.3d 802, 819 (Tex. 2005).

[360] *City of Keller v. Wilson*, 168 S.W.3d 802, 819 (Tex. 2005).

361 *City of Keller v. Wilson*, 168 S.W.3d 802, 820 (Tex. 2005).

362 *City of Keller v. Wilson*, 168 S.W.3d 802, 820 (Tex. 2005).

363 *City of Keller v. Wilson*, 168 S.W.3d 802, 820–21 (Tex. 2005).

364 *City of Keller v. Wilson*, 168 S.W.3d 802, 820–21 (Tex. 2005).

365 *City of Keller v. Wilson*, 168 S.W.3d 802, 821 (Tex. 2005).

366 *City of Keller v. Wilson*, 168 S.W.3d 802, 821 (Tex. 2005).

367 *Kingsaire, Inc. v. Melendez*, 477 S.W.3d 309, 317 (Tex. 2015) (quoting *Hancock v. Variyam*, 400 S.W.3d 59, 70 (Tex. 2013)).

368 *City of Keller v. Wilson*, 168 S.W.3d 802 (Tex. 2005).

369 *AutoZone, Inc. v. Reyes*, 272 S.W.3d 588, 592 (Tex. 2008) (citing *City of Keller v. Wilson*, 168 S.W.3d 802, 827 (Tex. 2005)); *see also Blaylock v. Holland*, 396 S.W.3d 720, 722 (Tex. App.—Dallas 2013, no pet.) (same); *Clear Lake City Water Auth. v. Clear Lake Country Club, L.P.*, 340 S.W.3d 27, 34 (Tex. App.—Houston [1st Dist.] 2011, no pet.) (same).

370 *Citizens Nat'l Bank in Waxahachie v. Scott*, 195 S.W.3d 94, 96 (Tex. 2006) (per curiam).

371 *Citizens Nat'l Bank in Waxahachie v. Scott*, 195 S.W.3d 94, 96 (Tex. 2006) (per curiam).

372 *Ortiz v. Jones*, 917 S.W.2d 770, 772 (Tex. 1996); *Cain v. Bain*, 709 S.W.2d 175, 176 (Tex. 1986).

373 *Ortiz v. Jones*, 917 S.W.2d 770, 772 (Tex. 1996).

374 *Bergene v. Community Bank of Tex., N.A.*, No. 09-12-00315-CV, 2013 WL 2732681, at *2 (Tex. App.—Beaumont June 13, 2013, no pet.) (mem. op.).

375 *Lanier v. E. Foundations, Inc.*, 401 S.W.3d 445, 455 (Tex. App.—Dallas 2013, no pet.).

376 Elaine A. Grafton Carlson, 6 McDonald & Carlson Tex. Civ. App. Prac. § 44:10 (2d ed., Westlaw, database updated Dec. 2012) (citations omitted).

377 Elaine A. Grafton Carlson, 6 McDonald & Carlson Tex. Civ. App. Prac. § 44:10 (2d ed., Westlaw, database updated Dec. 2012) (citations omitted).

378 *Gonzalez v. McAllen Med. Center, Inc.*, 195 S.W.3d 680, 681 (Tex. 2006); *see also Pool v. Ford Motor Co.*, 715 S.W.2d 629, 635 (Tex. 1986) (Intermediate courts overruling judgments on factual sufficiency grounds "should, in their opinions, detail the evidence relevant to the issue in consideration and clearly state why the jury's finding is factually insufficient or is so against the great weight and preponderance as to be manifestly unjust; why it shocks the conscience; or clearly demonstrates bias. Further, those courts, in their opinions, should state in what regard the contrary evidence greatly outweighs the evidence in support of the verdict.").

379 *Gonzalez v. McAllen Med. Center, Inc.*, 195 S.W.3d 680, 681 (Tex. 2006).

380 *Gonzalez v. McAllen Med. Center, Inc.*, 195 S.W.3d 680, 681 (Tex. 2006).

381 *In re Smith*, 192 S.W.3d 564, 568 n.3 (Tex. 2006).

382 *In re S.M.R.*, 434 S.W.3d 576, 586 (Tex. 2014) (quoting *Jaffee Aircraft Corp. v. Carr*, 867 S.W.2d 27, 29 (Tex. 1993)).

383 *In re S.M.R.*, 434 S.W.3d 576, 586 (Tex. 2014) (quoting *Jaffee Aircraft Corp. v. Carr*, 867 S.W.2d 27, 29 (Tex. 1993)).

384 *In re S.M.R.*, 434 S.W.3d 576, 586 (Tex. 2014).

385 *In re S.M.R.*, 434 S.W.3d 576, 586 (Tex. 2014).

386 *Diamond Shamrock Refining Co., L.P. v. Hall*, 168 S.W.3d 164, 170 (Tex. 2005) (quoting *Southwestern Bell Tel. Co. v. Garza*, 164 S.W.3d 607, 632 (Tex. 2004)).

387 *Diamond Shamrock Refining Co., L.P. v. Hall*, 168 S.W.3d 164, 170 (Tex. 2005).

388 *Diamond Shamrock Refining Co., L.P. v. Hall*, 168 S.W.3d 164, 170 (Tex. 2005) (quoting *In re J.F.C.*, 96 S.W.3d 256, 266 (Tex. 2002)).

[389] Tex. Civ. Prac. & Rem. Code § 41.003(a).

[390] Tex. Civ. Prac. & Rem. Code § 41.003(b).

[391] Tex. Civ. Prac. & Rem. Code § 41.003(c).

[392] Tex. Civ. Prac. & Rem. Code § 41.003(d).

[393] *Southwestern Bell Tel. Co. v. Garza*, 164 S.W.3d 607, 625 (Tex. 2004).

[394] *See, e.g., Safeshred, Inc. v. Martinez*, 365 S.W.3d 655, 662–63 (Tex. 2012) (spreading false rumors about a fired employee may establish malice because preventing the former employee from being rehired is a qualitatively different damage than the firing itself).

[395] *Diamond Shamrock Refining Co., L.P. v. Hall*, 168 S.W.3d 164, 170 (Tex. 2005) (quoting *In re J.F.C.*, 96 S.W.3d 256, 266 (Tex. 2002)).

[396] *Diamond Shamrock Refining Co., L.P. v. Hall*, 168 S.W.3d 164, 170 (Tex. 2005).

[397] *Diamond Shamrock Refining Co., L.P. v. Hall*, 168 S.W.3d 164, 170 (Tex. 2005).

[398] *Diamond Shamrock Refining Co., L.P. v. Hall*, 168 S.W.3d 164, 170 (Tex. 2005); *see also U-Haul Int'l, Inc. v. Waldrip*, 380 S.W.3d 118, 137–41 (Tex. 2012) (engaging in the same type of factual analysis).

[399] Tex. Civ. Prac. & Rem. Code § 41.003(a)(3).

[400] *Columbia Med. Center of Las Colinas v. Hogue*, 271 S.W.3d 238, 248–49 (Tex. 2008); *Diamond Shamrock Refining Co., L.P. v. Hall*, 168 S.W.3d 164, 170 (Tex. 2005).

[401] Tex. Health & Safety Code § 574.034.

[402] Tex. Health & Safety Code § 574.034.

[403] *State v. K.E.W.*, 315 S.W.3d 16, 20 (Tex. 2010).

[404] Tex. Fam. Code § 161.001.

[405] Tex. Fam. Code § 101.007.

[406] *In re B.G.*, No. 14-14-00729-CV, 2015 WL 393044, at *2 (Tex. App.—Houston [1st Dist.] 4 Jan. 29, 2015, no pet. h.) (mem. op.).

[407] *In re K.M.L.*, 443 S.W.3d 101, 112–13 (Tex. 2014); *In re J.F.C.*, 96 S.W.3d 256, 265–66 (Tex. 2002) (same); *see also In re E.N.C.*, 384 S.W.3d 796, 803 (Tex. 2012) (quoting *In re J.O.A.*, 283 S.W.3d 336, 346 (Tex. 2009)); *C.V. v. Tex. Dept. of Family & Protective Servs.*, 408 S.W.3d 495, 502–03 (Tex. App.—El Paso 2013, no pet.) (describing standard as "whether the evidence is such that a factfinder could reasonably form a firm belief or conviction about the truth of the State's allegations") (quoting *In re C.H.*, 89 S.W.3d 17, 25 (Tex. 2002)).

[408] *Bentley v. Bunton*, 94 S.W.3d 561, 596 (Tex. 1997).

[409] *Bentley v. Bunton*, 94 S.W.3d 561, 596 (Tex. 1997).

[410] *Catalina v. Blasdel*, 881 S.W.2d 295, 297 (Tex. 1994).

[411] *Worford v. Stamper*, 801 S.W.2d 108, 109 (Tex. 1990).

[412] *Vickery v. Comm'n for Lawyer Discipline*, 5 S.W.3d 241, 251 (Tex. App.—Houston [14th Dist.] 1999, pet. denied).

[413] *Vickery v. Comm'n for Lawyer Discipline*, 5 S.W.3d 241, 251 (Tex. App.—Houston [14th Dist.] 1999, pet. denied).

[414] Tex. R. Civ. P. 296, 297; *Cherne Indus., Inc. v. Magallanes*, 763 S.W.2d 768, 772 (Tex. 1989).

[415] *Tenery v. Tenery*, 932 S.W.2d 29, 30 (Tex. 1996) (quoting *Cherne Indus., Inc. v. Magallanes*, 763 S.W.2d 768, 772 (Tex. 1989)).

[416] *Liberty Mut. Fire Ins. v. Laca*, 243 S.W.3d 791, 794 (Tex. App.—El Paso 2007, no pet.).

[417] *Liberty Mut. Fire Ins. v. Laca*, 243 S.W.3d 791, 794 (Tex. App.—El Paso 2007, no pet.).

[418] *Mayhew v. Town of Sunnyvale*, 964 S.W.2d 922, 938 (Tex. 1998).

[419] *City of San Antonio v. TPLP Office Park Props.*, 218 S.W.3d 60, 65 (Tex. 2007).

420 *City of San Antonio v. TPLP Office Park Props.*, 218 S.W.3d 60, 65 (Tex. 2007).

421 *City of San Antonio v. TPLP Office Park Props.*, 218 S.W.3d 60, 65 (Tex. 2007).

422 *Klumb v. Hous. Mun. Emps. Pension Sys.*, 458 S.W.3d 1, 13 (Tex. 2015).

423 *Klumb v. Hous. Mun. Emps. Pension Sys.*, 458 S.W.3d 1, 13 (Tex. 2015).

424 *Klumb v. Hous. Mun. Emps. Pension Sys.*, 458 S.W.3d 1, 13 (Tex. 2015).

425 Tex. Civ. Prac. & Rem. Code §§ 27.003-.011.

426 Tex. Civ. Prac. & Rem. Code § 27.005(c).

427 *Rehak Creative Servs., Inc. v. Witt*, 404 S.W.3d 716, 726 (Tex. App.—Houston [14th Dist.] 2013, pet. denied) (quoting *McDonald v. Clemens*, 464 S.W.2d 450, 456 (Tex. Civ. App.—Tyler 1971, no writ)).

428 *Rehak Creative Servs., Inc. v. Witt*, 404 S.W.3d 716, 726 (Tex. App.—Houston [14th Dist.] 2013, pet. denied) (quoting *Duncan v. Butterowe, Inc.*, 474 S.W.2d 619, 621 (Tex. Civ. App.—Houston [14th Dist.] 1971, no writ)).

429 *In re C.E.*, 391 S.W.3d 200, 203 (Tex. App.—Houston [1st Dist.] 2012, no pet.) (citing *Baker v. Goldsmith*, 582 S.W.2d 404, 406 (Tex. 1979); *Nichols v. Jack Eckerd Corp.*, 908 S.W.2d 5, 7–8 (Tex. App.—Houston [1st Dist.] 1995, no writ)); *see also Elliott v. Elliott*, 21 S.W.3d 913, 917 (Tex. App.—Fort Worth 2000, pet. denied).

430 *Rehak Creative Servs., Inc. v. Witt*, 404 S.W.3d 716, 726 (Tex. App.—Houston [14th Dist.] 2013, pet. denied).

431 *See* Tex. Civ. Prac. & Rem. Code § 171.088; *CVN Group, Inc. v. Delgado*, 95 S.W.3d 234, 237–38 (Tex. 2002) (assuming continued viability of common-law grounds for vacating an arbitration award issued under the Texas General Arbitration Act). *But see Nafta Traders, Inc. v. Quinn*, 339 S.W.3d 84, 91–92 (Tex. 2011) (when reviewing arbitration awards issued under the Federal Arbitration Act, the court is constrained by the United States Supreme Court's decision in *Hall Street Assocs., L.L.C. v. Mattel, Inc.*, 552 U.S. 576, 578 (2008), that the federal statutory grounds are exclusive).

432 *In re Chestnut Energy Partners, Inc.*, 300 S.W.3d 386, 397 (Tex. App.—Dallas 2009, orig. proceeding [mand. denied]).

433 *See Bison Bldg Materials, Ltd. v. Aldridge*, 422 S.W.3d 582, 588 (Tex. 2012) (quoting *Wall St. Assoc., L.P. v. Becker Paribas Inc.*, 27 F.3d 845, 849 (2nd Cir. 1994)); *East Tex. Salt Water Disposal Co., Inc. v. Werline*, 307 S.W.3d 267, 271 (Tex. 2010) ("[J]udicial review of an arbitration award is extraordinarily narrow.").

434 *Corrections Prods. Co., Ltd. v. Gaiser Precast Constr.*, 394 S.W.3d 818, 824 (Tex. App.—El Paso 2013, no pet.).

435 Tex. Civ. Prac. & Rem. Code § 171.088(a).

436 *Xtria L.L.C. v. Int'l Ins. Alliance Inc.*, 286 S.W.3d 583, 598 (Tex. App.—Texarkana 2009, pet. denied); *Aspri Invs., L.L.C. v. Afeef*, No. 04-10-00573-CV, 2011 WL 384987, at *7 (Tex. App.—San Antonio Aug. 31, 2011, pet. dism'd) (mem. op.).

437 *Xtria L.L.C. v. Int'l Ins. Alliance Inc.*, 286 S.W.3d 583, 594 (Tex. App.—Texarkana 2009, pet. denied); *Aero Air, L.L.C. v. Sino Swearingen Aircraft Corp.*, 55 No. 07-07-00271-CV, 2009 WL 1940916, at *1–2 (Tex. App.—Amarillo July 7, 2009, no pet.) (mem. op.).

438 *CVN Group, Inc. v. Delgado*, 95 S.W.3d 234, 239 (Tex. 2002).

439 *Bennett v. Reynolds*, 315 S.W.3d 867, 873 (Tex. 2010) (quoting *State Farm Mut. Auto. Ins. Co. v. Campbell*, 538 U.S. 408, 417 (2003)).

440 *Bennett v. Reynolds*, 315 S.W.3d 867, 874 (Tex. 2010).

441 *Bennett v. Reynolds*, 315 S.W.3d 867, 874 (Tex. 2010).

442 *Bennett v. Reynolds*, 315 S.W.3d 867, 875–76 (Tex. 2010).

443 *Bennett v. Reynolds*, 315 S.W.3d 867, 877 (Tex. 2010).

[444] *Bennett v. Reynolds*, 315 S.W.3d 867, 877 (Tex. 2010).

[445] *Bennett v. Reynolds*, 315 S.W.3d 867, 879 (Tex. 2010) (quotation and citation omitted).

[446] *Exxon Shipping Co. v. Baker*, 554 U.S. 471, 514–15 (2008).

[447] *Bennett v. Reynolds*, 315 S.W.3d 867, 880–82 (Tex. 2010).

[448] *See* Tex. Gov't Code §§ 2001.001-.17 (prescribing the standards and procedures for judicial review of contested case).

[449] Tex. Gov't Code § 2001.172.

[450] Tex. Gov't Code § 2001.173(a).

[451] Tex. Gov't Code § 2001.174.

[452] Tex. Gov't Code § 2001.174.

[453] *Railroad Comm'n v. Pend Oreille Oil & Gas Co.*, 817 S.W.2d 36, 41 (Tex. 1991) (emphasis in original; citations omitted); *see also City of Jacksboro v. Tow Bush Cmty. Action Group*, No. 03-01-00860-CV, 2012 WL 2509804, at *7 (Tex. App.—Austin June 28, 2012, no pet.) (mem. op.) ("We must uphold an agency's finding even if the evidence actually preponderates against it, so long as enough evidence suggests the agency's determination was within the bounds of reasonableness.").

[454] Tex. Gov't Code § 2001.175(b), (e).

[455] Tex. Gov't Code § 2001.175(c).

[456] *Sierra Club v. Tex. Comm'n on Envtl. Quality*, 455 S.W.3d 214, 222–23 (Tex. App.—Austin 2014, pet. denied) (citing *Tex. Comm'n on Envtl. Quality v. City of Waco*, 413 S.W.3d 409, 424 (Tex. 2013) and *Tex. Comm'n on Envtl. Quality v. Bosque Rive Coal.*, 413 S.W.3d 403, 404 (Tex. 2013)).

[457] *Sierra Club v. Tex. Comm'n on Envtl. Quality*, 455 S.W.3d 214, 222–23 (Tex. App.—Austin 2014, pet. denied) (quoting *City of El Paso v. Public Util. Comm'n*, 883 S.W.2d 179, 184 (Tex. 1994), additional citations omitted).

CHAPTER 3

Reversible Error

3-1 Introduction

Litigation is not a game. It is not a law school examination. It is a real-world means of resolving disputes affecting real people or entities. It also costs taxpayer money. As a result, the law has evolved to require that an error be harmful before it can be reversible. The reversible-error rule "establishes a sound and common-sense policy of not reversing a judgment unless the error or errors can be said to have contributed in a substantial way to bring about the adverse judgment."[1] This rule applies to *all* errors.[2]

The doctrine of reversible error is a necessary compromise between the requirement of due process of law and the ability to decide a volume of cases expeditiously. "The rule recognizes that a litigant is not entitled to a perfect trial for, indeed, few trials are perfect."[3] In short, if an error probably made no difference in the outcome, neither the parties nor the system should be put to the burden of another trial.

As a result, only those errors that probably caused an improper judgment are held reversible.

3-2 General Considerations

3-2:1 Reversible Error vs. Harmless Error

The flip-side of reversible error is harmless error. The two terms require definition.

3-2:1.1 Definitions

Reversible error means that the error "probably caused the rendition of an improper judgment."[4] An error by the trial court that "probably prevented the appellant from properly presenting the case to the court of appeals" also is reversible.[5] But when the latter can be corrected, the appellate court orders the trial court to do so and then the appeal proceeds.[6] Harmless error is everything else.

3-2:1.2 Appellant's Burden to Demonstrate Probable Harm From Record as a Whole

Because of the need to move cases through the system, a judgment by the trial court is rebuttably presumed to be correct; thus, the burden is on the appellant to demonstrate reversible error from the entire record.[7]

Not all reversible errors, however, require the entire judgment to be reversed:

> If the error affects part of, but not all, the matter in controversy and that part is separable without unfairness to the parties, the judgment must be reversed and a new trial ordered only as to the part affected by the error.[8]

This has one important exception: "The court may not order a separate trial solely on unliquidated damages if liability is contested."[9]

3-2:1.3 Presumed Harm

Nevertheless, a few types of cases embrace the concept of presumed harm. One is incurable jury argument, usually an appeal to racial or national prejudice, or something outrageously inflammatory.[10]

A second is the "*Casteel*"[11] problem in the court's charge. That problem typically commingles valid and invalid theories in a single jury question, so that one cannot be sure that the jury answered the question on the basis of the valid theory. The Supreme Court has held that harm is presumed in those instances.[12]

A third involves improper jurors included on the panel. Appellate courts presume harm when improper jurors participate in deliberations.[13] Similarly, harm is presumed when the trial court excludes jurors by erroneously denying a *Batson*[14] challenge.[15]

3-2:2 Distinguishing Reversible Error From Preservation of Complaints

Many Texas cases confuse three distinct concepts: (1) preservation; (2) error; and (3) harm. So you see cases saying something like: "Because appellant made no objection, the trial court did not abuse its discretion; hence, there is no reversible error." Although that may occasionally save a lawyer from an adverse malpractice judgment, it risks serious analytical confusion.

3-2:2.1 Waived Errors

Whether an appellant preserved a complaint has nothing to do with whether an error occurred. And whether an error occurred simply begs the question whether the error is harmless. The logical analysis flows as follows:

Was the Complaint Preserved?

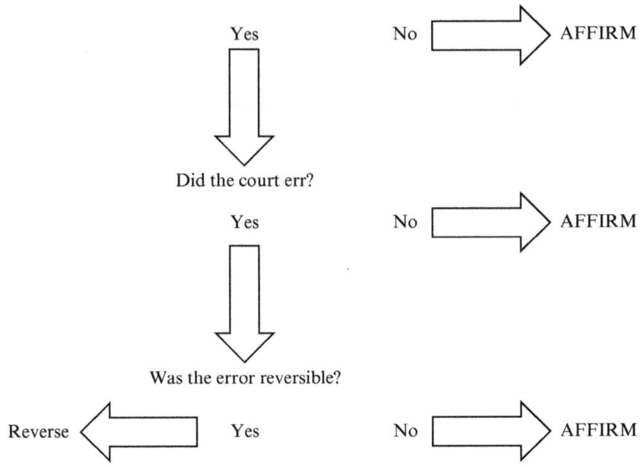

3-2:2.2 Invited Errors

You also find similarly loose language in some cases about the doctrine of invited error. "The invited error doctrine applies to situations where a party requests the court to make a specific ruling, then complains of that ruling on appeal."[16] The appellate courts rightly reject those challenges. But the analysis should not be on the basis of harmless error. Instead, the analysis should be one of preservation: a party is estopped to complain of a ruling the party asked the judge to make. First, a party may not schizophrenically complain about what it asked the court to do. Second, even if the party both invited the error and objected to it in the trial court, the complaint could not have been clearly and specifically presented to the trial court in light of the mixed signals stemming from the invitation. So the preservation requirement of Rule 33.1(a)(1)(A) is not met.

Similarly, an erroneous decision by a trial court can be rendered harmless by subsequent events.[17] So a party could possibly remove the harmful effect of an earlier erroneous ruling by subsequently introducing similar evidence, making a similar argument, requesting a similar charge, or having the court reconsider a ruling.

3-2:3 Distinguishing Reversible Error From Scopes and Standards of Review

The applicable scope and standard of review determines whether error has occurred. But they have no role in the analysis of reversible error.

3-2:3.1 Errors Affecting Fact Findings

Probably the most common type of reversible error affects the fact findings leading to the judgment. As will be discussed further, this can take many forms.

3-2:3.2 Cumulative Error

A reviewing court may reverse a lower court judgment under the cumulative-error doctrine when the record shows a number of instances of error, no one instance being sufficient to call for reversal, yet all the instances taken together may do so.[18] Yet the doctrine of cumulative error is somewhat superfluous. It is usually stated as errors that individually might be harmless can be accumulated to present reversible error. But the standard test for reversible error examines "the entire record."[19] The entire record includes all the other errors. So logically there is no need for a separate doctrine of cumulative error; it is just another subset of reversible error.

3-3 Pre-Trial Rulings

Pre-trial rulings are subject to the reversible-error doctrine. When they probably affected the validity of the judgment, they are reversible error.[20]

3-3:1 Subject-Matter Jurisdiction

An error involving subject-matter jurisdiction is always reversible, because it is a void judgment.[21] The proper remedy is to vacate, rather than reverse, the judgment.[22]

3-3:2 Personal Jurisdiction

An error involving personal jurisdiction is always reversible, because a judgment against a party over whom the court has no jurisdiction is void.[23] The proper remedy is to vacate, rather than reverse, the judgment.[24]

3-3:3 Venue and Forum

By statute and rule, an erroneous venue ruling is reversible:

> On appeal from the trial on the merits, if venue was improper it shall in no event be harmless error and shall be reversible error.[25]

An error regarding the proper forum also is reversible, because the wrong court cannot render a valid judgment. So the proper remedy is to dismiss the case.[26]

3-3:4 Sufficiency of Pleadings

If the court erred in striking pleadings, the error is reversible, because the judgment must conform to the pleadings.[27]

3-3:5 Docket Control and Discovery Rulings

Errors affecting docket control and discovery are reversible only if they probably caused an improper judgment.[28] That varies depending on what the entire record demonstrates about the probable effect of the particular ruling in question.

3-3:6 Summary Judgment

An error in granting summary judgment is always reversible, because it by definition resulted in an improper judgment.[29]

3-4 Trial Rulings

Trial rulings are reversible when they probably led to an improper judgment.[30]

3-4:1 Administration of Trial

Incidental trial court rulings have to be evaluated from the record as a whole with regard to the particular ruling under review. Unless those rulings probably caused an improper judgment, they are harmless error.[31]

3-4:2 Selection of Jury

Rulings about the selection of the jury now seem to turn on the facts. Because they potentially affect the fact-finding process, erroneous rulings regarding the questioning of prospective jurors and rulings on challenges for cause generally are reversible error.[32]

Harm is also presumed when a trial judge excludes jurors by improperly denying a *Batson*[33] challenge.[34]

When the trial court errs in allocating peremptory strikes, the harmless-error rule is "relaxed."[35] This is necessary because peremptory strikes reflect "intangibles not susceptible of precise description" rendering it difficult to establish how the absence of a particular juror might have made a difference.[36] The test is, instead, whether the trial was "hotly contested and the evidence sharply conflicting."[37] This depends on the number of witnesses, the number of jury questions, and whether the verdict was unanimous.[38]

3-4:3 Evidentiary Rulings

Evidentiary errors should be evaluated with care. Many cases state that the jury is the sole judge of the credibility of the witnesses and the weight to be given to their testimony.[39] They say this in the context of reviewing the sufficiency of the evidence. But logic dictates that the courts' inability to invade the province of the jury by weighing the sufficiency of the evidence and credibility of the witnesses also means the courts cannot invade the province of the jury's ability to weigh the evidence by declaring an erroneous evidentiary ruling to have been harmless. This logic is most in tension with the doctrine of cumulative evidence. That doctrine states that a court "will ordinarily not find reversible error for erroneous rulings on admissibility of evidence where the evidence in question is cumulative and not controlling on a material issue dispositive of the case."[40] The court reviews "the entire record to determine whether the judgment was controlled by the testimony that should have been excluded."[41] But "[t]he erroneous admission of testimony that is merely cumulative of properly admitted testimony is harmless error."[42]

Yet that oversimplifies the analysis if the jury truly has the "sole" right to decide the credibility of the witnesses. To avoid the logical tension, the courts might better analyze the issue not in terms of reversible error, but in terms of whether error occurred. A trial court has discretion to exclude cumulative evidence in the interests of expediting the trial.[43] Often, therefore, the exclusion of cumulative evidence does not amount to an abuse of discretion. So the issue of reversible error will rarely arise. When it does, however, a rebuttable presumption of harm would seem to comport better with the jury's right to weigh the evidence.

Non-jury trials, of course, are different, because there are no constitutional issues involved in second-guessing the thought processes of another judge. The deference afforded a trial court as fact-finder is simply one of administrative convenience and of practical recognition of the judge's ability to view the demeanor of the witnesses. So in a non-jury trial, there is a rebuttable presumption that the trial court disregarded any inadmissible evidence that was erroneously admitted into evidence.[44] When it is shown that the trial court did in fact rely on the evidence, then the presumption is rebutted.[45]

3-4:4 Directed Verdict

An erroneous ruling on a directed verdict is almost always reversible error, because it directly affects the judgment. An exception occurs, however, when the only damages a party sought were barred as a matter of law.[46] Thus, the Supreme Court has held that a trial court's error in granting a directed verdict before the party had presented all its evidence was harmless.[47]

3-4:5 Charge of the Court

Erroneous rulings regarding the court's charge usually constitute reversible error, because they are calculated to affect the fact-finding process that leads to the judgment. Charge error "is generally considered harmful if it relates to a contested, critical issue."[48] If it is a matter so incidental that it probably did not affect the judgment, then it often may not have been erroneous in the first place. And one can envision small, immaterial errors that surely misled no one.

Still, the appellate courts have at most limited powers to review a jury's thought processes.[49] So it is the rare case in which an appellate court can logically conclude that charge error is harmless. That is the principle at work in the *Casteel*[50] line of cases, and its analysis makes sense for other types of charge error, too.

A different analysis applies, however, when it can be determined with certainty what the jury followed:

> While *Casteel's* presumed harm analysis is necessary in instances where the appellate court cannot determine "whether the improperly submitted theories formed the sole basis for the jury's finding" because the broad-form question mixed valid and invalid theories of liability,[51] or when the broad-form question commingled damage elements that are unsupported by legally sufficient evidence,[52] an improper inferential rebuttal instruction and improper defensive theory of contributory negligence presented in a broad-form question with separate answer blanks in a single-theory-of-liability case does not prevent the harmed party from obtaining meaningful appellate review. When a trial court abuses its discretion by including erroneous charge questions or instructions in a single-theory-of-liability case, our traditional harmless error analysis applies and the appellate courts should review the entire record to determine whether the charge errors probably caused the rendition of an improper judgment.[53]

The *Casteel* presumed-harm holding has correctly been extended to a case involving a jury question that submitted a single claim, negligence, when some of the evidence would support liability under a particular theory of that claim that was legally or factually invalid, and the jury had not been instructed to disregard the invalid theory.[54]

3-4:6 Jury Argument

Incurable jury argument is presumed reversible.[55] Curable jury argument often will not have been preserved by timely objection and thus waived, or the ruling may not be erroneous either because the argument was invited or is within the wide latitude granted the attorneys in closing argument.[56] In either of those instances, the question of harm should not even arise.

If the complaint is merely that no evidence supports the argument, usually the error in allowing the argument is harmless because the jury is presumed to recall the evidence and is instructed to base its decision on the evidence.[57]

More troubling would be a trial court's erroneous ruling that counsel cannot argue a material matter that *was* admitted into evidence. This would probably constitute reversible error because it is akin to a prohibited comment on the weight of the evidence that there was no such evidence.[58]

3-4:7 Receipt of Verdict and Mistrial

Most errors regarding receipt of the verdict are reversible because they affect the fact findings that will underlie the judgment. If they are of a more clerical nature, however, they may not be harmful. Or a party may waive the error, so that no question of harm arises.

3-5 Post-Trial Rulings

Errors affecting the judgment, including post-trial motions, are reversible.[59]

3-5:1 Rendition of Judgment

By definition, reversible error exists wherever the error probably affected the judgment.[60]

3-5:2 Ruling on Whether to Disregard Jury Findings or to Render JNOV

An erroneous ruling on a motion to disregard findings or to render JNOV is reversible because it directly led to an improper judgment.[61]

3-5:3 Ruling on Whether to Grant a Motion for New Trial or Remittitur

An erroneous ruling on a motion for new trial or remittitur is reversible error because it improperly affected the judgment.[62]

3-5:4 Ruling on Whether to Modify, Correct, or Reform the Judgment

The same is true for a ruling on a motion to modify, correct, or reform the judgment.[63]

3-5:5 Findings of Fact and Conclusions of Law

When a party makes a proper and timely request for findings of fact and conclusions of law under Tex. R. Civ. P. 296, but the trial court fails to comply, harm is presumed unless the record affirmatively shows that the requesting party was not harmed by their absence.[64] Sometimes the judgment reversed on the basis that error is harmful if it prevents an appellant from properly presenting the case to the appellate court.[65]

Notes

1 *Lorusso v. Members Mut. Ins. Co.*, 603 S.W.2d 818, 819–20 (Tex. 1980).

2 *G & H Towing Co. v. Magee*, 347 S.W.3d 293, 297 (Tex. 2011).

3 *Lorusso v. Members Mut. Ins. Co.*, 603 S.W.2d 818, 819 (Tex. 1980).

4 Tex. R. App. P. 44.1(a)(1).

5 Tex. R. App. P. 44.1(a)(2).

6 *See* Tex. R. App. P. 44.4.

7 *E.g., Ford Motor Co. v. Castillo*, 279 S.W.3d 656, 667 (Tex. 2009); *Enterprise Leasing Co. of Houston v. Barrios*, 156 S.W.3d 547, 550 (Tex. 2004).

8 Tex. R. App. P. 44.1(b).

9 Tex. R. App. P. 44.1(b).

10 *Living Ctrs. of Tex., Inc. v. Penalver*, 256 S.W.3d 678, 681 (Tex. 2008) ("Such argument is not subject to the general harmless error analysis.").

11 *Crown Life Ins. Co. v. Casteel*, 22 S.W.3d 378, 381 (Tex. 2000).

12 *E.g., Romero v. KPH Consol., Inc.*, 166 S.W.3d 212, 226 (Tex. 2005); *Harris Cty. v. Smith*, 96 S.W.3d 230, 233–34 (Tex. 2002); *Crown Life Ins. Co. v. Casteel*, 22 S.W.3d 378, 381 (Tex. 2000).

13 *Cortez v. HCCI-San Antonio, Inc.*, 159 S.W.3d 87, 91 (Tex. 2005).

14 *Batson v. Kentucky*, 476 U.S. 79 (1986).

15 *See, e.g., Davis v. Fisk Elec. Co.*, 268 S.W.3d 508, 526 (Tex. 2008); *Powers v. Palacios*, 813 S.W.2d 489, 491 (Tex. 1991).

16 *In re Dep't of Family & Protective Servs.*, 273 S.W.3d 637, 646 (Tex. 2009).

17 *See, e.g., Progressive Cnty. Mut. Ins. Co. v. Boyd*, 177 S.W.3d 919, 921 (Tex. 2005).

18 *E.g., Sproles Motor Freight Lines, Inc. v. Long*, 140 Tex. 494 at 499, 168 S.W.2d 642 at 645 (1943).

19 *State v. Cent. Expressway Sign Assocs.*, 302 S.W.3d 866, 870 (Tex. 2009).

20 *See* Tex. R. App. P. 44.1(a)(1).

21 *Browning v. Prostok*, 165 S.W.3d 336, 346 (Tex. 2005).

22 *PNS Stores, Inc. v. Rivera*, 379 S.W.3d 267, 272 (Tex. 2012).

23 *Browning v. Prostok*, 165 S.W.3d 336, 346 (Tex. 2005).

24 *PNS Stores, Inc. v. Rivera*, 379 S.W.3d 267, 272 (Tex. 2012).

25 Tex. Civ. Prac. & Rem. Code § 15.064(b) (*quoted in Wilson v. Texas Parks & Wildlife Dep't*, 886 S.W.2d 259, 261 (Tex. 1994)).

26 *In re Gen. Elec. Co.*, 777 S.W.2d 681, 693–94 (Tex. 2008) (orig. proceeding).

27 Tex. R. Civ. P. 301. *See generally CRSS Inc. v. Montanari*, 902 S.W.2d 601, 612–13 (Tex. App.—Houston [1st Dist.] 1995, writ denied).

28 *See* Tex. R. App. P. 44.1(a)(1).

29 *See generally Guest v. Cochran*, 993 S.W.2d 397, 402 (Tex. App.—Houston [14th Dist.] 1999, no pet.).

30 *See* Tex. R. App. P. 44.1(a)(1).

31 *See* Tex. R. App. P. 44.1(a)(1).

[32] *See, e.g., Cortez v. HCCI-San Antonio, Inc.*, 159 S.W.3d 87, 91 (Tex. 2005).

[33] *Batson v. Kentucky*, 476 U.S. 79 (1986).

[34] *See, e.g., Davis v. Fisk Elec. Co.*, 268 S.W.3d 508, 526 (Tex. 2008); *Powers v. Palacios*, 813 S.W.2d 489, 491 (Tex. 1991).

[35] *See Lopez v. Foremost Paving, Inc.*, 709 S.W.2d 643, 644 (Tex. 1986); *Patterson Dental Co. v. Dunn*, 592 S.W.2d 914, 921 (Tex. 1980).

[36] *Patterson Dental Co. v. Dunn*, 592 S.W.2d 914, 921 (Tex. 1980) (quoting *Tamburello v. Welch*, 392 S.W.2d 114, 117 (Tex. 1965)).

[37] *Garcia v. Cent. Power & Light Co.*, 704 S.W.2d 734, 737 (Tex. 1986).

[38] *Garcia v. Cent. Power & Light Co.*, 704 S.W.2d 734, 737 (Tex. 1986).

[39] *E.g., City of Keller v. Wilson*, 168 S.W.3d 802, 819 (Tex. 2005); *see also* Tex. R. Civ. P. 226a (Jury Instructions, Court's Charge III).

[40] *Gee v. Liberty Mut. Fire Ins. Co.*, 765 S.W.2d 394, 396 (Tex. 1989).

[41] *Gee v. Liberty Mut. Fire Ins. Co.*, 765 S.W.2d 394, 396 (Tex. 1989).

[42] *Gee v. Liberty Mut. Fire Ins. Co.*, 765 S.W.2d 394, 396 (Tex. 1989).

[43] Tex. R Evid. 403.

[44] *Gillespie v. Gillespie*, 644 S.W.2d 449, 451 (Tex. 1982).

[45] *See Marshall v. Telecomms. Specialists, Inc.*, 806 S.W.2d 904, 906 (Tex. App.—Houston [1st Dist.] 1991, no pet.); *Solis v. Garcia*, 702 S.W.2d 668, 672 (Tex. App.—Houston [14th Dist.] 1985, no writ).

[46] *Tana Oil & Gas Corp. v. McCall*, 104 S.W.3d 80, 82 (Tex. 2003).

[47] *Tana Oil & Gas Corp. v. McCall*, 104 S.W.3d 80, 82 (Tex. 2003).

[48] *E.g., Thota v. Young*, 366 S.W.3d 678, 687 (Tex. 2012).

[49] *See* § 3-4:3.

[50] *Crown Life Ins. Co. v. Casteel*, 22 S.W.3d 378, 381 (Tex. 2000).

[51] *Crown Life Ins. Co. v. Casteel*, 22 S.W.3d 378, 389 (Tex. 2000).

[52] *Harris Cty. v. Smith*, 96 S.W.3d 230, 235 (Tex. 2002).

[53] *Thota v. Young*, 366 S.W.3d 678, 693 (Tex. 2012).

[54] *Benge v. Williams*, 548 S.W.3d 466, 475–76 (Tex. 2018); *see also Columbia Rio Grande Healthcare, L.P. v. Hawley*, 284 S.W.3d 851, 862–63 (Tex. 2009); *Texas Commission on Human Rights v, Morrison*, 381 S.W.3d 533, 535–37 (Tex. 2012) (per curiam).

[55] *Living Ctrs. of Tex., Inc. v. Penalver*, 256 S.W.3d 678, 681 (Tex. 2008).

[56] *See Standard Fire Ins. Co. v. Reese*, 584 S.W.2d 835, 839 (Tex. 1979).

[57] Tex. R. Civ. P. 226a (Jury Instructions, Court's Charge III).

[58] *See* Tex. R. Civ. P. 277; *In re M.S.*, 115 S.W.3d 534, 538 (Tex. 2003).

[59] *See* Tex. R. App. P. 44.1(a)(1).

[60] Tex. R. App. P. 44.1(a)(1).

[61] *See* Tex. R. App. P. 44.1(a)(1).

[62] *See* Tex. R. App. P. 44.1(a)(1).

[63] *See* Tex. R. App. P. 44.1(a)(1).

[64] *Tenery v. Tenery*, 932 S.W.2d 29, 30 (Tex. 1996).

[65] Tex. R. App. P. 44.1(a)(2); *Tenery v. Tenery*, 932 S.W.2d 29, 30 (Tex. 1996).

CHAPTER 4

Appealability and Notice of Appeal

4-1 Introduction

Generally, judgments and orders become appealable only when they are final. There are exceptions for certain types of judgments and orders, including interlocutory orders made appealable by statute.

To appeal a judgment, the first step is perfecting the appeal. Perfecting the appeal means invoking the jurisdiction of the court of appeals over the judgment or order appealed from.

4-2 Appealable Final Judgments or Orders

4-2:1 General Requirements for Finality

4-2:1.1 Express Statement or Actual Accomplishment of Finality

A judgment or order is final for purposes of appeal if it either (1) disposes of all claims and parties, or (2) expressly states that it disposes of all claims and parties, even if it does not actually do so.[1] An example of an express statement is: "This judgment finally disposes of all parties and all claims and is appealable."[2] If that precise language is present, the judgment or order constitutes a final judgment and is appealable, even if evidence indicates that the finality language was included by mistake and that the order was intended to be interlocutory.[3] Even without those words, if the judgment "states with unmistakable clarity that it is a final judgment as to all claims and parties," then it will begin the timetable for filing an appeal.[4]

4-2:1.2 Definiteness

To be final, a judgment must be definite. It cannot condition recovery on uncertain events.[5] If further proceedings are necessary, the judgment is final only if the ancillary matters are ministerial.[6] For instance, a judgment may be final, even it does not state the amount or means for calculating prejudgment interest so long as the rate and means of calculating interest are matters of law.[7] But prejudgment interest is not ministerial, and a judgment therefore is not final, if the record reflects facts that support the tolling of interest or if the award of interest is within the court's discretion.[8]

Also, a court has held that a judgment is final when it allows a party to obtain a credit on the judgment by reinstating an insurance policy because it concerns the *form*, not the *value*, of the compensation awarded.[9] Thus, the clerk preparing a writ of execution could ascertain the proper amount of the judgment.[10] As another court observed, "[a]lthough the amount of compensation differed depending on the circumstances, the amount was certain under all possible circumstances."[11] By contrast, a judgment that could be certain only if a single, uncertain event (e.g., the failure to object to an accounting) occurred is not final.[12]

A court has held that a judgment is not final when it does not include the amount recoverable, but incorporates a prior order that provides a range of recovery, but no certain amount and no manner for ascertaining it.[13] Interestingly, in this case the judgment also included the finality language that the Supreme Court of Texas, two years later, held established finality beyond doubt.[14] The *Blankenhagen* court resolved this conflict by concluding that an indefinite judgment was an exception that overrode finality language. It is unclear whether this conclusion survives the Supreme Court's decision in *Elizondo*.

4-2:2 Requirements for Specific Types of Judgments and Orders

4-2:2.1 Judgment After Conventional Trial on the Merits

There is a presumption that a judgment after a conventional trial on the merits disposes of all parties and claims and is final, even if there is no express statement to that effect.[15] If a judgment after trial contains a "Mother Hubbard" clause ("all relief not granted is denied"), that indicates finality.[16] But a "Mother Hubbard" clause does not establish finality when there has not been a conventional trial on the merits.[17]

4-2:2.2 Interlocutory Orders

Interlocutory orders are by definition not final and, thus, are not appealable unless statute or rule provides otherwise.[18] But interlocutory orders generally become final, and thus appealable, upon merger or severance.

Merger. An interlocutory order is merged into a final judgment when all remaining claims are resolved on the merits or dismissed.[19] Merger occurs even when the interlocutory orders are not mentioned in the judgment.[20]

Severance. An interlocutory order also becomes final if it is severed from unadjudicated claims.[21] Upon severance, the judgment is final even if there is no separate file or cause number.[22] If a party discovers that the judgment being appealed is interlocutory, it can ask the appellate court to abate the appeal to allow the trial court to sever.[23]

If finality unclear. If finality is not clear, then the appellate court can review the record to determine finality.[24] An appellate court also can abate an appeal to allow the trial court to clarify whether a judgment or order was intended to be final.[25]

Exception for mandatory interlocutory appeals. An exception to appealability occurs when an interlocutory order has been made appealable by statute or rule, and interlocutory appeal is mandatory. In that circumstance, the interlocutory order will not be appealable if merged or severed into a final judgment.[26]

4-2:2.3 Summary Disposition

There is no presumption that a judgment signed after summary disposition (e.g., summary judgment, default judgment, orders of dismissal) is final.[27] Such judgments are final if they actually dispose of all parties and all claims, or if they state unequivocally that they do.[28]

For example, if a defendant moves for summary judgment on only one claim, but the trial court signs a judgment that the plaintiff take nothing, then the judgment is erroneous but final.[29] A judgment granting more relief than a party is entitled to is not necessarily interlocutory, although it is erroneous.[30] A "Mother Hubbard" clause in a summary judgment is *not* an unequivocal expression of finality.[31]

Bottom line. Does the order or judgment say "This judgment finally disposes of all parties and all claims and is appealable?" If so, then it is a final and appealable judgment, no matter the character or intent behind it. And, if that precise language is not present, does the language of the judgment and the record as a whole indicate that the trial court intended to dispose of all parties and claims? If so, then the judgment is also final and appealable.

4-2:2.4 Bill of Review

A bill of review that does not dispose of all issues in the underlying case on the merits is interlocutory and not a final, appealable order.[32]

4-2:3 Certain Probate, Receivership, and Partition Orders

Generally, only one final judgment can be signed in a case.[33] But there are exceptions. The most common proceedings with multiple final judgments are probate, receivership, and partition cases.

If a statute provides that a discrete phase of a proceeding is final and appealable, the judgment or order signed in that phase is final.[34] If there is no statute, a judgment or order regarding a discrete phase can be appealable if it is not part of an unadjudicated phase.[35] Such orders often *must* be appealed *immediately*—not after the entire proceeding.[36]

4-2:4 Judgment or Order Not Appealable

If a judgment or order is not final and cannot be severed, there may be other options for an immediate appeal.

4-2:4.1 Options for Immediate Review

Interlocutory appeal as of right. First, the order may fall within one of the substantive categories for which interlocutory appeal is permitted by statute or rule.[37]

Permissive interlocutory appeal. Second, the court of appeals still may consider an interlocutory appeal if the trial court certifies it for interlocutory appeal and the court of appeals exercises its discretionary jurisdiction.[38]

Mandamus. Finally, the order may be reviewable by a petition for writ of mandamus. Generally, mandamus is not permitted to correct incidental trial court rulings, but rather is allowed only if the trial court commits a clear abuse of discretion for which there is no adequate remedy by appeal.[39]

4-2:4.2 Practical Considerations

Cost, delay, and unintended consequences. As a practical matter, even if an interlocutory order is appealable or otherwise reviewable, should you seek such review? Sometimes parties or attorneys are so incensed by an adverse ruling that they rush to file an interlocutory appeal or mandamus petition without carefully thinking through the implications. Sometimes, tens of thousands of dollars and several years later, the decision to seek such review may seem, in hindsight, to have been misguided. Although it can be difficult to predict the future, a cold assessment of the importance of the issue, the likely outcome, and the costs of pursuing immediate review will diminish the chances of buyer's remorse.

If the issue is not potentially case-dispositive or vitally important to damages, it is probably not worth pursuing a costly, lengthy interlocutory appeal or mandamus. Of course, if an interlocutory appeal is mandatory, it cannot be avoided.[40]

If the case is even moderately complex, costs can reach six figures in both the court of appeals and in the Texas Supreme Court. And these proceedings can take years. The costs and delay should be weighed against the likelihood of success. Also, there is always the possibility of unintended negative consequences. For example, in resolving a threshold issue on interlocutory appeal, an appellate court might include dicta that prejudices the client's position in the main case.

The record in the trial court. Finally, before deciding to file an interlocutory appeal or a mandamus petition, make sure the record will support a decision in your favor. Failure to make the proper record in the trial court can doom your appeal or mandamus, or, if you are defending an interlocutory order, could result in reversal.[41]

Often, deficiencies in the record can be corrected by submitting a new motion (or, in some cases, asking for reconsideration) and obtaining a ruling. If this opportunity exists, it is always best to take it, even if it involves admitting that a mistake was made in the initial motion. It is much better than having to tell the client later that its money and time were wasted on a futile appellate proceeding because the record was not sufficient at the outset. Be careful that any new motion or motion to reconsider is filed within the time limits of Section 51.014(b) of the Civil Practice and Remedies Code, if applicable, and that an order on the new motion or motion to reconsider is subject to interlocutory appeal.[42]

4-3 Perfecting the Appeal

Perfecting an appeal means invoking the jurisdiction of the court of appeals over the judgment or order appealed from.

4-3:1 What to File

4-3:1.1 Notice of Appeal

Under Texas Rule of Appellate Procedure 25.1, a written notice of appeal must be filed with the trial court clerk. It is a very short document and need only:

- identify the trial court;
- state the style and case number in the trial court;
- state the date of the judgment or order appealed from;
- identify the party filing the notice and state its desire to appeal;
- identify the court to which the appeal will be taken;
- for accelerated appeals, state that the appeal is accelerated, and whether it is a parental termination or child protection case, as defined in Tex. R. App. P. 28.4; and
- state, if applicable, that the appellant is presumed indigent and may proceed without advance payment of costs as provided in Texas Rule of Appellate Procedure 20.

Tex. R. App. P. 25.1(d).

In a restricted appeal, the notice of appeal must also:

- state that the appellant is a party affected by the trial court's judgment but did not participate in the hearing resulting in the judgment complained of;
- state that the appellant did not timely file either a post-judgment motion, request for findings of fact and conclusions of law, or notice of appeal; and
- be verified by the appellant if pro se.

Tex. R. App. P. 25.1(d). A notice of appeal that omits some of these requirements, or even one that is not a formal notice of appeal, can still be effective as long as it was filed "in a bona fide attempt to invoke appellate court jurisdiction."[43]

4-3:1.2 Appeals to the 1st and 14th Courts of Appeals

The First and Fourteenth Courts of Appeals have concurrent jurisdiction over appeals from the same 10 counties.[44] A notice of appeal from a trial court subject to their jurisdiction should state: "to the First or Fourteenth Court of Appeals."

When the notice of appeal is filed, and the case has not been the subject of a prior proceeding in the appellate court, the trial court clerk randomly assigns the appeal to one of the two courts.[45] But when a notice of appeal is filed for an appeal to the First or Fourteenth Court, local rules require that it contain "a statement indicating whether a related appeal or original proceeding has been previously filed in either the First or Fourteenth Court of Appeals and must include the caption, trial court case number, and appellate court case number of the related appeal or original proceeding."[46] If a related appeal or original proceeding has been previously filed or assigned to the First or Fourteenth Court of Appeals, the new proceeding will be assigned to the same court as the prior proceedings.[47]

4-3:1.3 Appeals From Hunt, Wood, Upshur, Gregg, and Rusk Counties

An appeal from a Hunt County trial court can be taken to either the Dallas or Texarkana Court of Appeals.[48] An appeal from a judgment entered in Wood, Upshur, Gregg, or Rusk Counties can be taken to either the Texarkana or Tyler Court of Appeals.[49]

If parties file competing notices of appeal to different appellate courts, they must confer about consolidating the appeals in a single court.[50] If they cannot agree, the trial court randomly selects one of the courts.[51]

4-3:1.4 Amending the Notice of Appeal

4-3:1.4a Notice of Appeal May Be Amended

A notice of appeal may be amended any time before the appellant's brief is filed.[52] After the appellant's brief is filed, the notice of appeal may be amended only by permission of the appellate court.[53] Other parties may move to strike the amendment for cause.[54]

4-3:1.4b Clerk Must Notify Parties of Defect

If the appellate court clerk determines that the notice of appeal is defective, he or she must notify the parties so that the defect can be remedied, if possible.[55] After such notice, parties are given 30 days to correct the defect.[56]

4-3:1.4c No Amendment Required if Judgment Modified

It is not necessary to amend the notice of appeal if the trial court modifies or replaces the judgment or order. The appellate court "must treat the appeal as from the subsequent order or judgment."[57]

4-3:1.5 Docketing Statement

The appellant must file a docketing statement with the court of appeals promptly upon perfecting an appeal.[58] The docketing statement gives the appellate court basic information about the case as well as contact information for the parties and their attorneys. The requirements are listed in Texas Rule of Appellate Procedure 32.1, but it is preferable to use the forms on each court's website. Although the Rules set no specific deadline for filing the docketing statement, some appellate courts have deadlines in their local rules. The failure to file a docketing statement can result in dismissal of an appeal.

4-3:2 Where to File the Notice of Appeal

The notice of appeal should be filed with the trial court clerk.[59] A courtesy copy should be sent to the court of appeals, but there is no specific deadline stated in the Rules.[60] If the notice of appeal is mistakenly filed in the court of appeals rather than the trial court, it is considered filed in the trial court on the same day.[61]

4-3:3 Who Must File a Notice of Appeal?

4-3:3.1 Any Party Complaining of the Judgment

Any party who seeks to alter the trial court's judgment (or appealable order) must file a notice of appeal.[62] This applies to appeals and cross-appeals.

For example, one court held that an appellee who won a jury verdict but wishes to complain that she also should have been awarded attorney fees must file a notice of appeal or else she waives her complaint.[63]

In another case, after a split judgment below on cross-motions for summary judgment, only one party filed a notice of appeal.[64] The court held that the non-appealing party should have prevailed on its motion for summary judgment but waived its complaint by not filing a notice of appeal.[65]

4-3:3.2 Excuse for Just Cause

A party's failure to file a notice of appeal can be excused if it shows just cause.[66] Just cause has been found to exist when a party's interests were closely interwoven with those of a party who filed a notice of appeal.[67]

4-3:3.3 No Notice Required for Alternative Ground for Affirmance

If an appellee is satisfied with the relief granted by the trial court but wants to present additional, independent grounds for affirming the trial court's judgment or order, no notice of appeal is required.[68]

4-3:4 When to File the Notice of Appeal

4-3:4.1 Final Judgments or Orders

4-3:4.1a No Post-Judgment Motions

Under Texas Rule of Appellate Procedure 26.1, if no post-judgment motions are filed that extend the appellate deadlines, the notice of appeal is due within 30 days of the signing (not entry) of the judgment. If any party timely files a notice of appeal, another party may file a notice of appeal within 30 days of the signing of the judgment or 14 days after the first-filed notice of appeal, whichever is later.[69]

4-3:4.1b Effect of Post-Judgment Motions

Under Texas Rule of Appellate Procedure 26.1(a), the deadline for filing a notice of appeal is 90 days after the judgment is signed if one of the following post-judgment motions is filed:

- *Motion for new trial.* This motion can be filed as a matter of right, for the sole purpose of extending appellate deadlines, even if supported by no sound or reasonable basis.[70] It extends the timetable for all parties, even if they do not file a motion for new trial.[71]
- *Motion to modify the judgment.* To extend the appellate deadlines, a motion to modify must seek to substantively alter the trial court's judgment.[72]
- *Motion to reinstate a case dismissed for want of prosecution.* To extend the appellate deadlines, this motion must be verified.[73]
- *A proper request for findings of fact and conclusions of law.* This request extends the appellate deadlines only if (1) the request is required by Rule 296 or (2) the appellate court could consider the findings.[74] The request is required by Rule 296 only in bench trials.[75] The findings are not required but may be considered in the following situations: default judgment involving unliquidated damages,

judgment for sanctions, and any judgment based on an evidentiary hearing.[76] The findings may not be considered in the following situations: summary judgment, judgment after directed verdict, judgment n.o.v., default judgment involving liquidated damages, dismissal for want of prosecution or jurisdiction with no evidentiary hearing, dismissal based on the pleadings or special exceptions, and any judgment rendered without an evidentiary hearing.[77]

Premature motions. A prematurely filed post-judgment motion or request for findings of fact and conclusions of law is considered effective on the same day, but after, the judgment or order it challenges was signed.[78] Prematurely filed motions for new trial and requests for findings of fact and conclusions of law still extend the appellate deadlines.[79] Other prematurely filed post-judgment motions *may* extend appellate deadlines, at the appellate court's discretion.[80]

4-3:4.2 Interlocutory or Other Accelerated Appeals

Under Texas Rule of Appellate Procedure 28, all appeals from interlocutory orders and quo warranto proceedings are accelerated.[81] In accelerated appeals, the deadlines for the notice of appeal, record, and briefs are shorter. And the courts are expected to decide accelerated appeals on an expedited basis, although for most types of cases there are no specific requirements.

One exception is family-law cases where parental rights have been terminated or the State has been named managing conservator. Rule of Judicial Administration 6 requires appellate courts, if reasonably possible, to dispose of those appeals within 180 days of the filing of the notice of appeal (in the courts of appeals) or the petition for review (in the Supreme Court).

Generally, in accelerated appeals, the notice of appeal must be filed within 20 days of the signing of the order being appealed.[82] Post-judgment motions do not extend this deadline.[83] If an appeal is governed by a statute, the statute may have its own filing deadlines and notice-of-appeal requirements.

4-3:4.3 Restricted Appeals

The notice of appeal must be filed within six months of the judgment or order appealed from.[84]

4-3:4.4 Extending Time to File Notice of Appeal

The notice of appeal is jurisdictional. But a party may move for additional time to file a notice of appeal, even if the deadline has expired.[85] The notice, along with a motion for extension of time, must be filed within 15 days of the deadline.[86] The motion must reasonably explain the need for an extension, must otherwise comply with Texas Rule of Appellate Procedure 10.5(b), and may need to be verified if it alleges facts not in the record.[87] The motion for extension of time should state that the failure to file was not deliberate or intentional.[88] If a notice of appeal or equivalent document is filed after the deadline but within the 15-day period for an extension, the court will imply a motion of extension of time.[89] Beware of appeals that have their own statutory filing deadlines and requirements. They may not allow for extension.

4-3:4.5 Premature Notice of Appeal

A prematurely filed notice of appeal becomes effective on the same day that the judgment or order it challenges is signed.[90]

Notes

1 *Lehmann v. Har-Con Corp.*, 39 S.W.3d 191, 192–93 (Tex. 2001).

2 *In re Daredia*, 317 S.W.3d 247, 248–49 (Tex. 2010).

3 *In re Elizondo*, 544 S.W.3d 824, 826 (Tex. 2018) (per curiam).

4 *Lehmann v. Har-Con Corp.*, 39 S.W.3d 191, 192–93 (Tex. 2001).

5 *Hinde v. Hinde*, 701 S.W.2d 637, 639 (Tex. 1985) (per curiam).

6 *Hinde v. Hinde*, 701 S.W.2d 637, 639 (Tex. 1985) (per curiam).

7 *Harris Cnty. Toll Rd. Auth. v. Sw. Bell Tel. Co.*, 263 S.W.3d 48, 54–55 (Tex. App.—Houston [1st. Dist.] 2006), *aff'd, Sw. Bell Tel. Co. v. Harris Cnty. Toll Rd. Auth.*, 282 S.W.3d 59 (Tex. 2009); *Olympia Marble & Granite v. Mayes*, 17 S.W.3d 437, 442 (Tex. App.—Houston [1st Dist.] 2000, no pet.).

8 *Olympia Marble & Granite v. Mayes*, 17 S.W.3d 437, 443 (Tex. App.—Houston [1st Dist.] 2000, no pet.); *In re Griffith*, No. 04–03–00322–CV, 2003 WL 21508337, at *3 (Tex. App.—San Antonio July 2, 2003, orig. proceeding [mand. denied]) (mem.op.).

9 *Hinde v. Hinde*, 701 S.W.2d 637, 639 (Tex. 1985) (per curiam).

10 *Hinde v. Hinde*, 701 S.W.2d 637, 639 (Tex. 1985) (per curiam).

11 *Sherer v. Sherer*, 393 S.W.3d 480, 488 (Tex. App.—Texarkana 2013, pet. denied).

12 *Sherer v. Sherer*, 393 S.W.3d 480, 488 (Tex. App.—Texarkana 2013, pet. denied).

13 *In re Blankenhagen*, 513 S.W.3d 97 (Tex. App.—Houston [14th Dist.] 2016, pet. dism'd, mand. denied).

14 *In re Elizondo*, 544 S.W.3d 824 (Tex. 2018) (per curiam).

15 *Vaughn v. Drennon*, 324 S.W.3d 560, 562–63 (Tex. 2010).

16 *See Lehmann v. Har-Con Corp.*, 39 S.W.3d 191, 203–04 (Tex. 2001).

17 *Lehmann v. Har-Con Corp.*, 39 S.W.3d 191, 203–04 (Tex. 2001).

18 *See generally* Chapter 5.

19 *See, e.g., Parking Co. v. Wilson*, 58 S.W.3d 742, 742 (Tex. 2001).

20 *Webb v. Jorns*, 488 S.W.2d 407, 408–09 (Tex. 1972).

21 *See* Tex. R. Civ. P. 41; *see, e.g., Harris Cnty. Flood Control Dist. v. Adam*, 66 S.W.3d 265, 266 (Tex. 2001).

22 *McRoberts v. Ryals*, 863 S.W.2d 450, 452–53 & n.4 (Tex. 1993).

23 *See* Tex. R. App. P. 27.2, 27.3; *State Farm Mut Auto. Ins. v. Leeds*, 981 S.W.2d 693, 693 (Tex. App.—Houston [1st Dist.] 1998, order).

24 *Lehmann v. Har-Con Corp.*, 39 S.W.3d 191, 205–06 (Tex. 2001).

25 *Lehmann v. Har-Con Corp.*, 39 S.W.3d 191, 206 (Tex. 2001).

26 *See Hernandez v. Ebrom*, 289 S.W.3d 316, 319–21 (Tex. 2009).

27 *See Crites v. Collins*, 284 S.W.3d 839, 840 (Tex. 2009).

28 *In re Burlington Coat Factory Warehouse*, 167 S.W.3d 827, 830 (Tex. 2005).

29 *Jacobs v. Satterwhite*, 65 S.W.3d 653, 655 (Tex. 2001); *Lehmann v. Har-Con Corp.*, 39 S.W.3d 191, 200 (Tex. 2001).

30 *Lehmann v. Har-Con Corp.*, 39 S.W.3d 191, 200 (Tex. 2001).

31 *Lehmann v. Har-Con Corp.*, 39 S.W.3d 191, 192 (Tex. 2001).

32 *Kiefer v. Touris*, 197 S.W.3d 300, 302 (Tex. 2006).

33 Tex. R. Civ. P. 301; *Logan v. Mullis*, 686 S.W.2d 605, 609 (Tex. 1985).

34 *Crowson v. Wakeham*, 897 S.W.2d 779, 783 (Tex. 1995).

35 *Crowson v. Wakeham*, 897 S.W.2d 779, 783 (Tex. 1995).

36 *See Long v. Spencer*, 137 S.W.3d 923, 925–26 (Tex. App.—Dallas 2004, no pet.) (partition order); *Roach v. Rowley*, 135 S.W.3d 845, 848 (Tex. App.—Houston [1st Dist.] 2004, no pet.) (probate order).

37 *See generally* Chapter 5.

38 *See generally* Chapter 5, § 5-3.

39 *Walker v. Packer*, 827 S.W.2d 833, 839 (Tex. 1992) (orig. proceeding); *see generally* Chapter 6.

40 *See* Chapter 5.

41 *See Hendee v. Dewhurst*, 228 S.W.3d 354, 377–78 (Tex. App.—Austin 2007, pet. denied) (declining to address substantive issue on appeal because appellee failed to submit supporting evidence to the trial court).

42 *See generally* Chapter 5.

43 *In re J.M.*, 396 S.W.3d 528, 530–31 (Tex. 2013) (per curiam).

44 Tex. Gov't Code § 22.201(b), (o).

45 Tex. Gov't Code § 22.202(h).

46 1st Tex. App. (Houston) Loc. R. 1.4(a); 14th Tex. App. (Houston) Loc. R. 1.4(a).

47 1st Tex. App. (Houston) Loc. R. 1.4(c); 14th Tex. App. (Houston) Loc. R. 1.4(c).

48 Tex. Gov't Code § 22.201(f), (g).

49 Tex. Gov't Code § 22.201(g), (m).

50 Tex. R. Judicial Admin. 15.3(a).

51 Tex. R. Judicial Admin. 15.4.

52 Tex. R. App. P. 25.1(f).

53 Tex. R. App. P. 25.1(f).

54 Tex. R. App. P. 25.1(f).

55 Tex. R. App. P. 37.1.

56 Tex. R. App. P. 37.1.

57 Tex. R. App. P. 27.3.

58 Tex. R. App. P. 32.1.

59 Tex. R. App. P. 25.1.

60 *See* Tex. R. App. P. 25.1(e).

61 Tex. R. App. P. 25.1(a).

62 Tex. R. App. P. 25.1(c).

63 *Chandler v. Chandler*, 842 S.W.2d 829, 834–35 (Tex. App.—El Paso 1992, writ denied).

64 *Lubbock Cty., Tex. v. Trammel's Lubbock Bail Bonds*, 80 S.W.3d 580, 583–84 (Tex. 2002).

65 *Lubbock Cty., Tex. v. Trammel's Lubbock Bail Bonds*, 80 S.W.3d 580, 583–84 (Tex. 2002).

66 Tex. R. App. P. 25.1(c).

67 *Welkener v. Welkener*, 71 S.W.3d 364, 368 (Tex. App.—Corpus Christi 2001, no pet.).

68 *Dean v. Lafayette Pl. (Section One) Council of Co-Owners, Inc.*, 999 S.W.2d 814, 818 (Tex. App.—Houston [1st Dist.] 1999, no pet.).

[69] Tex. R. App. P. 26.1(d).

[70] *Old Republic Ins. Co. v. Scott*, 846 S.W.2d 832, 833 (Tex. 1993) (per curiam).

[71] Tex. R. App. P. 26.1(a)(1).

[72] Tex. R. App. P. 26.1(a)(2); *Lane Bank Equip. Co. v. Smith S. Equip., Inc.*, 10 S.W.3d 308, 313 (Tex. 2000).

[73] *Butts v. Capitol City Nursing Home, Inc.*, 705 S.W.2d 696, 697 (Tex. 1986) (per curiam).

[74] Tex. R. App. P. 26.1; *Gene Duke Builders, Inc. v. Abilene Hous. Auth.*, 138 S.W.3d 907, 908 (Tex. 2004) (per curiam).

[75] *See Linwood v. NCNB Tex.*, 885 S.W.2d 102, 103 (Tex. 1994) (per curiam).

[76] *IKB Indus. (Nigeria) Ltd. v. Pro-Line Corp.*, 938 S.W.2d 440, 443 (Tex. 1997).

[77] *IKB Indus. (Nigeria) Ltd. v. Pro-Line Corp.*, 938 S.W.2d 440, 443 (Tex. 1997).

[78] Tex. R. App. P. 27.2; Tex. R. Civ. P. 306c.

[79] Tex. R. Civ. P. 306c.

[80] Tex. R. App. P. 27.2.

[81] The requirements and timing regarding permissive and agreed interlocutory appeals are discussed in Chapter 5.

[82] Tex. R. App. P. 26.1(b).

[83] Tex. R. App. P. 28.1.

[84] Tex. R. App. P. 26.1(c).

[85] Tex. R. App. P. 26.3.

[86] Tex. R. App. P. 26.3.

[87] Tex. R. App. P. 26.3; *Williams v. Flores*, 88 S.W.3d 631, 632 (Tex. 2002) (per curiam); Tex. R. App. P. 10.2.

[88] *See Garcia v. Kastner Farms*, 774 S.W.2d 668, 669–70 (Tex. 1989).

[89] *Verburgt v. Dorner*, 959 S.W.2d 615, 617 (Tex. 1997).

[90] Tex. R. App. P. 27.1.

CHAPTER 5

Interlocutory Appeals

5-1 Introduction

As a general rule, an appeal may be taken only from a final judgment.[1] But there are exceptions to this rule, "in narrow situations expressly authorized by statute."[2] Most of the statutory bases for interlocutory appeal are codified in Section 51.014 of the Texas Civil Practice and Remedies Code. These "narrow situations" were once quite rare, but they are becoming less so as the Legislature continues to add to the list of interlocutory orders that are appealable as of right.

Even if a particular interlocutory order is not appealable as of right, it can be the basis of a permissive interlocutory appeal when the trial court certifies that it meets certain statutory requirements and the court of appeals exercises its jurisdiction.

The statutes authorizing interlocutory appeals, including permissive appeals, are strictly construed, and an order must fit within the scope of the statute for the court of appeals to have jurisdiction.[3]

5-2 Interlocutory Orders Appealable as of Right

Orders expressly authorized by statute for interlocutory appeal are appealable as of right. Although Section 51.014(a) of the Texas Civil Practice and Remedies Code is the primary statute authorizing interlocutory appeals,[4] there are a number of other statutes that also do so. The list below includes many of the types of orders that are currently authorized by statute for interlocutory appeal.

- **Tex. Civ. Prac. & Rem. Code § 51.014(a)(1), (2).**

  Permits an interlocutory appeal from an order appointing a receiver or trustee or overruling a motion to vacate an order that appoints a receiver or trustee.[5]

- **Tex. Civ. Prac. & Rem. Code § 51.014(a)(3).**

  Permits an interlocutory appeal from an order certifying or refusing to certify a class in a suit brought pursuant to Tex. R. Civ. P. 42.

- **Tex. Civ. Prac. & Rem. Code § 51.014(a)(4).**

  Permits an interlocutory appeal from an order granting or refusing to grant a temporary injunction, granting or overruling a motion to dissolve a temporary injunction.[6]

- **Tex. Civ. Prac. & Rem. Code § 51.014(a)(5).**

  Permits an interlocutory appeal from an order denying a motion for summary judgment based on an assertion of official immunity.[7]

- **Tex. Civ. Prac. & Rem. Code § 51.014(a)(6).**

  Permits an interlocutory appeal from an order denying a motion for summary judgment based in whole or in part on a claim against or defense by the electronic or print media arising under the free speech or free press clauses of the U.S. or Texas Constitutions.

- **Tex. Civ. Prac. & Rem. Code § 51.014(a)(7).**

  Permits an interlocutory appeal from an order granting or denying the special appearance of a defendant. This provision does not apply to suits brought under the Texas Family Code.

- **Tex. Civ. Prac. & Rem. Code § 51.014(a)(8).**

  Permits an interlocutory appeal from an order granting or denying a plea to the jurisdiction of a governmental unit. This provision applies also to a plea to the jurisdiction of a governmental official sued in his or her official capacity.[8] An immunity-based motion to dismiss or motion for summary judgment is also appealable under this provision.[9]

- **Tex. Civ. Prac. & Rem. Code § 51.014(a)(9).**

  Permits an interlocutory appeal from an order denying all or part of the relief sought by a motion of a defendant physician or health care provider for the failure of the claimant in a health care liability claim to file an expert report within 120 days of filing the original petition.[10]

- **Tex. Civ. Prac. & Rem. Code § 51.014(a)(10).**

  Permits an interlocutory appeal from an order granting the relief sought by a motion challenging the adequacy of an expert report in a health care liability claim.[11]

- **Tex. Civ. Prac. & Rem. Code § 51.014(a)(11).**

  Permits an interlocutory appeal from an order denying a motion to dismiss a claimant's asbestos/silica-related claims for failure of the claimant to timely serve a physician report, or service of a report that does not comply with the requirements of Tex. Civ. Prac. & Rem. Code ch. 90.

- **Tex. Civ. Prac. & Rem. Code § 51.014(a)(12).**

  Permits an interlocutory appeal from an order denying an "anti-SLAPP" motion, which is a motion to dismiss a legal action based on the exercise of free speech, right to petition, or right of association.[12]

- **Tex. Civ. Prac. & Rem. Code § 51.014(a)(13).**

  Permits an interlocutory appeal from an order denying an electric utility's motion for summary judgment claiming limited liability pursuant to Tex. Civ. Prac. & Rem. Code § 75.0022.[13]

- **Tex. Civ. Prac. & Rem. Code § 51.016.**

  Permits an interlocutory appeal from an order in a matter subject to the Federal Arbitration Act:

  - refusing a stay of any action;
  - denying a petition to order arbitration to proceed;
  - denying an application to compel arbitration;
  - confirming or denying confirmation of an award or partial award;
  - modifying, correcting, or vacating an award or partial award; or
  - granting, continuing, or modifying an injunction against an arbitration.[14]

- **Tex. Civ. Prac. & Rem. Code § 171.098.**

  Permits an interlocutory appeal from an order in a matter subject to the Texas Arbitration Act:

  - denying an application to compel arbitration;
  - granting an application to stay arbitration;
  - confirming or denying confirmation of an award;
  - modifying or correcting an award; or
  - vacating an award without direction a rehearing.

- **Tex. Civ. Prac. & Rem. Code § 15.003(b).**

  Permits an interlocutory appeal in multi-plaintiff cases from an order:

  - determining that a plaintiff did or did not independently establish proper venue; or
  - if a plaintiff did not, determining that a plaintiff did or did not independently establish the following:

    (1) joinder or intervention is proper under the rules of civil procedure;

    (2) maintaining venue does not unfairly prejudice another party;

    (3) there is an essential need to have the plaintiff's claim tried in that venue; and

    (4) the venue is a fair and convenient venue for all parties.[15]

- **Tex. Civ. Prac. & Rem. Code § 150.002(f).**

  Permits an interlocutory appeal from an order granting or denying a motion to dismiss a suit for damages against a licensed architect, licensed professional engineer, registered professional land surveyor, or registered landscape architect based on the plaintiff's failure to file a third-party certificate-of-merit.[16]

- **Tex. Civ. Prac. & Rem. Code § 26.051(b).**

  In cases involving class certification, permits an interlocutory appeal from an order denying a plea to the jurisdiction asserting that a state agency has exclusive or primary jurisdiction of the action or a part of the action, or that a party has failed to exhaust administrative remedies.[17]

- **Tex. Civ. Prac. & Rem. Code § 27.008.**

  Permits an interlocutory appeal from an order denying an "anti-SLAPP" motion, which is a motion to dismiss a legal action based on the exercise of free speech, right to petition, or right of association. Tex. Civ. Prac. & Rem. Code § 27.003.[18]

- **Tex. Gov't Code §§ 1205.068, 1205.105.**

  In a public security declaratory judgment action, permits an interlocutory appeal from an order setting the amount of a bond; denying the issuer's motion to require a bond; and dismissing a party for failure to file a bond.

- **Tex. Bus. Orgs. Code § 2.106(b).**

  Permits an interlocutory appeal from an order denying or otherwise failing to grant summary judgment based on an assertion of immunity by a non-profit corporate trustee.

- **Tex. Ins. Code § 102.151.**

  Permits an interlocutory appeal from an order denying or otherwise failing to grant summary judgment based on an assertion of immunity by a party involved in the issuance of a qualified charitable gift annuity.

- **Tex. Ins. Code § 541.259(c).**

  Permits an interlocutory appeal from an order determining whether a class action may be maintained in a suit brought for unlawful insurance practices.

- **Tex. Health & Safety Code § 1101.104(e).**

  Permits an interlocutory appeal from an order requiring the disclosure of allegedly privileged environmental, health, and safety audit reports.[19]

- **Tex. Fam. Code §§ 56.01(c)(1)(A), (B), (D), (E); 56.01(c)(2).**

  Permits an interlocutory appeal by or on behalf of a child from an order under the Juvenile Justice Code transferring a child for prosecution as an adult; finding delinquent conduct or conduct indicating a need for supervision; modifying a previous juvenile court disposition; committing a child to a facility for the mentally ill or intellectually disabled; or transferring a child who become 16 years of age from a correctional facility to the Texas Department of Criminal Justice.

- **Tex. Health & Safety Code §§ 81.191, 574.070(b), 574.108(a).**

  Permits an interlocutory appeal from an order directing the management of a person with a communicable disease or requiring court-ordered mental health services, or modifying or renewing such an order.[20]

- **Tex. R. Civ. P. 76a(8).**

  Permits an interlocutory appeal from an order sealing or unsealing court records.[21]

5-3 Permissive Interlocutory Appeals

5-3:1 History

5-3:1.1 Enactment in 2001

In 2001, the Texas Legislature amended Section 51.014 of the Texas Civil Practice & Remedies Code to provide an avenue for appealing an interlocutory order not otherwise appealable.[22] Generally, the amendment permitted an appeal when the parties agreed that an interlocutory order involved a "controlling question of law as to which there is a substantial ground for difference of opinion" and that "an immediate appeal of the order may materially advance the ultimate termination of the litigation."[23] To pursue the appeal, the appealing party needed a written order from the trial court permitting the appeal, and the opposing party's agreement to the order.[24] If the trial court issued the agreed order, the court of appeals could permit the appeal upon application.[25]

5-3:1.2 Amendment in 2005

In 2005, the Legislature repealed the subsection of the 2001 amendment providing for the court of appeals to permit the appeal *upon application*.[26] Thus, for the six years from June 2005 to August 2011 (when again the statute was amended), there was no subsection expressly requiring a party to request the court of appeals to permit the appeal or granting the court of appeals discretion to deny the appeal. However, effective September 1, 2008, the Texas Supreme Court amended Rule 28.2 of the Texas Rules of Appellate Procedure to require the appellant in an agreed interlocutory appeal to state in the notice of appeal that the statutory requirements are met.[27] Additionally, under subsection (d) of that Rule, the court of appeals may require the appellant to demonstrate the court's jurisdiction by proving that the appeal meets the statutory requirements.[28]

During this time period, some courts of appeals accepted agreed interlocutory appeals without discussing the substantive requirements of the statute.[29] Others examined the requirements before accepting the appeal, with some noting that appellate jurisdiction is never presumed.[30]

Except for the 2005 repeal of the subsection requiring application to the court of appeals, the remaining provisions of the 2001 version of the statute were unchanged through August 31, 2011. The 2005 version currently governs permissive (agreed) appeals in cases filed before September 1, 2011.[31]

5-3:1.3 Amendment in 2011

In 2011, the Legislature again amended the permissive-appeal statute, and the 2011 amendment currently governs permissive appeals in cases filed on or after September 1, 2011.[32] Under current law, the parties no longer are required to agree to the appeal, but the interlocutory order still must "involve[] a controlling question of law as to which there is a substantial ground for difference of opinion," and the appeal must be one that "may materially advance the ultimate termination of the litigation."[33]

Rule 168 of the Texas Rules of Civil Procedure implements the 2011 amendment, and requires a trial court order that (i) expressly permits the appeal, (ii) identifies the controlling question of law as to which there is a substantial ground for difference of opinion, and (iii) states why an immediate appeal may materially advance the ultimate termination of the litigation.[34] The trial court's permission must be stated in the order to be appealed, and an order previously issued may be amended to include such permission.[35] If the trial court signs an order meeting these requirements, Rule 28.3 of the Texas Rules of Appellate Procedure requires the appealing party to file a petition in the court of appeals "explaining why an appeal is warranted."[36] This petition procedure is intended to be similar to the procedure governing petitions for review in the Texas Supreme Court.[37] If the court of appeals grants the petition, the appeal is governed by the accelerated-appeal procedures of the Texas Rules of Appellate Procedure[38], with the notice of appeal deemed filed on the date the petition is granted.[39]

5-3:2 The Interlocutory Order Must Strictly Comply With the Statute

Because interlocutory orders are immediately appealable only in limited situations, statutes authorizing interlocutory appeals are strictly construed.[40] This includes the permissive-appeal statute, and the courts of appeals routinely dismiss such appeals for want of jurisdiction when the statute's requirements are not strictly observed.[41]

For example, if the appellant in a case governed by current law fails to secure an order from the trial court granting permission to appeal, the interlocutory order is not appealable, and the court of appeals has no jurisdiction to review it.[42] The court of appeals also lacks jurisdiction if the order granting permission does not identify the controlling question of law, even if that question can be inferred from the reporter's record.[43] In cases governed by the 2005 amendment, the appellate court lacks jurisdiction if the parties do not agree to the trial court's order.[44]

In contrast, under the 2011 amendment, the fact that the parties agree to the permissive appeal does not permit the court of appeals to enlarge appellate jurisdiction by disregarding the appeal's statutory requirements.[45]

5-3:3 What Is a "Controlling Question of Law"?

The court of appeals has discretion to accept or reject a permissive appeal,[46] and that discretion often turns on whether the appeal involves a "controlling question of law." Such a question is "one that deeply affects the ongoing process of litigation."[47]

Although summary-judgment orders are frequently the subject of permissive appeals, they must involve a controlling *legal* issue.[48] The statute "does not contemplate permissive appeals of summary judgments where the facts are in dispute."[49] Thus, "if the trial court denies a motion for summary judgment based on the existence of fact issues or the movant's failure to meet its burden on summary judgment rather than a substantive ruling on a controlling legal issue," the court of appeals has no jurisdiction to review the trial court's ruling under section 51.014(d).[50]

5-3:3.1 Examples of Accepted Issues

Courts of appeals have accepted (either expressly or implicitly) the following issues as "controlling questions of law":

- Whether the causation standard under the Federal Employers Liability Act renders inapplicable the expert admissibility standards of *Robinson* and *Havner*;[51]

- Whether a plaintiff's medical authorization form for her health care claim met the legal requirements of the Texas Medical Liability Act;[52]
- Whether a prior judgment was valid;[53]
- Whether the trial court properly construed the Communication's Decency Act;[54]
- Whether an insurer owed insured a duty to defend under a commercial general liability insurance policy, or whether coverage was barred by exclusions in the policy;[55]
- Whether an insurer owed a duty to defend under the errors and omissions coverage of a commercial general liability insurance policy;[56]
- Whether an assignment of an oil and gas lease reserved a royalty interest and, if so, whether the reservation was a covenant that ran with the land;[57]
- Whether an automobile insurer may lawfully recoup from its policyholders a state-mandated fee that the insurer is required to pay ($1 per insured vehicle per year) to the Texas Automobile Theft Prevention Authority;[58]
- Whether a contract between a city and a contractor failed to comply with a local government code, rendering it void as against public policy;[59]
- Whether a tax-foreclosure sale of real property was valid, nullifying a pre-existing lien on the property;[60]
- Whether Mississippi law, rather than Texas law, should govern the issue of recoverable compensatory damages for wrongful death and personal injury claims arising from a pipeline explosion;[61]
- Whether summary-judgment evidence conclusively established that certain deed restrictions were valid;[62]
- Whether a remand order by the court of appeals in a prior appeal reversing a summary judgment was limited in scope;[63]
- Whether federal law preempted a city's claim for certain fees under a franchise agreement with a cable services provider;[64]
- Whether the plaintiff's health care liability claims were barred under conflicting statutes of limitations;[65]
- Whether the plaintiffs' pre-suit notice of their health care liability claims tolled the statute of limitations, when plaintiffs failed to accompany the notice with the statutorily required authorization form for the release of medical information;[66]
- Whether a damages expert utilized a proper measure of damages;[67]
- Whether a Rule 11 agreement was enforceable;[68]
- Whether the heightened burden of proof under Section 74.153 of the Texas Civil Practice & Remedies Code applies in a medical malpractice action against an emergency room physician and hospital in circumstances that allegedly involved treatment of a non-emergency condition;[69]
- Whether the trial court properly construed oil and gas leases;[70]
- "[W]hether the exclusive remedy defense provided by the Texas Workers' Compensation Act applies on a worksite that was subject to a contractor-controlled insurance program";[71]

- Whether a party "can invoke the open courts provision of the Texas Constitution to toll the statute of limitations in a wrongful death and survival claim" that was originally brought as a negligence claim prior to decedent's death;[72] and
- Whether a party is a "seller" and is eligible to seek indemnity under Chapter 28 of the Texas Civil Practice & Remedies Code.[73]

5-3:4 When Is There a "Substantial Ground for Difference of Opinion"?

A "substantial ground for difference of opinion" means there are "legitimate disagreements" regarding the controlling question of law.[74] This requirement is ***not*** met by default whenever a trial court rules on the question against the petitioner seeking permissive review.[75] It is also not met when the trial court's ruling comports with settled law.[76] Quoting a Texas Commentator looking to federal cases interpreting similar language in the federal counterpart to section 51.014 (28 U.S.C. § 1292(b)), the court of appeals in *Gulf Coast* wrote:

> Substantial grounds for disagreement exist when the question presented to the court is novel or difficult, when controlling circuit law is doubtful, when controlling circuit law is in disagreement with other courts of appeals, and when there simply is little authority upon which the district court can rely.[77]

5-3:5 The Trial Court Must Make a Substantive Ruling on the Controlling Question of Law

The permissive-appeal statute cannot be used as a mechanism to present, in effect, a "certified question" to the courts of appeals, similar to the procedure used by federal appellate courts in certifying a determinative question of state law to the Texas Supreme Court.[78] Unlike in the "certified question" scenario, where the purpose of the procedure is for the Supreme Court to answer a question of state law that has not previously been decided, the purpose of a permissive appeal is to obtain immediate review of a substantive ruling on a pivotal issue of law.[79] Thus, the trial court must make a substantive ruling on the legal issue presented on appeal, and the record must clearly reflect that ruling. A substantive ruling on the specific legal question presented for determination by the court of appeals is "a jurisdictional prerequisite to permissive appeals pursuant to section 51.014(d)."[80] The court in *Tommy Harral Construction, Inc.* explained:

> Because an appellate court may only address an action taken by the trial court, the record presented upon a permissive appeal must reflect the trial court's substantive ruling on the specific legal issue presented for appellate-court determination. Otherwise, this court's opinion with respect to the requested legal determination would be an advisory opinion. The court has no jurisdiction to issue an advisory opinion.[81]

The following are examples of summary-judgment rulings that were not subject to permissive appeal because of this defect:

- A trial court's ministerial ruling denying competing motions for summary judgment without making a substantive decision on the "matter of law" interpretation of a contract;[82]

- A trial court's ministerial ruling denying summary judgment without making a substantive decision on the legal issue of the proper construction of two statutes;[83]
- A trial court's denial of competing motions for summary judgment on the basis that each side "failed to meet their burden," when nothing in the record showed a substantive ruling by the trial court on any of the legal issues presented on appeal;[84] and
- A trial court's denial of summary judgment based generally "on the merits," when multiple bases for summary judgment were urged but nothing in the record showed the ground for the trial court's ruling or that the court ruled on the specific legal issue presented on appeal.[85]

On the other hand, a permissive appeal might be taken from an order that denies summary judgment without specifying the basis for the denial, when the motion for summary judgment asserts only a single ground.[86]

The best practice is to ask the trial court to include its substantive ruling in its order identifying the controlling legal issue and authorizing the permissive appeal.[87]

5-3:6 The Question of Law Presented to the Court of Appeals Defines the Scope of the Appeal

The question of law presented to the appellate court defines the scope of the permissive appeal,[88] and the parties may not add to the trial court's description of it.[89] Further, the question decided by the trial court and court of appeals must be the same.[90]

5-3:7 The Appeal Must Materially Advance the Ultimate Termination of the Litigation

A permissive appeal will facilitate final resolution of a case "when resolution of the legal question dramatically affects recovery" in it.[91]

5-3:8 The Court of Appeals Has Absolute Discretion to Permit or Deny the Appeal—But the Supreme Court Encourages Permitting the Appeal When the Statutory Requirements Are Met

The Texas Supreme Court recently clarified that the Texas Legislature modeled section 51.014(d) after the federal counterpart to permissive interlocutory appeals, which has been interpreted by the United States Supreme Court as "providing federal circuit courts absolute discretion to accept or deny permissive appeals."[92] Accordingly, Texas courts of appeals "have discretion to accept or deny permissive interlocutory appeals certified under section 51.014(d), just as federal circuit courts do."[93] However, the Supreme Court cautioned:

> [W]hile courts of appeals have discretion to deny acceptance of permissive interlocutory appeals, the Legislature in its enactment of section 51.014(d) and (f) has recognized the benefit of appellate courts accepting such appeals when the threshold for an exception to the final judgment rule is met. . . . Just because courts of appeals can decline to accept permissive interlocutory appeals does

not mean they should; in fact, in many instances, courts of appeals should do exactly what the Legislature has authorized them to do—accept permissive interlocutory appeals and address the merits of the legal issues certified.[94]

5-4 The Accelerated Nature of Interlocutory Appeals

When allowed by statute, appeals from interlocutory orders are accelerated.[95] In accelerated appeals, the deadlines are shortened for filing the notice of appeal, and motions for new trial, other post-trial motions, and requests for findings of fact and conclusions of law will ***not*** extend the time for perfecting the appeal.[96] The deadlines are jurisdictional. Unless the notice of appeal is timely, or the court of appeals has granted an extension of time for filing it, the appeal will be dismissed for lack of jurisdiction.[97]

Generally, the rules of procedure govern the deadlines for an interlocutory appeal.[98] However, the statute authorizing the interlocutory appeal may provide a different deadline for perfecting the appeal. When a statute provides the deadline, comply with the statutory deadline, not the rules of procedure, because the deadline in the rules of procedure—and the procedural rules for extending the deadline—do not apply.[99]

Although a request for findings of fact and conclusions of law will not extend the deadline for perfecting an accelerated appeal, a trial court may, but is not required to, file findings and conclusions. If the court chooses to do so, the deadline for the findings and conclusions is 30 days after the order being appealed is signed.[100]

The deadlines and procedures for filing the record and briefs in an accelerated appeal are also shortened.[101] Additionally, the court of appeals may dispense with the clerk's record altogether, and hear the appeal on the original papers, or on sworn and uncontroverted copies of those papers.[102]

An accelerated appeal is given precedence over other civil appeals pending before the court of appeals.[103]

5-5 Trial Court Activity While the Interlocutory Order Is on Appeal

5-5:1 Actions and Orders Permitted and Prohibited

Rule 29 of the Texas Rules of Appellate Procedure governs the trial court's activities while an interlocutory order is pending. The trial court retains jurisdiction during the appeal and, unless prohibited by law, may proceed with trial on the merits and make further orders, "including one dissolving the order complained of on appeal."[104] However, the trial court may not enter an order that "(a) is inconsistent with any appellate court temporary order; or (b) interferes with or impairs the jurisdiction of the appellate court or effectiveness of any relief sought or that may be granted on appeal."[105] If the trial court enters an interlocutory order concerning the same subject matter as the order already on appeal, or enters an interlocutory order that "interferes with or impairs the effectiveness of the relief sought or that may be granted on appeal," the appellate court may, on a party's motion or on the appellate court's own initiative, choose to review that order as well.[106]

5-5:2 Stay Pending Resolution of Interlocutory Appeal

5-5:2.1 General Rule and Exceptions

Generally, an interlocutory appeal does not have the effect of staying trial court proceedings. However, an appeal under Section 51.014(a)—other than appeals related to temporary injunctions—automatically stays the commencement of trial pending resolution of the appeal.[107] In certain instances, an appeal under Section 51.014(a) also stays all other trial court proceedings.[108] The chart below identifies whether and to what extent Section 51.014(a)'s interlocutory appeals are stayed:

	No stay	Stay of trial only	Stay of trial + all other proceedings	Stay only if deadlines met[109]
§ 51.014(a)(1) (receiver/trustee)		✓		
§ 51.014(a)(2) (receiver/trustee)		✓		
§ 51.014(a)(3) (class cert.)			✓	
§ 51.014(a)(4) (injunction)	✓			
§ 51.014(a)(5) (official immunity)			✓	✓
§ 51.014(a)(6) (media)		✓		
§ 51.014(a)(7) (special app.)		✓		✓
§ 51.014(a)(8) (personal juris. gov't unit)			✓	✓
§ 51.014(a)(9) (Med. Liab. Act expert report)		✓		
§ 51.014(a)(10) (Med. Liab. Act expert report)		✓		
§ 51.014(a)(11) (asbestos/silica)		✓		
§ 51.014(a)(12) (anti-SLAPP)			✓	
§ 51.014(a)(13) (electric utility)		✓		
Family Code Suit	✓			

A party's failure to object when a trial court proceeds despite a statutorily mandated stay waives any error in the trial court's failure to impose it.[110]

Most interlocutory appeals under statutes other than Section 51.014 require an order from the trial or appellate court granting a stay.

5-5:2.2 Strategies for Seeking a Stay Pending Resolution of Interlocutory Appeal

Although there are no specific guidelines for seeking a stay of trial court proceedings when a stay is not statutorily imposed, certain strategies increase the likelihood of obtaining a stay:

- Seek the agreement of the opposing party. A joint or unopposed motion is much more likely to be granted.

- Seek a stay from the trial court before seeking a stay from the court of appeals. The court of appeals expects a party to seek relief from the trial court before petitioning the court of appeals.
- Rather than arguing only that time and resources will be lost if there is no stay, attempt to demonstrate that a stay is required to protect the court of appeals' jurisdiction over the appeal, or that substantive rights of the parties will be lost without a stay.
- Present your request for a stay in a separate motion that complies with Rule 10.1 of the Texas Rules of Appellate Procedure.
- If you need the stay on an expedited basis, request emergency relief in your motion, and make that request clear on the front page, e.g.:

  EMERGENCY MOTION TO STAY ALL TRIAL

  COURT PROCEEDINGS

  (RELIEF NEEDED BY [specific date])

  In your motion, specify the grounds for needing expedited relief.[111]
- If possible, avoid seeking an emergency stay on a Friday, especially a Friday afternoon.

5-5:2.3 Mandamus May Be Appropriate if the Trial Court Refuses to Rule to Avoid an Interlocutory Appeal and Automatic Stay

Mandamus may be appropriate if a trial court refuses to rule on a pending motion in order to avoid triggering the right to appeal and the automatic stay that often accompanies it. However, before resorting to that measure, explain to the trial court that your client is being deprived of his statutory right to appeal immediately while trial is stayed and ask (on the record) for a ruling. If the trial court refuses to rule, seek mandamus relief.[112]

5-5:3 Enforceability of Interlocutory Order Pending on Appeal

An appeal of an interlocutory order does not suspend enforcement of the order being appealed.[113] However, the order may be suspended if the trial court permits it to be superseded in accordance with Rule 24 of the Texas Rules of Appellate Procedure,[114] or if "the appellant is entitled to supersede the order without security by filing a notice of appeal."[115] If the court refuses to allow the order to be superseded, the appellant may request appellate review of that decision for an abuse of discretion.[116] Although an appellate court "must not suspend the trial court's order if the appellant's rights would be adequately protected by supersedeas or another order made under Rule 24," the court may make any temporary order necessary to preserve the parties' rights until completion of the appeal.[117] During the appeal, only the appellate court may enforce the temporary order.[118] However, the court may refer any enforcement proceeding to the trial court with instructions to "(a) hear evidence and grant appropriate relief; or (b) make findings and recommendations and report them to the appellate court."[119]

5-6 Review by the Texas Supreme Court

For interlocutory appeals of orders entered prior to September 1, 2017, the Texas Supreme Court's jurisdiction is limited.[120] For those appeals, the Supreme Court "may only review the appellate court's interlocutory decision if (1) one or more justices dissented in the court of appeals, or (2) the court of appeals holds differently from a prior decision of another court of appeals or of the supreme court."[121] One court "holds differently from another when there is inconsistency in their respective decisions that should be clarified to remove unnecessary uncertainty in the law and unfairness to litigants."[122]

In 2017, the Texas Legislature substantially broadened the Texas Supreme Court's jurisdiction to review interlocutory appeals. Now, for orders entered after September 1, 2017, the Supreme Court has jurisdiction over all interlocutory appeals that it deems "important to the jurisprudence of the state."[123]

As discussed, the Supreme Court recently clarified that the Texas courts of appeals have virtually unfettered discretion to permit or deny a party's petition for permissive appeal.[124] But the Supreme Court clarified that a court of appeals' exercise of that discretion—even to *deny* a permissive appeal—does not deprive the court of jurisdiction over that same appeal if it meets the Legislature's threshold for an exception to the final judgment rule.[125] However, the Supreme Court's jurisdiction to accept an interlocutory appeal that was denied by the court of appeals does not "alter[] the requirement that a party advancing a permissive appeal must first petition the court of appeals for review before petitioning [the Supreme Court]."[126]

5-7 Use It or Lose It?

5-7:1 Interlocutory Appeals Permitted But Not Mandated—Sometimes

An issue that continues to brew in Texas jurisprudence is whether a party who did not utilize his right to appeal on an interlocutory basis may challenge the interlocutory order after final judgment. Section 51.014(a) of the Texas Civil Practice & Remedies Code provides that a person "may" appeal from one of the listed interlocutory orders. The Texas Supreme Court has construed this language to mean interlocutory appeal is permitted but not mandated—sometimes. Specifically, in *Hernandez v. Ebrom*,[127] a defendant-doctor failed to challenge the adequacy of the plaintiff's expert report by interlocutory appeal, as permitted by Section 51.014(a)(9), and instead waited to raise it in his appeal from the final judgment.[128] The Supreme Court concluded that the defendant's failure to pursue an interlocutory appeal did not waive his complaints about the expert report.[129]

However, the procedural posture of the case was important to the court's decision. The doctor was nonsuited six months after the trial court denied his motion to dismiss and the case was never tried on the merits.[130] The court explained that if the case had been tried and the defendant found liable, requiring post-trial dismissal of the case "would be construing the statute to yield an unjust and nonsensical result—one we presume the Legislature did not intend."[131] The purpose of requiring timely expert reports is to reduce frivolous claims, not to preclude meritorious claims.[132]

The Supreme Court's reasoning in *Ebrom* has been considered in other contexts. For example, the court in *Nalle Plastics Family Ltd. Partnership v. Porter, Rogers,*

Dahlman & Gordon, P.C.[133] concluded that the word "may" in the statute permitting interlocutory appeal of a venue ruling in a case involving multiple plaintiffs suggests that review of a pre-trial venue ruling is available on final appeal.[134] However, "transferring a case to a different forum for a new trial—after full trial proceedings have been completed in the initial forum—may well be considered an 'absurd result' that the Legislature could not have intended."[135]

The court in *In re Santander Consumer USA, Inc.*[136] considered *Ebrom*'s reasoning in the context of a party's failure to challenge on interlocutory appeal a trial court's denial of arbitration under the FAA. The court suggested that, under *Ebrom*, the failure to pursue the interlocutory appeal would not waive the right to challenge the ruling on final judgment.[137] The court in *In re S.M.H.*[138] reached the same result in the context of the TAA, where the losing party failed to pursue an interlocutory appeal of a trial court order vacating an arbitration award under the TAA.[139]

Citing *Ebrom*, the court in *DeWolf v. Kohler*[140] concluded that the appellant did not waive her right to challenge on appeal from the final judgment, the trial court's interlocutory order granting one defendant's special appearance, despite her failure to pursue an interlocutory appeal.[141]

Similarly, the court in *Am. Heritage Capital, LP v. Gonzalez*[142] concluded that the cross-appellant was not required to pursue an interlocutory appeal of the trial court's denial of her anti-SLAPP motion to dismiss, but instead could appeal that denial after final judgment.[143]

5-7:2 Some Interlocutory Orders Rendered Moot by Subsequent Orders

The Court in *Ebrom* additionally acknowledged that some interlocutory orders cannot be challenged after final judgment because they are rendered moot by subsequent orders.[144] For example, the appeal of a temporary injunction is rendered moot by entry of a permanent injunction.[145] Similarly, the appeal of class certification is rendered moot by the court's subsequent grant of the defendant's motion for summary judgment.[146] Normally, an interlocutory appeal of the trial court's decision to certify a class automatically stays all trial court proceedings. Thus, in circumstances like these, where a risk exists that a subsequent order will moot the interlocutory order, it is critical to object to the trial court's refusal to observe the statutory stay. The failure to object *waives* any error related to the stay, and the lack of the stay may moot the error in the interlocutory ruling once the case proceeds to final judgment.

In sum, under current jurisprudence, whether an interlocutory appeal is permissive or mandatory is unclear in many circumstances. Accordingly, in deciding to forego interlocutory appeal, carefully consider the risk that the right to challenge the ruling might be permanently lost.[147]

Notes

1 *See* Chapter 4, § 4-2.

2 *Gulley v. State Farm Lloyds*, 350 S.W.3d 204, 206 (Tex. App.—San Antonio 2011, no pet.).

3 *See City of Houston v. Estate of Jones*, 388 S.W.3d 663, 666 (Tex. 2012) (per curiam).

4 Section 51.014(a) permits appeals from interlocutory orders of a district court, county court at law, statutory probate court, or county court.

[5] Orders resolving distinct issues unrelated to appointment, such as resolving a claim, may not be challenged by interlocutory appeal.

[6] An order that substantially modifies a temporary injunction is also appealable under this provision. *Ahmed v. Shimi Ventures, L.P.*, 99 S.W.3d 682, 688–89 (Tex. App.—Houston [1st Dist.] 2003, no pet.)

[7] The denial of a motion to dismiss based on official immunity is also appealable under this provision. *Austin State Hosp. v. Graham*, 347 S.W.3d 298, 300–01 (Tex. 2011). *See Tex. Dept. of Aging and Disability Servs. v. Cannon*, 453 S.W.3d 411, 413 n.4 (Tex. 2015) (refusing to reconsider *Graham's* holding that Section 51.014 authorizes an interlocutory appeal of an order denying a motion to dismiss based on official immunity).

[8] *Texas A&M Univ. Sys. v. Koseoglu*, 233 S.W.3d 835, 845–46 (Tex. 2007).

[9] *City of Magnolia 4A Economic Dev. Corp. v. Smedley*, 533 S.W.3d 297, 299 (Tex. 2017).

[10] Tex. Civ. Prac. & Rem. Code § 74.351(b). An appeal may not be taken from an order granting an extension to file the report.

[11] Tex. Civ. Prac. & Rem. Code § 74.351(l).

[12] The anti-SLAPP statute also provides for an interlocutory appeal. *See infra* Tex. Civ. Prac. & Rem. Code § 27.008.

[13] Section 75.0022 provides limited liability for electric utilities in certain counties that have entered into an agreement with a political subdivision for the subdivision's use of the utilities' land for recreation, exercise, relaxation, travel, or pleasure.

[14] Section 51.016 permits an interlocutory appeal under the same circumstances that an appeal from a federal district court's order or decision would be permitted by 9 U.S.C. § 16.

[15] The court of appeals reviews the trial court's order based on an independent determination from the record, rather than under an abuse of discretion or substantial evidence standard. Tex. Civ. Prac. & Rem. Code § 15.003(c)(1). The court of appeals must render judgment not later than the 120th day after the date the appeal is perfected. Tex. Civ. Prac. & Rem. Code § 15.003(c)(2).

[16] This provision applies to any action or arbitration proceeding, regardless of the defendant's state of licensing.

[17] This provision applies only when the plea is denied and a class is subsequently certified; as part of an appeal of the order certifying the class, a party may obtain appellate review of the order denying the plea to the jurisdiction.

[18] Together, sections 27.008 and 51.014(a)(12) of Tex. Civ. Prac. & Rem. Code confirm that a party may take an interlocutory appeal from an order denying an anti-SLAPP motion, whether the motion is expressly denied by the trial court or denied by operation of law as a result of the court's failure to rule on it.

[19] This provision does not apply to orders refusing to require the disclosure of such reports.

[20] Each statute differs regarding whether the order remains in effect pending appeal; these appeals are given preference.

[21] These orders are deemed severed from the case and are therefore final and appealable. Nonetheless, they are labeled interlocutory appeals and are governed by the interlocutory-appeal rules.

[22] Act of June 16, 2001, 77th Leg., R.S., ch. 1389, § 1, eff. Sept. 1, 2001, 2001 Tex. Sess. Law Serv. ch. 1389 (current version at Tex. Civ. Prac. & Rem. Code § 51.014(d)).

[23] Act of June 16, 2001, 77th Leg., R.S., ch. 1389, § 1, eff. Sept. 1, 2001, 2001 Tex. Sess. Law Serv. ch. 1389 (current version at Tex. Civ. Prac. & Rem. Code § 51.014(d)).

[24] Act of June 16, 2001, 77th Leg., R.S., ch. 1389, § 1, eff. Sept. 1, 2001, 2001 Tex. Sess. Law Serv. ch. 1389 (current version at Tex. Civ. Prac. & Rem. Code § 51.014(d)).

[25] Act of June 16, 2001, 77th Leg., R.S., ch. 1389, § 1, eff. Sept. 1, 2001, 2001 Tex. Sess. Law Serv. ch. 1389 (current version at Tex. Civ. Prac. & Rem. Code § 51.014(d)).

[26] Act of June 18, 2005, 79th Leg., R.S., ch. 1051, § 2, eff. June 18, 2005, 2005 Tex. Sess. Law Serv. ch. 1051 (current version at Tex. Civ. Prac. & Rem. Code § 51.014(d)).

[27] Tex. R. App. P. 28.2(c) (eff. Sept. 1, 2008). For cases filed before September 1, 2011, there is no rule of civil procedure governing the procedure in the trial court for an agreed interlocutory appeal.

[28] Tex. R. App. P. 28.2(d).

[29] *See, e.g., Lyle v. Jane Guinn Revocable Trust*, 365 S.W.3d 341, 349 (Tex. App.—Houston [1st Dist.] 2010, pet. denied); *Stein v. Bridgepoint Prop. Owners Ass'n, Inc.*, No. 03-11-00311-CV, 2012 WL 987792, at *2 (Tex. App.—Austin Mar. 22, 2012, no pet.) (mem. op.).

[30] *See State Fair of Tex. v. Iron Mountain Info. Mgmt., Inc.*, 299 S.W.3d 261, 262–64 & n.3 (Tex. App.—Dallas 2009, no pet.) (dismissing appeal for want of jurisdiction because order being appealed did not present a controlling question of law as to which there was substantial ground for a difference of opinion); *State v. Ledrec, Inc.*, 366 S.W.3d 305, 306 (Tex. App.—Fort Worth 2012, no pet.) (accepting appeal); *Comcast Cable of Plano, Inc. v. City of Plano*, 315 S.W.3d 673, 677 (Tex. App.—Dallas 2010, no pet.) (accepting appeal). The court in *Iron Mountain* noted that Rule 28.2 of the Texas Rules of Appellate Procedure permits the court of appeals to dismiss an appeal for lack of jurisdiction at any stage of the appeal. 299 S.W.3d at 263. *See* Tex. R. App. P. 28.2(d).

[31] *See* Act of May 30, 2011, 82nd Leg., R.S., ch. 203, §§ 6.01-.02, eff. Sept. 1, 2011, 2011 Tex. Sess. Law Serv. ch. 203; *State v. Ledrec, Inc.*, 366 S.W.3d 305, 306 n.1 (Tex. App.—Fort Worth 2012, no pet.).

[32] Act of May 30, 2011, 82nd Leg., R.S., ch. 203, §§ 3.01, 6.01-.02, eff. Sept. 1, 2011, 2011 Tex. Sess. Law Serv. ch. 203.

[33] Tex. Civ. Prac. & Rem. Code § 51.014(d). *See Sabre Travel Int'l, Ltd. v. Deutsche Lufthansa AG*, __ S.W.3d __, No. 17-0538, 2019 WL 406062, at *4 (Tex. Feb. 1, 2019).

[34] Tex. R. Civ. P. 168; *see also, e.g., Rig Tools, Inc. v. Leamer*, No. 06-13-00001-CV, 2013 WL 177419, at *1 (Tex. App.—Texarkana Jan. 17, 2013, no pet.) (mem. op.) (Tex. R. Civ. P. 168 implements Tex. Civ. Prac. & Rem. Code § 51.014(d)).

[35] Tex. R. Civ. P. 168.

[36] Tex. Civ. Prac. & Rem. Code § 51.014(f); Tex. R. App. P. 28.3(a), (e).

[37] Tex. R. App. P. 28.3 cmt.; *see* Tex. R. App. P. 53. *See Sabre Travel Int'l, Ltd. v. Deutsche Lufthansa AG*, __ S.W.3d __, No. 17-0538, 2019 WL 406062, at *4 (Tex. Feb. 1, 2019).

[38] Tex. R. App. P. 28.3(k); Tex. Civ. Prac. & Rem. Code § 51.014(f). Consistent with the prior versions of the statute, a permissive appeal does not stay proceedings in the trial court unless the parties agree to a stay or the trial court or appellate court orders one. Tex. Civ. Prac. & Rem. Code § 51.014(e).

[39] Section 51.014(f) states: "The date the court of appeals enters the order accepting the appeal *starts the time applicable to filing the notice of appeal*." Tex. Civ. Prac. & Rem. Code § 51.014(f) (emphasis added). Thus, Section 51.014(f) appears to contemplate (but does not expressly require) that a notice of appeal will be filed after the petition is granted. However, under Rule 28.3(k), if the petition is granted, "a notice of appeal is deemed to have been filed under Rule 26.1(b) on that date, . . . [and] [a] separate notice of appeal need not be filed." Rule 28.3(k)'s provision that a notice of appeal is deemed filed presumably satisfies Section 51.014(f). The author was unable to find any case law expressly discussing this apparent discrepancy. However, the Texas Supreme Court recently cited Rule 28.3(k) as "clarifying that if a petition seeking interlocutory appeal is granted, the appeal is thereby perfected in the court of appeals." *See Sabre Travel Int'l, Ltd. v. Deutsche Lufthansa AG*, __ S.W.3d __, No. 17-0538, 2019 WL 406062, at *4 (Tex. Feb. 1, 2019).

[40] *King-A Corp. v. Wehling*, No. 13-13-00100-CV, 2013 WL 1092209, at *2 (Tex. App.—Corpus Christi Mar. 14, 2013, no pet.) (mem. op); *Rig Tools, Inc. v. Leamer*, No. 06-13-00001-CV, 2013 WL 177419, at *1 (Tex. App.—Texarkana Jan. 17, 2013, no pet.) (mem. op.).

[41] *See, e.g., King-A Corp. v. Wehling*, No. 13-13-00100-CV, 2013 WL 1092209, at *2 (Tex. App.—Corpus Christi Mar. 14, 2013, no pet.) (mem. op) (dismissing appeal for want of jurisdiction); *Rig Tools, Inc. v. Leamer*, No. 06-13-00001-CV, 2013 WL 177419, at *1 (Tex. App.—Texarkana Jan. 17, 2013, no pet.) (mem. op.) (same).

[42] *See, e.g., Colvin v. B. Spender & Assocs., P.C.*, No. 01-15-00247-CV, 2015 WL 2228728, at *1–2 (Tex. App.—Houston [1st Dist.] May 12, 2015, no pet.) (mem. op.); *Indemnity Ins. Co. v. Helix Energy Solutions Group, Inc.*, No. 01-13-00222-CV, 2013 WL 1932140, at *1 (Tex. App.—Houston [1st Dist.] May 9, 2013, no pet.) (mem. op.); *AMF Mech. Corp. v. Bermudez*, No. 13-13-00105-CV, 2013 WL 1791069, at *1–2 (Tex. App.—Corpus Christi, Apr. 25, 2013, no pet.) (mem. op.); *Rig Tools, Inc. v. Leamer*, No. 06-13-00001-CV, 2013 WL 177419, at *1 (Tex. App.—Texarkana Jan. 17, 2013, no pet.) (mem. op.); *Senegal v. McClendon*, No. 09-11-00497-CV, 2011 WL 6251069, at *1 (Tex. App.—Beaumont Dec. 15, 2011, no pet.) (mem. op.).

[43] *Long v. State*, No. 03-12-00437-CV, 2012 WL 3055510, at *1 (Tex. App.—Austin July 25, 2012, no pet.) (mem. op.). *See also Armour Pipe Line Co. v. Sandel Energy, Inc.*, No. 14-16-00010-CV, 2016 WL 514229, at *2 (Tex. App.—Houston [14th Dist.] Feb. 9, 2016, no pet.) (mem. op.)

[44] *See, e.g., Watson v. Moray*, 133 S.W.3d 877, 878 (Tex. App.—Dallas 2004, no pet.); *Tian Jia v. Hua Xu*, No. 14-12-01165-CV, 2013 WL 1154317, at *1 (Tex. App.—Houston [14th Dist.] Mar. 21, 2013, pet. denied) (mem. op.); *Ace Parking Mgmt., Inc. v. Main Street Parking, Ltd.*, No. 14-12-00262-CV, 2012 WL 1425098, at *1 (Tex. App.—Houston [14th Dist.] Apr. 24, 2012, no pet.) (mem. op.); *Glazer's Wholesale Drug Co. v. Ontiveros-Nietoi*, No. 08-11-00376-CV, 2012 WL 400356, at *1 (Tex. App.—El Paso Feb. 8, 2012, no pet.) (mem. op.); *Burch v. Fontenot*, No. 09-10-00030-CV, 2010 WL 728555, at *1 (Tex. App.—Beaumont Mar. 4, 2010, no pet.) (mem. op.).

[45] *Gulf Coast Asphalt Co., L.L.C. v. Lloyd*, 457 S.W.3d 539, 544 n.8 (Tex. App.—Houston [14th Dist.] 2015, no pet.).

[46] *Orion Marine Constr., Inc. v. Cepeda*, No. 01-18-00323-CV, 2018 WL 3059756, at *2 (Houston [1st Dist.] June 21, 2018, no pet.) ("Even if the statutory requirements are satisfied, whether to accept a permissive appeal rests in [the court of appeals'] discretion.").

[47] *Gulf Coast Asphalt Co., L.L.C. v. Lloyd*, 457 S.W.3d 539, 544–45 (Tex. App.—Houston [14th Dist.] 2015, no pet.) (quoting Renee Forinash McElhaney, *Toward Permissive Appeal in Texas*, 29 St. Mary's L.J. 729, 747–49 (1998)).

[48] *Diamond Prods. Int'l, Inc. v. Handsel*, 142 S.W.3d 491, 494 (Tex. App.—Houston [14th Dist.] 2004, no pet.) (attempted appeal from denial of summary judgment).

[49] *Diamond Prods. Int'l, Inc. v. Handsel*, 142 S.W.3d 491, 494 (Tex. App.—Houston [14th Dist.] 2004, no pet.); *King-A Corp. v. Wehling*, No. 13-13-00100-CV, 2013 WL 1092209, at *3 (Tex. App.—Corpus Christi Mar. 14, 2013, no pet.) (mem. op.) ("While diligence [in securing service of process] may be determined as a matter of law, it is generally a question of fact."). *See Orion Marine Constr., Inc. v. Cepeda*, No. 01-18-00323-CV, 2018 WL 3059756, at *2 (Houston [1st Dist.] June 21, 2018, no pet.); *Armour Pipe Line Co. v. Sandel Energy, Inc.*, No. 14-16-00010-CV, 2016 WL 514229, at *3 (Tex. App.—Houston [14th Dist.] Feb. 9, 2016, no pet.) (mem. op.).

[50] *Hartford Accident and Indem. Co. v. Seagoville Partners*, No. 05-15-00760-CV, 2016 WL 3199003, at *2 (Tex. App.—Dallas June 9, 2016, no pet.). *See In re Fisher*, 421 S.W.3d 682, 685 (Tex. App.—Texarkana 2014, no pet.) (no jurisdiction over permissive appeal that involved controlling issue of fact, rather than controlling issue of law).

[51] *BNSF Ry. Co. v. Baca*, No. 02-17-00168-CV, 2018 WL 1528573, at *1 (Tex. App.—Fort Worth March 29, 2018, no pet.) (accepting permissive appeal of order denying motion to exclude expert and citing 45 U.S.C. §§ 51–60; *E.I. Dupont de Nemours & Co. v. Robinson*, 923 S.W.2d 549 (Tex. 1995); *Merrell Dow Pharm., Inc. v. Havner*, 953 S.W.2d 706 (Tex. 1997)).

[52] *Borowski v. Ayers*, 524 S.W.3d 292, 296 (Tex. App.—Waco 2016, pet. denied) (citing Tex. Civ. Prac. & Rem. Code § 74.052).

[53] *Orca Assets, G.P., L.L.C. v. Dorfman*, 470 S.W.3d 153, 156, 159 (Tex. App.—Fort Worth 2015, pet. denied) (appeal from partial summary judgment).

[54] *Davis v. Motiva Ent., L.L.C.*, No. 09-14-00434-CV, 2015 WL 1535694, at *1–3 (Tex. App.—Beaumont Apr. 2, 2015, pet. denied) (mem. op.) (appeal from order granting motion to dismiss).

[55] *Mid-Continent Cas. Co. v. Krolczyk*, 408 S.W.3d 896, 901 (Tex. App.—Houston [1st Dist.] 2013, pet. denied) (appeal from denial of summary judgment). *See also St. Paul Fire & Marine Ins. Co. v. Petroplex Energy, Inc.*, 474 S.W.3d 454, 456, 461 (Tex. App.—Eastland 2015, pet. dism'd) (appeal from partial summary judgment).

[56] *Service Lloyd's Ins. Co. v. J.C. Wink, Inc.*, 182 S.W.3d 19, 23–24 (Tex. App.—San Antonio 2005, pet. dism'd) (appeal from partial summary judgment), *abrogated on other grounds by Lamar Homes, Inc. v. Mid-Continent Cas. Co.*, 242 S.W.3d 1 (Tex. 2007). *See also Mid-Continent Cas. Co. v. Krolczyk*, 408 S.W.3d 896, 901 (Tex. App.—Houston [1st Dist.] 2013, pet. denied); *Certain Underwriters at Lloyd's of London v. Cardtronics, Inc.*, 438 S.W.3d 770, 774 (Tex. App.—Houston [1st Dist.] 2014, no pet.) (proper interpretation of insurance policy constituted controlling issue of law under permissive-appeal statute).

[57] *Lyle v. Jane Guinn Revocable Trust*, 365 S.W.3d 341, 345, 348–49 (Tex. App.—Houston [1st Dist.] 2010, pet. denied) (appeal from partial summary judgment).

[58] *Liberty Mut. Ins. Co. v. Griesing*, 150 S.W.3d 640, 642–43 (Tex. App.—Austin 2004) (appeal from partial summary judgment), *dism'd w.o.j.*, 251 S.W.3d 471 (Tex. 2007).

[59] *City of San Antonio v. Casey Indus., Inc.*, 381 S.W.3d 589, 590–92 (Tex. App.—San Antonio 2012, pet. denied) (appeal from partial summary judgment).

[60] *WMC Mortg. Corp. v. Moss*, No. 01-10-00948-CV, 2011 WL 2089777, at *1 (Tex. App.—Houston [1st Dist.] May 19, 2011, no pet.) (mem. op.) (appeal from partial summary judgment).

[61] *Enterprise Prods. Partners, L.P. v. Mitchell*, 340 S.W.3d 476, 478–79 (Tex. App.—Houston [1st Dist.] 2011, pet. abated and subsequently dism'd by agr.) (appeal from order ruling that Texas law applied). *See also Am. Nat'l Ins. Co. v. Conestoga Settlement Trust*, 442 S.W.3d 589, 593 (Tex. App.—San Antonio 2014, pet. denied) (permitting permissive appeal to determine whether New Jersey or New York law governed issues relating to validity of insurance policy); *Winspear v. Coca-Cola Refreshments, USA, Inc.*, No. 05-13-00712-CV, 2014 WL 2396142, at *1 (Tex. App.—Dallas Apr. 9, 2014, pet. denied) (mem. op.) (permitting permissive appeal to determine whether Georgia law applied to construction of guaranty agreement).

[62] *Stein v. Bridgepoint Prop. Owners Ass'n, Inc.*, No. 03-11-00311-CV, 2012 WL 987792, at *2–3 (Tex. App.—Austin Mar. 22, 2012, no pet.) (mem. op.) (appeal from partial summary judgment declaring deed restrictions valid).

[63] *Maswoswe v. Nelson*, No. 09-11-00639-CV, 2012 WL 1448575, at *1–2 (Tex. App.—Beaumont Apr. 26, 2012, no pet.) (mem. op.) (appeal from denial of motion to dismiss).

[64] *Comcast Cable of Plano, Inc. v. City of Plano*, 315 S.W.3d 673, 675–76 (Tex. App.—Dallas 2010, no pet.) (appeal from denial of summary judgment).

[65] *Kimbrell v. Molinet*, 288 S.W.3d 464, 466 (Tex. App.—San Antonio 2008), aff'd, 356 S.W.3d 407 (Tex. 2011) (appeal from denial of summary judgment).

[66] *Jose Carreras, M.D., P.A. v. Marroquin*, 297 S.W.3d 420 (Tex. App.—Corpus Christi-Edinburg 2009), *rev'd on other grounds*, 339 S.W.3d 68 (Tex. 2011) (appeal from denial of summary judgment on limitations).

[67] *State v. Ledrec, Inc.*, 366 S.W.3d 305, 307, 309 (Tex. App.—Fort Worth 2012, no pet.) (appeal from partial summary judgment). The court in *Ledrec* implied that another controlling issue of law appropriate for permissive appeal would be whether an expert's testimony is unreliable because it is based on speculation and conjecture, and therefore constitutes no evidence. *State v. Ledrec, Inc.*, 366 S.W.3d 305, 309 n.3 (Tex. App.—Fort Worth 2012, no pet.).

[68] *General Metal Fabricating Corp. v. Stergiou*, 438 S.W.3d 737, 742 (Tex. App.—Houston [1st Dist.] 2014, no pet.) (discussing Tex. R. Civ. P. 11).

[69] *Crocker v. Babcock*, 448 S.W.3d 159, 162 (Tex. App.—Texarkana 2014, pet. denied).

[70] *Commissioner of the General Land Office of the State of Texas v. Sandridge Energy, Inc.*, No. 08-13-00145-CV, 2014 WL 6481855, at *1 (Tex. App.—El Paso Nov. 19, 2014, pet. filed).

[71] *Becon Constr. Co., Inc. v. Alonso*, 444 S.W.3d 824, 825 (Tex. App.—Beaumont 2014, pet. denied).

[72] *Gale v. Lucio*, 445 S.W.3d 849, 850 (Tex. App.—Houston [1st Dist.] 2014, pet. denied).

[73] *Centerpoint Builders GP, L.L.C. v. Trussway, Ltd.*, 436 S.W.3d 882, 885 (Tex. App.—Beaumont 2014), *aff'd*, 496 S.W.3d 33 (Tex. 2016).

[74] *King-A Corp. v. Wehling*, No. 13-13-00100-CV, 2013 WL 1092209, at *3 (Tex. App.—Corpus Christi Mar. 14, 2013, no pet.) (mem. op.).

[75] *King-A Corp. v. Wehling*, No. 13-13-00100-CV, 2013 WL 1092209, at *3 (Tex. App.—Corpus Christi Mar. 14, 2013, no pet.) (mem. op.).

[76] *Texas Farmers Ins. Co. v. Minjarez*, No. 08-12-00272-CV, 2012 WL 5359284, at *1 (Tex. App.—El Paso Oct. 31, 2012, no pet.) (mem. op.); *see also State Fair of Tex. v. Iron Mountain Info. Mgmt., Inc.*, 299 S.W.3d 261, 264 (Tex. App.—Dallas 2009, no pet.) (dismissing appeal when parties failed to demonstrate controlling question of law or a substantial ground for difference of opinion in contract dispute involving the application of well-settled law); *Target Corp. v. Ko*, No. 05-14-00502-CV, 2014 WL 3605746, at *1 (Tex. App.—Dallas July 21, 2014, no pet.) (mem. op.). (denying permission to appeal where law was well settled on controlling question of law); *Jones v. Neil*, No. 05-14-00617-CV, 2014 WL 3605747, at *1 (Tex. App.—Dallas July 21, 2014, no pet.) (same).

[77] *Gulf Coast Asphalt Co., L.L.C. v. Lloyd*, 457 S.W.3d 539, 544–45 (Tex. App.—Houston [14th Dist.] 2015, no pet.) (quoting Renee Forinash McElhaney, *Toward Permissive Appeal in Texas*, 29 St. Mary's L.J. 729, 747–49 (1998)).

[78] *Gulley v. State Farm Lloyds*, 350 S.W.3d 204, 207 (Tex. App.—San Antonio 2011, no pet.); *see* Tex. R. App. P. 58.1. *See also Eagle Gun Range, Inc. v. Bancalari*, 495 S.W.3d 887, 889 (Tex. App.—Fort Worth 2016, no pet.).

[79] *Gulley v. State Farm Lloyds*, 350 S.W.3d 204, 207 (Tex. App.—San Antonio 2011, no pet.).

[80] *City of San Antonio v. Tommy Harral Construction, Inc.*, 486 S.W.3d 77, 81 (Tex. App.—San Antonio 2016, no pet.). *See Colonial County Mutual Ins. Co. v. Amaya*, 372 S.W.3d 308, 310–11 (Tex. App.—Dallas 2012, no pet.) (dismissing appeal for want of jurisdiction); *Bank of N.Y. Mellon v. Guzman*, 390 S.W.3d 593, 597–98 (Tex. App.—Dallas 2012, no pet.) (same); *Borowski v. Ayers*, 432 S.W.3d 344, 348 (Tex. App.—Waco 2013, no pet.) (same); *Christina De La Torre v. AAG Properties*, No. 14-15-00874-CV, 2015 WL 9308881, at *2 (Tex. App.—Houston [14th] Dec. 22, 2015, no pet.) (same); *Hartford Accident and Indem. Co. v. Seagoville Partners*, No. 05-15-00760-CV, 2016 WL 3199003, at *2 (Tex. App.—Dallas June 9, 2016, no pet.) (same); *Eagle Gun Range, Inc. v. Bancalari*, 495 S.W.3d 887, 888–89 (Tex. App.—Fort Worth 2016, no pet.) (same); *Ewing v. Colia*, No. 02-18-00315-CV, 2018 WL 5289380, at *1 (Tex. App.—Fort Worth Oct. 25, 2018, no pet.) (same); *Orion Marine Constr., Inc. v. Cepeda*, No. 01-18-00323-CV, 2018 WL 3059756, at *2 (Houston [1st Dist.] June 21, 2018, no pet.) ("The courts of appeals are not statutorily authorized to decide controlling questions of law in the first instance."). *But see Gulley v. State Farm Lloyds*, 350 S.W.3d 204, 208 n.2 (Tex. App.—San Antonio 2011, no pet.) (denying agreed interlocutory appeal because trial court failed to make a substantive ruling but holding that the court of appeals had jurisdiction over the appeal); *Stewart Title Gty. Co. v. Vantage Bank Tex.*, No. 04-15-00228-CV, 2015 WL 2124802, at *1–2 (Tex. App.—San Antonio May 6, 2015, no pet.) (mem. op.) (denying (as opposed to dismissing) petition because trial court did not make substantive ruling).

[81] *City of San Antonio v. Tommy Harral Construction, Inc.*, 486 S.W.3d 77, 81 (Tex. App.—San Antonio 2016, no pet.).

[82] *Gulley v. State Farm Lloyds*, 350 S.W.3d 204, 208 (Tex. App.—San Antonio 2011, no pet.).

[83] *City of San Antonio v. Tommy Harral Construction, Inc.*, 486 S.W.3d 77 (Tex. App.—San Antonio 2016, no pet.).

[84] *Bank of N.Y. Mellon v. Guzman*, 390 S.W.3d 593, 596–98 (Tex. App.—Dallas 2012, no pet.). The result is the same, even if the issues raised on summary judgment were pure questions of law and there were no issues of material fact that could have served as the basis for the trial court's denial. The permissive-appeal statute cannot be used to avoid a trial court ruling and instead submit legal issues to the court of appeals for decision. *Bank of N.Y. Mellon v. Guzman*, 390 S.W.3d 593, 597 (Tex. App.—Dallas 2012, no pet.).

[85] *Colonial Cnty. Mut. Ins. Co. v. Amaya*, 372 S.W.3d 308, 310–11 (Tex. App.—Dallas 2012, no pet.). *See State Fair of Tex. v. Iron Mountain Info. Mgmt., Inc.*, 299 S.W.3d 261, 264 (Tex. App.—Dallas 2009, no pet.); *Borowski v. Ayers*, 432 S.W.3d 344, 348 (Tex. App.—Waco 2013, no pet.).

[86] *See, e.g., Comcast Cable of Plano, Inc. v. City of Plano*, 315 S.W.3d 673, 675–76 (Tex. App.—Dallas 2010, no pet.) (appeal from order denying summary judgment where motion asserted only that the plaintiff's claim was preempted by federal law).

[87] *See Eagle Gun Range, Inc. v. Bancalari*, 495 S.W.3d 887, 889 (Tex. App.—Fort Worth 2016, no pet.) (trial court order needs to show substantive ruling); *Ewing v. Colia*, No. 02-18-00315-CV, 2018 WL 5289380, at *1 (Tex. App.—Fort Worth Oct. 25, 2018, no pet.) (same); *Christina De La Torre v. AAG Properties*, No. 14-15-00874-CV, 2015 WL 9308881, at *2 (Tex. App.—Houston [14th] Dec. 22, 2015, no pet.) (same); *Hartford Accident and Indem. Co. v. Seagoville Partners*, No. 05-15-00760-CV, 2016 WL 3199003, at *4 (Tex. App.—Dallas June 9, 2016, no pet.) (same).

[88] *Comcast Cable of Plano, Inc. v. City of Plano*, 315 S.W.3d 673, 675–76, 684 (Tex. App.—Dallas 2010, no pet.) (refusing to review additional grounds for summary judgment where agreed issue presented an appeal encompassed only one ground). *See also Byrd v. Phillip Galyen, P.C.*, 430 S.W.3d 515, 521 (Tex. App.—Fort Worth 2014, pet. denied) (court of appeals may address only the claims disposed on in the trial court's interlocutory order).

[89] *Gulf Coast Asphalt Co., L.L.C. v. Lloyd*, 457 S.W.3d 539, 544 (Tex. App.—Houston [14th Dist.] 2015, no pet.).

[90] *Orion Marine Constr., Inc. v. Cepeda*, No. 01-18-00323-CV, 2018 WL 3059756, at *2 (Houston [1st Dist.] June 21, 2018, no pet.).

[91] *Gulf Coast Asphalt Co., L.L.C. v. Lloyd*, 457 S.W.3d 539, 545 (Tex. App.—Houston [14th Dist.] 2015, no pet.) (quoting Renee Forinash McElhaney, *Toward Permissive Appeal in Texas*, 29 St. Mary's L.J. 729, 747–49 (1998)).

[92] *Sabre Travel Int'l, Ltd. v. Deutsche Lufthansa AG*, __ S.W.3d __, No. 17-0538, 2019 WL 406062, at *4 (Tex. Feb. 1, 2019).

[93] *Sabre Travel Int'l, Ltd. v. Deutsche Lufthansa AG*, __ S.W.3d __, No. 17-0538, 2019 WL 406062, at *5 (Tex. Feb. 1, 2019) (court of appeals did not abuse its discretion in refusing to accept permissive appeal).

[94] *Sabre Travel Int'l, Ltd. v. Deutsche Lufthansa AG*, __ S.W.3d __, No. 17-0538, 2019 WL 406062, at *5 (Tex. Feb. 1, 2019) (citations omitted).

[95] Tex. R. App. P. 28.1(a).

[96] Tex. R. App. P. 28.1(b).

[97] *See In re K.L.V.*, 109 S.W.3d 61, 67 (Tex. App.—Fort Worth 2003, pet. denied); *Arismendez v. Vasquez*, No. 04-12-00624-CV, 2012 WL 5874478, at *1 (Tex. App.—San Antonio Nov. 21, 2012, no pet.).

[98] *See* Tex. R. App. P. 26.1(b).

[99] *In re D.B.*, 80 S.W.3d 698, 702 (Tex. App.—Dallas 2002, no pet.) (enforcing deadline under Texas Family Code); *Arismendez v. Vasquez*, No. 04-12-00624-CV, 2012 WL 5874478, at *1

(Tex. App.—San Antonio Nov. 21, 2012, no pet.) (enforcing deadline under election-contest statute).

100 Tex. R. App. P. 28.1(c).

101 *See* Tex. R. App. P. 35.1(b), 38.6(a), (b).

102 Tex. R. App. P. 28.1(e).

103 Tex. R. App. P. 40.1(b).

104 Tex. R. App. P. 29.5.

105 Tex. R. App. P. 29.5.

106 Tex. R. App. P. 29.6(a).

107 Tex. Civ. Prac. & Rem. Code § 51.014(b).

108 Tex. Civ. Prac. & Rem. Code § 51.014 (b) (identifying interlocutory appeals under subsections 51.014(a)(3), (5), (8), and (12)).

109 The automatic stay for these appeals applies only if the request for relief (i.e., the motion for summary judgment, special appearance, or plea to the jurisdiction) is filed and requested for submission or hearing not later than the later of (1) a date set by the trial court in a scheduling order; or (2) the 180th day after the defendant files its original answer or first other responsive pleading to the plaintiff's petition, or (3) the defendant raises a defense in response to an amended pleading by the plaintiff alleging a new cause of action under Section 51.014(a)(5), (7), or (8). Tex. Civ. Prac. & Rem. Code § 51.014(c).

110 *Roccaforte v. County*, 341 S.W.3d 919, 922 (Tex. 2011).

111 Although most appellate court local rules do not address the issue of expedited relief, the Waco Court of Appeals specifically requires that "[a] request for a more expeditious decision and grounds supporting same must be stated in the motion." 10th Tex. App. (Waco) Loc. R. 7(a). Regardless of which court of appeals you are in, specifying the grounds for needing expedited relief is the best practice and will increase your chances of success.

112 *See City of Galveston v. Gray*, 93 S.W.3d 587, 591–92 (Tex. App.—Houston [14th Dist.] 2002, orig. proceeding, pet. denied) (ordering mandamus relief when trial court refused to rule on defendants' pleas to the jurisdiction, which precluded defendants from pursuing their statutory right to an interlocutory appeal under Section 51.014(a)(8) of the Texas Civil Practice & Remedies Code).

113 Tex. R. App. P. 29.1.

114 Tex. R. App. P. 29.2.

115 Tex. R. App. P. 29.1(b).

116 Tex. R. App. P. 29.2.

117 Tex. R. App. P. 29.3.

118 Tex. R. App. P. 29.4.

119 Tex. R. App. P. 29.4.

120 *Pidgeon v. Turner*, 538 S.W.3d 73, 81 (Tex. 2017).

121 *Pidgeon v. Turner*, 538 S.W.3d 73, 81 (Tex. 2017) (citing Tex. Gov't Code § 22.225(c), *repealed by* Act of May 29, 2017, 85th Leg., R.S., ch. 150, 2017 Tex. Gen. Laws 291, 292 (incorporating Tex. Gov't Code § 22.001(a)(1)-(2)). *See* Act of May 29, 2017, 85th Leg., R.S., ch. 150, § 5, 2017 Tex. Gen. Laws 291, 292 ("The repeal of Section 22.225(d), Government Code, applies only to an interlocutory order signed on or after the effective date [Sept. 1, 2017] of this Act. An interlocutory order signed before the effective date of this Act is governed by the law applicable to the order immediately before the effective date of this Act, and that law is continued in effect for that purpose.").

122 *Pidgeon v. Turner*, 538 S.W.3d 73, 81 (Tex. 2017) (quoting former Tex. Gov't Code § 22.225(e)). *Melden & Hunt, Inc. v. East Rio Hondo Water Supply Corp.*, 520 S.W.3d 887, 889

n.1 (Tex. 2017) (holding that Supreme Court had jurisdiction pursuant to former Tex. Gov't Code §§ 22.225(c), (e)); *Columbia Valley Healthcare System, L.P. v. Zamarripa*, 526 S.W.3d 453, 459 (Tex. 2017) (same); *D Magazine Partners, L.P. v. Rosenthal*, 529 S.W.3d 429, 433 n.2 (Tex. 2017) (same); *see Levinson Alcoser Assocs., L.P. v. El Pistolon II, Ltd.*, 513 S.W.3d 487, 490–91 (Tex. 2017) (same). Former section 22.225 expressly excluded from the Texas Supreme Court's jurisdiction all interlocutory appeals allowed by law, except certain types. Tex. Gov't Code § 22.225(b)(3) (*repealed*). Those types included class certification orders, denials of summary judgment in media free-speech cases, denials of dismissal for the failure to file a timely medical report in an asbestosis or silicosis case, and permissive interlocutory appeals. Tex. Gov't Code § 22.225(d) (*repealed*). *See Sabre Travel Int'l, Ltd. v. Deutsche Lufthansa AG*, __ S.W.3d __, No. 17-0538, 2019 WL 406062, at *6–8 (Tex. Feb. 1, 2019) (holding that, for appeal of interlocutory order entered prior to September 1, 2017, (former) section 22.225(d) of the Texas Government Code gave the court jurisdiction over the interlocutory appeal of the order) (citing former Tex. Gov't Code § 22.225(d); Tex. Civ. Prac. & Rem. Code § 51.014(d)).

123 Tex. Gov't Code § 22.001(a) (eff. Sept. 1, 2017). Specifically, the Texas Supreme Court "has appellate jurisdiction, except in criminal law matters, of an appealable order or judgment of the trial courts if the court determines that the appeal presents a question of law that is important to the jurisprudence of the state. The supreme court's jurisdiction does not include cases in which the jurisdiction of the court of appeals is made final by statute." Tex. Gov't Code § 22.001(a). The Legislature left intact the section of the Government Code prohibiting the Supreme Court from reviewing factual sufficiency. Tex. Gov't Code § 22.225(a) ("A judgment of a court of appeals is conclusive on the facts of the case in all civil cases.").

124 *See supra* § 5-3:8; *Sabre Travel Int'l, Ltd. v. Deutsche Lufthansa AG*, __ S.W.3d __, No. 17-0538, 2019 WL 406062, at *4–5 (Tex. Feb. 1, 2019).

125 *Sabre Travel Int'l, Ltd. v. Deutsche Lufthansa AG*, __ S.W.3d __, No. 17-0538, 2019 WL 406062, at *5 (Tex. Feb. 1, 2019) ("While we recognize the discretion courts of appeals have to accept or deny permissive interlocutory appeals, we disagree with the suggestion that how a court exercises its discretion determines whether this Court has jurisdiction to consider the merits of an interlocutory order that meets the Legislature's threshold for an exception to the final judgment rule . . . ."). Although the Supreme Court's analysis in *Sabre* was under former section 22.225(d) of the Texas Government Code due to the date of the interlocutory order, the same analysis presumably would apply under current law (Tex. Gov't Code § 22.001(a) (eff. Sept. 1, 2017)), which eliminated the prior law's limitations of the Supreme Court's jurisdiction over all civil appeals, including the stringent limitations that had been placed on interlocutory appeals.

126 *Sabre Travel Int'l, Ltd. v. Deutsche Lufthansa AG*, __ S.W.3d __, No. 17-0538, 2019 WL 406062, at *8 (Tex. Feb. 1, 2019).

127 *Hernandez v. Ebrom*, 289 S.W.3d 316 (Tex. 2009).

128 *Hernandez v. Ebrom*, 289 S.W.3d 316, 318–19 (Tex. 2009).

129 *Hernandez v. Ebrom*, 289 S.W.3d 316, 318–19 (Tex. 2009).

130 *Hernandez v. Ebrom*, 289 S.W.3d 316, 317 (Tex. 2009).

131 *Hernandez v. Ebrom*, 289 S.W.3d 316, 318, 321 (Tex. 2009) ("Unambiguous statutory language is interpreted according to its plain language unless such an interpretation would lead to absurd results.").

132 *Hernandez v. Ebrom*, 289 S.W.3d 316, 321 (Tex. 2009).

133 *Nalle Plastics Family Ltd. Partnership v. Porter, Rogers, Dahlman & Gordon, P.C.*, 406 S.W.3d 186 (Tex. App.—Corpus Christi 2013, pet. denied) (mem. op.).

134 *Nalle Plastics Family Ltd. Partnership v. Porter, Rogers, Dahlman & Gordon, P.C.*, 406 S.W.3d 186, 196–97 (Tex. App.—Corpus Christi 2013, pet. denied) (mem. op.).

[135] *Nalle Plastics Family Ltd. Partnership v. Porter, Rogers, Dahlman & Gordon, P.C.*, 406 S.W.3d 186, 197 (Tex. App.—Corpus Christi 2013, pet. denied) (mem. op.) (citing *Hernandez v. Ebrom*, 289 S.W.3d 316, 318 (Tex. 2009)).

[136] *In re Santander Consumer USA, Inc.*, 445 S.W.3d 216 (Tex. App.—Houston [1st Dist.] 2013, orig. proceeding).

[137] *In re Santander Consumer USA, Inc.*, 445 S.W.3d 216, 220 (Tex. App.—Houston [1st Dist.] 2013, orig. proceeding).

[138] *In re S.M.H.*, 523 S.W.3d 783 (Tex. App.—Houston [14th Dist.] 2017, no pet.).

[139] *In re S.M.H.*, 523 S.W.3d 783, 788 (Tex. App.—Houston [14th Dist.] 2017, no pet.).

[140] *DeWolf v. Kohler*, 452 S.W.3d 373 (Tex. App.—Houston [14th Dist.] 2014, no pet.).

[141] *DeWolf v. Kohler*, 452 S.W.3d 373, 384 (Tex. App.—Houston [14th Dist.] 2014, no pet.). *See Southampton Ltd. v. Four Horseman Auto Group, Inc.*, No. 05-14-01415-CV, 2016 WL 3964731, at *3 (Tex. App.—Dallas July 20, 2016, no pet.).

[142] *Am. Heritage Capital, LP v. Gonzalez*, 436 S.W.3d 865 (Tex. App.—Dallas 2014, no pet.).

[143] *Am. Heritage Capital, LP v. Gonzalez*, 436 S.W.3d 865, 872–73 (Tex. App.—Dallas 2014, no pet.).

[144] *Hernandez v. Ebrom*, 289 S.W.3d 316, 319 (Tex. 2009).

[145] *Hernandez v. Ebrom*, 289 S.W.3d 316, 319 (Tex. 2009) (citing *Richards v. Mena*, 820 S.W.2d 372, 372 (Tex. 1991)); *see also Bayoud v. Bayoud*, 797 S.W.2d 304, 313 (Tex. App.—Dallas 1990, writ denied) (order granting preliminary injunction is only reviewable by interlocutory appeal); *Double Diamond-Delaware, Inc. v. Walkinshaw*, No. 05-12-01140-CV, 2013 WL 3327523, at *2 (Tex. App.—Dallas June 27, 2013, no pet.) (mem. op.) (appeal challenging temporary injunction mooted by trial court's grant of summary judgment seeking permanent injunction and ruling on the merits).

[146] *Hernandez v. Ebrom*, 289 S.W.3d 316, 319 (Tex. 2009) (citing *Lincoln Prop. Co. v. Kondos*, 110 S.W.3d 712, 715 (Tex. App.—Dallas 2003, no pet.)); *see also CitiMortgage, Inc. v. Hubener*, 345 S.W.3d 193, 195 (Tex. App.—Dallas 2011, no pet.); *Long v. Spencer*, 137 S.W.3d 923, 926 (Tex. App.—Dallas 2004, no pet.) (same) (order appointing a receiver must be challenged by interlocutory appeal).

[147] For an in-depth analysis of this issue, *see McKay Cunningham, Use It or Lose It: By Choosing Not to Pursue a Statutory Interlocutory Appeal, Do You Waive Appellate Review After Final Judgment?*, 22 App. Advoc. 134 (Winter 2009).

CHAPTER 6

Petitions for Writ of Mandamus

6-1 Introduction

In the Texas state court system, when review is desired before the entry of a final judgment, but none of the statutes authorizing an interlocutory appeal apply, appellate court review may be available by filing an original proceeding in a court of appeals or the Texas Supreme Court petitioning for the issuance of a writ. By far, the most common of these writs, and the only one addressed in depth in this book, is the writ of mandamus.

The issuance of a writ of mandamus is discretionary. To be entitled to the writ, the requesting party must show a clear abuse of discretion for which there is no adequate remedy by appeal.[1]

Generally, the odds of getting a petition for writ of mandamus granted are extraordinarily slim. If the decision is made to proceed with the mandamus action, exacting care must be taken to survive the initial screening process employed by the various courts of appeals and the Supreme Court of Texas. The appellate courts in Texas have experienced staff attorneys who act as gatekeepers in screening mandamus filings and separating those filings that are procedurally defective and of dubious merit from those that have a chance. Given this practice, a principal concern in preparing a mandamus filing is avoiding summary denial on the basis of a technical noncompliance with the rules.

6-2 Preliminary Considerations

6-2:1 Verify Jurisdiction

6-2:1.1 Court of Appeals

The mandamus jurisdiction of the court of appeals is set forth in section 22.221 of the Texas Government Code.[2] Section 22.221(a) confers jurisdiction on each court of appeals to issue a writ of mandamus to enforce the jurisdiction of the court. This provision permits, for example, a court of appeals to order a court reporter to prepare a reporter's record when the reporter's record is necessary for the court to exercise its jurisdiction to decide a pending appeal over which it has jurisdiction.[3]

Section 22.221(b) provides that a court of appeals may issue a writ of mandamus against a judge of a district or county court in the court of appeals' district.[4] But, like the Supreme Court, the intermediate appellate courts lack jurisdiction against those not listed in the statute, such as county and district clerks, except when issuing mandamus against court officers is necessary to enforce the jurisdiction of the court of appeals.[5]

Various statutes and rules also provide the appellate courts (and sometimes only the Supreme Court) with authority to grant mandamus relief in specific situations, including:

- to enforce mandatory venue requirements under chapter 15 of the Texas Civil Practice and Remedies Code;[6]
- in connection with the holding of an election or political party convention, even if the respondent is not a public officer;[7] and
- in connection with the granting of injunctive relief under certain Natural Resource Code provisions when a trial court does so without the statutorily required notice and hearing.[8]

When a statute, such as those listed in these examples, specifies that mandamus is available from a particular type of order, the relator is relieved of the obligation of demonstrating the second prong of mandamus relief—that the remedy by appeal is inadequate.[9]

6-2:1.2 Texas Supreme Court

The Texas Constitution provides that the Supreme Court and its justices have the power to issue writs of mandamus to enforce the Supreme Court's jurisdiction and "to issue writs of . . . mandamus in such cases as may be specified, except as against the Governor of the State."[10] In fact, the Texas Supreme Court's "original jurisdiction is derived solely from Article V, Section 3(a) of the Texas Constitution, which provides that '[t]he Legislature may confer original jurisdiction on the Supreme Court to issue writs of quo warranto and mandamus in such cases as may be specified, except as against the Governor of the State.'"[11]

In addition, section 22.002(a) of the Texas Government Code confers jurisdiction on the Supreme Court to issue writs of mandamus against a statutory county court judge, a statutory probate court judge, a district judge, a court of appeals or a justice of a court of appeals, or any officer of state government except the governor, the court of criminal appeals, or a judge of the court of criminal appeals.[12] Section 22.002(a) authorizes the Texas Supreme Court to "review a court of appeals' issuance of a writ of mandamus to determine if it constituted a clear abuse of discretion."[13] When the Texas Supreme Court reviews a court of appeals' issuance of the writ, "however, [the Supreme Court's] 'focus remains on the trial court's order.'"[14]

Only the Texas Supreme Court has jurisdiction to issue a writ of mandamus against any of the officers of the executive departments of the government of the state, such as the Lieutenant Governor and the Comptroller of Accounts.[15]

Other than when it is necessary to protect its own jurisdiction,[16] the Texas Supreme Court generally does not have jurisdiction to issue a writ of mandamus directed to those not specifically listed by statute. For instance, the Texas Supreme Court does not have jurisdiction to mandamus district clerks, justices of the peace, sheriffs and constables, and court reporters.[17]

Jurisdiction to mandamus a statutory county court judge or statutory probate court judge was extended to the Supreme Court by an amendment to section 22.002(a) of the Texas Government Code, which remedied a long-standing anomaly that prohibited parties from seeking mandamus relief against a statutory county court judge beyond the court of appeals.[18] However, the amendment does not completely wipe out the anomaly. The amendment extends the Supreme Court's mandamus jurisdiction only to statutory county court judges and statutory probate court judges.[19] The amendment does not extend the Supreme Court's mandamus jurisdiction to constitutional county courts.[20]

Various statutes and rules also provide the appellate courts (and sometimes only the Supreme Court) with authority to grant mandamus relief in specific situations. Like the appellate courts, the Supreme Court may issue mandamus to enforce mandatory venue requirements under chapter 15 of the Texas Civil Practice and Remedies Code;[21] in connection with the holding of an election or political party convention, even if the respondent is not a public officer;[22] and in connection with the granting of injunctive relief under certain Natural Resource Code provisions when a trial court does so without the statutorily required notice and hearing.[23] Examples of the statutes that provide for review by mandamus, but only to the Texas Supreme Court, include:

- to enforce the rule on judgments in attorney disciplinary proceedings;[24]
- to require performance of duties by the Legislative Redistricting Board;[25] and
- to enforce obligations of state officials with respect to public debt.[26]

Again, when a statute, such as those listed in these examples, specifies that mandamus is available from a particular type of order, the relator is relieved of the obligation of demonstrating the second prong of mandamus relief—that the remedy by appeal is inadequate.[27]

6-2:2 Develop Proper Record in Trial Court

The mandamus petition will not survive scrutiny if the relator—the party seeking relief—has failed to develop a proper record in the trial court.

6-2:2.1 Make Sure Record Reflects Right to Relief and Preservation of Complaint

Any break in the chain of preserving the complaint at issue will permit the appellate court to summarily deny the mandamus petition. For example, if relator is complaining of an order compelling discovery, but the record reflects that the objection to discovery was asserted outside the time limits permitted by the rules, the appellate court may deny the petition even though opposing counsel never complained of the delay. Indeed, the appellate court may deny the petition on that basis even though opposing counsel actually agreed to the late filing of objections, if that agreement was not incorporated into a Rule 11 agreement that was on file with the trial court and included in the mandamus record.

6-2:2.2 Safeguard Documents Submitted for In Camera Review

As a general rule, trial courts will safeguard documents submitted under seal for in camera review. But what happens when the trial court compels production of the documents tendered for in camera review and mandamus relief is sought in the court of appeals? If the documents are forwarded to the appellate court as part of the mandamus record but no sealing order is in place, the clerk of the appellate court might permit your opponent to view the documents upon request, under the rationale that the documents are nothing more or less than unsealed court records within the meaning of Rule 76a.

To safeguard against the inadvertent unsealing of documents that had been submitted for in camera review, ask the trial court to forward them to the appellate court under seal and to return them to the appropriate party. Failing that, ask the court of appeals to order the trial court to forward the documents to the court of appeals for its in camera review. A relator who does not possess the documents should follow the latter course or have the party in possession of the documents deliver the documents to the appellate clerk for in camera review or arrange for the trial court clerk to do so.

When the documents are actually transferred from the trial court to the court of appeals, make sure the clerk of the court of appeals understands that the documents are under seal and protected by an appropriate court order. Most courts of appeals will return in camera documents to the party who tendered them but some courts require a motion to withdraw exhibits after the court has disposed of the mandamus.

Practices may vary from court to court. If in doubt, contact the clerk of the reviewing court and ascertain the local practice.

6-2:2.3 Make Sure Trial Court Signed Complained-of Order

Trial courts will often make known their rulings on discovery disputes before the ruling is actually reduced to a written order. Resist the temptation to rush to the court of appeals before the ruling is reduced to a written order. One of the requirements of Rule 52 is that a certified or sworn copy of the order in question be presented to the court of appeals as part of the mandamus filing.[28]

When the complaint is that the trial court has failed to act on a matter within its jurisdiction, there is no written order to present with the mandamus petition. In that event, develop a record showing that the trial court was requested to rule on the matter and either expressly refused to do so or failed to do so within a reasonable time.[29]

6-2:3 Ripeness for Mandamus Review

Before the appellate court can be expected to grant mandamus relief, the matter must be ripe for mandamus review. Just as mandamus will not lie if the relator has an adequate remedy by appeal, mandamus also will not lie if the appellate court perceives that there is a possibility that the dispute can still be resolved in the trial court.

Some matters that may render mandamus unripe—such as the lack of a written order—are obvious; others are less so. The following are some of the less obvious matters.

6-2:3.1 Pending Motion to Reconsider in Trial Court

Don't pursue mandamus relief while a motion to reconsider the order complained of is still pending. A pending motion to reconsider deprives the challenged order of sufficient finality and leaves open the possibility of a remaining adequate remedy if the reconsideration motion were granted.

6-2:3.2 Other Circumstances Making Mandamus Premature

- *Mandamus complaining of order denying motion to quash.* Don't complain of a trial court order denying relator's motion to quash a deposition on the grounds of privilege before appearing at the deposition and lodging objections to specific questions.
- *In camera inspection.* Don't complain of a trial court's failure to recognize documents as privileged before the trial court has completed its in camera review. Your petition may conclusively show that the attorney–client privilege attaches to documents sought to be protected, but if the trial court orders an in camera inspection, nothing harmful has happened yet; the documents have not been ordered to be produced to the other side. After the inspection, the trial court may order the documents protected.
- *Order of visiting judge.* Don't complain of an order signed by a visiting judge without first presenting the matter to the duly elected judge.
- *Order of judge no longer holding office.* The Texas Rules of Appellate Procedure require an appellate court (either the court of appeals or the Texas Supreme Court) to abate an original proceeding when the judge or public officer who issued the disputed order ceases to hold office before the original proceeding is finally disposed of to allow the successor an opportunity to reconsider the decision.[30] If this change happens before an original proceeding is filed, a motion to reconsider should be filed before seeking mandamus. If this change happens after an original proceeding has been filed and is still pending, file a motion to abate the original proceeding to permit the filing of a reconsideration motion before the new officeholder.

6-2:4 Pursue Mandamus Relief Promptly

Just as the petition may be summarily denied for pursuing mandamus relief too early, it also may be denied for pursuing mandamus relief too late. Although the rules themselves do not limit the time within which mandamus relief must be sought, a relator can wait too long. The issuance of mandamus is largely controlled by equitable principles. As the court stated in the principal case discussing those limits, *Rivercenter Associates v. Rivera,*[31] "'[e]quity aids the diligent and not those who slumber on their rights.'"[32]

In *Rivercenter,* the relator was denied mandamus when it waited over four months after the triggering event to pursue relief and the record revealed no justification for the delay.[33] Because the question of unreasonable delay is controlled by equitable principles, what constitutes diligent pursuit of mandamus relief will ultimately turn on the circumstances of the particular case.[34]

To avoid a determination of unwarranted delay, you should pursue mandamus relief as quickly as possible, particularly when failing to do so may harm the opposing party or inconvenience the trial court. Seeking review on the eve of trial of an order issued a month or two earlier is frowned upon and forces the appellate court to act quickly when counsel or the client failed to do so.

If the pursuit of mandamus relief is delayed for any reason, that reason should be fully explained to the reviewing court, as well as the absence of harm to real parties in interest.

Pursuing mandamus diligently is particularly important when an emergency stay is requested. When possible, pursue mandamus relief and emergency relief promptly to avoid forcing the appellate court to act precipitously in issuing a stay before it has the chance to assess the merits of a mandamus petition.[35]

6-2:5 Provide Clerk's Office Advance Notice, Particularly for Temporary Relief

If emergency relief is sought, make a particular effort to make the request as painless as possible for the appellate court. Even before the papers are prepared, alert the clerk's office of the anticipated filing and need for emergency relief.[36] This advance notification will permit the court to line up the personnel necessary to review and act expeditiously on the motion once it is filed. And keep in mind that the worst time to file a request for emergency relief is on a Friday afternoon.

6-3 Anatomy of Petition for Writ of Mandamus

The mandamus filing package consists of the petition for writ of mandamus, the appendix, and the mandamus record.[37]

The most common reason for denial of a mandamus petition is for failure to comply with the requirements of a Texas Rules of Appellate Procedure. Rule 52 is the basic rule governing the formatting of mandamus petitions in both the courts of appeals and the Texas Supreme Court.

A petition for writ of mandamus must contain the following items:

- Cover
- Identity of Parties and Counsel
- Table of Contents
- Index of Authorities
- Statement of the Case
- Statement of Jurisdiction
- Issues Presented
- Statement of Facts
- Summary of the Argument
- Argument
- Prayer
- Signature

- Certificate of Service
- Certificate of Compliance
- Certification
- Appendix[38]

6-3:1 Caption and Cover

The petition is captioned "In re [name of relator]."[39] Under Rule 9.4(g), the required contents of the cover include the case style; the case number; the title of the document being filed (e.g., "Petition for Writ of Mandamus" or "Response to Petition for Writ of Mandamus"); and the name, mailing address, telephone number, fax number, if any, and State Bar number of the lead counsel for the filing party.[40] Rule 9.4(g) requires that the email address of lead counsel also be included on the cover.[41]

The State Bar Number of each listed attorney should be included immediately beneath his or her name. The clerk's office enters a notation on the computer system next to the name of the first signer to indicate that he or she is lead counsel. Only that attorney will receive official notices from the clerk's office, although anyone who signs up through the CaseMail system can receive notices electronically. The name of the attorney should be the "bar card" name of the attorney, not some interesting nickname. The name is cross-checked against the State Bar database and the clerk's office will investigate name variations.

When out-of-state attorneys are included on the cover, prudent practice dictates filing a *pro hac vice* motion prior to or contemporaneously with the filing of the brief. Although not required, some justices prefer (and the clerk's office appreciates) for the cover to reflect that the matter is "On Petition for Writ of Mandamus from the [number] Court of Appeals at [City], Texas, Cause No. ______."

The cover of a petition being filed in the court of appeals should request oral argument; the cover of a petition filed in the Texas Supreme Court should not.[42]

In those instances in which a paper copy is permitted to be filed, the rule specifically prohibits red, black, or dark blue covers.[43] The rule also expressly forbids the use of plastic covers.

6-3:2 Contents

Under appellate rule 52.3, the petition must contain the following sections and information, under appropriately named headings and in the order listed.

6-3:2.1 Identity of Parties and Counsel

The petition must list at the outset the names of all parties and the names and addresses of all counsel (and now counsels' email addresses).[44] The party seeking mandamus relief is the relator.[45] The person against whom relief is sought is the respondent.[46]

In the court of appeals, when the mandamus petition complains of a trial court order, the respondent is the trial judge who issued the order. In the Supreme Court, if the court of appeals denied the mandamus petition and the same relator continues to complain of the same trial court order, the respondent in the Supreme Court is still the trial judge. If, on the other hand, the court of appeals granted mandamus relief and the losing party (who becomes the new relator) complains of the court of appeals' decision by petition to the Supreme Court, the court of appeals becomes the new respondent.

A real party in interest in the mandamus proceeding is one "whose interest would be directly affected by the relief sought."[47] Under this definition, the parties to the mandamus proceeding may be fewer in number than the parties to the underlying action. For example, in a mandamus proceeding involving a discovery dispute in a multi-party case, it is conceivable that certain parties would be directly affected by the relief sought while others would not be affected at all. In such a case, the affected parties should be clearly identified as "Real Parties in Interest" and the names and addresses of their counsel should be provided pursuant to Rule 52.3(a).

Although not required by the rule, telephone and facsimile numbers and email addresses of the attorneys should also be provided to assist the clerks. Although also not required by the rule, the names of the remaining parties to the underlying proceeding, together with the names of their counsel, should be separately listed under the category "Parties and Counsel in the Underlying Action who are not Parties to the Mandamus Proceeding." This information may be of assistance to the judges evaluating potential disqualification or recusal.

6-3:2.2 Table of Contents

The petition must include a table of contents that indicates the subject matter of each issue or point.[48] Although not specified in the rules, the table of contents should include headings and subheadings in narrative form so that it presents a summary of the argument.[49]

6-3:2.3 Index of Authorities

The petition must include an index of authorities that is arranged alphabetically and indicate the pages where each authority is cited.[50] Although not spelled out in the rule, the alphabetical listing of cases should be without segregation by jurisdiction; statutes and rules should be listed in a separate category; and any miscellaneous sources should be listed in a third category. Some appellate justices examine the index of authorities in mandamus petitions to see how many mandamus cases are cited as a preliminary indicator of whether the complained-of act is one for which mandamus is the proper vehicle for review.

6-3:2.4 Statement of the Case

The governing rule spells out in detail the specific matters that must be contained in the statement of the case, including details concerning a petition to an intermediate appellate court as well as to the Supreme Court of Texas.[51] It should contain:

- a concise description of the nature of any underlying proceeding (e.g., a suit for damages, a contempt proceeding for failure to pay child support, or the certification of a candidate for inclusion on an election ballot);
- if the respondent is a judge, the name of the judge, the designation of the court in which the judge was sitting, and the county in which the court is located; and

if the respondent is an official other than a judge, the designation and location of the office held by the respondent; and

- a concise description of the respondent's action from which the relator seeks relief.[52]

If the petition is filed in the Supreme Court after a petition requesting the same relief was filed in the court of appeals, the statement of the case must also include:

- the date the petition was filed in the court of appeals;
- the district of the court of appeals and the names of the justices who participated in the decision;
- the author of any opinion for the court of appeals and the author of any separate opinion;
- the citation of the court's opinion; and
- the disposition of the case by the court of appeals, and the date of the court of appeals' order.[53]

Ideally, the statement of the case should be limited to one page. It should not address the facts or contain argument. Development of the pertinent facts and procedural background, as well as arguments or a summary of the argument in support of the requested relief, should be reserved for subsequent sections of the petition. The courts generally prefer the statement of the case to be presented in a tabular format.

6-3:2.5 Statement of Jurisdiction

The petition must state, without argument, the basis of the court's jurisdiction.[54] In the court of appeals, the jurisdictional statement should merely cite the appropriate provision of Texas Government Code section 22.002. When the Texas Supreme Court and an intermediate court of appeals have concurrent mandamus jurisdiction, Rule 52.3(e) requires that a party must first present an original proceeding to the appropriate court of appeals.

In the Supreme Court, unless the court of appeals is the respondent,[55] the statement should additionally recite that the petition was first presented to the court of appeals and describe the disposition by that court, or explain the "compelling reason" why the petition was not first presented to the court of appeals.[56]

6-3:2.6 Issue Presented

The petition must state the issues or points presented for relief.[57] Issues or points will be construed as covering every subsidiary question that is fairly included.[58]

Although the appellate rules provide counsel the option of presenting either issues or points,[59] the recommended practice is to present issues and, preferably, a single substantive issue.[60] First, by identifying a single issue at the very outset of the petition, you will immediately focus the attention of the screening attorneys and signal to them that this is not just another amorphous complaint of a party that was "wronged" by an "abusive" decision of a trial court.

Second, by carefully framing the issue as a discrete legal question, you will avoid the roadblock of the petition's characterization as one calling for the court of appeals to decide disputed fact questions.[61]

Third, if the issue can be fairly characterized as one of substantial importance to the jurisprudence of the state, you will enhance the chances for success in the Supreme Court should the initial effort in the court of appeals fail.[62]

Almost any complaint of trial court action can be reduced to one or, at most, two narrow issues for mandamus review. If the complaint cannot be narrowed, the matter probably is not worthy of mandamus review.

6-3:2.7 Statement of Facts

The statement of facts "must state concisely and without argument the facts pertinent to the issues or points presented."[63] The statement must be supported by references to the appendix or mandamus record. Merely providing the appellate court with a complete record is not sufficient. The statement of facts should develop the procedural background and facts necessary to demonstrate the right to mandamus relief.

The appellate court knows nothing about the case and will not indulge any presumptions. While it is not necessary to outline the entire history of the litigation, you should tell a complete story highlighting all of the essential facts and procedural history leading up to the complained-of order.

Take care to not omit relevant facts that are perceived to be unfavorable. If there has been delay in seeking mandamus relief, the statement of facts should explain the delay. For instance, if the time for complying with an order of the trial court has expired, such as when an order compelling production of documents requires action by a certain date, the statement of facts should explain why the issue is not moot.

In crafting the statement of facts, you should demonstrate that the relevant facts are not in dispute since the appellate courts cannot resolve disputed fact questions in a mandamus proceeding, and the trial court's resolution of a disputed fact question is ordinarily immune from mandamus review.[64] The statement of facts should also show that any disputed fact questions are not pertinent to the relator's right to mandamus relief.

6-3:2.8 Summary of Argument

The rules do not require a summary of argument for a petition for writ of mandamus or a response. But the rules do not prohibit a summary of the argument. Space permitting, consider adding a summary of the argument section before the argument section.

6-3:2.9 Argument

The petition must include "clear and concise argument" for the contentions made, and must include citations to appropriate authorities, the appendix, and the mandamus record.[65]

In addition to demonstrating that the trial court lacked the discretion to issue the subject order,[66] this section of the petition should establish precisely why the relator has no adequate remedy at law.[67]

In the Supreme Court, the argument should include a discussion of why the issue presented is of significance to the jurisprudence of the state.[68]

Like other appellate briefs, the argument in support of the petition should demonstrate the right to relief but do so as concisely as possible. If the mandamus petition can be presented in 15 to 20 pages, it will stand a greater chance of success than a lengthier petition making essentially the same arguments. The petition to the Supreme Court may not exceed 4,500 words.[69]

Appropriate headings and subheadings should be used to lead the reader through the argument. The tone of the argument should be neutral and respectful; you can, and should, complain of an "abuse of discretion" by the trial judge without disparaging the character of either that judge or opposing counsel. The chances of success will be enhanced to the extent that the argument can be depersonalized. For example, it is more effective to grapple with the legal question of whether trial courts, generally, have the authority to issue orders such as the one at issue, rather than to criticize the conduct of respondent, personally, in issuing that order.

6-3:2.10 Prayer

"The petition must contain a short conclusion that clearly states the nature of the relief sought."[70] The prayer should not merely request, in conclusory fashion, that a writ of mandamus be issued against respondent. It should clearly and specifically explain what actions the reviewing court should direct the respondent court to do. It is helpful to know before crafting the petition the precise relief you are requesting from the appellate court.

6-3:2.11 Certificate of Service

The mandamus petition must contain a certificate of service.[71] A general statement that service has been made on all counsel in compliance with the rules will not suffice. The certificate must be signed by the person who made the service and must state the date and manner of service, the name and address of each person served, and, if the person served is a party's attorney, the name of the party or parties represented by that attorney.

If emergency relief is sought, the party seeking temporary relief is required to notify the other parties by expedited means and certify that expedited notice was given.[72]

6-3:2.12 Certificate of Compliance

A computer-generated document must include a certificate by counsel or an unrepresented party stating the number of words in the document. The person certifying may rely on the word count of the computer program used to prepare the document.[73]

6-3:2.13 Certification

Although not listed among the contents of the petition, the rules require the person filing the petition to "certify that he or she has reviewed the petition and concluded that every factual statement in the petition is supported by competent evidence included in the appendix or [mandamus] record."[74] The prior version of the rule, formerly requiring verification by counsel's affidavit that all factual statements in the petition are true and correct, changed in 2008. The prescribed verification procedure under the old version of the rule no longer complies with the current certification requirement and subjects the mandamus petition to being struck for failure to comply with the rules.[75]

6-3:3 Appendix

The rules expressly require an appendix as part of the mandamus filing.[76] When electronically filed, the appendix should be combined with the petition into a single PDF as long as the combined document complies with the size limitations.[77] If it exceeds those limitations, it must be divided. The required paper copies, if any, of the appendix may be bound either with the petition or separately.[78]

Mandatory items that must be included in the appendix are:

- a certified or sworn copy of the order complained of or any other document showing the matter complained of;
- any order or opinion of the court of appeals, if relief is sought in the Supreme Court; and
- unless voluminous, copies of any rule, regulation, or similar law (except case law) relied on.[79]

The appendix may also include other items that were part of the record below,[80] or "copies or excerpts of relevant court opinions, statutes, constitutional provisions, documents on which the suit was based, pleadings, and similar materials."[81] For instance, the appendix should contain the portion of any contract that is central to the order complained of (e.g., forum-selection clause).

Use discretion when determining optional items to include so as to not overload the appendix. At the same time, the appendix should not be used to circumvent the length limitations on the petition.[82] Each item in the appendix must be bookmarked. Tex. R. App. P. 9.4(h).

6-3:4 Mandamus Record

The mandamus record is a required part of the mandamus filing package.[83] It is different from the appendix. The mandamus record must include (1) a certified or sworn copy of every document that is material to relator's claim for relief that was filed in any underlying proceeding and (2) a properly authenticated transcript of any relevant testimony from any underlying proceeding, including any exhibits offered in evidence, or a statement that no testimony was adduced in connection with the matter complained of.[84] That rule does not mean that relator files a copy of every document on file with the trial court, but only the ones that matter. In practice, most practitioners do not obtain certified copies of the documents to be included in the mandamus record. Instead, to satisfy the requirement of "sworn" copies, the common practice is to include an attorney affidavit with the mandamus record attesting that the documents are true and correct copies of documents filed with the trial court clerk's office or orders issued by the court.

Relator must also be mindful of any need for a reporter's record. If any evidence was presented at the hearing resulting in the order complained of, relator must secure a transcript of the hearing and present it to the appellate court. If the court reporter cannot prepare the transcript immediately, the petition should inform the appellate court when the transcript can be expected and should be supported by an affidavit from the court reporter.

If the hearing in question was not an evidentiary hearing, a reporter's record may not be needed. Nonetheless, relator must present an affidavit to the appellate court stating that no evidence was adduced at the hearing.[85] The governing rule contains no express requirement that the "statement" in question be sworn to by affidavit, but this is the recommended practice. The affidavit should include a statement that counsel for relator actually appeared at the hearing, in order to avoid the appellate court concluding that relator waived its complaint about the order resulting from the hearing.

Only the original of the record need be filed with the court.[86] After the record is filed, relator or any other party to the proceeding may file additional matters for inclusion in the record.[87] Each item in the electronic version of the mandamus record must be bookmarked.[88]

6-3:5 Motion for Emergency Relief

In addition to preparing the required petition, counsel should also evaluate whether to request emergency relief. Relator may file a motion to stay any underlying proceedings or for any other temporary relief pending the court's action on the petition.[89] The governing rule includes a special notification requirement. Relator must notify or make a diligent effort to notify all parties by expedited means, such as telephone or fax, that a motion for temporary relief has been filed. In addition, relator must certify in the petition compliance with this requirement.[90]

A request for emergency relief should not merely be included as part of the petition, as it may be overlooked. The recommended practice is to file a separate motion for emergency relief. Counsel should note that, in the mandamus context, the appellate courts cannot entertain a motion for emergency relief if the appellate court's jurisdiction has not been invoked through the filing of a mandamus petition. An anticipated, but yet-to-be filed petition is insufficient.

A motion for emergency relief should recite at the outset that it is filed not only pursuant to Rule 52.10(a) of the Texas Rules of Appellate Procedure, but also pursuant to Rule 10.3(a)(3). That rule permits the appellate court to decide emergency motions on less than the usual 10-day notice.

The motion for emergency relief should recite succinctly the facts and procedural background making necessary the relief sought. Certified or sworn copies of pertinent orders should be attached to the motion. The motion should concretely demonstrate the irreparable harm that relator would suffer should the motion be denied. The motion should also demonstrate, if possible, how little or no harm would result to the real parties in interest should the motion be granted. The motion should specify whether a stay is sought of the entire proceeding below or only of the order complained of. And, it is recommended that the motion state the date by which court action is required.

Although not expressly stated in Rule 52.10, the real justification for the appellate court granting emergency relief is usually for the court to protect its own jurisdiction to hear the matter. The motion should conclude with a succinct prayer, clearly stating the nature and scope of the emergency relief requested. Although not required, the motion should be verified by affidavit.

6-3:6 Response to Mandamus Petition

Any party may respond to a mandamus petition, but the rules do not require a response.[91] However a court may not grant a petition for writ of mandamus unless a response has been filed or requested.[92]

A response must comply with all the requirements applicable to mandamus petitions under the rules,[93] but need not contain certain items unless dissatisfied with, or there is a need to correct, those portions of the petition. Those sections that need not be in a response are:

- Identity of Parties and Counsel
- Statement of the Case
- Statement of Jurisdiction
- Issues Presented
- Statement of Facts
- Appendix[94]

The argument in the response should be limited to the issues or points presented in the mandamus petition.

6-3:7 Reply to Response to Mandamus Petition

The rules permit the relator to file a reply addressing any matter discussed in the response.[95] Because the appellate courts may rule on a mandamus petition before a reply is filed, a relator wishing to file a reply should do so expeditiously and should let the clerk's office know that a reply is forthcoming and an anticipated filing time.

6-3:8 Form

The appellate rules specify the form of all documents to be filed in the appellate courts.[96] These include a requirement that 14-point typeface be used for proportionately spaced documents (footnotes may be in 12-point font);[97] specifics concerning margin-width and the use of double and single spacing; and a prohibition against the use of red, black, dark blue, or plastic covers.[98]

6-3:9 Length Limitations

Texas appellate courts now use word limits (not page limits) for briefs produced on a computer. The limits listed below are exclusive of those pages containing the identity of parties and counsel, the table of contents, the index of authorities, the statement of the case, the statement of jurisdiction, the issues presented, the signature, the proof of service, the appendix, and the mandamus record, which is a separate document altogether.[99]

In the courts of appeals:

- Petitions and responses in original proceedings—15,000 words.[100]
- Reply briefs original proceedings—7,500 words.[101]
- Motions for rehearing and responses—4,500 words.[102]
- Aggregate of all briefs filed by a party—27,000 words.[103]

In the Supreme Court:

- Petitions and responses in original proceedings—4,500 words.[104]
- Reply briefs at petition stage in original proceedings—2,400 words.[105]

On the vote of three justices, the Supreme Court may request full briefing on the merits in an original proceeding.[106] In that event, the page limitations for the merits brief are the same as for the petition in the court of appeals, exclusive of the matters described above.

- Briefs on the merits for Relator and for brief on the merits for Real Party in Interest—15,000 words.[107]
- Reply briefs on the merits—7,500 words.[108]

6-3:10 Fees

Effective September 1, 2015, the following filing fees pertain to mandamus practice:

In the Courts of Appeals:	
Original proceeding	$155.00
Response	$ 0.00
Motion for Rehearing (including for en banc)	$ 15.00
Miscellaneous Motions	$ 10.00
Exhibits Tendered for Oral Argument	$ 25.00
In the Supreme Court:	
Original Proceeding	$155.00
Additional Fee if Original Proceeding Is Granted	$ 75.00
Waiver of Response	$ 0.00
Response	$ 0.00
All Other Briefs	$ 0.00
Motion for Rehearing	$ 15.00
Miscellaneous Motions	$ 10.00
Exhibits Tendered for Oral Argument	$ 25.00

6-3:11 Number of Copies

The number of copies for original proceedings filed with the intermediate courts of appeals is changing as the courts of appeals adopt electronic filing. Counsel should consult the website for the court in which the proceeding is being filed and call the clerk's office to verify that court's policies about filing original proceedings electronically, in paper only, or some combination of the two, and ask how many paper copies of the mandamus filing and the mandamus record the court requires.[109]

If a court permits electronic filing of the mandamus record, counsel should inquire about the electronic size limitations. The record may need to be broken into separate filings to fit within those limitations. Counsel should leave extra time in accomplishing the e-filing of large amounts of data. The process of uploading large amounts of data close to the size limits has sometimes resulted in the data size increasing over the electronic-size limits.[110]

In the Supreme Court, the relator must e-file the mandamus petition by entering the court of appeals' docket number in the electronic filing service provider and indicating that it is an original proceeding. The Supreme Court requires two paper copies of the petition and appendix (and only one paper copy of the mandamus record).[111]

6-4 Core Requirements for the Issuance of Mandamus

6-4:1 Clear Abuse of Discretion

It is almost an article of faith that mandamus may issue when the trial court "abuses its discretion." Unfortunately, nobody knows what "abuse of discretion" really means; the term is afforded differing interpretations depending on whether one is arguing that the trial court did or did not commit such abuse.

But there is an even more fundamental problem that routinely trips up counsel pursuing mandamus relief. Often counsel will complain that the trial court "abused its discretion" when, regardless of what that phrase actually means, this is simply not an accurate statement of the actual complaint.

To illustrate, what if the trial court had no jurisdiction to issue the order it did? In that event, the trial court could scarcely "abuse" discretion that it did not even possess. Or what if the trial court refused to act on a motion that the law required it to? In that event, the correct complaint is not that the trial court "abused its discretion," rather it is that the trial court failed to exercise its discretion by reaching and ruling on the motion in question. But the fact that the trial court did not "abuse" its discretion in either of these circumstances in no way means that mandamus does not lie. It merely means that if counsel were to improperly frame the complaint as one of "abuse of discretion," counsel might suffer a denial of an otherwise meritorious mandamus action. Simply stated, when counsel fails to properly articulate the basis for the complaint, the screening attorneys may justifiably conclude that counsel has failed to comply with Rule 52's requirement that the petition contain a clear and concise argument for the contentions made.

You can avoid this mistake by exercising extraordinary care in categorizing the precise basis of the complaint. Outlined below are some of the more common categories.

6-4:1.1 Exercise-of-Discretion Abuse

Abuse of discretion is divisible into two subcategories—exercise-of-discretion abuse and error-of-law abuse. Exercise-of-discretion abuse is the most widely recognized example of "abuse of discretion": The trial court has discretion to act but acts in a way wholly at odds with what common sense would seem to dictate.

This subcategory is paradoxical: On the one hand, this type of "abuse" is the one most likely to provoke outrage on the part of trial counsel and the client but, on the other hand, is the one least likely to secure mandamus relief from the court of appeals.

Why? Appellate courts are less receptive to this type of mandamus because the standard of review for this character of "abuse" is so exacting—the amount of deference owed the trial court is extraordinarily high. If the trial court has demonstrated what all would agree to be an utter lack of common sense in, for example, compelling expensive discovery relating to an issue of only marginal relevance, that is of little moment to the court of appeals.

Violation of "common sense" is not the yardstick by which the court of appeals measures whether mandamus relief can properly issue. Rather, the standard is a strict one: "whether the court acted without reference to any guiding rules and principles."[112] "The mere fact that a trial judge may decide a matter within his or her discretionary authority in a different manner than an appellate judge in a similar circumstance does not demonstrate that an abuse of discretion has occurred."[113]

An exercise-of-discretion abuse is effectively viewed as the equivalent of "no discretion." A relator stuck with this standard of review faces a difficult, but not necessarily impossible, burden.

Relator should do three things: (1) develop the parameters of the guiding rules and principles governing the question in dispute; (2) persuade the appellate court that the trial court's discretion is not unbridled and that the parameters developed constitute the outer boundary of the discretion the trial court may properly exercise; and (3) demonstrate that the trial court, by its order, has strayed beyond that outer boundary. By constructing such an argument, a relator can legitimately assert that the trial court had "no discretion" to issue the order it did. Supreme Court authority can be cited in support of this type of argument.[114]

Faced with such a difficult burden, counsel should also explore whether the complaint might fit into another category, one in which the standard of review is not as strict. One of these is the other subcategory of "abuse of discretion," discussed below.

6-4:1.2 Error-of-Law Abuse

This subcategory of "abuse of discretion" is addressed in *Walker v. Packer.*[115] There, the Supreme Court contrasted review of a matter truly committed to the trial court's discretion with review of the trial court's determination of the legal principles controlling the ruling. The Supreme Court concluded that review of the latter is much less deferential:

> [R]eview of a trial court's determination of the legal principles controlling its ruling is much less deferential. A trial court has no "discretion" in determining what the law is or applying the law to the facts. Thus, a clear failure by the trial court to analyze or apply the law correctly will constitute an abuse of discretion, and may result in appellate reversal by extraordinary writ.[116]

Thus, if the trial court's action can be characterized as one involving an improper determination of the law or an improper application of the law to the facts, the action should be characterized in that way—even if the law is unsettled.[117] When it can be so characterized, relator has only to demonstrate to the appellate court the trial court's error of law, a determination which, unlike the trial court's exercise of discretion, is accorded no material deference by the reviewing court reviewing court.[118]

6-4:1.3 Trial Court Exceeds Statutorily Granted Authority

Mandamus will lie to set aside the action of a trial court which, as a matter of law, is void because the trial court exceeded its statutorily granted authority. Although the question was unsettled for many years, the Supreme Court now expressly recognizes this category of complaint as an exception to the general rule that a relator must show that there is no adequate remedy by appeal.[119]

6-4:1.4 Trial Court Refuses to Act on Matter

Use this category when the trial court has refused to act on a matter. As a general rule, trial courts are "required to consider and rule on a properly filed motion within a reasonable period of time once a ruling has been requested."[120] There are some circumstances, however, in which a "trial court need not ever rule on a pending motion[,]" for instance, "if the issue that is the subject of the motion has previously been litigated."[121] In that circumstance:

> the trial court does not have a ministerial duty to rule on the motion, ever. No amount of time can pass after which the trial court should be compelled to rule on the pending motion. To hold otherwise would be to require a trial court to repeatedly engage in a useless act by requiring the trial court to repeatedly decide the same issue.[122]

In those instances in which mandamus is available to compel a trial court to issue a ruling, however, the appellate court cannot compel any particular outcome; it can simply compel the trial court to act.[123] "We start with the basic premise that although our appellate court lacks power to compel a trial judge to do a particular act involving or requiring discretion on his part, our court does have power to order a trial judge to exercise his discretion in some manner."[124]

A variety of trial court failures to act, for which mandamus was held to lie, fall within this category: failure of the trial court to rule on a motion for default judgment within a reasonable time,[125] failure of the trial court to rule on a motion to enforce Rule 11 discovery agreement,[126] failure of the trial court to rule on a motion for appointment of personal representative,[127] failure of the trial court to hear and render decision on a Rule 76a motion,[128] failure of the trial court to rule on a severance motion,[129] failure of the trial court to conduct an in camera inspection of certain documents in discovery dispute,[130] and failure of the trial court to rule on a recusal motion.[131]

The principal burden falling on relator invoking this category is to develop a proper record. Merely showing that the trial court has failed to act on a matter within its discretion will not be enough. Rather, you should develop a record demonstrating that: "(1) the motion was properly filed and had been pending for a reasonable time; (2) [relator] requested a ruling on the motion; and (3) the trial court has either refused to rule or failed to rule within a reasonable time."[132] Absent such a showing, the court of appeals may deny the requested mandamus relief as premature.[133]

6-4:1.5 Court of Appeals Acts to Enforce Jurisdiction

Power is conferred on the courts of appeals to issue mandamus to enforce their jurisdiction.[134] Invoke this category when mandamus relief is sought against a district clerk or a court reporter who does not provide the appellate court with the record necessary for the court of appeals to consider a pending civil appeal.[135]

6-4:1.6 Inviting Texas Supreme Court to Overrule Precedent in Denying Mandamus Relief

One of the most interesting mandamus decisions to come out of the Supreme Court in the past two decades discussing the clear-abuse-of-discretion requirement is *In re Smith Barney, Inc.*[136] The majority opinion and the four-justice concurring opinion remain vital to understanding differing trains of thought on mandamus jurisprudence.

In *Smith Barney,* relator sought mandamus relief from a trial court order overruling its motion to dismiss the lawsuit on the basis of forum non conveniens. After being denied mandamus relief in the court of appeals, relator proceeded to the Supreme Court.

The Supreme Court acknowledged that the trial court was bound to deny the forum non conveniens motion because of a "writ refused" appellate court decision holding that an action by a corporation qualified to do business in Texas cannot be dismissed on the basis of forum non conveniens.[137] In the Supreme Court's words: "Although we conclude that *Rouw* was wrongly decided and is no longer the law, the district court was bound to follow it."[138]

Thus, the Supreme Court concluded that the district court "did not abuse its discretion" in following *Rouw,* and "therefore we will not compel the district court to set aside its decision."[139] But then, the Supreme Court in denying the mandamus effectively gave relator precisely the relief it sought: "We do free the court, however, to consider the application of the forum non conveniens doctrine to this case unconstrained by *Rouw*."[140] The court articulated the following standard:

> [A]lthough a lower court ordinarily should not be said to have abused its discretion in following existing law, even if that law is no longer valid or should be significantly changed, in denying mandamus relief it is appropriate to state what the correct law is in order to permit the lower court to reconsider its decision.[141]

The four-justice concurring opinion authored by then-Justice Hankinson criticized the majority's decision, colorfully stating that "the Court's decision to consider the merits of *Rouw* gives relator the benefit of an ultra vires interlocutory appeal."[142] In the concurring opinion, the Supreme Court's conclusion that the trial court did not abuse its discretion by following binding legal precedent should have ended the inquiry.[143] Indeed, the concurrence identified another basis for denying mandamus relief—relator had an adequate remedy by appeal; a motion to dismiss is an incidental pre-trial ruling not ordinarily appropriate for mandamus relief.[144] The concurrence voiced its concern that, by effectively granting relator what it sought in denying mandamus relief, the Supreme Court would only encourage the filing of more petitions:

> When the Court makes relief available in the absence of a trial court's abuse of discretion and a showing that an ordinary appeal would be inadequate, litigants

> are unable to predict what they must show to obtain relief. In lieu of standards, and without guidance, litigants are simply put to guessing what issue will catch the attention of five justices at any given time. Unpredictability may well encourage more petitions, with the result that resources will have been wasted on mandamuses that should never have been filed.[145]

In the intervening years since *Smith Barney* was decided, however, few appellate courts have relied on the opinion to render an "ultra vires interlocutory appeal."[146] Nonetheless, creative counsel may look to *Smith Barney* as an avenue for obtaining interlocutory relief in the appropriate case. On occasion, the Supreme Court continues to effectively grant relief even though the mandamus is denied.[147]

6-4:1.7 Unsettled Law

A mandamus petition predicated on law that is uncertain may be denied. One view is that mandamus will not lie if the law is uncertain. Under this view, the only exception is "when the issue goes to the subject-matter jurisdiction of the trial court."[148]

This view is unduly restrictive. In a 1996 decision, *Huie v. Deshazo*,[149] the Supreme Court expressly rejected the argument that mandamus would not lie because the law at issue was unsettled. Writing for a unanimous court, Chief Justice Phillips analyzed the question as follows:

> [Real party in interest] argues that because the legal question confronting the trial court was an issue of first impression in Texas, the court could not have "abused its discretion" in resolving the issue, and thus mandamus relief is inappropriate. We disagree. "A trial court has no 'discretion' in determining what the law is or applying the law to the facts." Consequently, the trial court's erroneous legal conclusion, even in an unsettled area of law, is an abuse of discretion.[150]

A number of courts of appeals have since recited this language from *Huie*.[151] And the Texas Supreme Court continues to follow this rule.[152]

Counsel facing a mandamus proceeding involving an issue of first impression or an area of unsettled law should cite *Huie*[153] and its progeny in support of the proposition that mandamus is nonetheless appropriate. And counsel should be aware of an interesting paradox. While the fact that "the law is uncertain" may cause some courts of appeals to summarily deny the petition (although they should not), that fact may enhance the chances for success before the Supreme Court, particularly if the issue is one likely to recur. In that event, relator can effectively argue that the issue is one of importance to the jurisprudence of the state, warranting the Supreme Court's exercise of discretionary jurisdiction.

6-4:2 No Adequate Remedy by Appeal

With the exception of actions to set aside void orders, as a general rule, relator must demonstrate the lack of an adequate remedy at law in order to obtain mandamus relief.[154] Understanding that this is the general rule, however, is not the same thing as understanding how the rule actually works in practice.

For 12 years, Chief Justice Phillips's opinion in *Walker v. Packer* stood as the standard for determining whether the relator had an adequate remedy by appeal.[155] In 2004, however, the Supreme Court revisited and relaxed the *Walker v. Packer* standard.[156] *Walker* held that "an appellate remedy is not inadequate merely because it may involve more expense or delay than obtaining an extraordinary writ."[157] *In re Prudential* questioned this restrictive standard, observing that "the word 'merely' carries heavy freight."[158]

The Supreme Court in *In re Prudential* reexamined what constitutes an inadequate remedy by appeal. "The operative word, 'adequate', has no comprehensive definition; it is simply a proxy for the careful balance of jurisprudential considerations that determine when appellate courts will use original mandamus proceedings to review the actions of lower courts."[159]

The Supreme Court articulated the following test for determining when the "adequacy" analysis must be performed: "An appellate remedy is 'adequate' when any benefits to mandamus review are outweighed by the detriments. When the benefits outweigh the detriments, appellate courts must consider whether the appellate remedy is adequate."[160] Under this test, the "adequacy" analysis comes into play only when the benefits of mandamus review outweigh the detriments.

In the Supreme Court's view, the "adequacy" analysis must involve a flexible, rather than a rigid, approach: "Although this Court has tried to give more concrete direction for determining the availability of mandamus review, rigid rules are necessarily inconsistent with the flexibility that is the remedy's principal virtue."[161] Thus, the analysis depends heavily on the circumstances of the particular case, "and is better guided by general principles than by simple rules."[162]

What the court deems to constitute the "general principles" for determining whether an appellate remedy is "adequate" can be gleaned from a close reading of the opinion. The following are factors that *In re Prudential* suggests would support the conclusion that appeal constitutes an inadequate remedy and that mandamus should issue:

- Allowing the trial court's order to stand would make the trial "amount to little more than a fiction," and would result in an "irreversible waste of judicial and public resources."[163]
- There is "a complete lack of authority for the trial court's order," and the civil justice system would be adversely affected by allowing the proceeding to grind forward toward an inevitable reversal.[164]
- The case involves "exceptional" circumstances, and granting mandamus would permit the correction of a "clear error" and "afford appropriate guidance to the law."[165]
- The issue presented by the mandamus proceeding is a question of law, one that is unsettled but is likely to recur, and an issue that "eludes answer by appeal."[166]

Do not rely solely on the general principles articulated in *Prudential*.[167] Although the opinion appeared to loosen the standard for "no adequate remedy," it has not resulted in a significant increase in the granting of mandamus petitions. A more effective approach is to search for prior decisions involving similar fact patterns in which courts have determined that the relator had no adequate remedy by appeal.

Texas courts have wrestled with the "adequacy" rule in a variety of different contexts, generating more particularized statements of the rule with respect to those specific contexts.

In persuading the appellate court that relator has no adequate remedy, counsel should search for cases involving original proceedings. Citing "petition denied" or "no writ" decisions, without explaining their pertinence, may be an immediate, and fatal, tip off to the appellate court that the issue involved is one that can be resolved by appeal.[168]

6-4:3 In the Texas Supreme Court, Demonstrate Importance to the Jurisprudence

If the court of appeals denies mandamus relief, relator is not guaranteed review by the Supreme Court. Just as in the case of petitions for review, it is within the Supreme Court's discretion whether to exercise jurisdiction over the mandamus proceeding. The Supreme Court will decline to exercise its discretionary jurisdiction unless it is persuaded that the proceeding presents an issue of such importance to the jurisprudence of the state as to warrant review.[169]

How does relator demonstrate that the case is "important" to the state's jurisprudence? One approach is to draw on the factors that the court should consider in deciding whether to grant a petition for review.[170] Although these factors may not precisely fit the particular mandamus action at issue, they nonetheless provide useful guidelines.[171]

6-5 Examples of Cases in Which Mandamus Was the Proper Remedy

Many mandamus decisions explore the inadequate-remedy principle. The following list is not intended to be exhaustive, but it is representative.

6-5:1 Discovery Rulings

- *Order compelling discovery of document protected by privilege or attorney work-product protection*

An order compelling discovery of document protected by privilege or an attorney work-product protection is reviewable by mandamus.[172] Relator has no adequate remedy by appeal because, once the documents are produced, the privilege is lost; the appellate court cannot cure the trial court's discovery error.[173]

This category of orders reviewable by mandamus includes a trial court's ruling that a privilege has been waived.[174] Similarly, a trial court's refusal to conduct an in camera review, when such a review is needed to decide a privilege question, is also reviewable by mandamus.[175]

- *Order compelling overly broad, irrelevant discovery*

A trial court order that compels overly broad discovery, or irrelevant discovery not permitted by the rules, is an abuse of discretion,[176] and mandamus relief may be available.[177] Relator has no adequate remedy by appeal because, once the production is made, the harm is done.[178]

- *Order compelling disproportionate or overly burdensome discovery*

Discovery that is disproportionate,[179] or unduly burdensome or harassing,[180] is also beyond the scope of discovery permitted by the rules.[181] Relator has no adequate remedy by appeal from an order compelling such discovery because, once the production is made, the harm is done.[182]

- *Order compelling apex deposition*

A trial court order compelling the taking of an apex deposition is ordinarily reviewable by mandamus.[183]

- *Order compelling discovery of trade secrets*

A trial court order compelling the discovery of trade secrets without adequate protections to maintain the confidentiality of the information has been reviewed by mandamus. Relator has no adequate remedy by appeal because the appellate court would not be able to cure the trial court's discovery error.[184]

- *Order compelling discovery that violates First Amendment rights*

Relator has no adequate remedy by appeal because once the discovery is permitted, the constitutional harm is complete.[185]

- *Order compelling production of tax returns without showing of relevance*

"Compelling production of the returns leaves [relator] without an adequate remedy by appeal."[186]

- *Order imposing "death penalty" sanctions*

Relator has no adequate remedy by appeal when discovery sanctions have the effect of precluding the decision on the merits of the party's claims, unless the sanctions are imposed simultaneously with the rendition of a final, appealable judgment.[187] "Whenever a trial court imposes sanctions which have the effect of adjudicating a dispute, whether by striking pleadings, dismissing an action or rendering a default judgment, but which do not result in rendition of an appealable judgment, then the eventual remedy by appeal is inadequate."[188] Thus, when a sanctions order for discovery abuse excludes evidence that either completely vitiates or severely compromises the ability to present a viable claim or defense at trial, such order will be reviewable by mandamus like a death-penalty sanctions order.[189]

- *Order imposing monetary sanctions for discovery abuse*

Mandamus will lie for the trial court's imposition of monetary sanctions when the amount imposed "threatens a party's continuation of the litigation."[190] In that event, "appeal affords an adequate remedy only if payment of the sanctions is deferred until final judgment is rendered and the party has the opportunity to supersede the judgment and perfect his appeal."[191]

The Supreme Court also has held that a relator does not have an adequate remedy by appeal when a trial court's sanctions order serves as an improper deterrent to seeking appellate review, such as when a trial court's sanction order grants the opposing party an unconditional award of appellate attorney fees.[192] That type of award "essentially punishes [relator] for seeking mandamus relief."[193] Appeal is not an adequate remedy for such an order. "A monetary penalty for seeking mandamus relief takes something that cannot be restored by appeal: the unfettered right to seek any relief that may be available by mandamus."[194]

- *Order denying relator's request for discovery*

Relator has no adequate remedy by appeal only if relator can establish that denial of the discovery in question constitutes "the effective denial of a reasonable opportunity to develop the merits of his or her case, so that the trial would be a waste of judicial resources."[195] Stated another way, "a denial of discovery going to the heart of a party's case may render the appellate remedy inadequate."[196] This principle has been applied to permit review by mandamus when a trial court order postponed basic discovery requested by 30 defendants from more than 1,000 plaintiffs until just before trial.[197]

- *Order denying discovery when missing discovery cannot be made part of appellate record*

Mandamus may also be available from a trial court order denying discovery when the missing discovery cannot be made part of the appellate record.[198] In that scenario, the remedy by appeal is inadequate because the reviewing court is unable to evaluate the effect of the trial court's error on the record before it. Whether relator has an adequate remedy by appeal depends on the circumstances of the particular case. For example, when relator is denied certain discovery altogether, then the appellate court "must carefully consider all relevant circumstances, such as the claims and defenses asserted, the type of discovery sought, what it is intended to prove, and the presence or lack of other discovery, to determine whether mandamus is appropriate."[199]

- *Trial court finding of good cause for the late filing of discovery*

A trial court's finding of good cause for the late filing of discovery responses is reviewed for abuse of discretion.[200] But as a matter of law, inadvertence of counsel alone is not sufficient to support a trial court's finding of good cause.[201]

6-5:2 Forum- and Dispute-Resolution Related Rulings

- *Certain rulings on plea to the jurisdiction*

When the trial court denies a plea to the jurisdiction and the trial court's exercise of jurisdiction interferes with jurisdiction of a state agency or another court, the Texas Supreme Court has issued mandamus.[202]

- *Venue rulings based on mandatory venue provisions*

A trial court's denial of a motion to transfer venue based on a mandatory venue statute is, by statute, reviewable by mandamus.[203]

- *Order refusing to enforce forum-selection clause*

When a trial court refuses to enforce a venue provision in a commercial agreement, that order is reviewable by mandamus because the ruling forfeits for all time the contract rights the relator purchased and on which the parties agreed.[204] The remedy by appeal is inadequate because, once tried in Texas contrary to the venue provision, it would be impossible for the relator to receive the benefit of its bargain that any dispute would only be tried elsewhere.[205]

- *Order refusing to enforce contractual waiver of a jury trial*

Mandamus is proper when a trial court denies a party's attempt to enforce a contractual waiver of a jury trial.[206] Proceeding to trial would be a waste of judicial resources and a forfeiture of substantial rights. And if the relator were to obtain judgment on a favorable jury verdict, it could not appeal, and its contractual right would be lost forever because even if the relator "could somehow obtain reversal based on the denial of its contractual right, it would already have lost a part of it by having been subject to the procedure it agreed to waive."[207]

- *Forum non conveniens*

A trial court's order denying a forum non conveniens motion is reviewable by mandamus because "the movant cannot obtain a final judgment, and no immediate appeal is available."[208]

6-5:3 Orders During Course of Pre-Trial, Trial, and Post-Trial

- *Order Granting TRO*

While there are statutory provisions providing for interlocutory appeals from orders granting or denying temporary injunctions, those statutes do not apply to temporary restraining orders.[209] The Supreme Court has granted mandamus relief from a trial court's order granting a TRO when the TRO's duration violated Rule 680's time limits for TROs[210] and other procedural requirements.[211] As a practical matter, most TROs expire before any relief can be obtained by mandamus.[212]

- *Scheduling the docket*

A trial court has wide latitude in establishing a schedule for its docket and in enforcing that schedule through orders, including orders of dismissal. Such decisions are reviewed for abuse of discretion.[213] An appellate court may not arbitrarily interfere with that schedule.[214]

- *Jury demand*

Because the right to a trial by jury is constitutionally protected, trial courts have limited discretion to remove a case from the jury docket. Even when a party has not timely requested a jury and paid the fee, a jury trial should be permitted if it will not interfere with the court's docket, delay trial, or prejudice the opposing party.[215]

- *Order denying motion to disqualify or recuse judge*

When a judge denies a motion to disqualify and continues to sit in violation of a constitutional or statutory proscription, mandamus is available to compel the judge's mandatory disqualification. In that instance, the relator need not show that the remedy by appeal is inadequate.[216] By contrast, mandamus is generally not available for the denial of a motion to recuse, because that can be reviewed on appeal, unless a relator meets the *Prudential*[217] standard.[218]

- *Order granting motion to disqualify counsel*

Disqualification of counsel renders remedy by appeal inadequate.[219]

An order disqualifying counsel is reviewed for abuse of discretion.[220] However, because disqualification is such a severe remedy, the trial court must adhere to an exacting standard to ensure that a motion to disqualify is not a dilatory tactic.[221] Logically, this requires the court to consider the motion to disqualify within the context of the larger proceeding.[222]

- *Order denying motion to disqualify counsel*

Orders denying a motion to disqualify counsel are reviewable by mandamus.[223] The Supreme Court has expressly held that the appellate remedy is inadequate when the trial court erroneously overrules a motion to disqualify counsel.[224]

- *Consolidation*

An order consolidating cases, especially in mass tort suits, may be reviewable by mandamus when awaiting an appeal would be an enormous waste of judicial resources.[225]

- *Order refusing to grant a nonsuit*

A trial court's order refusing to grant a nonsuit when there is no pending claim by the defendant for affirmative relief is reviewable by mandamus.[226]

- *Order denying motion for continuance*

Ordinarily, the denial of a motion for continuance is not reviewable by mandamus because it is considered to be an incidental trial court ruling. But mandamus review has been available in narrow circumstances. For instance, when the continuance ruling interferes with an important legislative scheme or deprives a litigant of a peculiar right not generally available to all litigants, mandamus has issued, such as when a legislative continuance was denied.

The Supreme Court also ruled that mandamus relief was available to challenge a trial court order denying a motion for continuance in *General Motors Corp. v. Gayle.*[227] The Court limited its holding to the "special circumstances" of the case before it—General Motors had requested the continuance to allow its request for a jury trial to become timely and the Supreme Court already had before it another mandamus issue concerning the trial court's order regarding crash testing. The Supreme Court's attempt to limit its holding reads as follows:

> [T]he denial of a motion for continuance is an incidental trial ruling ordinarily not reviewable by mandamus. In the absence of any other error, we would not grant extraordinary relief merely to revise a trial judge's scheduling order, however perverse. This case, however, presents special circumstances, in that we must remedy the crash-test order by interlocutory mandamus review. Under these special circumstances, the interests of judicial economy dictate that we should also remedy the trial court's denial of the right of jury trial by mandamus.[228]

- *Sealing orders*

Because court records are presumptively open and public, an order sealing the record must strictly comply with the rules.[229] Such orders are subject to immediate interlocutory review for abuse of discretion, cabined by Rule 76a's requirements.[230]

- *Peremptory challenges*

Orders granting re-alignment of parties in connection with the allocation of peremptory strikes are reviewable by mandamus.[231]

- *Contempt order not involving confinement*

While contempt orders directing confinement of the contemnor are reviewable by habeas corpus, those not involving confinement are not reviewable through that avenue. Thus, the only possible relief is a writ of mandamus.[232]

- *Orders denying and granting leave to designate responsible third parties under section 33.004.*

Allowing a case to proceed to trial, despite erroneous denial of a responsible-third-party designation "would skew the proceedings, potentially affect the outcome of the litigation, and compromise the presentation of [the relator's] defense in ways unlikely to be apparent in the appellate record."[233] Because forcing a party to proceeding to trial and await a final-judgment appeal "impairs—and potentially denies—a litigant's significant and substantive right to allow the fact-finder to determine the proportionate responsibility of all responsible parties," mandamus is available.[234] The Supreme Court has extended the same reasoning to permit review by mandamus of a trial court's grant of a motion to designate responsible third parties.[235]

- *Order denying motion to abate second-filed action.*

When "inherently interrelated suits are pending in two counties and venue is proper in either county, the court in which suit was first filed acquires dominant jurisdiction," and the second-filed suit should be abated; "mandamus relief is available to secure this result."[236]

- *Order denying motion for summary judgment*

"[M]andamus is generally unavailable when a trial court denies summary judgment, no matter how meritorious the motion."[237] The Texas Supreme Court has explained why mandamus ordinarily is not an available vehicle for obtaining immediate review of interlocutory summary-judgment orders:

> [P]arties are not "entitled" to summary judgment in the same way they are entitled to arbitration, their chosen attorney, or an expert report like those here. Summary judgments were unknown at common law, and appeared in Texas cases only with adoption of the rule in 1949. Even if the merits could be decided only one way, jury trials may still be important both for justice and the appearance of doing justice. Moreover, trying a case in which summary judgment would have been appropriate does not mean the case will have to be tried twice—as it will if the first trial is conducted in the wrong time, place, or manner.[238]

A few exceptions have been made over the years. For instance, in *In re United States Automobile Association*,[239] the trial court denied summary judgment based on the statute of limitations in an employment-discrimination case.[240] There, the plaintiff re-filed suit in district court after his first suit—which had been tried to judgment in county court—was dismissed for lack of jurisdiction.[241] The Texas Supreme Court granted mandamus under the *Prudential* balancing standard.[242] It weighed the fact that the defendant had "already endured one trial in a forum that lacked jurisdiction," and that a second trial on a claim that was barred by limitations was a further waste of judicial resources.[243] The Court was also persuaded that denying mandamus review "would thwart the legislative intent that non-tolled TCHRA claims be brought within two years."[244]

Even before the adoption of the *Prudential* balancing test,[245] in *Tilton v. Marshall*,[246] the Supreme Court of Texas effectively reviewed a trial court's denial of a motion for summary judgment. The concurring and dissenting opinion noted the unprecedented nature of the decision: "up until now, this Court has never held that mandamus is available to review the denial of a motion for summary judgment."[247] But that is effectively what the Supreme Court held in *Tilton*: "Because we conclude that the trial court has abused its discretion in refusing to dismiss the plaintiffs' claims for intentional infliction of emotional distress and related conspiracy claims, and in ordering the production of certain documents which are therefore irrelevant, we conditionally grant a writ of mandamus."[248]

The Supreme Court was quick to dismiss the notion that mandamus will lie to review the denial of just any motion for summary judgment: "We are not, of course, granting mandamus relief to Tilton merely because we conclude that plaintiffs cannot prevail on certain claims."[249] The Supreme Court grounded its decision on the unique circumstances of the case, concluding that forcing relator to trial without dismissal of these claims would result in a violation of his First Amendment free exercise rights.[250]

> Adjudication of the claims for intentional infliction of emotional distress would necessarily require an inquiry into the truth or falsity of religious beliefs that is forbidden by the Constitution. The trial itself, therefore, and not merely the imposition of an adverse judgment, would violate relator's constitutional rights.[251]

- *Order granting new trial motion*

In 2009, the Texas Supreme Court in a landmark decision granted mandamus relief in *In re Columbia Medical Center*[252] when a trial court granted new trial without specifying its reasons. *Columbia* held that stating that a new trial is granted "in the interests of justice and fairness" is not sufficiently specific, and that a relator challenging that type of order has no adequate remedy by appeal.[253]

In 2013, In *In re Toyota Motor Sales, U.S.A., Inc.*, the Texas Supreme Court extended its holding in *Columbia* by granting mandamus from the trial court's grant of a new trial motion because the reasons articulated for granting new trial were not sufficiently supported by the record.[254] *Toyota* was a significant extension of *Columbia* because it stands for the proposition that an appellate court may conduct a merits-based mandamus review of a trial court's articulated reasons for granting a new trial.[255]

Appellate courts have also held that mandamus is available when a new trial is granted in violation of procedural and jurisdictional rules, such as a grant of new trial after plenary power has expired.[256] The Texas Supreme Court has also held that mandamus is available from an order granting a new trial "when the trial court erroneously finds that the jury's answers to special issues are irreparably conflicting."[257] And the Texas Supreme Court has reviewed the grant of a new trial motion based on juror conduct by mandamus.[258]

- *Void orders*

Void orders, such as actions taken after the trial court's plenary power has expired, may be challenged by mandamus.[259] When challenging a void order, the relator is excused from the necessity of showing that it lacks an adequate remedy by appeal.[260]

• *Exclusive agency jurisdiction*

When a state agency has exclusive jurisdiction over an action pending in a trial court, mandamus is available because "allowing those claims to proceed in the trial court would disrupt the orderly processes of government."[261]

Notes

1 *In re Prudential Ins. Co. of Am.*, 148 S.W.3d 124, 135–36 (Tex. 2004) (orig. proceeding); *Walker v. Packer*, 827 S.W.2d 833, 839 (Tex. 1992) (orig. proceeding).

2 Tex. Gov't Code § 22.221; *see* Tex. Const. art. V, § 6.

3 *See, e.g., Wolters v. Wright*, 623 S.W.2d 301, 305 (Tex. 1981) ("Since a statement of facts [now, Reporter's Record] is often necessary to the exercise of appellate jurisdiction, the court of appeals may issue a writ of mandamus to compel the court reporter to complete the statement of facts in order to protect that court's jurisdiction."); *Palacio v. Johnson*, 663 S.W.2d 490, 491 (Tex. App.—Houston [1st Dist.] 1983, orig. proceeding) ("This court has jurisdiction to mandamus a court reporter to prepare a statement of facts required to resolve questions raised on appeal, in order to protect our jurisdiction."). *Cf. In re Strickhausen*, 994 S.W.2d 936 (Tex. App.—Houston [1st Dist.] 1999, no pet.) (denying mandamus relief requested to compel preparation of reporter's record because First Court of Appeals lacked jurisdiction over appeal pending before the Fourteenth Court of Appeals).

4 Tex. Gov't Code § 22.221(b). This includes orders issued by probate courts. *See Qwest Microwave, Inc. v. Bedard*, 756 S.W.2d 426, 441 (Tex. App.—Dallas 1988, orig. proceeding) (probate court is county court within meaning of section 22.221(b)); *see, e.g., In re Marshall*, 515 S.W.3d 420, 421 (Tex. App.—Houston [14th Dist.] 2017, orig. proceeding) (granting mandamus relief against judge of probate court).

5 *See Lesikar v. Anthony*, 750 S.W.2d 338, 339 (Tex. App.—Houston [1st Dist.] 1988, orig. proceeding); *see, e.g., Click v. Tyra*, 867 S.W.2d 406, 407 (Tex. App.—Houston [14th Dist.] 1993, orig. proceeding) (district clerk).

6 Tex. Civ. Prac. & Rem. Code § 15.0642 (not restricted to Supreme Court); *see In re Tex. Ass'n of Sch. Bds., Inc.*, 169 S.W.3d 653, 656 (Tex. 2005) (orig. proceeding); *In re Mo. Pac. R.R.*, 998 S.W.2d 212, 215 (Tex. 1999) (orig. proceeding).

7 Tex. Elec. Code § 273.061 (not restricted to Supreme Court). Counsel should note that election-contest mandamus proceedings are governed by particular venue rules for the appellate court in which mandamus may be filed. *See* Tex. Elec. Code § 273.063.

8 Tex. Nat. Res. Code § 85.258 (not restricted to Supreme Court).

9 *See, e.g., In re Mo. Pac. R.R.*, 998 S.W.2d 212, 215–16 (Tex. 1999) (orig. proceeding) (holding that, because the statute expressly provides for review by mandamus, it would undermine the purpose of the statute if a relator were forced to show inadequate remedy by appeal).

10 Tex. Const. art. V, § 3(a).

11 *In re Occidental Chem. Corp.*, 18-0660, 2018 WL 4939073, at *5 (Tex. Oct. 12, 2018) (quoting Tex. Const. art. V, § 3).

12 Tex. Gov't Code § 22.002(a).

13 *In re State*, 556 S.W.3d 821, 826 (Tex. 2018) (orig. proceeding) (citing *Ginsberg v. Fifth Court of Appeals*, 686 S.W.2d 105, 107 (Tex. 1985) (orig. proceeding), and Tex. Gov't Code § 22.002(a)).

14 *In re State*, 556 S.W.3d 821, 826 (Tex. 2018) (orig. proceeding) (quoting *Johnson v. Fourth Court of Appeals*, 700 S.W.2d 916, 918 (Tex. 1985)).

15 Tex. Gov't Code § 22.002(c).

[16] Tex. Const. art. V, § 3.

[17] *See, e.g., HCA Health Servs. of Tex., Inc. v. Salinas*, 838 S.W.2d 246, 248 (Tex. 1992) (orig. proceeding) (district clerk); *Pat Walker & Co. v. Johnson*, 623 S.W.2d 306, 308 (Tex. 1981) (orig. proceeding) (mandamus jurisdiction of Supreme Court does not extend to court reporters or district officer other than district judge).

[18] Until the amendment, the Supreme Court routinely dismissed for want of jurisdiction mandamus filings against county court judges, citing *Pat Walker & Co. v. Johnson*, 623 S.W.2d 306, 308 (Tex. 1981) (orig. proceeding). The 1995 amendment statutorily overruled this limitation on the Supreme Court's jurisdiction recognized in *Pat Walker & Co. v. Johnson*, 623 S.W.2d 306, 308 (Tex. 1981) (orig. proceeding).

[19] Tex. Gov't Code § 22.002(a).

[20] Tex. Gov't Code §§ 22.001–002.

[21] Tex. Civ. Prac. & Rem. Code § 15.0642 (not restricted to Supreme Court); *see In re Tex. Ass'n of Sch. Bds., Inc.*, 169 S.W.3d 653, 656 (Tex. 2005) (orig. proceeding); *In re Mo. Pac. R.R.*, 998 S.W.2d 212 (Tex. 1999) (orig. proceeding).

[22] Tex. Elec. Code § 273.061 (not restricted to Supreme Court). Counsel should note that election-contest mandamus proceedings are governed by particular venue rules for the appellate court in which mandamus may be filed. Tex. Elec. Code § 273.063.

[23] Tex. Nat. Res. Code § 85.258 (not restricted to Supreme Court).

[24] Tex. Disciplinary Rules Prof'l Conduct R. 3.09, *reprinted in* Tex. Gov't Code tit. 2, subtit. G, app. A-1 (restricted to Supreme Court only).

[25] Tex. Const. art. III, § 28 (restricted to Supreme Court only).

[26] *See, e.g.*, Tex. Agric. Code § 58.036 (restricted to Supreme Court only); Tex. Gov't Code §§ 404.126, 1205.02(b) (same).

[27] *See, e.g., In re Mo. Pac. R.R.*, 998 S.W.2d 212, 215–16 (Tex. 1999) (orig. proceeding) (holding that, because the statute expressly provides for review by mandamus, it would undermine the purpose of the statute if a relator were forced to show inadequate remedy by appeal).

[28] Tex. R. App. P. 52.3(j)(1)(A) ("[The appendix must contain] a certified or sworn copy of any order complained of. . . .").

[29] For an example of a case in which mandamus was granted when the trial court refused to rule, see *City of Galveston v. Gray*, 93 S.W.3d 587, 592–93 (Tex. App.—Houston [14th Dist.] 2002, orig. proceeding, pet. denied).

[30] Tex. R. App. P. 7.2(b).

[31] *Rivercenter Assocs. v. Rivera*, 858 S.W.2d 366, 367 (Tex. 1993) (orig. proceeding); *see In re Laibe Corp.*, 307 S.W.3d 314, 318 (Tex. 2010) (orig. proceeding); *In re Int'l Profits Assocs., Inc.*, 274 S.W.3d 672, 676 (Tex. 2009) (orig. proceeding).

[32] *Rivercenter Assocs. v. Rivera*, 858 S.W.2d 366, 367 (Tex. 1993) (orig. proceeding) (quoting *Callahan v. Giles*, 155 S.W.2d 793, 795 (Tex. 1941) (orig. proceeding)).

[33] *Rivercenter Assocs. v. Rivera*, 858 S.W.2d 366, 367 (Tex. 1993) (orig. proceeding).

[34] Nonetheless, decisions following *Rivercenter* provide some guidance. *See, e.g., In re Oceanografia, S.A. de C.V.*, 494 S.W.3d 728, 730–31 (Tex. 2016) (orig. proceeding) (holding that nine-month delay in seeking mandamus relief from the denial of its motion to dismiss for forum non conveniens was not unreasonable "when to press ahead might have compromised its appeal of the denial of its special appearance"); *In re Int'l Profits Assocs., Inc.*, 274 S.W.3d 672, 676 (Tex. 2009) (orig. proceeding) (holding that held that neither a party's four-month delay in obtaining a hearing on its motion to dismiss based on a contractual forum-selection clause nor the following eight-month delay in obtaining a corrected order denying the motion precluded mandamus review because the delays were not the party's fault); *In re Sw. Bell Tel. Co.*, 235 S.W.3d 619, 624 (Tex. 2007) (orig. proceeding) (when underlying case had been removed to federal court in the interim, year-long delay did not

foreclose relief); *In re Gen. Elec. Capital Corp.*, 203 S.W.3d 314, 315 (Tex. 2006) (org. proceeding) (10-month delay in moving to quash jury demand did not bar mandamus relief; analyzing issue as one of waiver because of evidentiary uncertainty over whether defendant served notice of jury demand on plaintiff); *In re E.I. du Pont de Nemours & Co.*, 92 S.W.3d 517, 524–25 (Tex. 2002) (orig. proceeding) (holding that defendant's four-year delay in moving for dismissal for forum non conveniens under section 71.052 while challenging in personam jurisdiction did not preclude mandamus relief, especially when the delay had not prejudiced the plaintiffs).

35 *See Wadley Research & Blood Bank v. Whittington*, 843 S.W.2d 77, 83 (Tex. App.—Dallas 1992, orig. proceeding) ("[T]his Court cannot be forced into a position where it must issue a stay precipitously, before it has had an opportunity to assess the merits of an original proceeding.").

36 Parties and counsel may communicate with the appellate courts about a case only through the clerk's office. Tex. R. App. P. 9.6.

37 Sections 6-3:1 and 6-3:2 address the mandamus petition itself, while the appendix and the mandamus record are addressed in § 6-3:3 and § 6-3:4.

38 The appendix may be bound with the petition or separately. *See* § 6-3:3.

39 Tex. R. App. P. 52.1. The party seeking mandamus relief is the relator. Tex. R. App. P. 52.2.

40 Tex. R. App. P. 9.4(g).

41 The appellate rules formally incorporate the role of "lead counsel." Lead counsel for a petitioner is the first attorney to sign a pleading in the Supreme Court. Tex. R. App. P. 6.1. Although the rule technically requires only that identifying information for lead counsel appear on the cover, the cover may also contain other counsel of record for the petitioner.

42 Tex. R. App. P. 9.4(g).

43 Tex. R. App. P. 9.4(f).

44 Tex. R. App. P. 52.3(a).

45 Tex. R. App. P. 52.2.

46 Tex. R. App. P. 52.2.

47 Tex. R. App. P. 52.2.

48 Tex. R. App. P. 52.3(b).

49 In bookmarking the electronic copy of the sections of petitions, responses, and replies, counsel should pay particular attention to the way the headings and subheadings appear in the bookmark and either edit the content of the bookmark to shorten any headings or subheadings too lengthy to be useful, or shorten the text of the headings or subheadings in the document itself and generate new bookmarks.

50 Tex. R. App. P. 52.3(c).

51 Tex. R. App. P. 52.3(d).

52 Tex. R. App. P. 52.3(d).

53 Tex. R. App. P. 52.3(d).

54 Tex. R. App. P. 52.3(e).

55 In original proceedings filed at the Texas Supreme Court that are first presented to the court of appeals, if the court of appeals merely denied the petition, the respondent remains the same as it did in the filing to the court of appeals (e.g., the district court judge). But, if the court of appeals grants relief, and the real party in interest wishes to seek review of that ruling, the real party in interest becomes the relator, and the respondent becomes the court of appeals.

56 Tex. R. App. P. 52.3(e). While it is rare, the Texas Supreme Court has found bypassing the court of appeals appropriate in compelling circumstances, such as election-context cases. *See, e.g., In re State Bar of Tex.*, 113 S.W.3d 730, 732 n.1 (Tex. 2003) (orig. proceeding);

LaRouche v. Hannah, 822 S.W.2d 632, 633–34 (Tex. 1992) (orig. proceeding) (per curiam). On rare occasion, timing considerations make it necessary to file a mandamus petition in the court of appeals and the Supreme Court simultaneously. In those instances, the relator should explain the simultaneous filings and the reasons why it was necessary.

57 Tex. R. App. P. 52.3(f).

58 Tex. R. App. P. 52.3(f).

59 Tex. R. App. P. 52.3(f).

60 Many practitioners choose to list the vehicle question as a second issue, *i.e.*, whether mandamus is available to review the type of error listed in the substantive issue. Doing so is particularly important when there is no settled law holding that mandamus is the appropriate vehicle for review.

61 Mandamus relief is not available when a petition is based on disputed fact questions. *See In re Angelini*, 186 S.W.3d 558, 560 (Tex. 2006) (orig. proceeding).

62 *Walker v. Packer*, 827 S.W.2d 833, 840 (Tex. 1992) (orig. proceeding). Indeed, the issues presented section is critically important in a Supreme Court mandamus petition, since many justices read that section first to determine what the petition is about and whether the issues are worthy of a grant.

63 Tex. R. App. P. 52.3(g).

64 *See In re Angelini*, 186 S.W.3d 558, 560 (Tex. 2006) (orig. proceeding).

65 Tex. R. App. P. 52.3(h).

66 *See* § 6-4:1.

67 *See* § 6-4:2; *In re Prudential Ins. Co. of Am.*, 148 S.W.3d 124, 135–36 (Tex. 2004) (orig. proceeding).

68 *Walker v. Packer*, 827 S.W.2d 833, 840 n.7 (Tex. 1992) (orig. proceeding); *see* § 6-4:3.

69 Tex. R. App. P. 52.6. This word-count limitation was intended to approximate 15 pages in 13-point font, which was formerly the limit for Supreme Court petitions, including mandamus petitions. When the court amended the page-limit rule to adopt a word-count limit, the court required that the font size be a minimum of 14-point for text and 12-point for footnotes.

70 Tex. R. App. P. 52.3(i).

71 Tex. R. App. P. 9.5(d).

72 Tex. R. App. P. 52.10(a).

73 Tex. R. App. P. 9.4(i)(3); *see* Chapter 16, § 2:6.1.

74 Tex. R. App. P. 52.3(j).

75 Tex. R. App. P. 52.7.

76 Tex. R. App. P. 52.3(j). The appendix to the mandamus is distinct from the required mandamus record discussed further in § 6-3:4.

77 See Chapter 16 for more detailed information.

78 Tex. R. App. P. 9.4(h).

79 Tex. R. App. P. 52.3(k)(1).

80 Tex. R. App. P. 52.3(k)(2).

81 Tex. R. App. P. 52.3(k)(2).

82 Tex. R. App. P. 52.3(k)(2); *see Wal-Mart Stores, Inc. v. Sturges*, No. 98-1107, 43 Tex. Sup. Ct. J. 372 (Tex. Feb. 11, 1999) (striking mandamus appendix that included the briefing to the court of appeals; ordering it re-drawn).

83 Tex. R. App. P. 52.7(a)(1).

84 Tex. R. App. P. 52.7(a)(2) (requiring that record contain "a properly authenticated transcript of any relevant testimony from any underlying proceeding, including any exhibits offered

in evidence, or a statement that no testimony was adduced in connection with the matter complained").

[85] *See Barnes v. Whittington*, 751 S.W.2d 493, 495 (Tex. 1988) (orig. proceeding).

[86] Tex. R. App. P. 9.3(c).

[87] Tex. R. App. P. 52.7(b). See Chapter 16, § 16-3 for special considerations regarding e-filing a record in an original proceeding.

[88] Tex. R. App. P. 9.4(h).

[89] Tex. R. App. P. 52.10(a).

[90] Tex. R. App. P. 52.10(a).

[91] Tex. R. App. P. 52.4.

[92] Tex. R. App. P. 52.4.

[93] Tex. R. App. P. 9.4, 52.3.

[94] Tex. R. App. P. 52.4.

[95] Tex. R. App. P. 52.5.

[96] Tex. R. App. P. 9.4. Rules 9.1 through 9.8, containing the rules applicable to appellate filings generally (such as the number of copies required, guidelines governing service and signatures, and the form of the filings), also apply to original proceedings.

[97] The rule permits the use of Courier or some other nonproportionally spaced type face, in which case the font must be "printed in standard 10-character-per-inch" font, Tex. R. App. P. 9.4(e), but the use of nonproportionally spaced type face is not recommended. Instead, counsel should use proportionally spaced typeface, such as Times New Roman or Georgia.

[98] See Chapter 16 for a further discussion of filing procedures.

[99] Tex. R. App. P. 52.6.

[100] Tex. R. App. P. 9.4(i)(2)(B).

[101] Tex. R. App. P. 9.4(i)(2)(C).

[102] Tex. R. App. P. 9.4(i)(2)(D).

[103] Tex. R. App. P. 9.4(i)(2)(B).

[104] Tex. R. App. P. 9.4(i)(2)(D).

[105] Tex. R. App. P. 9.4(i)(2)(E).

[106] Tex. R. App. P. 52.8(b).

[107] Tex. R. App. P. 9.4(i)(2)(B).

[108] Tex. R. App. P. 9.4(i)(2)(C).

[109] Tex. R. App. P. 9.3(a)(1)(A), (a)(2).

[110] Issues regarding e-filing and electronic-size limits are discussed further in Chapter 16.

[111] Tex. R. App. P. 9.3(b).

[112] *Downer v. Aquamarine Operators, Inc.*, 701 S.W.2d 238, 241 (Tex. 1985).

[113] *Downer v. Aquamarine Operators, Inc.*, 701 S.W.2d 238, 242 (Tex. 1985).

[114] *See Texaco, Inc. v. Sanderson*, 898 S.W.2d 813, 815 (Tex. 1995) (orig. proceeding) (issuing mandamus to vacate overbroad discovery order because the request in question "is well outside the bounds of proper discovery").

[115] *Walker v. Packer*, 827 S.W.2d 833, 840 (Tex. 1992) (orig. proceeding).

[116] *Walker v. Packer*, 827 S.W.2d 833, 840 (Tex. 1992) (orig. proceeding); *see In re State*, 556 S.W.3d 821, 827 (Tex. 2018) (noting that a "court abuses its discretion . . . if it clearly fails to correctly analyze or apply the law" (quoting *In re Cerberus Capital Mgmt., L.P.*, 164 S.W.3d 379, 382 (Tex. 2005))); *see, e.g.*, *In re Mahindra, USA Inc.*, 549 S.W.3d 541, 545 (Tex. 2018) (orig. proceeding) ("The meaning of the Texas-residency exception [in the

statute] and other definitions and provisions in dispute are questions of law over which the trial court exercised no discretion. Our review of statutory interpretation questions is de novo.").

117 *See infra* § 6-4:1.7; *In re State Farm Lloyds*, 520 S.W.3d 595, 604 (Tex. 2017) (orig. proceeding) ("[W]ith regard to questions of law and mixed questions of law and fact, a trial court has no 'discretion' in determining what the law is or applying the law to the facts, even when the law is unsettled." (internal quotations omitted)).

118 *See, e.g., In re Ford Motor Co.*, 442 S.W.3d 265, 269 (Tex. 2014) (orig. proceeding).

119 *See In re Sw. Bell Tel. Co.*, 35 S.W.3d 602, 605 (Tex. 2000) (orig. proceeding) (holding that "because the order was void, the relator need not show it did not have an adequate appellate remedy, and mandamus relief is appropriate").

120 *In re Cunningham*, 454 S.W.3d 139, 143 (Tex. App.—Texarkana 2014, orig. proceeding) (quoting *In re Greenwell*, 160 S.W.3d 286, 288 (Tex. App.—Texarkana 2005, orig. proceeding)).

121 *In re Bannister*, 216 S.W.3d 555, 556 (Tex. App.—Waco 2007, orig. proceeding) (mem. op.) (Gray, C.J., concurring from denial of mandamus).

122 *In re Bannister*, 216 S.W.3d 555, 556 (Tex. App.—Waco 2007, orig. proceeding) (mem. op.) (Gray, C.J., concurring from denial of mandamus).

123 *See, e.g., Eli Lilly & Co. v. Marshall*, 829 S.W.2d 157, 158 (Tex. 1992) (orig. proceeding) (granting mandamus relief to order the trial court to rule on pending motion, but "express[ing] no opinion on any aspect of the merits of relators' motion").

124 *Greenberg, Benson, Fisk & Fielder, P.C. v. Howell*, 685 S.W.2d 694, 695 (Tex. App.—Dallas 1984, orig. proceeding).

125 *In re Holleman*, No. 04-04-00340-CV, 2004 WL 1393582, at *2 (Tex. App.—San Antonio June 23, 2004, orig. proceeding) (mem. op.).

126 *In re Salazar*, 134 S.W.3d 357, 357 (Tex. App.—Waco 2003, orig. proceeding).

127 *O'Donniley v. Golden*, 860 S.W.2d 267, 269 (Tex. App.—Tyler 1993, orig. proceeding).

128 *Eli Lilly & Co. v. Marshall*, 829 S.W.2d 157, 158 (Tex. 1992) (orig. proceeding).

129 *Cooke v. Millard*, 854 S.W.2d 134, 135 (Tex. App.—Houston [1st Dist.] 1992, orig. proceeding).

130 *Texas Utils. Elec. Co. v. Marshall*, 739 S.W.2d 665, 667 (Tex. App.—Dallas 1987, orig. proceeding).

131 *Greenberg, Benson, Fisk & Fielder, P.C. v. Howell*, 685 S.W.2d 694, 695 (Tex. App.—Dallas 1984, orig. proceeding); *see, e.g., Eli Lilly & Co. v. Marshall*, 829 S.W.2d 157, 158 (Tex. 1992) (orig. proceeding) (holding that trial court "abused discretion by refusing to conduct hearing and render decision on the motion in compliance with Rule 76a").

132 *In re Cunningham*, 454 S.W.3d 139, 143 (Tex. App.—Texarkana 2014, orig. proceeding). "However, if a reasonable time has not yet passed, the trial court's failure to rule may not be a clear abuse of discretion." *In re Greenwell*, 160 S.W.3d 286, 288 (Tex. App.—Texarkana 2005, orig. proceeding).

133 *In re Cunningham*, 454 S.W.3d 139, 143 (Tex. App.—Texarkana 2014, orig. proceeding).

134 Tex. Gov't Code § 22.221(a).

135 *See, e.g., Palacio v. Johnson*, 663 S.W.2d 490, 491 (Tex. App.—Houston [1st Dist.] 1983, orig. proceeding).

136 *In re Smith Barney, Inc.*, 975 S.W.2d 593 (Tex. 1998) (orig. proceeding).

137 *In re Smith Barney, Inc.*, 975 S.W.2d 593, 596 (Tex. 1998) (orig. proceeding) (citing *H. Rouw Co. v. Ry. Express Agency*, 154 S.W.2d 143 (Tex. Civ. App.—El Paso 1941, writ ref'd)).

138 *In re Smith Barney, Inc.*, 975 S.W.2d 593, 598 (Tex. 1998) (orig. proceeding).

139 *In re Smith Barney, Inc.*, 975 S.W.2d 593, 598 (Tex. 1998) (orig. proceeding).

140 *In re Smith Barney, Inc.*, 975 S.W.2d 593, 599 (Tex. 1998) (orig. proceeding).

[141] *In re Smith Barney, Inc.*, 975 S.W.2d 593, 599 (Tex. 1998) (orig. proceeding) (denying mandamus relief to allow reconsideration in light of alterations to the controlling law); *see, e.g., Crown Cent. Petroleum Corp. v. Garcia*, 904 S.W.2d 125, 128 (Tex. 1995) (orig. proceeding) (denying mandamus relief without prejudice to allow reconsideration in light of newly adopted guidelines for apex depositions); *Phoenix Founders, Inc. v. Marshall*, 887 S.W.2d 831 (Tex.1994) (orig. proceeding) ("Because we have modified the controlling legal standard, the writ of mandamus is denied without prejudice to allow the trial court to reconsider the disqualification motion in light of today's opinion."); *Nat'l Tank Co. v. Brotherton*, 851 S.W.2d 193, 207 (Tex. 1993) (orig. proceeding); *Borders v. Hartman*, 814 S.W.2d 389, 389 (Tex. 1991) (orig. proceeding) (denying request for relief from the trial court's sanctions order without prejudice to allow the court to reconsider rulings in light of *TransAmerican* factors).

[142] *In re Smith Barney, Inc.*, 975 S.W.2d 593, 600 (Tex. 1998) (orig. proceeding).

[143] *In re Smith Barney, Inc.*, 975 S.W.2d 593, 600 (Tex. 1998) (orig. proceeding); *see Bradshaw v. Bradshaw*, 555 S.W.3d 539, 554 (Tex. 2018) (Boyd, J. dissenting, joined by Green, Johnson and Lehrmann, JJ.) ("[E]ven if the Court adopted the plurality's view as a new generally applicable legal principle, it would not apply retroactively to render the trial court's decision an abuse of discretion in this case.").

[144] *In re Smith Barney, Inc.*, 975 S.W.2d 593, 601 (Tex. 1998) (orig. proceeding).

[145] *In re Smith Barney, Inc.*, 975 S.W.2d 593, 600 (Tex. 1998) (Hankinson, J., concurring).

[146] For an example of a decision that does appear to constitute an "ultra vires interlocutory appeal," see *In re Gillespie*, 124 S.W.3d 699, 704 (Tex. App.—Houston [14th Dist.] 2003, orig. proceeding). In that case, the court of appeals declined to grant mandamus relief, concluding that the trial court did not abuse its discretion because it followed binding precedent in declining to set aside its previous order granting a new trial.

Nevertheless, following the dictates of *In re Smith Barney*, 975 S.W.2d 593 (Tex. 1998), the court of appeals reached the merits of the case and concluded that the trial court's new-trial order was void because the filing of a request for findings of fact and conclusions of law did not extend the trial court's plenary power, and the order was issued after the expiration of the court's plenary jurisdiction. In so holding, the court of appeals effectively overruled its prior precedent to the contrary that the trial court had followed. Thus, although relator was denied mandamus relief, she was effectively granted precisely what she had sought—the court of appeals provided clear guidance to the trial court to declare void the order that relator attacked. *In re Gillespie*, 124 S.W.3d 699, 704–05 (Tex. App.—Houston [14th Dist.] 2003, orig. proceeding).

[147] *E.g., In re State Farm Lloyds*, 520 S.W.3d 595, 615 n. 88 (Tex. 2017) (orig. proceeding) ("Because the trial court and the parties lacked the benefit of our views on the matter, neither granting nor denying mandamus relief on the merits is appropriate. Accordingly, we deny the request for mandamus relief without prejudice to allow the relator to seek reconsideration by the trial court in light of this opinion.").

[148] *Qwest Microwave, Inc. v. Bedard*, 756 S.W.2d 426, 434 (Tex. App.—Dallas 1988, orig. proceeding).

[149] *Huie v. DeShazo*, 922 S.W.2d 920, 927–28 (Tex. 1996) (orig. proceeding).

[150] *Huie v. DeShazo*, 922 S.W.2d 920, 927–28 (Tex. 1996) (orig. proceeding) (emphasis added) (citations omitted); *see, e.g., Lunsford v. Morris*, 746 S.W.2d 471 (Tex. 1988) (orig. proceeding) (in a mandamus case, establishing rule that net-worth discovery is proper when plaintiff seeks punitive damages).

[151] *See, e.g., In re Compton*, 117 S.W.3d 548, 550 (Tex. App.—Texarkana 2003, orig. proceeding); *In re Wells Fargo Bank Minn. N.A.*, 115 S.W.3d 600, 605 n.4 (Tex. App.—Houston [14th Dist.] 2003, orig. proceeding); *In re Skiles*, 102 S.W.3d 323, 325 (Tex. App.—Beaumont 2003, orig. proceeding).

[152] *In re Shipman*, 540 S.W.3d 562, 565–66 (Tex. 2018) (orig. proceedings) ("[W]ith regard to questions of law and mixed questions of law and fact, a trial court has no discretion in determining what the law is or applying the law to the facts, even when the law is unsettled."); *In re State Farm Lloyds*, 520 S.W.3d 595, 604 (Tex. 2017) (orig. proceeding) (same); *In re Prudential Ins. Co. of Am.*, 148 S.W.3d 124, 135 (Tex. 2004) (orig. proceeding) (observing as established mandamus law that "[a] trial court has no discretion in determining what the law is or applying the law to the facts, even when the law is unsettled" (internal quotations omitted)).

[153] *Huie v. DeShazo*, 922 S.W.2d 920, 927–28 (Tex. 1996) (orig. proceeding).

[154] *See Walker v. Packer*, 827 S.W.2d 833, 842 (Tex. 1992) (orig. proceeding) ("The requirement that mandamus issue only where there is no adequate remedy by appeal is sound, and we reaffirm it today.").

[155] *Walker v. Packer*, 827 S.W.2d 833 (Tex. 1992) (orig. proceeding).

[156] *See In re Prudential Ins. Co. of Am.*, 148 S.W.3d 124, 136 (Tex. 2004) (orig. proceeding). That *In re Prudential* marks a substantial departure by the Court from its more restrictive standard in *Walker v. Packer* is illustrated by the fact that the author of the majority opinion in *Walker*, Chief Justice Phillips, was also the author of the dissenting opinion in *Prudential*. *See In re Prudential Ins. Co. of Am.*, 148 S.W.3d 124, 141 (Tex. 2004) (orig. proceeding) (Phillips, J., dissenting). He described *Prudential* as a "retreat" from the standards articulated in *Walker*.

[157] *Walker v. Packer*, 827 S.W.2d 833, 842 (Tex. 1992) (orig. proceeding).

[158] *In re Prudential Ins. Co. of Am.*, 148 S.W.3d 124, 136 (Tex. 2004) (orig. proceeding).

[159] *In re Prudential Ins. Co. of Am.*, 148 S.W.3d 124, 136 (Tex. 2004) (orig. proceeding).

[160] *In re Prudential Ins. Co. of Am.*, 148 S.W.3d 124, 136 (Tex. 2004) (orig. proceeding).

[161] *In re Prudential Ins. Co. of Am.*, 148 S.W.3d 124, 136 (Tex. 2004) (orig. proceeding); *see In re Team Rocket, L.P.*, 256 S.W.3d 257, 262 (Tex. 2008) (orig. proceeding).

[162] *In re Prudential Ins. Co. of Am.*, 148 S.W.3d 124, 137 (Tex. 2004) (orig. proceeding).

[163] *In re Prudential Ins. Co. of Am.*, 148 S.W.3d 124, 136–37 (Tex. 2004) (orig. proceeding).

[164] *In re Prudential Ins. Co. of Am.*, 148 S.W.3d 124, 137 (Tex. 2004) (orig. proceeding); *see, e.g., In re John G. & Marie Stella Kenedy Mem'l Found.*, 315 S.W.3d 519, 523 (Tex. 2010) (orig. proceeding).

[165] *In re Prudential Ins. Co. of Am.*, 148 S.W.3d 124, 138 (Tex. 2004) (orig. proceeding).

[166] *In re Prudential Ins. Co. of Am.*, 148 S.W.3d 124, 138 (Tex. 2004) (orig. proceeding).

[167] *In re Prudential Ins. Co. of Am.*, 148 S.W.3d 124 (Tex. 2004) (orig. proceeding).

[168] See § 6-5 for examples.

[169] *See Tilton v. Marshall*, 925 S.W.2d 672, 682 (Tex. 1995) (orig. proceeding) (noting that, under *Walker*, relator must show that "the petition raises important issues for the state's jurisprudence"); *Walker v. Packer*, 827 S.W.2d 833, 839 n.7 (Tex. 1992) (orig. proceeding) ("[T]his Court will not grant mandamus relief unless we determine that the error is of such importance to the jurisprudence of the state as to require correction.").

[170] *See* Tex. R. App. P. 56.1.

[171] These factors are discussed further in Chapters 14 and 15.

[172] *In re Silver*, 540 S.W.3d 530, 538 (Tex. 2018) (orig. proceeding) (privilege); *In re Nat'l Lloyds Ins. Co.*, 532 S.W.3d 794, 803 (Tex. 2017) (orig. proceeding) (word-product protection); *In re Christus Santa Rosa Health Sys.*, 492 S.W.3d 276, 279 (Tex. 2016) (orig. proceeding) (privilege); *Walker v. Packer*, 827 S.W.2d 833, 843 (Tex. 1992) (orig. proceeding).

[173] *See In re Univ. of Tex. Health Ctr.*, 33 S.W.3d 822, 827 (Tex. 2000) (orig. proceeding); *Irving Healthcare Sys. v. Brooks*, 927 S.W.2d 12, 21 (Tex. 1996) (orig. proceeding); *Memorial Hosp.—The Woodlands v. McCown*, 927 S.W.2d 1, 12 (Tex. 1992) (orig. proceeding); *see*

also Huie v. DeShazo, 922 S.W.2d 920, 928 (Tex. 1996) (orig. proceeding); *Ford Motor Co. v. Leggat*, 904 S.W.2d 643, 649 (Tex. 1995) (orig. proceeding); *Walker v. Packer*, 827 S.W.2d 833, 843 (Tex. 1992) (orig. proceeding).

174 *Transamerican Natural Gas Corp. v. Flores*, 870 S.W.2d 10, 12 (Tex. 1994) (orig. proceeding).

175 *See, e.g.*, *In re Does*, 337 S.W.3d 862, 864–65 (Tex. 2011) (orig. proceeding) (per curiam); *see also In re Silver*, 540 S.W.3d 530, 538 (Tex. 2018) (orig. proceeding) (after concluding that Texas recognizes a patent agent–client privilege when a patent agent serves at the direction of an attorney or when a registered patent agent qualifies as a lawyer for purposes of Texas Rule of Evidence 503, vacating the order compelling disclosure and ordering the trial court to conduct an in camera inspection to determine whether the communications were privileged).

176 *In re Nat'l Lloyds Ins. Co.*, 449 S.W.3d 486, 488 (Tex. 2014) (orig. proceeding) (order compelling production of documents beyond the liberal bounds of the rules of procedure); *In re Ford Motor Co.*, 427 S.W.3d 396, 397–98 (Tex. 2014) (orig. proceeding) (order compelling disclosure of financial and business records of its engineering experts' employers was overbroad, fishing expedition); *In re Deere & Co.*, 299 S.W.3d 819, 821 (Tex. 2009) (orig. proceeding) (per curiam) (discovery not limited by a reasonable time period); *In re Jorden*, 249 S.W.3d 416, 419–20 (Tex. 2008) (orig. proceeding) (order compelling presuit depositions in violation of statute); *In re Allstate Cnty. Mut. Ins. Co.*, 227 S.W.3d 667, 669–70 (Tex. 2007) (orig. proceeding) (observing that whether a request for discovery is overbroad is distinct from whether it is burdensome or harassing, and holding that "[o]verbroad requests for irrelevant information are improper whether they are burdensome or not"); *In re E.I. DuPont de Nemours & Co.*, 136 S.W.3d 218, 223 (Tex. 2004) (orig. proceeding); *In re CSX Corp.*, 124 S.W.3d 149, 152 (Tex. 2003) (orig. proceeding) ("Discovery orders requiring production from an unreasonably long period . . . are impermissibly overbroad."); *In re Am. Optical Corp.*, 988 S.W.2d 711, 713 (Tex. 1998) (orig. proceeding) (concluding that a discovery order was overly broad by requiring production of "virtually all documents regarding its products for a fifty-year period").

177 *In re Weekley Homes, L.P.*, 295 S.W.3d 309, 322 (Tex. 2009) (orig. proceeding) (mandamus relief is available to cure order compelling production beyond permissible bounds of discovery when appellate court cannot otherwise cure the error, such as when the order compels direct access to an opponent's electronic storage device).

178 *See In re N. Cypress Med. Ctr. Operating Co., Ltd.*, No. 16-0851, 2018 WL 1974376, at *2 (Tex. Apr. 27, 2018) (orig. proceeding), *reh'g denied* (Nov. 16, 2018); *In re CSX Corp.*, 124 S.W.3d 149, 152 (Tex. 2003) (orig. proceeding); *In re Am. Optical Corp.*, 988 S.W.2d 711, 713 (Tex. 1998) (orig. proceeding); *In re Colonial Pipeline Co.*, 968 S.W.2d 938, 942–43 (Tex. 1998) (orig. proceeding); *K Mart Corp. v. Sanderson*, 937 S.W.2d 429, 431–32 (Tex. 1996) (orig. proceeding); *Texaco, Inc. v. Sanderson*, 898 S.W.2d 813, 815 (Tex. 1995) (orig. proceeding); *Dillard Dep't Stores, Inc. v. Hall*, 909 S.W.2d 491, 492 (Tex. 1995) (orig. proceeding); *Walker v. Packer*, 827 S.W.2d 833, 843 (Tex. 1992) (orig. proceeding); *Gen. Motors Corp. v. Lawrence*, 651 S.W.2d 732, 734 (Tex. 1983) (orig. proceeding).

179 *In re State Farm Lloyds*, 520 S.W.3d 595, 604 (Tex. 2017) (orig. proceeding) (for electronically stored information (ESI), establishing the factors to be assessed on a case-by-case basis in performing balancing for proportionality inquiry).

180 *In re Alford Chevrolet-Geo*, 997 S.W.2d 173, 181 (Tex. 1999) (orig. proceeding) ("A party resisting discovery, however, cannot simply make conclusory allegations that the requested discovery is unduly burdensome or unnecessarily harassing. The party must produce some evidence supporting its request for a protective order.").

181 *See, e.g.*, *In re Shipman*, 540 S.W.3d 562, 566 (Tex. 2018) (orig. proceeding) ("'Intrusive discovery measures—such as ordering direct access to an opponent's electronic storage device—require, at a minimum, that the benefits of the discovery measure outweigh the burden imposed upon the discovered party.' *In re Weekley Homes, L.P.*, 295 S.W.3d 309, 322

(Tex. 2009) (orig. proceeding) (citing Tex. R. Civ. P. 196.4, 192.4). 'Providing access to information by ordering examination of a party's electronic storage device is particularly intrusive and should be generally discouraged, just as permitting open access to a party's file cabinets for general perusal would be.' *In re Weekley Homes, L.P.,* 295 S.W.3d 309, 317 (Tex. 2009).").

182 *See In re Weekley Homes, L.P.*, 295 S.W.3d 309, 322 (Tex. 2009) (orig. proceeding).

183 *In re Alcatel USA, Inc.*, 11 S.W.3d 173, 176 (Tex. 2000) (orig. proceeding) (agreeing with the court of appeals' issuance of mandamus to stop apex depositions); *Crown Cent. Petroleum Corp. v. Garcia*, 904 S.W.2d 125, 128 (Tex. 1995) (orig. proceeding) (denying mandamus without prejudice so that the trial court could reconsider its order in light of guidelines for apex depositions articulated in opinion); *see also In re BP Prod. N. Am., Inc.*, 244 S.W.3d 840, 848–49 (Tex. 2008) (orig. proceeding) (reviewing by mandamus order refusing to enforce Rule 11 agreement concerning an apex deposition, and concluding that the benefits outweigh the detriments of mandamus review because delaying review until appeal would defeat the purpose of the discovery agreement and the strong public policy encouraging parties to resolve their discovery disputes without court intervention).

184 *Walker v. Packer*, 827 S.W.2d 833, 843 (Tex. 1992) (orig. proceeding); *see In re Bridgestone/Firestone, Inc.*, 106 S.W.3d 730, 734 (Tex. 2003) (orig. proceeding); *In re Cont'l Gen. Tire, Inc.*, 979 S.W.2d 609, 615 (Tex. 1998) (orig. proceeding); *see also In re M-I L.L.C.*, No. 14-1045 (Tex. Jan. 13, 2016), *available at* http://www.texasbarcle.com/CLE/SCPlayer5.asp?sCaseNo=14-1045&bLive=&k=&T= (oral argument held in petition for writ of mandamus reviewing issue of first impression to set parameters for how the recently enacted Texas Uniform Trade Secrets Act can be used to keep rival and opposing party in trade-secrets action out of the courtroom during a key trade-secrets hearing).

185 *See In re Bay Area Citizens Against Lawsuit Abuse*, 982 S.W.2d 371, 375 (Tex. 2000) (orig. proceeding) ("When a discovery order violates First Amendment rights, the party seeking mandamus generally has no adequate remedy by appeal."); *see, e.g. In re Doe*, 444 S.W.3d 603, 604 (Tex. 2014) (orig. proceeding) (reviewing order granting corporation's request seeking to depose Internet host of Relator's blog as part of pre-suit discovery to acquire relator's identity and investigate potential libel and business disparagement claims).

186 *Hall v. Lawlis*, 907 S.W.2d 493, 495 (Tex. 1995) (orig. proceeding).

187 *See TransAm. Natural Gas Corp. v. Powell*, 811 S.W.2d 913, 919 (Tex. 1991) (orig. proceeding); *see also Chrysler Corp. v. Blackmon*, 841 S.W.2d 844, 849 (Tex. 1992) (orig. proceeding); *Walker v. Packer*, 827 S.W.2d 833, 843 (Tex. 1992) (orig. proceeding).

188 *TransAm. Natural Gas Corp. v. Powell*, 811 S.W.2d 913, 919 (Tex. 1991) (orig. proceeding).

189 *See, e.g., In re Garza*, 544 S.W.3d 836, 840, 843 (Tex. 2018) (orig. proceeding) (granting mandamus to set aside discovery sanctions order excluding testimony of medical provider and medical records where the excluded evidence pertained to a significant component of plaintiff's damages claim and thus significantly compromised that claim).

190 *Braden v. Downey*, 811 S.W.2d 922, 929 (Tex. 1991) (orig. proceeding).

191 *Braden v. Downey*, 811 S.W.2d 922, 929 (Tex. 1991) (orig. proceeding).

192 *In re Ford Motor Co.*, 988 S.W.2d 714, 722–23 (Tex. 1998) (orig. proceeding).

193 *In re Ford Motor Co.*, 988 S.W.2d 714, 722 (Tex. 1998) (orig. proceeding).

194 *In re Ford Motor Co.*, 988 S.W.2d 714, 722 (Tex. 1998) (orig. proceeding).

195 *Walker v. Packer*, 827 S.W.2d 833, 843 (Tex. 1992) (orig. proceeding).

196 *Walker v. Packer*, 827 S.W.2d 833, 843 (Tex. 1992) (orig. proceeding); *see also In re Colonial Pipeline Co.*, 968 S.W.2d 938, 942 (Tex. 1998) (orig. proceeding) (issuing mandamus directing trial court to vacate order abating discovery from all but 10 plaintiffs); *General Motors Corp. v. Tanner*, 892 S.W.2d 862, 864 (Tex. 1995) (orig. proceeding) (issuing mandamus directing trial court to allow defendant to examine allegedly defective part with

electron microscope); *Able Supply Co. v. Moye*, 898 S.W.2d 766, 771–72 (Tex. 1995) (orig. proceeding) (issuing mandamus directing trial court to compel plaintiffs to supplement interrogatory answer requesting identification of physicians who had attributed any plaintiff's alleged injury to specific product manufactured or supplied by any defendant). *Cf. Polaris Inc. Mgmt. Corp. v. Abascal*, 892 S.W.2d 860, 862 (Tex. 1995) (orig. proceeding) (holding that trial court's abatement of discovery did not go to heart of defendant's case).

197 *In re Allied Chem. Co.*, 227 S.W.3d 652, 658 (Tex. 2007) (orig. proceeding) (issuing mandamus when "the burden of making 30 defendants prepare in the dark for 1,900 claims is far out of proportion to the benefit of giving the plaintiffs more time (after five years) to decide who or what injured them"); *Able Supply Co. v. Moye*, 898 S.W.2d 766, 770 (Tex. 1995) (orig. proceeding) (granting mandamus to prevent monumental waste of judicial resources when the plaintiffs' intention—to withhold discovery responses until shortly before trial—meant the defendants could not prepare a viable defense).

198 *See Walker v. Packer*, 827 S.W.2d 833, 844 (Tex. 1992) (orig. proceeding).

199 *See Walker v. Packer*, 827 S.W.2d 833, 844 (Tex. 1992) (orig. proceeding).

200 *Remington Arms Co. v. Canales*, 837 S.W.2d 624, 625 (Tex. 1992) (orig. proceeding).

201 *Remington Arms Co. v. Canales*, 837 S.W.2d 624, 625 (Tex. 1992) (orig. proceeding) (citing *Alvarado v. Farah Mfg. Co.*, 830 S.W.2d 911, 915 (Tex. 1992)).

202 *In re Entergy Corp.*, 142 S.W.3d 316, 321–22 (Tex. 2004) (orig. proceeding); *In re State Bar of Tex.*, 113 S.W.3d 730, 734 (Tex. 2003) (orig. proceeding); *In re SWEPI, L.P.*, 85 S.W.3d 800, 807–08 (Tex. 2002) (orig. proceeding).

203 Tex. Civ. Prac. & Rem. Code § 15.0642; *see In re Fisher*, 433 S.W.3d 523, 528–29 (Tex. 2014) (orig. proceeding); *In re Tex. Dep't Transp.*, 218 S.W.3d 74, 76 (Tex. 2007) (orig. proceeding); *In re Tex. Ass'n of Sch. Bds., Inc.*, 169 S.W.3d 653, 656 (Tex. 2005) (orig. proceeding); *In re Mo. Pac. R.R.*, 998 S.W.2d 212 (Tex. 1999) (orig. proceeding); *In re Cont'l Airlines, Inc.*, 988 S.W.2d 733, 735 (Tex. 1998) (orig. proceeding).

204 *In re AIU Ins. Co.*, 148 S.W.3d 109, 115 (Tex. 2004) (orig. proceeding).

205 *In re AIU Ins. Co.*, 148 S.W.3d 109, 117–18 (Tex. 2004) (orig. proceeding).

206 *In re Prudential Ins. Co. of Am.*, 148 S.W.3d 124, 138–39 (Tex. 2004) (orig. proceeding).

207 *In re Prudential Ins. Co. of Am.*, 148 S.W.3d 124, 138 (Tex. 2004) (orig. proceeding).

208 *In re Mahindra, USA Inc.*, 549 S.W.3d 541, 545 (Tex. 2018) (orig. proceeding); *see In re Oceanografia, S.A. de C.V.*, 494 S.W.3d 728, 732 (Tex. 2016) (orig. proceeding) (under Tex. Civ. Prac. & Rem. Code § 51.014(b)); *In re Ford Motor Co.*, 442 S.W.3d 265, 269 (Tex. 2014) (orig. proceeding); *In re ENSCO Offshore Int'l Co.*, 311 S.W.3d 921, 923 (Tex. 2010) (orig. proceeding); *In re Gen. Elec. Co.*, 271 S.W.3d 681, 685, 694 (Tex. 2008) (orig. proceeding); *In re Pirelli Tire, L.L.C.*, 247 S.W.3d 670, 676 (Tex. 2007) (orig. proceeding); *see also In re Bridgestone Americas Tire Operations L.L.C.*, 459 S.W.3d 565 (Tex. 2015) (orig. proceeding) (granting mandamus relief from order denying motion to dismiss for forum non conveniens).

209 *See* Tex. Civ. Prac. & Rem. Code § 51.014(a)(4).

210 Tex. R. Civ. P. 680.

211 *See In re Office of Attorney Gen.*, 257 S.W.3d 695, 697–98 (Tex. 2008) (orig. proceeding); *In re TNRCC*, 85 S.W.3d 201, 207 (Tex. 2002) (orig. proceeding).

212 *In re Tex Dep't of Criminal Justice*, No. 14-0243 (Tex. May 16, 2014) (dismissing as moot mandamus petition that sought review of a TRO because the TRO had expired).

213 *Ho v. Univ. of Tex. at Arlington*, 984 S.W.2d 672, 693–94 (Tex. App.—Amarillo 1998, pet. denied) (citing *Clanton v. Clark*, 639 S.W.2d 929, 931 (Tex. 1982); Tex. R. Civ. P. 245).

214 *In re Elliott*, No. 06-10-00101-CR, 2010 WL 2683150, at *2 (Tex. App.—Texarkana July 7, 2010, orig. proceeding) (mem. op.).

215 *General Motors Corp. v. Gayle*, 951 S.W.2d 469, 476 (Tex. 1997) (orig. proceeding).

[216] *In re Union Pac. Res.*, 969 S.W.2d 427, 428 (Tex. 1998) (orig. proceeding); *Mitchell Energy Corp. v. Ashworth*, 943 S.W.2d 426, 427 (Tex. 1997) (orig. proceeding).

[217] *In re Prudential Ins. Co. of Am.*, 148 S.W.3d 124 (Tex. 2004) (orig. proceeding).

[218] *In re McKee*, 248 S.W.3d 164, 165 (Tex. 2007) (orig. proceeding).

[219] *In re Sanders*, 153 S.W.3d 54, 56 (Tex. 2004) (orig. proceeding); *In re Epic Holdings, Inc.*, 985 S.W.2d 41, 52 (Tex. 1998) (orig. proceeding); *NCNB Tex. Nat'l Bank v. Coker*, 765 S.W.2d 398, 400 (Tex. 1989) (orig. proceeding).

[220] *In re Cerberus Capital Mgmt., L.P.*, 164 S.W.3d 379, 382 (Tex. 2005) (orig. proceeding) (per curiam).

[221] *In re Nitla S.A. de C.V.*, 92 S.W.3d 419, 422 (Tex. 2002) (orig. proceeding).

[222] *See In re Garcia*, No. 13-12-00440-CV, 2012 WL 3792112, at *3 (Tex. App.—Corpus Christi Aug. 31, 2012, orig. proceeding [mand. denied]) (mem. op.).

[223] *In re Columbia Valley Healthcare Sys., L.P.*, 320 S.W.3d 819, 823 n.2 (Tex. 2010) (orig. proceeding); *In re Basco*, 212 S.W.3d 637, 638 (Tex. 2007) (orig. proceeding); *NCNB Tex. Nat'l Bank v. Coker*, 765 S.W.2d 398, 400 (Tex. 1989) (orig. proceeding); *see In re Thetford*, No. 02-17-00182-CV, 2017 WL 2590576, at *1 (Tex. App.—Fort Worth June 15, 2017, orig. proceeding [mand. pending]), *argument granted on pet. for writ of mandamus* (No. 17-0634, argued Oct. 10, 2018).

[224] *In re Turner*, 542 S.W.3d 553, 555 (Tex. 2017) (orig. proceeding) ("'Mandamus is available where a motion to disqualify is inappropriately denied as there is no adequate remedy on appeal.'" (quoting *In re Columbia Valley Healthcare Sys., L.P.*, 320 S.W.3d 819, 824 n.2 (Tex. 2010) (orig. proceeding))); *Nat'l Med. Enters., Inc. v. Godbey*, 924 S.W.2d 123, 133 (Tex. 1996) (orig. proceeding).

[225] *In re Van Waters & Rogers, Inc.*, 145 S.W.3d 203, 206 (Tex. 2004) (orig. proceeding) (reviewing order consolidating 20 cases for trial in mass tort case); *In re Gulf Coast Bus. Dev. Corp.*, 247 S.W.3d 787, 794 (Tex. App.—Dallas 2008, orig. proceeding); *Crestway Care Ctr., Inc. v. Berchelmann*, 945 S.W.2d 872, 873–74 (Tex. App.—San Antonio 1997, orig. proceeding); *see also In re Bristol-Myers Squibb Co.*, 975 S.W.2d 601 (Tex. 1998) (orig. proceeding) (declining to grant mandamus because the record was not sufficiently developed for court to determine if trial court abused its discretion in consolidating for trial the claims of a limited number of breast implant plaintiffs); *In re Ethyl Corp.*, 975 S.W.2d 606 (Tex. 1998) (orig. proceeding) (same, but in asbestos litigation).

[226] *In re Greater Houston Orthopedic Specialists, Inc.*, 295 S.W.3d 323, 325 (Tex. 2009) (orig. proceeding).

[227] *General Motors Corp. v. Gayle*, 951 S.W.2d 469 (Tex. 1997) (orig. proceeding).

[228] *General Motors Corp. v. Gayle*, 951 S.W.2d 469, 477 (Tex. 1997) (orig. proceeding).

[229] *See* Tex. R. Civ. P. 76a.

[230] *In re Samsung Telecommc'ns of Am., Inc.*, Nos. 05-99-01949-CV & 05-99-01960-CV, 1999 WL 1081387, at *1 (Tex. App.—Dallas Dec. 2, 1999, orig. proceeding) (not designated for publication).

[231] *Amis v. Ashworth*, 802 S.W.2d 379, 382–83 (Tex. App.—Tyler 1990, orig. proceeding).

[232] *In re Long*, 984 S.W.2d 623, 625 (Tex. 1998) (orig. proceeding); *see also Rosser v. Squier*, 902 S.W.2d 962, 962 (Tex. 1995) (orig. proceeding).

[233] *In re Coppola*, 535 S.W.3d 506, 509–10 (Tex. 2017) (orig. proceeding) (holding that, "ordinarily, a relator need only establish a trial court's abuse of discretion to demonstrate entitlement to mandamus relief with regard to a trial court's denial of a timely filed [Texas Civil Practice & Remedies Code] section 33.004(a) motion").

[234] *In re Coppola*, 535 S.W.3d 506, 509 (Tex. 2017) (orig. proceeding); *see In re McAllen Med. Ctr., Inc.*, 275 S.W.3d 458, 465 (Tex. 2008) (orig. proceeding) ("The most frequent use we

have made of mandamus relief involves cases in which the very act of proceeding to trial—regardless of the outcome—would defeat the substantive right involved.").

235 *In re Dawson*, 550 S.W.3d 625, 630 (Tex. 2018) (orig. proceeding) (extending *In re Coppola* to review by mandamus a trial court's grant of a motion under Texas Civil Practice & Remedies Code section 33.004(d) to designate a responsible third party, explaining that the defendant sought "to protect her right . . . to not have to try her case against an empty chair"); see *In re CVR Energy, Inc.*, 500 S.W.3d 67, 73 (Tex. App. 2016) (describing section 33.004(d) as a "procedural safeguard[] that prevent[s] a defendant from undercutting the plaintiff's case by belatedly pointing its finger at a time-barred responsible third party against whom the plaintiff has no possibility of recovery" (internal quotations omitted)).

236 *In re Red Dot Bldg. Sys., Inc.*, 504 S.W.3d 320, 322 (Tex. 2016) (orig. proceeding); *In re J.B. Hunt Transport, Inc.*, 492 S.W.3d 287, 299–300 (Tex. 2016) (orig. proceeding).

237 *In re McAllen Med. Ctr., Inc.*, 275 S.W.3d 458, 465 (Tex. 2008) (orig. proceeding).

238 *In re McAllen Med. Ctr., Inc.*, 275 S.W.3d 458, 465–66 (Tex. 2008) (orig. proceeding).

239 *In re United States Auto. Ass'n*, 307 S.W.3d 299, 314 (Tex. 2010) (orig. proceeding).

240 *In re United States Auto. Ass'n*, 307 S.W.3d 299, 314 (Tex. 2010) (orig. proceeding).

241 *In re United States Auto. Ass'n*, 307 S.W.3d 299, 314 (Tex. 2010) (orig. proceeding).

242 *In re United States Auto. Ass'n*, 307 S.W.3d 299, 314 (Tex. 2010) (orig. proceeding).

243 *In re United States Auto. Ass'n*, 307 S.W.3d 299, 314 (Tex. 2010) (orig. proceeding).

244 *In re United States Auto. Ass'n*, 307 S.W.3d 299, 314 (Tex. 2010) (orig. proceeding); *see In re McAllen Med. Ctr., Inc.*, 275 S.W.3d 458, 465 (Tex. 2008) (orig. proceeding).

245 *In re Prudential Ins. Co. of Am.*, 148 S.W.3d 124 (Tex. 2004) (orig. proceeding).

246 *Tilton v. Marshall*, 925 S.W.2d 672 (Tex. 1996) (orig. proceeding).

247 *Tilton v. Marshall*, 925 S.W.2d 672, 695 (Tex. 1996) (orig. proceeding) (Enoch, J., dissenting).

248 *Tilton v. Marshall*, 925 S.W.2d 672, 675 (Tex. 1996) (orig. proceeding).

249 *Tilton v. Marshall*, 925 S.W.2d 672, 681 (Tex. 1996) (orig. proceeding).

250 *Tilton v. Marshall*, 925 S.W.2d 672, 682 (Tex. 1996) (orig. proceeding).

251 *Tilton v. Marshall*, 925 S.W.2d 672, 682 (Tex. 1996) (orig. proceeding) (citations omitted).

252 *In re Columbia Med. Ctr.*, 290 S.W.3d 204, 212–13 (Tex. 2009) (orig. proceeding).

253 *In re Columbia Med. Ctr.*, 290 S.W.3d 204, 212–13 (Tex. 2009) (orig. proceeding).

254 *In re Toyota Motor Sales, U.S.A., Inc.*, 407 S.W.3d 746, 758 (Tex. 2013) (orig. proceeding) (permitting merits-based mandamus review of reasons articulated in new trial order).

255 *In re Toyota Motor Sales, U.S.A., Inc.*, 407 S.W.3d 746, 755–59 (Tex. 2013) (orig. proceeding) ("[I]t would make little sense to conclude now that the correctness or validity of the orders' articulated reasons cannot also be evaluated. To deny merits-based review would mean that a trial court could set aside a verdict for reasons that are unsupported by the law or the evidence, as long as those reasons are facially valid." (citing *In re United Scaffolding, Inc.*, 377 S.W.3d 685 (Tex. 2012) (orig. proceeding))); *see, e.g., In re Davenport*, 522 S.W.3d 452, 456 (Tex. 2017) (reviewing by mandamus the reasons for the trial court's new trial order that had turned on the construction of an attorney-fee agreement).

256 *In re Dickason*, 987 S.W.3d 570, 571 (Tex. 1998) (orig. proceeding).

257 *In re Davenport*, 522 S.W.3d 452, 456 (Tex. 2017) (orig. proceeding).

258 *See, e.g., In re Whataburger Rests. LP*, 429 S.W.3d 597, 598–99 (Tex. 2014) (orig. proceeding) (reviewing the trial court's grant of a motion for new trial based on a juror's failure to disclose information during pre-trial questioning); *In re Health Care Unlimited, Inc.*, 429 S.W.3d 600, 601–02 (Tex. 2014) (orig. proceeding) (reviewing the trial court's grant of a motion for new trial based on juror communications with a party's representative).

259 *In re Elizondo,* 544 S.W.3d 824, 829 (Tex. 2018) (orig. proceeding) (reviewing void order that was signed after plenary power expired and that attempted to amend final judgment containing *Lehmann* language to correct judicial error by removing the finality language); *In re Vaishangi, Inc.*, 442 S.W.3d 256, 260–61 (Tex. 2014) (orig. proceeding) (reviewing whether the trial court had jurisdiction to enforce a Rule 11 agreement nearly one year after the case was dismissed); *In re Daredia,* 317 S.W.3d 247, 250 (Tex. 2010) (orig. proceeding) (order granting default judgment after expiration of plenary power); *In re Sw. Bell Tel. Co.*, 35 S.W.3d 602, 605 (Tex. 2000) (orig. proceeding) (order vacating venue transfer order after expiration of plenary power); *In re Dickason*, 987 S.W.3d 570, 571 (Tex. 1998) (orig. proceeding) (order granting new trial after expiration of plenary power); *see also In re John G. & Stella Kenedy Mem'l Found.*, 315 S.W.3d 519, 522 (Tex. 2010) (orig. proceeding) (exhumation order issued by probate court lacking jurisdiction was void and subject to mandamus); *In re Discount Rental, Inc.*, 216 S.W.3d 831, 832 (Tex. 2007) (orig. proceeding) (order to sell property to satisfy a void judgment can be reviewed and corrected by mandamus).

260 *In re Sw. Bell Tel. Co.*, 35 S.W.3d 602, 605 (Tex. 2000) (orig. proceeding); *In re Dickason*, 987 S.W.3d 570, 571 (Tex. 1998) (orig. proceeding).

261 *In re Accident Fund Gen. Ins. Co.*, 543 S.W.3d 750, 754–55 (Tex. 2017) (orig. proceeding) ("Because the Division has exclusive jurisdiction over Sayaz's claims against Accident Fund and Sayaz did not exhaust administrative remedies through the workers' compensation system before filing suit, allowing those claims to proceed in the trial court would disrupt the orderly process of government. Thus, mandamus relief for Accident Fund is appropriate."); *In re Crawford & Co.*, 458 S.W.3d 920, 928 (Tex. 2015) (orig. proceeding) (granting mandamus "[b]ecause the . . . claims arise out of [the defendant]'s investigation, handling, and settling of workers' compensation claims, they fall within the Division [of Workers' Compensation]'s exclusive jurisdiction and the Act provides the sole process and remedies for those claims. Because the Johnsons failed to exhaust their administrative remedies under the Act prior to filing this action, the trial court lacked jurisdiction and should have dismissed it."); *In re Sw. Bell Tel. Co.*, 235 S.W.3d 619, 624 (Tex. 2007) (orig. proceeding) (granting mandamus to require dismissal of claims over which Public Utility Commission had exclusive jurisdiction because "[a]llowing the trial court to proceed if the PUC has exclusive jurisdiction would disrupt the orderly processes of government"); *In re Entergy Corp.*, 142 S.W.3d 316, 321 (Tex. 2004) (orig. proceeding) (same).

CHAPTER 7

The Record

7-1 Introduction

The appellate record consists of the Clerk's Record and, if necessary to the appeal, the Reporter's Record.[1]

The appellate record should include the following:

- Everything needed to show that the court of appeals has jurisdiction;
- For the appellant: everything needed to show a trial court decision or action that constitutes reversible error; and
- For the appellee: everything needed to (1) show that no error occurred; (2) show waiver or that any errors are harmless; and (3) support any cross-points.

7-2 The Clerk's Record

7-2:1 What Is the Clerk's Record?

The Clerk's Record contains the documents that have been filed in the case and designated by the parties for purposes of appeal.

7-2:1.1 Required Contents

Unless the parties agree otherwise,[2] the Clerk's Record in all civil cases must include:

(1) all pleadings on which any trial was held;

(2) the trial court's docket sheet;

(3) the court's charge and the jury verdict, or the court's findings of fact and conclusions of law;

(4) the trial court's judgment or other order being appealed;

(5) any request for findings of fact and conclusions of law, any post-judgment motions, and the trial court's order on such motions;

(6) the notice of appeal;

(7) any formal bill of exceptions;

(8) any request for a Reporter's Record, including any statement of points or issues under Rule 34.6(c) (governing partial Reporter's Records);

(9) any request for preparation of the Clerk's Record;

(10) certified bill of costs, including the cost of preparing the Clerk's Record, showing credits for payments made; and

(11) any additional items that a party designates under Rule 34.5(b) to have included in the record.[3]

7-2:1.2 Additional Items

At any time before the Clerk's Record is prepared, any party may file a designation of additional items for inclusion in the Clerk's Record with the trial court clerk.[4]

The designation must be specific enough to enable the clerk to "readily identify" the item.[5] To avoid confusion, the designation should track the name of the document as closely as possible and provide the date of filing or signature. The clerk is directed to ignore general designations, such as "all papers filed in this cause."[6]

7-2:1.3 Agreed Clerk's Record

Rule 34.5 permits the parties to vary the Clerk's Record from the standard contents by agreeing to the items to be included in it. The court of appeals will presume the agreed Clerk's Record contains "all evidence and filings relevant to the appeal."[7]

7-2:1.4 Trial and Hearing Exhibits

Exhibits admitted at a trial or hearing and filed with the trial court clerk are not part of the Clerk's Record. Instead, the court reporter includes them as part of the Reporter's Record.[8]

7-2:1.5 Form

The following is the format for the Clerk's Record, whether electronic or paper:

- start each new document on a new page;
- include the date of filing on each document;
- arrange in ascending chronological order, by date of filing or occurrence;
- use consecutive numbering regardless of the number of volumes;
- place each page number at the bottom of each page; and
- as far as practicable, include the date of signing by the judge on each order and judgment.[9]

A paper Clerk's Record must bind the documents together in one or more volumes, include no more than 500 pages in each volume, include only one-sided copies of documents, and number volumes sequentially.[10]

A supplemental Clerk's Record must also follow this form.[11]

7-2:1.6 Electronic Filing

Absent permission from the appellate court to file the record in paper form, the clerk of a court subject to mandatory civil electronic filing must file the Clerk's Record electronically.

Among other requirements, an electronically filed Clerk's Record must be in text-searchable Portable Document Format (PDF), have electronic bookmarks to mark the first page of each document, and be limited in size to 100 MB or less, if possible, for each computer file.[12]

7-2:1.7 Local Rules and Guidelines

The Clerk's Record must also comply with any local rules and guidelines of the particular court of appeals.

7-2:2 Triggering the Clerk's Duty to Prepare the Clerk's Record

When a party files a notice of appeal, and the party responsible for paying for the preparation of the clerk's record has paid the fee or made satisfactory arrangements with the clerk to pay the fee,[13] the clerk of the trial court is required to prepare and file the Clerk's Record with the clerk of the appellate court.[14]

If a trial court clerk refuses to prepare the Clerk's Record after receiving a proper request, mandamus relief may be available from the court of appeals.[15]

7-2:3 Deadlines

7-2:3.1 Generally

The trial and appellate courts are jointly responsible for ensuring that the appellate record is timely filed.[16] In an ordinary appeal, the Clerk's Record must be filed no later than 60 days after the judgment is signed.[17] If an extended appellate timetable applies due to certain post-judgment filings, the Clerk's Record is due 120 days after the judgment is signed.[18]

In accelerated appeals, the Clerk's Record must be filed no later than 10 days after the notice of appeal is filed.[19] However, Rule 28.1(e) provides an alternative by allowing the appellate court to hear an accelerated appeal on "the original papers forwarded by the trial court."[20] The "original papers" must be certified by the trial court clerk or attested to by counsel as being accurate.[21]

The rules for accelerated appeals also apply to permissive interlocutory appeals.[22]

In a restricted appeal, the record is due within 30 days after the notice of appeal has been filed.[23]

The deadlines for the Clerk's Record in accelerated and restricted appeals differ from a standard appeal. In these appeals, the clock begins to run when the notice of appeal is filed, rather than the signing of the judgment.

7-2:3.2 Extensions

Clerks have the duty to ensure the Clerk's Record is timely filed. There is no need for counsel to seek an extension of time for filing the Clerk's Record.

The court of appeals may extend the deadline for filing the record if requested by the trial court clerk.[24] No single extension may exceed 30 days for an ordinary or restricted appeal, or 10 days in an accelerated appeal.[25]

The appellate court must allow the appellate record to be filed late when the appellant was not the cause of the tardiness.[26] However, when the delay is caused by the appellant—for example, by failing to make arrangements to pay for the record—the court of appeals makes a discretionary decision whether to allow the Clerk's Record to be filed late.[27]

7-2:3.3 Late Filing

If a Clerk's Record is not timely filed, the appellate court must send a notice directing the trial court clerk to file the record within 30 days for an ordinary appeal or a restricted appeal, and within 10 days for an accelerated appeal.[28]

If the Clerk's Record is not filed within those deadlines, the appellate court clerk must refer the matter to the court of appeals for issuance of "whatever order appropriate to avoid further delay and to preserve the parties' rights."[29]

If the Clerk's Record is late because the appellant failed to pay or make arrangements to pay the fee for preparing the record, the court may dismiss the appeal for want of prosecution.[30] However, the court must give the appellant a reasonable opportunity to make or arrange for payment prior to dismissing the appeal.[31]

7-2:4 Paying for the Clerk's Record

7-2:4.1 Cost

By statute, trial court clerks currently may charge up to $1 per page for preparing the Clerk's Record.[32] Some clerks also charge an additional preparation fee.

7-2:4.2 Agreement for Payment

The clerk's responsibility to prepare and file the Clerk's Record does not arise until the appellant has filed a notice of appeal and paid the fee for the record or made arrangements for payment.[33] Thus, it is important to have a clear understanding with the trial court clerk regarding the financial arrangements.

7-2:5 Missing and Lost Documents

7-2:5.1 Pleadings Missing From Trial Court's File

If a pleading or document is missing from the trial court's file, the party wishing to include the document or item should try to locate a file-stamped copy. If one cannot be located, the party should attempt to resolve the issue with opposing counsel by agreeing to a copy of the document.

If a pleading has been lost or destroyed, the parties may submit an agreed copy to the trial court to be included in the Clerk's Record.[34] When the parties cannot agree on copies of missing items, the court of appeals or any party may ask the trial court to determine an accurate copy.[35]

7-2:5.2 Non-Replaceable Lost Items Needed for Appeal

When an item that is necessary to the appeal is lost and cannot be substituted or stipulated, a reversal of the entire case, or possibly the relevant part of the case, may result.[36]

7-2:6 Consequences of No Clerk's Record

When a document is not designated for inclusion in the Clerk's Record, any appellate complaint requiring that document cannot be reviewed, and the court of appeals will presume that the missing item supports the trial court's judgment.[37] As a result, the party urging error on appeal must ensure that the trial court clerk does not omit any designated items from the Clerk's Record.

If no Clerk's Record is filed, error cannot be demonstrated, and the case will either be dismissed or the judgment affirmed. A party may move to dismiss or affirm based on the absence of the Clerk's Record. The court may dismiss or affirm on its own initiative. However, the court must give the parties 10 days' notice prior to doing so.[38]

An appellee asserting cross-points to affirm the judgment on an alternative basis has the burden to make sure the Clerk's Record includes any necessary items to support appellate review of those points.[39]

7-2:7 Strategies for Bringing an Adequate Clerk's Record to the Court of Appeals

7-2:7.1 File Your Own Designation

Time for designation. Parties may designate additional items for the Clerk's Record any time before the record is prepared.[40] However, the court of appeals may not refuse to file the Clerk's Record or a supplemental Clerk's Record because of a party's failure to timely request additional items.[41]

7-2:7.1a Supplemental Designations

If items are overlooked in the original designation, any party, the trial court, or the court of appeals can request the trial court clerk to include the additional items in a supplemental Clerk's Record.[42] The courts of appeals are lenient about permitting supplementation of the Clerk's Record prior to submission of the case.[43] It is not uncommon for an appeal to include more than one supplemental Clerk's Record.

7-2:7.1b Items for Designation

Items that are not required to be included in the Clerk's Record but are needed to support challenges on appeal should be designated for inclusion. Every case varies, but examples of additional items to consider include:

- requests for admissions, responses to those requests, and deemed admissions;
- written stipulations;

- matters reflected only in superseded pleadings, such as a special appearance, plea in abatement, or special exceptions;
- pre-trial motions, such as motions for change of venue, continuance, or recusal;
- agreed statement of facts under Texas Rule of Civil Procedure 263;
- requests for findings of fact and conclusions of law, notices of past due findings and conclusions, and requests for amended findings and conclusions;
- written motions for instructed verdict and motions for entry of judgment n.o.v., and related orders;
- written objections to the judgment, motions to modify, correct and reform the judgment, and related orders;
- trial court motions and orders relating to filing a notice of appeal; and
- supersedeas bond.

7-2:7.1c Items Not Ordinarily Designated

Parties ordinarily should not designate:

- letters by counsel;
- letters from the trial court that do not constitute rulings;
- subpoenas;
- trial briefs; and
- discovery matters.

However, if these items may be important to the appeal, counsel should err on the side of inclusion. For instance, a party may wish to include a trial brief in the Clerk's Record to show that an argument was raised in the trial court, or to show that the opposing party maintained a different position in the trial court from its position on appeal.

7-2:7.1d Consequences of Unnecessary Designation

To the extent items included in the Clerk's Record are extraneous or irrelevant they are typically ignored by the court of appeals. However, the court has the authority to assess the costs of the unnecessary items on the party who requested their inclusion.[44]

7-2:7.1e Designate Agreed Statements of the Case for Inclusion

In the event the appeal proceeds on an agreed statement of the case in lieu of a Reporter's Record, the statement must be filed with the trial court clerk and included in the Clerk's Record.[45] Because the statement is not automatically included in the Clerk's Record, the appellant should be sure to designate it for the Clerk's Record.

7-2:7.2 Communication With the Clerk

Problems with the Clerk's Record often can be avoided by regularly communicating with the clerk to confirm that the record is being prepared and he or she is not having trouble locating any documents.

7-2:8 After the Clerk's Record Is Filed With the Court of Appeals

7-2:8.1 Review by Appellate Court Clerk

The clerk of the trial court sends (electronically or physically) the Clerk's Record to the court of appeals, not to the appellant. The clerk of the court of appeals then determines if the Clerk's Record was properly prepared.[46] If so, the clerk will endorse the date of receipt, file the record, and notify the parties of the filing.[47]

If the Clerk's Record was not properly prepared, the appellate court clerk will return it to the trial court clerk.[48] The appellate court clerk must specify the defects and instruct the trial court clerk to make the necessary corrections by a specified date.[49]

7-2:8.2 Promptly Review

Once the Clerk's Record is filed, promptly review it to make sure it is complete and contains all requested items. Attorneys of record in an appeal can obtain online access to most clerk's records through an "attorney portal," after registering with an attorney state bar number and email address.[50] Unsealed clerk's records are available through the portal. Non-PDF files like audio and video exhibits are not available and must be obtained through the clerk's office, as must sealed records.

If the record was submitted as a paper record, be aware that some courts do not allow counsel to remove a paper record from the building for copying but may allow counsel to bring a scanner and scan the record.

7-2:9 Inaccuracies in the Clerk's Record

7-2:9.1 Request Supplemental Clerk's Record

Items missing from the Clerk's Record can be included in a supplemental Clerk's Record, which becomes part of the appellate record.[51] The rules permit liberal supplementation.[52] If there is more than one supplemental Clerk's Record, the trial court will number the volumes of the Supplemental Record in the order in which they are filed.

7-2:9.2 No Time Limit

The rules do not impose a limit for requesting a supplemental Clerk's Record.[53] In fact, the rules prohibit a court of appeals from refusing to file a supplemental Clerk's Record based on a party's failure to include an item in an original request.[54]

7-3 The Reporter's Record

7-3:1 What Is the Reporter's Record?

A Reporter's Record includes the transcripts of hearings and trial proceedings, which can be either stenographically or electronically recorded.[55] The Reporter's Record also includes exhibits from hearings and trial proceedings.[56]

7-3:1.1 Contents

Typically, a court reporter creates either an electronic recording or contemporaneous handwritten or machine-aided stenographic notes of what is stated and by whom at court proceedings. Then, at the request of a party, the court reporter produces a transcript of the proceedings. The transcripts are forwarded to the appellate court, together with the exhibits, as the Reporter's Record.

When a court reporter uses electronic recording, certified copies of all tape recordings, designated exhibits, and logs prepared by the court reporter constitute the Reporter's Record.[57]

In the usual case, the Reporter's Record consists of the trial or hearing testimony of witnesses. But it can include transcripts of any court proceedings, including, for example: voir dire proceedings, arguments of counsel, oral motions, oral objections, oral rulings, oral agreements or stipulations between the parties, the reading of the charge to the jury, and offers of proof. The requests should be guided by an understanding that the appellate court cannot determine if an error occurred, an action should have been taken, or an argument was preserved if the relevant hearing and/or exhibits are not in the Reporter's Record.[58]

Exhibits are part of the Reporter's Record.[59] The court reporter receives the exhibits marked by the parties during hearings and trial, files them with the clerk of the court, and forwards copies of them to the court of appeals as part of the Reporter's Record.[60] If someone other than the trial court clerk has an original exhibit, the trial court or appellate court clerk may order that person to deliver the exhibit to the trial court clerk.[61]

The trial court or the court of appeals can order the original exhibits forwarded to the court of appeals for inspection.[62] A party may also request the appellate court to order an original exhibit from the trial court.[63]

7-3:1.2 Form

If recorded stenographically, the Reporter's Record must follow the electronic format of Section 8 of the Uniform Format Manual for Texas Reporters' Record.[64]

Among other requirements, the electronic format must duplicate, page by page, the record as it would have been filed in paper, be in text-searchable Portable Document Format (PDF), have electronic bookmarks in exhibit volumes to mark the first page of each exhibit document, and be limited in size to 100 MB or less, if possible, for each computer file.[65]

7-3:1.3 Electronic Filing

If the proceedings were recorded stenographically, the court reporter must file the reporter's record in the court of appeals via the Texas Appeals Management and E-filing System (TAMES), a records submission portal.[66] The format of the Reporter's Record must comply with the Uniform Format Manual For Texas Reporters' Records.[67] The manual includes specific rules for electronic format, any exhibits, and naming conventions. Sealed documents must be saved in a separate electronic file.[68]

7-3:1.4 Local Rules and Guidelines

The Reporter's Record must also comply with any local rules and guidelines of the particular court of appeals.[69]

7-3:2 Alternative to Reporter's Record: Agreed Statement of the Case

The parties may agree to a "brief statement of the case" in lieu of a Reporter's Record.[70] This agreed statement must be filed with the trial court clerk and forwarded to the appellate court as part of the Clerk's Record.[71] The appeal will then be decided on the agreed statement.

An agreed statement of the case may be appropriate when the controlling factual issues are undisputed and the core dispute is the legal effect of the undisputed facts. If proceeding on an agreed statement, the appellee should be sure that all facts needed to support the trial court's judgment are included in the stipulation, to avoid the case being reversed on factual-insufficiency grounds.

An agreed statement of facts is presumed to embrace every fact in the case and no other facts or findings may be presumed or inferred, except facts that are necessarily implied from those expressly stipulated.[72]

7-3:3 Requesting Reporter's Record

The appellant must make a written request to the official court reporter for preparation of the Reporter's Record, designating the particular proceedings and exhibits to be included.[73] The request must be sent to the court reporter with a copy filed in the trial court.[74]

The request must be made at or before the time for perfecting the appeal.[75]

The rules prohibit the court of appeals from refusing to file a Reporter's Record or supplemental Reporter's Record because of a failure to timely request it.[76]

7-3:4 Deadlines

7-3:4.1 Generally

In an ordinary appeal, the record must be filed in the appellate court within 60 days after the judgment is signed by the trial court.[77]

If an extended appellate timetable applies due to certain post-judgment filings, the Reporter's Record is due 120 days after the judgment is signed.[78]

The trigger for the deadlines in accelerated and restricted appeals is different than in an ordinary appeal. In those types of appeals, the timeline begins with the filing of the notice of appeal. In accelerated appeals, the record must be filed within 10 days after the notice of appeal has been filed.[79] With a restricted appeal, the record is due within 30 days after the notice of appeal has been filed.[80] Permissive interlocutory appeals are controlled by the same rules as accelerated appeals.[81]

7-3:4.2 Extensions

The court reporter may seek an extension of time from the court of appeals for filing the Reporter's Record.[82] No single extension should exceed 30 days for an ordinary or restricted appeal, or 10 days in an accelerated appeal,[83] but multiple extensions are regularly permitted.

7-3:4.3 Late Filing

If the Reporter's Record is not timely filed, the court of appeals must notify the court reporter that the record is late and request that the record be filed within 30 days for an ordinary appeal or restricted appeal and within 10 days for an accelerated appeal.[84]

If the Reporter's Record is not filed by the new deadline, the court of appeals may issue appropriate orders to avoid further delay and to preserve the parties' rights.

The appellate court must permit the record to be filed late when the delay is not the appellant's fault.[85] When it is appellant's fault, the court has the discretion to permit or disallow the filing of the Reporter's Record.[86] An appellant is at fault if he failed to request the preparation of the record, or failed to pay for it.[87] The court of appeals may not refuse a Reporter's Record or supplemental Reporter's Record based on an untimely request for its preparation.[88]

If the Reporter's Record is not filed due to the appellant's fault and the Clerk's Record has already been filed, the court of appeals may consider and decide those issues that do not require a Reporter's Record for decision.[89] But the court must first give the appellant notice and a reasonable opportunity to cure the problem.[90]

7-3:4.4 Compelling Court Reporter to Prepare the Reporter's Record

The court of appeals may issue any order necessary to ensure the timely filing of the Reporter's Record.[91] The court of appeals also may issue a writ of mandamus.[92] Although rare, contempt proceedings are also a possibility.[93]

7-3:5 Paying for the Reporter's Record

7-3:5.1 Cost

Generally the cost for the Reporter's Record is a per-page rate set by each court reporter. This can vary depending on the density of the proceeding, the technical or expert nature of the testimony, the number of exhibits, and the need to convert exhibits into searchable format.

A party dissatisfied with the cost of the Reporter's Record can file an objection with the trial court, which must then determine a reasonable fee.[94]

Ultimately, the costs of preparing the Clerk's Record and Reporter's Record may be taxed in the appellate judgment against the unsuccessful party on appeal,[95] or their surety on a supersedeas bond, if one was filed.[96] The court of appeals also has the discretion to assess costs against a party other than on the losing party when required by law or for good cause, or against a party who requested unnecessary items to be included in the record.[97]

7-3:5.2 Agreement for Payment

The court reporter is not responsible for preparing and filing the Reporter's Record until: (1) a notice of appeal is filed; (2) the appellant has requested preparation of the Reporter's Record; and (3) the appellant has paid the court reporter's fee[98] or made satisfactory arrangements to pay for it.[99]

There can be several court reporters in a case. If so, it may be necessary to communicate and make arrangements with more than one court reporter.

7-3:6 Consequences of Incomplete or Missing Reporter's Record

7-3:6.1 Omitted Evidence Presumed to Support Judgment

If the Reporter's Record is not filed or is incomplete, any omitted evidence is presumed to support the trial court's judgment.[100] However, issues of law still may be considered by the court of appeals in the absence of all or part of the Reporter's Record.[101]

Because exhibits admitted or tendered are also part of the Reporter's Record, the same rule applies. A missing exhibit may prevent the court of appeals from determining if reversible error occurred.

7-3:6.2 Reporter's Record Unavailable Through No Fault of Prejudiced Party

The presumption that missing evidence supports the judgment does not apply when the Reporter's Record is unavailable through no fault of the complaining party. Instead, an appellant is entitled to a remand for new trial if: (1) the appellant timely requested the Reporter's Record; (2) a significant exhibit or portion of the Reporter's Record is lost or destroyed, or inaudible, if it is an electronic recording; (3) the lost or destroyed portion is necessary to the appeal's resolution; and (4) the parties cannot agree on a complete Reporter's Record or the lost or destroyed exhibit cannot be replaced either by agreement of the parties or with a copy determined by the trial court to accurately duplicate the original exhibit with reasonable certainty.[102]

7-3:6.3 No Transcript Because of Court Reporter's Absence

A Reporter's Record cannot be prepared if the court reporter is not present for the hearing or trial. Unless excused through agreement of the parties, the court reporter is obligated to attend court sessions and make a complete record of the proceedings.[103]

To preserve a complaint that a court reporter failed to record proceedings, the complaining party must make a request in the trial court for a court reporter to appear and record the proceeding, and object on the record to the proceeding going forward without a court reporter.

As a practical matter, if no reporter is present to record the objection to the reporter's absence, counsel should immediately file a written objection, objecting to the proceeding going forward without a court reporter and seeking a continuance if one cannot be found. If necessary, handwrite the objection and request for a continuance, so that it can be filed immediately.[104] One way to avoid this situation is to call a few days before the proceeding to make sure a court reporter is scheduled to record it. It is not necessary to seek an agreed or reconstructed Reporter's Record to complain about a court reporter's failure to record a proceeding.[105]

7-3:6.4 Raising the Unavailability of All or Part of the Reporter's Record

The complaint of a missing Reporter's Record can be raised as a point of error in the brief to the court of appeals.[106] It also can be raised by filing a motion.[107]

In challenging the lack of a Reporter's Record, the complaining party should indicate the underlying grounds of error that require a Reporter's Record for proper review (e.g., a challenge to the sufficiency of the evidence, complaints regarding the admission or exclusion of evidence, waiver contentions).

7-3:7 Communicate With the Court Reporter

Regular communication with the court reporter to ensure the record is being prepared and the reporter is not having trouble locating exhibits can avoid delays in filing and inaccuracies in the content of the Reporter's Record.

7-3:8 After the Reporter's Record Is Filed With the Court of Appeals

7-3:8.1 Review by Appellate Court Clerk

Once the Reporter's Record is received from the court reporter, the court of appeals must determine if it complies with the rules.[108] If so, the clerk must endorse the date of receipt, file the record, and notify the parties that the Reporter's Record has been filed and the date of filing.[109]

If the Reporter's Record is defective, the court of appeals must endorse the record and return it to the court reporter with instructions to correct specified defects by a particular date.[110]

7-3:8.2 Promptly Review

Once the Reporter's Record is filed, promptly review it carefully to ensure it is complete and does not contain inaccuracies, particularly if it was electronically recorded. Attorneys of record in an appeal can obtain online access to most records through an "attorney portal," after registering with an attorney state bar number and email address.[111] Unsealed reporter's records are available through the portal. Non-PDF files like audio and video exhibits are not available and must be obtained through the clerk's office, as must sealed records.

A court reporter can usually provide the Reporter's Record to counsel in electronic format upon request or an electronic copy may be available upon request from the appellate clerk's office. If counsel plans to use a program such as Visionary or Case Notebook to review and annotate the record, counsel should take care to request an electronic copy in the proper format for the particular program.

7-3:9 Inaccuracies in the Reporter's Record

7-3:9.1 Attempt to Resolve Through Agreement

If there are inaccuracies in the Reporter's Record, attempt to resolve them by agreement with opposing counsel; otherwise, seek resolution by the trial court.[112] When the dispute over the accuracy occurs after the record already has been filed in the court of appeals, that court may submit the dispute to the trial court to resolve.[113] Once the trial court resolves the dispute, it must order the court reporter to conform the Reporter's Record, certify the amended version, and file the certified corrections in the appellate court.[114]

7-3:9.2 Request Supplemental Reporter's Record

If a proceeding or exhibit is missing from the Reporter's Record, the omission can be remedied by a supplemental Reporter's Record. The parties, the trial court, or the appellate court may request the court reporter to prepare, certify, and file a supplemental Reporter's Record.[115] The request must be done by letter.[116]

A supplemental Reporter's Record is not limited to curing omissions from an original request to the court reporter. If it becomes apparent while preparing a brief that there are additional transcripts or exhibits needed for the appeal, request that they be filed in a supplemental Reporter's Record.

7-3:10 Proceeding on a Partial Reporter's Record

To reduce the costs of the appellate record, an appellant may consider using a partial Reporter's Record.[117]

7-3:10.1 Presumed to Constitute Entire Record

Ordinarily, proceeding with an incomplete Reporter's Record gives rise to the presumption that all omitted evidence supports the trial court's judgment, which could make it difficult or impossible to demonstrate reversible error.[118] However, an appellant may proceed on a partial Reporter's Record and limit the appeal to specified points and issues by including in the request for the partial record the points or issues to be presented on appeal. The appellant will then be limited to those points or issues.[119] The Texas Supreme Court has indicated that substance should control over form, and the issues or points may be included either in the request for a partial Reporter's Record or in a separate document filed at the same time.[120]

If an appellant complies with Texas Rule of Appellate Procedure 34, the court of appeals must presume that the partial Reporter's Record is complete for purposes of the appeal.[121] The presumption permits a party to argue that error demonstrated in the record is reversible without the necessity of bringing forward the entire Reporter's Record.[122]

In many cases, the courts of appeals have strictly enforced the requirements for proceeding on a partial Reporter's Record,[123] and they will disregard points or issues that are not consistent with those stated in the designation.[124]

7-3:10.2 Legal or Factual Sufficiency

Even when the challenge on appeal is to the legal or factual sufficiency of the evidence, if a party properly designates pertinent portions of the Reporter's Record and includes the statement of issues and points on appeal, he can proceed on a partial Reporter's Record and enjoy the presumption that the record constitutes the entire record.[125]

7-3:10.3 Other Parties Not Limited to Partial Record

Proceeding on a partial Reporter's Record restricts the appeal to the points or issues presented in the request.[126] However, one party's decision to proceed on a partial Reporter's Record does not limit the points or issues of other parties to the appeal. Thus, any other party may designate additional transcripts and exhibits for inclusion in the Reporter's Record.[127] Cross or reply points may require a complete Reporter's Record.[128] As one court has explained:

> The purpose of Rule 34.6(c) is to protect an appellee from having to defend an appeal without parts of the record that support its defense. The statement of points or issues mandated by Rule 34.6(c) gives an appellee notice of the issues to be appealed, so that it can designate additional portions of the record that may be necessary for its case. . . . Absent such a specific statement [of points or issues], the Appellee is left to guess which additional portions of the evidence should be included in the statement of facts.[129]

Accordingly, all parties to the appeal have the opportunity to ensure that a sufficient record is brought forward that will support their points.

7-3:11 Agreed Appellate Record

The parties may agree on the contents of the appellate record by written stipulation filed with the trial court clerk. The stipulated record will be presumed by the court of appeals to contain "all evidence and filings relevant to the appeal."[130] Because of this presumption, take care in deciding the scope of the stipulation.

To request the portions to be included in the agreed record, the parties must comply with the procedures for requesting the Clerk's Record and the Reporter's Record.[131]

Notes

1 Tex. R. App. P. 34.1.

2 Tex. R. App. P. 34.2, 34.5(a).

3 Tex. R. App. P. 34.5(a).

4 Tex. R. App. P. 34.5(b)(1).

5 Tex. R. App. P. 34.5(b)(2).

6 Tex. R. App. P. 34.5(b)(2).

7 Tex. R. App. P. 34.2.

8 *See* Tex. R. App. P. 34.6(g); Tex. R. Civ. P. 75b(b).

9 Tex. R. App. P. 34.4 & Tex. R. App. P. App. C, Rule 1.1.

[10] Tex. R. App. P. App. C, Rule 1.3.

[11] Tex. R. App. P. App. C, Rule 1.4.

[12] Tex. R. App. P. App. C, Rule 1.2.

[13] A person unable to afford the costs of the appellate record can file a Statement of Inability to Afford Payment of Court Costs in the trial court. Tex. R. Civ. P. 145(a). Requirements for eligibility and the necessary steps to avoid being charged the fees for preparation of the appellate record are governed by Texas Rule of Civil Procedure 145. *See* Tex. R. App. P. 20.1(a).

[14] Tex. R. App. P. 35.3(a).

[15] *Click v. Tyra*, 867 S.W.2d 406, 408 (Tex. App.—Houston [14th Dist.] 1993, orig. proceeding).

[16] Tex. R. App. P. 35.3(c).

[17] Tex. R. App. P. 35.1.

[18] Tex. R. App. P. 35.1(a) (relying on Tex. R. App. P. 26.1(a)).

[19] Tex. R. App. P. 35.1(b).

[20] Tex. R. App. P. 28.1(e).

[21] Tex. R. App. P. 28.1(e).

[22] Tex. R. App. P. 28.3(k).

[23] Tex. R. App. P. 35.1(c).

[24] Tex. R. App. P. 35.3(c).

[25] Tex. R. App. P. 35.3(c).

[26] Tex. R. App. P. 35.3(c).

[27] Tex. R. App. P. 35.3(c).

[28] Tex. R. App. P. 37.3(a)(1).

[29] Tex. R. App. P. 37.3(a)(1).

[30] Tex. R. App. P. 37.3(b).

[31] Tex. R. App. P. 37.3(b).

[32] *See* Tex. Gov't Code § 51.318(b)(7).

[33] *See* Tex. R. App. P. 35.3(a).

[34] Tex. R. App. P. 34.5(e).

[35] Tex. R. App. P. 34.5(e).

[36] *See* Tex. R. App. P. 44.1 (explaining that trial court's acts or omissions are reversible error when they prevent an appellant from making a proper presentation of case to the court of appeals).

[37] *See, e.g., Pierson v. SMS Fin. II, L.L.C.*, 959 S.W.2d 343, 348 (Tex. App.—Texarkana 1998, no pet.) (when appellants challenged grant of summary judgment but failed to include a response to the motion for summary judgment, court had to presume that the missing response supported the judgment); *University of Tex. at Austin v. Hinton*, 822 S.W.2d 197, 202 (Tex. App.—Austin 1991, no writ) (appellate court could not find error in excluding testimony based on failure to supplement interrogatory answers when interrogatories and answers not included in record on appeal); *see also, e.g., Ahmed v. Sosa*, 514 S.W.3d 894, 896 (Tex. App.—Fort Worth 2017, no pet.) ("[I]t is axiomatic that we may not consider a document cited in a brief and attached as an appendix if it is not formally included in the record on appeal.").

[38] Tex. R. App. P. 42.3.

[39] *See, e.g., Sammons v. Elder*, 940 S.W.2d 276, 285 (Tex. App.—Waco 1997, no writ) (noting appellee's burden to bring forward a record to support cross-point); *see also* Tex. R. App. P. 38.2(b).

[40] Tex. R. App. P. 34.5(b)(1).

[41] Tex. R. App. P. 34.5(b)(4).

[42] Tex. R. App. P. 34.5(c).

[43] Tex. R. App. P. 34.5(c).

[44] Tex. R. App. P. 34.5(b)(3).

[45] Tex. R. App. P. 34.3.

[46] Tex. R. App. P. 37.2.

[47] Tex. R. App. P. 37.2.

[48] Tex. R. App. P. 37.2.

[49] Tex. R. App. P. 37.2.

[50] https://attorneyportal.txcourts.gov/Account/Login (last visited Feb. 10, 2019).

[51] Tex. R. App. P. 34.5(c)(3).

[52] Tex. R. App. P. 34.5(c).

[53] Tex. R. App. P. 34.5(c)

[54] Tex. R. App. P. 34.5(b)(4).

[55] Tex. R. App. P. 34.6(a).

[56] Tex. R. App. P. 34.6(a).

[57] Tex. R. App. P. 34.6(a)(2).

[58] *See, e.g., Michiana Easy Livin' Country, Inc. v. Holten*, 168 S.W.3d 777, 782–83 (Tex. 2005) (although pre-trial hearings are generally nonevidentiary, if trial court's order, proceeding's nature, or other indications show there was an evidentiary hearing, reporter's record is necessary to preserve error); *Mitchell v. Newton*, No. 02-15-00340-CV, 2016 WL 7010926, at *1 (Tex. App.—Fort Worth Dec. 1, 2016, no pet.) ("Without a reporter's record of the bench trial upon which to review Appellants' evidentiary-based arguments, we must presume that the evidence supports the trial court's judgment."); *In re Marriage of Spiegel*, 6 S.W.3d 643, 646 (Tex. App.—Amarillo 1999, no pet.) (without a reporter's record of temporary injunction hearing, "we do not know what, if any, evidence was presented to the trial court" and "the reporter's record is so pivotal to our review that its absence obligates us to presume that the missing evidence actually supported the trial court's ruling"); *Juarez v. United Parcel Serv. de Mexico S.A. de C.V.*, 933 S.W.2d 281, 283 (Tex.App.—Corpus Christi 1996, no writ) (when order on a special appearance referred to "other evidence" and there was no reporter's record, court presumed evidence supported order). *But see Crawford v. XTO Energy, Inc.*, 509 S.W.3d 906, 910 (Tex. 2017) (no reporter's record of hearings needed when "[n]othing in those orders indicates that the trial court took evidence at the pertinent hearings or relied on any such evidence in ruling on the motions").

[59] Tex. R. App. P. 34.6(a), (b).

[60] Tex. R. App. P. 34.6(g)(1); 13.1(b), (c); Tex. R. Civ. P. 75b(b) (court reporter may withdraw the exhibits from trial court clerk as required for forwarding copies to court of appeals).

[61] Tex. R. App. P. 34.6(g)(1).

[62] Tex. R. App. P. 34.6(g)(2).

[63] Tex. R. App. P. 34.6(g)(2).

[64] Tex. R. App. P. App. C Rule 2(b).

[65] *www.txcourts.gov/media/190785/Uniform-Format-Manual-07012010.pdf* (last visited Feb. 10, 2019).

[66] Tex. R. App. P. App. C, Rule 2(b).

[67] Tex. R. App. P. App. C, Rule 2(b).

[68] Tex. R. App. P. App. C, Rule 2(b) at § 8.7.

[69] Tex. R. App. P. App. C, Rule 2(a).

[70] Tex. R. App. P. 34.3.

[71] Tex. R. App. P. 34.3.

[72] *Preston v. Sears, Roebuck & Co.*, 573 S.W.2d 560, 563 (Tex. Civ. App.—Texarkana 1978, writ ref'd n.r.e.) (reviewing Tex. R. App. P. 34.3's predecessor, former Tex. R. Civ. P. 378).

[73] Tex. R. App. P. 34.6(b)(1).

[74] Tex. R. App. P. 34.6(b).

[75] Tex. R. App. P. 34.6(b)(1); *see also Rodriguez v. Am. Gen. Fire & Cas. Co.*, 788 S.W.2d 581, 583 (Tex. App.—El Paso 1989, no writ) (timely request can be made up to the final day appeal could have been perfected, even though appeal actually perfected prior to the deadline).

[76] Tex. R. App. P. 34.6(b)(3).

[77] Tex. R. App. P. 35.1.

[78] Tex. R. App. P. 35.1(a).

[79] Tex. R. App. P. 35.1(b).

[80] Tex. R. App. P. 35.1(c).

[81] Tex. R. App. P. 28.3(k).

[82] Tex. R. App. P. 35.3(c).

[83] Tex. R. App. P. 35.3(c).

[84] Tex. R. App. P. 37.3(a)(1); Tex. R. App. P. 28.3(k).

[85] Tex. R. App. P. 35.3(c).

[86] Tex. R. App. P. 35.3(c).

[87] Tex. R. App. P. 37.3(c).

[88] Tex. R. App. P. 34.6(b)(3).

[89] Tex. R. App. P. 37.3(c).

[90] Tex. R. App. P. 37.3(c).

[91] *See In re Ryan*, 993 S.W.2d 294, 298–300 (Tex. App.—San Antonio 1999, no pet.) (orig. proceeding) (recounting coercive orders issued to obtain a sufficiently complete record from court reporter).

[92] *Wolters v. Wright*, 623 S.W.2d 301, 305 (Tex. 1981) (court of appeals can issue mandamus requiring a court reporter to prepare and file the Reporter's Record in connection with an appeal since Reporter's Record is often necessary to the exercise of appellate jurisdiction).

[93] *Wolters v. Wright*, 623 S.W.2d 301, 305 (Tex. 1981) (disobedience of a writ of mandamus commanding preparation of a Reporter's Record is punishable as contempt); *In re Ryan*, 993 S.W.2d 294, 298–300 (Tex. App.—San Antonio 1999, no pet.) (orig. proceeding) (citing inherent powers to find court reporter in criminal contempt for willfully and intentionally failing to comply with order requiring the filing of Reporter's Record).

[94] Tex. Gov't Code § 52.047(b).

[95] Tex. R. App. P. 43.4, 60.4.

[96] Tex. R. App. P. 43.5, 60.5.

[97] Tex. R. App. P. 34.6(c)(3), 43.4, 60.4.

[98] A person unable to afford the costs of the appellate record can file a Statement of Inability to Afford Payment of Court Costs in the trial court. Tex. R. Civ. P. 145(a). Requirements for eligibility and the necessary steps to avoid being charged the fees for preparation of the appellate record are governed by Texas Rule of Civil Procedure 145. *See* Tex. R. App. P. 20.1(a). When the statement was not filed in the trial court, an appellate court may permit the filing. *See* Tex. R. App. P. 20.1(c).

[99] Tex. R. App. P. 35.3(b)(1)-(3).

[100] *See, e.g., Bennett v. Cochran*, 96 S.W.3d 227, 230 (Tex. 2002); *Haut v. Green Cafe Mgmt., Inc.*, 376 S.W.3d 171, 180 (Tex. App.—Houston [14th Dist.] 2012, no pet.). However, this presumption does not arise where an appealing party invokes and follows the procedures to proceed on a partial Reporter's Record. *See* § 7-3:10.1.

[101] *See, e.g., In re L.C.H.*, 80 S.W.3d 689, 691 (Tex. App.—Fort Worth 2002, no pet.) (in the absence of a Reporter's Record, the trial court's findings of fact are conclusive, but the court may still consider issues of law).

[102] Tex. R. App. P. 34.6(f); *see also, e.g., Villagomez Invs., L.L.C. v. Magee*, 294 S.W.3d 687, 689 (Tex. App.—Houston [1st Dist.] 2009, no pet.); *Adams v. Transp. Ins. Co.*, 845 S.W.2d 323, 327–28 (Tex. App.—Dallas 1992, no writ) (reversal and remand for new trial required when missing exhibits could not be reconstructed and were needed to review sufficiency of the evidence).

[103] Tex. R. App. P. 13.1.

[104] *See, e.g., In re Estate of Arrendell*, 213 S.W.3d 496, 502 (Tex. App.—Texarkana 2006, no pet.) (error based on absence of court reporter and lack of transcript of proceeding not preserved for appellate review when counsel did not object to the failure to report the proceedings); *Reyes v. Credit Based Asset Servicing & Securitization*, 190 S.W.3d 736, 740 (Tex. App.—San Antonio 2005, no pet.) (to preserve complaint of court reporter's failure to transcribe proceedings, party must object on the record to the absence of the court reporter).

[105] *Weaver v. Westchester Fire Ins. Co.*, 739 S.W.2d 23, 24 (Tex. 1987).

[106] *See, e.g., Villagomez Invs., L.L.C. v. Magee*, 294 S.W.3d 687, 688–89 (Tex. App.—Houston [1st Dist.] 2009, no pet.).

[107] *See, e.g., In re Funk*, No. 07-99-0247-CV, 1999 WL 680379 (Tex. App.—Amarillo Sept. 1, 1999, no pet.) (not designated for publication) (motion supported by court reporter affidavit).

[108] Tex. R. App. P. 37.2.

[109] Tex. R. App. P. 37.2.

[110] Tex. R. App. P. 37.2.

[111] https://attorneyportal.txcourts.gov/Account/Login (last visited Feb. 10, 2019).

[112] Tex. R. App. P. 34.6(e).

[113] Tex. R. App. P. 34.6(e)(3).

[114] Tex. R. App. P. 34.6(e)(2).

[115] Tex. R. App. P. 34.6(d).

[116] Tex. R. App. P. 34.6(d).

[117] Tex. R. App. P. 34.6(c); *CMM Grain Co., Inc. v. Ozgunduz*, 991 S.W.2d 437, 439 (Tex. App.—Fort Worth 1999, no pet.) (noting this procedure can "reduce the expense of an appeal by abridging the reporter's record and thereby limit the appellate court's review to only those portions of the record that are relevant to the points raised in the appeal").

[118] *Christiansen v. Prezelski*, 782 S.W.2d 842, 843 (Tex. 1990); *Smith v. Karanja*, 546 S.W.3d 734, 739 (Tex. App.—Houston [1st Dist.] 2018, no pet.) ("Without a reporter's record, it is impossible for Smith to prevail on his sufficiency challenges because we must presume the evidence supports the trial court's judgment."); *Petterson v. JGMS Invs. L.L.C.*, No. 05-15-01286-CV, 2016 WL 6124134, at *2 (Tex. App.—Dallas Oct. 20, 2016, no pet.) ("Without a record of the bench trial, we must assume the 'evidence' admitted at the trial was sufficient to support the trial court's judgment.").

[119] Tex. R. App. P. 34.6(c)(1).

[120] *See Furr's Supermarkets, Inc. v. Bethune*, 53 S.W.3d 375, 377 (Tex. 2001) (appellee's issue statement in its notice of appeal was sufficient to invoke the presumption that the partial Reporter's Record constituted the entire record for purposes of reviewing the appellate

issue); *Schafer v. Conner*, 813 S.W.2d 154, 155 (Tex. 1991) (disapproving the court of appeals' "hypertechnical" interpretation that would require the appellate points to be stated *in* the request for a partial Reporter's Record rather than *with* the request).

121 Tex. R. App. P. 34.6(c)(4).

122 *Sandoval v. Comm'n for Lawyer Discipline*, 25 S.W.3d 720, 722 (Tex. App.—Houston [14th Dist.] 2000, pet. denied) ("a party who properly designates certain portions of the Reporter's Record may appeal a sufficiency point without a complete record—and the appellate court is to presume the incomplete record is complete for purposes of the appeal . . . .").

123 *See, e.g., Bailey v. Gallagher*, 348 S.W.3d 322, 325 (Tex. App.—Dallas 2011, pet. denied) ("the appealing party must comply strictly with rule 34.6(c) to activate this presumption that the omitted portions of the record are irrelevant"); *Wheeler v. Greene*, 194 S.W.3d 1, 4–5 (Tex. App.—Tyler 2006, no pet.) (appellant was not entitled to presumption where statement of points were so broad that appellees could not anticipate the portions of the record they needed to designate); *Mason v. Our Lady Star of Sea Catholic Church*, 154 S.W.3d 816, 818–21 (Tex. App.—Houston [14th Dist.] 2005) (because statement of points of errors or issues was untimely when not presented until four months after briefing, court of appeals had to presume the omitted portions of the record were relevant and supported trial court's judgment); *Hilton v. Hillman Distr. Co.*, 12 S.W.3d 846, 848 (Tex. App.—Texarkana 2000, no pet.) (a general description of the proposed contentions of error is insufficient to provide necessary level of particularity); *In re R.C.*, 45 S.W.3d 146, 148 (Tex. App.—Fort Worth 2000, no pet.) ("Strict compliance with rule 34.6(c) is necessary to activate the presumption that the omitted portions of the record are irrelevant to the issues on appeal and appellate disposition."). *But see Bennett v. Cochran*, 96 S.W.3d 227, 229 (Tex. 2002) (adopting a "more flexible approach in certain cases—like this one—when a rigid application of Rule 34.6 would result in denying review on the merits, even though the appellee has not established any prejudice from a slight relaxation of the rule").

124 *See, e.g., In re R.C.*, 45 S.W.3d 146, 149 (Tex. App.—Fort Worth 2000, no pet.).

125 Tex. R. App. P. 34.6(c)(4). *Bennett v. Cochran*, 96 S.W.3d 227, 228 (Tex. 2002). *But see Candelier v. Ringstaff*, 786 S.W.2d 41, 44 (Tex. App.—Beaumont 1990, writ denied) (appellants could not attack the sufficiency of all of the evidence to support the trial court's findings of fact and also avail themselves of the presumption that nothing omitted from the record was relevant to the appeal).

126 Tex. R. App. P. 34.6(c)(1).

127 Tex. R. App. P. 34.6(c)(2).

128 *See Cowling v. Colligan*, 312 S.W.2d 943, 947 (1958) (when appellee brings cross-points regarding the sufficiency of the evidence, the appellee must bring the statement of facts forward if the appellant does not, or the points are waived).

129 *W & F Transp., Inc. v. Wilhelm*, 208 S.W.3d 32, 38 (Tex. App.—Houston [14th Dist.] 2006, no pet.) (quotation and citation omitted).

130 Tex. R. App. P. 34.2.

131 Tex. R. App. P. 34.2; *see* Tex. R. App. P. 34.5, 34.6.

CHAPTER 8

Staying Execution and Superseding the Judgment

8-1 Introduction

Ancillary to an appeal is the important matter of staying execution of the judgment during the appeal. If you are the judgment debtor seeking reversal of the judgment, knowing Texas supersedeas jurisprudence and the procedures required to effectively stay enforcement of the judgment is critical to your appeal.

The primary sources for Texas supersedeas law are:

- Chapter 52 of the Texas Civil Practice and Remedies Code;
- Rule 24 of the Texas Rules of Appellate Procedure; and
- Case law interpreting and applying these provisions.

8-1:1 What It Means to "Supersede" a Judgment

"Supersedeas" in Latin means "you shall desist," and is defined as "[a] writ or bond that suspends a judgment creditor's power to levy execution. . . ."[1] Therefore, a properly superseded judgment suspends the enforcement process and permits the parties to maintain the status quo during the pendency of the appeal. This is so because, in addition to staying enforcement of the judgment, supersedeas at the same time provides the judgment creditor assurance that the judgment will be satisfied if the appeal is unsuccessful. If a writ of execution has been issued, the court clerk must immediately issue a writ of supersedeas once proper security is made.[2]

8-1:2 Voluntary Nature of Supersedeas

Superseding the judgment is voluntary and not necessary to perfect an appeal—an appeal may proceed without an appeal bond or other appellate security.[3] A judgment debtor, therefore, may forgo the right to supersede the judgment when appealing the judgment. Of course, the judgment debtor runs the risk of the judgment creditor executing on the judgment during the appellate process. Even if execution occurs, the appeal will proceed.[4]

8-1:3 Final Judgment Necessary for Enforcement

The prevailing party may execute only on a final judgment. A judgment is final when it disposes of all claims, issues, and parties before the court, and no further action is required to determine the controversy.[5] Such a judgment is final for purposes of appellate review.[6] As a general rule, interlocutory orders may not be executed upon.[7] However, as discussed below, under some limited circumstances, a trial court may permit a party to supersede an order granting temporary relief pending an appeal of that order.

8-1:4 Interlocutory Orders

8-1:4.1 Discretion to Permit Supersedeas

Under Rule 29.2, a "trial court may permit an order granting interlocutory relief to be superseded pending an appeal from the order. . . ."[8] If that occurs, the party may supersede the order in the same manner as a final judgment.[9] If the trial court refuses to allow suspension, the appellant may seek review of that ruling in an appellate court under an abuse-of-discretion standard.[10] Additionally, during an appeal of an interlocutory order, the appellate court "may make any temporary orders necessary to preserve the parties' rights until disposition of the appeal and may require appropriate security."[11] But if supersedeas would adequately protect an appellant's rights, the appellate court "must not suspend the trial court's order."[12] An interlocutory order *denying* relief may not be suspended.[13]

8-1:4.2 Stay Pending Appeal

An appeal of an interlocutory order under section 51.014 of the Texas Civil Practice and Remedies Code stays the trial in the trial court "pending resolution of the appeal," except for appeals of temporary injunctions.[14] If there is an appeal from class-certification orders, a denial of a summary-judgment motion based on immunity, or the granting or denial of a plea to the jurisdiction by a governmental unit, the appeal "also stays all other proceedings in the trial court pending resolution of that appeal."[15] Regardless of whether a stay is in effect, a trial court may not act in a manner that impairs or interferes with the jurisdiction of the appellate court.[16]

8-1:5 Orders and Judgments That May Not Be Stayed

Execution of the following judgments may not be stayed:

- orders denying interlocutory relief;[17]
- appointment of receivers in a shareholder-derivative suit;[18]
- child support or custody orders, unless the trial court orders otherwise;[19]
- suspension of a license to practice law;[20] and
- final judgments of a district court regarding an order of the Texas Alcoholic Beverage Commissioner "refusing, cancelling, or suspending a permit or license."[21]

8-1:6 Pending Appeal

Only judgments or appealable orders that are the subject of an actual pending appeal may be superseded. But the mere filing of a notice of appeal does not suspend enforcement of a judgment.[22] If an appeal is not perfected during the time period for perfecting an appeal, enforcement of a judgment may not be stayed. Therefore, if the unsuccessful party does not perfect an appeal, the judgment may not be superseded.

And once all appellate remedies have been exhausted, the judgment can no longer be superseded.

8-1:7 Time to Supersede

A judgment debtor is not required to supersede a judgment at any particular time. Nevertheless, to avoid execution on the judgment, the judgment debtor should file the security promptly. The timing of the filing of the security is largely dictated by the timetable for execution. The time when a party may begin efforts to collect (but not actually execute) on the judgment—such as garnishment and turnover proceedings—and hence the deadline for suspending these efforts begins to run when the trial court signs a final and appealable judgment.[23] A judgment creditor may not actually execute on a final judgment until 30 days after it is signed, or 30 days after a timely motion for new trial is overruled.[24] However, a timely filed motion to modify the judgment, alone, does not extend the date on which a party may execute on the judgment.

To avoid a potential writ of garnishment, the judgment debtor should file the security to suspend execution on the judgment immediately after it is rendered. A plaintiff may obtain a writ of garnishment immediately after the judgment is signed unless a proper supersedeas bond is filed.[25] Also, in some cases a turnover order may be issued immediately after the judgment is signed.[26] Lastly, the judgment debtor may wish to supersede the judgment immediately in order to prevent post-judgment discovery.

8-1:8 Actions Not Stayed by a Properly Superseded Judgment

8-1:8.1 Abstract of Judgment

Not all actions by the judgment creditor regarding possible future enforcement of the judgment are precluded by the posting of proper security. For example, the successful party may record an abstract of judgment in the deed records of any county in which the judgment debtor has property even if the judgment is superseded, unless prohibited by court order.[27] The filing of the abstract does not constitute an *enforceable* lien on the real property if enforcement is stayed.

The lien will nonetheless remain unless:

- the defendant has posted proper security; and
- "the trial court finds that the creation of a lien would not substantially increase the degree to which the judgment creditor's recovery under the judgment would be secured when balanced against the costs to the defendant after the exhaustion of all appellate remedies."[28]

A certified copy of the court's finding must be recorded in the real-property records in each county in which the abstracted judgment or certified copy of the judgment has been filed.[29] A lien on personal property of the judgment debtor is improper after the judgment is superseded.[30]

8-1:8.2 Injunction to Prevent Dissipation of Assets

Even when a judgment debtor posts security in the maximum amount required, a judgment creditor may seek and obtain an injunction against the judgment debtor from dissipating or transferring assets to avoid satisfaction of the judgment.[31] And the judgment debtor may pursue post-judgment discovery related to such an injunction.[32]

8-1:8.3 Discovery Regarding the Security

Although all parties may conduct discovery any time after final judgment to obtain information regarding collection—such as discovering assets of the judgment debtor—or security on appeal, the prevailing party may not conduct post-judgment discovery to aid collection after the judgment is superseded.[33] But post-judgment discovery is permissible during the pendency of the appeal to determine whether the posted security continues to be sufficient to protect the judgment creditor, or when the discovery relates to certain motions allowed under the appellate rules.[34] Sometimes circumstances arise that require modification of the amount or method of security, and that determination may be a factual inquiry necessitating discovery. Discovery also is permitted after supersedeas to discover the net worth of the judgment debtor when the amount of security posted is based on net worth.[35]

8-2 Amount of Security

8-2:1 Money Judgment

The trial court clerk has the ministerial duty to approve the bond or deposit, including the amount. The amount of security for a money judgment must cover:

- the amount of compensatory—but not punitive—damages;
- interest for the estimated duration of the appeal, and costs.[36]

The "interest" that must be included in the amount of security is interest only on the compensatory damages that are being superseded—interest on the sums that do not have to be superseded (such as punitive damages and non-compensatory attorney's fees) is *not* included.[37]

The amount of the bond cannot exceed the lesser of:

- 50% of the debtor's current net worth; or
- $25 million.[38]

8-2:2 "Compensatory Damages"

"Compensatory damages" are commonly defined as "damages sufficient in amount to indemnify the injured person for the loss suffered."[39] This phrase is interchangeable with "actual damages," which is defined as "[a]n amount awarded to a complainant to compensate for a proven injury or loss; damages that repay actual losses."[40]

8-2:2.1 Pre-judgment Interest

These definitions do not expressly include pre-judgment interest. Noting that "[n]ot every amount, even if compensatory, can be considered damages," the Texas Supreme Court has concluded that "neither costs nor interest qualify as compensatory damages."[41] Two intermediate appellate courts have agreed, as well as a highly respected commentator.[42]

8-2:2.2 Attorney Fees

Attorney fees incurred in the prosecution or defense of a claim are not compensatory damages or costs.[43] Nevertheless, if attorney fees are an element of damages, such as in a breach-of-contract claim for unpaid attorney fees, those fees are compensatory damages.[44]

Where a contract between the parties allows for the recovery of attorney's fees "related to the breach [of that contract]," the fees are not compensatory and do not need to be superseded should the non-breaching party recover them against the breaching party.[45]

8-2:3 Proving "Net Worth"

8-2:3.1 Burden on Judgment Debtor

The judgment debtor who seeks to apply the statutory net-worth cap to the amount of security required has the burden to prove net worth.[46]

8-2:3.2 Affidavit Required

When the superseding party posts security, it "must simultaneously file with the trial court clerk an affidavit that states the debtor's net worth and states complete, detailed information concerning the debtor's assets and liabilities from which net worth can be ascertained."[47] This affidavit is prima facie proof of net worth, but is subject to challenge by the judgment creditor, who may conduct "reasonable" discovery concerning the judgment debtor's net worth.[48]

8-2:3.3 Hearing and Order Required

Once discovery is complete, the trial court is required to (1) hold a hearing at which the judgment debtor must prove its net worth, and (2) issue an order that specifically states the debtor's net worth and provides with particularity the factual basis for the court's determination.[49]

8-2:3.4 Meaning of "Net Worth"

8-2:3.4a Assets Minus Liability

Although neither Texas Rule of Appellate Procedure 24 nor Texas Civil Practice and Remedies Code Chapter 52 defines "net worth," courts have held the term is unambiguous and means the difference between total assets and total liabilities determined according to generally accepted accounting principles (GAAP).[50]

8-2:3.4b Current *Net Worth*

Under Rule 24.2(a)(1), the cap is based on the judgment debtor's *current* net worth. But whether the value of assets is based on book value—i.e., historic costs—or current fair-market value is uncertain. The net-worth evidence upon which the court in *Ramco Oil* relied in determining net worth was based on book value.[51] Of course, assets that have appreciated will produce a greater net worth under the latter accounting method. The court in *Ramco Oil* acknowledged that determining net worth under GAAP "may be quite complicated and may involve different considerations based on the circumstances of the judgment debtor and based on GAAP."[52] And Texas courts have not yet addressed whether net worth includes inventory reserves and liability-insurance coverage available for the damages at issue.

8-2:3.4c Judgment Not Included in Net-Worth Calculation

Two appellate courts have indicated that the judgment being appealed is not counted as a liability in determining net worth under GAAP.[53]

8-2:3.4d Exempt Assets Not Included

The trial court does not abuse its discretion in excluding exempt homestead in determining the judgment debtor's net worth.[54]

8-2:3.4e Interest and Costs Not Included

If the judgment debtor posts security at the net-worth cap, it is not required to further secure the interest and costs awarded in the judgment.[55]

8-2:3.4f Jointly and Severally Liable Judgment Debtors

Jointly and severally liable judgment debtors who are posting security on the basis of their respective net worth may file a joint bond that secures compensatory damages, interest, and costs in the aggregate. In any event, no appellant is individually responsible on the bond in an amount that would exceed the supersedeas cap as to that appellant.[56]

Once the trial court makes its finding of the judgment debtor's net worth, it can then be determined whether the amount of the security will be capped below the amount otherwise required, under Rule 24.2(a)(1) or under Rule 24.2(b) (determining the substantial-economic-harm factors).[57] In the event the judgment debtor has a negative net worth, the amount of the bond under Rule 24.2(a)(1) would be zero.

8-2:3.5 Calculating Court Costs

The amount of the bond should include an amount for court costs.[58] The amount of court costs, however, is frequently not known at the time the bond must be prepared and filed. Some courts will provide a bill of costs that may be used to calculate court costs. Appellate counsel may wish to consult with trial counsel to obtain an estimate of the amount of court costs, which often is all that is available. To avoid a potential challenge to the bond, deposit, or other security, the judgment debtor would be wise to overestimate the amount of court costs.

8-2:4 Reducing Security Amount Based on "Substantial Economic Harm"

8-2:4.1 Reduction Mandatory

The trial court is *required* to order a reduced amount of the bond, deposit, or security if the amount otherwise required by Rule 24 will cause the judgment debtor "substantial economic harm":

> The trial court must lower the amount of security required by [Rule 24.2(a)] to an amount that will not cause the judgment debtor substantial economic harm if, after notice to all parties and a hearing, the court finds that posting a bond, deposit, or security in the amount required by [Rule 24.2(a)] is likely to cause the judgment debtor substantial economic harm.[59]

8-2:4.2 "Substantial Economic Harm"

Although undefined, "substantial economic harm" under the current rule is more favorable to the judgment debtor than under the prior rule. Then, the trial court had the discretion to reduce the amount of security if the court found: (1) that posting a bond, deposit, or security in the full amount required would irreparably harm the judgment debtor; and (2) that posting a bond, deposit, or security in a lesser amount would not substantially impair the judgment creditor's ability to recover under the judgment after all appellate remedies are exhausted.[60] The current rule eliminates the second prong of the prior rule.

Although "irreparably harm" was not defined in the prior law either, cases construing that standard held that the test was met if the judgment debtor demonstrated that posting the full security would place it in bankruptcy.[61] The possibility of bankruptcy is one of several factors courts now consider in determining "substantial economic harm," as discussed in the following section.

8-2:4.3 Factors Courts May Consider

In determining whether "substantial economic harm" to the judgment debtor is "likely," "a number of factors that could affect the judgment debtor's ability to post bond or other security based on the facts and circumstances specific to the case" are considered.[62] The primary issues concern what resources are available to the judgment debtor and whether it is able to use them to post security:

- How much cash or other resources would it take to post a supersedeas bond in the amount in question?
- Does the judgment debtor have sufficient cash or other assets on hand to post a bond in this amount or to post a deposit in lieu of bond in this amount?
- Does the judgment debtor have any other source of funds available?
- Does the judgment debtor have the ability to borrow funds to post the requisite security?
- Does the judgment debtor have unencumbered assets to sell or pledge?
- What economic impact is such a transaction likely to have on the judgment debtor?
- Would requiring the judgment debtor to take certain action likely trigger liquidation or bankruptcy or have other harmful consequences?
- To what extent would the attorney fees and other costs of appeal drain the judgment debtor's resources?[63]

Although these factors certainly are not exhaustive, a judgment debtor seeking to show substantial economic harm would be wise to marshal and present evidence on as many of them as possible.

8-2:5 Interest Computation

In the case of a money judgment, the bond, deposit, or security must include "interest for the estimated duration of the appeal."[64] Generally, most court clerks will approve security that includes interest on the judgment for a one-year period. If more than a year passes without the appeal being resolved, the judgment creditor may force the judgment debtor to amend the bond to cover the additional interest.[65] Most bonds automatically renew for another year, thereby covering the original bond amount, including interest for the second year, provided the bond premium is paid. But by including interest for a period of two years, the judgment debtor may avoid a challenge to the amount of the bond and the attorney fees resulting from the challenge.

8-2:6 Non-Monetary Judgments

If the judgment is for recovery of an interest in real or personal property, the trial court must determine the amount of security required.[66]

8-2:6.1 Real Property

If the judgment is for an interest in real property, the amount of the bond, deposit, or security must be the value of the property interest's rent or revenue.[67] The amount of the bond should not be measured by the potential loss of profit or loss of future sales to the judgment creditor.[68]

8-2:6.2 Personal Property

If the judgment is for an interest in personal property, the amount of the bond, deposit, or security must be the value of the property interest on the date the court rendered judgment.[69]

8-3 Methods of Superseding the Judgment

There are five methods to supersede a judgment:

- written agreement with the judgment creditor;
- supersedeas bond;
- deposit in lieu of bond;
- alternate security ordered by the trial court; and
- notice of appeal, for certain governmental entities, agencies, and public servants.[70]

Any of these methods is acceptable to suspend enforcement unless otherwise provided in the appellate rules or by law.

8-3:1 Written Agreement

The judgment debtor and creditor may agree between themselves to suspend enforcement of the judgment during the appeal.[71] The agreement need only be in writing and filed with the trial court. The trial court's (or clerk's) approval is not necessary. The rules do not address the form of the agreement. Therefore, the right to make a private agreement opens a world of possibilities for the parties, limited only by their imagination and that of their counsel.

8-3:2 Supersedeas Bond

8-3:2.1 General Principles and Tips

8-3:2.1a Purpose and Parties

Under a supersedeas bond, an obligor is bound to pay the judgment and damages for the delay of the appeal—including interest and costs (up to the cap)—to the judgment creditor if the judgment is affirmed or the appeal is dismissed. The principal on the bond is the judgment debtor; the surety is a third party who guarantees payment of the judgment if the judgment debtor fails to satisfy the judgment. The judgment debtor or the judgment debtor's agent must sign the bond.[72] The bond is defective on its face—and subject to challenge—if it is not signed in this manner.

The judgment debtor pays an annual premium to the surety in an amount based on the amount of the bond. The premium rate for the bond varies among sureties and is affected by the amount required for the bond and financial position of the judgment debtor. Usually, the surety requires liquid collateral before issuing the bond. The type and amount of collateral usually depends on the credit-worthiness of the judgment debtor.

8-3:2.1b Contract Principles Apply

Because a supersedeas bond is a contract, it is "construed as any other contract, and the cardinal rule of construction is to ascertain the intent of the parties."[73] Sureties are "no further bound than they have contracted to be."[74] The bond is not itself property owned by the judgment debtor.[75] It is not an unconditional agreement to pay a stated sum of money; it imposes only a conditional or contingent liability.

8-3:2.1c Approval

To stay enforcement, a supersedeas bond must be approved by the trial court clerk before it is filed.[76] Generally, the clerk will determine whether the amount of the bond is proper and whether the surety is sufficient for the amount of the bond. Accordingly, it is critical for the superseding party to ensure at the outset that the surety is "approved" for the amount of the bond. If efforts to collect on the judgment are imminent, making the need for supersedeas immediate, failure of the bond because of insufficient surety can result in execution on the judgment while another surety is being obtained.

8-3:2.2 When Multiple Parties Supersede

In the case of multiple judgment debtors, each one must file a bond in order to protect itself from execution unless exempted by statute. If any relief or award in the judgment is joint and several, the filing of a bond by only one of the judgment debtors will not inure to the benefit of the other judgment debtors.[77] Each judgment debtor must either separately file a bond or deposit for the full amount of the judgment against it (inclusive of the joint and several amount), or the joint-and-several judgment debtors may file a single, joint bond.[78] This requirement is necessary to ensure adequate protection of the judgment creditor in the event the judgment is reversed as to only one of the judgment debtors, or if the judgment creditor is unable to collect against one of the judgment debtors.[79] Because the amount of the bond is connected to the judgment debtors' net worth, it is possible that the bond amount for each jointly and severally liable judgment debtor may be different.[80]

8-3:2.3 Form of Bond

8-3:2.3a Basic Requirements

A bond must conform with certain specified requirements of form and amount before the trial court clerk will approve it and before it will operate to suspend enforcement. It must be in the amount required by Rule 24.2, and must be:

- payable to the judgment creditor;
- signed by the judgment debtor or its agent;
- signed by a sufficient surety or sureties as obligors; and
- properly conditioned.[81]

The trial court clerk may refuse to approve a bond that fails to recite that it is payable to the judgment creditor. If such a bond is approved, it is subject to challenge.[82] In the case of a corporate judgment debtor, the bond should be signed by the corporation's principal or authorized representative.

8-3:2.3b Conditioning Language

A bond must contain proper conditioning language by which the surety or sureties subject themselves to liability for all damages and costs that may be awarded against the judgment debtor up to the bond amount. The surety or sureties bind themselves to liability for all damages and costs if:

- the debtor does not perfect an appeal or the debtor's appeal is dismissed, and the debtor does not perform the trial court's judgment;
- the debtor does not perform an adverse judgment final on appeal; or
- the judgment is for the recovery of an interest in real or personal property and the debtor does not pay the creditor the value of the property interest's rent or revenue during the pendency of the appeal.[83]

Failure to include this conditioning language may result in the bond being rejected or successfully challenged.

8-3:2.4 Sufficiency of Sureties

8-3:2.4a Solvency

The surety requirement is critical to providing the judgment creditor proper security during the appeal. The bond must be signed by a "sufficient" surety or sureties as obligors because the surety binds itself equally with the judgment debtor to be liable in the event the judgment is affirmed and the judgment debtor fails to perform.[84]

Some Texas district court clerks maintain a list of companies that are "sufficient" as sureties, as provided in the Notice of Companies Holding Certificates of Authority as Acceptable Sureties in Federal Bond, and as Acceptable Reinsuring Companies, published by the United State Department of Treasury in the Federal Register every July 1st.[85] Before selecting a surety, or once the surety is selected—and before obtaining the signature of the surety—counsel should confer with the trial court clerk to determine if the particular surety is acceptable. The trial court has jurisdiction, upon proper motion, to review and determine the sufficiency of sureties, including the relationship between the sureties and the appellant and the likelihood that the sureties will in fact be able or willing to satisfy the judgment. Little or no direct guidance is given in the rules on this issue.

The following rules govern the sufficiency of a surety:

- A surety is sufficient only if it is an entity that is legally separate from the judgment debtor;[86] a nonparty;[87] and one whose ability to pay is not in dispute;[88] and
- The surety is insufficient if its only asset is stock in the judgment debtor.[89]

The person signing the bond must be authorized by a valid power of attorney or corporate resolution.[90] Counsel should ask to review any side-agreements or indemnity arrangements related to the bond. Often, such agreements will be referenced in the power of attorney.

8-3:2.4b Relationship to Defendant

A surety is one "who is primarily liable for paying *another's* debt or performing another's obligation."[91] Accordingly, a surety is a third party—legally separate from the debtor and not a party to the suit—that contracts to pay the judgment plus interest if the appeal is unsuccessful.[92] "The relationship between the principal (judgment debtor) and surety as applied to individuals necessarily involves separate personalities."[93] A person cannot be a surety for himself.[94]

8-3:2.4c Multiple Sureties

Some judgments are so large that they require multiple sureties. But the greater the number of sureties, the greater the burden of establishing their sufficiency. Additional proof of solvency might be required under articles 6.16 and 7.19-1(b) of the Texas Insurance Code if multiple sureties are jointly liable.[95] If the liability is joint and several, however, each surety would likely be required to independently satisfy the Insurance Code provisions. Obviously, if multiple sureties are used and their liability is joint and several, then proof that one of the sureties is solvent to pay the judgment should be sufficient.[96]

8-3:3 Cash Deposit in Lieu of Bond

In lieu of filing a bond, a judgment debtor has the option of filing a deposit with the trial court clerk for the same amount that would be required if a bond were filed.[97] Three types of deposits are acceptable:

- cash;
- a cashier's check payable to the court clerk drawn on a federally insured and federal-chartered or state-chartered bank or savings-and-loan association; or
- upon leave of court, a negotiable obligation of the federal government or of any federally insured and federal-chartered or state-chartered bank or savings-and-loan association.[98]

The actual negotiable instrument must be filed with the clerk, rather than a receipt for the instrument.[99] A letter of credit does not qualify as a proper negotiable obligation under the provisions governing deposits in lieu of bond.[100] A certificate of deposit may qualify.[101]

In the case of the deposit of cash or a cashier's check, the clerk is required to "promptly" deposit the money "in accordance with law."[102] This rule does not state any further parameters regarding the deposit. In some Texas courts, the deposits are deposited into the registry of the court. A cash deposit in lieu of bond is not deposited into any other type of account unless a court orders otherwise. In other Texas courts, the money is deposited into an interest-bearing account, which accrues interest until the money is withdrawn. The clerk is required to hold the deposit until the conditions of liability provided in Rule 24.1(d) are satisfied.[103]

In calculating the amount of the deposit, the judgment debtor should use the same formula for calculating the bond amount.[104] Judgment debtors seldom make use of this method of suspending enforcement for the obvious reason that it rarely makes economic sense to tie up money in a non-interest-bearing account or a low-interest-bearing account for months or even years. In other cases, the judgment debtor is insured and the insurer can obtain a bond, often at discounted rates.

8-3:4 Alternate Security

8-3:4.1 Broad Scope

Parties may supersede a judgment by providing alternate security—as to both the type *and* amount of security in question—upon securing a court order permitting it.[105] For example, although Rule 24.1(a)(3) does not permit the filing of non-negotiable instruments, such as letters of credit, "alternate security"—which is undefined—is broad enough to permit the filing of a letter of credit. The term is also sufficiently broad to permit, for example, a judgment debtor to pledge unencumbered assets toward securing the judgment.

8-3:4.2 Motion

If the judgment debtor seeks to post alternate security, it should file a motion for alternate security as soon as possible to obtain a ruling before execution may issue. The judgment debtor would have the burden to demonstrate how alternate security sufficiently supersedes the judgment, such as the value and liquidity of unencumbered assets.

8-3:5 Supersedeas by Notice of Appeal for Certain Litigants

The legislature has exempted certain judgment debtors from filing a bond; for such defendants the filing of a notice of appeal suspends enforcement of the judgment.[106] The courts liberally construe statutes exempting persons from filing bonds.[107] Although many of the statutes addressing this issue refer to the filing of bonds for costs, the courts interpret these statutes as including supersedeas bonds.[108] When the legislature exempts a judgment debtor from filing security for appeal, the trial court has no discretion to require the judgment debtor to post security to supersede the judgment.[109] Mandamus will issue if the court requires security.[110]

8-3:5.1 The Government

Many government officials and governmental entities are exempt from filing a supersedeas bond. Section 6.001 of the Texas Civil Practice and Remedies Code provides that the following governmental entities or officers are exempt from the requirement of filing a bond:

- the State;
- a department of the State;
- the head of a department of the State;
- a county of the State;
- the Federal Housing Administration;
- the Federal National Mortgage Association;
- the Government National Mortgage Association;
- the Veterans' Administration;
- the Administrator of Veterans Affairs;
- any national mortgage savings and loan insurance corporation created by an act of Congress as a national relief organization that operates on a state-wide basis; and
- the Federal Deposit Insurance Corporation in its capacity as receiver or in its corporate capacity.[111]

Included in this category of parties who are not required to file a bond to appeal is the district clerk,[112] the prison commission and its individual members sued in their official capacities,[113] the Texas Liquor Control Board and its administrator,[114] the state commissioner of insurance and banking and his special agent acting in his official capacity,[115] the Teacher Retirement System of Texas and its board of trustees,[116] the Texas Department of Human Resources,[117] the Railroad Commission and its members when sued in their official capacity,[118] the Public Utilities Commission,[119] the Texas banking commissioner,[120] a county board or agency,[121] the state comptroller,[122] county judges and county commissioners sued in their official capacities,[123] and the county treasurer and the county auditor.[124]

Although the statute's liberal construction ordinarily operates in favor of individuals sued in their official capacities, when the person is suing or being sued in an *individual* capacity, the statute does not operate to exempt the individual from filing a bond.[125]

Section 6.001 does not exempt the United States of America or other unnamed departments of the United States.[126] Notably, federal law exempts the U.S. government from filing bond in appeals taken in federal courts.[127] The federal statute does not exempt the United States or any department thereof, however, from filing a supersedeas bond in state court.[128]

A number of other agencies, entities, and individuals do not fall within section 6.001. In particular, section 6.001 does not apply to appeals by other states.[129] It does not apply to appeals by the University Interscholastic League (UIL) or its officials.[130] Further, although it ordinarily applies to the Texas Department of Insurance and its commissioner, section 6.001 does not operate to exempt the liquidator of an insurance company in receivership.[131] Although acting with the Department's approval, the liquidator stands in the shoes of the insolvent insurance corporation.[132]

8-3:5.2 Certain Public Servants

Certain public servants who are sued because of conduct or omissions occurring in the course of their office or employment are exempt from filing a supersedeas bond if the suit is defended by the attorney general.[133] Included in this class of persons are: (1) an employee, a member of the governing board, or any other officer of a state agency, institution, or department; (2) a former employee, former member of the governing board, or any other former officer of a state agency, institution, or department who was an employee when the act or omission on which the damages are based occurred; (3) a physician or psychiatrist licensed in Texas who was performing services under a contract with any state agency, institution, or department when the act or omission on which the damages are based occurred; (4) a racing official who was performing service under a contract with the Texas Racing Commission when the act or omission on which the damages are based occurred; (5) a person serving on the governing board of a foundation, corporation, or association at the request and on behalf of an institution of higher education, not including a public junior college; (6) a state contractor who signed a waste manifest as required by a state contract; and (7) the estate of any of the aforementioned individuals.[134]

8-4 Trial Court's Continuing Jurisdiction to Review Security

Even after it has lost plenary power, the trial court has continuing jurisdiction to review the security for: (1) amount, (2) type of security, (3) sufficiency of the sureties, and (4) consideration of any changes in circumstances that may alter the amount or type of security.[135] The judgment debtor has the duty to notify the appellate court of any modifications to the bonding requirements.[136]

Challenges to the security in the trial court are generally made in a motion to review sufficiency of, or a motion to modify, the posted security. Motions challenging the sufficiency of the security should be supported with proof or be verified and heard before the trial court. Whether seeking or opposing modification, a party should present competent evidence either attached to the motion or in the form of testimony at the hearing and must obtain a ruling.

If the court of appeals reverses or reduces the judgment, an issue arises as to whether the trial court may reduce the amount of security according to the court of appeals' judgment then, even if a judgment creditor plans to pursue a petition for review in the Texas Supreme Court. The general rule is that a trial has no authority to either increase or decrease the amount of security based on a court of appeals' judgment when that judgment is subject to further appellate review and no mandate has issued.[137] This rule is based on the premise that until the appeal has concluded and the mandate has issued, the court of appeals' judgment cannot be enforced.[138]

8-5 Appellate Review of Security Orders

Review of a trial court order regarding supersedeas is made by motion in the court of appeals.[139] Review of a court of appeals' ruling in the Texas Supreme Court is by petition for writ of mandamus.[140]

8-5:1 Reviewable Orders

Under Rule 24.4, Texas appellate courts have broad power to review trial court-security orders, including orders regarding:

- the sufficiency or excessiveness of the security amount;
- the sufficiency of sureties;
- the type of security; and
- whether to suspend enforcement.[141]

This review is based both on conditions existing at the time of the trial court order and changes occurring afterward.[142] The appellate court must hear the motion for review "at the earliest practicable time."[143] Appellate courts review the trial court's determination of both the amount of security and whether the judgment debtor will likely suffer "substantial harm" for abuse of discretion.[144] The Supreme Court also has the power of review, but it does not have jurisdiction to review the factual sufficiency of the evidence supporting the order.[145]

Appellate courts also may review a trial court order disposing of a supersedeas bond after the mandate has issued.[146] In addressing the appellate courts' jurisdiction to review a trial court's disposition of a supersedeas bond after the mandate has issued, the Texas Supreme Court has explained that the proper method of review depends on whether the post-mandate order imposes obligations beyond those expressly articulated in the judgment.[147] "[I]f a post judgment order imposes obligations in addition to or in excess of those in the judgment, an appeal from the post judgment order is permissible, provided the order disposes of all pending issues and parties."[148] When an order requires a party to pay an amount of the supersedeas bond that goes beyond what the provisions of the judgment awarded, the appropriate method of review is direct appeal of that post-judgment order.[149]

8-5:2 Scope of Appellate Review

The scope of the appellate court's action is also very broad. The court may:

- increase or reduce the amount of security;
- alter type of security;
- require another bond or security to be filed; and
- require "other changes in the trial court's order."[150]

The court cannot modify the amount of security so as to exceed the caps. Although it may issue its own modification order, the court also may remand to the trial court for the entry of findings of fact or for the taking of evidence.[151]

8-5:3 Complying With Appellate Modification

Rule 24.4 provides a critically important stay of enforcement of *20 days* after the appellate court orders additional or other security to enable the judgment debtor to comply with the order.[152] The appellant's failure to timely comply with the order could result in the judgment's enforcement.[153] Modifications, such as an increase in the amount of the security, are effected through the filing of security just for the additional required amount. The posting of additional security itself does not release or affect previously posted security unless otherwise ordered by the appellate court.[154]

8-6 Effect of Execution During Appeal or Voluntary Payment

Because a party may appeal without superseding the judgment, the judgment creditor may execute on the judgment without affecting the appellate court's jurisdiction. But if the judgment is reversed on appeal, the judgment debtor has a right to recover in restitution against the judgment creditor the fair-market value of the property taken by execution.[155] The fair-market value may (and usually will) differ from the value received from the execution sale, so the executing party runs the risk of having to pay in restitution more than it obtained at execution.

Although a voluntary and *unconditional* payment of the judgment moots the appeal,[156] satisfaction of the judgment will not moot the appeal if the appellant expresses the intent to pursue the appeal.[157]

8-7 Effect of Mandate on Collection and Bond

8-7:1 Liability of Surety and Procedures to Collect on Bond

8-7:1.1 Mandate

Once the appeal is final, the clerk of the appellate court must prepare a mandate consistent with the judgment and send it to the trial court clerk.[158] When the mandate issues to the trial court, the judgment of the appellate court "must be enforced," and the trial court clerk may issue a writ of execution "as in any other case."[159]

Enforcement cannot occur until the appeal has concluded and the mandate has issued.[160] However, one Texas intermediate appellate court has held that—even where the trial court judgment was superseded by a bond, and before the mandate had issued—the judgment creditor could proceed directly against the surety through a turnover proceeding to enforce the judgment that had been affirmed by the Texas Supreme Court when no timely motion for rehearing had been filed.[161]

8-7:1.2 Affirmance of the Judgment

If the appellate court affirms the judgment, or modifies and renders judgment against the appellant, the surety is potentially liable to pay the judgment up to the amount of the bond, deposit, or security if the judgment debtor fails to perform or pay the judgment. Texas Rule of Appellate Procedure 43.5 says that, upon affirmance, the court of appeals "must render judgment against the sureties on the appellant's supersedeas bond . . . for the performance of the judgment and for any costs taxed against the appellant."

Rule 24.1(d) requires the surety's performance on the bond if:

- the judgment debtor does not perfect an appeal or the appeal is dismissed, and the debtor does not perform the trial court judgment; or
- the debtor does not perform an adverse judgment final on appeal.

Enforcement of the bond can therefore be accomplished through:

- amendment of the judgment to include the surety so that collection may be undertaken;
- a breach-of-contract action brought against the surety; or
- a motion made to the appellate court for judgment against the sureties on the bond.[162]

8-7:1.3 Reversal of the Judgment

On the other hand, if the judgment is either reversed, vacated, or rendered in favor of the judgment debtor, the surety has no obligation, and the bond will be released and the surety discharged. A reversal and remand for new trial has the same effect.[163]

8-7:1.4 *Certiorari* Proceedings to the Supreme Court

A party may seek a stay of the issuance of the mandate pending the United States Supreme Court's disposition of a petition for writ of *certiorari*.[164] The motion must state the grounds for the petition and the circumstances justifying a stay.[165] The appellate court has the discretion to grant the stay "if it finds that the grounds are substantial and that the petitioner or others will incur serious hardship" if the mandate were to issue and the Supreme Court later reverses the judgment.[166]

8-7:2 Collecting Against the Judgment Debtor

Once an appeal in which the judgment is affirmed is final, the judgment creditor may recover either from the surety on its contractual promise under the bond or from the judgment debtor as principal.[167] However, the trial court cannot order the judgment debtor or surety to perform under the bond if such performance goes beyond the provisions of the mandate.[168] The same remedies available to the judgment creditor to collect on the judgment before a proper bond is filed are available when the judgment becomes final.[169]

8-8 Practical Steps and Considerations

Below are some practical steps and considerations when helping your client suspend enforcement of an adverse judgment.

8-8:1 Preliminary Considerations

- Confirm that the judgment or order is appealable and that your client desires to appeal.
- Seek and obtain a Rule 11 agreement with opposing counsel not to attempt collection efforts or execution on the judgment during the time period needed to supersede the judgment.
- Continue to check whether the judgment creditor has abstracted the judgment. A judgment is "abstracted" when the judgment creditor files a copy of the judgment in the deed records of the county where any real property owned by the judgment debtor is located, which acts as a judgment lien on that property.
- Calculate the amount of security required to supersede.
- Evaluate the various methods available to supersede and the costs.
- Contact a reputable bond broker to begin the process of obtaining a bond. If you do not know of one, a source is the National Association of Surety Bond Producers, a national trade association of surety brokers and producers.[170]

8-8:2 Net-Worth Issues

- If superseding a money judgment, ask your client if it believes that the amount of required security exceeds 50% of its current net worth.
- If yes, or if possibly, have the client:
  - gather its current financials, if any, preferably audited financials;
  - make a list of current assets and liabilities; and
  - secure accounting expertise to calculate net worth under GAAP.
- If the amount of security will be based on the client's current net worth:
  - assist the client and accountant to ensure the net-worth affidavit complies with Rule 24.2(c)(1);
  - ensure that the necessary supporting documentation is attached to the affidavit;
  - determine if the client wants the court to seal the record, limited to the net-worth information being filed, and pursue a court order and a protective order or confidentiality agreement with the judgment creditor;
  - file a motion to order security based on net worth, with the affidavit attached;
  - secure a hearing as soon as possible;
  - anticipate and prepare for net-worth discovery by the judgment creditor;
  - ensure the hearing is on the record;

- ensure the court's order complies with Rule 24.2(c)(3);
- if the court denies the motion, evaluate the merits of seeking appellate review; and
- if you appeal, seek a stay of execution during the appellate process in either the trial court or appellate court.

8-8:3 Substantial-Economic-Harm Issues

- Ask the client if posting the required security will cause it "substantial economic harm," obtaining answers and evidence addressing the factors courts may consider in determining whether substantial economic harm is likely.[171]
- Use the assistance of accounting or economic experts, if possible.
- Ask the client to identify all competent witnesses regarding the harm the client will likely suffer if the full amount of security is posted.
- If the standard can be met:
  - prepare and file a motion to reduce the amount of required security;
  - set the motion for hearing as soon as possible;
  - ensure the hearing is on the record;
  - ensure the court's order complies with Rule 24.2(b);
  - if the court denies the motion, evaluate the merits of seeking appellate review; and
  - if you appeal, seek a stay of execution during the appellate process in either the trial court or appellate court.

8-8:4 Supersedeas Bonds

- Ask the client if it has a relationship with a surety.
- Use a surety bond broker to assist in finding a sufficient surety, after informing the broker as to the bond amount.
- Once a surety is proposed:
  - explore whether the surety will require collateral, and, if so, the type and amount (liquid collateral in the full bond amount is usually required, depending on the principal's financial position); and
  - call the appropriate department at the court to determine whether the surety is approved for the amount of the bond.
- Craft the proper language for the bond.
  - set out the amount (and how it was calculated) of:
    - the principal amount;
    - pre-judgment interest;
    - post-judgment interest, the rate and term;

- specify the aggregate amount of the bond and that the surety and principal (judgment debtor) are liable for the aggregate amount and no more.
- set out the required conditions for the bond and certificate of cash deposit.

- Personally "walk" the bond through the approval process at the clerk's office:
  - observe the clerk signing the bond as approved; and
  - ensure it is filed and obtain a file-marked copy.

8-8:5 Cash Deposits

- If filing a cash deposit in lieu of bond, draft a notice of filing cash deposit in lieu of bond:
  - set out the calculations provided above for bonds;
  - set out the conditioning language; and
  - request that the deposit be placed in an interest-bearing account, if possible.
- Prepare an order for the court to place the funds in an interest-bearing account.
- Personally file the notice and order to ensure that the clerk approves the amount and will provide the order to the court for placing the funds in an interest-bearing account.

8-8:6 Non-Monetary Judgments

- Work with the client to determine:
  - the value of the rent or revenue of the client's property interest, if the judgment is for the recovery of an interest in real property; and
  - the value of the property interest, if the judgment is for the recovery of personal property.
- Gather the documentary support and identify any persons with personal knowledge of the foregoing values.
- File a motion to determine the amount of security required as soon as possible, and request a hearing.
- Present evidence on the record of the foregoing values.
- Obtain a written order finding the values and the amount of total security required.
- If dissatisfied, proceed with appellate review as described above.

8-8:7 Upon Conclusion of the Appellate Process

- If you succeed in reversing the judgment:
  - upon issuance of the mandate, file a motion to release the supersedeas bond or cash deposit in lieu of bond;

- prepare an agreed order (if it is not an agreed order, some sureties may wait until the time period to challenge the order in the court of appeals has run to effectively terminate the bond on the surety's end), stating:
  - that the bond is released;
  - that the surety and principal are discharged and released from any obligations under the bond; and
  - that the court clerk is to return the original bond to the attorney for the judgment debtor (some sureties require that the original bond be returned to them).

- If the judgment is affirmed:
  - communicate with opposing counsel that your client will perform the judgment, so as to dissuade them from attempting to execute on the bond;
  - alternatively, attempt to settle and compromise the amount of judgment instead of providing full performance (there may be some ambiguity on what "full performance" is, values of non-monetary judgments may have changed, and it may be a matter of convenience for the judgment creditor);
  - once performance or settlement occurs or is agreed-upon, proceeding with a motion to release bond or cash deposit described above.

8-9 Conclusion

Although an appeal can proceed without staying or superseding the judgment, most appellants will want a stay. The rules for obtaining a stay in Texas are very specific and must be carefully followed. Because of the urgency surrounding the entry of a judgment, counsel should familiarize themselves with the rules *before* an adverse judgment is entered. Advance preparation also should be made to comply with the strict requirements required by many bonding companies.

Notes

1 Black's Law Dictionary 1576 (9th ed. 2009).

2 Tex. R. App. P. 24.1(f).

3 *See* Tex. R. App. P. 24.1(a) (stating that "a judgment debtor *may* supersede the judgment") (emphasis added).

4 *See Miga v. Jensen*, 96 S.W.3d 207, 211–12 (Tex. 2002).

5 *See Lehmann v. Har-Con Corp.*, 39 S.W.3d 191, 200 (Tex. 2001).

6 Tex. Civ. Prac. & Rem. Code § 51.012.

7 *See Nalle v. Harrell*, 12 S.W.2d 550, 551 (Tex. Comm'n App. 1929, holding approved); *Rose v. Dominguez*, 669 S.W.2d 866, 868 (Tex. App.—Corpus Christi 1984, orig. proceeding).

8 Tex. R. App. P. 29.2.

9 Tex. R. App. P. 29.2.

10 Tex. R. App. P. 29.2.

11 Tex. R. App. P. 29.3.

12 Tex. R. App. P. 29.3.

13 *See* § 8-1:5.

[14] Tex. Civ. Prac. & Rem. Code § 51.014(b).

[15] Tex. Civ. Prac. & Rem. Code § 51.014(b).

[16] Tex. R. App. P. 29.5(b); *Perry v. Del Rio*, 66 S.W.3d 239, 259 (Tex. 2001).

[17] Rule 29.2 expressly permits supersedeas in interlocutory orders *granting* relief. Tex. R. App. P. 29 cmt. 1. The predecessor appellate rule expressly prohibited suspension of an order denying relief. Tex. R. App. P. 43(a) (1997).

[18] *See Providential Inv. Corp. v. Dibrell*, 320 S.W.2d 415, 418 (Tex. Civ. App.—Houston 1959, orig. proceeding).

[19] Tex. Fam. Code § 109.002(c).

[20] *State Bar of Tex. v. Heard*, 603 S.W.2d 829, 834 (Tex. 1980) (orig. proceeding).

[21] Tex. Alco. Bev. Code §§ 11.67(a), (b)(4).

[22] Tex. R. App. P. 25.1(h).

[23] *Hood v. Amarillo Nat'l Bank*, 815 S.W.2d 545, 548 (Tex. 1991).

[24] Tex. R. Civ. P. 627.

[25] Tex. R. Civ. P. 657; *see* Tex. Civ. Prac. & Rem. Code § 63.001(3).

[26] Tex. Civ. Prac. & Rem. Code § 31.002(b)(1).

[27] *See* Tex. Prop. Code § 52.0011; *Group Purchases, Inc. v. Lance Invs., Inc.*, 685 S.W.2d 729, 731 (Tex. App.—Dallas 1985, writ ref'd n.r.e.).

[28] Tex. Prop. Code § 52.0011(a).

[29] Tex. Prop. Code § 52.0011(a)(2); *see* Tex. Prop. Code § 52.0011; *Group Purchases, Inc. v. Lance Invs., Inc.*, 685 S.W.2d 729, 731 (Tex. App.—Dallas 1985, writ ref'd n.r.e.).

[30] *Powell v. Powell*, 822 S.W.2d 181, 185 (Tex. App.—Houston [1st Dist.] 1991, writ denied).

[31] *Emeritus Corp. v. Ofczarzak*, 198 S.W.3d 222, 226 (Tex. App.—San Antonio 2006, no pet.).

[32] *In re Emeritus Corp.*, 179 S.W.3d 112, 117 (Tex. App.—San Antonio 2005, orig. proceeding); *see* Tex. R. Civ. P. 621a.

[33] Tex. R. Civ. P. 621a.

[34] Tex. R. Civ. P. 621a; *see* Tex. R. App. P. 24, 29.

[35] *In re Smith*, 192 S.W.3d 564, 569 (Tex. 2006).

[36] Tex. R. App. P. 24.2(a)(1).

[37] *In re Teresa Corral-Lerma*, No. 12-0485, 2014 WL 6612872, at *2 (Tex. Nov. 21, 2014) (orig. proceeding).

[38] Tex. R. App. P. 24.2(a)(1).

[39] Black's Law Dictionary 445 (9th ed. 2009).

[40] Black's Law Dictionary 445 (9th ed. 2009); *see In re Nalle Plastics Family Ltd. P'ship*, No. 11-0903, 2013 WL 2150717, at *3 (Tex. May 17, 2013) (applying these definitions).

[41] *In re Nalle Plastics Family Ltd. P'ship*, 406 S.W.3d 168, 173 (Tex. 2013).

[42] *See Eagle Oil & Gas. Co. v. Shale Exploration, L.L.C.*, 510 S.W.3d 92, 94 (Tex. App.—Houston [1st Dist.] 2016) ("[T]he trial court was not required to include prejudgment interest in setting the security amount."); *Kennedy Con., Inc., v. Forman*, 493 S.W.3d 103, 105 (Tex. App.—Houston [14th Dist.] 2014) ("[T]he trial did not abuse its discretion in omitting prejudgment interest from the calculation of the amount of security. . . ."); 5 McDonald & Carlson, *Texas Civil Practice* § 30:27 & n.307.15 (2d ed.) (updated Dec. 2015).

[43] *In re Nalle Plastics Family Ltd. P'ship*, 406 S.W.3d 168, 174 (Tex. 2013).

[44] *In re Nalle Plastics Family Ltd. P'ship*, 406 S.W.3d 168, 174–75 (Tex. 2013).

[45] *Highland Capital Mgmt., L.P. v. Daugherty*, No. 05-14-01215-CV, 2014 WL 6559001, at *1–2 (Tex. App.—Dallas Oct. 22, 2014, (order) no pet.) (mem. op.).

[46] Tex. R. App. P. 24.2(c)(3).

[47] Tex. R. App. P. 24.2(c)(1).

[48] Tex. R. App. P. 24.2(c)(2).

[49] Tex. R. App. P. 24.2(c)(3).

[50] *See, e.g., Ramco Oil & Gas, Ltd. v. Anglo Dutch (Tenge) L.L.C.*, 171 S.W.3d 905, 913 (Tex. App.—Houston [14th Dist.] 2005, no pet.).

[51] *Ramco Oil & Gas, Ltd. v. Anglo Dutch (Tenge) L.L.C.*, 171 S.W.3d 905, 912, 916 (Tex. App.—Houston [14th Dist.] 2005, no pet.).

[52] *Ramco Oil & Gas, Ltd. v. Anglo Dutch (Tenge) L.L.C.*, 171 S.W.3d 905, 915 (Tex. App.—Houston [14th Dist.] 2005, no pet.).

[53] *See Anderton v. Cawley*, 326 S.W.3d 725, 727 (Tex. App.—Dallas 2010, orig. proceeding [mand. denied]); *Montelongo v. Exit Stage Left, Inc.*, 293 S.W.3d 294, 299 (Tex. App.—El Paso 2009, no pet.).

[54] *Montelongo v. Exit Stage Left, Inc.*, 293 S.W.3d 294, 299 (Tex. App.—El Paso 2009, no pet.).

[55] *Ramco Oil & Gas, Ltd. v. Anglo Dutch (Tenge) L.L.C.*, 171 S.W.3d 905, 921 (Tex. App.—Houston [14th Dist.] 2005, no pet.).

[56] *O'Quinn v. Wood*, No. 12-08-00011-CV, 2009 WL 2367133, at *8 (Tex. App.—Tyler, June 10, 2009, orig. proceeding) (mem. op.).

[57] *See* § 8-2:4.

[58] Tex. R. App. P. 24.2(a)(1).

[59] Tex. R. App. P. 24.2(b).

[60] Tex. R. App. P. 24.2(b) (Tex. 1997, 2003); *see also McDill Columbus Corp. v. Univ. Woods Apts., Inc.*, 7 S.W.3d 923, 924–25 (Tex. App.—Texarkana 2000, no pet.) (applying the pre-2003 amended Rule 24.2(b)).

[61] *See, e.g., Isern v. Ninth Court of Appeals*, 925 S.W.2d 604, 606 (Tex. 1996) (orig. proceeding); *Mudd v. Mudd*, 665 S.W.2d 128, 129 (Tex. App.—San Antonio 1983, no writ) (holding insufficiency of personal assets to post a bond supported reduction in the bond amount).

[62] *Ramco Oil & Gas, Ltd. v. Anglo Dutch (Tenge) L.L.C.*, 171 S.W.3d 905, 917 (Tex. App.—Houston [14th Dist.] 2005, no pet.).

[63] *Ramco Oil & Gas, Ltd. v. Anglo Dutch (Tenge) L.L.C.*, 171 S.W.3d 905, 917 (Tex. App.—Houston [14th Dist.] 2005, no pet.).

[64] Tex. R. App. P. 24.2(a)(1).

[65] *See Kennesaw Life & Accident Ins. Co. v. Streetman*, 644 S.W.2d 915, 916–17 (Tex. App.—Austin 1983, writ ref'd n.r.e.).

[66] Tex. R. App. P. 24.2(a)(2).

[67] Tex. R. App. P. 24.2(a)(2)(A).

[68] *Culbertson v. Brodsky*, 775 S.W.2d 451, 454 (Tex. App.—Fort Worth 1989, writ dism'd w.o.j.).

[69] Tex. R. App. P. 24.2(a)(2)(B).

[70] Tex. R. App. P. 24.1(a). *See* § 8-3:5.

[71] Tex. R. App. P. 24.1(a)(1).

[72] Tex. R. App. P. 24.1(b).

[73] *Amwest Sur. Ins. Co. v. Graham*, 949 S.W.2d 724, 726 (Tex. App.—San Antonio 1997, writ denied).

[74] *Trent v. Rhomberg*, 18 S.W. 510, 512 (Tex. 1886).

[75] *Universe Life Ins. Co. v. Giles*, 982 S.W.2d 488, 491 (Tex. App.—Texarkana 1998, pet. denied).

[76] Tex. R. App. P. 24.1(b)(2).

77 *Valerio v. Laughlin*, 307 S.W.2d 352, 353 (Tex. Civ. App.—San Antonio 1957, orig. proceeding).

78 *Gullo-Haas Toyota, Inc. v. Davidson, Eagleson & Co.*, 832 S.W.2d 418, 419 (Tex. App.—Houston [1st Dist.] 1992, no writ); *Fortune v. McElhenney*, 645 S.W.2d 934, 935 (Tex. App.—Austin 1983, no writ).

79 *Fortune v. McElhenney*, 645 S.W.2d 934, 935 (Tex. App.—Austin 1983, no writ).

80 *See also* § 8-2:3.4f.

81 Tex. R. App. P. 24.1(b)(1).

82 *See Mercantile Bank & Trust v. Cunov*, 733 S.W.2d 717, 718 (Tex. App.—San Antonio 1987, no writ).

83 Tex. R. App. P. 24.1(d).

84 Tex. R. App. P. 24.1(b)(1)(D).

85 Financial Management Service, Dep't of Treasury, Department of the Treasury's Listing of Approved Sureties (Department Circular 570), *available at* http://www.fms.treas.gov/c570.

86 *Universal Automobile Ins. Co. v. Culberson*, 51 S.W.2d 1071, 1073 (Tex. Civ. App.—Waco 1932, no writ).

87 *Elliott v. Lester*, 126 S.W.2d 756, 759 (Tex. Civ. App.—Dallas 1939, no writ).

88 *Brown & Root, Inc. v. DeSautell*, 554 S.W.2d 764, 771 (Tex. Civ. App.—Houston [1st Dist.] 1977, writ ref'd n.r.e.).

89 *See TransAmerican Natural Gas. Corp. v. Finkelstein*, 905 S.W.2d 412, 414 (Tex. App.—San Antonio 1995, no writ).

90 *See, e.g., Kantor v. Herald Publ'g Co.*, 632 S.W.2d 656, 658 (Tex. App.—Tyler 1982, no writ).

91 Black's Law Dictionary 1579 (9th ed. 2009) (emphasis added).

92 *Amwest Sur. Ins. Co. v. Graham*, 949 S.W.2d 724, 726 (Tex. App.—San Antonio 1997, writ denied); *see* Tex. R. App. P. 24.1(a), (b)(1)(D), (d).

93 *Universal Automobile Ins. Co. v. Culberson*, 51 S.W.2d 1071, 1073 (Tex. Civ. App.—Waco 1932, no writ).

94 *Universal Automobile Ins. Co. v. Culberson*, 51 S.W.2d 1071, 1073 (Tex. Civ. App.—Waco 1932, no writ).

95 Tex. Ins. Code arts. 6.16, 7.19-1(b).

96 *See, e.g., Ruiz v. Watkins*, 701 S.W.2d 688, 691 (Tex. App.—Amarillo 1985, orig. proceeding).

97 Tex. R. App. P. 24.1(a)(3).

98 Tex. R. App. P. 24.1(c)(1); Tex. R. Civ. P. 14c.

99 *Mercantile Bank & Trust v. Cunov*, 733 S.W.2d 717, 718 (Tex. App.—San Antonio 1987, no writ).

100 *Heritage Hous. Corp. v. Ferguson*, 651 S.W.2d 272, 273 (Tex. App.—Dallas 1983, no writ) (per curiam).

101 *Southwestern States Gen. Corp. v. McKenzie*, 658 S.W.2d 850, 852 (Tex. App.—Dallas 1983, writ dism'd w.o.j.).

102 Tex. R. App. P. 24.1(c)(3).

103 Tex. R. App. P. 24.1(c)(3).

104 Tex. R. App. P. 24.1(c)(2).

105 Tex. R. App. P. 24.1(a)(4).

106 *See* Tex. R. App. P. 25.1(g)(2).

107 *Herring v. Houston Nat'l Exch. Bank*, 253 S.W.2d 813, 816 (Tex. 1923) (construing general governmental exemption); *Board of Adjustment v. Stovall*, 216 S.W.2d 171, 174–75 (Tex. 1949) (construing incorporated cities exemption).

108 *See Ammex Warehouse Co. v. Archer*, 381 S.W.2d 478, 481–82 (Tex. 1964).

109 *In re Dallas Area Rapid Transit*, 967 S.W.2d 358, 360 (Tex. 1998) (orig. proceeding) (per curiam).

110 *In re Dallas Area Rapid Transit*, 967 S.W.2d 358, 360 (Tex. 1998) (orig. proceeding) (per curiam).

111 Tex. Civ. Prac. & Rem. Code § 6.001; *see Ammex Warehouse Co. v. Archer*, 381 S.W.2d 478, 481–82 (Tex. 1964).

112 *In re Long*, 984 S.W.2d 623, 625 (Tex. 1999).

113 *Herring v. Houston Nat'l Exch. Bank*, 253 S.W.2d 813, 815–816 (Tex. 1923).

114 *Ammex Warehouse Co. v. Archer*, 381 S.W.2d 478, 480–82 (Tex. 1964).

115 *Collier v. Smith*, 169 S.W. 1108, 1109–10 (Tex. Civ. App.—Amarillo 1914, writ ref'd); *see Hall v. Eastland County*, 254 S.W. 1113, 1114 (Tex. Civ. App.—El Paso 1923, no writ).

116 *Teacher Retirement Systems v. Duckworth*, 260 S.W.2d 632, 633 (Tex. Civ. App.—Fort Worth 1953), *aff'd*, 264 S.W.2d 98 (Tex. 1954).

117 *Holder v. Holder*, 582 S.W.2d 598, 600 (Tex. Civ. App.—Texarkana 1979, no writ).

118 *Railroad Comm'n v. Roberts*, 332 S.W.2d 745, 749 (Tex. Civ. App.—Austin 1960, no writ).

119 *Public Utilities Comm'n v. Coalition for Affordable Utility Rates*, 776 S.W.2d 221, 222 (Tex. App.—Austin 1989, no writ).

120 *Gossett v. L.G. Balfour Co.*, 111 S.W.2d 1119, 1121 (Tex. Civ. App.—Fort Worth 1937), *rev'd on other grounds*, 115 S.W.2d 595 (Tex. 1938).

121 *Dallas Cnty. Bail Bond Bd. v. Mason*, 773 S.W.2d 586, 587 (Tex. App.—Dallas 1989, no writ).

122 *Lane v. Hewgley*, 155 S.W. 348, 350 (Tex. Civ. App.—San Antonio 1913, no writ).

123 *Parker v. White*, 815 S.W.2d 893, 895 (Tex. App.—Tyler 1991, no writ); *but see Valerio v. Laughlin*, 307 S.W.2d 352, 353 (Tex. Civ. App.—San Antonio 1957, no writ).

124 *Weber v. Walker*, 591 S.W.2d 559, 563 (Tex. Civ. App.—Dallas 1979, no writ).

125 *City of Ranger v. Comm'n on Law Enforcement Officer Standards & Educ.*, 599 S.W.2d 693, 694 (Tex. Civ. App.—Austin 1980, writ ref'd n.r.e.).

126 *Southland Life Ins. Co. v. Barrett*, 172 S.W.2d 997, 1001 (Tex. Civ. App.—Fort Worth 1943, writ ref'd w.o.m.); *Thomas v. Cowan*, 153 S.W.2d 509, 509–10 (Tex. Civ. App.—Fort Worth 1941, no writ); *United States v. Branson*, 147 S.W.2d 286, 287 (Tex. Civ. App.—San Antonio 1941, writ ref'd).

127 28 U.S.C. § 2408.

128 *United States Dep't of Air Force v. Wilhelm*, 555 S.W.2d 498, 499 (Tex. Civ. App.—Houston [14th Dist.] 1977, no writ); *United States v. Branson*, 147 S.W.2d 286, 287 (Tex. Civ. App.—San Antonio 1941, writ ref'd).

129 *Arkansas v. Sabo*, 559 S.W.2d 124, 126 (Tex. Civ. App.—Texarkana 1977, writ ref'd n.r.e.).

130 *University Interscholastic League v. Hardin-Jefferson I.S.D.*, 648 S.W.2d 770, 773 (Tex. App.—Beaumont 1983, no writ); *University Interscholastic League v. Payne*, 635 S.W.2d 754, 756–57, 758 (Tex. App.—Amarillo 1982, writ dism'd w.o.j.); *Marshall v. Brown*, 635 S.W.2d 578, 580 (Tex. App.—Amarillo 1982, writ ref'd n.r.e.).

131 *Eagle Life Ins. Co. v. Hernandez*, 743 S.W.2d 671, 671–72 (Tex. App.—El Paso 1987, writ denied).

132 *Eagle Life Ins. Co. v. Hernandez*, 743 S.W.2d 671, 671 (Tex. App.—El Paso 1987, writ denied).

133 Tex. Civ. Prac. & Rem. Code § 104.006.

[134] Tex. Civ. Prac. & Rem. Code § 104.001.

[135] Tex. R. App. P. 24.3(a).

[136] Tex. R. App. P. 24.3(b).

[137] 5 Roy W. McDonald & Elaine A. Grafton Carlson, McDonald & Carlson Texas Civil Practice § 30:20 (2d ed. 2013).

[138] *See* Tex. R. App. P. 51.1(b) ("When the trial court clerk receives the mandate, the appellate court's judgment must be enforced."); *see also Dignowity v. Fly*, 210 S.W. 505, 506 (Tex. 1919) (holding that court of civil appeals' judgment is not final while subject to review by the Texas Supreme Court).

[139] Tex. R. App. P. 24.4(a).

[140] Tex. R. App. P. 24.4(a).

[141] Tex. R. App. P. 24.4(a).

[142] Tex. R. App. P. 24.4(b).

[143] Tex. R. App. P. 24.4(d).

[144] *Ramco Oil & Gas, Ltd. v. Anglo Dutch (Tenge) L.L.C.*, 171 S.W.3d 905, 909 (Tex. App.—Houston [14th Dist.] 2005, no pet.).

[145] *City of Keller v. Wilson*, 168 S.W.3d 802, 822 (Tex. 2005).

[146] *See infra* § 8-8.

[147] *McFadin v. Broadway Coffeehouse, L.L.C.*, 539 S.W.3d 278, 283–85 (Tex. 2018).

[148] *McFadin v. Broadway Coffeehouse, L.L.C.*, 539 S.W.3d 278, 284 (Tex. 2018).

[149] *McFadin v. Broadway Coffeehouse, L.L.C.*, 539 S.W.3d 278, 284–85 (Tex. 2018).

[150] Tex. R. App. P. 24.4(d).

[151] Tex. R. App. P. 24.4(d).

[152] Tex. R. App. P. 24.4(e).

[153] Tex. R. App. P. 24.4(e).

[154] Tex. R. App. P. 24.4(e).

[155] Tex. Civ. Prac. & Rem. Code § 34.022.

[156] *Continental Cas. Co. v. Huizar*, 740 S.W.2d 429, 430 (Tex. 1987).

[157] *Miga v. Jensen*, 96 S.W.3d 207, 211–12 (Tex. 2002).

[158] Tex. R. App. P. 18.1.

[159] Tex. R. App. P. 51.1(b), 65.2.

[160] Tex. R. App. P. 51.1(b), 65.2; *see In re Long*, 984 S.W.2d 623, 626 (Tex. 1998) (refusing to hold party in contempt for violating a lower court judgment that was superseded on appeal until the issuance of mandate enforcing the lower court judgment); *see also supra* § 8-4.

[161] *Universe Life Ins. Co. v. Giles*, 982 S.W.2d 488, 490 (Tex. App.—Texarkana 1998, pet. denied); *see* Elaine A. Carlson, *Reshuffling the Deck: Enforcing and Superseding Civil Judgments on Appeal After House Bill 4*, 46 S. Tex. L. Rev. 1035, 1117 (2005) (citing *Universe Life Ins. Co. v. Giles*, 982 S.W.2d 488, 490 (Tex. App.—Texarkana 1998, pet. denied)).

[162] *Universe Life Ins. Co. v. Giles*, 982 S.W.2d 488, 492 n.21 (Tex. App.—Texarkana 1998, pet. denied).

[163] *E.g., Amwest Sur. Ins. Co. v. Graham*, 949 S.W.2d 724, 727 (Tex. App.—San Antonio 1997, writ denied); *Edlund v. Bounds*, 842 S.W.2d 719, 732 (Tex. App.—Dallas 1992, writ denied).

[164] Tex. R. App. P. 18.2.

[165] Tex. R. App. P. 18.2.

[166] Tex. R. App. P. 18.2.

[167] *Universe Life Ins. Co. v. Giles*, 982 S.W.2d 488, 493 (Tex. App.—Texarkana 1998, pet. denied).

[168] *See McFadin v. Broadway Coffeehouse, L.L.C.*, 539 S.W.3d 278, 285 (Tex. 2018) (trial court's order "requiring [defendant] to pay the amount of the bond went beyond the provisions of the 2014 judgment," and that order was a final, appealable order).

[169] *Universe Life Ins. Co. v. Giles*, 982 S.W.2d 488, 493 (Tex. App.—Texarkana 1998, pet. denied).

[170] Their website is www.nasbp.org. Click on the tab "Find a Producer," which is listed on the left side of the home page, and type in the required information.

[171] *See* § 8-2:4.3.

CHAPTER 9

Appellate Motions

9-1 General Rules

During the course of an appeal, the advocate often files more motions than briefs. Although the appeal is presented through the briefs (and oral argument), motions can, and usually do, play an important part in accomplishing that goal. This chapter presents several general principles of appellate-motion practice, and then addresses specific motions, providing the purposes, requirements, and practical pointers for each.

9-1:1 Organizing the Content of the Motion

Like briefs, motions should be brief, and should quickly state what the movant wants the court to do. To that end, the following steps in organizing the motion's content may be helpful:

- Know the general requirements of appellate motions contained in Texas Rule of Appellate Procedure 10;[1]
- Determine which specific rule governs your motion and knows its requirements;
- Specifically write out the desired relief;
- Think about the explanation you need to present to obtain the desired relief; and
- Determine what, if any, evidentiary support you will need to make that explanation, and whether it is contained in the appellate record (if filed) or outside the record.

9-1:2 Requirements of Rule 10

Rule 10 provides the general requirements for appellate motions, and expressly states that additional requirements may exist for certain motions.[2] Also, always check the local rules for the court of appeals in which your appeal has been filed for additional requirements.

Content of the motion. A party seeking "an order or other relief" must file a motion, which must:

- "contain or be accompanied by any matter specifically required by a rule governing such a motion;"

- "state with particularity the grounds on which it is based;"
- "set forth the order or relief sought;"
- "be served and filed with any brief, affidavit, or other paper filed in support of the motion;" and
- in civil cases (and except for motions for rehearing and en banc reconsideration), contain a certificate of conference—that the filing party "conferred, or made a reasonable attempt to confer, with all other parties about the merits of the motion and whether those parties oppose the motion."[3]

9-1:3 Evidence

Rule 10.2 addresses evidence supporting appellate motions. Essentially, factual support for motions comes from four general sources:

1. the appellate record;
2. sources outside the record;
3. the court's "knowledge in its official capacity;" and
4. the signing attorney's personal knowledge.

Facts from sources 1, 3, and 4 do *not* need to be verified by affidavit or other evidence.[4] Facts supported by sources outside the record *must* be supported by an affidavit "or other satisfactory evidence."[5] For example, if a motion is relying on an order filed in the trial court but not yet filed in the appellate record, the motion should attach that order and an affidavit signed by an attorney who can authenticate it.

9-1:4 Rulings on Motions

9-1:4.1 Timing

Courts generally wait to rule on a motion until after a response is filed (if opposed) or 10 days.[6] Courts "should not" rule on a motion until 10 days have passed unless:

- the motion is for an extension of time to file a brief, petition for review, or petition for discretionary review;
- the motion is unopposed; or
- it is an emergency motion.[7]

9-1:4.2 Reconsideration

If the court prematurely rules on a motion, the party adversely affected may request the court to reconsider its order.[8]

9-1:4.3 Ruling by One Judge

Most motions may be ruled upon by one judge.[9] But in civil cases, one judge should not do the following:

- rule on a petition for extraordinary relief (e.g., a mandamus petition); or
- "dismiss or otherwise determine an appeal or a motion for rehearing."[10]

9-1:4.4 Ruling by Panel

Rule 10.4(b) provides that the appellate court may provide by order or a local rule that a panel or the en banc court must determine any motion or "class of motions."

9-1:5 Local Rules

Before filing any motion in a court of appeals, consult that court's local rules to determine whether that court has additional requirements for the motion.

9-1:6 Filing Fees

Most motions require a filing fee, which must be paid by the filing party unless it is excused by statute or the appellate rules.[11] Consult the court's web site and/or local rules for a list of motions requiring a filing fee and the amount of the fee. If the motion is not listed, or if you have doubt about the category which applies to your motion, telephone the clerk's office.

9-2 Specific Motions

9-2:1 Motion to Extend Time to File Notice of Appeal

A party that fails to timely file a notice of appeal in the trial court may, within 15 days of the missed deadline, file *in the court of appeals* (i) a motion to extend the time for filing the notice of appeal, and (ii) the notice of appeal.[12] The motion must state:

- the deadline for filing the notice of appeal in the trial court;
- a reasonable explanation as to why the notice of appeal was not timely filed;
- the identity of the trial court;
- the date of the trial court's judgment or appealable order; and
- the case number and style of the case in the trial court.[13]

The "reasonable explanation" can be simply that the attorney inadvertently missed the deadline, or miscalculated the due date for the notice of appeal.[14] If these requisites are met, the court of appeals should grant the extension and deem the notice of appeal timely when filed.

9-2:2 Motions Regarding Counsel

9-2:2.1 Motions to Admit Counsel Pro Hac Vice

A non-resident attorney should consult several sources before seeking admission pro hac vice to participate in a proceeding in any court in Texas, including an appellate court:

- Rule XIX of the State Bar of Texas Rules Governing Admission to the Bar;
- Section 82.0361 of the Texas Government Code; and
- The Texas Board of Law Examiners (BLE) web site addressing the procedures and providing a link for the application that must precede the motion.[15]

A non-resident attorney must complete the procedures outlined below for *each proceeding* in which the attorney desires admission. These procedures are specific and mandatory, and therefore must be carefully followed.

9-2:2.1a Application

The non-resident attorney must first make application before moving for admission pro hac vice by following these steps:

- Obtain and complete a copy of the Application for Pro Hac Vice Admission from the website listed above (if *any* question is not answered, the Application will be rejected);
- Mail a completed Application (which must be notarized) to the BLE ***with a check for $250*** made payable to the BLE (this fee must accompany each application); and
- Wait for receipt by mail of an acknowledgment issued by the BLE.[16]

9-2:2.1b Motion by Non-Resident Attorney

After receipt of the acknowledgment, the non-resident attorney must file with the applicable court a sworn motion requesting permission to participate in a particular proceeding, providing:

1. the office address, telephone number, and fax number of the non-resident attorney;
2. the name and State Bar number of a duly licensed Texas attorney with whom the non-resident attorney will be associated in the proceeding and the same contact information for that attorney;
3. a list of all Texas cases and causes, including cause number and caption, in which the non-resident attorney has appeared or sought leave to appear or participate within the past two years;
4. "a list of jurisdictions in which the non-resident attorney is licensed, including federal courts, and a statement that the non-resident attorney is or is not an active member in good standing in each of those jurisdictions;"
5. "a statement that the non-resident attorney has or has not been the subject of disciplinary action by the Bar or courts of any jurisdiction in which the attorney is licensed within the preceding five years, with a description of any such disciplinary action;"
6. "a statement that the non-resident attorney has or has not been denied admission to the courts of any State or to any federal court during the preceding five years;"
7. "a statement that the non-resident attorney is familiar with the State Bar Act, the State Bar Rules, and the Texas Disciplinary Rules of Professional Conduct," and that the attorney will abide by and comply with the foregoing as long as the attorney participates in the proceeding; and
8. a copy of the acknowledgment from the BLE, which provides proof that the non-resident attorney paid the mandatory fee.[17]

9-2:2.1c Motion by Texas Attorney

The non-resident attorney's motion must be accompanied by a separate motion of the "resident practicing Texas attorney with whom the non-resident attorney shall be associated in the proceeding of a particular cause."[18] The motion must provide:

1. a statement that the resident attorney finds the non-resident attorney to be a reputable attorney; and
2. a recommendation that the non-resident attorney be granted permission to participate in the proceeding at issue.[19]

Unlike the motion by the non-resident attorney, this motion is not a sworn motion.

In practice, the motions by the non-resident attorney and the Texas attorney are filed separately, but contemporaneously. If more than one non-resident attorney is seeking permission to participate in a particular proceeding, each non-resident attorney must file his or her own motion, and the Texas attorney should file a separate supporting motion for each non-resident attorney.

9-2:2.2 Motions to Withdraw/Substitute Counsel

9-2:2.2a Mandatory Content When No Attorney Substitutes

When no attorney is immediately substituting for the withdrawing counsel, Rule 6.5(a) provides that the motion to withdraw by the current attorney *must* contain:

- "a list of current deadlines and settings in the case;"
- "the party's name and last known address and telephone number;"
- "a statement that a copy of the motion was delivered to the party;" and
- "a statement that the party was notified in writing of the right to object to the motion."[20]

9-2:2.2b Delivery of Motion

The motion must be delivered to the party in person or by *both* certified and first-class mail to the party's last known address.[21]

9-2:2.2c Withdrawal Granted

If the court grants the motion, the withdrawing attorney must immediately notify the party in writing of any deadlines or settings known by the attorney at the time of withdrawal but not previously disclosed to the client. A copy of the written notice must be filed with the court clerk.

9-2:2.2d Exception for Substitution of Counsel

If an attorney substitutes for the withdrawing attorney, the motion to withdraw need not comply with the four requirements in Rule 6.5(a). The motion to withdraw need only state the substituting attorney's:

- name,
- mailing address,

- telephone number,
- facsimile number, and
- State Bar of Texas identification number.[22]

The withdrawing attorney must still deliver the motion to withdraw as provided above, but he or she need not provide the party notice of impending deadlines or settings.[23] Rule 6.5(d) does not provide that the substituting attorney is required to sign this motion.

9-2:3 Motions Regarding Briefs

9-2:3.1 Motions for Extension of Time

Rules 10.5(b)(1) and 38.6(d) address motions to extend the time to file briefs.

9-2:3.1a Preliminary Steps

Before filing, the moving attorney should first:

- review the court's local rules to determine if any rules apply to requests for extensions;
- determine the amount of time required—it should be no more than 30 days from the due date, as most courts do not grant longer extensions;
- outline with specificity the reasons for the extension, such as the attorney's work schedule and other time impediments to completing the brief; and
- ask opposing counsel whether he or she will oppose the requested extension.

9-2:3.1b Mandatory Contents of All Motions

Under Rule 10.5(b)(1), the motion must state:

- the deadline for filing the brief;
- the length of extension requested;
- "the facts relied on to reasonably explain the need for an extension;" and
- the number of prior extensions granted regarding the particular brief at issue.

The Tenth Court of Appeals Local Rule 7 expressly addresses motions for extensions. It requires a statement of the dates the clerk's record and reporter's record were filed in motions related to the appellant's brief.[24]

9-2:3.1c Motions Regarding Petitions for Review

Motions for extension to file a petition for review or petition for discretionary review must also specify:

- the court of appeals;
- the date of the court of appeals' judgment;

- the case number and style of the case in the court of appeals; and
- the date every motion for rehearing or en banc reconsideration was filed, and either the date and nature of the court's ruling or that the motion remains pending.[25]

9-2:3.1d Facts That "Reasonably Explain"

The explanation should be candid and with some detail. For a first extension, the general reason is the moving attorney's work load and schedule. Therefore, identifying the style, case number, task, and deadline related to another proceeding that is part of the reason for an extension is strongly recommended. Dates of non-refundable travel or a reasonably specific description of an event are also advised. For a second extension, more than "busyness" of counsel is advised, although that may be sufficient.

9-2:3.1e When to File

Rule 38.6(d) states the motion "may be filed before or after the date the brief is due." The better practice is to file the motion several days before the due date, assuming the reasons for the extension are apparent at that time. If a motion will be opposed, filing it as early as possible is particularly important, allowing time for a response and for the court to rule.

9-2:3.1f Ruling

As a general rule, Texas appellate courts grant the first request for extension, provided a reasonable explanation is given. Further extensions may be granted, particularly if unopposed, but counsel should not think it will be automatic.[26]

9-2:3.1g Accelerated Appeals

Some courts of appeals will grant extensions in increments of only 20 days rather than 30 days in accelerated appeals. Also, in parental-termination cases, extensions may be particularly difficult to obtain because the courts are subject to a legislative 180-day deadline (starting from the date of the notice of appeal) for issuing an opinion. Look carefully at the calendar to ascertain a reasonable number of days to request, and acknowledge the accelerated nature of the case in your motion.

9-2:3.2 Motion to Enlarge Page or Word Limit

Appellate briefs, petitions for review, briefs on the merits, and motions for rehearing now have word limits, as opposed to page limits, if produced on a computer.[27] But whether a party requires an enlargement of a word limit or a page limit, the motion must state a compelling reason for the enlargement, as courts very rarely grant such relief.

9-2:3.2a Content

In addition to general rules for all motions, such a motion should also state:

- the status of the appeal, such as whether other briefs have been filed, and when, and the submission date, if known;

- the page or word limit required under Rule 9.4;
- the number of additional words or pages requested; and
- the reason for the request.

9-2:3.2b Timing of Motion

The motion should be filed as soon as counsel realizes during the preparation process that additional words or pages will be required. A motion filed on the eve of, or soon before, the filing date will carry less credibility than if filed relatively early in the preparation process.

9-2:3.2c Attaching the Completed Document

The rule does not require that the completed document be attached to the motion, particularly if the motion is filed close to the filing date, but doing so will show the court that the filing attorney has been diligent in preparing the document and what is contained in the extra words or pages. But this is in no way a guarantee that the motion will be granted. If the motion is denied, the filing party will of course need to shorten the document and timely file it.

9-2:3.3 Motion for Leave to Amend or Supplement the Brief

9-2:3.3a Briefs in the Courts of Appeals

Rule 38.7 states that "[a] brief may be amended or supplemented whenever justice requires, on whatever reasonable terms the court may prescribe." Although the rule does not require a motion for leave, the local rules of several courts of appeals expressly require one.[28] Even if not required by a local rule, the better practice is to file a motion for leave.

9-2:3.3b Petitions and Briefs in the Supreme Court

Rules 53.8 and 55.8 address amending petitions for review and briefs on the merits, respectively. Both rules require the motion to show "good cause" for amending.

9-2:3.3c Attachments

Always attach to a motion for leave a copy of the amended or supplemented document. Even if only one or a few pages have been modified or supplemented, the better practice is to file the entire modified document and rename it "Amended Brief," "Amended Petition," etc. That way, the court will have to review only one document.

9-2:3.4 Motion for Leave to File Post-Submission Brief

Periodically, events occur during oral argument raising the need to address an issue in a post-submission brief. Some of the reasons to file a post-submission brief include:

- clarifying an answer given during argument;
- expanding on an answer to a question;

- providing full citations to authorities mentioned or addressed at oral argument that are not contained in any of the briefs;
- addressing a new case decision issued after oral argument; and
- responding to an argument raised by opposing counsel not made in his or her briefs and to which time did not permit the opportunity to respond.

Although the Rules do not specifically address post-submission briefs, they are essentially supplemental briefs and therefore are governed by the rules addressed in the preceding section. A party should always move for leave to file if leave was not expressly given during oral argument. Some courts of appeals have local rules specifically addressing post-submission briefs.[29]

9-2:4 Motions Regarding Oral Argument

9-2:4.1 Motion to Postpone

Under Rule 10.5(c), a party may move to postpone the oral argument date. Unless all parties agree to postpone or "sufficient cause" is apparent to the court, the motion "must be supported by sufficient cause." This phrase is not defined in the rules, but appears to be a higher standard than "reasonable explanation" for motions for extension to file briefs. Because the courts provide notice to counsel well in advance of argument and generally have full dockets, the motion, if opposed, must clearly state why counsel cannot present argument that day, such as a scheduling conflict that cannot be altered. In addition to the standard requirements, the motion should provide these basic facts:

- the date of the argument;
- the reason counsel cannot present argument that date, stating that the conflict cannot be remedied and/or an unsuccessful attempt was made to reschedule the conflicting event; and
- the time period of the postponement.

9-2:4.2 Motion for Additional Time

A party seeking additional time to present oral argument has a high burden, as courts rarely enlarge the time allotted for argument. It may help if the motion is unopposed and a compelling reason exists. The motion should be filed immediately after the case is set for argument, or arguably before then.

9-2:4.3 Motion to Allow Additional Counsel or Amicus

The rules provide that only two counsel can argue for the same side.[30] You need a motion for leave to allow more, although this is disfavored by courts and in most cases is not a good idea.[31] If an amicus desires to participate, it must file a motion for leave stating that one of the parties is willing to divide its time with the amicus, or asking the court to enlarge the time for argument to allow the amicus to participate.[32] Consent of all parties is not required for the latter but strongly recommended if the motion is to succeed.[33]

9-2:5 Motion to Disqualify or Recuse a Judge

The grounds for disqualifying and recusing an appellate judge are generally the same as for trial judges.[34] Differences exist between disqualification and recusal. This chapter will not extensively address Texas jurisprudence regarding disqualification or recusal, but will provide the practitioner with the procedural framework for seeking both types of relief.

9-2:5.1 Motion to Disqualify

Disqualification of a judge in Texas is governed by Texas Rule of Civil Procedure 16.1, 18a(a) and 18b(a), the Texas Constitution, and various statutes.

9-2:5.1a Timing

A motion to disqualify may be filed at any time and is not waivable, even as a collateral attack on the judgment.[35] This is so because orders and judgments issued by a judge who is constitutionally disqualified are void.[36]

9-2:5.1b Supporting Facts

In addition to the requirements for all motions, the motion to disqualify must state sufficient facts with particularity and in a form that would be admissible in evidence.[37] The facts must be based on personal knowledge or on information and belief if the basis for the latter is stated.[38] The motion should be verified.[39]

9-2:5.1c Grounds

The motion must specify the ground(s) upon which disqualification is sought. In general, a judge may be disqualified and removed from a case if he or she is (i) disqualified under Article V, section 11 of the Texas Constitution, (ii) disqualified under a statute, or (iii) disqualified or recused under rules promulgated by the Texas Supreme Court.[40] Appellate judges, however, may be disqualified only on constitutional or statutory grounds, not on the basis of the rules of civil procedure.[41] The following are the primary grounds for disqualification:

- the judge previously served as counsel[42] in the case;
- the judge "may be interested" in the outcome of the case to such a degree that it might influence or impair his or her judgment or create a conflict of interest; and
- the judge is related to one of the parties by affinity or the third degree of consanguinity.[43]

For a discussion about disqualification of an appellate judge, read *Tesco American, Inc. v. Strong Industries*.[44]

9-2:5.1d Appellate Relief

Should the judge continue to sit once constitutionally disqualified, mandamus relief is available, and the party seeking disqualification need not prove the lack of an appellate remedy.[45]

9-2:5.2 Motion to Recuse

9-2:5.2a Timing

A party should file a motion to recuse as soon as it learns of facts providing a reasonable basis for recusal.[46] This is because a party can waive the ability to seek recusal.[47]

9-2:5.2b Supporting Facts

As with motions to disqualify, a motion to recuse must state sufficient facts with particularity and in a form that would be admissible in evidence.[48] The fact must be based on personal knowledge or on information and belief if the basis for the latter is stated.[49] The motion should be verified.[50]

9-2:5.2c Grounds

The motion must specify the ground(s) upon which recusal is sought. A judge should be recused when:

- "the judge's impartiality might reasonably be questioned;"
- "the judge has a personal bias or prejudice concerning the subject matter or a party;"
- "the judge has personal knowledge of disputed evidentiary facts concerning the proceeding;"
- "the judge or a lawyer with whom the judge previously practiced law has been a material witness concerning the proceeding;"
- "the judge participated as counsel, adviser, or material witness in the matter in controversy, or expressed an opinion concerning the merits of it, while acting as an attorney in government service;"
- "the judge knows that the judge, individually or as a fiduciary, or the judge's spouse or minor child residing in the judge's household, has a financial interest in the subject matter in controversy or in a party to the proceeding, or any other interest that could be substantially affected by the outcome of the proceeding;"
- "the judge or the judge's spouse, or a person within the third degree of relationship to either of them, or the spouse of such a person:
    - is a party to the proceeding or an officer, director, or trustee of a party;
    - is known by the judge to have an interest that could be substantially affected by the outcome of the proceeding; or
    - is to the judge's knowledge likely to be a material witness in the proceeding[;] [or]"
- "the judge or the judge's spouse, or a person within the first degree of relationship to either of them, or the spouse of such a person, is acting as a lawyer in the proceeding."[51]

9-2:5.2d Procedure and Ruling

The motion is initially presented to the challenged judge. Upon the filing of the motion, the challenged judge must either remove himself or herself from all participation in the case, or alternatively, refer the matter to the entire court, which will decide the motion en banc by majority vote.[52]

9-2:5.2e Appellate Relief

An order of recusal is not reviewable, but an order denying a motion to recuse is reviewable.[53]

9-2:6 Dispositive Motions

9-2:6.1 Motion to Dismiss Appeal for Lack of Jurisdiction

Under Texas Rule of Appellate Procedure 42.3(a), a party may move to dismiss the appeal or affirm the judgment or appealable order based on lack of jurisdiction. A challenge to the court's jurisdiction cannot be waived, and may be raised at any time. But once a practitioner can demonstrate that the court lacks jurisdiction, it should move immediately, saving the time and resources of the client and the court. Although a challenge to the court's jurisdiction may be made in the brief, the better practice is to file a separate motion.

9-2:6.1a Circumstances Resulting in Lack of Jurisdiction

The following circumstances will support a motion to dismiss for lack of jurisdiction:

- the appellant never filed a notice of appeal;
- the notice of appeal was untimely, and no motion to extend the time to perfect the appeal was filed, or was filed untimely;
- the trial court's judgment was not final;
- the interlocutory order that is the subject of the appeal is not appealable;
- the appellant lacks standing to appeal;
- the petition for review was untimely, and no motion to extend the time to file the petition for review was filed, or was filed untimely; and
- the appeal is moot.

9-2:6.1b Content/Evidence

The motion must state the specific reason why the court lacks jurisdiction, providing references to the appellate record, if possible, attaching verified copies of documents not in the record, and ample briefing in support of the argument.

9-2:6.2 Motion to Dismiss Appeal for Want of Prosecution

Rule 42.3(b) permits a motion to dismiss for want of prosecution. Circumstances supporting this motion include:

- the appellant fails to timely file its opening brief;[54] and
- no clerk's record is filed because the (non-indigent) appellant did not pay or make arrangements to pay for the clerk's record.[55]

9-2:6.2a Content/Evidence

The appellant's failure to prosecute the appeal under these circumstances will be obvious, but the motion nevertheless should briefly state the specific ground and point to the lack of either the appellant's brief and/or the clerk's record. Regarding the failure to file a brief, the moving party should explain how it has been "significantly injured" by such failure, if possible (see below). As for the failure to file the clerk's record, the motion should state that the appellant has not filed an affidavit of indigence in compliance with Rule 20.1.

9-2:6.2b Ability to Cure

Because the court generally cannot act on a motion before the expiration of 10 days,[56] the appellant will have time to cure the defect. For example, if the appellant provides a reasonable explanation for its failure to file the brief, and the appellee is not "significantly injured" by such failure, the appellant may avoid dismissal.[57]

9-2:6.3 Motion to Voluntarily Dismiss Appeal

Under Rule 42.1(a), a party may voluntarily move to dismiss its appeal—a type of appellate nonsuit.[58] This may occur when the party simply does not wish to pursue the appeal or after settlement. Whatever type of dismissal motion is filed, the motion should specify how costs of appeal are to be taxed.[59]

9-2:6.3a Simple Dismissal

A motion that seeks a simple dismissal should:

- state that it is unopposed (or that it is filed jointly by all parties, particularly if there are multiple appellants separately represented);
- state that "the appellant (or petitioner) no longer desires to pursue this appeal;"
- ask the court to dismiss the appeal; and
- ask the court to "tax costs against the appellant (or petitioner)," unless the parties agree that each party will bear its own costs.

The motion may also ask the court to affirm the judgment or order, but unless that request is part of an agreement between the parties, the motion should simply ask for a dismissal.

9-2:6.3b Dismissal by Agreement

Rule 42.1(a)(2) permits the parties to ask the court to dispose of the appeal according to the parties' signed, written agreement. The relief sought under an agreement is usually more than a simple dismissal. The procedures for effecting the parties' agreement are:

- the parties' agreement must be signed and filed with the court, which is best effected by attaching it to a motion; and
- the title of the motion should reflect the disposition sought, such as "motion to reverse the judgment and remand pursuant to settlement."

9-2:6.3c Scope of Relief Beyond Dismissal

Rule 42.1(a)(2) provides three general types of relief the court may grant under the parties' agreement:

- "*render judgment* effectuating the parties' agreement;"
- "*set aside the trial court's judgment* without regard to the merits and remand the case to the trial court for rendition of judgment in accordance with the agreement;" or
- "*abate the appeal* and permit proceedings in the trial court to effectuate the agreement."[60]

New trial. According to the comments to Rule 42.1, an appellate court cannot order a new trial as requested in an agreement "absent reversible error."[61]

Vacate. The comments also provide that the appellate court cannot vacate the trial court's judgment unless there is reversible error or a settlement agreement.[62]

9-2:6.3d Effect on Issued Opinion

If dismissal is sought after the appellate court has issued its opinion, the parties may request the court to withdraw the opinion. The court has discretion whether to grant that request. Rule 42.1(c) provides: "[i]n dismissing a proceeding, the appellate court will determine whether to withdraw any opinion it has already issued."[63] This rule also states that a motion for dismissal cannot be conditioned on a withdrawal of the opinion. The same is true if the case is in the Supreme Court when settlement occurs. Also, the Supreme Court will vacate the court of appeals' judgment upon agreement of the parties, but will not vacate the court of appeals' opinion.

Notes

1 *See* § 9-1:2.

2 *See* Tex. R. App. P. 10.

3 Tex. R. App. P. 10.1(a).

4 *See* Tex. R. App. P. 10.2.

5 *See* Tex. R. App. P. 10.2.

6 *See* Tex. R. App. P. 10.3(a).

7 *See* Tex. R. App. P. 10.3(a).

8 Tex. R. App. P. 10.3(b).

9 Tex. R. App. P. 10.4(a).

10 Tex. R. App. P. 10.4(a).

11 Tex. R. App. P. 5.

12 Tex. R. App. P. 10.5(b)(2), 26.3.

[13] Tex. R. App. P. 10.5(b)(2).

[14] *See, e.g., Hernandez v. Lopez*, 288 S.W.3d 180, 184 (Tex. App.—Houston [1st Dist.] 2009, no pet.) (that attorney miscalculated the deadline to perfect an appeal was a reasonable explanation).

[15] http://www.ble.state.tx.us/atty_us/rule19notice2.htm.

[16] Tex. R. Governing Bar Admission XIX(a); Tex. Gov't Code § 82.0361(b).

[17] State Bar Rule XIX(a), (c).

[18] State Bar Rule XIX(b).

[19] State Bar Rule XIX(b).

[20] Tex. R. App. P. 6.5(a).

[21] Tex. R. App. P. 6.5(b).

[22] Tex. R. App. P. 6.5(d).

[23] Tex. R. App. P. 6.5(d).

[24] 10th Tex. App. (Waco) Loc. R. 7(b).

[25] Tex. R. App. P. 10.5(b)(3).

[26] *See, e.g.*, 10th Tex. App. (Waco) Loc. R. 7(d) ("A motion requesting an extension of more than 60 days to file a brief and successive motions for extensions of time to file a brief will rarely be granted.").

[27] Tex. R. App. P. 9.4 cmt.

[28] *See* 2nd Tex. App. (Fort Worth) Loc. R. 1.C; 4th Tex. App. (San Antonio) Loc. R. 8.4; 10th Tex. App. (Waco) Loc. R. 12(f) (pre-submission supplemental briefs raising "new issues" may be filed only with leave of court; otherwise, no leave is required).

[29] *See, e.g.*, 2nd Tex. App. (Fort Worth) Loc. R. 1.C; 4th Tex. App. (San Antonio) Loc. R. 8.5; 10th Tex. App. (Waco) Loc. R. 12(f).

[30] Tex. R. App. P. 39.4, 59.5.

[31] Tex. R. App. P. 39.4, 59.5.

[32] Tex. R. App. P. 39.5, 59.6.

[33] *See* Tex. R. App. P. 39.5, 59.6 (only one party need consent).

[34] *See* Tex. R. App. P. 16.

[35] Tex. R. App. P. 16 cmt.; *Gulf Mar. Warehouse Co. v. Towers*, 858 S.W.2d 556, 560 (Tex. App.—Beaumont 1993).

[36] *In re Union Pac. Res.*, 969 S.W.2d 427, 428 (Tex. 1998) (orig. proceeding).

[37] Tex. R. Civ. P. 18a(a)(4)(B).

[38] Tex. R. Civ. P. 18a(a)(4)(A).

[39] Tex. R. Civ. P. 18a(a)(1).

[40] *In re Union Pac. Res.*, 969 S.W.2d 427, 428 (Tex. 1998) (orig. proceeding); *see also* Tex. Gov't Code § 74.053 (removal of former trial and appellate judges); Tex. Gov't Code § 74.059 (removal of district, statutory probate, and county court judges).

[41] Tex. R. App. P. 16.1.

[42] For purposes of this rule, a judge was "counsel" in the case if he or she was a member of a firm who was counsel for a party at the time of the firm's representation. *Tesco Am., Inc. v. Strong Indus.*, 221 S.W.3d 550, 554 (Tex. 2006).

[43] *See* Tex. Const. art. V, § 11; Tex. R. Civ. P. 18b(a) (incorporating the constitutional grounds for disqualification).

[44] *Tesco Am., Inc. v. Strong Indus.*, 221 S.W.3d 550 (Tex. 2006).

[45] *In re Union Pac. Res.*, 969 S.W.2d 427, 428 (Tex. 1998) (orig. proceeding).

[46] Tex. R. App. P. 16.3.

[47] Tex. R. App. P. 16.3.

[48] Tex. R. Civ. P. 18a(a)(4).

[49] Tex. R. Civ. P. 18a(a)(4).

[50] Tex. R. Civ. P. 18a(a)(1).

[51] Tex. R. Civ. P. 18b(b).

[52] Tex. R. App. P. 16.3(b).

[53] Tex. R. App. P. 16.3(c).

[54] *See* Tex. R. App. P. 38.8(a)(1).

[55] *See* Tex. R. App. P. 37.3(b).

[56] Tex. R. App. P. 10.3(a).

[57] Tex. R. App. P. 38.8(a)(1).

[58] Tex. R. App. P. 42.1(a).

[59] *See* Tex. R. App. P. 42.1(d) ("Absent agreement of the parties, the court will tax costs against the appellant.").

[60] Tex. R. App. P. 42.1(a)(2).

[61] Tex. R. App. P. 42.1 cmt.

[62] Tex. R. App. P. 42.1 cmt.

[63] Tex. R. App. P. 42.1(c).

CHAPTER 10

Court of Appeals Briefs

10-1 Introduction

This chapter addresses the rules for briefing in the courts of appeals, a framework for thinking about briefing strategy, and strategies for each part of a court of appeals brief. Many of these strategies also apply to other types of briefs, including briefs in the Texas Supreme Court, amicus briefs, and briefing in support of an original proceeding. We present these here because the court of appeals brief is the most common appellate brief. In other chapters, we discuss strategies specific to the Texas Supreme Court proceedings, amicus briefs, and original proceedings.

10-2 General Rules

10-2:1 Deadlines

Deadlines for filing briefs in the courts of appeals are dictated by the rules.

10-2:1.1 Ordinary Appeal

- *Appellant's brief:* 30 days after the clerk's and reporter's record have both been filed.[1]
- *Appellee's brief:* 30 days after the appellant's brief is filed.[2]
- *Reply brief:* 20 days after the appellee's brief is filed.[3]
- *Briefs in a cross-appeal:* Because the rules do not distinguish between deadlines for an appeal and a cross-appeal, the deadlines are the same for a cross-appellant as for the appellant and the same for a cross-appellee as for the appellee.

10-2:1.2 Accelerated Appeal of Interlocutory Order

- *Appellant's brief:* 20 days after the clerk's and reporter's record have both been filed.[4]
- *Appellee's brief:* 20 days after the appellant's brief is filed.[5]
- *Reply brief:* 20 days after the appellee's brief is filed.[6]

The court of appeals may extend these deadlines on a motion complying with Rule 10.5(b).[7] Or it may shorten the deadlines in the interest of justice.[8]

If either party discovers that it has missed a briefing deadline, it should file a motion to extend the deadline as soon as possible. The rules expressly allow a motion to extend a court of appeals briefing deadline "before or after the date the brief is due."[9]

10-2:2 Format

Briefs are subject to the formatting rules of all appellate filings in Rule 9.4.

10-2:2.1 Margins

The rules require one-inch margins on both sides, top, and bottom of the page.[10]

10-2:2.2 Typeface

The rules require a 14-point font or larger, except for footnotes, which may be 12-point or larger.[11] Although no particular typeface or font is required, the typeface must be "conventional."[12]

10-2:2.3 Maximum Word Count

- *Appellant's and appellee's briefs:* 15,000 words
- *Reply briefs:* 7,500 words
- *Aggregate of all briefs filed by a party:* 27,000 words.[13]

The word count does not include these parts of the brief: caption, identity of parties and counsel, statement regarding oral argument, table of contents, index of authorities, statement of the case, statement of issues presented, statement of jurisdiction, statement of procedural history, signature, proof of service, certification, certificate of compliance, and appendix.[14]

It is particularly important for briefs to follow the rules that are designed to make it easier for judges and court staff to use briefs. In particular, briefs should be:

- in text-searchable, PDF, format;
- directly converted to PDF rather than scanned, if possible; and
- combined with any appendix into a single computer file unless that would exceed the size limit for electronic filing.[15]

Following these rules will make a brief easier to navigate on the court's computer screens.

10-2:3 Failure to File Brief

If an appellant in a civil appeal fails to file a brief, the court of appeals may:

1. dismiss the appeal for want of prosecution, unless the appellant reasonably explains the failure to file and the appellee has not been significantly injured by the failure to timely file a brief;

2. retain the appeal and give further direction to the case as it considers proper; or
3. if an appellee's brief has been filed, affirm the trial court judgment on the appellee's brief without examining the record.[16]

If the appellee fails to file a brief, the court will accept as true the facts stated in the appellant's brief.[17]

10-3 General Principles

10-3:1 Writing to the Reader's Perspective

To win, an advocate must think of a brief differently from other writing. A brief should not be written in the same way as a law-review article. Because the purpose of a brief is to persuade the reader, writing a successful brief requires understanding the unique perspective, and the needs, of the judicial reader.

Too many appellate briefs are written for the wrong audience.

Wrong audience #1: the audience in the writer's own head. It is human nature to write from our own perspective. When we write a document, we understand exactly what we mean. But it is a mistake to assume that readers will understand it simply because we do.

The problem is that advocates who write from their own perspective often stop editing to make their arguments clearer when they reach the point where they persuade themselves. It requires much more work to make a brief understandable and persuasive to someone else because most of us write with a voice in our head that provides all of the necessary emphasis and explanation for our own writing. For instance, a long, complex sentence can make perfect sense to the writer, yet be completely incomprehensible to the reader. It takes work to make our writing as clear as possible so that our audience will understand it.

Wrong audience #2: the perfect judge. The perfect judge has full knowledge of the law and great interest in the case. This perfect judge has infinite time to read, research, and consider the arguments. This perfect judge also reads briefs in a quiet, library-like setting. Many authors routinely write briefs under the assumption that, if the judges are smart and fair, the judges will certainly agree with the author's side of the issue because they will understand and be persuaded by it.

The reality, of course, is that judges rarely meet this ideal. Judges, like the rest of us, are distracted readers. As Third Circuit Judge Ruggero J. Aldisert explained:

> Briefs usually must compete with a number of other demands on the judge's time and attention. The telephone rings. The daily mail arrives with motions and petitions clamoring for immediate review. The electronic mail spits out an urgent message. . . . The law clerks buzz you on the intercom because they have hit a snag in a case. So the deathless prose that you have been reading . . . must await another moment. Or another hour. Or another day.[18]

Judges also are rarely the substantive experts we expect. Advocates often know much more about the issue that they have researched and crafted into an argument than the judge does. Advocates also usually have more interest in the issue than most judges will. For the advocate, understanding the issue and winning the argument may help them keep the client, establish a reputation, and earn a bonus or contingency fee. Judges rarely have the same personal incentives.

Judges do want to do a good job, but they need help from advocates. In their speeches and papers, more and more judges are asking advocates to give them more assistance in the brief itself. As Supreme Court Justice Ruth Bader Ginsburg advised:

> The cardinal rule: it should play to the audience. . . . The best way to lose that audience is to write the brief long and cluttered. . . . The concentration of court of appeals sittings means that the judges will lack time to ferret out bright ideas buried in complex sentences.[19]

To understand how judges read our briefs, it is important to place ourselves in the shoes of real judges and the circumstances in which they typically read briefs. Real judges want to be able to understand the argument quickly, and they need to quickly understand the most persuasive reasons why you should win.

10-3:2 Helping Readers Work Less

This may seem counterintuitive. When we write to courts, we want courts to work; we want courts to act. We praise judges and court staff who are hard workers. Why, then, would we want to help judges and court staff work less? The answer is that we want them to spend their time effectively—deciding the legal rule in our favor, writing an opinion in our favor.

You should not force courts to do extra, unnecessary work. You do not want courts to waste their limited time trying to determine what your argument or support is. So your brief should not force courts to spend extra time identifying the brief's structure and locating its main points. Headings in a brief should enable readers to know what to expect from each part of the brief. The brief should not make the court do any work that the document can do for the court.

Judges and court staff have a limited amount of energy and patience that they are willing to devote to understanding a brief. You should not squander their patience by requiring them to spend 10 minutes to comprehend the meaning of a contract provision, or 20 minutes trying to find the structure of an argument. You want courts to save their mental energy for processing and acting on that information.

10-3:3 Persuasion

Appellate briefs differ from some other forms of legal writing—such as law-review articles and memoranda to clients—in that their purpose is to persuade. To persuade a court to rule favorably, you must understand the court's perspective. You should put yourself in the shoes of a judge.

The key to understanding the court's perspective is understanding what courts do. The job of courts is not just to hear one side's argument and determine whether it is correct. It is the court's job to weigh competing arguments—which often both have merit—and then decide which argument is better.

As a result, the job of an advocate is not just to explain the client's position. It is to explain why that position is better than the other side's position.

The problem with much advocacy is that it is oblivious to the best arguments made by the other side. This is because advocates often are locked in the point of view of their own side. And they believe that, if they just ignore or mischaracterize the other side's better arguments, maybe the court will ignore or not understand them. But that is unlikely to happen. Instead, you should directly address the other side's best arguments and give the judges a road map to weigh the arguments in your clients' favor.

10-3:4 Structure

For legal readers, visible structure is an important aid to understanding a brief's primary arguments. Readers look for arguments in the structure of a brief to orient themselves quickly.

Visible structure also helps a reader see and understand the logic of an argument. For instance, a primary heading followed by three numbered points tells the reader that the primary heading is the main argument, and the three numbered points are support.

10-3:4.1 Structural Tools

Useful structural tools include:

- *Frequent headings.* Particularly in an argument, headings are very useful to give the reader the overall logical structure. Because a tablet screen is smaller, tablet readers need frequent headings to remind them of their place in the argument.
- *Outlines.* Outlines help show the overall structure of the argument.
- *Topic sentences.* Readers use the first sentence of a paragraph to understand the point of the paragraph. Plus, when readers are reading quickly, they are more likely to read the first sentence of a paragraph than later sentences. Readers often read the topic sentence to decide whether they want to read the remainder of the paragraph. A useful topic sentence helps the reader quickly understand the argument of the paragraph.
- *Lists/bullets.* Lists are useful to delineate separate arguments or support. Lists show structure-oriented readers how many points support an argument and where each new point begins. Bullets points are similar but are better suited for examples or support where the number of points is not important.

10-3:5 Thorough Editing

Editing may be the most important part of the writing process. Of course, editing corrects many errors, from grammatical mistakes and misspellings to incorrect citations. But the greatest value of editing is something more. Editing helps bridge the gap between the writer and the reader. It helps create a document that is easier to understand, more persuasive, and more useful.

The biggest challenge for any writer is to overcome our natural instinct to write to ourselves—that is, to write from our own perspective. When we write a document, we understand exactly what we mean. But readers do not always understand.

The best solution for this problem is to use editing tools to review a brief from a reader's perspective. The best editing tool is to ask someone else to edit the brief. The best editor is usually a reader who is largely a stranger to the case, like the readers on the court will be. It may be helpful to get substantive feedback from a lawyer who is a specialist in the subject matter. But any intelligent person—with or without a law degree—can give valuable feedback about how a document reads.

10-3:5.1 Editorial Feedback

The key to effective editing is not only to ask your editor to make corrections, but to have the editor give feedback. Ask your reader questions about his or her experience in reading the brief:

- Were any parts of the brief hard to read?
- Which parts of the argument did not make sense?
- Which parts of the argument were not persuasive? Why?
- What questions did you still have after you finished reading?

If your brief is an appellee's brief or a reply, have your test reader read both sides' arguments. Ask additional questions, such as:

- What do you take from the briefs as the primary disputes between the parties?
- What are the most persuasive points for each side?
- Did the other side make any arguments that our side did not address?

In big cases, our firm often assembles a panel of mock judges, unfamiliar with the case, to read both sides' briefs and sometimes even to deliberate. This provides great insight into how real judges are likely to view the case. You cannot get the same sort of insight by simply circulating the briefs to lawyers who are involved in the case.

In addition to providing feedback, an editor also corrects mistakes and suggests different structure, arguments, or wording. The goal of editing should be to approach the document from the reader's perspective. The editor should try to place herself in the shoes of a reader and identify questions or concerns readers might have.

The editor may flag problems for the author. Or the editor may suggest fixes. Either way, the decision to make the edit should be a decision in which the original author participates. If the editor misunderstands the author, and tries to edit the text, the result may be quite different from what the author intended. The author's intent will be protected only if the author has a say in whether to make an edit.

10-3:5.2 Employing an Editorial Team

A critical part of editing is deciding who should edit. In most cases our firm uses a team of three editors:

1. another lawyer familiar with the case;
2. a stranger to the case; and
3. the author.

Editor 1—another lawyer familiar with the case—provides many benefits. She may think of additional arguments, defects in an argument, or responses the other side may raise. Because she has more knowledge, she can engage more in the substance of the argument.

Yet there is a drawback to relying solely on the familiar lawyer. She also is detached from the perspective of the ultimate reader. The familiar lawyer knows the case. She will not approach the document with the same fresh eyes as the ultimate audience, who is likely to be someone unfamiliar with the case when reading the document for the first time.

Editor 2—the stranger to the case—may not know the facts. The stranger may not even understand the substance of the law. But the stranger's perspective is essential to better predict how the document will be read by a law clerk or judge.

Editor 3—the author—is in some respects the worst person to review the brief. Authors cannot see the issue freshly. They know too much. They cannot read their own writing in the same way as another reader. They had the original thought that led to the sentence and will remember that thought when they re-read it. The author's perspective is a poor indicator of whether the reader will understand the same thought.

But there are techniques an author can use to bridge the gap with the reader. The best technique for the author to edit is to put down the draft for as a long as possible—at least a few days—before editing. You probably have had the experience of going back to something you wrote weeks earlier and not being able to understand it. That is the perspective you want. It replicates as closely as possible the experience of a first-time reader.

10-3:6 Unwritten Conventions

In addition to following the Rules of Appellate Procedure, it also is important to follow unwritten conventions for appellate briefs—unless there is a good reason to break them. Unwritten conventions include the format for the cover page of a brief, the use of a heading outline in the argument section, the use of Bluebook citation form for cases, and the use of a standard record-citation form (i.e., CR 3:124).

The rules do not require lawyers to follow these conventions. But it is a good practice to be aware of them and follow them most of the time for a few reasons.

First, a brief that follows conventions helps the reader know where to locate particular information. For instance, if the court wants to know whether an appellant has requested oral argument, the court is likely to look first at the bottom center of the cover page for the words "Oral Argument Requested." The Texas Rules of Appellate Procedure do not require those particular words or that location, but only that the request appear somewhere on the cover of the brief. The convention tells most readers where to look first. And if it does not appear there, they may miss it.

Second, a brief that follows conventions gives the reader some assurance that the advocate knows what he or she is doing. A brief that contains the oral argument request in the upper right corner suggests that the advocate has not done many appeals. And that may hurt the court's view of the writer's competence.

It is important to be aware of conventions. If you are preparing your first brief in a particular appellate court, look at other briefs that have been filed by respected appellate firms. Sample briefs may be easily located on the courts' websites. They can serve as a guide for conventions to follow.

10-3:7 The Screen-Friendly Brief

The biggest change in recent years in Texas appellate courts is the switch from reading on paper to reading on screens. Five years ago, most judges read appellate briefs on paper. Today, it is far more likely that a brief will be read on some sort of screen.

Although the words on a screen are the same, the reading experience is different. One of the primary differences is that screen readers must scroll up or down to find other parts of the document, rather than flipping to particular pages. They also cannot open more than one page at a time. And their visible screen is often smaller than a paper page, especially on tablet screens.

Studies have shown that readers have a harder time navigating and understanding a text on screen versus the same text on paper.[20] It is easier to flip pages looking for a particular argument than it is to scroll down a PDF document on a screen.

A digital brief should be designed to be easy to navigate and use. The following are a few suggestions for designing the brief to help screen readers.

10-3:7.1 Bookmarks

Judges who read briefs on screens report that one of the most important tools for navigation is the bookmark. A bookmark is a feature in many programs that allows a user to jump from a heading or exhibit in a table of contents to the corresponding heading or exhibit in the document. Some Texas appellate judges have stated at seminars that advocates should always include bookmarks in their electronic filings.

It does not require much additional work to create bookmarks. When Microsoft Word or Word Perfect converts an outline-structured document to Acrobat, they convert the full text of marked headings to bookmarks. If the brief uses argument headings that appear in the table of contents, they also will show up as bookmarks. But sometimes the full text of long argument headings may not show up on the court's screen, particularly if the judge is using a smaller tablet screen. For this reason, edit bookmarks in Adobe so that the essence of the heading is reduced to a short, visible bookmark.

For instance, when this argument heading appears in a table of contents, the entire sentence will automatically be converted into a bookmark:

> The statute of limitations bars Sharpwell's claim of minority-shareholder oppression.

On a PC, the entire bookmark would be visible in the outline navigation pane. But on a tablet, it is too long. The solution is to truncate the bookmark to:

Limitations—oppression.

Remember to review the appearance of the brief, not only on paper, but also on a screen and on a tablet. In most briefs, bookmarked headings will need to be edited for tablet readers.

10-3:7.2 Moderate Hyperlinking

Hyperlinking serves a similar function to bookmarks. It allows a reader to jump from a citation in the text of a brief to the document itself in the appendix. It is an especially useful tool for readers who want to review an important document, such as the contract that is the subject of the case or the trial court's judgment.

As useful as hyperlinking can be for readers, it is best used sparingly. If readers are given the opportunity to jump to every citation, they may do so, resulting in a disjointed reading process. For this reason, hyperlinks are best reserved for the most important documents and cases.

10-3:7.3 Avoid Footnotes

At the end of the 20th century, there was a robust debate about the use of footnotes in appellate briefs, particularly for citations. Today, the transition to screen reading has largely resolved that debate. On most screens, footnotes are hard to read. Viewers typically do not view the entire "page" at a time on a screen. Particularly on a small screen, a reader must scroll down the page to see the text of a footnote, and then scroll back to the location of the footnote in the text. This is a time-consuming process. Judges who read briefs on tablets report that they almost never read footnotes.

Footnotes should be avoided except for material that you believe should be included, but that do not need or want the court to read. Most briefs should have few if any footnotes.

10-4 Sections of an Appellant's Brief

The rules require an appellant's brief to include the portions of the brief that are listed in this section in the order they are listed here.[21]

10-4:1 Cover

10-4:1.1 Requirements

Rule of Appellate Procedure 9.4(g) dictates the information that must be included on a brief cover.[22] The required contents include:

- the case style;
- the case number;
- the title of the brief;

- the filing party's name; and
- lead counsel's name, state bar number, email address, mailing address, phone number, and fax number.[23]

If a party would like to request oral argument, that request must appear on the front cover.[24] Usually, that request is designated with the phrase "Oral Argument Requested" centered at the bottom of the cover.

10-4:1.2 Conventions

It is a mistake to give a brief cover no more thought than whether it satisfies the required information in Rule 9.4. The cover is the first part of the brief that the reader sees. It is the first step in persuasion. It can give an advocate credibility, or it can

Illustration—a conventional brief cover

No. 14-14-00816-CV

In the Fourteenth Court of Appeals
Houston, Texas

Dominion Insurance Company,
Appellant

v.

Coastal Manufacturers, Inc., Coastal Piping Corp.,
Appellees

On Appeal from the 335th Judicial District Court
Harris County, Texas
Cause No. 2010-34526

BRIEF OF APPELLANT

Douglas W. Alexander Texas Bar No. 00992350 ALEXANDER DUBOSE JEFFERSON & TOWNSEND LLP 515 Congress Avenue, Suite 2350 Austin, Texas 78701 Telephone: (512) 482-9300 Facsimile: (512) 482-9303	Robert Dubose Texas Bar No. 00787396 ALEXANDER DUBOSE JEFFERSON & TOWNSEND LLP 1844 Harvard Street Houston, Texas 77008 Telephone: (713) 523-2358 Facsimile: (713) 522-4553

Counsel for Appellant Dominion Insurance Company

Oral Argument Requested

detract from credibility. When a cover looks professional and follows standard formatting conventions, it suggests that the advocate is professional and has experience in the court of appeals. When a cover is not professionally formatted or when it fails to follow standard conventions, it gives the opposite impression.

The conventional format for a cover includes information in this order: (1) the case number, (2) the court of appeals to which the brief is addressed, (3) the parties, separated by a "v." with the labels "appellant" and "appellee," (4) the trial court from which the case is appealed, and (5) the title of the document. These items are centered on the page and typically separated by solid horizontal lines. Below this information, information about counsel appears indented slightly to the right of the center of the page. If additional counsel are listed, counsel information typically appears in two columns, one on the left side of the page, and the other slightly to the right of center. "Oral Argument Requested" appears centered at the bottom of the page.

10-4:2 Identity of Parties and Counsel

Rule 38.1 requires that an Appellant's Brief include "a complete list of all parties to the trial court's judgment or order appealed from, and the names and addresses of all trial and appellate counsel."[25] A list of parties and counsel is not required in an Appellee's Brief "unless necessary to supplement or correct the appellant's list."[26]

From the court's perspective, this list serves several purposes. It helps the court identify the parties. It provides the court with contact information for counsel. And it provides the necessary information for the court of appeals to check possible conflicts of interest.

It can be a serious problem for the court when the list of parties and counsel is not a complete list of all parties and counsel, including all former counsel in the case. An illustration of this problem is *Tesco American, Inc. v. Strong Industries, Inc.*[27] In *Tesco* a law firm had briefly appeared in the case for the Appellee before being replaced by other counsel. In the court of appeals, the case was assigned to a panel that included a justice who had worked at the same firm at the time it had appeared in the case, but the justice had no involvement with the case when she worked for the firm. Because the briefs did not mention that firm's short involvement in the case, the justice was not aware of a potential conflict of interest. Nonetheless, the Texas Supreme Court held that the justice was disqualified, and the opinion she wrote was reversed.[28]

The lesson of *Tesco* is that judges may have no way to learn of possible conflicts of interest unless the parties list all former counsel in the list of parties and counsel.

In organizing an identity of parties and counsel page, a useful format for readers is typically a table, listing trial and appellate counsel for each party or groups of parties.

Illustration—identity of parties and counsel

IDENTITY OF PARTIES AND COUNSEL

Appellant

Dominion Insurance Company

Trial counsel:

Stacy Miller
MILLER AND SEIFORTH
P.O. Box 3845
Austin, Texas 78767

Appellate counsel:

Robert Dubose
ALEXANDER DUBOSE JEFFERSON & TOWNSEND LLP
1844 Harvard Street
Houston, Texas 77008

Appellees

Coastal Manufacturers, Inc., Coastal Piping Corp.

Trial and Appellate Counsel:

Rebecca Roy
Lashawn Brown
ROY & BROWN, L.L.P.
Three Riverway, Suite 5200
Houston, Texas 77057

Ronald Crest
CREST & JONES
24 Greenway Plaza, Suite 4050
Houston, Texas 77046

10-4:3 Table of Contents

The rules of procedure require that all briefs include a "table of contents with references to the pages of the brief."[29]

Several aspects of the table of contents and index of authorities are important. First, the table of contents is required to "indicate the subject matter of each issue or point, or group of issues or points."[30] If the issues are short, the best practice is to copy them into the table of contents.

Second, although not required by the rules, the standard convention is for the "Argument" section of the table of contents to include the outline of all of the argument headings from the argument section in the brief. This not only helps judges locate the page on which a specific argument is made, it also allows judges to see an outline of the entire argument in one place. It allows judges to see the logical relationship between primary argument headings in the outline and the subordinate headings.

Third, a clean and accurate table of contents and index of authorities add credibility to the advocate and the brief. It should look professional, follow standard conventions, and provide accurate page numbers. The table can be difficult to format, and usually must be prepared after all other parts of the brief are completed because page numbers often change with editing. Thus, it is always important to complete the rest of the brief early enough to allow time for the table of contents to be accurately prepared and proofread.

Illustration—table of contents

TABLES OF CONTENTS

10-4:4 Index of Authorities

The rules of procedure require that all briefs include an "index of authorities arranged alphabetically and indicating the pages of the brief where the authorities are cited."[31]

Like the table of contents, the index of authorities should be clean, professional, and accurate. And because the index also is difficult to format, it is important to complete the rest of the brief with enough time to ensure that the index can be accurately prepared and proofread.

It is a convention of an index of authorities to group certain types of authorities in different categories. The best approach for readers is usually general categories, such as "cases," "rules," "statutes," and "other."

Illustration—index of authorities

INDEX OF AUTHORITIES

Cases

City of Keller v. Wilson,
168 S.W.3d 802 (Tex. 2005)........ 7, 16
FFE Transp. Servs., Inc. v. Fulgham,
154 S.W.3d 84 (Tex. 2004)........ 9, 10, 11, 13
Greater Houston Transportation Co. v. Phillips,
801 S.W.2d 523 (Tex. 1990)........ 16, 17, 20, 21
Requena v. Otis Elevator Co.,
305 S.W.3d 156 (Tex. App.—Houston [1st Dist.] 2009, no pet.)........ 9, 12
Travis v. City of Mesquite,
830 S.W.2d 94 (Tex. 1992)........ 16
Turbines, Inc. v. Dardis,
1 S.W.3d 726 (Tex. App.—Amarillo 1999, pet. denied)........ 8, 9, 12

Rule

Tex. R. App. P. 43.2........ 19

Statutes

Tex. Civ. Prac. & Rem. Code § 37.009........ 18
Tex. Civ. Prac. & Rem. Code § 38.001........ 15, 16

10-4:5 Statement of the Case

10-4:5.1 Requirements

Rule 38.1 requires that this section of the brief "must state concisely" this information:

- the nature of the case (e.g., whether it is a suit for damages, on a note, or involving a murder prosecution);
- the course of proceedings; and
- the trial court's disposition of the case.

The rule also provides that the statement "should be supported by record references, should seldom exceed one-half page, and should not discuss the facts."[32]

10-4:5.2 Tabular Information vs. Procedural Narrative

There are two common approaches to the statement of the case.

One approach is to provide the required information and only the required information in a simple table. A table is organized by the categories of information required in Rule 38.1.

This is often the best approach because the rule requests particular information, prohibits the discussion of facts, and suggests that the length of this section in the court of appeals should be no more than one-half a page.[33] A table format makes it easier for the reader to locate and quickly process the required information.

Illustration—tabular statement of the case

STATEMENT OF THE CASE

Nature of Case	Insurance-coverage dispute involving a claim for declaratory judgment and counterclaims for breach of contract and subrogation. CR 1:78-91, 92-100.
Trial Court	Judicial District Court, Harris County, Texas, Hon. Nancy Ginsler presiding
Course of Proceedings	After the trial court granted summary judgment on grounds not at issue in this appeal, CR 1:101, this Court reversed and remanded for further proceedings. *Coastal Mfg., Inc. v. Dominion Ins. Co.*, 218 S.W.3d 279 (Tex. App.—Houston [14th Dist.] 2007, pet. denied). After a jury trial, Judge Ginsler rendered final judgment. CR 7:1625-28.
Trial Court's Disposition	Judgment that Coastal recover from Dominion: • Actual damages of $4 million • Attorney fees through trial of $839,054.92 • Attorney fees for post-judgment motions and appeal of $350,000 • Pre- and post-judgment interest CR 7:1625-28.

A different approach is a procedural narrative. A narrative must include the same information, but is typically in paragraph form. The goal of the narrative is to tell a story.

A procedural narrative can be a useful tool when the appeal turns on procedural issues. It can tell a story of an unfair trial, particularly when the appellant is arguing there were cumulative errors. Yet it should be concise so that it does not exceed Rule 38.1's suggested half-page limit.

Illustration—narrative statement of the case

STATEMENT OF THE CASE

This appeal involves an insurance claim by Eastside Hospital against Dominion Insurance for property damage caused by Hurricane Ike.

The case was tried before Hon. Ronald Wilson of the 136th District Court. The trial court denied Dominion Insurance's motion for separate trials on (1) contractual and bad-faith liability, and (2) punitive damages. CR 4:169. Over objection, the court admitted evidence about Dominion's net worth, as well as the struggling hospital's financial condition. RR 2:245-59; RR 310-15; RR PX-1, pp. 2-10. Then, over objection, the trial court admitted testimony from the hospital's expert witness about the legal requirements for a bad-faith claim against an insurer. RR 5:20-36.

The trial court entered judgment on the jury verdict for $32 million in actual damages and $10 million in punitive damages. CR 5:198-200.

10-4:6 Statement Regarding Oral Argument (Optional)

The required method for requesting oral argument is to place the request on the cover of the brief.[34] The rules also permit, but do not require, a statement inside the brief regarding oral argument.[35] The statement must not exceed one page.[36] It should address how the court's decisional process would, or would not, be aided by oral argument.[37]

The statement regarding oral argument serves two purposes. First, it allows a party who desires argument to make a case for having an oral argument. This can be helpful because, even when argument is requested, courts of appeals frequently do not grant it. Typically, the statement focuses on why a dialogue may help the court's decision process. For instance, it may help explain that the issue is one of first impression, or that the deciding legal rule is the subject of disagreement among other courts of appeals and worthy of discussion.

Second, a party may not believe argument is necessary, but would like to preserve the right to participate in argument if the Court would like one. In this case, the best approach is to request argument on the cover and explain in the statement why argument is not necessary, but that the party would like to participate if the court schedules an argument.

Illustration—statement regarding oral argument

STATEMENT REGARDING ORAL ARGUMENT

Oral argument would assist the Court. A threshold issue is whether a person not named as a beneficiary in a life insurance policy has standing to sue an insurer for failure to make a change of designated beneficiary. The issue is unsettled in Texas.

The standing issue overlaps with the question of whether interpleader extinguished the insurer's liability. The insurance company interpleaded all funds it owed under the policy. The real dispute was between purported beneficiaries. Ordinarily, interpleading the funds in dispute extinguishes the interpleading parties' liability. Although Smith argues that the life insurance context is different, Texas courts have never addressed that specific issue. The interplay among these issues suggests that this Court would benefit from oral argument.

10-4:7 Issues Presented

Rule 38.1 provides: "The brief must state concisely all issues or points presented for review."[38] Detail about sub-parts of an issue is not required. The rule instructs courts to treat a statement of an issue or point as "covering every subsidiary question that is fairly included."[39]

The framing of an issue can determine the outcome of the case. As Justice Frankfurter wrote, "In law the right answer usually depends on putting the right question."[40] Similarly, one lawyer—it is not clear today who it was—notably said "that he would gladly take either side of any case as long as he could pick the issues."[41]

Despite the importance of issues, there are considerable differences of opinion among practitioners about how to craft them.

10-4:7.1 Number of Issues

In practice, the number of issues in an appellant's brief varies widely, from one to far too many. The better practice is to reduce the number of issues as much as possible. Briefs rarely should have more than three or four issues.

First, most cases do not have more than four winning issues. It is rare to see a court of appeals opinion that holds that a trial court committed more than one or two reversible errors. Of course, most trial court proceedings are not error-free. But to obtain a reversal, the error must meet the high standard for reversible error.[42] Few cases involve many reversible errors.

Second, arguing too many issues can limit the space and attention devoted to the best issues. To fit within the brief length limits, counsel may be forced to choose between briefing an extra issue and providing additional support to the best issue in the appeal. More importantly, judges and law clerks bring a finite amount of energy and time to an appeal. An advocate who raises too many issues is forcing the court to decide too many issues. This may reduce the time that the court will spend addressing the best issue.

Third, when there are too many issues, courts lose patience and the advocate loses credibility. Courts assume the advocate has not made the effort to distill the appeal to winnable points. As one judge explained, when a brief lists six or more issues, there is a "strong presumption that no point is worthwhile."[43]

In rare instances, an advocate may have a strategic interest in demonstrating that the trial judge made many errors and that the cumulative effect of those errors resulted in an unfair trial. For example, an advocate may wish to complain about the admission of multiple documents, as well as trial testimony, pertaining to a single subject. In these instances, the best approach may not be using multiple issues, but instead raising the cumulative errors under a single issue.[44]

10-4:7.2 Issue Length—One Sentence vs. the "Deep Issue"

Since the 1997 amendments to the Texas Rules of Appellate Procedure, appellate lawyers have had more freedom in framing the issues. Part of that freedom is the ability to depart from the prior convention of one-sentence issues. That freedom has led to two common approaches to statements of the issues.

The one-sentence issue. The rules provide that this issue may be stated as a question or a positive statement about the error the trial court committed.[45] This is the more common, and the most traditional, approach.

Bryan Garner's "deep issue." A Garner deep issue consists of separate sentences, contains no more than 75 words, incorporates enough detail to convey a sense of the story, and ends with a question mark.[46] In practice, most deep issues include one or two sentences about the relevant law or the key facts of the case, followed by a question that poses the legal issue.

In choosing the best approach for your case, consider two goals. First, issues should not be too long. Similarly, remember that issues must be stated "concisely."[47] There will be an opportunity to summarize the ***argument*** in the summary of argument section of the brief. There is no need to summarize the entire argument in the statement of the issue.

Second, an issue is an opportunity to frame the legal issue in terms of the most persuasive reasons for ruling in favor of your side. An issue that is too general tells the court nothing. For instance, consider an issue that asks:

> Did the trial court err in entering judgment in favor of Smith, and against Black?

Apart from telling the court that the case concerns a judgment, this issue is so general that it tells the court nothing about the nature of the dispute. It is neither helpful nor persuasive.

The best issue is both short and detailed enough to persuade. But one size does not fit all issues. In many cases, one sentence is sufficient to clearly frame the issue with some persuasive details.

Illustration—issue presented (one sentence)

ISSUE PRESENTED

May an individual who was not a party to a will sue the attorney for failing to make changes to his client's will that the client had requested eight hours before he died?

In this illustration, the issue is framed persuasively with specific facts in one sentence that requires no more than 30 seconds to read and understand. In this case, a "deep issue" format may be counterproductive when it makes an issue longer than it needs to be.

But in some instances, an issue may be so complex that more than one sentence may be required to adequately explain and frame the issue. In these instances, the "deep issue" format may be the best approach.

Illustration—issue presented

ISSUE PRESENTED

The Dominion excess policy and the Assurance excess policy each provide excess insurance coverage for the same loss. Each policy contains "other insurance" provisions providing that it is excess to all other insurance. Under the pro-rata rule in *Hardware Dealers*, which addresses these types of provisions, did the trial court err by ruling the Dominion policy must be exhausted before the Assurance policy was reached, rather than allocating coverage between the excess policies pro rata?

10-4:7.3 Objective vs. Persuasive Tone

A final strategic consideration in drafting an issue is whether to phrase the issue (1) objectively, or (2) positively and persuasively. The rules do not speak to this issue.[48]

The best approach is usually to use the question to persuasively suggest the answer. A survey of Texas appellate judges indicated that 58 percent preferred a positive statement of the issue that suggests the answer.[49]

While the issue should be persuasive, it also should be fair. The issue should not raise evidence that should not be considered under the standard of review. It should not misstate the other side's position. The best issue is often one that appears objective but subtly nudges the reader toward the answer, without the reader being consciously aware that they are being nudged.

Similarly, advocates should avoid overstatement. An issue should avoid adjectives and adverbs and instead focus on relevant, persuasive details. It is less persuasive to characterize an award as "excessive punitive damages" than to characterize the award as "$40 million in punitive damages based on $2 million in actual damages."

10-4:8 Statement of Facts

Rule 38.1 provides that the appellant's brief in the court of appeals "must state concisely and without argument the facts pertinent to the issues or points presented."[50]

10-4:8.1 "Without Argument"

The best statement of facts tells a persuasive story without argument. In fact, Rule 38.1(f) prohibits "argument" in the statement of facts.[51]

It is a mistake to read this prohibition on argument as a requirement that the statement of facts should be a neutral recitation of facts. As Justice Scalia and Bryan Garner explain: "To say that the Statement of Facts must not contain argument is not to say that it cannot be designed to persuade. Like everything else in your brief, it *must* be."[52] An effective statement should persuade, but it should do so without legal argument. There are several methods to avoid improper argument.

First, the statement should avoid argumentative reasoning. The most obvious type of argument is an inference or legal conclusion made from a fact. For instance, it is permissible to state in a statement of facts:

> Jenny Francis testified that she saw Smithers' car run the red light.

It is improper argument, however, to conclude that Smithers ran the red light based on an inference from the evidence:

> Because Francine Jones had a green light as she crossed the intersection from the cross street, Smithers necessarily ran a red light when he entered the intersection from the perpendicular direction.

This sort of inferential reasoning usually needs to be reserved for the argument section.

Second, the statement should rarely reference legal standards. For instance, some judges believe a sentence such as the following would be improper in a statement of facts:

> Undisputed witness' testimony that she saw Smithers' car run the red light conclusively establishes Smithers' negligence.

When legal concepts, such as negligence, appear in a statement of facts, it sounds as though the advocate is making an argument, which runs afoul of Rule 38.1(f).

Third, advocates should avoid the improper use of adjectives and adverbs in a statement of facts. Adjectives and adverbs are a less obvious type of argument but are just as improper when they reflect the opinion or viewpoint of the advocate rather than facts in the record. Steven Stark counsels that "[a]djectives are opinions about facts and therefore generally don't belong in a fact section."[53] Similarly, adverbs often are opinions about facts.

Of course, adjectives and adverbs are appropriate when they are supported by the record. For instance, a statement may include adjectives and adverbs that are contained in quotes from witnesses' testimony. They are also appropriate when the adjective or adverb is not a characterization of the fact, but an objective, observable fact supported by the record, such as "the light was red."

10-4:8.2 Persuasive Organization of Facts

If a statement does not contain argument, how can it be persuasive? The key to persuasion is the effective selection and ordering of facts. The statement is an opportunity to organize the facts so that they tell a story that supports the legal argument that the advocate will make later.

A statement of facts should tell a story. Readers best process a series of facts when the facts are connected as a story. Unless the brief can tell a story that will attract the readers' attention, many readers will simply skip over the statement to get to the argument.

The advocate should carefully consider the organization of facts at the macro level of the larger narrative as well as in the structure of each sentence.

On the level of the larger narrative, advocates often make two mistakes. The first mistake is summarizing testimony witness by witness. This approach almost never serves the purpose of giving the reader a coherent narrative of events because it jumps from one perspective to another.

Another mistake is to fall back on a chronological ordering of facts, when a non-chronological ordering is more persuasive. For instance, consider the following paragraph with a non-chronological ordering:

> On September 17, 2005, WidgetCorp.'s President, Thurston Grey, announced in a shareholder meeting that the corporation's financial health "is excellent and is almost certain to improve for the remainder of the year." One week earlier, Grey received a memo from WidgetCorp.'s CEO stating "WidgetCorp. may face a serious financial crisis in October 2005 when the government releases its safety report." Only a few days before the September 17 meeting, Grey was told by the company's Vice President of regulatory compliance that, "this safety report may do us in."

This narrative moves around in time, but it does so with a purpose. The President's representation is immediately followed by earlier events that demonstrate he knew his representation was false.

In some cases, chronology is important and is a useful organizational tool. But in many cases, the exact chronology simply does not matter. Before reciting the dates of each event by habit, consider whether the court needs the date information. Eliminating the dates can free the advocate to organize the story more persuasively.

Organization can be equally important at the sentence level. Readers remember best the information at the end of a sentence.[54] Readers remember least the information in the middle of a sentence.[55] Thus, if it is important to emphasize a fact, it should appear at the end of a sentence. If it is important to disclose but minimize a fact, the writer may want to place that fact in the middle of a sentence. Professor Gopen offers a useful example:

4a. Although Fred's a nice guy, he beats his dog.

4b. Although Fred beats his dog, he's a nice guy.[56]

Although these sentences use almost identical words, sentence 4b paints a much more positive picture of Fred. It buries the bad fact that Fred beats his dog in a subordinate clause in the middle of the sentence. It emphasizes a good fact, that Fred is a nice guy, at the end of the sentence. In contrast, sentence 4a buries Fred's niceness in the middle of the sentence and emphasizes that he beats his dog.

10-4:8.3 Disclosing Bad Facts

The example about Fred raises a question: If you are defending Fred, why tell the reader that he beats his dog? The reason is to maintain credibility for the advocate and client by disclosing relevant bad facts.

In the statement of facts, it is important to disclose bad facts when they may be important to the court because the other side will almost certainly inform the court of them. If you do not disclose it, you lose credibility because it looks like you are trying to hide from important facts. "One would think that after Watergate, Iran-contra, and the Lewinsky matter, lawyers would realize that the coverup is almost always worse than the crime."[57] The most effective approach is often to disclose the bad facts, but use the organization of the statement of facts to minimize their importance in the story. Then, once the brief discloses bad facts, it should immediately explain or minimize them. This is preferable to the court learning of the bad facts for the first time in your opponent's argument without the benefit of explanation or minimization.

10-4:8.4 Keeping in Mind the Scope of Review

Especially in sufficiency cases, it is important to write the statement of facts with the scope of review in mind.

In a legal-sufficiency case, the scope of review often limits the facts the reviewing court should consider. The scope has been stated differently by Texas courts. The Texas Supreme Court has stated that the reviewing court must disregard evidence that a reasonable juror could disregard.[58]

Of course, any argument about how the scope of review applies should be made in the argument section, not the statement of facts. But the statement of facts should be written in light of the scope of review, and it occasionally makes sense to reference it.

For instance, a statement of facts by an appellant in a legal-sufficiency case should mention all facts that the other side might argue to support the verdict. The appellant ordinarily should not discuss evidence that favors the appellant when it is evidence that a reasonable juror could disregard—such as witness testimony that is directly contradicted by other witness testimony.

To bolster credibility, while reminding the court that there were two sides to the story at trial, an appellant may preface the narrative with a statement such as:

> Although there was conflicting evidence at trial, we only recite the evidence that favors the verdict.

Of course, when the appellant makes this promise, the appellant must stick to it.

Similarly, the appellee should take full advantage of the scope of review. It is appropriate in a legal-sufficiency review to focus on the facts that support the verdict. And the appellee may want to briefly remind the court of the standard of review, without argument, when explaining which facts it selected to include in the statement of facts.

10-4:8.5 Choice of Subjects and Perspective

When writing and editing a statement of facts, the advocate should carefully consider whose story is being told throughout the statement of facts. A statement should be the story of at least one person or thing—what that person or thing did and what happened to him, her, or it. That person or thing is the subject.

Readers expect that a sentence, or a clause, will tell the story of whomever or whatever shows up first in the subject position.[59] For instance, consider whose story is being told in these illustrations:

1. Acme hired Coastal to work on different construction jobs for Acme from 2009 to 2012. Acme hired Coastal to work on eight different Acme sites around

Houston under seven different contracts. Acme hired Coastal to perform only one job, a discrete project in February 2011, under a contract that contained an arbitration clause.

2. Coastal was hired to work on different construction jobs for Acme from 2009 to 2012. Coastal worked at eight different Acme sites around Houston under seven different contracts. Coastal performed only one job for Acme, a discrete project in February 2011, under a contract that contained an arbitration clause.

3. The contracts between Acme and Coastal applied to various construction jobs that Coastal was hired to perform for Acme from 2009 to 2012. Under these seven contracts, Coastal worked for Acme on eight different sites around Houston. The contract for only one of these jobs, a discrete project in February 2011, contained an arbitration clause.

Each story is almost identical, except the identity of the subject throughout each paragraph. Each sentence in paragraph 1 tells the story of Acme, which is in the subject position in each sentence. Paragraph 2 tells the story of Coastal. And paragraph 3 tells the story of the contracts. The same paragraph can be structured different ways to tell the story of Acme, Coastal, or the contracts.

It is important to decide who or what should be the subject for each sentence. You may choose to tell your client's story, which can be an especially useful tool to explain the injuries or damages that the client suffered. Or you may focus on the other side as a subject, especially when the other side's conduct is reprehensible. Or you may want to deemphasize the conduct of particular individuals by using a thing as the subject, such as a contract, an accident, or a trial. Your choice of a subject should be a conscious choice of whose story it is most important to tell.

Neither a statement of facts, nor a single paragraph, must repeat the same subject in each sentence. A paragraph also may tell the story of more than one subject, or it may tell the story of the relationship between subjects. For instance, the subject in this paragraph changes logically from one sentence to the next:

> Emerson looked up from his smart phone too late as his car collided with the back of Dora Jameson's car. Jameson's car then struck Aldo Smith's motorcycle. Smith was thrown 100 feet and landed against the median, killing him. Smith was not wearing a helmet.

The subject in this paragraph shifts from Emerson to Jameson's car to Smith. The progression makes sense as the action is conveyed from Emerson and his car to Jameson's car to Smith. As a whole, this paragraph tells the story of the relationship between the three subjects.

A change in subjects makes sense when the action flows from one to the next. But a change can be confusing when the subject jumps from one to the next without a logical connection between subjects. This can cause the reader to lose the thread of the narrative and stop reading the statement of facts as a story. For instance:

> Acme hired Coastal to work on different construction jobs for Acme from 2009 to 2012. There were eight different sites around Houston on which Coastal was

hired to work. An arbitration clause was contained in a contract for a discrete project that Acme hired Coastal to perform in February 2011.

The subjects in this paragraph jump from "Acme" to "eight different sites" to "an arbitration clause," without any immediately apparent relation between each subject. The last sentence, for instance, begins with a completely new subject—"an arbitration clause"—which is not mentioned previously in the paragraph. The result is disorienting.

To tell an effective story in the statement of facts, the writer should keep in mind who or what is the subject of each sentence, how the subject changes throughout the statement, and whether or not that flow of subjects makes sense.

10-4:8.6 Pros and Cons of Active Verbs

At some point most of us were taught to use active verbs and to avoid passive voice and nominalizations. This is usually good advice for creative writers. Yet it is not always the best advice for brief writers who, at times, should emphasize action, but at other times should deemphasize it.

The best way to forcefully express action is in a verb:

Asbestos causes cancer.

This can be an effective sentence if you represent a cancer patient who is complaining about asbestos. But if you represent the asbestos manufacturer, you may want to explain the same concept in a way that does not convey the action so forcefully.

One way to minimize action is the passive voice:

Cancer is caused by asbestos.

As Strunk and White explained, the passive voice is "less direct, less bold, and less concise."[60] In describing some events, advocates should want to be less direct, less bold, and less concise. The passive voice also can be useful when the action is less important than the author's need to make a particular word the subject of the sentence. Or the passive voice can be used to divorce an action from any subject, such as "Mistakes were made."

Another way to minimize action is nominalization. A writer can deemphasize action by taking it out of the verb and placing it in the noun. For instance:

Studies have established the causation of cancer by asbestos.

This minimizes the action of causing cancer. The sentence conveys less action than, "Studies have established that asbestos causes cancer." Yet authors may prefer the nominalization if they wish to deemphasize the action.

Passive voice and nominalization should not be overused because they can make a statement of facts too dull and lifeless. A bored reader may be more likely to rely on the other side's statement of facts. Passive voice and nominalization also should not be overused because they may alert the reader that the writer is trying to minimize the action of the story. But used selectively, they can tone down the most harmful actions of the story.

10-4:8.7 Effective Storytelling

The statement of facts is the part of the brief that is most like fiction. It tells a story. It begins by introducing the characters and setting. Then it describes what happens—the conflict. It concludes with the resolution, or the end of the conflict, whether that is the conclusion of events before trial or the trial itself.

In approaching the statement, the initial question the writer should ask is: "What story should I tell?" That story should depend on the legal issues in the argument section of the brief. For instance, if an appellant's only issue is the sufficiency of the evidence of damages, the story should be the *damages* story, not the *liability* story. The writer should briefly discuss the liability facts as part of the setting of the story. But the story itself should be about the evidence of damages.

In a multi-issue appeal, the statement may need to tell more than one story. The writer will need to decide whether those stories should be integrated or told separately. For instance, in a case where the issues are (1) the existence of a duty, and (2) exclusion of evidence by the trial court, the author probably should tell the story of the facts concerning the existence of a duty first, and then tell the story of the evidentiary rulings at trial.

10-4:8.8 Organization: Summary and Topic Headings

Two organizational tools are especially useful for a reader in reading a statement of facts: summaries and topic headings.

Summary of the facts. A fact summary is usually a paragraph or introductory section of no more than a half a page that gives an overview of the story before going into details. The summary also may briefly and generally introduce the issues in the appeal, only for the purpose of orienting the reader to understand the facts. This introduction of issues is not a replacement for the statement of issues, and usually should be no more than a sentence. The fact summary or overview can be particularly helpful for the reader who has not first read the issues to identify what to look for in the facts.

Topic headings. Topic headings are as useful in a statement of facts as they are in an argument. They tell the reader where to find different parts of the story. They also serve as chapter breaks, informing the reader when the story transitions from one part to another.

Illustration—portion of a statement of facts with summary and headings

STATEMENT OF FACTS

Overview

Eloise Smith owned a taxi cab, which she drove as an independent contractor. Her cab had dispatch equipment installed by Green Taxi Company.

Smith collided with John Garza's motorcycle after crossing into the wrong lane of traffic as she approached a blind turn. This appeal concerns whether Green Taxi's placement or maintenance of dispatch equipment breached its standard of care.

(*Continued*)

The accident

Smith conceded the accident was "my fault." RR 2:284-85. It occurred when she was driving home, approaching a blind curve on Blanco Road. RR 2:274, 291-93; PX 17-19. PX 17. When Smith's car crossed the line into the oncoming lane, she collided with Garza's motorcycle, coming from the opposite direction. RR 2:275-76.

Smith told Garza that the accident happened because she was looking at her computer screen. RR 3:95, 123-24, 215. An accident report by a state trooper indicates that the accident was caused by "distraction in the vehicle" or "driver inattention," but the trooper did not remember what the distraction was. RR 3:32-33.

The placement of the computer screen

Smith's taxi had dispatch equipment installed by Green Taxi. RR 2:271-73.

10-4:9 Summary of Argument

A summary of argument is required in every appellate brief.[61] A summary of argument should be "a succinct, clear, and accurate statement of the arguments made in the body of the brief."[62] It "must not merely repeat the issues or points presented for review."[63]

The summary of argument is one of the most important parts of the brief. It should orient the reader to the arguments that follow. It should crystallize the best arguments as to why the advocate's client should win. And it should do all of that quickly.

10-4:9.1 Road Map

The road map tells readers what the document is about. It provides the framework that allows readers to process the details of the document. As Steven Stark explains:

> Unless readers know right up front where you're heading and why, it's very difficult for them to follow a complicated explanation or argument, much less be convinced by it.[64]

In most briefs, the road map aspect of the summary is as simple as a listing of the primary arguments in the brief, in the order in which they appear. But in appeals where the court's decision tree is not immediately clear, it can be helpful to explain which issues should be decided first, which issues are in the alternative to other issues, which issues might be rendered moot by the resolution of other issues, and which issues must be decided regardless of the court's decision on other issues.

10-4:9.2 Specific Arguments

The problem with many legal summaries is that they stop with the listing of the primary arguments in the brief. They do not persuade because they are too general, too conclusory.

A summary is the part of the brief that the judges on the panel and law clerks are most likely to read. For that reason, it is the best place to highlight your best arguments, argue your best facts, and make your most persuasive legal points. A summary should provide the two or three specific, persuasive reasons that support the main position, even if the legal and factual support will require substantial development later in the body of the document.

10-4:9.3 Brevity

Summaries should be short. The goal is to orient the reader with an overview and give the highlights. If a summary is too long, then the reader may get bogged down in the details, rather than receiving an overview. If the summary includes too many details, then the focus on the true highlights is lost.

For most appellate briefs, a summary of argument should be no more than one page. But if a brief has more than two issues, the summary may run longer. As a rule of thumb, the summary rarely should include more than half of a page of summary per issue. And when a brief has more than two issues, it may be helpful for each issue to be identified with a short, bold-type issue label.

Illustration—summary of argument

SUMMARY OF ARGUMENT

The judgment should be affirmed because Upco did not conclusively establish that Tucker breached his fiduciary duties. Upco's argument is mistaken about both the legal rule and the evidence.

First, the rule of law proposed by Upco's brief would expand the fiduciary duties of a departing employee beyond any duties recognized by Texas courts. Previously, Texas law has recognized that a departing employee has the right to make plans to compete with his employer, the right to join other employees in the endeavor, and the right to keep these plans secret from his employer. However, Upco would change Texas law by requiring the departing employee to disclose the plans to compete.

Second, Upco's Brief violates the scope of review by omitting evidence and inferences that favor the jury's verdict. There was substantial evidence to support the jury's verdict that Tucker did not breach any fiduciary duty when other employees joined his new company after he resigned. For instance, there was substantial evidence that the employees, all Latino, left Upco, not because of any inducement by Tucker, but because they perceived Upco's management as racist.

In this illustration, the summary acts as a road map because it tells the reader that the fiduciary-duty argument will be addressed in two parts: (1) a legal argument about the applicable rule of law, and (2) a factual argument about the testimony at trial. The summary also provides the most important details about the argument—both specific arguments about the correct legal rule and the most important facts. Finally, the summary does all of this concisely, in less than one page.

10-4:10 The Argument

The rules require that the argument section "must contain a clear and concise argument for the contentions made, with appropriate citations to authorities and to the record."[65] This rule provides few constraints, and little guidance, about how to draft an effective argument. But there are a number of practical guidelines that help make an effective argument.

10-4:10.1 Leading With the Best Issue and Best Arguments

Apart from exceptional circumstances, the best, most persuasive arguments should appear first.

There are several reasons for this approach. First, if the judge has limited time, the judge is likely to devote the most attention to the argument that appears first. Because the first argument may be the best chance to catch the judge's attention, it should be the argument that is most likely to succeed.

Second, the advocate's credibility declines with each issue that fails to persuade the reader. For that reason, it is important to establish credibility early in the written argument, rather than giving the judge the impression his or her time is being wasted by considering weaker arguments.

Third, most judges expect lawyers to lead with their best argument. If a good argument appears after a weaker argument, the judge may have rejected the first argument, and then may assume that the second argument is even weaker.

There are a few limited exceptions to this rule. It may make sense to argue first any issue that concerns the court of appeals jurisdiction because the court of appeals must decide jurisdiction first. Or if the outcome of an issue depends on winning another issue first, then the primary issue should appear before the dependent one.

The "best issue first" rule also applies to arguments within a particular issue. An advocate should lead with the best arguments when possible for the same reasons that the advocate should lead with the best issue.

10-4:10.2 Joining the Issue

The job of a judge is not limited to understanding the legal arguments in favor of both sides. The ultimate job of the judge goes one step further. The judge must choose which arguments are better and which side should prevail.

Advocates often miss the opportunity to help the judge choose which argument is better. They miss this opportunity because they fail to even acknowledge the best arguments for the other side. Advocates often make the mistake of seeing only their own arguments, from their own point of view, without acknowledging the best aspects of the other side's argument, let alone acknowledging that a point raised by the other side may have some merit.

The best way to help judges make a decision is to directly clash with the other side's arguments. In other words, the brief should "join the issue." Joining the issue is a method to focus the judge on the primary reason why your arguments are superior. It involves three steps:

1. Make the best arguments for your position;
2. Briefly acknowledge the best arguments for the other side's position; and

3. Explain why your arguments should prevail over the best arguments for the other side.

Most advocates accomplish the first step—explaining their own arguments. The second and third steps, however, appear all too rarely in legal writing. This is unfortunate because an advocate who skips the second and third steps often loses an opportunity to persuade the judge.

The second step, acknowledging the other side's best arguments, makes your position sound more credible, more honest, and more intelligent. Acknowledging the other side's arguments demonstrates that you do not fear those arguments. But most importantly, it is necessary to give you the opportunity to move to the crucial third step in the process—explaining why your position should prevail.

In the third step in this process, weigh the arguments for both sides and explain why the scales tip in your client's favor. This may involve explaining why the other side's arguments are weaker, or it may involve explaining why your arguments are stronger, or both.

Illustration—joining the issue

The *Maritime Overseas* waiver rule does not apply here. In *Maritime Overseas*, this Court held that, when scientific testimony is admitted without objection, a party may not challenge the legal sufficiency of that testimony on the grounds that it is scientifically unreliable. *Maritime Overseas v. Ellis*, 971 S.W.2d 402, 409 (Tex. 1998). But no objection to expert testimony is needed to preserve an appellate complaint that the testimony lacks probative value on the face of the record. *Schaefer v. Tex. Employers' Ins. Assoc.*, 612 S.W.2d 199, 204 (Tex. 1980). These rules are consistent. An objection is only required if a party seeks to show with evidence outside of the record that expert testimony was unreliable.

AmeriTool argues that a party must object before expert testimony is admitted in order to preserve an argument that the testimony is no evidence. There are two problems with AmeriTool's approach. First, it is based on a view that prior Texas cases are incoherent, even though they can be easily harmonized. As demonstrated above, *Maritime Overseas* can easily be squared with *Schaefer*. Second, AmeriTool's proposed rule would require courts to make a difficult, and false, distinction between "reliability" challenges and "no-evidence" challenges. But AmeriTool does not even attempt to define this purported distinction.

This example goes beyond mere argument to acknowledge the heart of the other side's position and explain why the Court should reject it. The first paragraph explains the advocate's position. This is where many briefs stop. But the second paragraph goes on to address the essence of the other side's position briefly and then to give reasons why it is wrong. It joins the issue because it gives the judge reasons to choose one side's arguments over the other side's arguments.

It is more difficult to join the issue in an appellant's brief when the other side has not presented any arguments to the appellate court. Often, however, the other side has previously stated its position in the trial court. In that situation, you can use the other side's arguments in the trial court in your appellant's brief as a foil for comparison.

10-4:10.3 The Most Defensible Winning Position

The best way to winning an appeal is usually not the most aggressive position, but rather the most defensible winning position.

Avoid assuming too high a burden. You should avoid taking on a burden to prove more than you need to prove. For instance, if your client prevailed with the jury on an issue, there is no need to argue on appeal that there is no evidence to support the other side's position. You only need to show that there was some evidence to support a reasonable jury's answer to that question. Assuming the higher burden could lead the court to mistakenly believe that you have to meet the higher burden to prevail.

Avoid arguing too many elements or factors. When an argument only requires you to win one of multiple elements there is no need to argue every element. Often the best approach is focus on the elements that you are most likely to win.

Concede minor skirmishes that are irrelevant to victory. Particularly when lawyers have worked a long time on a contentious case, there is a tendency to fight the other side on every assertion, regardless of whether it matters to the result of the appeal or not. There is no point in doing so, and it only distracts the court's attention from the issues that matter.

Although it may be counterintuitive, making concessions often can help win an appellate argument. Concessions focus the court on an advocate's most defensible route to victory and help avoid wasting time on issues that the advocate need not win. Of course, the trick to concessions is knowing which concessions should be made, and which concessions may doom your case. Lawyers should not be so eager to make concessions that they give up an argument on appeal that has a reasonable chance of success.

10-4:10.4 Write an Argument, Not a Law-Review Article or Court Opinion

Many brief writers had early experiences as a legal writer doing one of two jobs: writing for law review or drafting opinions as a law clerk for a judge. Although these experiences are helpful, the writing styles for those experiences are different from the style you should use in writing a brief.

The purpose of writing a brief is different. Most law-review articles offer an academic, objective summary of the law, even if they advocate a particular position on changing the law. Similarly, judicial opinions are designed, not only to explain a result, but also to provide a set of neutral rules that serve as precedent in later cases. In contrast, the purpose of a brief is to persuade. Although judges expect that brief to be honest about the law and facts, there is no requirement or expectation by judges that an argument in a brief will sound academic, objective, or neutral. Rather, an argument in a brief should provide an "argument" for "contentions."[66]

There are a few specific conventions from law-review articles and judicial opinions that should not be followed in briefs. First, unlike a thorough law-review article, a brief need not include every authority for a proposition or long string cites. Usually, one authoritative citation is sufficient.

Second, unlike the "law" portion of an opinion, an argument should not begin with a long list of broad, neutral legal principles that apply generally to the issue.

Rather, a brief should jump right into the argument. For instance, one opinion began a discussion in an insurance case with a neutral summary of construction rules:

> In interpreting these insurance policies as any other contract, we must read all parts of each policy together and exercise caution not to isolate particular sections or provisions from the contract as a whole. *State Farm Life Ins. Co. v. Beaston*, 907 S.W.2d 430, 433 (Tex.1995); *Gen. Am. Indem. Co. v. Pepper*, 161 Tex. 263, 339 S.W.2d 660, 661 (1960); *see Am. Mfrs. Mut. Ins. Co. v. Schaefer*, 124 S.W.3d 154, 156, 157 (2003). Viewing the policy in its entirety furthers our objective to give effect to the written expression of the parties' intent. *Tex. Farmers Ins. Co. v. Murphy*, 996 S.W.2d 873, 879 (Tex.1999) (*citing Balandran v. Safeco Ins. Co. of Am.*, 972 S.W.2d 738, 741 (Tex.1998); *Forbau v. Aetna Life Ins. Co.*, 876 S.W.2d 132, 133 (Tex.1994)).[67]

This type of discussion is completely appropriate in a judicial opinion. But it is not persuasive argument. It is neutral and detached from the parties in the case. It cites more authority than is necessary to persuade a court that the legal principles are correct.

In contrast, even when it relies on the same principles, an effective brief sounds very different:

> Dominion's interpretation relies solely on one clause in a policy provision, and ignores other language in the same clause, as well as two other provisions that contradict its interpretation. Thus, Dominion violates this Court's admonition against isolating "particular sections or provisions from the contract as a whole."[68]

This example is far more persuasive because it does not waste space espousing general legal principles, but instead concisely applies the relevant principle to explain why one side should win.

10-4:10.5 Authorities, Other Jurisdictions, Policy, and Common Sense

The best authority for an argument is usually a recent case from the highest court in the jurisdiction. But in most appeals, there is rarely an authoritative opinion that clearly applies and resolves the issue on appeal. If there were such a case, the appeal would be unnecessary.

For this reason, appellate lawyers should think creatively about authorities and other support for an argument. Sometimes the best support is not an authoritative, on-point case, but something else.

Other jurisdictions. Cases from other jurisdictions are not authoritative on Texas, but they are often persuasive. Some of the best arguments for citing cases from other jurisdictions include:

- *Persuasive reasoning:* A court from another jurisdiction may help explain why the holding of some Texas cases makes sense, or why Texas should adopt a similar rule when the issue is undecided here.

- *Fifty-state survey:* Despite the diversity of common law among different states, there is some judicial desire for consistency. When a majority of states has adopted a particular rule, there is at least a presumption that it is the better rule. It may be problematic for commerce or the rule of law if a different rule is followed in Texas.
- *The trend:* Similarly, even when the majority of jurisdictions may not favor your position, it may be helpful to show a trend, such as that 10 of 12 of the most recent jurisdictions to address the issue have decided in your favor. Again, the most recent movement of courts is a better indication of where the law is heading, and it may suggest that contemporary policy concerns may favor the trending rule.

Policy arguments and adjudicative facts. Policy arguments can be among the most effective appellate arguments, but they also can be the most misused. On one hand, judges are concerned about the consequences that the legal rule they apply will have in the real world. A policy argument can be an effective way to demonstrate to the court the consequences of a ruling.

On the other hand, many judges are wary of naked policy arguments. Most court of appeals judges do not see themselves as policy makers, instead deferring that role to the legislature or the Supreme Court. So the trick of making an effective policy argument is to frame it in terms that are consistent with the proper judicial role.

One way to make a policy argument is to identify a policy that a court or the legislature already has recognized as embodied in the law. This type of argument usually requires a citation.

Illustration—policy argument based on a policy embodied in the law

Industrial argues that Standard Insurance did not comply with the prompt-payment statute because it responded to a claim through an agent rather than responding directly. This argument would discourage insurers from hiring outside claims handlers in situations such as hurricanes where a high volume of claims are made in a short time. Yet the prompt-payment statute expressly provides that it is to be "liberally construed to promote the prompt payment of insurance claims." Tex. Ins. Code § 542.054. Industrial's argument would contradict the purpose of the statute by requiring insurers to handle their obligations in house, thus slowing their claims response time.

In most briefs, any policy arguments should be made after arguments based on precedent. Your first job is to persuade the court that your position is the most consistent with existing law. The policy argument is the one final persuasive nudge in case the court still has doubts. This order of arguments usually works best because most judges' first concern is to follow precedent, not to make the best policy.

In rare cases, it makes sense to assert the policy argument as the principal argument in the brief. This approach is best when existing law is clearly against your position, but there is a very strong policy argument that can be made against it. Although it happens rarely, Texas courts have changed existing law on the basis of public-policy arguments.[69]

Common sense. There are times when the best argument is not a particular authority, or a policy argument, but simple common sense. You may be able to demonstrate that the other side's argument is inconsistent with other legal rules, violates basic logic, creates absurd results, or contradicts the ordinary meaning of the words at issue.

10-4:10.6 Weaving Together Facts and Law

Judges often find it easier to read an argument that weaves together the law and facts, rather than one that addresses them separately. It is more difficult to read a summary of the relevant legal rules without first knowing how those rules will be relevant to the facts of the author's case. Similarly, it is more difficult to read a long argument about the facts, without first knowing the relevant legal rules that will be applied to that argument.

Consider this example which discusses legal rules without any explanation of how those rules bear on the author's case:

> A party can de-designate a testifying expert and re-designate the expert as a "consulting only" expert as long as they do not do so for an improper purpose.[70] Re-designating a witness as "consulting only" in order to suppress testimony or to conceal facts is considered an improper purpose.[71]

This statement of the legal rules can be much more effective if it is framed in terms of the parties and the facts of the particular case:

> Federated can de-designate its testifying expert and re-designate her as a "consulting only" expert only if it does not do so for an improper purpose.[72] Federated, however, re-designated the witness as "consulting only" in order to suppress testimony or to conceal facts, which Texas courts have held is an improper purpose.[73]

If the legal rule is presented in the context of the particular facts of the author's case, then it is easier for the court to see immediately how the rule should be applied.

10-4:10.7 Incorporating the Standard of Review

An appellate argument should incorporate the standard of review because that is the standard from which the appellate court will decide the case. Yet how the standard should be used and how much it should be emphasized will depend from case to case.

In many cases, the standard of review does not favor the appellant. For instance, the appellant may have to show that the trial court abused its discretion in order to prevail. The appellant in this situation should cite the standard of review and should frame the error in terms of the abuse of discretion. For instance:

> The trial court abused its discretion by admitting the Tanner Report.

Other than framing the argument in terms of the standard of review, the appellant probably will not want to place much emphasis on the standard of review in the argument.

In some cases, the standard of review favors neither party. A "de novo" standard allows the appellate court to revisit the issue from scratch; the way the trial court ruled should be largely irrelevant to the court of appeals' decision. Appellants in this situation may want to place more emphasis on the standard, simply to stress that the court of appeals need not defer to the trial court's ruling.

In other cases, the standard of review favors the appellant. Where the trial court granted a JNOV, for instance, the appellant must show only some evidence from which a reasonable jury could have found for the appellant in order to reverse. In this situation, the appellant should repeatedly emphasize and incorporate the standard of review, reminding the court that a reasonable jury could consider specific evidence that supports the verdict.

10-4:10.8 Organizing the Argument Around Effective Headings

Although not required by any rule, the convention for appellate briefs in Texas is to organize an argument with argument headings arranged in an outline format.

A heading is short text—no longer than a sentence—that summarizes the text that follows it. Headings usually are set apart from the rest of the text. For instance, in a double-spaced appellate brief, it is helpful to distinguish headings from the rest of the text with single-spacing and bold font.

10-4:10.8a Headings Serve a Number of Purposes

Headings help readers locate arguments. Most briefs include a number of different arguments. Most judges and law clerks do not simply read those arguments once, from beginning to end. Rather, they work with the briefs in drafting a study memo, preparing for argument, and writing an opinion. For these readers, it is a frustrating waste of time to "misplace" an argument. Headings help solve that problem. When a heading appears both in the table of contents and in the argument section of the brief, the reader can quickly locate the portion of the brief that addresses a particular argument.

Headings summarize the argument. Judges should be able to read only the headings in the argument section of the brief and have a good overall idea of the argument, even if they have only a few minutes to look at the brief before a conference or oral argument.

Headings help readers structure their mental processing of details. Headings help the reader understand the detailed facts and argument they are about to process. By telling the reader quickly at the beginning of a section of the argument what the argument is, the judicial reader can evaluate how the "proof"—the evidence and authorities—supports that argument. But if the reader does not immediately see what the argument is, then it is more difficult to evaluate whether the support is persuasive.

Headings give readers a break. Like a chapter break in a book, headings are a welcome pause in a long stream of legal text. The break allows readers to briefly rest and summon the mental energy to tackle the next batch of argument. When readers do not get frequent breaks, they can become tired.

Headings help readers switch gears. Many readers have the experience of reading a long text and finding themselves thinking about a particular argument. They notice that, as they think about the previous point, their eyes continue to move over the sentences that follow without processing them. Readers fail to realize that the argument has ended and the writer has moved on to the next argument. Headings signal a new argument. They prevent readers from missing it. They alert readers to shift their mental gears because the writer is beginning a new point.

10-4:10.8b Make the Heading More Than a Label

For an argument heading to accomplish all of these purposes, it should be more than just a label. It should be a concise, one-sentence argument that summarizes the points that follow.

Illustration—argument headings

This heading functions only as a label, not an argument:

A. Standard of Review

It does not convey any argument that helps the judge understand the argument of the brief. A more effective heading is a complete sentence that makes a persuasive point, such as:

A. Unless the trial court abused its discretion, the Court should not reverse the trial court's exclusion of the Tanner Report.

This heading places the discussion of the standard of review in the context of the main argument of the brief. The sentence is not a mere label that says the following discussion will concern the standard of review. It is an argument that the standard of review weighs in favor of affirming the trial court.

In an appellate brief, consider a new heading when the argument has continued for more than three pages without a break. For instance, if a section of a brief addresses a single argument, but is five or six pages long, consider whether the argument may be broken down into two or three easily digestible sub-parts, each with its own heading.

10-4:10.9 Organizing Headings Into a Logical Outline

Because an outline is a collection of headings, it serves the same purposes as an organization based on headings or lists. But an outline has two additional purposes that go beyond headings and lists.

First, an outline *shows* readers the logic of the argument. An outline is not just a list of points. It is a list of points arranged by their hierarchy. It helps readers see the relationship between the points because its shows which points are primary, and which points are secondary or supporting. By showing the logic in a visible structure, an outline is particularly useful for judges. It allows judges to see the conclusion that you want them to reach, then provides the support. By giving the conclusion first, it helps judges determine whether the supporting points support the conclusion.

Second, an outline gives readers a map to follow. Because an outline provides a hierarchical ordering of points, it helps readers get a quick overview of a document's contents. For this reason, an outline should be reproduced under the argument section in a table of contents.

10-4:10.9a Five Guidelines for Creating an Outline

To be useful to readers, an outline should follow five guidelines.

- *1: An outline should follow conventional outline structure*

Over time, outlines have developed a conventional structure of letters and numbers that most readers expect. The structure is organized with this hierarchy:

I.

    A.

        1.

            a.

This hierarchy is a map of main and supporting points. The points further to the left, such as point I, are the main points, or conclusions. Each point that falls under a main point supports it. In other words, point I is supported by A. In turn, point A is supported by 1.

Another convention of outlines is this: for every A, there should be a B; for every 1, there should be a 2. Each supporting level of an outline is a list of supporting points. A single point is not a list. Readers will be confused when they see a point 1 that is not followed by a point 2.

The one exception to this rule is a text with a single main point. Point I will not necessarily be followed by a point II if the text only makes a single main point.

- *2: Each subsidiary heading should directly support the primary heading under which it falls*

Although this guideline is part of the conventional outline structure, it deserves separate emphasis.

When most readers see an outline, they expect a particular relationship between points. For instance, most readers implicitly understand the relationship between points when they see this structure:

II.

    A.

    B.

Readers expect that Point I is the main point or the conclusion of the argument. Readers expect that points A and B directly support point I. Legal readers prefer to see the conclusion first, followed by the support, so that they can evaluate whether the subsidiary points support the conclusion.

Although this structure is useful for readers, it can be difficult for writers. The problem is that we are used to writing in the same order in which we think—working toward a conclusion rather than working backward from it.

The solution comes in editing an outline. Consider whether each subsidiary point is direct support for the conclusion under which it falls. If not, the outline needs reworking.

- *3: Each subsidiary heading should directly support the primary heading under which it falls*

When preparing an outline, it is important to consider the progression of points.

A poorly organized outline jumps from point to point, without any logic behind the ordering of points. In a well-organized outline, the ordering of points follows a logic that is clear to readers.

- *4: An outline should appear in the table of contents and bookmarks*

In an appellate brief, the argument outline should appear in several places: the table of contents page, the bookmarks, and headings placed throughout the argument section. When an outline is not reproduced in a table of contents, readers cannot view the entire outline on a page and see its logic. But when the outline is reproduced at the beginning of a document in the table of contents, readers can visualize the outline as a stand-alone map or summary of the document.

Similarly, when an outline is not reproduced in the bookmarks, screen readers must scroll from page to page in an effort to locate a particular argument, rather than jumping right to it. Bookmarks help screen readers pull up the outline of the argument at any time to remind them of the structure of the argument and to help them navigate from one argument to another.

- *5: An outline should not be too long*

In the case of outlines, there can be too much of a good thing. When an outline has too many headings, or too many levels of detail, it stops acting as a summary.

Ideally, most outlines in a table of contents should be less than a page long. Readers should be able to see the outline on a single screen, without having to scroll. If the outline is longer than a screen, screen readers can no longer get a map of the document with a single look.

10-4:10.9b Example of Full-Sentence Outline in Table of Contents

This is how the full-sentence outline would appear in the table of contents.

Illustration—argument outline in table of contents

I. Because there was some evidence of minority shareholder oppression, the summary judgment was error 7
  A. Minority shareholder oppression requires evidence of either of two measures of oppression 7
  B. There was evidence of at least one of the two tests for minority shareholder oppression 9
    1. There was evidence that Waltham's reasonable expectations as a minority shareholder were defeated 9

(*Continued*)

The same outline should be edited in the PDF bookmarks so that headings are shortened and readable by tablet users.

Illustration—edited argument outline for bookmarks

10-4:10.10 Lists and Bullet Points

Two other helpful tools for organizing arguments in a brief are lists and bullet points.

10-4:10.10a Lists

Lists serve many of the same functions as headings, but at the micro level of specific reasons. A listing of points is particularly helpful in argument because it helps the reader see each numbered point as a separate reason that must be evaluated independently. Numbering the reasons makes it easier to see the separate reasons.

Illustration—lists

Of these versions of the same legal argument, which one makes it easier to see the number of separate reasons that support the argument?

Version 1—no numbering, no list

Under the permissive-use exclusion, there is no automobile insurance coverage for accidents in which the insured is driving a vehicle without the permission of its owner.

The permissive-use exclusion is recognized by the Transportation Code. *See* Tex. Transp. Code Ann. § 601.076 (Vernon 1999) (providing that an auto insurer must pay on behalf of a named insured who "uses a covered motor vehicle with the express or implied permission of the named insured. . . ."). Further, the permissive-use exclusion has been recognized by the State Board of Insurance, which has limited standard policy coverage to a "temporary substitute automobile"—a term defined as an automobile "temporarily used with the permission of the owner." App. 1. This position also conforms to the rulings in most other states. *See, e.g., Allied Mut. Ins. Co. v. Webb*, 111 Cal. Rptr. 2d 426, 430 (Cal. Ct. App. 2001); *St. Paul Fire & Marine Ins. Co. v. Mid-Century Ins. Co.*, 18 P.3d 854, 855 (Colo. Ct. App. 2001).

Seeing the number of reasons is hard work in this paragraph. Most readers do not immediately *see* the structure of this paragraph, which is a conclusion supported by three reasons. Instead, readers must read the entire paragraph, word for word.

Version 2—numbered sentences

Under the permissive-use exclusion, there is no automobile insurance coverage for accidents in which the insured is driving a vehicle without the permission of its owner for several reasons. First, the permissive-use exclusion is recognized by the Transportation Code. *See* Tex. Transp. Code Ann. § 601.076 (Vernon 1999) (providing that an auto insurer must pay on behalf of a named insured who "uses a covered motor vehicle with the express or implied permission of the named insured. . . .").

Second, the permissive-use exclusion has been recognized by the State Board of Insurance, which has limited standard policy coverage to a "temporary substitute automobile"—a term defined as an automobile "temporarily used with the permission of the owner." App. 1. Third, the permissive-use exclusion conforms to the rulings in most other states. *See, e.g., Allied Mut. Ins. Co. v. Webb*, 111 Cal. Rptr. 2d 426, 430 (Cal. Ct. App. 2001); *St. Paul Fire & Marine Ins. Co. v. Mid-Century Ins. Co.*, 18 P.3d 854, 855 (Colo. Ct. App. 2001).

The structure is easier to find in Version 2 than in Version 1 because Version 2 makes the structure explicit. The first sentence promises "several reasons." The remaining sentences use the textual words "First, Second, and Third." Still, the structure is not apparent at first glance. Readers must read through most of the paragraph to find the words "First," "Second," and "Third."

Version 3—a list

Under the permissive-use exclusion, there is no automobile insurance coverage for accidents in which the insured is driving a vehicle without the permission of its owner for three reasons:

(1) The permissive-use exclusion is recognized by the Transportation Code. *See* Tex. Transp. Code Ann. § 601.076 (Vernon 1999) (providing that an auto insurer must pay on behalf of a named insured who "uses a covered motor vehicle with the express or implied permission of the named insured. . . .").

(2) The permissive-use exclusion has been recognized by the State Board of Insurance, which has limited standard policy coverage to a "temporary substitute automobile"—a term defined as an automobile "temporarily used with the permission of the owner." App. 1.

(*Continued*)

(3) The permissive-use exclusion conforms to the rulings in most other states. *See, e.g., Allied Mut. Ins. Co. v. Webb*, 111 Cal. Rptr. 2d 426, 430 (Cal. Ct. App. 2001); *St. Paul Fire & Marine Ins. Co. v. Mid-Century Ins. Co.*, 18 P.3d 854, 855 (Colo. Ct. App. 2001).

In this version, the reasons are organized as a list. A reader can immediately see from the structure, without reading a word, that there are three separate reasons to support the point.

10-4:10.10b Bullet Points

Bullet points are similar in structure to lists but have a slightly different purpose. Bullet points signal a list where the number of points is not important and is therefore omitted. Bullet points are particularly useful for giving illustrations, such as the identification of particular evidence, a list of cases with analogous facts, or a list of analogous legal rules.

Illustration—bullet points

Texas courts have permitted negligence claims for the recovery of economic injuries in a number of other circumstances:

- economic losses resulting from an accountant's negligence, *see, e.g., Logan & Co. v. Burgess Marketing, Inc.*, 744 S.W.2d 170, 187–88 (Tex. App.—Waco 1987, writ denied);
- lost profits resulting from attorney negligence, *see, e.g., Holland v. Hayden*, 901 S.W.2d 763, 765–66 (Tex. App.—Houston [14th Dist.] 1995, writ denied);
- lost profits resulting from a bank's negligence, *see, e.g., Allied Bank West Loop, N.A. v. C.B.D. & Associates, Inc.*, 728 S.W.2d 49, 54–55 (Tex. App.—Houston [1st Dist.] 1987, writ ref'd n.r.e.); and
- lost profits resulting from negligent damage to property, *see, e.g., City of Tyler v. Fowler Furniture Co.*, 831 S.W.2d 399, 406–08 (Tex. App.—Tyler 1992, writ denied).

To decide between a numbered list and bullet points, consider your purpose. Do you need readers to consider each listed point separately? If so, use a list. Do you only need readers to see that you have a number of different items of support, without reading each of them? If so, use bullet points.

10-4:10.11 Leading With Conclusions/Topic Sentences

It is helpful to think of each paragraph of an argument as making its own separate argument. Each paragraph is a building block for the overall argument.

In writing a legal argument, it is important to begin with the conclusion and follow with support. Judges need to know the paragraph's conclusion before they can evaluate its support. If the judge reads all of the support before first understanding the conclusion of the argument, the judge may not know how to evaluate the support.

It is particularly important for a brief to lead with a conclusion when it includes a long discussion about case authority. In most instances, it is not necessary to write more than one or two sentences about a case. Many legal rules are well-established and do not need more support than a citation to a single case. In these instances, it is enough to state the rule, cite the case, and perhaps provide a short quote from the case.

But in some instances, the details of a particular case are very important and need to be developed in depth. You may need to develop a cited case in depth because its facts are highly similar to your case. You may need to explain why that similar case should be followed or distinguished. At other times, you may need to discuss a cited case in depth because the scope of the legal rule announced in that case is not clear, and the details of the case help explain the proper scope of the legal rule.

If a brief discusses a cited case for a paragraph or more, the judge needs to know as quickly as possible why the case is being discussed. The first or second sentence of that discussion should explain how you are using the cited case.

If the judge sees only a detailed summary of the facts of the cited case, without first seeing any explanation about why those facts are relevant, the judge probably will fail to understand why case discussion is necessary. And the judge may even ignore that factual discussion altogether.

Illustration—topic sentence

Version 1

What is the point of this paragraph? Why is the writer discussing *Mesa*?

> In Mesa, there was a breach of a barrier followed by a continuous flow of water containing the pollution into the body of water that became polluted. Mesa had disposed of salt water captured along with oil and gas in an underground well. *Mesa Operating Co. v. California Union Ins. Co.*, 986 S.W.2d 749, 755 (Tex. App.–Dallas 1999, pet. denied). The casing of the well corroded and breached, resulting in the escape of salt water into a fresh water aquifer supply. Id. The contaminated water migrated into the fresh water supply gradually, over a period of time. Id. at 757. The court held that the pollution was not "sudden" within the meaning of the insurance policy and that "a discharge that continues over a lengthy period of time cannot be considered 'sudden' as a matter of law." Id.

The problem is that the writer gives no explanation for why he or she is citing Mesa. Most readers become frustrated at being expected to read details about Mesa when they do not know what to do with those details.

Version 2

How long does it take to determine the point of this paragraph?

> In Mesa, the one Texas case with facts most like this case, the court held that, because the leak was not abrupt, the pollution was not sudden as a matter of law and therefore not covered under the insurance policy. *Mesa Operating Co. v. California Union Ins. Co.*, 986 S.W.2d 749, 757 (Tex. App.–Dallas 1999, pet. denied). In Mesa, there was a breach

(*Continued*)

> of a barrier followed by a continuous flow of water containing the pollution into the body of water that became polluted. Mesa had disposed of salt water captured along with oil and gas in an underground well. Id. at 755. The casing of the well corroded and breached, resulting in the escape of salt water into a fresh water aquifer supply. Id. The contaminated water migrated into the fresh water supply gradually, over a period of time. Id. at 757. The court held that the discharge was not "sudden" within the meaning of the insurance policy and that "a discharge that continues over a lengthy period of time cannot be considered 'sudden' as a matter of law." Id.
>
> In this version, the writer explains in the first sentence why the Mesa case matters to this case. This makes the significance of the following details about Mesa much easier to process.

10-4:10.12 Omit Unnecessary Arguments, Law, and Facts

Judges often complain about legal writing that includes too much information—too many arguments, citations, or facts. For instance, judges frequently complain about string cites. String cites are only useful in a few circumstances, such as when it is important to demonstrate that a legal rule is a majority rule or to demonstrate a trend. But string cites are never useful to demonstrate that you found more than one case. Worse, unnecessary string cites are a waste of space and a waste of the reader's time when a single citation is sufficient to state the law. As Steven Stark explained, "I've yet to meet the judge who looks at the fifth case cited in a long string cite and exclaims, 'I love that case! You win!'"[74]

Similarly, a good argument can be lost in a sea of mediocre arguments. When 10 arguments are listed in a legal motion or brief and the third and fourth arguments are weak, many readers will assume that the later arguments are also weak. Thus, the poor arguments can detract from the credibility of the better arguments.

When writing or editing a written argument, decide what information the court needs to decide the issue. When information is not necessary, delete it.

10-4:10.13 White Space Creates a Helpful Pause

White space is any blank part of a page.[75] White space has a great effect on how much a user enjoys reading a page.[76]

This makes sense. White space gives our eyes and brain a rest. It is a pause.

Writing Professor George Gopen explains that readers must summon a certain amount of energy to begin to read any sentence or paragraph.[77] Gopen compares this energy to taking in a breath.[78] When a sentence takes too long to process the structure and absorb the words, the reader runs out of that mental breath. This helps explain why unnecessarily long or complex sentences and paragraphs are hard to read. The brain needs a rest between thoughts. If the sentence or paragraph requires too much work to read, readers run out of breath.

This problem is amplified when your brief is read on a computer screen. Reading from a screen is difficult—more difficult than reading from paper. Readers prefer even more frequent breaks between paragraphs than they do when reading from paper. The easiest way to make a brief hard to read on a screen is to include large, uninterrupted blocks of text.

The solution is to use techniques to break long, unbroken text into bite-sized chunks. Techniques to increase white space include:

1. shorter paragraphs,
2. shorter sentences,
3. frequent headings,
4. lists, and
5. visuals, such as diagrams or images.

Each of these techniques creates a break in the middle of a block of text. They not only create extra space, but they also give readers a mental pause.

10-4:10.14 Visuals

Trial lawyers understand the importance of visual tools in persuading juries during oral presentations. Visuals also can help appellate readers understand some kinds of information in ways that words cannot.

Strangely, lawyers seem reluctant to use visuals in written arguments. Even when the appellate record contains useful or persuasive visual representations, many advocates lose an opportunity to persuade by simply citing the record without incorporating the visual into the brief.

What explains this hesitance to use visual tools in legal documents? Perhaps the answer is old habits. Lawyers did not have the technology to insert images into documents until fairly recently. Because visuals were hard to incorporate, lawyers had a habit of *writing* arguments to judges without ever *showing* arguments to judges.

Using visuals in appellate briefs is easier than most lawyers think. It can be as simple as cutting and pasting. It is possible to insert relevant diagrams and even photos into the text of a legal document. Programs also make it easy to create charts or graphs to explain complex legal rules, case law holdings, facts, and data.

Illustration—visuals

Version 1—no visuals

This is an attempt to explain separate towers of underlying and excess insurance coverage using the traditional paragraph form:

> The Contractor's tower of insurance included three policies. The first is the XI Primary Policy, which required Contractor to pay a self-insured retention for the first $500,000 in losses. After the $500,000 self-insured retention, the XI Primary Policy provided $500,000 in coverage, but it also had a $500,000 deductible. The second was the XI Excess Policy, which provided $1 million of excess coverage. This coverage was for losses in excess of the XI Primary Policy, and it followed the terms and

(*Continued*)

conditions of the Primary Policy. The third is the Bentley Excess Policy, which provided $10 million of excess coverage. This coverage was not for losses in excess of any particular underlying policy, but instead was excess of the underlying amount of $2 million. The Subcontractor had two policies with Domus, a $1 million primary policy and a $5 million umbrella policy.

For most readers, this is very difficult to follow.

Version 2—visual

The Contractor and Subcontractor each had multiple layers of insurance coverage, as demonstrated by this chart:

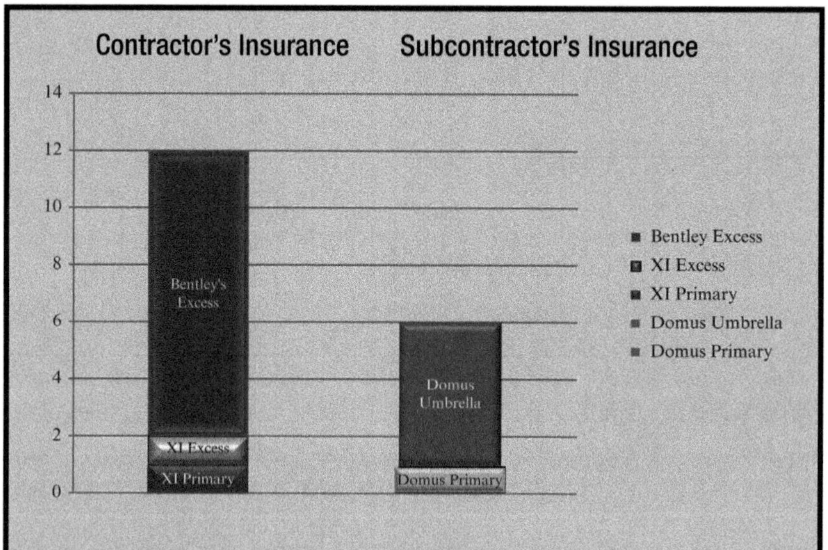

For most readers, it is much easier to see and understand the insurance picture in this second version than in the text version.

10-4:10.15 Respectful Argument

One of the biggest complaints by appellate judges about briefs is that advocates fail to respect the advocates and arguments on the other side. Judges are persuaded by reasoned arguments, not personal attacks. "An attack on opposing counsel undercuts the persuasive force of any legal argument. The practice is uncalled for, unpleasant, and ineffective."[79]

At the same time, advocates should not hesitate to attack the other side's legal arguments and to correct misstatements about the facts. An appeal is a battle that the advocate seeks to win. The question is where to draw the line.

This is a list of do's and don'ts that help strike the most persuasive balance:

- Don't characterize the other side's argument with derogatory adjectives.

  Jackson's argument is feeble and spurious.

- Do explain why the other side's argument is wrong.

  Jackson's argument fails to address the leading Texas Supreme Court case on this issue.

- Don't accuse the other side of lying.

  Jackson misleads this Court by falsely asserting that the light was red.

- Do point out inaccuracies with record citations.

  Contrary to Jackson's statement that the light was red, the only evidence in the record was that it was green. RR 3:142.

- Don't ascribe motives to opposing counsel.

  In an attempt to distract this Court with a red herring, Jackson argues that fiduciaries owe a duty to disclose all material facts.

- Do explain why the other side's arguments are flawed.

  Although Jackson argues that fiduciaries owe a duty to disclose all material facts, this duty never arose because Jackson admitted that Smith was not a fiduciary.

It is much more effective to persuade with reason, rather than characterization of the other side's arguments and speculation about their motives.

Advocates also should treat lower courts with civility, even though the purpose of an appellant's brief is to argue that the trial court erred. An advocate should almost never argue that the trial judge was unintelligent, dishonest, or partial. There are, of course, rare instances when the trial court may have been any one of these. But the advocate's role should be to present the facts and argument demonstrating why the trial court's ruling was erroneous without characterizing its actions or speculating on its motives.

10-4:11 Prayer for Relief

"The brief must contain a short conclusion that clearly states the nature of the relief sought."[80] It is important for the prayer for relief to specify the relief requested. In an appellant's brief, the prayer ordinarily should be for reversal and rendition, reversal and remand, reversal and remittitur, or reversal and modification. In the brief of an appellee or respondent, the prayer should be that the judgment below be affirmed, unless that party has urged cross-points. When a party fails to request the correct relief, the court may hold that the relief was waived because it was not requested.

10-4:12 Certificate of Compliance

The brief should include a certificate stating the number of words in the document.[81] The person certifying may rely on the word count feature of the computer program used to prepare the document.[82] The word count should include every word in every part of the document including headings, footnotes, and quotations, *except* the following: caption, identity of parties and counsel, statement regarding oral argument, table of contents, index of authorities, statement of the case, statement of issues presented, statement of jurisdiction, statement of procedural history, signature, proof of service, certificate of compliance, and appendix.[83]

10-4:13 Certificate of Service

The certificate of service must be signed by the person who made the service and must state:

1. the date and manner of service;
2. the name and address of each person served; and
3. if the person served is a party's attorney, the name of the party represented by that attorney.[84]

Note that this rule requires more than the certificate-of-service requirement in trial courts.[85] Appellate certificates are often defective because they omit the name and address of each person served and the parties they represent.

10-4:14 Appendix

Rule 38.1(j) requires that an appellant's brief in a civil case contain an appendix that includes: the trial court's judgment or other appealable order; the jury charge and verdict, if any, or the trial court's findings of fact and conclusions of law, if any; and the text of any rule, regulation, ordinance, statute, constitutional provision, or other law on which the argument is based and any contract or other document that is central to the argument.[86] The appendix may include optional contents such as excerpts from relevant court opinions, and documents from the record.[87]

The purpose of an appendix is to attach the key documents that the judges are likely to need to review, without having to review the entire record. With the statewide adoption of e-filing, the role of the appendix in briefs is likely to expand. Because the brief and appendix are filed as a single PDF document, citations in the brief can be hyperlinked to documents in the appendix making them easy to access. So it makes sense to include not only the required documents from the record, but all record documents that the court is likely to want to review.

When filing an e-brief with a large appendix, be aware of the e-filing limits on document size. If an appendix includes too many pages, it may be too large for the e-filing portal.

10-5 Appellees' Briefs

10-5:1 Optional Contents

An appellee's brief must contain the same sections as an appellant's brief, except that the rules do not require it to include:

- the list of parties and counsel "unless necessary to supplement or correct the appellant's list;"
- appendix items already contained in the appellant's appendix; and
- a statement of the case, a statement of the issues presented, or a statement of facts, "unless the appellee is dissatisfied with that portion of the appellant's brief. . . ."[88]

Notwithstanding this rule, appellees should almost always be "dissatisfied" with the appellant's statement of issues and statement of facts. Parties need to be able frame the issues in their favor and tell their side of the story. Appellees who omit these portions of the brief lose a valuable opportunity to persuade. Likewise, appellees who are e-filing and expect their briefs to be read on a screen may want to repeat appendix items and include hyperlinks to them in order to facilitate the judge's access to pertinent rulings or evidence.

10-5:2 Structural Considerations—When and How to Restructure

An appellee's brief is ordinarily easier for the court to use when it follows the same order of issues and supporting arguments as the appellant's brief. It is easier for a judge or briefing attorney to follow opposing arguments when they are in the same order. And it may be easier for them to overlook an appellee's responsive argument when the brief does not follow the same order.

But that does not mean that the appellee always should follow a structure that corresponds to the appellant's brief. There are several situations in which an appellee's structure should diverge from the appellant's structure.

10-5:2.1 Disagreement Over the Order of Decision

An appellee generally should follow the order of *issues* in the appellant's brief, unless the appellee disagrees with the order in which the appellate court must decide the issues. If the appellee believes that there is a jurisprudential or logical reason why the court should consider one issue before another issue, then the appellee should restructure the issues—probably with an explanation in the summary of argument or an introductory paragraph to explain the different order.

10-5:2.2 Rearranging Arguments Within an Issue to Make the Best Argument First

Within a particular issue, an appellee should not feel constrained to respond to the appellant's points in the order of the appellant's brief when the appellee believes that a different argument is the more important or better argument for the appellee to put first. Keep in mind the argument guideline that readers expect your best argument to appear first.

10-5:2.3 New Structure Within an Issue

An appellee may reject the appellant's structure altogether for strategic reasons. For instance, an appellant may have structured the argument around the four parts of a four-factor test that some courts have used when applying a particular doctrine. In response, the appellee may believe that the court must first address a threshold argument that disposes of the issue before the court reaches the four factors, such as whether the argument was preserved for appeal. Before the appellee discusses the four-factor test, the appellee should argue the threshold point, even though it does not have a place in the appellant's structure.

10-5:3 When to "Drop" a Prior Argument

Although most advocates become creative at crafting some response to any argument that the other side may make, there are situations when the better strategy may be to avoid, or concede, particular arguments.

For instance, in a car accident case, the plaintiff may appeal the trial court's no-evidence summary judgment against him by filing a brief that addresses each element of negligence. If there was at least some summary-judgment evidence that the appellee negligently caused the accident, but no evidence that the accident caused the plaintiff's only alleged injury—a cancer that developed two years later—then the appellee may want to focus the entire brief on causation. In this situation, the appellee would effectively drop the arguments about a breach of the duty of care.

The primary reason to drop an argument is to preserve credibility. If an appellee begins a brief with an argument that it is not likely to win, it detracts from a better argument later in the brief.

There can be consequences of dropping an argument. If the case continues to the Texas Supreme Court, the appellee may waive an argument by failing to present it to the court of appeals. The decision to drop an argument should not be made lightly.

10-5:4 Cross-Point

If an appellee responds to an appellant's issue by complaining about an error of the trial court, appellee should raise that response as a cross-point or conditional cross-point in the appellee's brief. Cross-points are proper, and a notice of appeal is unnecessary, when an appellee seeks to preserve its right to an equal or lesser judgment based on an alternate ground. *See* Tex. R. App. P. 25.1(c) (requiring a notice of appeal be filed by a party "who seeks to alter the trial court's judgment or other appealable order"); *Boyce Iron Works, Inc. v. Southwestern Bell Tel. Co.*, 747 S.W.2d 785, 787 (Tex. 1988) (holding cross-point need not be raised in trial court).

Specifically, if the trial court renders a judgment notwithstanding the verdict on one or more questions, the appellee must raise by cross-point any issue that would have vitiated the verdict or that would have prevented the affirmance of the judgment if the trial court had rendered judgment on the verdict. Tex. R. App. P. 38.2(b)(1).

In contrast, if an appellee plans to seek to alter the relief granted in the trial court's judgment, it should also timely file a notice of appeal and a cross-appellant's brief in the time required for filing an appellant's brief. *See* Tex. R. App. P. 25.1(c), 38.6(a).

10-6 Reply Briefs

Reply briefs are by their nature shorter than earlier briefs in the appeal. They are limited to 7,500 words, versus 15,000 words for an appellant's or appellee's brief. A reply brief ordinarily should not include an identity of parties and counsel, statement of the case, statement on oral argument, issues presented, and statement of facts. The focus of the reply brief should be on responding to arguments in the appellee's brief.

10-6:1 Structural Considerations

If the appellee's brief has diverged from the structure of the appellant's brief, then you will need to decide whether the reply brief should follow your original structure or the other side's.

If the other side has raised completely new argument headings that do not correspond to your appellant's brief, you will need to decide whether it is important to include your own separate heading in response. For instance, if the appellee has included a heading arguing that your client failed to preserve its appellate argument in the trial court, then you will want a heading to respond to that point.

But if the other side has simply restructured the argument, it often is advisable to follow the original structure of your Appellant's Brief, particularly if that structure is more persuasive for your position.

10-6:2 Balancing Reply Points and Restatement of Key Arguments

An effective reply brief should remind the court of the themes and most important arguments of the appellant's brief without sounding like the brief is merely repeating or restating them. And it should respond to the arguments of the appellee's brief without conceding that the appellee's choice of points and consideration are the most important ones.

These often are difficult balances to strike. But the following techniques may help.

10-6:2.1 Review Your Appellant's Brief for Themes and Arguments to Repeat

In writing a reply, it is easy to become mired in responding to the other side's arguments without remembering and reminding the court of your best points. For this reason, it is important to review your appellant's brief before drafting a reply. Identify your best themes and arguments. And if the other side did not address them, point them out briefly. But do not make the mistake of merely repeating the arguments of your appellant's brief, which will only cause the court to ignore your reply. The reply should address the appellee's arguments and explain why the appellant still wins in spite of, or even because of, the appellee's arguments.

10-6:2.2 Outline the Other Side's Arguments and Possible Responses

It is difficult to read an appellee's brief objectively, with a clear head. As advocates, most of us are too emotionally involved to do so. So we focus on minor inaccuracies while sometimes missing the other side's best points. For this reason it is important to outline the other side's brief, listing every argument, on the left side of a page. Then, on the right side of the page, it is useful to brainstorm possible responses, leaving no stone unturned. This reply outline is a useful tool in drafting the reply.

10-6:2.3 Identify the Arguments to Which You Are Responding

Often advocates are so focused on responding, that they forget to guide the reader to understand which arguments respond to particular arguments on the other side. A reply brief should make this clash of arguments as easy to follow as possible.

10-7 Supplemental and Post-Submission Briefs

The rules do not provide for or prohibit supplemental briefs before submission, or post-submission briefs after argument. Yet these briefs are commonly filed in Texas appeals.

A supplemental or post-submission brief is most appropriate in these situations:

- when the opposing party has raised a new argument or issue in a reply brief;
- when a new case has been decided that is relevant to an issue on appeal; and
- when a court has raised new questions or concerns in oral argument that are not fully addressed in the briefs.

In each of these situations, a supplemental brief can be helpful to the court. A supplemental brief is not helpful to the court when the advocate files one simply to repeat earlier points or arguments. Advocates should resist the urge to file another brief not authorized by the rules solely in order to "have the last word" on appeal.

It also is important to keep in mind the limits on total briefing that a party may file in an appeal. In a civil case in the court of appeals, the aggregate of all briefs filed by a party must not exceed 27,000 words.[89]

It is common for a supplemental brief to be filed in the form of a letter to the clerk. This format is more likely to be appropriate for a very short supplemental argument, such as a one-paragraph argument about a new case. For a longer brief, the traditional double-spaced argument with a table of contents and index of authorities is more likely to be useful to the court.

Also, before filing a letter brief, counsel should be aware of the rules and preferences of the particular court of appeals. Historically, some Texas appellate courts have discouraged briefs in letter form. Before filing a post-submission brief in letter form, it is advisable to call the clerk to ask whether the court prefers a letter or brief format.

Notes

1 Tex. R. App. P. 38.6(a).

2 Tex. R. App. P. 38.6(b).

3 Tex. R. App. P. 38.6(c).

4 Tex. R. App. P. 38.6(a).

5 Tex. R. App. P. 38.6(b).

6 Tex. R. App. P. 38.6(c).

7 Tex. R. App. P. 38.6(d).

8 Tex. R. App. P. 38.6(d).

[9] Tex. R. App. P. 38.6(d).

[10] Tex. R. App. P. 9.4(c).

[11] Tex. R. App. P. 9.4(e).

[12] Tex. R. App. P. 9.4(e).

[13] Tex. R. App. P. 9.4(i)(2).

[14] Tex. R. App. P. 9.4(i)(1).

[15] Tex. R. App. P. 9.4(j).

[16] Tex. R. App. P. 38.8.

[17] Tex. R. App. P. 38.1(g); *see, e.g., Cravens v. Skinner*, 626 S.W.2d 173, 174 (Tex. App.—Fort Worth 1981, no writ).

[18] Judge Ruggero J. Aldisert, Winning on Appeal: Better Briefs and Oral Argument 24–25 (rev. 1st ed. 1996).

[19] Justice Ruth Bader Ginsburg, *Appellate Advocacy: Remarks on Appellate Advocacy*, 50 S.C. L. Rev. 567, 568 (1999).

[20] Ferris Jabr, *The Reading Brain in the Digital Age: The Science of Paper Versus Screens*, Scientific American, April 11, 2013, http://www.scientificamerican.com (search for "science paper screens").

[21] *See* Tex. R. App. P. 9.4(g), 38.1.

[22] Tex. R. App. P. 9.4(g).

[23] Tex. R. App. P. 9.4(g).

[24] Tex. R. App. P. 21(f)(2).

[25] Tex. R. App. P. 38.1(a).

[26] Tex. R. App. P. 38.2(a)(1)(A).

[27] *Tesco Am., Inc. v. Strong Indus., Inc.*, 221 S.W.3d 550 (Tex. 2006).

[28] *Tesco Am., Inc. v. Strong Indus., Inc.*, 221 S.W.3d 550, 553 (Tex. 2006).

[29] Tex. R. App. P. 38.1(b), 38.2(a)(1).

[30] Tex. R. App. P. 38.1(b).

[31] Tex. R. App. P. 38.1(c); Tex. R. App. P. 38.2(a)(1).

[32] Tex. R. App. P. 38.1(d).

[33] Tex. R. App. P. 38.1(d).

[34] Tex. R. App. P. 9.4(i)(1).

[35] Tex. R. App. P. 38.1(e).

[36] Tex. R. App. P. 38.1(e).

[37] Tex. R. App. P. 38.1(e).

[38] Tex. R. App. P. 38.1(f).

[39] Tex. R. App. P. 38.1(f).

[40] *Estate of Rogers v. Comm'r*, 320 U.S. 410, 413 (1943).

[41] Antonin Scalia & Bryan A. Garner, Making Your Case: The Art of Persuading Judges 83 (2008).

[42] *See* Tex. R. App. P. 44.1; reversible error is discussed in Chapter 3.

[43] Judge Ruggero J. Aldisert, Winning on Appeal: Better Briefs and Oral Argument 129 (2003).

[44] *See* Tex. R. App. P. 38.1(e).

[45] Tex. R. App. P. 38.1(e).

46 Bryan A. Garner, *The Deep Issue: A New Approach to Framing Legal Questions*, 5 Scribes J. Legal Writing 1, 1 (1994/1995).

47 Tex. R. App. P. 38.1(e).

48 *See* Tex. R. App. P. 38.1(e).

49 Daryl L. Moore & Amy Hennessee, *Judicial Response to the Questionnaire*, State Bar of Texas 17th Annual Advanced Civil Appellate Practice Course, ch. 5 at 1–2 (2003).

50 Tex. R. App. P. 38.1(f).

51 Tex. R. App. P. 38.1(f).

52 Antonin Scalia & Bryan A. Garner, Making Your Case: The Art of Persuading Judges 94 (2008).

53 Steven D. Stark, Writing to Win 106 (1999).

54 George D. Gopen, The Sense of Structure: Writing From the Reader's Perspective 35 (2004).

55 George D. Gopen, The Sense of Structure: Writing From the Reader's Perspective 35 (2004).

56 George D. Gopen, The Sense of Structure: Writing From the Reader's Perspective 51 (2004).

57 Steven D. Stark, Writing to Win 101–02 (1st ed. 1999).

58 *City of Keller v. Wilson*, 168 S.W.3d 802, 811 (Tex. 2005). For more discussion of the scope of review, *see* Chapter 2.

59 George D. Gopen, The Sense of Structure: Writing From the Reader's Perspective 35 (2004).

60 William Strunk Jr. & E. B. White, The Elements of Style 18 (1979).

61 *See* Tex. R. App. P. 38.1(g), Tex. R. App. P. 38.2(a)(1).

62 Tex. R. App. P. 38.1.

63 Tex. R. App. P. 38.1.

64 Steven D. Stark, Writing to Win 6–7 (1st ed. 1999).

65 Tex. R. App. P. 38.1(h).

66 *See* Tex. R. App. P. 38.1(h).

67 *Provident Life and Acc. Ins. Co. v. Knott*, 128 S.W.3d 211, 216 (Tex. 2003).

68 *State Farm Life Ins. Co. v. Beaston*, 907 S.W.2d 430, 433 (Tex. 1995).

69 *See, e.g., Elbaor v. Smith*, 845 S.W.2d 240, 241 (Tex. 1992) (holding that Mary Carter agreements are void as against public policy).

70 *Castellanos v. Littlejohn*, 945 S.W.2d 236, 239 (Tex. App.–San Antonio 1997, no pet.).

71 *In re State Farm Mut. Automobile Ins. Co.*, 100 S.W.3d 338 (Tex. App.–San Antonio 2002, no pet.).

72 *Castellanos v. Littlejohn*, 945 S.W.2d 236, 239 (Tex. App.–San Antonio 1997, no pet.).

73 *In re State Farm Mut. Automobile Ins. Co.*, 100 S.W.3d 338 (Tex. App.–San Antonio 2002, no pet.).

74 Steven D. Stark, Writing to Win 132 (1st ed. 1999).

75 Robert Hoekman, Jr., Designing the Obvious: A Common Sense Approach to Web Application Design, 214 (2007).

76 Robert Hoekman, Jr., Designing the Obvious: A Common Sense Approach to Web Application Design, 214 (2007).

77 George D. Gopen, Expectations: Teaching Writing From the Reader's Perspective 19 (2004).

[78] George D. Gopen, Expectations: Teaching Writing From the Reader's Perspective 19 (2004).

[79] Morey L. Sear, *Briefing in the United States District Court for the Eastern District of Louisiana*, 70 Tul. L. Rev. 207, 224 (1995).

[80] Tex. R. App. P. 38.1(i).

[81] Tex. R. App. P. 9.4(i)(3).

[82] Tex. R. App. P. 9.4(i)(3).

[83] Tex. R. App. P. 9.4(i)(1).

[84] Tex. R. App. P. 9.5(e).

[85] *Compare* Tex. R. App. P. 9.5(e) *with* Tex. R. Civ. P. 21 (requiring only certification of "compliance with this rule. . . .").

[86] Tex. R. App. P. 38.1(j).

[87] Tex. R. App. P. 38.1(j).

[88] Tex. R. App. P. 38.2(a)(1)(B).

[89] Tex. R. App. P. 9.4.

CHAPTER 11

Oral Argument

11-1 Introduction

Oral argument is the court's opportunity to question counsel about the case and positions taken in the brief. Oral argument also has a ritualistic effect of enhancing a feeling that a party has had its day in court before actual judges who have studied the case. Accordingly, oral argument is usually a combination of prepared remarks and answers to questions. Which predominates will vary from court to court and case to case. An oral argument must be much more focused, and much simpler, than the detailed presentation in the written briefs. This is due to the short time for oral argument, the probability of using much of that time by answering questions, and the nature of oral remarks.

11-2 Preliminary Considerations

11-2:1 Deciding Whether to Request Oral Argument and How to Obtain It

Oral argument is granted in only a small percentage of cases. Although the court decides whether to conduct oral argument, it almost never will unless at least one party has requested oral argument.

"A party who has filed a brief and who has timely requested oral argument may argue the case to the court . . ." unless the court decides that oral argument is unnecessary because:

(a) the appeal is frivolous;

(b) the dispositive issue or issues have been authoritatively decided;

(c) the facts and legal arguments are adequately presented in the briefs and record; or

(d) the decisional process would not be significantly aided by oral argument.[1]

An appellant should usually request oral argument. The only exception should be if the client cannot afford it, and financial arrangements are impossible. An appellant's request for oral argument demonstrates to the court that the client is serious about the appeal and willing to invest the resources necessary to reverse the judgment. Because the burden is on the appellant to establish reversible error, oral argument is usually necessary to remove doubts the court may have after reading the briefs.

An appellee also may want to request oral argument. This usually occurs in large, complex cases when oral argument is a virtual certainty. Unless there is a lengthy, well-reasoned opinion from a well-respected trial judge, the appellee could lose credibility by suggesting oral argument is unnecessary. But an appellee should almost never request oral argument when the appellant has waived it. To do otherwise would suggest there are problems in the case. And the court is unlikely to reverse a judgment without setting the case for oral argument on its own initiative.

In many cases, however, the appellee can appropriately state that oral argument is unnecessary. This may be because the issues on appeal involve settled law and challenges to the sufficiency of the evidence, or allegations that well-respected judges abused their discretion in trial-administration issues.

To request oral argument in the court of appeals, state that request on the cover of the brief, usually at the bottom, e.g., "Appellant Requests Oral Argument."[2] The briefing rule gives either party the option to explain in more detail why oral argument is, or is not, necessary.[3] Although this statement is not counted in computing word limits, it should not be abused by including overt arguments on the merits here to circumvent the rules. Usually one paragraph is sufficient, or at most one page. It is unnecessary to request oral argument in the Texas Supreme Court.

11-2:2 Deciding Who Should Argue and Whether to Split the Argument

Appellate judges express a strong preference that the lawyer who is primarily involved in writing the brief argue the case. The reason is based on the purpose of oral argument—to answer the court's questions about the case and the positions taken in the brief. As a result, a "big name" senior partner, or an academic is usually a poor choice unless that lawyer has been heavily involved in the briefing process and has mastered the appellate record. Although trial counsel may know "what really happened," too often that knowledge includes matters not in the appellate record. Similarly, trial counsel often find it difficult to jettison weak positions, to appreciate the effect of the standard of review, and to answer the questions asked by the court rather than telling the court what trial counsel wants to argue. Unlike a passive jury that forms a captive audience for trial counsel's eloquence and persuasion, an appellate court actively, and often continually, interrupts counsel with questions requiring precise answers.

The appellate lawyer most involved in writing the brief will—by necessity—be familiar with the appellate record and the authorities. That appellate lawyer also will have decided which issues to discard for not having been preserved, for not meeting the standard of review, or for not amounting to reversible error. That appellate lawyer also will have considered the limits on any logical extension of the argument, concessions that can be safely made, and the pragmatic consequences of the competing rules. Finally, the appellate lawyer is more likely to be attuned to nuances in other areas of the law that may influence generalist appellate judges.

Dividing an oral argument between two lawyers is almost always a bad idea. The court is not bound to respect counsel's division of issues. So both counsel will have to be prepared on the entire case, which is a needless expense. Moreover, the first counsel may wind up spending most of the time intended for the second. The Rules reflect the preference for one advocate: "Generally, only one counsel should argue for each side. Except on leave of court, no more than two counsel on each side may argue. Only one counsel may argue in rebuttal."[4]

A more logical, though usually ineffective, division is for one lawyer to present the opening argument for the appellant and another lawyer to present the rebuttal. One problem with this approach is that any credibility gained by the opening argument will not carry over to the second advocate. The other problem is more serious: As discussed below, the most effective rebuttal is extremely limited in scope, usually only one or two points made in two to three minutes. It is very hard for a second advocate to be effective in that role.

A difficulty arises, however, when there are multiple parties on one side with separate counsel. The difficulty is exacerbated when the parties also have separate issues. Some courts are willing to allow counsel to divide the case to accommodate the discussion of issues unique to one party. But most courts frown on having two counsel discuss the same issues, even though they represent different parties. In that situation, the parties and their counsel should try to decide on one lawyer to argue the common issues.

11-2:3 Deciding Whether to Move to Extend Time Limits

The history of oral argument demonstrates a continual shortening of the allotted time. Limits of 20 minutes per side are usual for the Texas Supreme Court, and 15 minutes is not uncommon in the courts of appeals. So it is not uncommon for some clients, many trial lawyers, and even a few appellate lawyers to want to expand the time allotted for oral argument.

The desire to expand argument time is usually misplaced. The principal purpose of oral argument today is *not* to allow counsel to argue orally to the court. Instead, despite its name, the purpose of oral argument is to succinctly answer the court's questions. While the due-process ritual of having one's day in court remains relevant for many justices, they seem to believe 15 minutes is adequate.

So there rarely is a reason to move for additional time. Almost all courts in Texas will allow counsel to exceed the time limit when the court continues to be active in its questioning after the red light comes on. In other words, as long as the court has questions, counsel will likely be allowed to argue. But when the court is finished with its questions, it's time to stop. The relatively short time limits, therefore, encourage both the justices and the advocates to focus and compress their remarks.

If there ever is an occasion to seek additional time, it is when there are multiple parties with discrete issues or cross-appeals involving different issues. In that event, counsel should agree to a joint motion to expand the time allotted for oral argument and file it as soon as practicable after notice of the submission date. The motion should describe specifically why additional time is necessary.

11-3 Preparation for Oral Argument

Preparation is the key to a successful oral argument. Although the outcome in the case will turn on the court's view of the law and facts, the success of oral argument will turn on counsel's preparation.

11-3:1 When to Begin Preparing

Counsel should begin preparing for oral argument as counsel begins working on the first appellate brief. During record review and legal research, ideas will come into focus that could be useful at oral argument. These ideas should be saved in a separate oral-argument folder.

As the last brief is written, appellant's counsel should again consider what points might arise in oral argument. Appellant's counsel should try to include these in the reply brief, since there is no certainty that oral argument will be allowed. While reading the appellant's reply brief, the appellee's counsel should think of responses that could be made during oral argument.

Serious preparation should begin upon receiving notice that oral argument has been granted. This does not mean that every moment between receipt of notice and oral argument will be spent preparing. But it does mean that counsel should begin thinking about oral argument, reviewing key materials, and trusting the subconscious to activate itself.

11-3:2 Suggested Structure for Reviewing Materials and Preparation

Every lawyer prepares for oral argument differently. And preparation can vary depending on the vagaries of the case. But what follows is one useful method for structuring and planning preparation. The benefits from this method not only include thorough preparation, but also ensure adequate time for preparation.

First, generate a list of preparation steps, arrange them in a logical sequence, estimate the amount of time each step will take, and then schedule them, working in reverse order from the argument date. Whether each step is necessary, and the amount of time required for each step, will vary from case to case. For instance, an appeal from a summary judgment is unlikely to have much of a reporter's record to review. Or a case with settled legal issues may have few cases to be studied.

Here is a logical sequence for a sample list of preparation steps, which are discussed in more detail below:

- Review treatises
- Outline all briefs
- Review outlines of briefs
- Identify and collect key cases—those likely to arise during oral argument
- Identify and collect key record excerpts—those likely to be questioned during oral argument
- Identify a theme—the 20-second combination of law, facts, and justice that permeates your case and demonstrates why your side should prevail
- List affirmative points—the logical steps in your argument
- Outline oral argument
- Prepare an opening—the first 60 seconds of what you hope to say before the questions begin

- Draft a text for oral argument, which will be used only during practice, not at the podium
- Prepare a mantra—a short phrase summarizing a key theme that you will repeat often during the argument
- Identify likely questions
- Participate in an informal moot court to generate more ideas and see concerns of others
- Draft answers to anticipated questions
- Review the key cases and key-cite them
- Review the key record excerpts and exhibits
- Assemble a draft podium binder—the notebook that will contain all your materials at the podium
- Prepare argument modules—the key phrases that will remind you of key points for each argument, arranged by issue
- Rehearse
- Practice segues to transition between issues, in case the court takes you away from your planned order
- Identify more likely questions and develop answers to them
- Revise the draft of the text for the oral argument
- Present a formal moot court with active questioning, preferably from newcomers to the case who have read only the briefs
- Revise answers to the anticipated questions
- Revise the draft of the text for oral argument
- Conduct further legal research if necessary; update existing research
- Revise the podium binder, if necessary
- Rehearse and record or even videotape your practice session
- Key-cite the leading cases again
- Assemble other items to take: Pads, pens, post-it notes, lozenges, markers, glasses, mints, etc.
- Review the briefs a final time, especially your briefs
- Review the abstract of the record and the key record excerpts
- Listen to the recording of the argument and then rehearse

11-3:3 Selecting the Issues for Argument and Creating the Theme and Opening

The short time limits for oral argument rarely allow counsel to argue all issues in the briefs. Nevertheless, counsel must be prepared to answer questions on all of them. But counsel should select one or two issues to focus any prepared remarks on.

If the briefs have properly prioritized the issues, then usually the first one or two issues in the briefs will be the choices for oral argument. Some issues just don't come across well orally. So they may have to be left for the briefs, regardless of their importance, unless a simple way to present them orally can be discovered.

You generally will want to play to your strengths. As a result, the standard of review may influence your decision. Or the state of the settled law may lead you toward or away from a particular issue. Occasionally, moreover, one issue has all the sex appeal. Even if not argued, it will be on everyone's mind and prove a distraction.

The theme of the argument should track the theme of the briefing. To choose a new theme at oral argument is almost always unwise: at worst, it is a disaster that appears waived; at best, a confusion that is soon forgotten. A good theme is simple, interesting, and supported by the facts and law (or trends in the law), encompasses fairness, reveals the implications of the decision for future cases, and is conducive to the court deciding the case. To develop a theme, determine the clash points in the law and facts. The parties will agree about most matters; only on a few will they differ. If you have broad legal principles, then the theme may be fact-intensive. In any event, the theme will classify your legal and factual principles into an articulable description of justice.

After you have decided on the issues to argue and your theme, you should draft a 30–60 second opening. The opening will quickly summarize the essence of your position and show the court the structure of your planned presentation. Of course the court is free to take you in a completely different direction. But after your opening, any diversion from your road map will be deliberate rather than accidental. Advocates who are known and respected by the appellate court may be given some deference in their choice of issues and structure—at least for a few minutes.

Here is an example of a good opening in a Texas appellate court:

> This is ultimately a case about sanctity of contract. The first issue is that the contract bars justifiable reliance. This case boils down to whether one suffering from seller's remorse in hindsight can allege fraud to undo his written contract. We know that fraud vitiates everything it touches. But we also know that a party cannot allege fraud based on matters contradicted by the written agreement. This Court barred that fraud claim in its *DRC Parts* case, and other courts throughout Texas have held the same way for the same reason. The reason is that parties are charged with the knowledge of what they sign. Specific representations in a written contract negate the effect of any earlier representations. Without that rule, every contract could be turned into a swearing match, requiring a trial—with the winner often turning on what a jury thinks is fair in hindsight, rather than on what the parties actually bargained-for in foresight.
>
> This case is the archetype for that rule. [Appellee] signed a contract stating that opinions about value were merely estimates, that opinions about value could differ, and that value could increase in the future, but he was agreeing to sell at that price nonetheless. And he said he was releasing all claims that he should have been paid more. But when subsequent market changes made [X] more valuable, he sued, alleging that he had been misled about value. If [appellee] prevails, then every contract is subject to the same renegotiation in hindsight at the courthouse.

11-3:4 Organizing the Argument Using an Outline of Affirmative Points

Be sure that your oral argument is logically sound. Again, you probably have done a lot of this work while preparing your written brief. Yet, because oral argument is so abbreviated, it's wise to verify the logic of your planned oral remarks. Studying the logic of your argument should give you clues into what questions the court may ask at oral argument.

First, review the formal structure of the argument. Usually, your major premise will be taken from legal authority—case law, a statutory text, or constitutional prohibition. Your minor premise, usually, will be taken from the facts in the record, as viewed through the standard of review. You must then determine whether your conclusion is logically compelled from the application of the minor premise to the major premise. For example: "Texas law vitiates a contract for fraud in the inducement. Here, Jones told Smith that the car was new when in fact it already had 20,000 miles on the odometer. Smith relied on that false misrepresentation in buying the car. Texas law requires that the contract be rescinded as void." The formal logic of that argument is sound.

Second, you must ensure the validity of your major and minor premises. More often than not, this will be the focus of the appellate court's questions. "Is that *really* the law?" "Aren't there contrary facts we must take as true?" In some cases the law is unsettled, and in others the facts are unsettled (though this is rare). Many questions concern the application of the facts to the law: Should they be viewed under this rule, or under another rule, or should the rule be changed? In the above example, ask whether Texas law really vitiates all contracts for fraud. Ask whether Smith reasonably relied on the misrepresentation. Was it even a misrepresentation? And did Jones know it was false and intend to deceive Smith? The standard of review regarding the facts may essentially answer some of these questions.

Next, create an outline of affirmative points. Affirmative points are the logical reasons why your side should prevail. These are *not* the flaws in your adversary's argument; rather, these are your affirmative reasons based on the logical structure of your argument.

Next to each affirmative point note the key support for it—whether legal or factual. This list of affirmative points and supporting evidence should be with you at the lectern during your oral argument. By having ready support for each point, you can quickly field the court's challenges.

11-3:5 Preparation of Scripts, Textual Outlines, or Notes of Key Points

Lawyers differ in their choice of textual material to use at the lectern. While a script has its usefulness during preparation for oral argument, it is not useful at the lectern. Because the main purpose of oral argument is to answer the court's questions, a script will only get in the way.

A textual outline can suffer from similar problems. The exception is the outline of affirmative points. This list, however, is not the basis for your planned remarks, but a checklist to make sure you've covered all your important points and to use as a quick reference for citations to primary authority.

Some advocates argue without notes. This allows great spontaneity and constant eye contact with the justices. But effectively arguing without notes requires an exceptional, almost photographic, memory. Even then, it should be attempted only in single-issue cases with a short appellate record. And even in those cases, it should be attempted only by experienced advocates. The stress of arguing and the demands of rapid questioning can cause anyone to forget something. When effectively done, it can lead to an impressive argument. But one mistake can lead to disaster. Because appellate courts are more interested in correct answers to their questions than in an impressive show, you will almost always be better-off taking some notes to the lectern.

One of the best techniques is to use key points arranged in modules on a sheet of paper. Rather than textual sentences, these are pithy phrases that will call the point to mind. The advocate may elaborate for one to three paragraphs based on a two-word key point.

Further, the key points are arranged in a logical order and grouped by issue. This enables the advocate to switch issues in response to the court's questions. By glancing at the key points in that issue's module, the advocate can give the entire argument on the issue in response to a question. The advocate can then return to the issue module being discussed when the question intervened. Again, a quick glance at the key points will enable the advocate to resume seamlessly—particularly if thought and practice have been given to segues.

11-3:6 Anticipating Questions and Thinking Through Concessions

During the complete review of the briefs, record, and authorities, counsel should note questions that arise. Then, while the textual outline and script are being prepared, counsel should also think about likely questions and begin developing answers to them. This process will usually continue until the day of argument.

Another paramount concern is identifying what to concede and what can be conceded. In some cases, counsel may wish to make an express concession early in the argument. For instance, "I concede that the *Jones* case is controlling on the first issue. But we plan to ask the Supreme Court to overrule *Jones*." In many cases, counsel will need to make a concession under relentless questioning. Unless concessions are carefully thought out in advance, there is a grave danger of conceding under pressure something fatal to your position.

One way to think about concessions is to study the logic of the affirmative points. If something is a major or minor premise, it cannot be conceded unless the conclusion can also be conceded.

Other concessions may involve legal authorities or the record. These almost always affect the major or minor premises. So they can be handled as just described.

More dangerous are concessions about the policy implications of your proposed rule. Some justices may favor those implications, but some may not. Since these concessions may affect actual votes, they need to be carefully considered in advance. Proper preparation for oral argument and for briefing includes a thorough consideration and discussion of policy considerations. You need to think ahead of time about where to draw the line under pressure.

Similarly, but perhaps even more dangerous, are concessions about the logic of the argument. Unlike attacks on major and minor premises, these attack the formal structure of your logic. In other words, given A and B, the conclusion is not C, but D. If you have carefully thought through the logic of your argument in writing the brief, your conclusion should be defensible. If not, your argument is flawed anyway, and the case should be settled.

11-3:7 Moot Courts

11-3:7.1 Why?

No oral argument should be presented without at least one moot court. The advocate typically is so wrapped up in the client's perspective of the case that he cannot view it the way objective, generalist newcomers—appellate justices—will view the case. An advocate presenting an oral argument without a moot court runs the risk of encountering a surprise, often a bad one, at oral argument. In oral-argument preparation, two heads are better than one, and three are better than two.

11-3:7.2 How?

The informal moot court consists of sitting around a table, usually with lawyers who have been involved in the case at trial and on appeal. Problems should be openly discussed, and suggestions offered about which issues to argue and which to avoid. If cost is not a concern to your client, you can even ask another lawyer or former judge to review the briefs and give first reactions to them as cold readers. The arguing advocate can then use this information in preparing for the argument.

The formal moot court is simply that—a formal run-through of the argument. Even then, approaches may vary from case to case. In some cases, the advocate may prefer first to give the "canned" remarks, and then take questions afterward. The advantage to this approach is that it allows feedback about the opening and the structure of the planned argument. If this approach is used, however, the advocate should then have another presentation that is "hot" from the beginning, meaning the mock judges can interrupt with questions at any time.

11-3:7.3 Who?

The moot court judges ideally should consist of three lawyers, diverse like the appellate panel, who are unfamiliar with the case. Ideally, one lawyer would be relatively inexperienced in order to simulate an appellate briefing attorney. Another would be a senior lawyer with little or no experience in the main issue on appeal. And the third would be a lawyer with experience in the relevant area of law. The mock judges can also be former appellate judges or former appellate law-clerks. This composition will maximize your chances of getting all possible perspectives.

You should also include the other lawyers who have worked on the brief. They may be aware of problems lurking beneath the surface of the briefing. These problems might not arise during oral argument, but might arise during the drafting of the opinion. The advocate needs to know them (1) to be able to address them if they do arise, and (2) to assess whether to address them anyway while there is a chance to do so. Rehearing may be too late.

11-3:7.4 When?

The moot court should occur several days before oral argument for two reasons. First, counsel will need time to revise the argument, develop better answers to questions, and research or review additional materials in light of the moot court. Second, counsel will need some "down time" simply to relax from the stress of the moot court, to become comfortable with the revised argument, and to "re-psyche" for the real argument.

Yet a formal moot court too far in advance of oral argument can be a waste of time. Until counsel is pretty far along in the preparation process, counsel will not benefit from a formal moot court. On the other hand, an early informal moot court can be beneficial in alerting the advocate to fresh readers' initial concerns after reading the briefs.

So the best practice is to hold an initial informal moot court relatively early in the preparation process, followed by a formal moot court 2–7 days before oral argument.

11-3:8 Final Preparation

Following the formal moot court, final preparation will include continued thinking and rehearsal, with several important goals.

11-3:8.1 What to Leave for Rebuttal

As an appellant, there may be matters that are bound to arise during the appellee's argument for which you may have a zinger reply. Those might be saved for rebuttal. This is to be distinguished from affirmative points, which must be made during the opening argument. These are simply devastating replies to arguments that the appellee might be induced to make. Knowing your case, the panel, and your opposing counsel will help you make the judgment call about what is safe to leave for rebuttal. Experience also helps.

11-3:8.2 Demonstrative Aids and Bench Exhibits

It is important to determine whether any sort of demonstrative exhibit would be useful. Generally, blow-ups on poster boards are a waste of time, since they are hard to see unless huge and hard to set up if huge. Bench exhibits may be more useful, though there is little need to include things that already are in the appendix to the briefs. Occasionally, however, juxtaposing certain parts of the record may be useful in a bench exhibit.

Some advocates try to find a way to leave the court with a summary of the key points of their argument. Because most arguments are recorded, it is questionable how valuable this practice is. Others want to use a chart, picture, or graph concocted from the evidence. Some judges may resent this as trying to add to the record, while others will welcome the advocate's attempt to explain the case more easily.

On rare occasions, advocates use PowerPoint presentations during oral argument. The results have been mixed. Usually, the court—not the advocate—is in control of the argument. It is unusual for the court to sit passively while the advocate lectures from the slides in a pre-determined order. In some cases, the tactic might work. But in most cases, it backfires.

11-3:8.3 Final Review of Materials and Updating of Research

During the two or three days before the argument, it is wise to review the important authorities, the briefs, and key record materials. These are the items that will most need to be fresh in the advocate's memory during the argument.

Research needs to be updated, especially with regard to keyciting for overruled or vacated authorities or criticized cases. Embarrassing episodes during oral argument can result from omitting this important step.

11-3:8.4 Final Rehearsals and Rest

Counsel should consider avoiding alcohol for a couple of days before the argument, simply because it dulls the mind and impairs memory. Exercise is particularly useful for working off nervous energy. You should try to have completed most of your preparation so that you can spend the final day simply with a few private rehearsals and checking on answers to a few questions that may pop into your head.

The evening before the argument is best spent quietly reviewing notes of the argument and then relaxing with something that takes your mind away from the case. Most important is a good night's rest, to the extent possible. Consider avoiding caffeine during the day before the argument, since it often interferes with sleep. The same is true for alcohol, which can affect sleep and memory for several days after its consumption. Consider stop drinking alcohol about a week before a scheduled argument.

11-3:8.5 Logistics, Appearance, and Behavior on the Day of Argument

If you are not familiar with the courtroom, you should try to visit it the day before, possibly observing an argument. If the argument is out of town, arrive the day before. The last thing you need to be worrying about is a travel snafu.

Even for an in-town argument, give yourself plenty of time to reach the courthouse, park, clear security, and get comfortably situated. This may require you to have awakened earlier than usual. That is not a bad thing, because it gives you a final chance to review your notes or even to go through a final rehearsal. That will give you the confidence that you know your argument as thoroughly as you thought you did before going to sleep the night before.

Your appearance should be traditional and conservative, such as a dark-colored, formal suit. Your briefcase should also be conservative, and the materials in it easily accessed. If you are a woman, your hair style, makeup, neckline, purse, and jewelry should be subdued. Don't wear high heels if you are likely to trip in them. The key is: Nothing snappy or distracting. You want the court to focus on what you are saying, not on what you are wearing.

If listening to other arguments before your case is called, maintain a respectful attitude. If, instead, you need to review your notes, do it outside the courtroom. Many appellate courts have nearby rooms for just that purpose.

11-4 Delivery of the Argument

11-4:1 Credibility of the Speaker and Delivery

Aside from having a good case on the facts and law, the most important thing you can do for your client is to have credibility with the court. This begins with past appearances. But it includes having a serious attitude on the day of argument, as shown by respectful attire, confidence in your remarks, and direct answers to the court's questions.

Body language is important. It must convey sincerity. Because body language is often unconscious, it is important to believe in what you say. Periodically reviewing a videotape of your practice sessions may help you identify and eliminate mannerisms that detract from the impression you wish to make.

11-4:2 The Opening

The ritualistic opening "May it please the Court" is still the best way to begin. Varying from that phrase will simply be a distraction that you don't need at the beginning of the argument. Whether to introduce yourself depends on whether the marshal does so as you stand up. Only in multi-party appeals should it be necessary to remind the court who you represent. And there is no reason to say you represent the appellant, appellee, petitioner, or respondent. The court surely knows at least that much from where you were sitting and when you stood up.

Usually an opening sentence or two that summarizes the case and your argument is a good idea. At worst, it lets the court call to mind the issues that it will be hearing about. At best, it lets you get your key point out before being bombarded with questions. It also is advisable to inform the court which issues you plan to focus on.

In contrast, the appellee may be better-off by beginning with a point that has arisen during the appellant's argument. Perhaps a justice has expressed skepticism about a certain argument. The appellee can elaborate on the appellant's problems with that argument. Or perhaps there is a jurisdictional or waiver point that renders moot most of what the appellant argued. The appellee should be prepared to go off-script depending on what the appellant actually argued and how it was received by the court.

11-4:3 Role of Sound Bites

With short times for arguments, using sound bites has become increasingly important. Rarely is there time to fully develop all the paragraphs of a cogent argument. Instead, topic sentences should be the norm for all but the most important parts of the argument. These should be carefully crafted during your preparation, not off-the-cuff. The key words in each module in your podium binder should remind you of those prepared sentences.

11-4:4 Integrating Law, Text, Facts, and Policy

The art of oral advocacy primarily consists of two aspects. The first is integrating the governing law, and any controlling textual materials, with the facts that animate the policies underlying the governing law so as to lead to the conclusion that your client should prevail on appeal. This is usually easier said than done, but it is a worthwhile goal.

The best argument convinces the court that the facts and law favor a ruling for your client in two respects. The first is that the result for your client is fair under the facts in the appellate record. The second is that the result for your client will be fair for most other parties in a similar situation. The latter requires some knowledge of the practical effects of the decision on the industry at issue or society in general. And it may also involve a slightly tangential consideration of the administrative convenience of the judicial system or even separation-of-powers issues.

11-4:5 Handling Questions and Making Concessions

The second aspect of the art of oral advocacy is how counsel handles the court's questions. Because the primary purpose of oral argument is simply to allow the justices to ask questions that arose while reading the briefs, the most important part of oral argument is handling questions. These are two suggestions for handling questions.

First, answer a question directly. If at all possible, the answer should begin with a "yes," "no," or "it depends." Sometimes the court may ask you about a reference or authority, which of course would call for a different answer. Then, if necessary, explain your answer.

The second suggestion is to use the court's questions to advance the points the advocate wanted to make anyway. This requires great preparation, a cool head, and some degree of mental flexibility and quickness. Some people are naturally better at it than others. But everyone can improve by preparing thoroughly and thinking about the case in detail.

11-4:6 Transitioning to Other Issues

Ideally, you will have only one issue to argue. But more often, you will have two to three issues, or two to three points to make under the one issue. This will require you to signal that you are transitioning to another point or issue. Usually an explicit transition is best. But at times, the court's questions will take you there anyway. In that event you should go with the flow. If you need to return to an earlier point, be explicit about doing so. Clarity is the key.

11-4:7 Concluding

A formal summation is usually unnecessary and often precluded by the red light. But a simple reminder that the requested relief is "reversed," "modified," or "affirmed," followed by a "thank you," is fine.

Be careful, however, to know the protocol of your court. Some courts require counsel to stop in mid-syllable when the red light comes on. Before those panels, do just that. But most panels will allow you to finish that sentence, so long as it's not prolonged.

11-5 Special Tips for Appellee

The key for the appellee is to listen and respond directly to appellant's arguments rather than sticking to a prepared script. The appellant may have argued matters not in the brief, or more likely may not have argued certain issues at all. The appellee looks foolish arguing things not raised by the appellant's argument, unless they are dispositive of the argument the appellant made. More often, the court's questioning will reveal its tentative views about the issues. The appellee who is listening attentively can either jump on the bandwagon or try to shore up a position that seems to be losing ground.

Many judges report that the most critical part of an entire oral argument is the first two minutes of the appellee's argument. This is because many of the appellant's remarks may have tracked the reply brief, to which the appellee's response has not been heard. This raises a dilemma, requiring judgment. Sometimes it's best for an appellee to open with the last thing said by the appellant, so it's fresh in the court's mind. Or the appellee may wish to quickly brush away a waiver or jurisdictional argument to which there is an easy answer. But more often, the appellee should go straight to the heart of the matter, which (with luck) will have been indicated by the court's questioning of the appellant, or at least by the focus of the appellant's remarks and reply brief.

11-6 Rebuttal

Effective rebuttals are the hardest part of oral argument. They typically last only three to five minutes, the court has largely indicated its leanings and concerns, and there are usually a dozen things the appellant wants to say. To lessen the stress, however, recall that rebuttal rarely changes anything.

The best rebuttal raises one to three points—each of which contains only one or two pithy sentences—at most. Rebuttal is not the time to reargue disputed points. Rather, rebuttal is the time to correct a misstatement of the record, a misquotation of the law, or to follow-up on a judge's question. Limiting rebuttal to "silver bullets" will help you identify which two or three points are worth making. Let the others go.

11-7 Follow-Up

Counsel may accidentally say something wrong at oral argument. The pressures are too intense, the time is too short, and the questioning is too fast. If you said something incorrect, fix it that day or the next day at the latest. A short letter to the clerk correcting the mistake will be appreciated. Silence will not.

11-8 The Possible Future of Oral Argument

Given the changes in oral argument, and the reductions in both the number of arguments granted and the time allotted, it might someday vanish.

While it does have a due-process ritualistic value, could that value be served in other ways? Would it be less of a strain on the court's budget, and client resources, to turn oral argument into something akin to an open-book examination?

For instance, a court could issue a few questions by email, asking for a response of no more than 100 words within two days. The other side could then have a similar chance to reply. This would enable counsel to look up the correct answer from the record or the case law. If the question required a different type of answer, counsel could at least craft it in a succinct manner and think through its implications.

Although handling oral argument is a key technique for appellate advocates to master, the rapid-fire question and answer of modern oral arguments does not always fully serve the function of providing the court with the most helpful responses. So it remains for the future to what extent oral argument will remain viable.

Notes

1 Tex. R. App. P. 39.1.

2 *See* Tex. R. App. P. 9.4(g) ("If a party requests oral argument in the court of appeals, the request must appear on the front cover of that party's first brief.").

3 *See* Tex. R. App. P. 38.1(e).

4 Tex. R. App. P. 39.4.

CHAPTER 12

Briefs of Amicus Curiae

12-1 Introduction

"Amicus curiae" literally means "friend of the court" in Latin. Originally, an author of an amicus brief was just that—a disinterested "friend" who helped the court by offering a unique legal perspective or helpful fact. Indeed, the term "amicus curiae" once "applied to a bystander, who without having an interest in the cause, of his own knowledge makes suggestion on a point of law or of fact for the information of the presiding judge."[1] Over the years, however, the role of the amicus changed, and today, the "institution of the amicus curiae brief has moved from neutrality to partisanship, from friendship to advocacy."[2]

Use of amicus briefs is on the rise. The number of amicus filings in the United States Supreme Court increased by more than 800 percent in the years 1946–1995.[3] In the Court's 2017–2018 term, 100% of cases with signed majority opinions included at least one amicus brief at the merits stage.[4] Likewise, the submission of amicus briefs in state courts of last resort has consistently increased.[5]

Whether and how much amicus briefs influence a court is the source of debate. Studies show that the United States Supreme Court increasingly cites amicus briefs. During the 1986–1995 terms, 37% of the Court's decisions referenced an amicus brief.[6] By the Court's 2017–2018 term, that number had increased to 59%, up from 50% the previous term.[7] The majority of those briefs cited were filed by the Office of the Solicitor General.[8] Closer to home, both the Texas Supreme Court and Texas courts of appeals favorably cite helpful amicus briefs, occasionally noting the excellent assistance they provide.[9] A survey of Texas appellate courts reveals that while rarely outcome-determinative, amicus briefs often can shape the reasoning of a decision.[10]

So amicus briefs can, and do, make a difference in some cases. But the evidence suggests that amicus briefs serve an important, and even critical, role only if they are well-written and bring something new to the table. Judges and law clerks alike have made clear that poorly written amicus briefs or ones that only mirror the parties' briefs are a burden, rather than a help, to the court. As Justice Posner famously stated:

> After 16 years of reading amicus curiae briefs the vast majority of which have not assisted the judges, I have decided that it would be good to scrutinize these motions in a more careful, indeed a fish-eyed, fashion. The vast majority of amicus curiae briefs are filed by allies of litigants and duplicate the arguments

> made in the litigants' briefs, in effect merely extending the length of the litigant's brief. Such amicus briefs should not be allowed. They are an abuse.[11]

And a survey of law clerks for the United States Supreme Court revealed that amicus briefs are too often "duplicative, poorly written, or merely lobbying documents not grounded in sound argument."[12] Thus, before deciding whether to recruit amicus support—or whether to author an amicus brief on behalf of another—one must consider whether the brief will serve a useful function for the court.

12-2 Functions of an Amicus Brief

The Texas Supreme Court's opinions over the last 15 years reveal that amicus briefs are most effective if they perform one of the following functions.

12-2:1 Examining Public Policy Implications

An amicus frequently occupies a unique position in the non-profit, government, business, or legal world and can shed important light on the public policy implications of a decision. An amicus brief serving this role can provide invaluable information to the court regarding the potential dangers or unintended consequences of a particular decision. Indeed, a survey of the Texas appellate judiciary revealed that one of the best ways to improve the quality of an amicus brief is to further develop the public policy issues involved in the case.[13] An amicus is often uniquely qualified to provide such information because of its intimate familiarity with the matter at issue—and for the same reason may capture the attention of the court more effectively than the party.

For example, in one recent opinion, the Texas Supreme Court noted that pet-welfare amici, who "understand the deep emotional bonds between people and their animals," made a "forceful case" that public policy weighed against permitting non-economic damages for the loss of a pet.[14] The Court extensively cited the public policy arguments made by animal welfare organizations regarding the dangers of permitting such recovery and ultimately held that such recovery was prohibited.[15] In another case, the Court noted that the plethora of amicus briefs "from every corner of the [oil and gas] industry—regulators, landowners, royalty owners, operators, and hydraulic fracturing service providers—all oppose liability for hydraulic fracturing, almost always warning of adverse consequences in the direst language."[16] The Court cited at length the long-term ramifications of a contrary decision as set forth by the various amici and held that damages for drainage by hydraulic fracturing were precluded by the rule of capture.[17]

Alerting the court to the potential ramifications of a recent decision can also be influential at the motion for rehearing stage. For example, Justice Hecht, in a dissenting opinion on motion for rehearing, stated: "Centex moved for rehearing, supported by twenty-three amici curiae representing virtually the entire Texas home building industry, which counts among its ranks thousands of small businesses as well as four of the five biggest home builders in America. Centex and the amici argue that the Court has misunderstood their industry—no doubt, they say, because of the spare factual record in this case—and that its decision is likely to cause unintended harm. . . . I would grant the motion for rehearing."[18] Justice Owen likewise dissented on the basis of the amicus briefs: "I have become convinced by the amicus briefs filed in this case that the Court would benefit from granting rehearing and scheduling another argument. . . . We have no idea what the practical impact of our holding will be on consumers."[19]

12-2:2 Providing Information From First-Hand Experience or Specialized Expertise

An amicus typically has day-to-day experience with how a particular law or statute operates in the real world, and thus can provide useful information to the court that a party does not have or that is more credible coming from an amicus. For example, in one recent case, the Texas Supreme Court repeatedly cited amici who weighed in on the deleterious effects of single-use plastics.[20] In another, the Court noted that a "well-established practice" regarding assignment of acreage was supported by the fact that "the numerous amici who filed briefs in this case nearly all agree that the operator, not the [Railroad] Commission, 'assigns' lands to proration units."[21] In another case, the Court noted the anecdotal evidence provided by amici City of Fort Worth, City of Sulphur Springs, and City of Mesquite that property owners rarely invoke the right to appeal nuisance findings by city standards boards.[22] And in another, the Court noted that amicus Property Casualty Insurers Association of America, "a trade association representing more than 1,000 property casualty insurance companies doing business throughout the nation," held the view that parties to an automobile liability policy reasonably expect the policy to cover against the risk of automobile accidents, not the injury-producing event in this case—negligent exposure to a communicable disease on a bus.[23]

12-2:3 Providing Non-Record Statistical or Empirical Information

An amicus often can provide factual or empirical data relevant to the appeal, which can be helpful to the court in determining the potential ramifications of its decision. For example, in a recent case, the Court determined that a patent agent who "stays within the sphere of patent law," has no need for a supervising attorney because the agent can provide all the same services.[24] In support, the Court cited the Intellectual Property Owners Association's amicus brief, which stated that non-attorney patent agents working without attorney involvement or supervision make up "roughly 13% of the practitioners who appear before the Patent and Trademark Office."[25] In another case, the Court reaffirmed that a railroad's duty is not to clear its right-of-way of things that may obstruct sight at a crossing but rather to give adequate warning of approaching trains given whatever obstructions or other conditions exist.[26] In so holding, the Court noted that amicus Association of American Railroads "cites data indicating that the regulation of railroad crossings has, from 1980 to 2004, coincided with a 71% decrease in collisions and a 56% decrease in collision fatalities."[27] The court stated: "Public policy does not require us to disturb a positive regulatory scheme."[28] In another case, the Court considered a suit for declaratory judgment that use of staff attorneys to represent insureds did not constitute the unauthorized practice of law.[29] The Court stated that an amicus curiae brief, "submitted by five insurers who use staff attorneys to defend insureds, states that fifteen insurers employ 220 staff attorneys in Texas in 39 offices. Another amicus curiae brief, received from insurance, corporate counsel, and business interests, estimated that in September 2005, over 10,000 cases in Texas were being defended by staff attorneys."[30]

12-2:4 Providing Support for a Party's Legal Arguments

Often, the amicus will focus on a particular legal issue, and its analysis of that issue can come into play in a number of different ways. Rather than repeating the party's brief, however, an amicus should focus only on the aspects of the legal issue pertinent to its position.

12-2:4.1 Supporting a Party's Primary Legal Argument

If the case involves a complex area of the law with which the amicus is uniquely familiar, an amicus may provide specialized background information, discuss how other jurisdictions have decided the issue, or provide unique insight on how the law should be analyzed in a particular context. Sometimes, the court will simply note that a particular amicus supports a party's legal argument.[31]

12-2:4.2 Shoring Up a Weak Area of a Party's Brief

An amicus may shore up a legal argument that it feels has not been handled effectively by the party, either because the party has mishandled the legal argument or has ignored controlling authorities. An amicus also may be aware of other cases pending before the court that deal with the same issue and should point those out to the court if the party has not done so.

12-2:4.3 Adding Depth to a Particular Legal Issue

If a party has neglected a legal argument, whether for lack of space or other, tactical reasons, an amicus brief may fill the void by adding analysis of that particular legal issue. As explained above, an amicus often is able to amplify an argument based on its first-hand experience with the matter at issue. However, the issue to which the legal argument relates must have been preserved.[32]

12-2:4.4 Making Riskier Legal Arguments

Sometimes an amicus can make a riskier legal argument than the party is willing to make simply because it is not a party to the case.

12-2:5 Expressing Concern Over the Uncertainty Resulting From a Decision

Amicus briefs are sometimes useful in obtaining further clarification from the court regarding a prior decision. These briefs often are filed in support of a motion for rehearing. For example, in one case, the Court noted that the Harris County Domestic Relations Office had submitted a brief requesting clarification of the Court's original opinion.[33] The Court responded by explaining its prior opinion.[34] In another case, the Court denied the motion for rehearing but addressed, in a supplemental opinion, the arguments made in the amicus brief filed by the Texas Secretary of State in support of rehearing.[35]

12-2:6 Explaining Why a Court Should Correct or Limit the Effect of a Decision

Again, because of its unique role, an amicus can effectively communicate to the court how a prior legal decision has affected the amicus itself, as well as its constituents, in the real world, and often can back up its argument with empirical data. For example, Justice Guzman, in a dissenting opinion, stated: "Amici assert that the Court's decision restricts the ability of municipalities to control and regulate nuisances through their police power and in turn restricts municipalities from protecting their communities' health and safety. Evidencing the debilitating effects the Court's holding has had in the mere six months since it was handed down, many cities have brought their substandard structure and nuisance enforcement procedures to a stand-still. And many are concerned that this new requirement will delay an already agonizingly slow process. I believe the cities' concerns warrant closer examination."[36]

12-2:7 Challenging Errors Made by the Parties or Other Amici

Sometimes amicus briefs challenge errors made by the parties or other amici. An example of this is a brief filed by social scientists in the United States Supreme Court.[37] In that brief, the amici, described as "leaders in the field of social science and statistical methodology," filed a brief in support of the University of Texas at Austin, pointing out "substantial methodological flaws in the research" discussed by other amici.[38] The brief of the Empirical Scholars argued that the research on which the other brief relied in arguing that affirmative action in higher education often undermines minority achievement was "unreliable, failing basic tenets of research design."[39]

12-3 Obtaining Amicus Support

12-3:1 Will an Amicus Brief Be Helpful?

An amicus brief can either be of tremendous help to a case or it can be a waste of time and money. Whether you are a party potentially seeking amicus support, or the potential author of an amicus brief, the first consideration is whether an amicus brief can fulfill one of the important functions listed above. If not, then it is probably not worth the time and money it will take to solicit or prepare the brief.

In addition, consider the nature of the case at hand:

> The lawyer should not seek amicus support in a routine appellate matter. In such cases, courts are likely to resent any proliferation of the briefing. The case that is appropriate for amicus support is the policy-laden case that raises novel issues or challenges the validity of a long-standing but controversial rule of law. Amicus support is also appropriate when it is best for someone other than the party to address the broader policy issues, or when there are larger issues at stake than those the parties desire to argue. A countervailing consideration is whether the filing of an amicus brief may result in attracting powerful amicus support for the opposing party. In such a situation, the lawyer should conduct a risk-benefit analysis before seeking amicus support.[40]

12-3:2 Who Should Provide Amicus Support?

Amicus support can come from various sources. Frequent amici include non-profit organizations, business associations, and governmental entities. Legal scholars and practitioners interested in a particular issue often serve as amici as well. Sometimes, parties in other cases that have similar legal issues at stake will weigh in with amicus support. Occasionally, organizations will file amicus briefs sua sponte, but the attorney for a party always has the option of, and should consider, seeking amicus support. In addition, the court itself sometimes makes known that the assistance of a particular amicus would be helpful.[41] Below are a few general guidelines to aid in finding appropriate help.

12-3:2.1 Seek Influential or Well-Known Organizations or Individuals

Well-known and respected organizations can provide significant amicus help. Likewise, legal scholars and well-known practitioners are often highly regarded amicus-brief authors. Online research, review of applicable case law, consultation with colleagues, and anecdotal information often can help point attorneys in the right direction for amicus assistance. If you would like to know which organizations have filed amicus briefs in particular cases before the Supreme Court of Texas, Austin appellate attorney Don Cruse's docket information database contains that information.[42] In addition, the client often may be an excellent source of ideas for potential amicus support.

Potential amici generally can be divided into the following groups:

- Special interest organizations, such as civil rights organizations, consumer associations, criminal justice organizations, labor and employment organizations, legal foundations, environmental organizations, and religious liberties groups;
- Business associations and trade groups;
- Parties in other, similar cases;
- The government, or an agency or official of the government;
- Persons affected by, but not parties to, the litigation;
- Law professors and attorneys practicing in a specialized field; and
- National, state, and local bar associations.[43]

12-3:2.2 Seek Organizations or Individuals That Can Fulfill the Functions of an Amicus Brief

As shown above, the Texas Supreme Court cites the briefs of amici who serve an important function for the Court. Thus, organizations or individuals are good choices for amicus assistance when they can do the following:

- *Explain how the law works in the real world.* Almost any type of amicus that has day-to-day experience with the law or regulation at issue can perform this function.
- *Explain the public policy implications of the case.* Examples include non-profit organizations, trade associations, governmental entities, and legal scholars.
- *Relay first-hand experience with the matter at issue.* Examples include promulgating authorities, persons or entities charged with enforcement of rules or laws, drafters of legislation, or persons or entities subject to the law at issue in the case.

- *Provide non-record statistical data to provide context for the decision.* Examples include trade associations, governmental units, non-profit groups, and individual experts in a particular field.

12-3:2.3 Seek Organizations With a Reputation for Writing Effective Amicus Briefs

Some organizations are known for high-quality amicus submissions, and their briefs tend to be cited more frequently than others. In the United States Supreme Court's recent terms, organizations known particularly for writing effective amicus briefs had multiple briefs cited by the justices.[44] Likewise, some legal scholars are well-known for writing effective amicus briefs. It is not often that amicus briefs are quoted at length by a court. But the Texas Supreme Court did just that with a brief authored by Professor Linda Eads, Associate Professor of Law at SMU's Dedman School of Law.[45] Investigating effective authors of amicus submissions is a worthwhile task when seeking amicus support.

Organizations that hire outside counsel to write amicus briefs may be open to recommendations about who to hire. Being ready to suggest the name of a skilled author can mean the difference between a great amicus brief and a mediocre one.

12-4 Writing an Effective Amicus Brief

12-4:1 Follow Applicable Rules

12-4:1.1 Follow Applicable Court Rules

Amicus briefs are governed by Texas Rule of Appellate Procedure 11.[46] Rule 11 provides that an amicus curiae brief must (a) comply with the briefing rules for parties; (b) identify the person or entity on whose behalf the brief is tendered; (c) disclose the source of any fee paid or to be paid for preparing the brief; and (d) certify that the brief has been served on all parties.[47]

An amicus need not file a motion for leave to submit an amicus brief. An appellate clerk may receive—but not file—an amicus brief.[48] The court may, for good cause, refuse to consider the brief and order that it be returned.[49]

Always be sure to check the rules applicable to the court in which you intend to file an amicus brief. For example, amicus briefs filed in the United States Supreme Court are governed by Supreme Court Rule 37.[50] Federal Rule of Appellate Procedure 29 governs amicus briefs filed in federal court.[51] You should always check all applicable rules, including local court rules.

12-4:1.2 Follow Organizational Rules and Procedures of the Amicus Curiae

Some organizations have a formal amicus curiae program that governs (1) whether amicus support will be provided, (2) authorship of the brief, and (3) review of the brief.

Some organizations have a formal application procedure that must be followed by someone seeking amicus support. For example, requests for amicus support from the Texas Municipal League must include a description of the legal issue to be resolved and how it relates to the relevant criteria, a summary of the facts of the case, the background of the litigants or other parties, a summary of past and projected administrative and/or legal proceedings, other sources of legal support, and how the organization's support will increase the probability of obtaining a favorable result and the basis for that conclusion.[52]

Some organizations also dictate who will author the brief. For example, the International Association of Defense Counsel's amicus guidelines provide that if the Association decides to participate as an amicus, the amicus committee chair will appoint counsel to draft the brief.[53]

Some organizations have guidelines governing the timing and contents of the brief itself. For example, the American Bar Association's amicus guidelines state that six weeks is the standard time needed from submission of an application to the filing of the brief. The guidelines provide a week-by-week analysis of drafting and review deadlines, a description of required contents, detailed drafting tips, and regulations governing the content of the briefs.[54]

Regardless of who the amicus is, an attorney seeking amicus support must begin the process early and comply with any rules or procedures that the organization or individual provides.

12-4:2 File the Most Effective Type of Brief

Typically, a single organization or individual will file an amicus brief on its own behalf. Generally, the brief will be a full brief that analyzes the pertinent legal issue in the context of the case at hand.

In some cases, if the legal issue is of widespread concern and interests are aligned, it will make more sense to present the court with a joint brief from multiple amici. It will take a considerable amount of time to coordinate a joint brief, so early communication and coordination is of utmost importance.

In some cases, a short letter brief is all that is required for effective amicus support. Consider how much the amicus really needs to say and whether a letter brief is the more effective way to handle the argument. This decision should also be made early on, and in conjunction with the party requesting amicus support.

12-4:3 Bring Something New to the Table

It is important not to merely duplicate the party's brief. In fact, filing a "me-too" brief is one of the biggest mistakes an amicus can make. As the rules of the United States Supreme Court explain: "An amicus brief that brings to the attention of the Court relevant matter not already brought to its attention by the parties may be of considerable help to the Court. An amicus curiae brief that does not serve this purpose burdens the Court, and its filing is not favored."[55] A review of the Texas Supreme Court's opinions in recent years reveals that an amicus brief is much more likely to be cited by the Court if it adds new, additional information and serves a useful function for the court.[56]

12-4:4 Avoid Legal Errors

Obviously, it is important to avoid committing legal errors in a brief. Sending a complete draft to the party and any other amici well in advance of the filing deadline will help ensure that the brief does not impermissibly expand on the legal arguments at issue, and that the legal arguments in the amicus brief do not conflict with arguments made by the party or other amici.

If an amicus raises an issue not raised by the parties or not relevant to the appeal, that legal argument is likely to be dismissed. In addition, raising extraneous issues looks sloppy and threatens to color the way the court views the rest of the brief. Courts will not miss the fact that an amicus has raised extraneous legal arguments that the court may not consider. For example, the Texas Supreme Court recently stated that an argument by an amicus suffered from several deficiencies, including that the issue "was not raised by any party in this litigation in federal or state court."[57]

12-4:5 Avoid Factual Errors

Perhaps nothing is as detrimental to an amicus brief as misrepresenting the facts of the case itself. Arguing about or misrepresenting the facts of the case before the court will do nothing but frustrate the court and likely will affect the way the court views the rest of the amicus brief. An amicus also must be sure to rely only upon proper evidence.[58]

An amicus must likewise take special care to avoid misrepresenting any extra-record factual information provided to the court. While, if accurate, such information can be invaluable, providing inaccurate information reflects poorly on the amicus and the party, and can affect the judicial process itself. Common examples of misrepresenting data include "not following research norms, over-generalizing limited data, selectively distorting findings, making normative statements that appear to be empirical, and citing questionable research produced specifically for litigation."[59] Ignoring data that is adverse to the amicus position should also be avoided.[60]

Courts are wary of the potential dangers of relying on data provided by amici that cannot readily be confirmed: "When an amicus brief recites facts and empirical data that fall outside the judicial notice doctrine and lie outside the record, special problems arise because judges have a limited ability to evaluate such evidence and they may approach it with skepticism."[61] Indeed, the Texas Supreme Court has specifically noted the dangers inherent in "factual missteps" made by amici: "Unless challenged by opposing counsel, such inaccuracies, however inadvertent, carry real potential to mislead judges and skew judicial decisionmaking."[62]

12-4:6 Carefully Consider Timing

Unlike in federal court, in Texas courts there is no deadline for submitting an amicus brief. However, it is important to coordinate the timing of the filing of an amicus brief with the filing of the party's brief, with attention paid to the court's timeline for consideration and to which party the brief supports. While it is important to put the best brief forward, no one wants to risk the court not considering the brief because of timing issues.

A survey of Texas courts of appeals reveals that amicus briefs filed in an intermediate appellate court are most effective if filed prior to oral argument.[63] A survey of justices on the Texas Supreme Court shows that amicus briefs supporting petitioners are most effective if filed after the petitioner has filed a petition for review, but before briefs on the merits have been requested, or at least before the decision has been made to grant or deny review.[64] If the amicus brief supports the respondent, the calculus changes.

Respondents wish to downplay the importance of the case so as to avoid review. Any amicus brief—even if it supports the respondent—tends to raise the profile of a case and increase its importance in the eyes of the Court. Therefore, amici supporting respondents generally should not submit a brief unless the Court grants review.

Sometimes, the need for amicus support does not become apparent until the motion for rehearing stage. Again, it is important to coordinate with the party and any other amici to be sure the brief is ready at the appropriate time. Also, amici cannot request rehearing on their own. If an amicus desires rehearing, it must convince the losing party to file a motion.

As mentioned above, some organizations have a procedure that must be followed before they will even agree to provide amicus support. And good practitioners are busy ones—they will need plenty of time to research and prepare a good amicus brief. To end up with a useful amicus brief that is filed on time, a party must begin the search for amicus support very early on in the appellate process. Also, in Texas courts, amici are not limited to one brief. For example, an amicus that files a brief at the petition for review stage in the Texas Supreme Court may—and should—consider filing a merits brief if the amicus has additional points to make.

12-4:7 Be Organized and Be Respectful

When writing, remember the particular function of the amicus brief, and resist the urge to cover the waterfront. Leave that to the party, unless the party has done a poor job. Because amicus briefs are "extra" briefing, they, in particular, need to be well-organized and brief. Let the function of the brief dictate the content and length of the brief. All briefing should be fair and respectful, but again, because amici are not parties, amicus briefs, in particular, should be even-handed, honest, and respectful.

12-4:8 Work Closely With the Party You Are Supporting

Amicus counsel should work closely with the party they are supporting. The party can give valuable input about areas the amicus brief may cover. Also, an amicus's goals may be broader or slightly different than the party's, but the amicus should take care not to inadvertently and unnecessarily undermine the party's position. For the same reasons, the attorney for the party should make every effort to work closely with amicus counsel.

12-5 The Contents of an Amicus Brief

The contents of an amicus brief may vary from those of the party's brief, given the nature and purpose of an amicus submission. An amicus may delete some elements that are required for a party's brief, but also may decide to include them for various reasons. Below is a description of the potential elements of an amicus brief and whether each element is required to be included in such a brief.

12-5:1 Cover (Required)

The cover of an amicus brief should look much like the cover of the parties' briefs. However, it should identify the amicus and reflect which of the parties the brief supports.

12-5:2 Identity of Parties and Counsel (Not Required)

Because the purpose of this part of the brief is to allow the Justices to decide whether to recuse themselves, this section is not necessary in an amicus brief. The Justices can learn what they need to know from the cover of the brief.

12-5:3 Table of Contents (Required)

The amicus brief should include a table of contents.

12-5:4 Index of Authorities (Required)

The amicus brief should include an index of authorities.

12-5:5 Statement of the Case (Not Required)

The parties' briefs typically will include an adequate statement of the case; the amicus brief need not include one.

12-5:6 Statement of Jurisdiction (Not Required)

While an amicus is permitted to include a statement of jurisdiction, it has been recommended that the amicus leave "jurisdictional battles" for the parties.[65]

12-5:7 Introductory Statement (Required)

The amicus brief should begin with a brief introductory statement. If the purpose of the brief is to urge the Texas Supreme Court to grant review, the introductory statement can be quite short; it need merely identify the amicus and explain why the amicus urges the Court to grant review.[66] If the purpose of the amicus brief is to persuade the Court on the merits, however, an introductory statement should include (1) the identity of the amicus, (2) why the case is of interest to the amicus, and (3) the ruling the amicus urges the Court to adopt on the merits.[67]

12-5:8 Interest of Amicus Curiae (Required)

This is one of the most important sections of the amicus brief. In this section, the amicus explains to the court who it is, why it cares about the ruling in the case, and who is paying the fee for the brief.

12-5:8.1 Description of the Amicus

The brief should describe the amicus in detail. Only by this description can the court get a sense of such things as the size of the organization, the purpose of the organization, the number of members that it has, or the amount of money that it generates.

A general overview of the nature of the organization also is important to give the court a sense upfront about how the organization and its constituents would be affected by a decision in the case.

12-5:8.2 Interest in Decision

This part of the brief also should inform the court why the amicus is interested in the decision. This is sometimes best achieved by providing an illustration of how an adverse result would affect the amicus or its members.[68]

12-5:8.3 Fee Disclosure

Texas Rule of Appellate Procedure 11(c) requires the disclosure of the source of payment for the amicus brief.[69]

12-5:9 Issues Presented (Not Required)

The amicus may decide to include issues for various reasons. If the parties have not done a satisfactory job of framing the issues, the amicus will want to do so. In addition, the amicus may wish to frame the issues specifically to reflect the concerns set forth in its brief.

12-5:10 Statement of Facts (Not Required)

While an amicus is not required to include a statement of facts, there are reasons to do so. First and foremost, the amicus may want to include a short statement of only those facts that are relevant to the legal arguments included in the amicus brief.[70] In this way, the amicus can focus the court upfront on a shorter set of facts that are pertinent to the amicus brief.

12-5:11 Summary of Argument (Not Required)

The amicus brief need not include a summary of argument. However, because a good amicus brief should present a different argument, either in terms of a new legal angle, a new policy argument, or helpful factual information, it generally makes sense for the amicus to summarize its position early on in the brief.

12-5:12 Argument (Required)

The amicus brief should include an argument section. The argument will be tailored to the particular function of the brief, as discussed above. Thus, this section of the brief may (1) discuss the widespread policy implications of a particular decision in the case, (2) explain the experience of the amicus with the legal issue at hand, (3) provide the court with extra-record facts or statistical data and explain how that impacts the case, and/or (4) bolster the legal arguments made by the party.

If the purpose of the amicus brief is merely to encourage the Texas Supreme Court to grant review, the argument section can be quite short and simply illuminate for the Court why the amicus believes review should be granted, without a legal analysis of the facts of the case.

12-5:13 Conclusion and Prayer (Required)

The amicus brief should include a conclusion and prayer for relief.

12-5:14 Signature Block (Required)

The amicus brief should include a signature block in the same format as the parties' briefs.

12-5:15 Certificate of Service (Required)

The amicus brief should follow the same format as the parties' briefs, reflecting service on counsel for both the petitioner and the respondent.

12-6 Oral Argument Considerations

With leave of court obtained before the argument, and with a party's consent, an amicus curiae may share allotted time for oral argument with a party.[71] Some courts will also consider granting extra time for an amicus. Because this is extraordinary, requests for extra time should be limited to five or possibly 10 minutes. Otherwise, counsel for an amicus may not argue.[72] Rarely will counsel for an amicus argue. While there is a chance that splitting time with an amicus may hinder a party's ability to make its desired points and/or result in a disjointed presentation, in some cases argument by an amicus may be quite helpful. A wise attorney will think of it from the court's perspective—would it help the court to hear from this amicus at oral argument? If so, consider permitting argument by the amicus if the advocate is skilled and the amicus respected.

Even if not arguing, however, one should always consider including amicus counsel in moot courts. Just as an amicus can add depth and breadth to the actual appeal, it can do the same in a moot court.

12-7 Ethical Considerations

Various ethical issues surround the preparation and filing of amicus briefs. Historically, the primary concern was whether the party was actually authoring and paying for the brief, either to get around the page limitations for the principal brief or to make it appear that there was widespread support for the party's position in the case.[73] In 1997, Texas Rule of Appellate Procedure 11 was amended to require disclosure of the person or entity on whose behalf the brief is filed as well as the source of any fee paid.[74] United States Supreme Court Rule 37 also requires that amicus briefs indicate whether counsel for a party authored the brief in whole or in part.[75] A survey of the Texas appellate judiciary indicates that many Texas judges believe the Texas rule should be modified to include a similar requirement.[76]

Notes

1 Samuel Krislov, *The Amicus Curiae Brief: From Friendship to Advocacy*, 72 Yale L.J. 694, 694 (1963) (quoting Abbot's Dictionary of Terms and Phrases).

2 Samuel Krislov, *The Amicus Curiae Brief: From Friendship to Advocacy*, 72 Yale L.J. 694, 704 (1963).

3 Sarah F. Corbally et al., *Filing of Amicus Curiae Briefs in State Courts of Last Resort: 1960–2000*, 25 Just. Sys. J. 39, 42 (2004) (citing J.D. Kearney & T.W. Merrill, *The Influence of Amicus Curiae Briefs on the Supreme Court*, 148 U. Penn. L. Rev. 743, 749 (2000)).

[4] R. Reeves Anderson & Anthony J. Franze, *Supreme Court Amicus Curiae Review: "Friends of the Court" Roared Back in 2017–18 Term,* Nat'l L. J. (Oct. 16, 2018), at 1, https://www.arnoldporter.com/-/media/files/perspectives/publications/2018/10/supreme-court-amicus-curiae-review.pdf?

[5] Sarah F. Corbally et al., *Filing of Amicus Curiae Briefs in State Courts of Last Resort: 1960–2000,* 25 Just. Sys. J. 39, 53 (2004) (also noting that the extent to which amicus briefs are used in the different states varies greatly).

[6] Joseph D. Kearney & Thomas W. Merrill, *The Influence of Amicus Curiae Briefs on the Supreme Court,* 148 U. Penn. L. Rev. 743, 757 (2000).

[7] R. Reeves Anderson & Anthony J. Franze, *Supreme Court Amicus Curiae Review: "Friends of the Court" Roared Back in 2017–18 Term,* Nat'l L. J. (Oct. 16, 2018), at 2, https://www.arnoldporter.com/-/media/files/perspectives/publications/2018/10/supreme-court-amicus-curiae-review.pdf?

[8] R. Reeves Anderson & Anthony J. Franze, *Supreme Court Amicus Curiae Review: "Friends of the Court" Roared Back in 2017–18 Term,* Nat'l L. J. (Oct. 16, 2018), at 2, https://www.arnoldporter.com/-/media/files/perspectives/publications/2018/10/supreme-court-amicus-curiae-review.pdf?

[9] *See, e.g., Strickland v. Medlen,* 397 S.W.3d 184, 195 (Tex. 2013) ("[T]he pet-welfare amici make a forceful case."); *Reed v. Wylie,* 597 S.W.2d 743, 750 (Tex. 1980) (Spears, J., concurring) ("[S]everal excellent amicus curiae briefs filed in this case have offered pertinent and helpful observations and suggestions."); *Marmon v. Mustang Aviation, Inc.,* 416 S.W.2d 58, 63 (Tex. Civ. App.—Austin 1967), *aff'd* 430 S.W.2d 182 (Tex. 1968) ("In examining the law and the record of this case we have been ably aided by . . . painstaking and persuasive works of competent amici curiae.").

[10] Sherry Radack, Peter Kelly & David Furlow, *Questionnaire Regarding Amicus Curiae Briefs,* State Bar of Texas 22nd Annual Advanced Civil Appellate Practice Course, ch. 12 at 4 (2008).

[11] *Ryan v. Commodity Futures Trading Comm'n,* 125 F.3d 1062, 1063 (7th Cir. 1997).

[12] Kelly J. Lynch, *Best Friends? Supreme Court Law Clerks on Effective Amicus Curiae Briefs,* 20 J. L. & Pol. 33, 44–45 (Winter 2004).

[13] Sherry Radack, Peter Kelly & David Furlow, *Questionnaire Regarding Amicus Curiae Briefs,* State Bar of Texas 22nd Annual Advanced Civil Appellate Practice Course, ch. 12 at 13 (2008).

[14] *Strickland v. Medlen,* 397 S.W.3d 184, 195 (Tex. 2013).

[15] *Strickland v. Medlen,* 397 S.W.3d 184, 193–95 (Tex. 2013).

[16] *Coastal Oil & Gas Corp. v. Garza Energy Trust,* 268 S.W.3d 1, 16 (Tex. 2008).

[17] *Coastal Oil & Gas Corp. v. Garza Energy Trust,* 268 S.W.3d 1, 16 & n.56 (Tex. 2008); *see also U.S. Metals, Inc. v. Liberty Mut. Grp., Inc.,* 490 S.W.3d 20, 27–28 (Tex. 2015) (noting competing policy concerns highlighted by various amici but finding it was a conflict "we cannot resolve"); *KCM Fin. L.L.C. v. Bradshaw,* 457 S.W.3d 70, 86 (Tex. 2015) ("The Texas Oil & Gas Association argues in an amicus brief that a lessee should not be tasked—directly or indirectly—with policing the executive's duty to non-executive interest holders. Nor should a lessee be expected to give weight to a non-participating royalty interest holder's economic interests; as we have held, that is the executive's responsibility. We agree with the Association that 'in negotiating with the executive, a lessee should not fear liability for doing nothing more than getting a good deal closed.'"); *Excess Underwriters at Lloyd's, London v. Frank's Casing Crew & Rental Tools, Inc.,* 246 S.W.3d 42, 47 (Tex. 2008) ("Several amici also warn that recognizing a reimbursement right risks weakening the insurer's incentive to negotiate a settlement most favorable to its insured."); *Miller v. Keyser,* 90 S.W.3d 712, 719 (Tex. 2002) ("We decline to judicially create an exemption that does not exist in the statute for agents acting solely on behalf of their employers. In doing so, we also acknowledge the amicus brief received from the Attorney General, in which the General asserts that

judicially creating such an exemption would adversely affect the General's ability to enforce the statute, which ultimately will affect the protections afforded to consumers."); *Bryant v. United Shortline Inc. Assur. Servs., N.A.*, 972 S.W.2d 26, 29 (Tex. 1998) ("The Texas Department of Insurance has filed amicus briefs in support of the Liquidator's position, arguing that there is a strong public policy interest in affording full faith and credit to liquidation proceedings in other states . . . We agree with the Liquidator and the Department of Insurance that Texas recognizes a compelling policy interest in having claims against an insolvent insurer's estate resolved in a single proceeding."); *Murphy v. Campbell*, 964 S.W.2d 265, 273 (Tex. 1997) (noting that amicus Texas Society of Public Accountants viewed the rule adopted by the majority in accounting malpractice cases as "fair" to both plaintiffs and defendants and thus rejecting Justice Abbott's dissent).

18 *Centex Homes v. Buecher*, 95 S.W.3d 266, 275–76 (Tex. 2002) (Hecht, J., dissenting).

19 *Centex Homes v. Buecher*, 95 S.W.3d 266, 281 (Tex. 2002) (Owen, J., dissenting).

20 *City of Laredo v. Laredo Merchants Ass'n.*, 550 S.W.3d 586, 600–02 (Tex. 2018).

21 *Endeavor Energy Res., L.P. v. Discovery Operating, Inc.*, 554 S.W.3d 586, 602–03 (Tex. 2018).

22 *City of Dallas v. Stewart*, 361 S.W.3d 562, 580 n.28 (Tex. 2012).

23 *Lancer Ins. Co. v. Garcia Holiday Tours*, 345 S.W.3d 50, 56 (Tex. 2011).

24 *In re Silver*, 540 S.W.3d 530, 536 (Tex. 2018).

25 *In re Silver*, 540 S.W.3d 530, 536 (Tex. 2018).

26 *Missouri Pac. R.R. Co. v. Limmer*, 299 S.W.3d 78, 92 (Tex. 2009).

27 *Missouri Pac. R.R. Co. v. Limmer*, 299 S.W.3d 78, 92 (Tex. 2009).

28 *Missouri Pac. R.R. Co. v. Limmer*, 299 S.W.3d 78, 92 (Tex. 2009).

29 *Unauthorized Practice of Law Comm. v. Am. Home Assur. Co.*, 261 S.W.3d 24, 29 (Tex. 2008).

30 *Unauthorized Practice of Law Comm. v. Am. Home Assur. Co.*, 261 S.W.3d 24, 29 (Tex. 2008); *see also City of Rockwall v. Hughes*, 246 S.W.3d 621, 633 n.11 (Tex. 2008) (Willett, J., dissenting) ("Judging by the myriad amicus briefs filed by Texas cities, expedited annexations under (h)(1) are so common that (h)(1) is actually the rule. TML's brief admits as much. . . ."); *Texas Dep't of Protective and Regulatory Servs. v. Mega Child Care, Inc.*, 145 S.W.3d 170, 175–76 (Tex. 2004) (quoting portion of amicus brief filed by the Texas Licensed Child Care Association, which asserted that the Austin Court of Appeals was the only state appellate court (out of 25 states with similar laws) that interpreted the subject language to be merely procedural and insufficient to confer jurisdiction).

31 *See, e.g., In re State Farm Lloyds*, 520 S.W.3d 595, 603–04 (Tex. 2017) ("State Farm, supported by several amici, characterize the lower court rulings as granting requesting parties 'essentially unlimited power' to dictate how the responding party must conduct electronic discovery under the Texas Rules of Civil Procedure."); *Natural Gas Pipeline Co. of Am. v. Justiss*, 397 S.W.3d 150, 159 (Tex. 2012) ("The Company and the amici urge us to apply *Coastal's* rule to the landowner's testimony here, and we agree that *Coastal* provides the appropriate standard for judging the adequacy of testimony offered under the Property Owner Rule."); *American Zurich Ins. Co. v. Samudio*, 370 S.W.3d 363, 368 (Tex. 2012) ("Samudio contends that the trial court properly dismissed this case because section 410.306(c) deprived it of any power to set aside the impairment rating assigned by the Division, even if the rating was invalid. American Zurich and amicus curiae Texas Department of Insurance Workers' Compensation Division . . . maintain that, if the trial court concluded that the assigned rating was invalid, it could reverse the Division's decision and remand to the agency. We agree with American Zurich and the Division.").

32 *See ExxonMobil Corp. v. Lazy R Ranch, LP*, 511 S.W.3d 538, 545–46 (Tex. 2017) (noting that "[w]hile amici have thoroughly examined . . . issues [relating to availability of injunctive relief,] the parties have not" and declining to address that issue because it was not properly presented to the trial court).

[33] *In re Zandi*, 270 S.W.3d 76, 78–79 (Tex. 2008) (supp. op. on reh'g).

[34] *In re Zandi*, 270 S.W.3d 76, 78–79 (Tex. 2008) (supp. op. on reh'g).

[35] *In re Sanchez*, 81 S.W.3d 794, 798–99 (Tex. 2002) (orig. proceeding); *see also Texas Rice Land Partners, Ltd. v. Denbury Green Pipeline-Tex., L.L.C.*, 381 S.W.3d 465, 468 n.3 (Tex. 2012) (Wainright, J., concurring) (noting receipt by the Court of briefing from 14 amici who "expressed concern over confusion, lack of predictability and the risk of variant judicial opinions that could arise from some of the language of the opinion").

[36] *City of Dallas v. Stewart*, 361 S.W.3d 562, 598–99 (Tex. 2012) (opinion on rehearing) (Guzman, J., dissenting).

[37] *See* Brief of Empirical Scholars as Amici Curiae in Support of Respondents, No. 14-981, *Fisher v. University of Texas at Austin* (Nov. 2, 2015), *available at* https://www.scotusblog.com/wp-content/uploads/2015/11/LCCR-and-Mintz-Fisher-Amicus-Empirical-Scholars.pdf

[38] Brief of Empirical Scholars as Amici Curiae in Support of Respondents at 1, No. 14-981, *Fisher v. University of Texas at Austin* (Nov. 2, 2015), *available at* https://www.scotusblog.com/wp-content/uploads/2015/11/LCCR-and-Mintz-Fisher-Amicus-Empirical-Scholars.pdf

[39] Brief of Empirical Scholars as Amici Curiae in Support of Respondents at 1, No. 14-981, *Fisher v. University of Texas at Austin* (Nov. 2, 2015), *available at* https://www.scotusblog.com/wp-content/uploads/2015/11/LCCR-and-Mintz-Fisher-Amicus-Empirical-Scholars.pdf

[40] Reagan Wm. Simpson & Mary Vasaly, The Amicus Brief: How to Write It and Use It Effectively 26 (3d ed. 2010).

[41] *See, e.g., In re E.R.*, 385 S.W.3d 552, 558 n.13 (Tex. 2012) ("We called for the views of the Solicitor General, who submitted a brief on behalf of the State of Texas as amicus curiae."); *State v. Naylor*, 466 S.W.3d 783, 792 (Tex. 2015) ("[I]t likely would have required relatively little effort for the State to file a petition in intervention or submit an amicus letter informing the trial court of its concerns. Yet there is no record that the State made any such effort until after the trial court rendered judgment.").

[42] The Supreme Court of Texas Blog, https://www.scotxblog.com (last visited Jan. 14, 2019). Information regarding amicus support in cases before the United States Supreme Court can be found in a similar database. *See* The Cert Pool, https://certpool.com/ (last visited Jan. 14, 2019).

[43] *See* Reagan Wm. Simpson & Mary Vasaly, The Amicus Brief: How to Write It and Use It Effectively 22–26 (3d ed. 2010).

[44] R. Reeves Anderson & Anthony J. Franze, *Supreme Court Amicus Curiae Review: "Friends of the Court" Roared Back in 2017–18 Term*, Nat'l L. J. (Oct. 16, 2018), at 2, https://www.arnoldporter.com/-/media/files/perspectives/publications/2018/10/supreme-court-amicus-curiae-review.pdf?

[45] *Anglo-Dutch Petroleum Int'l, Inc. v. Greenberg Peden, P.C.*, 352 S.W.3d 445, 450 (Tex. 2011).

[46] Tex. R. App. P. 11.

[47] Tex. R. App. P. 11(a)-(d).

[48] Tex. R. App. P. 11.

[49] Tex. R. App. P. 11.

[50] U.S. Sup. Ct. R. 37.

[51] Fed. R. App. P. 29.

[52] Robert Fugate, *Seeking Effective Amicus Support*, "Appendix A," http://www.texascityattorneys.org/2010speakerpapers/SeekingEffectiveAmicusSupport.pdf (last visited Jan.14, 2019) (Materials provided during 2010 TCAA Summer Conference).

53 IADC International Association of Defense Counsel, https://www.iadclaw.org/publications-news/Publications/Amicus-Curiae-Briefs/ (last visited Jan. 14, 2019).

54 Memorandum from ABA Standing Comm. on Amicus Curiae Briefs to Those Interested in Submitting an Application for an ABA Amicus Curiae Brief, *available at* https://www.americanbar.org/content/dam/aba/administrative/amicus/application_amicus_curiae_brief2.authcheckdam.pdf

55 U.S. Sup. Ct. R. 37(1).

56 *See* Sherry Radack, Peter Kelly & David Furlow, *Questionnaire Regarding Amicus Curiae Briefs*, State Bar of Texas 22nd Annual Advanced Civil Appellate Practice Course, ch. 12 at 3 (2008).

57 *Severance v. Patterson*, 370 S.W.3d 705, 711 n.7 (Tex. 2012); *see also Dallas Cnty. Mental Health & Mental Retardation v. Bossley*, 968 S.W.2d 339, 341 (Tex. 1998) ("The Attorney General has filed an amicus curiae brief, arguing that '[n]egligence in the use or condition of real property does not state a cause of action under the Act, unless it is a premise defect claim under section 101.022(1)'. . . . Defendants do not make this argument, however, and we find it unnecessary to address it. We confine our consideration to the parties' contentions.").

58 *See, e.g., Fink v. Anderson*, 477 S.W.3d 460, 464 (Tex. App.—Houston [1st Dist.] 2015, no pet.) ("[T]o the extent the [amicus] brief relies on an affidavit submitted after the trial court ruled on [appellant's] motion, we do not consider it."); *Fredericksburg Care Co., L.P. v. Perez*, 461 S.W.3d 513, 528 n.4 (Tex. 2015) ("Because there is no evidence that [appellant] operates as an HMO, amici's concerns are not properly before the Court at this time.").

59 Sarah F. Corbally & Donald C. Bross, *A Practical Guide for Filing Amicus Curiae Briefs in State Appellate Courts* 4 (2001), https://cdn.ymaws.com/naccchildlaw.site-ym.com/resource/resmgr/amicus_curiae/amicuspracticalguide.pdf (citing Michael Rustad & Thomas Koenig, *The Supreme Court and Junk Social Science: Selective Distortion in Amicus Briefs*, 72 N.C. L. Rev. 91, 100 (1993)).

60 Sarah F. Corbally & Donald C. Bross, *A Practical Guide for Filing Amicus Curiae Briefs in State Appellate Courts* 4 (2001), https://cdn.ymaws.com/naccchildlaw.site-ym.com/resource/resmgr/amicus_curiae/amicuspracticalguide.pdf

61 Reagan Wm. Simpson & Mary Vasaly, The Amicus Brief: How to Write It and Use It Effectively 61 (3d ed. 2010).

62 *Entergy Gulf States, Inc. v. Summers*, 282 S.W.3d 433, 473 n.61 (Tex. 2009).

63 Sherry Radack, Peter Kelly & David Furlow, *Questionnaire Regarding Amicus Curiae Briefs*, State Bar of Texas 22nd Annual Advanced Civil Appellate Practice Course, ch. 12 at 2 (2008).

64 Sherry Radack, Peter Kelly & David Furlow, *Questionnaire Regarding Amicus Curiae Briefs*, State Bar of Texas 22nd Annual Advanced Civil Appellate Practice Course, ch. 12 at 3 (2008).

65 *See* Douglas W. Alexander, *Crafting an Effective Amicus Brief to the Supreme Court of Texas*, State Bar of Texas 20th Annual Advanced Civil Appellate Course, ch. 18 at 2 (2006).

66 Douglas W. Alexander, *Crafting an Effective Amicus Brief to the Supreme Court of Texas*, State Bar of Texas 20th Annual Advanced Civil Appellate Course, ch. 18 at 2–3 (2006).

67 Douglas W. Alexander, *Crafting an Effective Amicus Brief to the Supreme Court of Texas*, State Bar of Texas 20th Annual Advanced Civil Appellate Course, ch. 18 at 3 (2006).

68 Douglas W. Alexander, *Crafting an Effective Amicus Brief to the Supreme Court of Texas*, State Bar of Texas 20th Annual Advanced Civil Appellate Course, ch. 18 at 4 (2006).

69 Tex. R. App. P. 11(c).

70 Douglas W. Alexander, *Crafting an Effective Amicus Brief to the Supreme Court of Texas*, State Bar of Texas 20th Annual Advanced Civil Appellate Course, ch. 18 at 4 (2006).

71 Tex. R. App. P. 39.5.

72 Tex. R. App. P. 39.5.

[73] *See* Reagan Wm. Simpson & Mary Vasaly, The Amicus Brief: How to Write It and Use It Effectively 64 (3d ed. 2010).

[74] Tex. R. App. P. 11 (comment to 1997 change).

[75] U.S. Sup. Ct. R. 37.

[76] Sherry Radack, Peter Kelly & David Furlow, *Questionnaire Regarding Amicus Curiae Briefs*, State Bar of Texas 22nd Annual Advanced Civil Appellate Practice Course, ch. 12 at 5–6 (2008).

CHAPTER 13

Wrapping Up the Appeal

13-1 Introduction

The appellate process includes much more than preparing the brief, making the necessary motions, and presenting oral argument. Some of the most critical aspects of the appellate process are ensuring that the judgment, including costs and attorney's fees, is collectible and in fact collected after the appeal is finished. For example, it is important to the successful party to ensure that the court allocates costs properly and in accordance with the final disposition of the case. These costs can be significant, especially if the case was fully tried below. Further, the parties cannot execute the judgment without a mandate issued by the appellate court. Thus, ensuring that the mandate is both correctly and timely issued is important to wrapping up the appeal. Full satisfaction of the judgment is dependent on technical compliance with these requisites.

This chapter describes the process of wrapping up the appeal by focusing on the appellate process from the appellate court's decision to the ultimate termination of the appeal, which includes seeking rehearing, correcting the judgment, issuing the mandate, and collecting the judgment. It also provides practical advice to assist practitioners with those particular aspects of the appellate process.

13-2 The Appellate Court's Decision

13-2:1 The Opinion

13-2:1.1 Written Opinions

Rule 47.1 requires the court of appeals to "hand down a written opinion that is as brief as practicable but that addresses every issue raised and necessary to final disposition of the appeal."[1] The opinion must be distributed to the parties, the trial court (both the judge and clerk of court), and the regional administrative judge.[2] And the clerk of the trial court must file the opinion of record.[3]

There are two official forms of opinions: "opinions" and "memorandum opinions." Opinions are either signed by a justice or designated as "per curiam," and a majority of the participating justices will make that determination.[4] Memorandum opinions are addressed in § 13-2:1.2. All justices participating in an opinion or order must be named in the document.[5]

A justice who participated in the decision may file a concurring or dissenting opinion.[6] And any justice on the court may file a concurring or dissenting opinion as to the denial of rehearing en banc.[7] But a justice who did not participate in the decision may not file a concurring or dissenting opinion from the judgment of the court of appeals.[8]

13-2:1.2 Memorandum Opinions

When the decision of the court of appeals applies settled precedent to a particular case, it "should write a brief memorandum opinion no longer than necessary to advise the parties of the court's decision and the basic reasons for it."[9] So, the opinion can be designated as a memorandum opinion unless it:

- establishes a new rule of law, alters or modifies an existing rule, or applies an existing rule to a novel fact situation likely to recur in future cases;
- involves issues of constitutional law or other legal issues important to the jurisprudence of Texas;
- criticizes existing law; or
- resolves an apparent conflict of authority.[10]

Cases involving concurrences and dissents are generally not appropriate for this designation, and an opinion cannot be designated as a memorandum opinion if the concurring or dissenting justice disagrees with the designation.[11]

13-2:1.3 Publication and Citation

Before 2002 there was a serious debate nationwide as to whether unpublished opinions could be cited as authority. Constitutional challenges were made to many court rules prohibiting citation to unpublished opinions.[12] The Texas Rules of Appellate Procedure now make clear that all opinions of the courts of appeals should be made freely and publicly available—going so far as to mandate that they "are open to the public and must be made available to public reporting services, print or electronic."[13] Opinions are no longer designated as published or unpublished.

Rule 47.2(c) ended the practice of designating certain opinions as unpublished by mandating that opinions issued on or after January 1, 2003, shall not be designated as "do not publish."[14] Those earlier opinions designated as unpublished "have no precedential value," but they can be cited "with the notation '(not designated for publication).'"[15] When citing unpublished opinions that are not easily accessible, practitioners should provide the court and opposing counsel with copies.[16]

Memorandum opinions in civil cases after the 2003 amendment have precedential value.[17]

13-2:2 The Judgment

13-2:2.1 Outcomes

When the appeal is entirely concluded, the court of appeals will issue a separate judgment, which is usually no more than a page. The judgment is often overlooked in the interest of reading the opinion, but it is vitally important and should be carefully reviewed. By rule, the courts of appeals are to render judgment "promptly" after submission of a case.[18]

13-2:2.1a Court of Appeals

There are six basic actions that may be taken by the intermediate court of appeals:

- affirm the trial court's judgment (where there is no reversible error);
- modify the judgment and affirm it as modified (where the decision does not warrant reversal, but needs changes);
- reverse the trial court's judgment in whole or in part and render the judgment the trial court should have rendered (where a new decision is substituted for that of the trial court);
- reverse and remand for further proceedings consistent with the opinion;
- vacate the trial court's judgment (when the trial court lacked jurisdiction or the parties have settled); and
- dismiss the appeal (for want of prosecution or appellate jurisdiction).[19]

If the appellate court finds reversible error, the presumption is that it should render the judgment the trial court should have rendered unless a remand is necessary either to entertain further proceedings or in the interests of justice for a new trial.[20]

A much less frequent option is a remittitur, which is more of a conditional outcome. In such situations, if the court of appeals or a party believes that the evidence supports a damages award, but not as much as the damages awarded in the judgment, it can suggest a lower amount. When the court of appeals suggests a remittitur, it essentially tells the losing party that it has found reversible error in a portion of the damages award but would uphold the award if it were reduced to a specified amount.[21] If the remitting party accepts the reduction and timely files the remittitur, the court of appeals reforms and affirms the judgment; if no remittitur is filed, it must reverse the judgment.[22] A party can also make a voluntary remittitur within 15 days after the court of appeals renders judgment by remitting "the amount that the party believes will cure the reversible error."[23] The court of appeals can accept the voluntary remittitur and affirm the modified judgment, reject it, or counter with a different amount.[24] In either scenario, the remitting party can reserve its rights to challenge the remittitur in the Supreme Court.[25]

13-2:2.1b Supreme Court of Texas

The Supreme Court's disposition of appeals is addressed in Rule 60. The Supreme Court has the same six basic options as the courts of appeals, except that its decision operates on the "lower court's judgment," meaning that it can act on either the trial court's or appellate court's judgment and it can also remand to either the trial court or the court of appeals for further proceedings consistent with its opinion.[26] The Supreme Court can also reverse and remand to the trial court "in the interest of the justice . . . even if rendition of judgment is otherwise appropriate."[27] It uses this authority, for example, when announcing a new rule of law that would be unfair to impose on the parties before it who had not had the benefit of its pronouncement during their proceedings in the courts below.[28]

13-2:2.2 Inconsistencies Between the Opinion and Judgment

The operative language is contained in the court's judgment. As a result, if there is an inconsistency between the two documents, the judgment controls.[29]

It is imperative that you check the court of appeals' judgment immediately to determine whether it is consistent with the opinion, whether the costs are inappropriately taxed, or whether the parties or sureties are omitted. If any of these issues are present, you should raise the arguments in a timely motion for rehearing.

13-2:2.3 Costs of Appeal

Generally, recoverable costs are fees and charges the law requires parties to pay to the courts, the amount of which is fixed by statute or court rule,[30] unless they are indigent.[31] Appellate costs are typically the filing fees in the court of appeals and the costs of preparing the record.[32] In Texas, an appealing party cannot recover its premiums for obtaining a supersedeas bond as appellate costs, even if successful on appeal.[33]

Except for cases involving exempt government entities, the judgment in a civil appeal should contain an order for the prevailing party to pay the costs of appeal.[34] However, the appellate court has authority to tax costs differently if "required by law or for good cause."[35] Situations where the "prevailing" party only succeeded on a small part of the appeal or engaged in conduct that was inappropriate can warrant taxing costs against it.

In cases involving supersedeas bonds, if the court of appeals affirms the judgment against the appellant or modifies it and renders judgment against the appellant, it must also render judgment against the surety or sureties on the bond "for the performance of the judgment and for any costs taxed against the appellant."[36]

If costs were inappropriately taxed or the judgment erroneously omitted the sureties, those arguments must be raised in a timely motion for rehearing.

13-2:2.4 Damages for Frivolous Appeals

The appellate courts may also impose penalties by way of awarding costs. For example, if a party has pursued a frivolous civil appeal, the appeals court may award to the appellee "just damages" as part of its judgment.[37] The courts need not await a motion by the parties and can order sanctions on their own initiative, but the grounds for such an award must be "in the record, briefs, or other papers filed in the court of appeals" or the Supreme Court.[38]

13-3 Rehearing

13-3:1 Court of Appeals

A party dissatisfied with the decision of the court of appeals has three options to seek further review:

- file a motion for rehearing by the panel of justices that decided the appeal;
- seek rehearing by the full "en banc" appellate court; or
- pursue a petition for review by the Supreme Court.

Motions for rehearing are rarely granted by the appellate courts, and they are not required for filing a petition for review.[39] These are important considerations when deciding whether to spend the time and expense on a motion for rehearing in the court of appeals. Another is that—even in the infrequent case where the court of appeals grants relief—the court of appeals may use the rehearing to shore up weaknesses in its original opinion, making it harder to obtain review by the Supreme Court.

Once a party files a petition for review, it no longer can file a motion for rehearing or reconsideration en banc unless the court of appeals changes its original judgment or opinion.[40] But it cannot prevent another party from doing so or the court of appeals from ruling; instead, the petition for review is stayed pending the final outcome of any pending motions for rehearing or reconsideration en banc.[41] And the party that filed the petition for review must "immediately" notify the Supreme Court's clerk (1) that a rehearing motion was filed in the court of appeals and (2) when the last timely filed motion is overruled.[42]

13-3:1.1 Panel Rehearing

Any party can seek rehearing by filing a motion for rehearing within 15 days of the judgment or order is rendered.[43] The motion must comply with the rules governing motion practice, including a word limit of 4,500 words,[44] except that no certificate of conference is required.[45] And the motion can be amended without leave of court during the 15-day period under Rule 49.1 or with leave of court any time before the court of appeals rules on the motion.[46] In an accelerated appeal, the court may shorten the 15-day period for seeking rehearing or deny the right to file a motion altogether.[47] The court of appeals can also extend the filing period if the party files a motion for extension "no later than 15 days" after the motion for extension is due.[48]

The motion must specifically point out the grounds for reconsideration[49] and, although the rules do not specify it, it should not merely "rehash" the arguments previously made. Having spent significant time considering the case and writing an opinion, the court will not be easily persuaded that its decision was wrong. And new arguments raised at the rehearing stage are generally considered untimely. However, if the court of appeals' decision fails to address all of the arguments raised by the losing party or creates a new error in its consideration or disposition of the issues, bringing that problem to its attention in a respectful and persuasive way may convince the court to correct the opinion. Successful strategies for rehearing also include enlisting the help of amicus curiae briefs.

The non-moving party need not file a response unless the court of appeals requests one. The motion should not be granted without first receiving a response, and the court of appeals can request one if it has not already been filed.[50]

The courts of appeals generally hear and decide cases by panels of three justices. A majority of the justices who participated in the decision can grant a motion for rehearing; otherwise, it will be denied.[51] If granted, the court may consider and resolve the case "with or without further briefing and argument."[52] If the appellate court modifies its judgment, vacates and renders a new judgment, or issues a different opinion, the parties may file further motions for rehearing.[53] Otherwise, the court will not entertain further motions for panel rehearing.

13-3:1.2 Reconsideration En Banc

A party dissatisfied with the result can also seek reconsideration by the full court, called reconsideration en banc.[54] This option is only practically available when the court has more than three justices. In addition, the court itself may order reconsideration en banc. Reconsideration en banc is a significant request because it requires all of the justices of the court to review the motion and the opinion.

The motion must be filed within 15 days of the court of appeals' judgment or order or 15 days after the court of appeals' denial of the party's last timely motion for rehearing or en banc reconsideration.[55] If a majority of the justices agree, the court of appeals can order en banc reconsideration—either on the party's motion or on its own—as long as it has plenary power.[56] Such an order prevents the panel's judgment or order from becoming final, and the case is then "resubmitted to the court for en banc review and disposition,"[57] either on the existing briefs or, more typically, with instruction to the parties for further briefing and possibly a new oral argument.

13-3:2 Supreme Court of Texas

A party seeking rehearing may file a motion for rehearing with the Supreme Court within 15 days of the Court's rendition of judgment on a cause or order disposing of a petition for review.[58] Extensions of time for filing are available for up to 15 days after the motion was due, but second motions will not be entertained unless the Court changes its opinion or judgment in a significant way.[59]

The motion for rehearing "must specify the points relied on for the rehearing"[60] and comply with the rules regarding motion practice, including a word-count limit of 4,500 words.[61] Former Supreme Court Chief Justice Wallace Jefferson has described obtaining rehearing in that court as "daunting and difficult."[62] These motions are rarely granted and should not be filed as a matter of course. It is generally advisable to obtain amicus support for your motion.

The opposing party need not file a response unless one is request, and the Court will not grant a motion for rehearing without providing an opportunity to respond except in "exceptional circumstances."[63]

13-4 The Mandate

13-4:1 Role of the Mandate

A "'[m]andate' is the official notice of the action of the appellate court, directed to the trial court, advising the trial court of the appellate court's action."[64] A mandate formally commands a lower court to obey a higher court's judgment.[65] "Upon receipt of the mandate, the trial court has no discretion to review, interpret, or enforce the mandate."[66] The trial court's jurisdiction is limited to the issues specified in the mandate.[67] The scope of the mandate is determined by referring to both the court of appeals' opinion and the mandate itself.[68]

Although the mandate is a necessary prerequisite to enforcing the judgment, the rules do not require the clerk to provide the parties with copies of the mandate. Thus, it is advisable that the parties request a copy of the mandate from the clerk of the court and carefully review it to ensure that it is consistent with the judgment. If not, the court of appeals can vacate, modify, correct, or reform the mandate. The vehicle to raise defects in the mandate is a timely motion for rehearing, or if after that time, motion to recall the mandate.

The appellate clerk's role in issuing the mandate is ministerial, not discretionary.[69]As the mandate of the court must issue "in accordance with the judgment,"[70] the judgment must conform to the mandate. If it does not, the appellate court may issue a writ of mandamus or prohibition to correct it.[71]

13-4:2 Timing of the Mandate

13-4:2.1 Court of Appeals

Rule 18 requires the appellate clerk to issue the mandate 10 days after the period for filing a motion to extend time to file a petition for review (typically 60 days after the court of appeals' judgment or disposition of the last pending motion for rehearing) if no petition has been filed or timely motion for extension is pending in the Supreme Court.[72] When a petition for review is filed and denied, refused, or dismissed by the Supreme Court, the court of appeals will issue the mandate after disposition of that petition.[73] In practice, Rule 18.1 is treated as the first possible date for issuance, and the mandate is frequently delayed due to the heavy workload of the intermediate courts of appeals. Often a courtesy call to the clerk's office will be sufficient to get the mandate issued. But in some cases, you may need to file a motion to expedite the mandate either based on the parties' agreement or showing "good cause" for an earlier issuance.[74]

13-4:2.2 Supreme Court of Texas

If the Supreme Court grants review, it will issue its own mandate at the conclusion of the appeal—10 days after the last day for filing a motion to extend time for seeking rehearing, assuming that no timely motion for rehearing or extension of time is pending.[75]

13-4:3 Motion Practice Regarding the Mandate

13-4:3.1 Motion to Expedite

As noted, the parties can agree to issue the mandate earlier than the rules provide or a party can file a motion to expedite the mandate demonstrating "good cause" for an earlier issuance.[76]

In expedited appeals from interlocutory orders, the appellate court may issue the mandate "immediately on announcing its decision if the circumstances require," or it can delay the mandate until the final disposition of the appeal.[77]

13-4:3.2 Motion to Stay

A party can move to stay issuance of the mandate while it seeks review from the United States Supreme Court.[78] The motion for stay is directed to the court that is authorized to issue the mandate and must show that "the grounds [for the stay] are substantial and . . . the petitioner or others would incur substantial hardship from the mandate's issuance if the United States Supreme Court were later to reverse the judgment."[79] This standard is quite demanding, and both the Texas Rules and the United States Supreme Court rules on the subject should be consulted.

13-4:3.3 Recalling the Mandate

Rule 18.7 provides that if a new or modified judgment or order is handed down after the mandate issues, the clerk should notify the clerk of court receiving the mandate that the mandate has no effect "and a new mandate may issue."[80] Although not specified in the rules, a party may file a motion to recall the mandate to correct an error, although the timing of this motion may determine whether that relief is limited to clerical or substantive corrections.

13-5 Enforcement of the Judgment

13-5:1 Timing of Enforcement

Because a party may appeal without superseding the judgment, the judgment creditor may execute on the judgment without affecting the appellate court's jurisdiction so long as no supersedeas is in place. But execution is not without risks—if the judgment is reversed on appeal, the judgment debtor has a right to recover in restitution against the judgment creditor the fair-market value of the property taken by execution.[81] The fair-market value often differs from the value received from the execution sale, so the executing party runs the risk of having to pay in restitution more than it obtained at execution.

If the trial court's judgment has been superseded pending the appeal, that suspension of enforcement ends after the mandate is received by the trial court. The mandate is directed to the trial court (or court of appeals)—not to the clerk of court. Therefore, the trial court is the appropriate forum for the initial enforcement of the mandate.[82] If the judgment of the appellate court either affirms the trial court's judgment, modifies it, or renders the judgment the trial court should have rendered, then the trial court need not make any further orders, and the judgment as mandated can be enforced as any other judgment.[83]

In the usual interlocutory appeal, "the appellate court's judgment on an appeal from an interlocutory order takes effect when the mandate is issued. The court may issue the mandate with its judgment or delay the mandate until the appeal is finally disposed of."[84]

13-5:2 Collecting From the Judgment Debtor

13-5:2.1 Individual Debtors

If the judgment debtor posted a supersedeas bond, the judgment creditor may recover either from the surety on its contractual promise under the bond or from the judgment debtor as principal.[85] However, the trial court cannot order the judgment debtor or surety to perform under the bond if such performance goes beyond the provisions of the mandate.[86] The same remedies available to the judgment creditor to collect on the judgment before a proper bond is filed are available when the judgment becomes final.[87] Those enforcement methods include levy and execution, creation of judgment liens, garnishment, turnover, and receivership.[88]

13-5:2.2 Governmental Entities

Several entities, including the State of Texas and its governmental subdivisions, are not required to post a bond to suspend execution of a judgment.[89] A judgment is automatically stayed when an exempt entity perfects an appeal and thus, there is no supersedeas bond or cash deposit to collect.

A judgment against a governmental entity presents additional concerns because the entity generally has sovereign immunity unless the legislature or the entity expressly waives it. Governmental immunity prevents an entity from being sued without its consent.[90] Even if the legislature allows a governmental unit to be sued and a judgment is rendered, the legislature must also appropriate the money to pay it.[91] Further, even where the government has waived liability, it may set caps on the amount of liability.[92] Consequently, even if the plaintiff can get the legislature's permission to sue the state and the plaintiff ultimately prevails, collecting the judgment from the governmental entity can be difficult.

13-5:3 Collecting From Third Parties

13-5:3.1 Supersedeas Bonds

Supersedeas bonds are typically written to permit the surety to collect on the bond only if the judgment is ultimately against the judgment debtor and the judgment debtor fails to perform the judgment. Therefore, the judgment creditor will typically have to seek payment from the debtor before proceeding against the surety.

If the debtor pays the judgment, then the bond can be released, generally through an agreed motion. If the judgment debtor either does not pay or fails to pay in full, the creditor may proceed to execute on the bond.

Although the general rule is that no collection efforts may go forward until the mandate is received by the trial court, one Texas intermediate appellate court has held that—even where the trial court judgment was superseded by a bond and before the mandate had issued—the judgment creditor could proceed directly against the surety through a turnover proceeding to enforce the judgment that had been affirmed by the Texas Supreme Court when no timely motion for rehearing had been filed.[93]

13-5:3.2 Cash Deposits

The clerk of the court cannot draw a check on trust funds except to pay a person entitled to those funds. And payment must be made under order from the court that deposited the funds. So, when the appellant posted a cash deposit with the clerk of the trial court to suspend execution of the trial court's judgment, the judgment creditor should obtain an order from the trial court to pay over the amount necessary to satisfy the judgment. The simplest process is to obtain an agreed order, but a formal motion may be necessary.

13-5:4 Collecting Costs

When sending out the mandate, the appellate clerk is directed to prepare and transmit a statement of costs on appeal, including the costs of preparing the appellate record and any appellate filing fees, designating the party responsible for those costs, and indicating whether they have been paid and by whom.[94]

If unpaid appellate costs are collected through enforcement of the judgment, the trial court clerk is to remit those fees directly to the court of appeals.[95]

13-6 Conclusion

Whether the result of an appeal is favorable or unfavorable to your client, you will want to be ready to take action or respond, and the times for doing so are generally short. Both sides need to take a close look at the opinion and judgment to address potential errors, ensure there are no unintended consequences, and take corrective action through motions for rehearing or further review while those remedies are available. The losing party should prepare for the worst, and the winning party should prepare for a potentially long road to execution on the final judgment during the interim. Having a clear road map of the items necessary to wind up the appeal in advance of the decision will undoubtedly help manage the clients' expectations and lead to the best results.

Notes

1 Tex. R. App. P. 47.1.

2 Tex. R. App. P. 48.1.

3 Tex. R. App. P. 48.3.

4 Tex. R. App. P. 47.2(a).

5 Tex. R. App. P. 47.2(a).

6 Tex. R. App. P. 47.5.

7 Tex. R. App. P. 47.5.

8 Tex. R. App. P. 47.5.

9 Tex. R. App. P. 47.4.

10 Tex. R. App. P. 47.4(a)-(d).

11 Tex. R. App. P. 47.4.

12 *E.g., Anastasoff v. United States*, 223 F.3d 898, 900 (8th Cir. 2000) (holding rule permitting unpublished opinions violates Article III of the United States Constitution), *opinion vacated on reh'g en banc*, 235 F.3d 1054 (8th Cir. 2000).

13 Tex. R. App. P. 47.3

14 Tex. R. App. P. 47.2(c).

15 Tex. R. App. P. 47.7.

16 Tex. R. App. P. 47 (comment to 2002 change).

17 *Hudson v. Paxton*, No. 03-13-00368-CV, 2015 WL 739605, at *3 (Tex. App.—Austin Feb. 20, 2015, pet. denied) (mem. op.); Tex. R. App. P. 47.7 cmt.

18 Tex. R. App. P. 43.1.

19 Tex. R. App. P. 43.2.

20 Tex. R. App. P. 43.3(a) & (b).

21 *See Samuels v. Nasir*, 445 S.W.3d 886, 894 (Tex. App.—El Paso 2014, no pet.).

22 Tex. R. App. P. 46.3.

23 Tex. R. App. P. 46.5.

[24] Tex. R. App. P. 46.5.

[25] Tex. R. App. P. 46.5.

[26] Tex. R. App. P. 60.2.

[27] Tex. R. App. P. 60.3.

[28] *See, e.g.*, *Union Pac. R.R. Co. v. Seber*, 477 S.W.3d 424, 436 (Tex. App.—Houston [14th Dist.] 2015, no pet.).

[29] *Continental Airlines v. Kiefer*, 920 S.W.2d 274, 277 (Tex. 1996).

[30] *Westech Engineering, Inc. v. Clearwater Constructors, Inc.*, 835 S.W.2d 190, 206 (Tex. App.—Austin 1992, no writ).

[31] Tex. R. App. P. 20.1(b)(1), 43.4.

[32] Tex. R. App. P. 43.4.

[33] *Hammonds v. Hammonds*, 313 S.W.2d 603, 606 (Tex. 1958); *Pilgrim's Pride Corp. v. Burnett*, No. 12-10-00037-CV, 2012 WL 381714, at *16 (Tex. App.—Tyler Feb. 3, 2012, no pet.); *Shenandoah Assoc. v. J & K Properties, Inc.*, 741 S.W.2d 470, 486–87 (Tex. App.—Dallas 1987, writ denied).

[34] Tex. R. App. P. 43.4.

[35] Tex. R. App. P. 43.4.

[36] Tex. R. App. P. 43.5.

[37] Tex. R. App. P. 45 (court of appeals); Tex. R. App. P. 62 (Supreme Court).

[38] Tex. R. App. P. 45 (court of appeals); Tex. R. App. P. 62 (Supreme Court).

[39] Tex. R. App. P. 49.9.

[40] Tex. R. App. P. 49.11.

[41] Tex. R. App. P. 49.11.

[42] Tex. R. App. P. 49.11.

[43] Tex. R. App. P. 49.1.

[44] Tex. R. App. P. 9.4(i)(2)(D).

[45] Tex. R. App. P. 10.1, 49.12.

[46] Tex. R. App. P. 49.6.

[47] Tex. R. App. P. 49.4.

[48] Tex. R. App. P. 49.8.

[49] Tex. R. App. P. 49.1.

[50] Tex. R. App. P. 49.2.

[51] Tex. R. App. P. 49.3.

[52] Tex. R. App. P. 49.3.

[53] Tex. R. App. P. 49.5.

[54] Tex. R. App. P. 49.7.

[55] Tex. R. App. P. 49.7.

[56] Tex. R. App. P. 49.7.

[57] Tex. R. App. P. 49.7.

[58] Tex. R. App. P. 64.1.

[59] Tex. R. App. P. 64.4, 64.5.

[60] Tex. R. App. P. 64.2.

[61] Tex. R. App. P. 9.4(i)(2)(D).

[62] Hon. Wallace B. Jefferson, *Motions for Rehearing on Denial of Petitions*, State Bar of Texas Practice Before the Supreme Court (2002).

63 Tex. R. App. P. 64.3.

64 *In re Kintz*, No. 01-02-00276-CV, 2002 WL 538975, at *1 (Tex. App.—Houston [1st Dist.] 2002, orig. proceeding) (not designated for publication).

65 *See* Tex. R. App. P. 51.1(b) ("When the trial court clerk receives the mandate, the appellate court's judgment must be enforced.").

66 *In re Elite Door & Trim, Inc.*, 362 S.W.3d 199, 200–01 (Tex. App.—Dallas 2012, orig. proceeding) (internal quotations and citations omitted).

67 *In re Elite Door & Trim, Inc.*, 362 S.W.3d 199, 201 (Tex. App.—Dallas 2012, orig. proceeding) (internal quotations and citations omitted).

68 *In re Elite Door & Trim, Inc.*, 362 S.W.3d 199, 201 (Tex. App.—Dallas 2012, orig. proceeding) (internal quotations and citations omitted); *see also Hudson v. Wakefield*, 711 S.W.2d 628, 630 (Tex. 1986) ("In interpreting the mandate of an appellate court . . . the courts should look not only to the mandate itself, but also to the opinion of the court.").

69 *Myers v. Myers*, 515 S.W.2d 334, 335 (Tex. Civ. App.—Houston [1st Dist.] 1974, writ dism'd w.o.j.).

70 *Continental Airlines v. Kiefer*, 920 S.W.2d 274, 277 (Tex. 1996) (quoting Tex. R. App. P. 86(a)).

71 *In re Castle Texas Prod. Ltd. P'ship*, 563 S.W.3d 216, 219 (Tex. 2018) (orig. proceeding) (citation omitted); *Lee v. Downey*, 842 S.W.2d 646, 648 (Tex. 1992) (orig. proceeding).

72 Tex. R. App. P. 18.1(a)(1).

73 Tex. R. AppPP. P. 18.1(a)(2).

74 Tex. R. App. P. 18.1(c).

75 Tex. R. App. P. 18.1(b).

76 Tex. R. App. P. 18.1(c).

77 Tex. R. App. P. 18.6.

78 Tex. R. App. P. 18.2.

79 Tex. R. App. P. 18.2.

80 Tex. R. App. P. 18.7.

81 Tex. Civ. Prac. & Rem. Code § 34.022.

82 *In re Long*, 984 S.W.2d 623, 626 (Tex. 1998) (citation omitted).

83 Tex. R. App. P. 51.1(b), 65.2; *see In re Long*, 984 S.W.2d 623, 626 (refusing to hold party in contempt for violating a lower court judgment that was superseded on appeal until the issuance of mandate enforcing the lower court judgment).

84 Tex. R. App. P. 18.6.

85 *Universe Life Ins. Co. v. Giles*, 982 S.W.2d 488, 493 (Tex. App.—Texarkana 1998, pet. denied).

86 *See McFadin v. Broadway Coffeehouse, L.L.C.*, 539 S.W.3d 278, 285 (Tex. 2018) (trial court's order "requiring [defendant] to pay the amount of the bond went beyond the provisions of the 2014 judgment," and that order was a final, appealable order).

87 *Universe Life Ins. Co. v. Giles*, 982 S.W.2d 488, 493 (Tex. App.—Texarkana 1998, pet. denied).

88 A detailed discussion of these various methods can be found in Chapters 31 and 32 of 5 Roy W. McDonald & Elaine A. Grafton Carlson, McDonald & Carlson Texas Civil Practice (2004).

89 Tex. Civ. Prac. & Rem. Code § 6.001.

90 *See, e.g., Texas Dept. of Human Servs. v. Green*, 855 S.W.2d 136, 141, n.5 (Tex. App.—Austin 1993, writ denied) (former employee who brought successful whistleblower case and recovered $13.6 million in damages was unable to collect for over two years because state legislature refused to appropriate the funds).

[91] Tex. Civ. Prac. & Rem. Code § 109.002.

[92] *See, e.g.*, Tex. Civ. Prac. & Rem. Code § 101.023 (Texas Tort Claims Act); Tex. Gov't Code Ann. § 554.003(c) (Texas Whistleblower Act).

[93] *Universe Life Ins. Co. v. Giles*, 982 S.W.2d 488, 490 (Tex. App.—Texarkana 1998, pet. denied); *see* Elaine A. Carlson, *Reshuffling the Deck: Enforcing and Superseding Civil Judgments on Appeal After House Bill 4*, 46 S. Tex. L. Rev. 1035, 1117 (2005) (citing *Universe Life Ins. Co. v. Giles*, 982 S.W.2d 488, 493 (Tex. App.—Texarkana 1998, pet. denied)).

[94] Tex. R. App. P. 51.1(a), 65.2.

[95] Tex. R. App. P. 51.1(b), 65.2.

CHAPTER 14

Texas Supreme Court: Petition for Review, Response, and Reply

14-1 Introduction

In the Texas Supreme Court, the petition for review is the vehicle by which a party seeks discretionary review of an adverse decision by an intermediate court of appeals. Few petitions are granted—approximately one in ten. As a result, a petition for review to the Supreme Court is fundamentally different from a brief of an appellant to a court of appeals. Whereas the primary goal of an appellant's brief is to persuade the court of appeals to rule for the client on the merits, the primary goal of the petition for review is to persuade the Supreme Court to take the case.

This distinction impacts the crafting of not only the petition itself, but also the response to the petition (urging the Court not to take the case), and the reply in support of the petition. This chapter addresses each of these three filings, the basic requirements applicable to all of them, and the Supreme Court's internal procedures.

14-2 Petition for Review

14-2:1 Goal of the Petition

The petitioner's ultimate goal at the petition-for-review stage is straightforward: getting through the door. Persuading the Supreme Court that the client should prevail on the merits is a secondary consideration at this stage. The petitioner must persuade at least three justices that the case is worthy of review to get to the next stage—full briefing on the merits.[1] And, ultimately, for the Court to grant review, the petitioner must persuade at least four justices that the case merits exercise of the Court's discretionary jurisdiction.

14-2:1.1 Demonstrating Substantial Importance

Unless the petitioner is angling for a per curiam opinion to correct error on a narrow legal point, getting through the door requires persuading the Court that the case involves a legal issue of substantial importance to the jurisprudence of the state. The task is complicated by the fact that the sheer volume of petitions the justices must review each week means, in all likelihood, that very little time will be devoted by the justices to any given petition.

One former justice has observed that due to the sheer volume of petitions, "the review is necessarily cursory."[2] Another justice has remarked that in reviewing a petition, "the judge can look at it in 90 seconds and realize that there is not a chance in the world that anybody on this Court is going to be interested in granting this case."[3] Although it may vary somewhat, most justices say they spend a maximum of 15 minutes per petition, which includes reviewing the petition, court of appeals' opinion, response (if any), and any amicus submissions. Some justices also rely on summaries of petitions written by law clerks.

14-2:1.2 The "Hook"—Grabbing the Supreme Court's Attention

With so little time being devoted by the justices to actually reviewing any given petition, the petitioner's initial goal must be to grab the Court's attention. This challenge is exacerbated by the fact that there is no guarantee that all of the justices will actually read every section of the petition or will read front to back. Some start with the court of appeals' opinion, since the Court is reviewing the opinion for error. Some start with the issue statements and then look at the court of appeals' opinion. Some start with the summary of the argument and then read only those portions of the court of appeals' opinion relevant to the issues presented. Some rely on summaries of petitions prepared by law clerks. The practical reality of this discretionary review process calls for a fundamental shift in strategy from briefing to the court of appeals, where there is an assurance that the case will be heard and that the entire brief will be read by at least one of the justices and, in all probability, by all three.

An effective technique to grab the Court's attention in the petition is the "hook." Developing a hook requires boiling down the principal argument to a simple statement, ideally a single sentence, which not only captures the argument but also reveals its importance. The hook is then incorporated into various sections of the petition, so that no matter which section a particular justice actually looks to, the chances are enhanced of the hook being set.

This technique will not appeal to those writers who rely on a thesaurus to avoid repeating themselves. It is nonetheless an effective technique for those writers whose practical goal is simply to grab the attention of justices who may give the petition no more than a cursory review.

14-2:1.3 Brevity Is the Soul of an Effective Petition

Above all, the petition should be short. The body of the petition for review (statement of facts, summary of the argument, argument, and prayer) may contain no more than 4,500 words.[4] Because many required sections of the petition do not fall within that limit, the temptation to use the preliminary sections to circumvent that page limitation may be strong. Resist that temptation. On average, the justices will have about three petitions to review each weekday, 52 weeks a year, to keep up with the inflow of petitions. Their time is valuable, and an effective petition will reflect respect for that fact. Attaching briefing in the appendix to circumvent the page limitations will ensure that the appendix gets struck.

Since a given petition is likely to receive no more than a cursory review, it is ultimately counterproductive to file a verbose petition. A streamlined, tightly focused petition is more likely to grab the attention of the justices. A former chief justice of the Supreme Court has emphasized that the length limit "is a maximum, not a recommendation or suggestion."[5] He has even gone Biblical in driving home this point:

> My own view is that writing to the page limits does not increase your chances for review or send any indication to the judges as to the seriousness of your case. To paraphrase St. Luke, "What profiteth a writer to use all his pages, but to lose his audience."[6]

The chief justice's view is shared by the other justices: "I rarely heard from other members of the court that the petition was too short."[7]

Technically, on motion, the Court may permit a longer petition, response, or reply.[8] As a practical matter, however, the Court routinely denies such motions. Accordingly, counsel should comply with the word limitations on the initial filing since, virtually without exception, these limitations will ultimately be enforced.

14-2:2 Anatomy of the Petition

With minor exception, a petition for review must contain the following sections, in the order listed and "under appropriate headings:"

- Identity of Parties and Counsel
- Table of Contents
- Index of Authorities
- Statement of the Case
- Statement of Jurisdiction
- Issues Presented
- *Statement of Facts*
- *Summary of the Argument*
- *Argument*
- *Prayer*
- Signature
- Certificate of Service
- Certificate of Compliance
- Appendix

Tex. R. App. P. 53.2. Only the italicized sections are included in the petition's 4,500-word limit.[9]

14-2:2.1 Cover

The cover should be clean and simple. The required cover contents for the petition are the case style; the case number; the title (e.g., "Petition for Review"); and the name, mailing address, telephone number, fax number, if any, email address, and State Bar number of the lead counsel for the filing party.[10] Though the rules require that only the email address of lead counsel be included on the cover the clerk's office prefers that the email address of each attorney listed on the cover be included.

Though not required under the rule, the State Bar Number of each listed attorney should be included immediately beneath his or her name. The clerk's office enters a notation on the computer system next to the name of the first signer to indicate that he or she is lead counsel. Only that attorney will receive official notices from the clerk's office, although anyone who signs up can receive CaseMail. The name of the attorney should be the "bar card" name of the attorney, not some interesting nickname. The name is cross-checked against the State Bar database, and the clerk's office will investigate name variations.

When out-of-state attorneys are included on the cover, prudent practice dictates filing a pro hac vice motion prior to or contemporaneously with the filing of the brief.

Although not required, some justices prefer that the cover reflect that the matter is "On Petition for Review from the [number] Court of Appeals at [City], Texas, Cause No. ______" And the clerk's office appreciates including this information.

The cover of a petition should not request oral argument. Only in the court of appeals must a request for oral argument appear on the cover.[11]

Now that e-filing is universally required in all appellate courts, the rule governing the colors and materials to be used for the cover has effectively been rendered obsolete.[12]

14-2:2.2 Identity of Parties and Counsel

Rule 53.2(a) requires a complete list of all parties to the trial court's judgment, and the names and addresses of all trial and appellate counsel.[13] The clerk's office also prefers inclusion of the email address for each listed attorney. It is not necessary under the rules to provide the addresses of the parties to the trial court's final judgment; only the addresses of trial and appellate counsel must be provided. Counsel should also provide the addresses of any pro se litigants.

Although not required, it is helpful to the Court to indicate the parties' procedural posture in the trial court, the court of appeals, and the Supreme Court (e.g., defendant/appellee/petitioner).

Under the rule governing petitions for review, both trial and appellate counsel must be listed. Clearly designate whether listed attorneys served as trial counsel, appellate counsel, or both.

The identity of parties and counsel page need not contain a stock introductory sentence as suggested by some appellate form books (e.g., "This list is being provided pursuant to Rule 53.2(a) so that the members of the Court may determine whether they are recused.").

This section of the petition does not count against the 4,500-word limit.[14]

14-2:2.3 Table of Contents

Rule 53.2(b) requires a table of contents.[15] Because of the sheer volume of petitions that each justice reviews, the importance of a well-drafted table of contents assumes greater importance under petition practice. Properly crafted, the table of contents may serve as an effective overview of the issues presented and the reasons that those issues merit the Court's attention. The table of contents is also an ideal place to incorporate the "hook" one or more times.[16]

The table of contents should contain page references for every required section. The primary advantage of providing a thorough table of contents is to aid the justices to go to the section in which they are interested. A secondary benefit is that the table of contents can then serve as a quick cross-check against Rule 53.2 to ensure that the petition includes all required sections in the correct order. Some justices also look to the table of contents as a summary.

The rules also require that the table of contents "indicate the subject matter of each issue or point, or group of issues or points."[17]

With electronic filing, parties have the option of linking each entry in the table of contents to the section of the petition/brief to which that entry corresponds. In addition, parties can create a "bookmark" for each section of the brief, and the justices may use those bookmarks to navigate within an electronic brief. The justices have commented that they find such links and bookmarks to be helpful, and they have come to expect them.

This section of the petition does not count against the 4,500-word limit.[18]

14-2:2.4 Index of Authorities

Rule 53.2(c) requires an alphabetical index of authorities indicating the pages where the authorities are cited.[19] The index of authorities should not be cumbersome. Over-categorization makes it difficult for the reader to find a case by simple alphabetical reference. To avoid this problem, the authorities should be listed alphabetically under the following headings or an appropriate variation thereof: (1) Cases (without grouping by jurisdiction); (2) Constitutional Provisions, Statutes and Rules; and (3) Miscellaneous Authorities.

The better practice is to provide page references for every page in the petition on which the authority is cited. Unless unduly cumbersome, avoid the use of "passim" in lieu of providing page numbers, even for a frequently cited authority. Although counsel should always provide pinpoint page references for authorities cited, delete the pinpoints in the index of authorities.

Follow Bluebook and Greenbook citation form meticulously. Many staff attorneys and law clerks are former law-review and journal editors to whom citation mistakes may be distracting and even credibility-reducing. Be particularly mindful to provide accurate subsequent histories.

This section of the petition does not count against the 4,500-word limit.[20]

14-2:2.5 Statement of the Case

Rule 53.2(d) requires a statement of the case containing specified information.[21] The statement of the case provides one of the greatest invitations for abuse under petition practice. Rule 53.2(d) provides a suggested page limit for the statement of the case (one page), but not a mandatory one. Compounding the risk of abuse is the fact that the statement of the case is excepted from the 4,500-word limit.

Practitioners who follow the format preferred by virtually all of the justices, however, will face no such temptation. The justices almost uniformly prefer that the statement of the case be presented in tabular form. The statement of the case should serve as a simple reference page, to which the justices can turn for basic information about the case. The tabular format resembles the study memo format that the Court's staff is currently required to use. Employing this format is, therefore, helpful to the chambers assigned to the case and can enhance credibility. Plus, any argument that counsel might really want to put in a narrative can be included more effectively in an introduction or the summary of argument.

Practitioners may be reluctant to abandon the traditional, narrative statement of the case for fear of losing an opportunity to persuade the Court. The expressed preferences of the justices and the ease of reference provided by the suggested format, however, outweigh any incremental persuasive value of a narrative statement of the case.

The nine items required by Rule 53.2(d) to be included in the statement of the case in a petition for review can easily be collapsed into five headings:

- Nature of the Case and Parties
- Trial Court
- Trial Court Disposition
- Court of Appeals
- Court of Appeals' Disposition

14-2:2.5a Nature of the Case and Parties

Rule 53.1(d)(1) gives as examples of the "concise description of the nature of the case:" "whether it is a suit for damages, on a note, or in trespass to try title." Being a little more specific, though not more lengthy, may be helpful. For example, "a suit for damages" can take many different forms, such as a product-liability suit, a medical-malpractice action, or a simple personal-injury suit. Provide enough information so that the statement of the nature of the case will distinguish this petition from others.

The rule also requires identifying "the parties in the court of appeals."[22] This information can be included as part of the description of the nature of the case.[23] In a multi-party appeal, of course, this could conceivably be an unmanageably long list. In that event, make reference to the appendix and include the list there. Because the statement of the case is not included in the page limit, this should not be construed as a violation of the rule precluding the inclusion of matters in the appendix in an attempt to avoid the page limits.[24]

14-2:2.5b Trial Court

Provide the full name of the trial judge who signed the order or judgment appealed from, as well as the designation of the trial court and the county in which it is located.[25]

14-2:2.5c Trial Court's Disposition

A one-line statement of the trial court action suffices.[26]

14-2:2.5d Court of Appeals

Include here the district of the court of appeals; the names of the justices who participated in the decision of the court of appeals; the author of the opinion for the court, and the author of any separate opinion; and the citation for the court of appeals' opinion.[27] Although it is best to identify the trial judge by his or her first and last names, including the first names of court of appeals justices is unnecessary unless there is more than one judge with the same last name on the court. Be sure to indicate if a lower court judge was sitting "by designation."

14-2:2.5e Court of Appeals' Disposition

Simply state what the court of appeals ultimately adjudged.[28] Reserve any details, including when the court of appeals acted on any motion for rehearing that may have been filed, for the statement of facts, which expressly calls for inclusion of the procedural background.[29]

If the practitioner chooses to provide a statement of the case in narrative form, it should be as short as practicable and should rarely exceed one-half page. The purpose of the statement of the case is to provide the Court with orientation. A simple litmus test can be employed to determine whether a statement of the case, provided in narrative form, is appropriate: could the Court include the statement verbatim in its opinion? If not, it is overly argumentative and should be redrafted.

14-2:2.6 Statement of Jurisdiction

Rule 53.2(e) requires that the petition state, without argument, the basis of the Court's jurisdiction.[30] In 2017, the Legislature eliminated the six jurisdictional grounds long contained in Texas Government Code section 22.001(a).[31] Now, the only remaining jurisdictional ground is the one previously housed in section 22.001(a)(6)—whether the "appeal presents a question of law that is important to the jurisdiction of the state."[32]

In many cases, a single sentence will suffice for the statement of jurisdiction. For example: "The Supreme Court has jurisdiction of this suit under Government Code section 22.001(a), because this case presents an important issue of constitutional law of first impression to this Court that is likely to recur in future cases."

While conflicts among the courts of appeals are no longer strictly jurisdictional, they nevertheless may show that an issue is one of statewide import. Consequently, if a case presents what would have traditionally been termed, "conflicts jurisdiction," the jurisdictional statement could include a single sentence stating the point on which the courts of appeals disagree, as well as citations to the conflicting opinions with appropriate signals.

The statement of jurisdiction is specifically accepted from the 4,500-word limit.[33]

Any argument that the practitioner may be tempted to include in the statement of jurisdiction, however, should be avoided. If argument is included in the statement of jurisdiction, at best it will go unread and at worst it will be perceived as an abusive attempt to circumvent the length limit and could result in the petition being struck.[34]

Only if jurisdiction truly is an issue in the case—such that the petition might be a legitimate target for a motion to dismiss for want of jurisdiction—should the statement of jurisdiction contain a substantive discussion of the jurisdictional issue. Even then, the bulk of the jurisdictional argument should be reserved for the Argument section of the petition.

14-2:2.7 Issues Presented

Rule 53.2(f) requires the petition to "state concisely all issues or points presented for review."[35] Although this allows the petitioner to present the Court with either points of error or issues, the justices prefer the use of issues over points. Moreover, issue practice lends itself much better to seizing the attention of the Court; it is more readily apparent that an issue is of substantial importance to the jurisprudence of the state when it is stated as an issue rather than as a point of error. Some justices have commented that they usually can spot a petition that is not "grant-worthy" from the issues.[36] On the other hand, "an issue presented can also attract judicial attention and encourage a justice to spend more time reviewing the case."[37]

Because the grant or denial of a petition can be determined by a justice reviewing nothing more than the issues presented, the importance of carefully selecting and framing the issues cannot be overstated.[38] Much has been written on issue practice.[39] Unfortunately, some of the advice is conflicting. Outlined below is the key advice, including conflicting advice, as well as our views on which path to take when the recommendations cannot be reconciled.

14-2:2.7a Limiting Briefed Issues

All agree that it is a good idea to limit the number of points or issues presented to the Supreme Court for review. The word-count limitations of the petition make limiting the number of issues even more critical; only one or two issues can be briefed effectively in the argument portion of the petition. As one justice has put it, "the best points, and only the best points, should be in the petition."[40]

The petitioner should critically evaluate whether to even preserve those issues as to which the available space does not permit meaningful discussion.

14-2:2.7b Preserving Unbriefed Issues in the Petition for Review

The rules do not require the petitioner to address in the argument section of the petition every issue listed in the issues presented.[41] If one or more issues in the petition are not addressed in the argument, to preserve them, the petitioner should include in the list of issues presented the parenthetical reference "(unbriefed)" immediately following each such issue, or group them under the heading "Unbriefed Issues."

14-2:2.7c Listing Issues

Simply listing the issues numerically is sufficient. It is not necessary to follow the traditional format for points of error, e.g., "Issue No. 1." The issues may be single-spaced.[42] The issues should not be typed in all capital letters as that makes them difficult to read.

14-2:2.7d Framing Issues

The issues should be framed in such a way that they present concrete, legal questions for the Court's resolution, reveal the importance of the question for the Court's consideration, and place the issue in the context of the actual case before the Court. This is easier said than done: "Preparing an effective issue statement is one of the most important, and difficult, tasks facing the author of an appellate brief."[43]

(i) Frame to demonstrate importance

An experienced Texas Supreme Court practitioner has developed a number of thoughtful suggestions for preparing issues. First, "[t]here are significant differences between the intermediate courts of appeals and the Texas Supreme Court that should be taken into account when drafting issues."[44] Unlike in the court of appeals, where the court must hear the case, in drafting issues to the Supreme Court, the petitioner "must try to incorporate the concept of importance—such as the need for the state's highest court to decide the case, the widespread effect that resolution of the issue has, or a need to resolve a conflict among courts of appeals."[45] To highlight importance, "a good issue is framed as broadly as the case will permit—like a good law school question. The broader the question, the broader its applicability, and the more likely the Court will determine the issue is important."[46] The petitioner should avoid framing the question in a manner that is overly fact-specific. "If the issue is fact-intensive, it suggests that the issue is not important to the jurisprudence of the state but only to resolution of the particular case."[47]

(ii) Frame neutrally

At the petition stage, the issue should be stated neutrally because the answer does not matter—yet.[48] Again, the goal at this stage is to just get through the door; persuading the Court that the client should prevail on the merits can be accomplished if the Court requests full briefing on the merits, which is what the petitioner should be angling for. At the petition phase, it is more important to convince the Court that the issue is interesting and in need of resolution by the state's highest authority. As one article co-authored by a Supreme Court justice has observed, "'the first review is to determine the cases that obviously have no merit; the review is not designed to resolve any apparent questions.' An interesting issue very often has more than one possible answer. It may do more to get a grant to state the issue in a neutral way."[49]

(iii) Frame for disposition sought

How the issue is framed may differ depending on whether the petitioner is seeking disposition after full oral argument or by per curiam opinion.[50] "If the petitioner seeks a short opinion correcting error without argument, obviously the issues will differ significantly from those asking the Court to review a broad issue of statewide importance."[51]

14-2:2.7e Split of Opinion on Single vs. Multi-Sentence Issues

There is split of opinion among practitioners and commentators as to whether issues should be framed using single sentences or multiple sentences. The most prominent proponent of the multi-sentence issue is Bryan Garner.[52] Garner is harshly critical of the single-sentence issue, at least as conventionally framed: "The one-sentence version of an issue doesn't seem to be required anywhere, but it's a widely followed convention. And it's ghastly in its usual form because it leads to unreadable issues that are deservedly neglected. They're either surface issues that are either too abstract, or else they're meandering, unchronological statements that can't be understood on fewer than three very close readings."[53]

Despite Garner's criticism of the single-sentence approach, depending on the case, this approach may be preferable at the petition stage.

First, the single-sentence approach conforms with the format that the law clerks employ in preparing the study memo.[54] In the study memo, the law clerk is instructed to list the issues presented. This list of issues is almost invariably presented in a single-sentence format. If that format is used in the petition and, ultimately, in the brief on the merits, the law clerk will be more inclined to adopt the issue as framed by the petitioner. If, on the other hand, the petitioner presents a multi-sentence issue, it falls to the law clerk to synthesize it into a single sentence—one not crafted by petitioner's counsel and one with which counsel might not be pleased. In short, counsel who use multi-sentence issues in their briefing to the Court risk losing control of the manner in which the issues are ultimately presented to the justices who will be making the grant/deny decision.

Second, using multi-sentence issues in the petition creates the danger of the justices on taking the time to digest the issues. According to some of the staff attorneys, when faced with a list of multi-sentence issues the reader is inclined to skip to the Table of Contents to divine what the case is actually about.

Garner's multi-sentence approach to issues raises an additional concern: it fails to account for the fundamental distinction between issue-framing in the court of appeals and issue-framing in the Supreme Court. The multi-sentence approach lends itself to being too case-specific. This detracts from demonstrating the importance of the issue to the jurisprudence of the state. The lead example of a multi-sentence issue in Garner's paper illustrates the point:

> As Hannicut Corp. planned and constructed its headquarters, the general contractor, Lawrence Construction Co., repeatedly recommended a roof membrane and noted that the manufacturer also recommended it. Even so, the roof manufacturer warranted the roof without the membrane. Now that the manufacturer has gone bankrupt and the roof is failing, is Lawrence Construction jointly responsible with the insurer for the cost of reconstructing the roof?[55]

While this approach cleanly frames the issue, it in no way indicates why the issue is jurisprudentially interesting. This syllogistic multi-sentence approach also leads logically to only one answer, which is precisely what Garner advocates: "Write fair but persuasive issues that have *only one answer*."[56] Although this approach makes good sense in a brief to a court of appeals, it is problematic at the petition stage before the Texas Supreme Court. Thus, we generally side with the following approach: "At the petition phase, it is more important to convince the Court that the issue is interesting and in need of resolution by the state's highest authority. . . . An interesting issue very often has *more than one possible answer*."[57]

The single-sentence approach does not lead logically to only one answer, although it can be couched so as to nudge the reader toward the desired answer.

The following are some suggestions for those who prefer the multi-sentence approach. First, Garner suggests limiting the issues to 75 words apiece, even where multiple sentences are used.[58] This suggestion is particularly important at the petition stage when the petitioner cannot reasonably expect more than a "cursory" review. Second, avoid making the issue sound too fact-specific, which is particularly challenging when multiple sentences are used. Third, incorporate the concept of importance.

A paper co-authored by a former Texas Supreme Court justice provides an example of an effective multi-sentence issue in a petition. This two-sentence issue "identifie[s] for the court not only the importance of the issue, but also the existence of both a dissent and a split among courts considering the issue at hand:"

> Contrary to precedent established by both the United States Court of Appeals for the Fifth Circuit and a sister court of appeals, and over the dissent of its Chief Justice, the majority of the El Paso Court of Appeals' panel held that Dr. Rennels, who never had nor sought an employment relationship with Sierra Medical Center, nevertheless had standing under the Texas Commission on Human Rights Act ("TCHRA" or "the Act") to sue the Hospital for employment discrimination. Is the existence of an employment relationship between the plaintiff and the defendant a jurisdictional prerequisite to the maintenance of an employment discrimination action under TCHRA, or does TCHRA confer standing to sue employers other than one's own for employment discrimination?[59]

At 119 words, this issue is not tightly framed, but it does satisfy the basic criteria for attracting the interest of the justices.

14-2:2.8 Reasons to Grant Review

The threshold decision before the Court on petition for review is whether to grant review. Accordingly, it may be useful to commence the body of the petition with a stand-alone section that focuses on a concrete question: why should the Court grant review? By including such a section in the bookmarks to the electronic version of the petition, a reviewing justice can simply click on that section and be transported to a set of enumerated reasons for the Court to take the case.

The single most common complaint among the justices has been that many, if not most, petitions "lack focus." A "Reasons to Grant Review" section should avoid this complaint by incorporating the "hook" and setting the "hook" early.[60] Such a section will not only provide the focus that the justices desire at the outset but also force the practitioner to identify and crystallize the reasons that the Court should grant review.

The rules enumerate specific factors that the Court should consider in deciding whether to grant a petition for review.[61] Rule 53.2(h) requires that the petition make specific reference to these factors. The better practice is to incorporate citations to the relevant provisions into the body of the argument rather than give the Court a laundry list of reasons from Rule 56.1 as to why it should exercise jurisdiction. The factors enumerated in Rule 56.1 are:

1. whether the justices of the court of appeals disagree on an important point of law;
2. whether there is a conflict between the courts of appeals on an important point of law;

3. whether a case involves the construction or validity of a statute;
4. whether a case involves constitutional issues;
5. whether the court of appeals appears to have committed an error of law of such importance to the state's jurisprudence that it should be corrected; and
6. whether the court of appeals has decided an important question of state law that should be, but has not been, resolved by the Supreme Court.

Rule 56.1 is not an exclusive list of factors. Other standards may be looked to in demonstrating that a case is "important" to the state's jurisprudence.

A paper authored by Ginger Rodd, a former Supreme Court staff attorney, provides excellent guidance on this point.[62] She explains that with the adoption of the study-memo procedure, a training program was developed for new law clerks. In developing that program, the justices were interviewed to obtain their views on what kinds of cases they consider "grant-worthy."[63] Although the Court's composition has changed since those interviews were taken, the types of cases that will interest justices remain the same. The following are factors identified by the justices as weighing in favor of a grant:[64]

1. The case presents an issue of first impression for the Court, particularly if the issue is likely to recur. Since some justices prefer that novel issues have the opportunity to "percolate" through the courts of appeals, Rodd suggests that if the issue in question has not previously reached many Texas courts of appeals, the petitioner might try to convince the Court that the issue has been well developed in other jurisdictions.[65]
2. The case involves the construction or interpretation of a statute of statewide importance. Statutory interpretation cases have, statistically, been one of the hottest areas for the granting of review.
3. The case presents an issue on which statewide uniformity is important.
4. The court of appeals' opinion is likely to mislead or confuse other courts of appeals if the petition were denied. Rodd writes that "[a]t least one justice took the view that a court of appeals' opinion that is *not* 'blatantly outlandish' would be more worthy of a grant than one that is, on the theory that other courts of appeals would be likely to recognize truly egregious analysis."[66] Petitioners should take note of this observation—while it is somewhat counterintuitive, blasting a court of appeals' opinion as "egregious" could ultimately prove counterproductive in trying to secure review and detracts from the petition's credibility. The better approach is to depict the court of appeals' opinion as reflecting confusion in the law—confusion that, unless corrected, is bound to engender confusion among other courts of appeals as well.
5. The case presents a genuine constitutional issue for review. "Uniformly, the justices consider constitutional issues generally important."[67]
6. The case involves an issue that is emerging nationally, and allows the Court to decide whether Texas will participate in a nationwide trend. Rodd advises that "[a] practitioner who wishes to rely on a nationwide trend to pique the Court's interest might consider including a tabular compilation describing the other 50 states' treatment of the issue. The law clerk who is ultimately directed

to conduct a 50-state search will undoubtedly be grateful for the assistance. Moreover, the Court is generally interested in knowing what, if anything, the relevant Restatement would say about a particular issue."[68]

7. The case allows the Court to clarify one of its own opinions that is being misinterpreted by the trial courts or courts of appeals. Since this is the type of case that would appropriate for a per curiam opinion, Rodd advises that "[a] litigant might improve his or her chances of obtaining relief from an unfavorable court of appeals' decision by arguing that the case would be appropriate for per curiam disposition."[69]

Another argument for a "grant" is to point out that there is already a granted petition pending before the Court involving the same controlling issue. Properly crafted so as to flag the attention of the Court to the pending case, a "me too" petition may well be pulled from the conveyor belt and "held" until resolution of that case.

Statistics suggest that many of the justices believe that the Court has an error-correction responsibility. Per curiam opinions, which are an ideal vehicle for error correction, have comprised a substantial portion of the Court's decisions in recent years. If counsel for a petitioner is faced with a case calling for error correction, the best practice may be to angle for a per curiam opinion. The recommended approach is to make any such suggestion gingerly or, even better, implicitly, by crafting the petition so that a per curiam opinion could be readily drafted based on the petition.

Angling for a per curiam opinion can be accomplished by focusing the petition on a single issue and demonstrating that the court of appeals' decision on that point is clearly erroneous and requires reversal, rather than arguing that the issue is worthy of a grant. There could be an unintended downside to directly arguing that the case should be resolved by per curiam opinion—such an opinion requires six votes and, thus, in a close case counsel could be shooting the client in the foot by asking for a disposition that requires more than a simple majority of votes.

If this optional section is included in the petition, it will count against the petition's 4,500-word limit.[70]

14-2:2.9 Statement of Facts

Rule 53.2(g) provides, "The petition must affirm that the court of appeals correctly stated the nature of the case, except in any particulars pointed out. The petition must state concisely and without argument the facts and procedural background pertinent to the issues or points presented. The statement must be supported by record references."[71]

The statement of facts is the first required section that counts against the petition's 4,500-word limit.[72]

The rules require that the petitioner either state agreement with the court of appeals' rendition of the facts or specify which facts are contested. But the petition should not rely too heavily on the court of appeals' rendition of the facts.

The petition's statement of facts should be freestanding. Several of the justices read the petition first and then turn to the court of appeals' opinion only if something in the petition sufficiently attracts their interest to proceed further. For these justices, a petition is inadequate if it merely refers the Court to the court of appeals' opinion for a recitation of the facts—in effect, the petition provides no factual context for these justices, and they may be disinclined to accept the invitation to turn elsewhere to find that context.

The statement of facts should include only those facts necessary to frame the issues presented in the petition and demonstrate the importance of those issues to the jurisprudence of the state. The facts should be presented in an uncomplicated fashion but should not be oversimplified.

Each fact stated in the statement of facts must be supported by a record reference.

Although every portion of the petition should be designed to persuade the Court to exercise its jurisdiction, the statement of facts must not include any argument,[73] and should disclose all key facts, even the important facts favorable to the respondent. Of course, the petitioner should always avoid exaggerating or inaccurately describing any facts. With nine chambers reviewing each petition, the ever-present danger inherent in misrepresenting the record is magnified. Nothing threatens to torpedo a petition more quickly than misrepresenting the record, and nothing places more at risk the credibility of a practitioner in future proceedings than playing fast and loose with the facts in the present one. The justices do remember.

The statement of facts must include a brief summary of the relevant procedural history. The practitioner should use the required recitation of the case's procedural history to reassure the justices that the issues presented to the Court in the petition were preserved for appeal in the courts below, if preservation was necessary. Under the rules, a motion for rehearing in the court of appeals is not required to preserve error.[74] Nonetheless, if a motion for rehearing was filed and disposed of, this procedural development should be described in the statement of facts.

14-2:2.10 Summary of the Argument

A petition for review must include a "succinct, clear, and accurate" summary of the argument.[75]

Because of the word limitations for the petition for review, the summary of the argument should seldom exceed one page. The summary should succinctly explain how the court of appeals or trial court or both got it wrong and why the Supreme Court should care. At this juncture in the proceedings, the facts of the particular case are less important. You should not challenge the court of appeals' decision as being unjust to your client, but rather as constituting an erroneous and unjust application of the law, which will be applied to future litigants.

The summary should not just regurgitate the headings in the argument section—the summary needs to be independently crafted. Because of the constraints on their time, certain justices may scrutinize this section in particular to determine whether the petition merits being pulled from the conveyor belt.

14-2:2.11 Argument

Rule 53.2(h) requires that the petition include a "clear and concise" argument for the parties and "the reasons why the Supreme Court should exercise jurisdiction to hear the case with specific reference to the factors listed in Rule 56.1(a)."[76] The argument need not address every issue in the statement of issues.[77]

In the petition the space actually available for the argument will be 4,500 words, *less* whatever space is consumed by the Reasons to Grant Review, Statement of Facts, Summary of Argument, and Prayer, all of which also count toward the page limitation.[78] Moreover, given that the justices would prefer to receive even shorter petitions, if possible, the argument should ultimately be even tighter still.

Incorporating charts or tables into a petition for review can help grab a justice's attention. Incorporating them into full briefing also increases the chances of the law clerk incorporating the relevant chart or table into the study memo.

The rule regarding petitions for review expressly states that "[t]he argument should state the reasons why the Supreme Court should exercise jurisdiction. . . ."[79] Given the importance of showing jurisprudential importance, as described above, it may be useful to include a stand-alone section at the outset of the petition entitled Reasons to Grant Review. That section can be devoted to explaining why the Court should exercise its discretionary jurisdiction.

Rule 53.2(h) states that the petition "must contain a clear and concise argument for the contentions made. . . ." If the petition contains a section such as "Reasons to Grant," the Argument section can be devoted to addressing the merits of the case.

For practical reasons, counsel should limit the argument of issues to the best one or two. If an attempt is made to brief more than that in the limited space available, the argument will suffer; it will appear granulated and superficial. Fact-specific issues are better left for the brief on the merits stage because they won't jump out to the justices as being issues of importance at the petition stage.

In crafting the merits argument, counsel should be particularly mindful of the forest rather than the trees. The goal at the petition stage is not to address all issues fully. Rather, the goal is to capture the attention of the Court and secure an invitation from the Court to provide a full brief on the merits under Rule 55. This does not mean, however, that the argument can afford to touch only lightly on the merits of the case. Counsel must carefully craft both the Reasons to Grant Review and the Argument on the merits. They are ultimately inextricably related. Collectively, they should be calculated to persuade the Court to hear the case.

14-2:2.12 Prayer

Rule 53.2(j) requires a short conclusion stating "the nature of the relief sought."[80] The prayer should be crafted with extraordinary care. The Court's power to grant the petitioner relief is circumscribed by the relief requested.[81] The petitioner must consider carefully what the Court must do to grant the petitioner effective relief and then request just that.

If the Court can render judgment in favor of petitioner, the petitioner should request a rendition. If effective relief requires that all or part of the case be remanded, the petitioner should request that action specifically. In those cases in which various issues give rise to various dispositions, the prayer should include alternative requests for relief. Care should be taken to draft a prayer that does not conflict with the relief suggested by the argument and does not ask for relief that the Court cannot grant.

A prayer for an invitation to file a brief on the merits is not necessary to preserve an opportunity to do so. If it wants full briefing, the Court will request it.

A prayer for general relief is not necessary. If the petitioner fails to ask the Court for the necessary relief, a general prayer will not help.

14-2:2.13 Signature

Under petition practice, *who* signs first matters. The rules incorporate the concept of "lead counsel" for purposes of receiving any notice and copies of documents filed in the appellate court.[82] In the Supreme Court, unless another attorney is designated, lead counsel for the petitioner is the attorney whose signature first appears on the first document filed in the Supreme Court which, in most cases, will be the petition.[83] Other attorneys may sign the petition as well, although the presence or absence of such signatures has no practical consequences under the rules.

This signature does not count against the 4,500-word limit.[84]

With mandatory electronic filing, few documents require an actual signature.[85] For paper filings, the clerk's office strongly encourages signing documents in blue ink so that they can distinguish the original from copies. It is difficult to distinguish copies of felt-tip black signatures from the original.

14-2:2.14 Certificate of Service

Rule 9.5(e) requires detailed information in the certificate of service. It must be signed by the person who made the service and must state:

(1) the date and manner of service;

(2) the name and address of each person served; and

(3) if the person served is a party's attorney, the name of the party represented by that attorney.[86]

The certificate of service does not count against the 4,500-word limit.[87]

Now that electronic copies of all petitions for review documents must be filed with the Court, in addition to the methods of service permitted by Rule 53.6, the certificate should reflect that a copy of the petition or other document is being served by email.

14-2:2.15 Certificate of Compliance

Rule 9.4(i)(3) requires:

> A computer-generated document must include a certificate by counsel or an unrepresented party stating the number of words in the document. The person certifying may rely on the word count of the computer program used to prepare the document.[88]

This rule was added as part of the Court's new word-count limitations.[89]

14-2:2.16 Appendix

As reflected in the rules quoted below, the appendix to a petition for review includes both necessary and optional contents. Rule 53.2(k) provides:

(1) *Necessary contents.* Unless voluminous or impracticable, the appendix must contain a copy of:

(A) the judgment or other appealable order of the trial court from which relief in the court of appeals was sought;

(B) the jury charge and verdict, if any, or the trial court's findings of fact and conclusions of law, if any;

(C) the opinion and judgment of the court of appeals; and

(D) the text of any rule, regulation, ordinance, statute, constitutional provision, or other law on which the argument is based (excluding case law), and the text of any contract or other document that is central to the argument.

(2) *Optional contents.* The appendix may contain any other item pertinent to the issues or points presented for review, including copies or excerpts of relevant court opinions, statutes, constitutional provisions, documents on which the suit was based, pleadings, and similar material. Items should not be included in the appendix to attempt to avoid the page limits for the petition.[90]

The appellate rules require the petition and appendix to be combined into a single computer file.[91] Before mandatory electronic filing, several justices expressed their displeasure at parties filing particularly bulky appendices. With electronic filing, however, the size of and number of items in an appendix are generally no longer problems.[92]

An electronically filed appendix must contain bookmarks to assist in locating each item.[93] When the petition refers to materials in the appendix, be sure to include the tab number or letter in the citation for ease of reference. Specifically, in the statement of the case, refer the Court to the tab numbers or letters where the order of the trial court and the opinion and judgment of the court of appeals are attached. Incorporating hyperlinks to the index tab for these items will be helpful to the screen reader.

Include copies of constitutional provisions, statutes, regulations, and ordinances only if the petition may require the justices to look at the text of the statute.[94] As a general rule, though, do not include copies if the argument is not based on the interpretation of the text of these provisions. On the other hand, if the resolution of an issue requires the interpretation of a controlling statute, regulation, or ordinance—and most especially one that has been superseded and, thus, is difficult to find—a copy should be included in the appendix.

The rule specifically excludes case law from the necessary contents of the appendix. But with the transition to e-filing, it can be helpful to include key cases in the appendix that can be readily accessed through the inclusion of hyperlinks in the text.

If the argument turns on the language of a contract or other document, it is sufficient to include the text of the pertinent provisions; it is not necessary to attach the entire document. However, if it is important to view the controlling language in context, counsel should include a copy of the entire document at issue, rather than merely quote the pertinent text. If the Court is being asked, for example, to interpret a clause in an insurance policy, it helps see a copy of the entire policy.

With mandatory electronic filing, counsel should be mindful of another recurring problem—PDFs of documents such as contracts and leases are frequently barely legible. Thus, counsel must be mindful to review electronic appendices before the brief is e-filed. If it is worth attaching to your brief, it is worth making sure it can be read. If only a portion of a lengthy oil and gas lease is relevant to your case, think about retyping that portion under a separate appendix tab, or within a text box added to the original document. The justices and staff will always appreciate efforts to ensure that the content of the appendix is readable.

All electronically filed appendix sources must be text-searchable.[95] Counsel should ensure that optical character recognition (OCR) software is run on any scanned document that must be included within an appendix. Otherwise, the scanned document will not be text-searchable. Also, it is helpful to the justices if each reference to an appendix in the text is hyperlinked to the appendix itself.

14-3 Response to Petition

A party may, but is not required to, file a response to a petition for review.[96] The petition will not be granted without a response being filed or requested by the Court.[97] Thus, one does not risk a grant of review by failing to respond to a petition. The expressly voluntary nature of the response under petition for review practice raises a number of strategic issues, which are addressed below.

14-3:1 Whether to File a Response

The justices of the Supreme Court are accustomed to parties electing not to file a response to the petition unless requested. Thus, a party need not fear offending the justices or appearing to concede the merits of the petition by electing not to file a response. Many petitions are disposed of after the justices have reviewed the petition and the court of appeals decision, without a response having been filed or requested by the Court. Moreover, one should not view with alarm a request for a response—it takes the vote of only one justice to request one.

Because there is no material downside to declining to file a response, and the responding party can save attorney's fees by not filing one, the presumption should be against filing one. However, there are a number of "stopper" factors that may rebut this presumption—factors which, if available, should preclude the Court from reaching the merits of the case. The late and legendary appellate practitioner Rusty McMains referred to these as the "pillars of affirmance."[98]

If the petition self-evidently involves no issue of substantial jurisprudential importance, the presumption should remain not to file a response. If, on the other hand, the petition appears to involve a jurisprudentially important issue and one or more of the "stopper" factors are legitimately available, counsel should seriously consider filing a response to address them. Each of the factors is addressed below.

14-3:1.1 Respond if Petitioner Failed to Preserve Error

The Supreme Court has substantially relaxed the technical requirements for preserving legal issues for review by the Court. Nonetheless, it is not unknown for overzealous petitioner's counsel to seek relief in the Supreme Court by presenting legal complaints that were not presented to the court of appeals. In such a case, the lack of preservation should be cleanly presented to Court as a factor that precludes its review.

14-3:1.2 Respond if Petitioner Cannot Survive Correct Standard of Review

In some cases, the petitioner will advocate a position that, at least superficially, sounds compelling, but cannot survive appellate scrutiny when the correct standard of review is applied. For example, petitioner may argue that a particular issue presents solely a legal question governed by a de novo standard of review, when, in fact, the issue was one relegated to the trial court's sound discretion, and the much more exacting abuse-of-discretion standard applies.[99]

14-3:1.3 Respond if, Though the Courts Below May Have Erred, the Error Is Harmless

It is not uncommon for a petition for review to argue how the court of appeals erred in affirming the trial court but fail to take the additional step of demonstrating how the error was reversibly harmful.[100]

In arguing harmless error, a respondent should not merely state in conclusory fashion that the petitioner has failed to demonstrate how the error is reversibly harmful. Counsel should go further and provide the Court with sufficient context to demonstrate how the result in the case probably would have been the same even if the claimed error had not occurred.

14-3:1.4 Respond if Stare Decisis Compels Affirmance of Court of Appeals' Decision or Denial of Review

Angling for a grant, the petition may argue that the case presents a legal issue of first impression when, in fact, controlling precedent compels affirmance of the court of appeals' decision. In making a stare decisis argument, however, respondent should exercise caution. First, the Texas Supreme Court does not view decisions by intermediate courts of appeals as binding on the Court. Second, even if there is Supreme Court precedent supporting denial of review, it may not be enough to point out, in conclusory fashion, that the precedent exists and compels that result. It is more effective to point out the controlling effect of the precedent and explain why the Court should decline to depart from that precedent.

14-3:1.5 Respond if an Independent Ground for Affirmance Exists

Assume, for example, that the petitioner has made a superficially compelling argument for reversal of a summary judgment based on ground X, but simply ignores independent grounds for affirmance Y and Z. This affords a ripe opportunity for the respondent to argue that, regardless of what the Court might feel about ground X, the Court should decline to grant review on that basis because other grounds compel affirmance. In every case, the respondent should analyze whether the petitioner has overlooked a ground for affirmance that torpedoes the petition.

14-3:1.6 When to File a Waiver of Response

Under the rules, the response or response waiver is due 30 days after the petition for review is filed.[101] Alternatively, the respondent can elect to do nothing in response to the petition. The petition will be forwarded to the justices for review upon either (1) the filing of the response or response waiver, or (2) allowing 30 days to pass without filing either. If the respondent elects to file a response waiver, the question arises of when to file it.

If the respondent elects to file a response waiver and desires the Court to review and dispose of the petition as quickly as possible, a response waiver should be filed immediately.

If, on the other hand, the respondent would like to take as long as possible to prepare and file the response if one is requested later, the respondent can wait until the last day of the 30-day deadline to file the waiver. The clock will not start ticking anew on the deadline for filing the response unless and until the Court requests a response.

An intermediate approach is to wait some "tasteful" period of time (e.g., two weeks) before filing the response waiver, so as not to give the appearance to the justices of trying to drag out the process as long as possible. Even under this intermediate approach, the clock will not start ticking anew unless and until the Court requests a response.

The justices agree that the response waiver need not be elaborate. A simple letter to the clerk, filed electronically, stating that the respondent waives the filing of a response will suffice.

14-3:2 How to Respond

In the event the respondent elects to file a response, or if the Court requests one, the next issue counsel faces is how to respond. The initial goal of the response is to dissuade the Court from granting review. The secondary goal is to persuade the Court that the court of appeals reached the correct result on the merits. These two goals serve the same ultimate purpose—to persuade the Court that it should decline to exercise its discretionary jurisdiction.[102]

14-3:2.1 Additional Arguments to Dissuade the Court From Granting Review

As discussed above, if a "stopper" argument is available—one of the "pillars of affirmance"—then that argument should be included in the response. But there are other arguments that can be made as well. The principal additional dissuasive arguments are discussed below.

14-3:2.1a The Case Is Fact-Intensive

If the case is fact-intensive, the likelihood of the Court granting review is substantially diminished. A case is fact-intensive if its outcome turns not on some over-arching legal dispute that is likely to recur, but rather on how the fact-finder weighed and resolved the disputed evidence or discretionary issue in this isolated case. However, counsel must be judicious in arguing that the case is fact-intensive, given that at least some justices believe there is still an error-correction role for the Court in cases involving what is perceived to be truly egregious error. Thus, arguing that the case is not "jurisprudentially important" may not be sufficient—counsel should go further and explain how at least rough justice was achieved in the decision below so that it should not be disturbed.

14-3:2.1b The Purported Conflict Among Appellate Courts Is Illusory

It is common for a petitioner to argue that the Supreme Court should grant review to resolve a purported conflict among appellate court decisions. If, in fact, the purported conflict is illusory, counsel should forcefully demonstrate this point as a ground for the Court to deny review. For example, if two courts of appeals reached different results simply because differing facts compelled those results, counsel should explain how the decisions can be reconciled and do not present a conflict.

14-3:2.1c The Issue of First Impression Should "Percolate"

The petitioner may well argue that the case presents an issue of first impression in Texas when, in fact, it does not. But what if the case does genuinely present an issue of first impression? In that case, the responding party may be able to persuasively argue that the issue should be allowed to "percolate" by being addressed by more than one intermediate appellate court before being addressed by the Supreme Court. The "percolation" argument should be made when the legal issue, while interesting, is not of immediate importance to the state's jurisprudence.

In evaluating whether it is important, counsel should consider two key questions. If the decision below is left undisturbed, is that likely to serve as a beacon to other litigants, encouraging similar suits? For example, if the court of appeals' decision recognizes a new tort duty in Texas that is likely to give rise to a whole new arena of litigation, it will usually be implausible to argue that the Supreme Court should simply disregard the issue until other courts have weighed in. Have other jurisdictions confronted and resolved the legal issue? If the issue is one that has received attention in a large number of other courts throughout the country, it is more difficult to argue that the Supreme Court should stay out of the debate until other intermediate courts of appeals in Texas have expressed their views.

But if the court of appeals' decision adopts what is a clear majority position, or one that is part of an unmistakable trend, it becomes more plausible to argue that other intermediate courts of appeals should address the issue before the Supreme Court does, particularly if the issue is not one that arises with great frequency. If the argument can credibly be made, it can be effective to show why this particular case is not the best case to resolve the question.

14-3:2.1d The Issue of Jurisprudential Importance Does Not Permit a Clean Review

It is not uncommon for an issue of jurisprudential importance to be properly preserved for the Supreme Court's review, but, nevertheless, the Court cannot reach and resolve that issue cleanly. For example, there may be alternative grounds for affirmance that preclude the court from reaching the "interesting" ground. In such a case, counsel should argue in the response that the Court should await another case that more cleanly presents the "important" issue for the Court's review.

14-3:2.1e The Court of Appeals Correctly Resolved the Legal Issue

This is the argument that should be resorted to in seeking to dissuade the Court from taking the case, when a candid review of the petition leads to the conclusion that none of the other dissuasive arguments can legitimately be asserted. When the other arguments are not available, and the respondent is the fortunate beneficiary of a solid court of appeals' decision, counsel should forcefully argue that the court of appeals not only reached the right result on the merits, but that its legal analysis is sound and should stand as the correct statement of Texas law on the point. Properly asserted and supported in the right case, this argument can dissuade the Court from taking the case, even when all other factors appear to point toward a grant.

14-3:2.2 Developing a Persuasive Response

If the practitioner elects to file a response, or if the Court requests one, the contents are the same as that of the petition, with enumerated exceptions.[103] Like the petition, the response is limited to a total of 4,500 words, exclusive of the same specified sections.[104]

The various sections of the response should be developed in a fashion that creates a persuasive whole. Selected sections of the response are discussed below with discussion of the strategy considerations associated with each.

14-3:2.2a Table of Contents

The response must include a table of contents.[105] The headings should be in narrative format, and when read as a whole, should clearly convey why the case does not merit the Court's review and why the responding party prevails on the merits.

14-3:2.2b Statement of the Case

Technically, the response need not include a statement of the case "unless the responding party is dissatisfied with that portion of the petition."[106] As a practical matter, however, the responding party should rarely be "satisfied" with the petitioner's statement.

The re-tooled statement of the case should be in tabular form. It should be brief and non-argumentative. However, the various elements of the statement should be drafted in such a fashion that the case sounds unexceptional and does not warrant review.

14-3:2.2c Statement of Jurisdiction

The rule regarding the response to a petition for review provides that "a statement of jurisdiction should be omitted unless the petition fails to assert valid grounds for jurisdiction, in which case the reasons why the Supreme Court lacks jurisdiction must be concisely stated."[107] Whether to include a jurisdictional statement presents a strategy decision on which there is a split of opinion.

Under one school of thought, including a jurisdictional statement in the response should be reserved for that relatively rare case which is a bona fide candidate for dismissal for want of jurisdiction. Under another school of thought, the statement of jurisdiction should be used by the responding party as a means to dissuade the Court from granting review.

As a general rule, we incline toward the first view. The justices can be irritated when a respondent abuses the reader's valuable time by using the jurisdiction section to make arguments that should be reserved for the argument section of the brief. In their view, contesting jurisdiction should be reserved for the exceptional case when it would be worth a separate motion to dismiss for want of jurisdiction. If a conflict of decisions among the courts of appeals is a basis for granting review invoked by the petitioner and the conflict is illusory, it suffices to say in the statement of jurisdiction in the response that the conflict is illusory and will be discussed in greater detail in the argument section.

14-3:2.2d Issues Presented

The rule regarding issues in a response to a petition for review is complicated—"a statement of the issues presented need not be made unless: (1) the respondent is dissatisfied with the statement made in the petition; (2) the respondent is asserting independent grounds for affirmance of the court of appeals' judgment; or (3) the respondent is asserting grounds that establish the respondent's right to a judgment that is less favorable to the respondent than the judgment rendered by the court of appeals but more favorable to the respondent than the judgment that might be awarded to the petitioner (e.g., a remand for a new trial rather than a rendition of judgment in favor of the petitioner)."[108]

Each of these exceptions is addressed below.

(i) Dissatisfaction with the Statement of Issues in the Petitioner's Brief

In most cases, the party responding to a petition for review will want to recast the issues framed by the petitioner. A possible exception is when the petitioner is the beneficiary of a favorable standard of review—for example, when the court of appeals has affirmed a summary judgment against the plaintiff-petitioner. In such a case, if the petitioner has fairly framed the issue, it may be more powerful for the respondent to argue that, even with the standard of review favoring the petitioner, the respondent nonetheless wins.

When the exception does not apply, the responding party should recast the issue in a manner designed to dissuade the Court from granting review. In this regard, it is useful to revisit the list of arguments militating against the Court's exercise of discretionary jurisdiction.[109]

(ii) Asserting independent grounds for affirmance

The "pillars of affirmance" addressed above implicate the second of the reasons for the respondent to present issues—"asserting independent grounds for affirmance." An example was provided above—the petitioner makes a compelling argument for reversal of a summary judgment on ground X, but ignores independent grounds for affirmance Y and Z.[110]

(iii) Entitlement to judgment less favorable than that rendered by the court of appeals but more favorable than that sought by petitioner

The third of the reasons for a response to present issues is more technical than the first two. The following hypothetical illustrates its operation: Assume (1) respondent was the defendant in the trial court, (2) the jury returned a verdict in favor of the plaintiff for $1 million, (3) the trial court granted defendant's motion for judgment n.o.v. that plaintiff take nothing, (4) the court of appeals affirmed the take-nothing judgment, and (5) the petitioner complains to the Supreme Court that the take-nothing judgment was erroneous and that the Court should reverse and render judgment in favor of petitioner on the jury's verdict.

Under these circumstances, in addition to arguing that the take-nothing judgment was proper, the respondent may wish to argue that even if the take-nothing judgment were set aside, rather than reversing and rendering judgment in favor of the petitioner, legitimate grounds exist for remand for a new trial. If this path is taken, the respondent should set forth as issues in response those grounds entitling the respondent to a new trial in the event the Supreme Court sets aside the take-nothing judgment.

14-3:2.2e Introduction to Body of Response

Although this section is not mentioned in the rules, as a matter of strategy, the responding party will generally want to include on the first page of the body of the response an introduction that hits the Court between the eyes with why the Court should decline to take the case. This section can be captioned "Reasons to Deny Review."

14-3:2.2f Statement of Facts

The governing rules provide that a statement of facts need not be included unless the responding party is dissatisfied with that portion of the petition.[111] Rarely should the responding party be satisfied with the petitioner's statement of facts. The response will generally include a newly crafted statement of facts that frames the issues from the responding party's perspective. It can be effective to point out where the parties disagree on the facts.

One exception is when the governing standard of review effectively compels the Court to review the record facts in the light most favorable to the petitioner. In such a case, it can be strategically powerful to expressly accept the petitioner's statement of facts (assuming it fairly characterizes the record) and argue that the petitioner loses as a matter of law in any event. On the other hand, if the standard of review precludes the petitioner's reliance on contested or contradicted facts, the responding party should use the statement of facts to establish that the petitioner's statement does not meet that standard, by pointing out the disputed facts on which the petitioner relies.

14-3:2.2g Summary of the Argument

The response to the petition for review must include a summary of the argument.[112] The summary should succinctly explain why the case is not worthy of the Court's exercise of its discretionary jurisdiction or, failing that, why the decision below was correct. Due to word-count constraints, the responding party should endeavor to limit the summary to one page.

14-3:2.2h Argument

The responding party's argument should follow the same basic format as that suggested for the petition. The argument must be confined to those issues raised in the petition or those raised by the respondent in the statement of issues section of the response.[113] The overarching objective of any response is, of course, to persuade the Court that the relief requested in the petition should be denied. In developing the argument section of the response, the responding party should consider each of the various arguments discussed above for dissuading the Court from taking the case.

14-3:2.2i Prayer

The rules provide that the response "must contain a short conclusion that clearly states the nature of the relief sought."[114] In most cases, the response's prayer will simply request the Court to deny the petition for review. When, however, the respondent is asserting grounds that establish the respondent's right to a judgment less favorable than that rendered by the court of appeals but more favorable than the disposition sought by the petitioner, the prayer should include an appropriate alternative request for relief.

A strategy question associated with the prayer is whether to include any argument that serves as a final punctuation of the core reason(s) that the Court should deny review. Properly crafted and kept short, such a concluding statement right before the requested relief can make for an effective conclusion to the response.

14-3:2.2j Appendix

The burden falls on the petitioner to prepare an appendix that includes the "necessary" contents prescribed by the governing rules, as well as any "optional" ones.[115] In many cases, the responding party will elect not to include any additional matters in the response. The responding party must be mindful of the potential backfiring effect of independently providing a lengthy appendix: it may make an otherwise "ungrantworthy" case appear "weighty" and therefore "important."

That cautionary note aside, a well-focused appendix can be effective in the right case. For example, in a case involving a contract dispute, if a particular provision of the contract blows the petitioner's argument out of the water, not only should that provision be quoted in the argument section of the response, but it should also be attached as an appendix.

14-3:2.3 Filing a Cross-Petition

Any party that seeks to alter the court of appeals' *judgment* must file a petition for review.[116] Under the rules, if one party has filed a petition, any other party may file a successive petition within 30 days thereafter or within 45 days after the overruling of the last timely filed motion for rehearing, whichever is later.[117] There may well be occasions when a respondent elects to file both a response to a petition and a cross-petition independently complaining of some portion of the court of appeals' judgment—for example, where the court of appeals affirms a judgment in the respondent's favor for actual damages but strikes an award of attorney fees.

In those circumstances when the respondent elects to file both, the question arises whether the response should be filed with the cross-petition in a single document or whether the two should be filed separately. The rules provide no guidance on this point. But the clerk's office has—the documents should be separately filed.

14-4 Reply in Support of Petition for Review

The rules provide no guide as to what should be included in the reply. As a practical matter, it need include nothing more than argument—a complete petition will have provided the Court with everything else necessary to furnish the requested relief. Rather than repeat matters already set forth in the petition, the reply should hone in directly on matters set forth in the response begging attack. The 2,400-word limit encourages focused attack.[118]

An important exception to this general rule is when the response fails to join issue on an important argument made in the petition. In such a case, the response should highlight the argument(s) to which the respondent failed to meaningfully respond.

Like the response, the filing of a reply is not mandatory. If nothing meaningful would be added to the Court's consideration of the petition by filing a reply to the response, none should be filed. This, however, will infrequently be the case. The Court is free to act on the petition before receiving the reply.[119]

To ensure that the reply is actually considered by the Court, the petitioner should not unduly delay in filing it. But if petitioner's counsel absolutely needs extra time to reply, a motion for extension of time (ideally not exceeding 15 days) should be filed as soon as reasonably possible so that the Court can adjust the date for action on the petition to accommodate the justice's consideration of the reply under the extended deadline.

14-5 Basic Requirements for Supreme Court Filing

14-5:1 Formatting and E-Filing

Chapter 16 addresses formatting and e-filing requirements that now apply in all Texas appellate courts, including the Supreme Court.

14-5:2 Deadlines

The following deadlines apply to the various filings under petition for review practice unless the clerk's notice directs otherwise. The Court can shorten the briefing deadlines if it wishes.

- *Petition for review:* 45 days from the later of the date of the court of appeals' judgment or its last ruling on a timely filed motion for rehearing or rehearing en banc.[120]
- *Successive petitions:* 45 days after the last timely motion for rehearing is overruled or 30 days after any preceding petition is filed, whichever date is later.[121]
- *Response to petition:* 30 days after the petition is filed.[122]
- *Reply to response:* 15 days after the response is filed.[123]
- *Petitioner's brief on the merits:* 30 days after the date of the clerk's notice that the Court has requested briefs on the merits.[124]
- *Respondent's brief on the merits:* 20 days after receiving petitioner's brief.[125]
- *Reply brief:* 15 days after receiving respondent's brief.[126]
- *Motion for rehearing:* 15 days from the date when the Court renders judgment or makes an order disposing of a petition for review.[127]

"Unless a document must be filed by a certain time of day, a document will be considered filed timely if it is electronically filed at any time before midnight (in the court's time zone) on the filing deadline."[128] If a document is electronically filed on Saturday, Sunday, or an official holiday, then it will be deemed filed on the next day that is not a Saturday, Sunday, or legal holiday.[129]

14-5:3 Motions to Extend Time (METs)

The Court has assigned most METs to the clerk for disposition. Motions should have a certificate of conference and make clear in the body of the motion whether the motion is opposed or unopposed.[130] If the motion is unopposed, that should also be noted in the title of the motion to assist the clerk in expediting it. Also, it is helpful to the clerk for the first paragraph of the motion to state (1) when the document is due; (2) the length of the extension sought; and (3) the new deadline if the extension is granted. If a MET is opposed, the clerk's office will inquire whether opposing counsel intends to file any opposition. No MET to file a petition for review is ever denied without the Court's approval.

Technically, the rules permit extension motions to be filed even after expiration of the various deadlines for filing. However, no practitioner should ever take advantage of the grace periods because the clerk's office and the Court would view that with disfavor. Similarly, while the Court is relatively generous with granting extensions, counsel should avoid taking undue advantage of that generosity. Subject to those caveats, the following are deadlines involving petition for review filings, and the clerk's general rules applicable to unopposed METs:

- *Petition for review:* No later than 15 days after the last day for filing the petition.[131] If the MET is unopposed, the first extension will generally be granted for up to 30 days. A second will also be granted for up to 30 days, but the grant notice will include "standard" language informing the movant that further requests for extension will be disfavored.
- *Response to petition:* At any time before or after the response is due.[132] An unopposed MET will be granted for up to 30 days; the grant notice will include the standard language about further requests being disfavored.
- *Reply to response:* At any time before or after the reply is due.[133] An extension of up to 15 days for filing the reply will routinely be granted. The Court will adjust the date for action on the petition to accommodate the justices' consideration of the reply under the extended deadline.
- *Petitioner's brief on the merits:* At any time before or after the brief is due.[134] Unopposed METs will be granted for up to 30 days and the standard language about further requests being disfavored is included.
- *Respondent's brief on the merits:* At any time before or after the brief is due.[135] Unopposed METs will be granted for up to 30 days and the standard language about further requests being disfavored is included.
- *Reply brief on the merits:* At any time before or after the brief is due.[136] The clerk's office will inform the chambers to which the study memo is assigned about the MET and will grant an unopposed MET for up to 30 days (although 15 days is preferred), unless instructed not to do so. If granted, the notice will contain the standard language about further requests being disfavored.
- *Motion for rehearing:* No later than 15 days after the last date for filing a motion for rehearing.[137] If rehearing is sought of a cause or per curiam decision, the chambers that authored the majority or per curiam opinion will decide whether to grant the MET. If rehearing is sought of the denial of a petition, the clerk's office processes the MET. The first unopposed MET is granted for up to 30

days; the letter includes the standard language about further requests being disfavored.

14-5:4 Amendment

On motion showing good cause, the Court may allow a party to amend, on such reasonable terms as the Court may prescribe, the petition for review, response, reply, or any of the briefs on the merits.[138] As with any appellate motion under the rules, the movant must comply with the requirements of Rule 10, including the provision of a certificate of conference.

14-6 Internal Procedures

14-6:1 Routing of Petitions

The clerk of the Supreme Court holds each petition for review for 30 days before forwarding it to the justices, unless a response or response waiver is filed before the expiration of 30 days. The first of these events to occur makes the petition "ripe" for review.

Once a petition is ripe, it will be forwarded to the justices electronically the next Tuesday morning. To trigger the forwarding of a petition to the justices on any given Tuesday, the response or waiver should be filed by around 4:00 p.m. the day before. When the petition is forwarded, it will be accompanied by the response or response waiver (if filed), and amicus submissions.

When the petition is electronically forwarded to the justices, the justices are also provided a pink vote sheet for that particular case.[139] The Court's administrative assistant also distributes to each member of the Court a purple vote sheet, which lists all matters being forwarded to the Court that week, including petitions for review, original proceedings, and other matters requiring action by the entire Court.[140]

The matters forwarded to the chambers each Tuesday morning include, on average, 15 petitions for review.

14-6:2 Action on Petitions

The Court employs a "conveyor belt" system in acting on petitions for review. Once a petition is placed in the hands of the justices on a given Tuesday, it begins moving along the conveyor belt. Unless it is affirmatively removed from the belt by one or more of the justices, the petition is automatically denied on the Court's Friday orders, 31 days after the justices first received it.

One or more of the justices can remove a petition from the conveyor belt by voting to take some action other than denying it. If any of the justices requests that a response be filed, that is sufficient to pull the case from the conveyor belt. The case is placed on a status-report list until the response is received or the deadline for filing the response has passed. At that point the case is placed on the Court's conference agenda for the first conference after the expiration of 30 days from the date the response is filed.

With the advent of mandatory electronic filing,[141] most of the justices obtain and read electronic copies of petitions on a personal computer or tablet. In addition, with courts of appeals opinions being available online, justices are often aware of matters that may come before the Court before a petition is filed.

14-6:3 Pink, Purple, and Yellow Vote Sheets

The Court employs vote sheets to note the justices' preferences about actions on petitions. The Court uses three different vote sheets, which serve three different functions. Under the Court's increasing use of technology, all of the justices ultimately mark their votes electronically. Thus, the sheets are mainly reflections of their electronic votes, although yellow sheets are always printed with the justices' votes before conference as a guide during conference when the justices discuss petitions. However, for purposes of understanding how the process works, it remains useful to refer to "pink," "purple," and "yellow" vote sheets, even though at least some of those physical sheets are being rendered obsolete by the ever-developing use of technology at the Court.

14-6:3.1 Pink Vote Sheet

A pink vote sheet accompanies each petition for review and motion for rehearing, and is the vote sheet for that particular case. The sheet is intended to be used by each of the justices reviewing the petition. It provides blanks for the reviewing justice to indicate the action deemed appropriate:

- deny;
- request response;
- request record;
- discuss at conference;
- request study memo;
- issue per curiam opinion;
- grant;
- dismiss for want of jurisdiction;
- refuse petition;
- hold; and
- dismiss petition on motion of party

The pink vote sheet also provides space for "remarks" by the reviewing justice—essentially space for notes the justice can use to refresh recollections about the case when the petition proceeds to conference. Some justices make notes on their computers. If briefs on the merits are requested in a particular case, the assigned law clerk is provided the pink vote sheets or electronically recorded notes of each of the justices to assist the clerk in preparing the study memo. Each justice's remarks may inform the law clerk as to which particular issues the justices are interested.

14-6:3.2 Purple Vote Sheet

Every Tuesday, each justice also receives a purple vote sheet on all matters forwarded to chambers that week. The sheet lists for action not only petitions for review, mandamus, and habeas corpus, but also rehearing motions, and other matters requiring action by the full Court. The purple vote sheet includes the same blanks as the pink vote sheet for the justices to record their preferred disposition.

The deadline for the purple vote sheet to be returned to the Court's administrative assistant is noon Tuesday, four weeks after the petition is first forwarded to the justices. If any justice votes to take any action other than denying a petition, the petition is removed from the conveyor belt. A justice's failure to mark a vote on a petition is treated as a vote to deny it.

As previously noted, virtually all of the justices nowcast their votes electronically. This has had an impact on the Court's deliberative process. With the use of a computerized system to record votes—votes which all of the justices can see—it is now possible for a justice to look over the shoulders of his or her colleagues to see how the voting is going on a particular matter. As the deadline for voting approaches, if a particular matter has attracted the interest of several justices, that may cause the reviewing justice to take a harder look at the petition and any response. If, on the other hand, no one has expressed interest in the case or there are a large number of votes for "deny," that may cause the reviewing justice to either review that petition in only cursory fashion or not at all.

The practical implications for counsel for petitioner are that even greater effort must be made today to craft a petition designed to attract the interest of the justices. If the initial group of justices to review the petition and cast votes is not interested, the herd effect may reduce the odds of the remaining justices developing interest.

14-6:3.3 Yellow Vote Sheet

The yellow vote sheet assists the Court's disposition of petitions and rehearing of denials of petitions. It is used to allow the justices, in advance of conference, to see how the other justices voted on matters previously recorded on purple vote sheets, and to record votes on circulated study memos due to be discussed at conference. The votes of the justices may change after circulation of study memos.

Petitions and rehearing motions that failed to make the initial cut—due to lack of a vote for anything other than "deny" on the purple vote sheets—will not be included on the yellow vote sheet. As for those petitions and rehearing motions that do make the initial cut, how the justices marked their purple vote sheets determines to which conference the matter proceeds. If any of the justices requests a response to a petition or rehearing motion, the matter is scheduled for the conference following the expiration of 30 days from the date the response is filed, with two exceptions. If a reply is filed before that 30 days expires, the matter may be scheduled for the next conference after the reply has been on file for as few as five days. If the petitioner obtains an extension of time to file the reply, the matter will be scheduled for the first conference following the filing of the reply. If the justices mark their purple vote sheets with anything other than "deny," the petition is placed on the conference agenda.

Those petitions and motions for rehearing of denial of a petition that make the initial cut and are ripe for discussion at the next scheduled conference are listed on the yellow vote sheet for that conference, along with any study memos that will be discussed at that conference. The Court's administrative assistant, by consulting the purple vote sheets, records on the yellow vote sheet how each justice voted on each petition and rehearing motion listed. With respect to study memos that are to be discussed, the administrative assistant lists the initial votes that had been cast before the study memo was prepared.

The yellow vote sheet is then circulated to all the justices. The justices, once they have had a chance to see how other justices have voted and review any study memos that have been circulated, are then at liberty to change their vote on a petition or rehearing of denial of petition motion. A new cumulative yellow vote sheet is then prepared, reflecting the updated votes, which is then used to guide the Court through the conference. Counsel should note that achieving a consensus by the justices that a petition should be denied is the quickest and easiest disposition for the Court.

14-6:4 Votes Required for Specific Actions

The following are the votes required for the Supreme Court to take specific actions on petitions for review:

Request Response	1
Request Record	1
Discuss	1
Request Briefs on the Merits	3
Grant Petition for Review	4
Dismiss Petition WOJ	5
Refuse Petition	6
Hold Petition	6
Deny Petition as Improvidently Granted	6
Issue Per Curiam Opinion	6
Issue Majority Opinion	5
Grant Rehearing of Denial of Petition	4
Grant Rehearing of Cause	6

Deny Petition: Automatic unless at least one vote for something other than "deny"

14-6:5 Odds of the Court Taking Specific Actions

Although the statistics vary some from year to year, the following are the odds of the Court taking the specific actions listed:

Requesting Petition for Review (PFR) response if not voluntarily filed:	1/3
Requesting Briefs on the Merits (BOM):	1/4
Granting PFR:	1/10
Granting PFR after response:	1/4
Granting PFR if BOM requested:	1/2
Affirming if granted:	1/5
Reversing if granted:	4/5
Granting motion for rehearing of PFR denial:	1/25
Granting motion for rehearing of cause:	1/33

Notes

1 *See* generally Chapter 15.

2 Justice Craig T. Enoch & Michael S. Truesdale, *Issues and Petitions: The Impact on Supreme Court Practice*, 31 St. Mary's L.J. 565, 568 (2000).

3 Remarks of Justice Hecht to the Supreme Court Advisory Committee, Transcript of May 10, 1994, at 4763–64 (quoted in Pamela Stanton Baron, *Drafting Issues in the Texas Supreme Court*, State Bar of Tex. Prof. Dev. Program, 15th Annual Advanced Civil Appellate Practice Course, ch. 6 at 2 (2001).

4 Tex. R. App. P. 9.4(i)(2)(D).

5 Chief Justice Thomas R. Phillips, *Thinking Inside the Box: A Review of the Supreme Court's Caseload Statistics and What Those Numbers Mean in Real Life*, State Bar of Tex. Prof. Dev. Program, Practice Before the Supreme Court of Texas, ch. 1 at 5 (2002).

6 Chief Justice Thomas R. Phillips, *Thinking Inside the Box: A Review of the Supreme Court's Caseload Statistics and What Those Numbers Mean in Real Life*, State Bar of Tex. Prof. Dev. Program, Practice Before the Supreme Court of Texas, ch. 1 at 5 (2002).

7 Chief Justice Thomas R. Phillips, *Thinking Inside the Box: A Review of the Supreme Court's Caseload Statistics and What Those Numbers Mean in Real Life*, State Bar of Tex. Prof. Dev. Program, Practice Before the Supreme Court of Texas, ch. 1 at 5 (2002).

8 *See* Tex. R. App. P. 9.4(i)(4).

9 Tex. R. App. P. 9.4(i)(1).

10 Tex. R. App. P. 9.4(g).

11 Tex. R. App. P. 9.4(g).

12 Tex. R. App. P. 9.4(f).

13 Tex. R. App. P. 53.2(a).

14 Tex. R. App. P. 9.4(i)(1).

15 Tex. R. App. P. 53.2(b).

16 *See* § 14-2:1.2.

17 Tex. R. App. P. 53.2(b).

18 Tex. R. App. P. 9.4(i)(1).

19 Tex. R. App. P. 53.2(c).

20 Tex. R. App. P. 9.4(i)(1).

21 Tex. R. App. P. 53.2(d).

22 Tex. R. App. P. 53.2(d)(5).

23 Tex. R. App. P. 53.2(d)(1).

24 Tex. R. App. P. 53.2(k)(2).

25 *See* Tex. R. App. P. 53.2(d)(2), (3).

26 *See* Tex. R. App. P. 53.2(d)(4).

27 *See* Tex. R. App. P. 53.2(d)(6), (7), (8).

28 *See* Tex. R. App. P. 53.2(d)(9).

29 Tex. R. App. P. 53.2(g).

30 Tex. R. App. P. 53.2(e).

31 Tex. H.B. 1761, § 1, 85th Leg., R.S. (2017), *codified at* Tex. Gov't Code § 22.001(a).

32 Tex. Gov't Code § 22.001(a).

33 Tex. R. App. P. 9.4(i)(1).

[34] *See Daimler-Benz Aktiengsellschaft v. Olson*, 53 S.W.3d 308 (Tex. 2000) (Hecht, J. dissenting) (striking a petition for review because it contained a five-page jurisdictional statement detailing the alleged conflict). Besides, it looks like a rookie move.

[35] Tex. R. App. P. 53.2(f).

[36] *Accord* Justice Craig T. Enoch & Michael S. Truesdale, *Issues and Petitions: The Impact on Supreme Court Practice*, 31 St. Mary's L.J. 565, 588, 590–91 (2000) ("Frequently, a justice may decide to deny a petition based solely on a review of the issue presented by a petition." . . . "A justice reviewing a petition may be able to tell immediately, based on review only of the issue presented, that the case is not one warranting supreme court review.").

[37] Justice Craig T. Enoch & Michael S. Truesdale, *Issues and Petitions: The Impact on Supreme Court Practice*, 31 St. Mary's L.J. 565, 591 (2000).

[38] Justice Craig T. Enoch & Michael S. Truesdale, *Issues and Petitions: The Impact on Supreme Court Practice*, 31 St. Mary's L.J. 565, 590 (2000) ("[T]he supreme court presumes that a petition for review will be denied, and the denial is automatic absent any action from members of the court. Given that presumption and the sparse amount of time the court can dedicate to reviewing each petition, the importance of the issues presented cannot be overestimated. In fact, one commentator suggests that the issue presented 'is as important as anything that follows in the petition.'") (quoting Charles B. Lord, *Understanding the New Petition for Review Process*, State Bar of Tex., Practicing Under the New Texas Appellate Rules, Tab I at 4 (1997)).

[39] *See, e.g.*, Justice Craig T. Enoch & Michael S. Truesdale, *Issues and Petitions: The Impact on Supreme Court Practice*, 31 St. Mary's L.J. 565, 568 (2000); Pamela Stanton Baron, *Drafting Issues in the Texas Supreme Court*, State Bar of Tex. Prof. Dev. Program, 15th Annual Advanced Civil Appellate Practice Course, ch. 6 (2001); Bryan A. Garner, *Issue-Framing: The Upshot of It All*, State Bar of Tex. Prof. Dev. Program, Advanced Civil Appellate Practice Course, Tab O (1997).

[40] Justice Craig T. Enoch & Michael S. Truesdale, *Issues and Petitions: The Impact on Supreme Court Practice*, 31 St. Mary's L.J. 565, 587, 603 (2000) ("[G]iven the page constraints of a petition, a party can only adequately brief one or two issues at most."); Justice Deborah Hankinson, *Framing Issues Under the New Rules: A View from the Supreme Court*, 5 The Appellate Lawyer 4 (Houston Bar Ass'n Appellate Practice Section Winter 1998–1999) ("Realistically, only one or two issues can be briefed effectively in a petition, so you need to focus even more carefully on choosing your strongest and most important issues.").

[41] *See* Tex. R. App. P. 53.2(i).

[42] *See* Tex. R. App. P. 9.4(d).

[43] Justice Craig T. Enoch & Michael S. Truesdale, *Issues and Petitions: The Impact on Supreme Court Practice*, 31 St. Mary's L.J. 565, 593 (2000).

[44] Pamela Stanton Baron, *Drafting Issues in the Texas Supreme Court*, State Bar of Tex. Prof. Dev. Program, 15th Annual Advanced Civil Appellate Practice Course, ch. 6 at 1 (2001).

[45] Pamela Stanton Baron, *Drafting Issues in the Texas Supreme Court*, State Bar of Tex. Prof. Dev. Program, 15th Annual Advanced Civil Appellate Practice Course, ch. 6 at 2 (2001).

[46] Pamela Stanton Baron, *Drafting Issues in the Texas Supreme Court*, State Bar of Tex. Prof. Dev. Program, 15th Annual Advanced Civil Appellate Practice Course, ch. 6 at 4 (2001).

[47] Pamela Stanton Baron, *Drafting Issues in the Texas Supreme Court*, State Bar of Tex. Prof. Dev. Program, 15th Annual Advanced Civil Appellate Practice Course, ch. 6 at 4 (2001).

[48] Pamela Stanton Baron, *Drafting Issues in the Texas Supreme Court*, State Bar of Tex. Prof. Dev. Program, 15th Annual Advanced Civil Appellate Practice Course, ch. 6 at 7 (2001).

[49] Pamela Stanton Baron, *Drafting Issues in the Texas Supreme Court*, State Bar of Tex. Prof. Dev. Program, 15th Annual Advanced Civil Appellate Practice Course, ch. 6 at 7 (2001)

(quoting Justice Craig T. Enoch & Michael S. Truesdale, *Issues and Petitions: The Impact on Supreme Court Practice*, 31 St. Mary's L.J. 565, 588 (2000)).

[50] Pamela Stanton Baron, *Drafting Issues in the Texas Supreme Court*, State Bar of Tex. Prof. Dev. Program, 15th Annual Advanced Civil Appellate Practice Course, ch. 6 at 1 (2001).

[51] Pamela Stanton Baron, *Drafting Issues in the Texas Supreme Court*, State Bar of Tex. Prof. Dev. Program, 15th Annual Advanced Civil Appellate Practice Course, ch. 6 at 3 (2001).

[52] Bryan A. Garner, *Issue-Framing: The Upshot of It All*, State Bar of Tex. Prof. Dev. Program, Advanced Civil Appellate Practice Course, Tab O (1997).

[53] Bryan A. Garner, *Issue-Framing: The Upshot of It All*, State Bar of Tex. Prof. Dev. Program, Advanced Civil Appellate Practice Course, Tab O at 5 (1997).

[54] *See* Chapter 15.

[55] Bryan A. Garner, *Issue-Framing: The Upshot of It All*, State Bar of Tex. Prof. Dev. Program, Advanced Civil Appellate Practice Course, Tab O at 4 (1997).

[56] Bryan A. Garner, *Issue-Framing: The Upshot of It All*, State Bar of Tex. Prof. Dev. Program, Advanced Civil Appellate Practice Course, Tab O at 7 (1997) (emphasis added).

[57] Pamela Stanton Baron, *Drafting Issues in the Texas Supreme Court*, State Bar of Tex. Prof. Dev. Program, 15th Annual Advanced Civil Appellate Practice Course, ch. 6 at 7 (2001) (emphasis added).

[58] Bryan A. Garner, *Issue-Framing: The Upshot of It All*, State Bar of Tex. Prof. Dev. Program, Advanced Civil Appellate Practice Course, Tab O at 6 (1997).

[59] Justice Craig T. Enoch & Michael S. Truesdale, *Issues and Petitions: The Impact on Supreme Court Practice*, 31 St. Mary's L.J. 565, 599–600 (2000).

[60] *See* § 14-2:1.2.

[61] Tex. R. App. P. 56.1.

[62] *See* Elizabeth V. Rodd, *What Is Important to the Jurisprudence of the State?*, State Bar of Tex. Prof. Dev. Program, Practice Before the Supreme Court of Texas 4 (2002).

[63] Elizabeth V. Rodd, *What Is Important to the Jurisprudence of the State?*, State Bar of Tex. Prof. Dev. Program, Practice Before the Supreme Court of Texas 4 (2002).

[64] *See* Elizabeth V. Rodd, *What Is Important to the Jurisprudence of the State?*, State Bar of Tex. Prof. Dev. Program, Practice Before the Supreme Court of Texas 3–4 (2002).

[65] *See* Elizabeth V. Rodd, *What Is Important to the Jurisprudence of the State?*, State Bar of Tex. Prof. Dev. Program, Practice Before the Supreme Court of Texas 3 (2002).

[66] Elizabeth V. Rodd, *What Is Important to the Jurisprudence of the State?*, State Bar of Tex. Prof. Dev. Program, Practice Before the Supreme Court of Texas 3 (2002).

[67] Elizabeth V. Rodd, *What Is Important to the Jurisprudence of the State?*, State Bar of Tex. Prof. Dev. Program, Practice Before the Supreme Court of Texas 4 (2002).

[68] Elizabeth V. Rodd, *What Is Important to the Jurisprudence of the State?*, State Bar of Tex. Prof. Dev. Program, Practice Before the Supreme Court of Texas 4 (2002).

[69] Elizabeth V. Rodd, *What Is Important to the Jurisprudence of the State?*, State Bar of Tex. Prof. Dev. Program, Practice Before the Supreme Court of Texas 4 (2002).

[70] Tex. R. App. P. 9.4(i)(1).

[71] Tex. R. App. P. 53.2(g).

[72] Tex. R. App. P. 9.4(i)(1).

[73] Tex. R. App. P. 9.4(g).

[74] Tex. R. App. P. 49.9.

[75] Tex. R. App. P. 53.2(h).

[76] Tex. R. App. P. 53.2(h).

77 Tex. R. App. P. 53.2(h).

78 Tex. R. App. P. 9.4(i)(1).

79 Tex. R. App. P. 53.2(h).

80 Tex. R. App. P. 53.2(j).

81 *See Continental Coffee Prods. Co. v. Cazarez*, 937 S.W.2d 444, 455 (Tex. 1996).

82 Tex. R. App. P. 6.

83 Tex. R. App. P. 6.1.

84 Tex. R. App. P. 9.4(i)(1).

85 *See* Chapter 16, § 16-2:6.2.

86 Tex. R. App. P. 9.5(e).

87 Tex. R. App. P. 9.4(i)(1).

88 Tex. R. App. P. 9.4(i)(3).

89 *See* Chapter 16, § 16-2:6.1.

90 Tex. R. App. P. 53.2(k).

91 Tex. R. App. P. 53.2(j)(4).

92 Blake A. Hawthorne, *Supreme Court of Texas Internal Operating Procedures*, State Bar of Tex. Prof. Dev. Program, Practice Before the Texas Supreme Court 9 (April 2009).

93 Tex. R. App. P. 9.4(h).

94 Tex. R. App. P. 53.2(k)(1)(D).

95 Tex. R. App. P. 9.4(j)(1).

96 Tex. R. App. P. 53.3.

97 Tex. R. App. P. 53.3.

98 Russell H. McMains, *Drafting a Respondent's Brief*, State Bar of Tex. Prof. Dev. Program, Practice Before the Supreme Court of Texas, ch. 8 at 1 (2002).

99 Chapter 2 addresses specific standards of review.

100 *See* Tex. R. App. P. 44.1 ("No judgment may be reversed on appeal on the ground that the trial court made an error of law unless the court of appeals concludes that the error complained of: (1) probably caused the rendition of an improper judgment; or (2) probably prevented the appellant from properly presenting the case to the court of appeals.").

101 Tex. R. App. P. 53.7(d).

102 Arguments aimed at dissuading the Court from exercising its discretionary jurisdiction are discussed in § 14-3:2.1. Strategies for developing various portions of the response in a persuasive fashion are discussed in § 14-3:2.2.

103 *See* Tex. R. App. P. 53.3.

104 Tex. R. App. P. 9.4(i)(1), (2).

105 *See* Tex. R. App. P. 53.3.

106 *See* Tex. R. App. P. 53.3.

107 Tex. R. App. P. 53.3(d).

108 Tex. R. App. P. 53.3(c).

109 *See* § 14-3:2.1.

110 *See* § 14-3:1.5.

111 Tex. R. App. P. 53.3(b).

112 Tex. R. App. P. 53.3, 53.2(h).

113 Tex. R. App. P. 53.3(e).

114 Tex. R. App. P. 53.2(j), 53.3.

[115] *See* § 14-2:2.16.

[116] Tex. R. App. P. 53.1.

[117] Tex. R. App. P. 53.7(c).

[118] *See* Tex. R. App. P. 9.4(i)(2)(E).

[119] *See* Tex. R. App. P. 53.5.

[120] Tex. R. App. P. 53.7(a).

[121] Tex. R. App. P. 53.7(c).

[122] Tex. R. App. P. 53.7(e).

[123] Tex. R. App. P. 53.7(e).

[124] Tex. R. App. P. 55.7.

[125] Tex. R. App. P. 55.7.

[126] Tex. R. App. P. 55.7.

[127] Tex. R. App. P. 64.1.

[128] Tex. R. App. P. 9.2(c)(4).

[129] Tex. R. App. P. 9.2(c)(4)(A).

[130] Tex. R. App. P. 10.1(a)(5).

[131] Tex. R. App. P. 53.7(f).

[132] Tex. R. App. P. 53.7(f).

[133] Tex. R. App. P. 53.7(f).

[134] Tex. R. App. P. 55.7.

[135] Tex. R. App. P. 55.7.

[136] Tex. R. App. P. 55.7.

[137] Tex. R. App. P. 64.5.

[138] Tex. R. App. P. 53.8, 55.8.

[139] *See* § 14-6:3.1.

[140] *See* § 14-6:3.2.

[141] *See* Chapter 16.

CHAPTER 15

Texas Supreme Court: Briefs on the Merits and Oral Argument

15-1 Briefs on the Merits

A brief on the merits to the Texas Supreme Court is substantially different from a brief to an intermediate court of appeals. In the court of appeals, it is not necessary to persuade the court to take the case—as a court of non-discretionary jurisdiction the court is required to decide the matter. The Texas Supreme Court, in contrast, gets to pick and choose which cases it decides. And almost invariably the Court does not make that decision until *after* it requests and receives full briefing on the merits.

As a result, the brief on the merits must not only address the merits of the case, but also, depending on who is filing it, the brief must seek to persuade or dissuade the Court from granting review. More specifically, from the perspective of the petitioner, the goal of the brief on the merits is to: (1) persuade the Court to grant review, and (2) persuade the Court that the petitioner should prevail on the merits. From the perspective of the respondent, the goal of the brief on the merits is to: (1) persuade the Court to deny review, or, alternatively, (2) persuade the Court that the court of appeals correctly ruled for respondent on the merits. Accordingly, this chapter will address the process of the Court's review of briefs on the merits first in order to explain the strategy for crafting a persuasive brief.

15-1:1 Internal Procedures and Deadlines

Technically, the Court can grant the petition for review without first requesting full briefing on the merits.[1] As a practical matter, however, this rarely, if ever, occurs under the Court's internal operating procedures—the Court requests full briefing as part of its continuing evaluation of whether to grant review.

Before full briefing is granted, certain justices may take an interest in a petition and circulate memoranda recommending the Court take a certain action. Sometimes, even after a petition receives sufficient votes to be automatically denied, a justice may pull the petition from orders and issue a memorandum or speak at conference in an effort to convince the other justices of another course of action.

A request for briefs on the merits requires the vote of three justices. When full briefing is requested, the Court also simultaneously (1) requests the court of appeals to transfer the record to the Court, and (2) assigns the case in rotation to one of the chambers for the preparation of a study memo. The study memo procedure is described in the following sub-section.

Unless the Court sets a different schedule, the rules provide that the petitioner's brief on the merits is due 30 days after the Court's request for full briefing; the respondent's brief on the merits is due 20 days after the petitioner's brief is filed; and the petitioner's reply brief is due 15 days after the respondent's brief is filed.[2]

15-1:2 Preparing the Brief Sensitive to the Study Memo Procedure

The most significant development since the Court switched to the petition practice has been the Court's adoption of the "study memo" procedure. When the Court requests briefing on the merits, the petition is assigned in rotation to one of the chambers for preparation of a study memo, which is typically prepared by one of the law clerks. The law clerk assigned to prepare the study memo is charged by the Court to study the case and prepare a memorandum addressing the pertinent law and facts. The study memo is prepared within 30 days of the filing of the respondent's brief on the merits. However, the grant of briefing extensions for any of the briefs will also delay the internal circulation of the study memo. The study memo will not be circulated until the filing of the reply brief, waiver of reply, or passage of the deadline for filing the reply.

The study memo's cover identifies the parties and counsel, lower courts, and issues in the case. The law clerk is charged with presenting the issue and the arguments on each side, and analyzing how each argument contributes to their recommended disposition. First, the law clerk must collect the "pink sheets" (the justices' handwritten notes on the case)[3] and the justices' electronic notes from each chambers for the relevant petition. The law clerk will be able to glean from these, and the discussion at Conference, which issues the Court is interested in, and what the law clerk should focus on in the study memo. If jurisdiction is questionable, if a particular issue is dispositive and the result is clear, or if an argument has been waived so that the Court is precluded from reaching it, the author is instructed to flag that for the Court in the study memo.

Although the author will typically frame the issues as presented by the parties, the author has freedom to consolidate or reframe the issues so they are presented in a concise manner, especially when numerous cross-issues or unbriefed issues are raised. Law clerks will typically frame the issues with single sentences, so an attorney who wants a law clerk to mimic their own framing of the issues should use the single-sentence style of issue framing. In addition, a law clerk will be more willing to borrow from a non-argumentative recitation of the facts rather than one laced with argument. The law clerk will check the record on disputed facts and often include citations to the record in the study memo.

Law clerks are also asked to recommend a disposition, generally either granting or denying the petition. Additionally, if the law appears to solidly support a more specific disposition, such as reversal by per curiam opinion, the law clerks are encouraged to provide that recommendation. Often, the law clerk may even draft a per curiam opinion and attach it to the study memo for discussion at Conference. If six justices vote for a per curiam disposition, or to at least consider one, the per curiam opinion is assigned to the chambers that drafted the study memo.

A law clerk may also recommend that the petition be held until another petition or cause before the Court with the same issue(s) is disposed of. When petitions become "linked" in this manner, a law clerk will often address the lead case in a full study memo, with shorter study memos for the linked petitions. However, when petitions arise from the same facts, or similar facts, one study memo may address several petitions with the same issue. Counsel can assist in this process by bringing to the Court's attention any pending petitions or causes with similar issues.

The recommendations by the study memo's author are not rigidly adhered to—it is not uncommon for a justice to note disagreement with the disposition recommended in a study memo emanating from his or her own chambers. A law clerk will typically attend the Conference(s) during which his or her study memo is discussed, and answer any questions the justices may have regarding the issues or record in the case.

Because the justices typically make the decision about whether to grant review based on the study memo, the primary target audience for the brief on the merits is someone fresh out of law school. Although the law clerk is undoubtedly bright, the briefing should be sensitive to their relative inexperience. However, the briefing also should be careful not to offend the law clerk. One law clerk tells of a brief that declared, "This issue is so simple that even a recent law grad could figure it out," ignoring that a "recent law grad" was preparing the study memo for the Court.

Counsel also should make every effort to assist the law clerk. One way to do that is to include detailed and accurate cites to the appellate record. Law clerks understandably become frustrated if they are forced to dig through a voluminous record to address a legal issue because counsel haven't done their job of providing record support for legal arguments.

The justices and law clerks have come to expect the electronic brief to include hyperlinks to key authorities and key record materials in the appendix.

15-1:3 To File or Not to File

Just because the justices have requested the parties to file briefs on the merits does not mean the parties are required to do so. But if the Court calls for briefing, someone at the Court wants to know something. Thus, the strong presumption should be in favor of filing a brief on the merits if the Court requests one.

Some petitioners elect not to file a brief but, instead, to stand on the petition. There is nothing inherently wrong with that decision, as long as counsel promptly advises the Court of that decision. Some justices are impressed with the confidence in the initial filing that this communicates. However, in most cases something additional can be done to improve on the petition, and counsel should take the opportunity to do so.

There are exceptions. For example, if the petition for review constitutes nothing more than a "me too" filing—advising the Court that the controlling issue on appeal is governed by another case on which the Court has granted review and that remains pending—there may be no reason to provide additional briefing. If no exceptions apply, however, counsel should consider the following guidelines.

15-1:3.1 Unbriefed Issues

The petitioner can preserve issues for review by raising them in the petition but reserving briefing until the brief on the merits.[4] Just because the petitioner has preserved an unbriefed issue for review does not mean that the petitioner is required to address it in the brief on the merits. The issue should be closely scrutinized afresh at this stage in the proceeding. Weak issues that could detract from the strength of others should be abandoned at this point. However, if the petitioner determines an issue to be worthy of pursuing, the brief on the merits is the last opportunity to brief it.

15-1:3.2 Authorities From Other Jurisdictions, Treatises, and Public-Policy Issues

Even issues that were briefed in the petition often merit further briefing beyond the scope permitted by the word limits of the petition. The more generous word limits for the brief on the merits allow for a more extended discussion. If an argument would benefit from a 50-state search of authorities or a discussion of the law in other jurisdictions, the brief on the merits is the ideal place to develop that discussion. Similarly, if a discussion of treatises would be helpful, the brief on the merits affords the opportunity for that discussion. Finally, if public-policy issues need to be developed, the brief on the merits is the place for that.

In discussing these arguments, however, counsel should not wear out their welcome. The opportunity to brief up to 15,000 words should not challenge counsel to come close to that limit. As always, the more concise the brief, the better.

15-1:4 Supplement to Petition or Stand-Alone Document

Another question that often arises is whether the brief on the merits merely supplements the petition, to avoid repetition, or should it be a stand-alone document, even if it is repetitive? Although the rules provide no answer to that question, the evolution of petition practice has made the answer clear: the brief on the merits should be a stand-alone document, even if it incorporates portions of the petition.

15-1:5 Differences (Besides Length) Between Petition and Brief on the Merits

The rules setting forth the contents of the petition for review and the brief on the merits are almost identical.[5] The relatively few differences are discussed below.

15-1:5.1 Issues Presented

In most cases, the issues presented in the brief on the merits will be identical to those presented in the petition. The petitioner may elect, however, to abandon issues that were presented in the petition. The petitioner also may elect to word one or more issues differently, so long as the substance remains the same and no new issues are added.[6]

Some commentators suggest that "[t]he petitioner may want to rewrite the issues in the brief to make them more argumentative."[7] That will often be the case if the issues in the petition are stated neutrally.[8]

15-1:5.2 Argument

The argument section of the petition must include a statement of the reasons why the Supreme Court should exercise jurisdiction to hear the case.[9] An independent section at the outset of the body of the petition entitled "Reasons to Grant Review" may be advisable to provide this information.[10]

The rules contain no comparable requirement with respect to the brief on the merits. The provision concerning argument in the brief on the merits simply states: "The brief must contain a clear and concise argument for the contentions made, with appropriate citations to authorities and to the record."[11]

The variance between the two provisions is explained by the different purposes of the petition and the brief. The petition is calculated to persuade the Court to exercise its discretionary jurisdiction to hear the case. The brief on the merits is intended to flesh out the discussion of the merits. But because the brief will invariably be filed before the Court has decided whether to exercise its discretionary jurisdiction, it remains important to continue to persuade the Court to take the case. Accordingly, like the petition, the petitioner's brief on the merits should include a stand-alone section addressing why the Court should hear the case.

In preparing the argument section of the brief on the merits, counsel should also be mindful of the fact that the law clerks are instructed to include in their study memos a section addressing preservation of error. Petitioner's counsel can assist the law clerk by addressing preservation in the merits brief, with citation to the record showing the issue was preserved below. Because many law schools do not educate students about issue preservation, counsel are advised to present the preservation argument in a fashion that is understandable to first-year lawyers.

15-1:5.3 Appendix

The rules governing the petition contain a lengthy section concerning the appendix.[12] In contrast, the rules governing the brief on the merits contain no provision concerning an appendix.[13] This discrepancy is because the appendix to the petition serves as a substitute for the record, which is not before the Court when it reviews the petition. When the Court receives the briefs on the merits, however, it will have the record itself—whenever the Court sets a briefing schedule for briefs on the merits, the Court also requests the record from the court of appeals. Thus, an appendix is not required as part of the filing of the brief on the merits.

Nonetheless, including an appendix to the brief on the merits with key documents is highly advisable—the justices expect to see an appendix, and they expect to see hyperlinks from references to the appendix in the brief to the actual documents in the appendix. Thus, the mere fact that an appendix is not required for a brief on the merits should not dissuade counsel from critically evaluating whether one would be helpful to the review process.

15-1:6 Response Brief

The rules governing the contents of the response brief on the merits are virtually identical to those governing the contents of the response to the petition for review.[14] The same criteria for deciding which matters to agree with or dispute apply equally with respect to the respondent's brief on the merits.

Notably, if the petitioner elects not to file a brief on the merits requested by the Court, the respondent is seemingly precluded from filing one—the respondent files a brief in response only "[i]f the petitioner files a brief on the merits . . . ."[15] Nonetheless, because the Court's request for briefing on the merits indicates a strong interest in the case and, in all probability, an interest that favors the petitioner, the respondent cannot afford to forgo the opportunity to brief the merits fully, particularly if the respondent did not fully brief the issues in response to the petition. In this circumstance, the respondent should simply file a brief on the merits. The Court is happy to receive whatever assistance it can get.

Like the petitioner's brief on the merits, the respondent's brief need not include an appendix.[16] But it is almost invariably helpful to include one, with hyperlinks between appendix references in the brief and the appendices themselves. The response should continue the effort to persuade the Court that the case does not merit its exercise of discretionary review. And it should address the merits of the arguments presented in the petitioner's merits brief.

15-1:7 Reply Brief

The petitioner may file a reply brief on the merits addressing any matter in the brief in response.[17] Under the Court's internal operating procedures, the study memo will not be circulated until the reply brief has been filed or the deadline for filing that brief has passed.

The reply brief on the merits is important. It provides petitioner the chance to distinguish the respondent's authority, cite new case law, and point out what the respondent could not refute. Thus, counsel for petitioner should take great care in preparing the reply.

15-2 Submission and Argument

15-2:1 Submission Without Oral Argument

By the vote of six of the nine justices, the petition may be granted and the case decided without oral argument.[18] Such cases are usually, but not always, disposed of by per curiam opinion. Summary disposition without oral argument provides a means for the Court to engage in error correction in cases not involving issues of substantial jurisprudential importance. It also provides a means for the Court to resolve cases involving a narrow legal question, such as the applicability of a rule to given circumstances.

15-2:2 Submission With Argument

If the Court decides to take the case and determines that argument would be helpful, it will set the case for oral argument and notify the parties of the submission date.[19] In the unlikely event that the Court has not already requested briefs on the merits, it will provide the parties with the opportunity to fully brief the case before argument.

15-2:3 Time for Argument

The Court determines the amount of time allotted for oral argument in each case.[20] Typically, the Court allows 20 minutes per side, of which the petitioner may reserve up to half the allotted time for rebuttal. While rarely granted, by motion filed before the day of argument, the Court may extend the time for argument.[21] The Court may also re-align the parties for purposes of presenting argument.[22]

A red and a green light are on the top of the podium to signal to counsel and the justices when the time remaining is growing short, or has expired. The green light comes on when five minutes remain for the argument. The red light is illuminated when time has expired. In a case in which the Court's interest has been sufficiently piqued, it is not uncommon for the justices to continue to address questions to counsel after the red light has come on and counsel will be afforded the opportunity to respond. Nonetheless, counsel should be careful not to unduly protract the argument and should be prepared to stop talking immediately if the Court has no further questions after time has expired.

15-2:4 Number of Counsel

The Court prefers that only one attorney argue per side.[23] Except on leave of Court, no more than two counsel on each side may argue.[24] And only one counsel may argue in rebuttal.[25]

Although not stated in the rules, Court practices dictate that only two counsel may sit at counsel table without leave of court. A motion must be filed for additional counsel to sit at counsel table. As a practical matter, no more than three counsel can comfortably sit at the table.

Strategically, splitting an argument by subject matter is almost always a bad idea. If, for instance, the Court has little or no interest in addressing one aspect of the case and profound interest in another, splitting argument by subject matter can run the risk of annoying the Court. Similarly, the justices may not feel constrained to confine their questions to the particular subject matter being presented. If that happens, it is not acceptable for counsel to ask the Court to defer the question until the other counsel speaks. In short, counsel should avoid splitting argument, if possible. If time is split, counsel should be prepared to address any question that might be raised by the Court.

15-2:5 Argument by Amicus Curiae

An amicus may share allotted time with a party only with that party's consent and with leave of Court obtained before the argument.[26] Otherwise, counsel for amicus curiae are not permitted to argue.[27] As discussed above, counsel should hesitate before deciding to split argument and, if a decision is made to split, be prepared to present argument in a fashion that will be helpful rather than cumbersome for the justices.

15-2:6 Purpose of Argument

Oral argument should clarify the written arguments in the briefs.[28] Reading from a prepared text is discouraged because it is both ineffective and impractical. Generally, the Court is active at oral argument, and counsel must be prepared to answer questions. Counsel should assume that justices have read the briefs before argument, although the level of preparation may vary among the justices.

Because the Court is, at least generally speaking, well prepared, it is not necessary to provide extensive factual background before turning to the actual arguments in the case. As a practical matter, because the justices are prone to be active in their questioning, it is best to get into the substantive arguments as quickly as possible.

15-2:7 Oral Argument Exhibits

Counsel may use exhibits to assist with a presentation of oral argument.

15-2:7.1 Blow-Ups

Generally speaking, blow-ups or posterboards are not effective in oral argument; handouts are better. If blow-ups are used, care should be taken to ensure that they will be legible from the bench and will not interfere with the argument. The blow-ups must be presented to the clerk's office before the argument, together with a $25 filing fee. The clerk will deliver the blow-ups to the courtroom. After the argument, the blow-ups must be removed by counsel. If blow-ups are used, they should also be duplicated as handouts for the Court (12 copies); no additional fee will be required in this event.

15-2:7.2 Handouts

If handouts for the individual justices are used, an original and 11 copies must be filed with the clerk, with a $25 filing fee, before the argument. The handouts must be electronically filed with the court as well. The clerk is responsible for placing the handouts on the bench; counsel submitting the handouts is responsible for delivering copies to opposing counsel. Counsel should avoid using too many handouts because the justices are active in questioning, leaving little time for discussion of individual handouts. Counsel should spiral bind the handouts like a brief, with each handout appearing under a separately numbered tab. The cover should look the same as the brief, and be properly labeled, e.g., "Petitioner's Oral Argument Exhibits." By using separately numbered tabs, counsel can easily refer the justices to a particular document during the argument.

15-2:7.3 Telestrator

In certain cases, counsel may find it useful to use the Court's telestrator to assist with oral argument. The telestrator is a sophisticated electronic device located on the podium. It not only permits electronic exhibits to be displayed on a large monitor in the courtroom, but also permits counsel, by the drag of a finger on a screen, to manipulate the exhibits by highlighting, circling, or crossing out certain language.

To use the telestrator, counsel will need to load the exhibits onto a thumbdrive and bring a laptop computer to argument to be connected to the telestrator. Because oral argument can be fast paced, counsel should plan on practicing with the telestrator one or more days before the argument. Counsel should contact the clerk's office to set up the practice session.

15-2:8 Webcasts of Oral Argument

Live webcasts of the Court's oral arguments can be accessed through a link on the Court's website. The arguments can also be viewed later through the archives section of the Court's website.

Webcasts enable clients and interested parties to view the oral argument live, without having to come to Austin. Viewing the archives of oral argument can also be helpful in several ways. First, counsel presenting oral argument can watch the video recording to evaluate whether a post-submission brief should be submitted. Counsel can observe things while watching the video that went unnoticed during the presentation of argument. Also, when other counsel have pending cases that involve issues similar to a case that has been orally argued, insights about the Court's views on those issues can be greatly informed by watching oral argument.

15-2:9 Post-Submission Brief

The appellate rules make no provision for the filing of post-submission briefs. Yet, they frequently are filed with the Court and no leave of Court is required. Thus, whether to file such a post-submission brief presents an important strategy question.

The rebuttable presumption should be *against* filing a post-submission brief since it can signal weakness or a lack of confidence in the offering party's position. But several factors can rebut the presumption.

First, if a justice requested a post-submission brief during oral argument, counsel should honor that request.

Second, if debriefing of the argument, including a review of the video, reveals that a material question was answered incorrectly or incompletely, a post-submission brief can provide an opportunity to correct or complete that answer.

Third, if the opposing party made an important argument that requires a response and either no response was made or the response was incorrect or incomplete, a post-submission brief can clear up the confusion.

The post-submission brief should be concise, direct, and specific. At some point, a party can cross the line from being helpful to the Court to being annoying.

Finally, the timing of any post-submission brief is important. The Court will discuss the case at the first conference following the oral argument. Counsel should consult the calendar on the Court's website to determine the date of the next scheduled conference, and should aim to file the post-submission brief sufficiently in advance of the conference for it to be meaningfully considered.

Notes

1 *See* Tex. R. App. P. 55.1.

2 Tex. R. App. P. 55.7.

3 For a complete description of the "pink sheet," *see* Chapter 14, § 14-6:3.1.

4 *See* Tex. R. App. P. 53.2(f), (i).

5 *Compare* Tex. R. App. P. 53.2 *with* Tex. R. App. P. 55.2.

6 *See* Tex. R. App. P. 55.2(f) ("The phrasing of the issues or points [in the brief on the merits] need not be identical to the statement of issues or points in the petition for review, but the brief may not raise additional issues or points or change the substance of the issues or points presented in the petition.").

7 *See* Pamela Stanton Baron, *Drafting Issues in the Texas Supreme Court*, State Bar of Texas 15th Annual Advanced Civil Appellate Practice Course, Tab 6 at 8 (2001).

[8] *See* Chapter14, § 14-2:2.7d.

[9] Tex. R. App. P. 53.2(i).

[10] *See* Chapter 14, § 14-2:2.8.

[11] Tex. R. App. P. 55.2(i).

[12] *See* Tex. R. App. P. 53.2(k).

[13] *See* Tex. R. App. P. 55.2.

[14] *Compare* Tex. R. App. P. 53.3 *with* Tex. R. App. P. 55.3.

[15] Tex. R. App. P. 55.3.

[16] Tex. R. App. P. 55.3.

[17] Tex. R. App. P. 55.4.

[18] Tex. R. App. P. 59.1.

[19] Tex. R. App. P. 59.2.

[20] Tex. R. App. P. 59.4.

[21] Tex. R. App. P. 59.4.

[22] Tex. R. App. P. 59.4.

[23] Tex. R. App. P. 59.5.

[24] Tex. R. App. P. 59.4.

[25] Tex. R. App. P. 59.4.

[26] Tex. R. App. P. 59.6.

[27] Tex. R. App. P. 59.6.

[28] Tex. R. App. P. 59.3.

CHAPTER 16

Filing Procedures

16-1 Introduction

The filing of documents has changed more than any other aspect of Texas appellate practice in the last decade. The new rules governing electronic filing now apply statewide. In some respects, they make appellate practice easier. In other respects, they make it more challenging.

As practitioners, we need to keep in mind the needs of judges and court staff who may read our filings on screen, rather than paper. The reading experience is different when the audience is reading on paper versus a PC screen. And the experience differs when the audience is reading on a PC screen versus a tablet. It is important to communicate with the courts in which you practice and find out how judges are reading briefs. Then, make sure you review your documents before filing, keeping in mind the media in which it is likely to be read.

16-2 Electronic Filing Rules

16-2:1 Attorneys Must E-File in Civil Appeals

Attorneys must e-file all documents through eFileTexas.gov, the e-filing portal provided by the Office of Court Administration. E-filing is still new in some appellate courts, and the rules remain in flux. Refer to the Texas Rules of Appellate Procedure (the most current version is available on the Texas Supreme Court website) and the applicable court's website for any requirements that may post-date this chapter.

Most e-filing rules are contained in the Texas Rules of Appellate Procedure. Minor differences remain. For example, a handful of courts still require paper copies. It is important to look at *all* of the local rules of the particular court to make sure that your brief will comply. And, it is always a good idea to call the clerk's office if you have any questions.

16-2:2 Exceptions

There are a few exceptions to mandatory e-filing.

16-2:2.1 Pro Se Parties

Pro se filers may e-file but are not required to do so.[1]

16-2:2.2 Emergencies

Attorneys may be permitted to use alternative electronic transmission systems (e.g., fax) in the event of emergency. Check the local rules of your court.

16-2:2.3 Sealed Materials

Documents filed under seal, or subject to a pending motion to seal, or presented to the court in camera, or to which access is restricted by law or court order must not be e-filed.[2] If you plan to file sealed or restricted documents, contact the clerk's office, as each court has its own procedures.

Some clerks will instruct counsel to e-file sealed documents notwithstanding the prohibition in the rules. If you do not want to be found in contempt of a sealing order, or find your client's private information inadvertently posted on the court's website, insist on compliance with the rules and file your documents in hard copy only.

16-2:2.4 By Permission

Appellate courts may grant a motion for leave to file in paper form for a particular case if good cause is shown.[3]

16-2:3 Mechanism

16-2:3.1 Use eFileTexas.gov

E-filing must be done through eFileTexas.gov, the portal established by the Office of Court Administration.[4]

16-2:3.2 Select an EFSP

You must first register with an Electronic Filing Service Provider (EFSP), an approved list of which is on the eFileTexas.gov website. You will receive a confidential, secure username and password.

16-2:3.3 File Your Document

EFSPs have step-by-step instructions to guide you through the e-filing process. Only minimal technical knowledge is necessary, e.g., how to browse through your own computer files to locate your document. Following these directions will transmit your document to the EFSP, which will send it to eFileTexas.gov, which will in turn transmit it to the clerk of the court. Unless you use the State's free EFSP, eFile.TXCourts.gov, a fee is charged for e-filing in addition to the customary filing fee.

Finally, plan ahead. Even though filing is not technically complex, problems sometimes arise that need technical assistance. Do not leave your filing until the last minute.

16-2:3.4 Receive Confirmation

The e-filer should receive up to four emails after filing:

- the EFSP's acknowledgment of the e-filing;
- confirmation that the document was successfully transmitted to the court;

- proof of service, if used; and
- confirmation of the clerk's acceptance of the filing (which will include a link to the file-stamped copy) or a notice of rejection.

16-2:4 Format

Texas Rule of Appellate Procedure 9.4 governs the format of e-briefs, paper briefs, and paper copies of e-briefs.

16-2:4.1 Paper and Printing

Use white paper, 8½ by 11 inches. Printing must be a "distinct black image."

16-2:4.2 Margins

One-inch margins are required on both sides, top, and bottom.

16-2:4.3 Spacing

Double spacing is required for all text except block quotations, footnotes, short lists, and issues presented, which may be single-spaced.

16-2:4.4 Typeface

Proportionally spaced fonts must be no smaller than 14 point, except that footnotes can be as small as 12 point.[5]

16-2:4.5 PDF Requirements

Texas Rule of Appellate Procedure 9.4(j) requires a text-searchable portable document format (PDF). If you create the document with a word processing program, then the e-filed document may not be a scan of the original. Rather, you must convert the electronic version of the document directly into PDF format. If you must use scanned documents, make them text searchable using optical-character-recognition (OCR) software, such as Adobe Acrobat, and use a resolution of 300 dots per inch (dpi). The document must not be locked.

16-2:4.6 Technology Standards

All e-filed documents must comply with the Technology Standards promulgated by the Judicial Committee on Information Technology and approved by the Texas Supreme Court. These can be found on the Court's website.

16-2:4.7 Maximum Word Count

Texas appellate courts now use word limits (not page limits) for briefs produced on a computer.[6]

In the courts of appeals:

- Appellant's and appellee's briefs; petitions and responses in original proceedings—15,000 words

- Reply briefs (including original proceedings)—7,500 words
- Motions for rehearing and responses—4,500 words
- Aggregate of all briefs filed by a party—27,000 words

In the Supreme Court:

- Petitions for review and responses, petitions and responses in original proceedings—4,500 words
- Reply briefs at petition stage and in original proceedings—2,400 words
- Opening briefs and response briefs on the merits—15,000 words
- Reply briefs on the merits—7,500 words
- Motions for rehearing and responses—4,500 words

16-2:4.8 Nonconforming Documents

If a document does not comply with the formatting rules, the court may strike the document or identify the error and give a deadline for the party to redraw and refile a compliant brief.[7] That deadline is customarily included in the email notification of noncompliance.

16-2:5 Deadlines

Texas Rule of Appellate Procedure 9.2(c) states that a document is considered filed timely if it is e-filed at any time before midnight (in the Court's time zone) on the deadline. If a document is electronically filed on Saturday, Sunday, or an official holiday, then it will be deemed filed on the next day that is not a Saturday, Sunday, or legal holiday. If a document requires a motion and order to allow its filing, it is deemed filed on the date the motion is granted.

16-2:6 Additional Requirements

16-2:6.1 Certificate of Compliance

Include a certificate of compliance stating the number of words in any document subject to word limits. Every word in the document must be counted except the parts excluded by Texas Rule of Appellate Procedure 9.4(i)(1). You may rely on a computer program, such as Microsoft Word, to calculate the word count.

CERTIFICATE OF COMPLIANCE

This brief complies with the type-volume limitations of Rule 9.4 because it contains 11,338 words, excluding the portions of the brief exempted by Texas Rule of Appellate Procedure 9.4(i)(1).

/s/ Name of Attorney
Name of Attorney

16-2:6.2 Signature

To sign an e-filed document, type "/s/" on the signature line with the filing attorney's name typed beside it, as shown in the box above. An electronic image or scanned image of a signature can also be used, and is required when the document is notarized or sworn.[8]

16-2:6.3 Attorney Contact Information

A party must list the following information for its own lead counsel on the cover of the brief: name, email address, State Bar number, mailing address, telephone number, and fax number, if any.[9] The same information also must be included somewhere in the document for all other attorneys appearing on the document as representing that party.[10]

Additionally, for the convenience of court clerks, counsel should include this information any place that an attorney's (even opposing counsel's) contact information is given, e.g., cover, identity of parties and counsel, signature block, certificate of service.

16-2:6.4 Pro Se Filer Contact Information

A pro se party must sign a document and provide the party's mailing address, phone number, email address, and fax number, if any.[11]

16-2:7 Appendices

If you wish to include cases or statutes in your appendix, you can download them from Westlaw or Lexis as PDFs. The Supreme Court prefers cases in single column format (for easier reading on a small screen), double spaced, and in 14-point font.

Minimize the size of the appendix by using native electronic documents whenever possible. If you must scan, the setting should be 300 dpi in black and white. You also should save it as a "reduced-size PDF" before filing.

16-2:8 Finishing Touches

16-2:8.1 File Size

To comply with rules. Your brief and appendix must be combined into one PDF document unless the file would exceed the size limitations of the e-filing portal.[12] Currently, the size limit for the portal is 35 megabytes. It is best not to approach the limit too closely. Thus, if your filing exceeds 30–32 MB, you should divide it into two parts.

To make reviewing your brief easier for the justices. Keep in mind that appellate justices travel frequently, and many of them read briefs on tablets. To reliably download filings to a tablet at present, the brief and appendix should be in one PDF (now called an "envelope") no larger than 5 MB. Thus, you may wish to limit the optional contents of your appendix to ensure that the entire envelope is smaller than 5 MB. The importance of facilitating tablet reading may change depending on the type of brief. For example, in the Supreme Court, it is more important for petition-stage briefs, in which the audience includes the justices, and less important for merits briefs, for which the first audience is typically a law clerk.

16-2:8.2 Bookmarking

You must bookmark each item in your appendix and in a record in an original proceeding.[13] Most courts prefer that you also bookmark all of the headings in your brief.

16-2:8.3 Optimization

Optimizing your PDF will make your readers' lives easier by making your brief readable with any device. In the Document Properties dialogue box, make sure the following are selected:

- *Navigations tab:* Bookmarks Panel and Page (this makes the document open with bookmarks visible, except that it does not work with some EFSPs) [File > Properties > Initial View > Navigation tab > Bookmarks Panel and Page > OK]
- *Page layout:* Single Page Continuous
- *Magnification:* Fit Page
- *Open to page:* 1
- *Windows options:* Open in Full Screen Mode

16-2:9 Redaction

16-2:9.1 Sensitive Data

Texas Rule of Appellate Procedure 9.9 identifies certain personal information as "sensitive data." Examples are social security number, birth date, driver's license number, passport number, tax ID number, other government-issued identification number, bank account number, credit card number, other financial account number, or the name, birth date, or home address of any person who was a minor when the underlying suit was filed. A document cannot be e-filed unless sensitive data is redacted. Texas Rule of Appellate Procedure 9.9(c) contains specific requirements for the manner of redaction, and the Supreme Court website contains further instructions.

16-2:9.2 Identity of a Minor

In parental-rights-termination or juvenile-court appeals, a child's identity is especially protected.[14] In some circumstances, parents' names must also be redacted and aliases used.[15]

16-2:10 Hyperlinking

16-2:10.1 Recommended but Not Required

Hyperlinking is not required, but many appellate justices encourage it—even though the Texas appellate courts now have software that automatically hyperlinks citations to cases and statutes. If you hyperlink, you should link to documents in your appendix whenever possible. It is permissible to link to outside sources, but such links may be less convenient for the justices. They may be unable to review outside sources when they are away from the office and lacking Westlaw or Lexis passwords or Internet access.

16-2:10.2 Strategies for Hyperlinking

The main debate about hyperlinking is how much to do it. Extensive hyperlinking can be convenient for the reader, but some research indicates that it interrupts the flow of the argument and can diminish comprehension.[16] Additionally, extensive hyperlinking can require a large appendix, which may exceed the file-size limits for e-filing portals and for reliable tablet viewing.

In the end, the degree of hyperlinking is a strategy call. Many practitioners opt for limited hyperlinking, i.e., linking only to key authorities or record excerpts. This approach can also be a persuasive tool, directing the court to the authorities that you believe are most important. Your approach may also differ depending on the type of brief. To use the Supreme Court as an example, limited hyperlinking may be the best choice for petition-stage briefs because the justices may be more likely to read those on tablets, which necessitate a smaller document. By contrast, extensive hyperlinking may be more useful in merits briefing, which is first reviewed by a law clerk likely working at a desktop computer in the office.

Many courts also allow the filing of a hyperlinked brief sometime after the filing of the "official" brief. This can be useful if you or your staff is unable to complete the hyperlinking by the filing deadline, or if you are using an outside service for hyperlinking.

16-2:11 Final Check Before Filing

When the final, combined PDF document is ready, check the functionality of your bookmarks and hyperlinks on your computer, tablet, or any other available device before filing. Also, consider shortening the bookmark headings so that the reader can see them at a glance.

16-2:12 Electronic Service

16-2:12.1 E-Service for Attorneys With Email Address on File

Service must be accomplished through eFileTexas.gov if the email addresses of the attorneys or parties to be served are on file with eFileTexas.gov. Tex. R. App. P. 9.5(b)(1).

16-2:12.2 Alternative Service

If an email address is not on file, service may be accomplished by email, hand-delivery, mail, commercial delivery, or fax. Texas Rule of Appellate Procedure 9.5 requires service on lead counsel for each party, not every attorney listed on a brief. However, it is a customary courtesy to serve all attorneys listed.

16-2:13 Paper Copies of E-Filed Documents

Paper copies are not required unless mandated by local rule.[17] Check the specific court's website and/or call the clerk's office to confirm. Paper copies, if any, are usually due one to three days after the filing date. These courtesy copies must be the printed version of the file-stamped e-filed document. The appendix to the paper copy need only include content required by Texas Rule of Appellate Procedure 52.3(k) and 53.3(f).

In addition to the format requirements listed above for e-filed documents, paper copies must have durable covers (not red, black, or white) and be appropriately bound.[18] Printing must be on one side only.[19]

16-2:14 Notifications

Two types of notifications are available to counsel to keep track of events in appellate cases. The first is CaseMail, an automated information system that will send registrants emails regarding any filings or other activity in any appellate court for a particular matter. The system has a number of additional useful features, including notice of when a court has calendared a due date and a tickler one week in advance of a calendared due date. In the Supreme Court, lead counsel must register for CaseMail.[20] Of course, you should not rely exclusively on this service and should always double-check any due dates and calendar those due dates independently of this system. The system can also provide notices of new filings and opinions. The Supreme Court's website contains information on registering to receive CaseMail.

The second type of notification is an e-notice from the appellate court. The scope of this notice is narrower than CaseMail: it provides notice of court actions only, not filings or deadlines. Generally, e-notices are sent the same day as the court's action, whereas CaseMail notices issue one or two days after the triggering event. Another difference is that e-notices are sometimes sent to lead counsel only, but there is no need to register, as the court issues the e-notices automatically. E-notice procedures may differ among appellate courts.

16-2:15 Creating an E-Brief

- For step-by-step instructions on how to create electronic briefs, Austin appellate attorney Don Cruse's blog is an excellent resource: http://www.scotxblog.com/ebrief-workflow
- The Supreme Court's website also has a very helpful document: www.txcourts.gov/media/124903/guidetocreatingelectronicappellatebriefs.pdf

16-2:16 Fees

Fees for electronically filed documents are paid through the filer's EFSP. EFSPs may accept credit cards for payment of fees for electronic filings. Consult with an individual EFSP to determine whether that EFSP accepts credit card payments. EFSPs may charge electronic filing fees in addition to the courts' filing fees.

For filings that are not electronic, the clerk will accept fees paid in cash, by check, or by money order. Checks and money orders should be made payable to the clerk of the particular court. Courts do not accept credit cards.

The clerk's office may file and hold (i.e., not forward to the Court) items received without adequate fees or a proper affidavit of indigence, unless the party is exempt from payment or allowed by law to delay payment. The clerk's office sends a letter informing the party that the item has been filed but that, if the fee or affidavit is not received within 10 days, the item will be dismissed under Texas Rule of Appellate Procedure 5. The current fee schedules can be found on each appellate court's website.

16-3 Special Considerations for Original Proceedings

In an original proceeding, the difficulties of e-filing are magnified largely because of the need to compile and file your own record. If the record is large, its compilation should begin days or weeks before the filing date. You must compile it early to ascertain whether it will exceed the portal's 35 MB limit. If so, it should be divided into separate parts for filing. Each part must contain an index. Avoid approaching the 35 megabyte limit too closely because some documents increase in size when they are e-filed or even when they are optimized. It typically is safe to a file a document with 32 MB or less. Work closely with the clerk of the court in which you are filing to ensure that you meet that court's requirements.

Remember that you must serve the record on opposing counsel in most appellate courts. And be aware of any need for sealing, as documents subject to sealing cannot be e-filed. Also, any sensitive information must be properly redacted before filing.[21]

An e-filed record must be bookmarked, and any required paper copies must be tabbed and indexed.[22]

16-4 Paper Filing

If you are filing documents under seal, or you are otherwise not subject to e-filing, the requirements for paper filing are the same as for paper copies with the following exceptions and additions:

- You do not have to use the file-stamped copy of your e-filed document because you did not e-file.
- A document produced on a typewriter (rather than a computer) must be printed in 10 character-per-inch (cpi) monospaced typeface.[23]
- The Supreme Court requires 11 paper copies of any document (except a motion, response, and reply) that is not electronically filed.[24] The courts of appeals require one unbound copy, unless provided otherwise by local rule.[25]
- Filing will be by hand delivery or mail.[26]
- Service will be by email, hand delivery, mail, commercial delivery, or fax.[27]
- Local rules may also apply. Call the clerk's office to ascertain any additional requirements, such as a flash drive containing the filed documents.

Notes

1 Tex. R. App. P. 9.2(c)(1).

2 Tex. R. App. P. 9.2(c)(3).

3 Tex. R. App. P. 9.2(c)(3).

4 Tex. R. App. P. 9.2(c)(2).

5 Times New Roman and New Century Schoolbook are good choices, and Georgia was specially designed for reading on a screen.

[6] Tex. R. App. P. 9.4(i)(2).

[7] Tex. R. App. P. 9.4(k).

[8] Tex. R. App. P. 9.1(c).

[9] Tex. R. App. P. 9.4(g).

[10] Tex. R. App. P. 9.1(a).

[11] Tex. R. App. P. 9.1(b).

[12] Tex. R. App. P. 9.4(i).

[13] Tex. R. App. P. 9.4(h).

[14] *See* Tex. R. App. P. 9.8.

[15] *See* Tex. R. App. P. 9.8.

[16] Nicholas Carr, The Shallows: What the Internet Is Doing to Our Brains 126–34 (2010).

[17] Tex. R. App. P. 9.3(a)(2).

[18] Tex. R. App. P. 9.4(b), (f).

[19] *See* Tex. R. App. P. 9.4(a).

[20] Order of Aug. 13, 2011, R. 10, Misc. Dkt. No. 11-9152, Supreme Court of Texas.

[21] *See* Tex. R. App. P. 9.9.

[22] Tex. R. App. P. 9.4(h).

[23] Tex. R. App. P. 9.4(e).

[24] Tex. R. App. P. 9.3(b)(1).

[25] Tex. R. App. P. 9.3(a)(1).

[26] Tex. R. App. P. 9.2(a), (b).

[27] Tex. R. App. P. 9.5.

CHAPTER 17

Appellate Ethics

17-1 Introduction

Like all lawyers, advocates practicing in Texas appellate courts are bound by the Texas Disciplinary Rules of Professional Conduct, and guided by the Texas Lawyer's Creed. So why are the ethical expectations of lawyers practicing in appellate courts addressed here as a separate topic? Because Texas appellate courts have developed a culture in which a higher degree of ethical conduct is expected, one characterized by greater civility, decorum, and candor than is typically seen in the trial courts.

This cultural difference between trial courts and appellate courts is not necessarily a reflection of the different personalities of those who choose those respective specialty areas. It is more a function of the different roles that counsel play in the different levels of the litigation process.

The outcome of a trial often depends on a jury making credibility determinations to resolve disputed facts. One of the best ways to persuade the jury that the other side's version of disputed facts is not credible is to attack the credibility of the person presenting those facts: opposing counsel. Persuading the jury that your position is more believable often involves questioning the character and credibility of the person advocating the opposite position.

However, on appeal credibility determinations already have been made in the trial court, and are given great deference. The primary emphasis becomes applying the law, given the facts found by the jury or trial judge. Appellate courts consider this process a more intellectual, scholarly exercise. They view the advocates' function as assisting the court in arriving at a just result in that case, as expressed in a written opinion that may affect outcomes in future cases. Attacking opposing counsel, or attempting to manipulate the court through inaccurate or incomplete representations about the appellate record or the applicable law, is not perceived as acceptable zealous advocacy. Rather, it is perceived as irrelevant or inappropriate at best, or unethical and counter-productive at worst. Attorneys who do not appreciate this fundamental characteristic of the appellate culture are doing a disservice to themselves and their clients.

17-2 The Standards for Appellate Conduct

As a reflection of the appellate bar's heightened sensitivity to ethics and professionalism, in 1999 the Texas Supreme Court and the Texas Court of Criminal Appeals jointly promulgated the Standards for Appellate Conduct (the Standards). The adoption of the Standards made Texas the first jurisdiction in the country to endorse ethical standards specifically applicable to appellate courts.

17-2:1 History

17-2:1.1 Genesis

In 1999, the Texas Supreme Court and Texas Court of Criminal Appeals jointly promulgated *The Texas Lawyer's Creed—A Mandate for Professionalism*. Largely a response to the rise of "Rambo litigation tactics" among trial lawyers in the 1980s, the Creed was specifically tailored to a trial court litigation practice.

At the same time, appellate CLE courses began featuring presentations on ethical issues unique to an appellate practice. The adoption of the Creed for trial lawyers and the treatment of similar issues in appellate CLE courses triggered discussions among appellate lawyers about whether it might be useful to have a similar body of guidelines aimed at an appellate practice.

In 1995, the State Bar of Texas Appellate Practice and Advocacy Section formed an "Appellate Lawyers' Creed Committee," charged with drafting standards for professional conduct in the appellate courts.[1]

17-2:1.2 Drafting

The Committee began by considering the sources and motivations for unprofessional conduct, the reasons that conduct seems to be less prevalent in the appellate courts, examples of unprofessionalism in appellate courts, and how best to address the problem. The primary theme that emerged from those discussions was that unprofessional conduct is often justified by lawyers as fulfilling a duty to zealously represent their clients. This view fails to recognize that lawyers have multiple duties, not only to their clients, but also to the court system and to opposing counsel. The essence of professionalism is the balancing of these conflicting duties. This concept is articulated in the preamble to the Standards, and is further underscored in the structure of the document, which is ordered around the separate duties owed by appellate counsel and the courts.

The Committee also studied approximately 40 standards for professionalism adopted in other jurisdictions, including states, counties, and the Seventh Circuit. In doing so, the Committee realized that all of these standards targeted litigation in the trial courts, and none specifically addressed appellate ethical issues.

The Committee eventually completed a final draft of what it called "Standards for Appellate Conduct." It submitted the draft to the Council of the Appellate Practice and Advocacy Section of the State Bar of Texas, and the Council approved the draft in August 1996.

17-2:1.3 Promulgation Process

The Standards were provided to, and comments solicited from, every judge in Texas, trial and appellate, state and federal, and all former appellate Chief Justices. They also were sent to representatives of every State Bar Section, to former members of the *Texas Lawyers Creed* Committee, the State Bar's General Counsel, and various local bar leaders.

Comments were received from around the State, mostly favorable, and minor changes were made. After this process, the State Bar Board of Directors, unanimously approved the Standards for Appellate Conduct, and the Standards were submitted to the Texas Supreme Court and the Texas Court of Criminal Appeals. Those courts then studied and discussed the Standards. On February 1, 1999, the Texas Supreme Court and Texas Court of Criminal Appeals issued an order jointly promulgating the Standards for Appellate Conduct for all Texas appellate courts.

17-2:1.4 Place in History

The Standards for Appellate Conduct are the first ethical guidelines in the United States specifically targeting practice in the appellate courts. As of this writing, no other jurisdiction has followed suit, though appellate lawyers from some jurisdictions have requested copies or the standards and appear to be considering something similar.

17-2:2 Philosophy of the Standards

17-2:2.1 Balancing Conflicting Duties

The drafters of the Standards recognized that unprofessional conduct often arises because of the tendency to overemphasize one duty to the exclusion of others. This principle is expressed in the preamble to the Standards:

> Problems that arise when duties conflict can be resolved through understanding the nature and extent of a lawyer's respective duties, avoiding the tendency to emphasize a particular duty at the expense of others, and detached common sense. To that end, the following standards of conduct for appellate lawyers are set forth by reference to the duties owed by every appellate practitioner.[2]

17-2:2.2 Suggestions for Civility, Not a Tool for Sanctions

The Committee felt strongly that the Standards *not* be used as a hammer to increase contentious bickering between appellate lawyers. Accordingly, it included a provision in the preamble prohibiting the offensive use of the standards. "Use of these standards for appellate conduct as a basis for motions for sanctions, civil liability or litigation would be contrary to their intended purpose and shall not be permitted."[3] Despite this clear admonition, some litigants have attempted, without success, to use the Standards as a tool for obtaining sanctions.[4]

17-2:2.3 Duty to Educate Clients About Standards

The drafters of the Standards wanted to avoid the possibility of appellate lawyers trying to justify unprofessional behavior by claiming to be acting under instructions from clients who are not aware of the Standards. So the section of the Standards entitled "Lawyers' Duties to Clients" contains numerous references to the duty of lawyers to inform their clients about the contents of the Standards.

The first standard in the section on Lawyers' Duties to Clients states this principle broadly: "Counsel will advise their clients of the contents of these Standards of Conduct when undertaking representation."[5] Lawyers are not directed to wait until a problem arises, but to advise their clients of the Standards "when undertaking representation." Prudent lawyers should include a copy of the Standards with their engagement letter or fee agreement.

Four other standards in this section begin with the words "Counsel will advise their clients . . ." or "Counsel will advise clients. . . ."[6] These standards address advising clients that civility and courtesy are expected, that reasonable requests by opposing counsel should be granted, that an appeal should only be taken upon a good faith belief that it is warranted, and that frivolous positions will not be taken.[7]

17-2:3 Structure and Summary of the Standards

The Standards for Appellate Conduct are structured according to the duties that lawyers owe to the participants in the appellate process.

The Standards begin with a *Preamble* that addresses the role that lawyers play in the appellate process, and acknowledges the different duties owed by lawyers, and the need to balance them. It acknowledges that these duties "are generally well-defined and understood by the appellate bar." It also cautions that the Standards are not intended to be grounds for sanctions or civil liability, and that they are not intended to alter existing ethical and professional guidelines like the Texas Disciplinary Rules of Professional Conduct or the Code of Judicial Conduct.

The section called *Lawyers' Duties to Clients* addresses the responsibility to keep clients informed about the Standards and their emphasis on civility, courtesy, cooperation, and accommodation. It also instructs lawyers to inform clients about the appellate process in general so they will have reasonable expectations about timing, costs, and possible outcomes. This section also contains several admonitions that the appellate process should be used only in good faith to pursue legitimate legal positions.

The next section is about *Lawyers' Duties to the Court*, and emphasizes proper decorum, civility, and respect. This section repeats the admonition against using the appellate process to assert frivolous positions or for the purpose of delay. It also encourages thorough preparation to assist the court, scrupulous honesty to avoid misleading the court, and punctuality so as to not inconvenience the court. It also emphasizes the duty to disclose relevant authority, even when it is adverse to the lawyer's position.[8]

The next section is *Lawyers' Duties to Lawyers*. It addresses the importance of treating opposing counsel—and parties—with respect. It encourages lawyers not to oppose reasonable requests for cooperation or scheduling accommodations, and to refrain from personal attacks or the attribution of bad motives, improper conduct, or other impropriety.

The final section addresses *The Court's Relationship With Counsel*. There was some resistance to including this section at all, because some judges questioned whether the Bar had authority to draft standards advising judges about their duties. In response to that, this section was not called "The Court's Duty to Counsel," which would have mirrored the other sections of the Standards, but instead is called "The Court's Relationship With Counsel."

This section encourages judges to show the same civility, respect, and courtesy to lawyers and other judges who are expected of lawyers. It also recognizes that the best way to encourage professional conduct among lawyers is for appellate judges to refrain from rewarding unprofessional conduct when it does occur, and to reward exemplary conduct. It encourages appellate judges to exercise integrity and professionalism in their treatment of the factual record, the applicable law, and the arguments of counsel. It even states that courts will "endeavor to avoid the injustice that can result from delay after submission of a case."[9]

17-3 Specific Suggestions for Ethical Appellate Practices

17-3:1 Refrain From Personal Attacks

Taking issue with arguments is appropriate and advisable. However, attacking the integrity, intelligence, sanity, or character of the person who made the argument is always a bad idea. Appeals are about legal issues, not personalities. The fact that our legal system is an "adversarial process" means that opposing litigants desire different ultimate outcomes. It does not mean that counsel must behave in an adversarial manner to each other. The opposing counsel is not your enemy; he or she is merely another professional trying to do their job of representing their client, and should be treated with respect and dignity.

STANDARDS FOR APPELLATE CONDUCT

Lawyers' Duties to Lawyers (No. 1). Counsel will treat each other and all parties with respect.

Lawyers' Duties to Lawyers (No. 5). Counsel will not make personal attacks on opposing counsel or parties.

17-3:2 Refrain From Accusing Opposing Counsel of Intentionally Misrepresenting the Record or the Law

Accusing opposing counsel of dishonesty is a serious charge that should never be made without unassailable proof. Making the charge in error can counter-productively tarnish the reputation of the accuser. An attorney is not lying when making an argument that is supported by the record, just because support can be found in the record for the contrary position. Making arguments based on conflicting evidence does not constitute lying. Similarly, conflicting interpretations of the same evidence is not lying. A typographical error may be a good faith mistake that should not be grounds for an accusation of a deliberate attempt to deceive.

Moreover, in order to justify the risk of accusing someone of lying, the perceived discrepancy should pertain to a matter that goes to the substance of an argument that the case may turn on. It should not be about a trivial matter that is unlikely to affect the outcome of the case, included simply to make opposing counsel look bad.

Finally, even if the evidence of dishonesty is beyond reproach and the subject matter is pivotal, most appellate courts still do not want to hear appellate counsel accuse each other of deliberately lying. The preferred approach is to dispassionately compare the statement by opposing counsel to the record or to a controlling authority, and trust appellate judges and their staff attorneys to draw their own conclusions on their own.

STANDARDS FOR APPELLATE CONDUCT

Lawyers' Duties to Lawyers (No. 6). Counsel will not attribute bad motives or improper conduct to other counsel without good cause, or make unfounded accusations of impropriety.

17-3:3 Refrain From Opposing Reasonable Requests for Extensions of Time or Word Counts

Requests for extension of time and word count are matters between the court and the party seeking a discretionary favor. Although the adversary of the party seeking a favor is not completely uninterested, there is little to be gained by turning these pleas for accommodation into a cat fight. Regardless of what clients may think, appeals are rarely decided by one party gaining a tactical advantage from an extension of time or page limits. If you believe that the granting of an extension will unfairly disadvantage your client, wait until an accommodation has been granted to the other side, and then request the same treatment for your client, and the court will always grant it.

Of course, this principle is limited by the word "reasonable." A first request for a 30-day extension should never be opposed. When opposing counsel moves for a fourth extension and seeks an additional 120 days, opposition may be warranted—although chances are that the court will take care of requests like that for you. A motion to extend the word count by 250 words should not be opposed. A request for an extension of 5,000 words may warrant opposition.

Moreover, parties that ask for an extension of the word count are often shooting themselves in the foot anyway, because appellate judges who are pressed for time and overwhelmed with lengthy filings do not want to read several thousand more words. If your adversaries want to hang themselves in that way, you should gladly give them plenty of rope.

STANDARDS FOR APPELLATE CONDUCT

Lawyers' Duties to Lawyers (No. 2). Counsel will not unreasonably withhold consent to a reasonable request for cooperation or scheduling accommodation by opposing counsel.

Lawyers' Duties to Clients (No. 10). Counsel will advise their clients that counsel reserves the right to grant accommodations to opposing counsel in matters that do not adversely affect the client's lawful objectives. A client has no right to instruct a lawyer to refuse reasonable requests made by other counsel.

17-3:4 Enter Into Reasonable Agreements

Most rules for repairing a broken appellate record provide two ways to supply the missing pieces: an easy way, based on the agreement of the parties, and a more difficult way necessitated by the failure of the parties to agree.[10] Parties who are victimized by deficiencies in the record can usually achieve what they want eventually, it is just a matter of whether that will be done the hard way or the easy way. Try to choose or facilitate the easy way. It will save time and money, and building some good will by being agreeable will not hurt either. You may need a favor yourself someday.

STANDARDS FOR APPELLATE CONDUCT

Lawyers' Duties to Clients (No. 10). Counsel will advise their clients that counsel reserves the right to grant accommodations to opposing counsel in matters that do not adversely affect the client's lawful objectives. A client has no right to instruct a lawyer to refuse reasonable requests made by other counsel.

17-3:5 Provide Specific and Accurate Citations to the Record and Legal Authorities

Any statement about the facts of the case must be supported by a citation to the record. It should be to a specific page that the court can find easily, and it must be accurate. Any statement about controlling law must be supported by a citation to case law, statute, or secondary authority, should include a pinpoint cite or jump cite to a specific page of a case or section of a statute, and, again, must be accurate. This is partly about helping the court to find the information and resources it needs quickly and easily, so it can properly and efficiently reach a decision, write an opinion, and resolve the case. It also is about making it easy for the court to verify the truth of the representations made by appellate lawyers in their briefing.

Both record citations and legal citations should be checked by a person who did not write the brief to make sure numbers did not get transposed or copied incorrectly, and that the person who did the research did not shade the meaning of the source as a natural manifestation of wishful thinking. If the court discovers citation errors, it does not know whether they were innocent and inadvertent or a deliberate attempt to mislead the court. Either way, having to spend time to find the source inaccurately cited slows down the process for everyone.

STANDARDS FOR APPELLATE CONDUCT

Lawyers' Duties to the Court (No. 3). Counsel should not misrepresent, mischaracterize, misquote, or miscite the factual record or legal authorities.

Lawyers' Duties to the Court (No. 4). Counsel will advise the Court of controlling legal authorities, including those adverse to their position, and should not cite authority that has been reversed, overruled, or restricted without informing the court of those limitations.

Lawyers' Duties to the Court (No. 7). Counsel will conduct themselves before the Court in a professional manner, respecting the . . . integrity of the judicial process.

Lawyers' Duties to the Court (No. 9). Counsel will . . . be prepared to assist the Court in understanding the record, controlling authority, and the effect of the Court's decision.

The Court's Relationship with Counsel (No. 2). The court will take special care not to reward departures from the record.

17-3:6 Avoid Weak Arguments

Never make an argument that you are fairly sure you cannot, or should not, win. You waste your time in making it, opposing counsel's time in responding to it, and the court's time in reading it, hearing it, and writing about it. Moreover, the credibility that you lose in making weak arguments can diminish the effectiveness of your strong arguments. It is better to make no argument at all than to make a weak argument. Or, as the old saying goes, "It is better to keep your mouth closed and be thought a fool than to open it and remove all doubt."

STANDARDS FOR APPELLATE CONDUCT

Lawyers' Duties to the Court (No. 1). An appellate remedy should not be pursued unless counsel believes in good faith that error has been committed, that there is a reasonable basis for the extension, modification, or reversal of existing law, or that an appeal is otherwise warranted.

Lawyers' Duties to the Court (No. 2). An appellate remedy should not be pursued primarily for purposes of delay or harassment.

17-3:7 Communicate Cordially With Opposing Counsel

Sad—but not uncommon—is the case in which appellate counsel meet each other for the first time at oral argument. Counsel should call each other as soon as they have been identified, introduce themselves if necessary, and try to establish an air of mutual cordiality. In most cases, appellate counsel should at least explore the possibility of settlement discussions if there is a possibility of saving the client time and money, and avoiding risk. Do not assume that opposing counsel will oppose everything that you want to do, or that you should oppose everything that they want to do. Try to agree to everything you can that will not jeopardize the interest of your client. These agreements are more likely to happen if appellate counsel are in regular communication with each other.

STANDARDS FOR APPELLATE CONDUCT

Lawyers' Duties to Clients (No. 9). Counsel will advise their clients of proper behavior, including that civility and courtesy are expected.

Lawyers' Duties to Clients (No. 10). Counsel will advise their clients that counsel reserves the right to grant accommodations to opposing counsel in matters that do not adversely affect the client's lawful objectives. A client has no right to instruct a lawyer to refuse reasonable requests made by other counsel.

Lawyers' Duties to Lawyers (No. 1). Counsel will treat each other and all parties with respect.

Lawyers' Duties to Lawyers (No. 2). Counsel will not unreasonably withhold consent to a reasonable request for cooperation or scheduling accommodation by opposing counsel.

17-4 Reasons to Comply With the Standards of Appellate Conduct

17-4:1 It's the Right Thing to Do

In this instance, the old saying that "Virtue is its own reward," has some truth. Treating other appellate lawyers in a more civilized and accommodating manner usually makes you feel better about yourself. It will certainly make them feel better about you when they have to deal with you in other cases, or when considering people for appellate referrals. It will undoubtedly make the appellate court personnel feel better if they perceive that they are engaged in the dignified task of resolving disputes and meting out justice rather than refereeing a cat fight. As the preamble to the Texas Lawyer's Creed states: "Professionalism requires more than merely avoiding the violation of laws and rules. I am committed to this Creed for no other reason than it is right."[11]

17-4:2 It Enhances the Client's Chance of Achieving a Favorable Result

Uniformly, appellate justices find the conduct cautioned against in the Standards to be offensive. Although those judges decide cases based on the law and the facts rather than on the personalities of the advocates, they are also human beings whose perception of the message cannot avoid being influenced by their feelings about the messenger. Credibility plays a role in decision-making, and human beings do not tend to place much credibility in those persons they consider to be offensive. Moreover, the judges may conclude, consciously or unconsciously, that persons who resort to unprofessional tactics are doing so in order to gain an unfair advantage because they lack the conviction in their substantive arguments to prevail if they play the game fairly.

In an opinion by the Fourteenth Court of Appeals, now Chief Justice Kem Thompson Frost eloquently expressed the court's frustration with unethical conduct and the adverse impact it can have on the client's case: "When counsel misrepresent the facts on which their legal arguments are based, they not only delay the entire process by unnecessarily adding to the court's workload, but also render a tremendous disservice to their clients. It is also a very poor strategy to misrepresent the record because any material misstatements and/or omissions will almost certainly be detected by opposing counsel, the appellate panel, and/or the court's alert and able staff."[12]

Thus, even if you are cynical enough to not be motivated to do the right thing simply because it is right, you should at least do the right thing because it is calculated to improve your client's chances of winning.[13]

17-4:3 Unconvincing Reasons to Disregard These Suggestions

Appellate advocates may choose to disregard the Standards for a variety of reasons. The most common explanations, and the reasons that they are unconvincing are as follows:

"My clients expect me to play hardball with their despised enemies."

Clients who are uneducated about the appellate process and the ethical standards of the profession may sincerely believe that their position is best served by an aggressive, combative, uncooperative posture in all aspects of the appeal. However, just as lawyers have a duty to educate their clients about the substantive law, they also have a duty to educate their clients about the way that the game is, or should be, played. The Standards recognize this problem of clients who want to vent their spleen through the conduct of their lawyer, and place the burden on the attorney to educate the client about the inappropriateness of these expectations.

The Standards approach this problem in two ways: (1) by specifying what an appellate attorney must advise their clients regarding professionalism and (2) by limiting what clients have a right to expect from their attorneys. Attorneys must "advise their clients of the contents of the Standards of Conduct when undertaking representation."[14] They must advise their clients "of proper behavior, including that civility and courtesy are expected,"[15] and that the attorney "reserves the right to grant accommodations to opposing counsel in matters that do not affect the client's lawful objectives."[16] The client has no right to "instruct a lawyer to refuse reasonable requests made by other counsel,"[17] or to "demand that counsel abuse anyone or engage in any offensive conduct."[18]

Thus, although the lawyer owes the client a duty to abide by the client's wishes, that duty does not override the concurrent duty to behave in a professional manner. If the client demands unprofessional conduct, and the attorney is unable to persuade the client otherwise, withdrawal may be the only alternative.[19]

"They did it first."

This justification for misconduct often is heard when fighting breaks out between children. It is considerably more disappointing to hear a similar argument from grown professionals. The lawyer's version of this whine usually goes something like, "I can be pretty easy to get along with as long as the other attorney plays fair with me, but if they mess with me I have the right to get them back."

This may be understandable as an initial emotional response to unprofessional conduct. However, the temptation to respond in kind should be resisted. Wait a couple of days to cool off before firing off an angry response. Go ahead and draft the venomous retort, but throw it away or edit it severely when cooler reason prevails. When one party to a dispute stoops to unprofessional conduct, but the other party adheres strictly to the high standards that should be expected of a professional, the contrast is vividly apparent to the appellate court, which will be more impressed by the attorney who takes the high road. When it comes to professionalism, "turn the other cheek" is a better rule than "an eye for an eye, and a tooth for a tooth."

17-5 Conclusion

Appellate courts really do expect a higher level of professionalism and ethical conduct than what is often seen in the trial courts. Any lawyer who comes into the appellate courts and behaves in a manner that is perceived as overly adversarial, non-cooperative, or less than completely candid is likely to be noticed and remembered, to the detriment of the current client and future clients. Ethical conduct in the appellate courts is not only a good idea, it is undeniably expected by the appellate courts. And frustrating that expectation increases the likelihood of unfavorable results.

Notes

[1] The Committee was chaired by Charles "Skip" Watson, and also included: the Hon. Gene Cook (former Texas Supreme Court Justice), the Hon. Ann McClure (Justice, El Paso Court of Appeals), Jesse Amos (Court of Appeals Staff Attorney), Stephen Tatum, David Gunn, David Hricik, Shane Sanders, and Kevin Dubose.

[2] Standards for Appellate Conduct, Preamble.

[3] Standards for Appellate Conduct, Preamble.

[4] *See In re A.M.B.V.*, No. 13–13–00081–CV, 2015 WL 127891, at *11 (Tex. App.—Corpus Christi-Edinburg January 8, 2015, no pet.) (mem. op.) (party sought sanctions for misrepresentation and omission of critical facts, based in part of Standards; sanctions denied because of possibility that errors were not made in bad faith).

[5] Standards for Appellate Conduct, Lawyers' Duties to Clients at 1.

[6] *See* Standards for Appellate Conduct, Lawyers' Duties to Clients at 9, 10, 12, 13.

[7] *See* Standards for Appellate Conduct, Lawyers' Duties to Clients at 9, 10, 12, 13.

[8] *See also Jones v. WKB Value Partners, L.P.*, No. 04-07-00865-CV, 2008 WL 2261192 at *2, n. 1 (Tex. App—San Antonio June 4, 2008, no pet.) (mem. op.) (citing Standards in support of duty to cite adverse authority).

[9] Standards of Appellate Conduct, The Court's Relationship With Counsel at 5.

[10] *See* Tex. R. App. P. 34.5(e) (regarding clerk's record, copies substituted if parties agree, court must resolve disputes and substitute copies if parties cannot agree); *but see* Tex. R. App. P. 34.6(f) (if a "significant exhibit" or a "significant portion of the court reporter's notes and records" is lost or destroyed, and the lost or destroyed portion of the reporter's record is "necessary to the appeal's resolution," if the parties cannot agree on substitution the appellant is entitled to a new trial).

[11] The Texas Lawyer's Creed–A Mandate for Professionalism, *reprinted in* TEXAS RULES OF COURT 723 (West 2017), *available at* http://www.txcourts.gov/media/276685/texas lawyerscreed.pdf.

[12] *Schlafly v. Schlafly*, 33 S.W.3d 863, 873 (Tex. App.—Houston [14th Dist.] 2000, pet. denied).

[13] *See* Kevin Dubose & Jonathan E. Smaby, *The Power of Professionalism: Civility as a Strategy for Effective Advocacy*, 79 Tex. Bar J. 432 (2016).

[14] Standards for Appellate Conduct, Lawyers' Duties to Clients at 1.

[15] Standards for Appellate Conduct, Lawyers' Duties to Clients at 9.

[16] Standards for Appellate Conduct, Lawyers' Duties to Clients at 10.

[17] Standards for Appellate Conduct, Lawyers' Duties to Clients at 10.

[18] Standards for Appellate Conduct, Lawyers' Duties to Clients at 11.

[19] *See* Texas Disciplinary Rule of Professional Conduct 1.02*2 cmt. 8.

CHAPTER 18

Building an Appellate Practice

18-1 Introduction: A Mindset for Business

Appellate lawyers tend to be an intellectual, introverted, self-selected group. Most of us would rather research the law or work on a brief than attend a client-development function. But the truth for most of us is that work will not come in the door simply because we write good—even great—briefs.

Building a self-sufficient appellate practice requires a marketing mindset. To develop that mindset, appellate lawyers should focus on ways to gain experience, build personal contacts, grow a reputation, and then find ways to connect with potential clients and appellate work. This chapter outlines some approaches to that process.

18-2 Gaining Experience

The first step in building an appellate practice is to gain appellate experience. Without experience, it is hard for attorneys to build a reputation or market their skills as an appellate lawyer.

The following are some ways in which successful Texas appellate lawyers have gained experience:

18-2:1 Working for a Court or Solicitor General's Office

One way to gain appellate experience early in a legal practice is to work for an appellate court. Most law clerks and briefing attorneys gain intensive practice with the primary tools of an appellate lawyer—reading, researching, and writing. They are exposed to good and bad appellate briefs and oral arguments by a range of advocates. So they see which approaches and types of arguments work and which do not.

More importantly, clerks and briefing attorneys learn how judicial decisions are made. They gain the experience of viewing a case from the audience's perspective. They read briefs and listen to arguments as someone involved in the decision between two positions, rather than as an advocate pursuing only one position. And they learn about court procedures and the decision-making process.

A clerkship is not necessary for an appellate practice. Many of Texas's most successful appellate attorneys never check for a court. But it does give a starting attorney valuable experience and a head start.

Working in the office of the Texas Solicitor General is another avenue for rapid experience of a different type. That position provides rapid experience as an *advocate*. Compared to most positions in private-sector firms, working for the solicitor general can give attorneys the opportunity to handle more appeals, and give more oral arguments. Historically, this has been one of the best positions for quickly meeting the experience requirements for Board Certification in Civil Appellate Law.

18-2:2 Expressing Interest and Asking for Appeals

For lawyers who seek to transition from a litigation practice to an appellate practice, a useful way to start is by expressing an interest in appellate work. Within a firm it often helps spread the word that you would like to work on appeals. In larger firms, the best way to get appellate work usually is to speak with an appellate or litigation partner about your interest in working on appeals. In midsized firms, or litigation boutiques, it often helps inform other litigators of your interest in handling appeals. Many litigators do not like the research or writing required to handle an appeal and will gladly seek your help when they have an appeal.

Even for small-firm or solo lawyers seeking to build an appellate practice, it helps talk with other lawyers about your interest. Discuss your interest in appellate work at local bar or other networking events. Express your interest on social-media sites. Or send a letter or email directly to small-firm litigators who may want to bring in help on an appeal.

18-2:3 Pro-Bono and "Almost" Pro-Bono Appeals

Pro-bono appeals are a great way to get experience as a lead appellate attorney for lawyers who have little prior experience. Paying clients are often reluctant to have their appeal handled by a lawyer who has never handled one. But indigent clients are often happy to have any lawyer take their case.

The State Bar of Texas Appellate Section and many local bar groups offer active pro-bono programs, often in conjunction with the court of appeals. Appeals typically are made available to volunteering attorneys through a listserv process. When bar organizations announce potential appeals by emails, usually with some information about the type of case, volunteering attorneys respond with their interest in handling it. Many of these pro-bono bar programs also offer the chance to work with an experienced appellate mentor while handling the appeal.

One body of underrepresented clients consists of small businesses or individuals who are not impoverished but cannot afford a high-priced appellate specialist. Less-experienced appellate lawyers often can gain work by offering discounted or low flat-fee rates to handle appeals. This approach is a useful way to get a broader range of substantive experience than is provided by most pro-bono appeals.

One way to find these types of potential clients is to express your interest to more experienced appellate lawyers who may refer potential clients who cannot afford their rates. Many potential clients are referred from one appellate lawyer to another until the potential client finds the right "fit." When referring lawyers know that your rates are lower than their rates, they often will be willing to send potential clients who cannot afford them.

18-2:4 Amicus Briefs

For more experienced appellate lawyers who are interested in developing a substantive subspecialty within appellate law or particular types of clients, one helpful vehicle is to write amicus-curiae briefs. Amicus briefs allow the lawyer to go beyond the perspective of parties in a particular case and address the shape of a particular substantive area of the law from the standpoint of a particular group or industry.

Writing amicus briefs help a lawyer develop a specialty in two respects. First, it allows the lawyer to deepen his or her substantive knowledge and experience of the law. Second, it allows the lawyer to develop a reputation as an advocate for a group or industry. This often opens opportunities to be hired on other appeals.

Although some lawyers occasionally write amicus briefs on behalf of themselves, the more common approach is to write the brief for an organization or industry group or for individual businesses. The best way to find amicus clients is often through legal organizations or industry groups such as the Texas Trial Lawyers Association, the Texas Association of Defense Counsel, or the U.S. Chamber of Commerce. Many of these groups have amicus committees who screen cases and then retain lawyers to represent the group.

Some amicus work is for a fee, but that sort of work is harder to find. A lawyer also may find long-term rewards by volunteering to write amicus briefs on behalf of particular groups. It is easier to find amicus work as a volunteer. And individuals in the group are likely to see the amicus volunteer as a "friend" advocating for their interests.

18-2:5 Studying the Law

Some appellate lawyers are known for their encyclopedic knowledge of the law. Most of those lawyers did not develop all of their knowledge simply by working on appeals for clients. Instead, they develop an extracurricular habit of studying the law.

One way to study the law is to make a daily or weekly habit of setting aside time to read new opinions or developments in the law. Some appellate lawyers read every new decision from the Texas Supreme Court, as well as their other local courts. Others focus on particular substantive areas of the law. For instance, the State Bar of Texas's Insurance Law Section circulates weekly emails with newly reported insurance decisions. If you do not have this much time, then try making a weekly habit of reading newsletters about recent cases from particular courts or subjects.

One great way to get into the habit of studying is to write a newsletter or a blog about decisions of a particular court or about a narrower subject-matter area. There are many opportunities to participate in writing newsletters for the State Bar, local bar associations, or substance-specific newsletters. Writing a newsletter typically requires the author to review many decisions and choose the most important decisions to highlight. Writing a newsletter makes it easier to understand trends and developments in the law.

18-3 Making Personal Connections

Many appellate lawyers hope to develop a practice, build a reputation, and find appellate clients simply by doing high-quality work. Unfortunately, doing high-quality work alone may not be sufficient. For most successful appellate lawyers, a key part of building a reputation and client base is making personal connections.

18-3:1 Build on Contacts in the Legal Community

Mentors. For starting appellate lawyers, the most important personal connection is often a mentor who teaches the sort of skills that are not taught in law school, such as how to interact with opposing counsel and court staff, how to keep clients informed and happy, and how to manage a practice.

Bar associations. To grow a reputation, it also is important to meet other lawyers. Not only may they become referral sources, but they can help you build a reputation. This is especially important because good clients often check an attorney's reputation with other attorneys. A lawyer who is well known in the bar usually has an advantage.

Bar associations are often the best way to meet other lawyers. Simply attending meetings or luncheons is a good way to meet other lawyers. Participating in bar work is even better.

Bar associations also create a good environment to meet and socialize with judges. For instance, bar luncheons or bench/bar conferences often act as a forum where judges can discuss advocacy skills that work and skills that do not. They also allow lawyers to develop a professional relationship with courts.

Opposing counsel. Many lawyers overlook the importance of developing a positive relationship with opposing counsel. Opposing lawyers who witness your advocacy and respect your professionalism can be a great source of business. It adds even more credibility to a referral when the referring lawyer says that you were a tough and professional opponent.

Online networking. A few appellate lawyers have helped develop a reputation as an appellate lawyer through online networking. Tom Goldstein, for instance, became well known as a United States Supreme Court advocate through his blog about the Court.

For most of us, though, online networking rarely brings in clients or builds a reputation standing alone. But when done effectively it can help. When a lawyer recommends colleagues on LinkedIn or makes positive, intelligent, and professional comments on Facebook, it can help keep them on the mind of potential clients or referral sources.

One-on-one meals and social events. There is no better way to make a personal connection with potential referral sources or clients than one-on-one breakfasts, coffee breaks, lunches, drinks, or dinner. Eating and drinking together is the most common form of social interaction. This is often the best way to cement a lasting professional relationship. Some of the best generators of appellate business never lose an opportunity to share a meal with others in the community.

18-4 Building a Good Reputation

There are two key components to building a reputation: (1) making your name known, and (2) making sure that reputation is good. For appellate lawyers, a good reputation is invaluable. It helps bring in business from referrals. It brings respect from opposing counsel and judges. And it helps a lawyer's sense of well-being to be thought of highly in the community.

Doing good work is the first step in building a good reputation. But many lawyers do good work without ever being widely known. Today, building a good reputation requires more.

18-4:1 CLE Speaking and Writing

There are many benefits to writing a paper and giving a presentation at a continuing-legal-education course. It helps build substantive knowledge; writing a continuing legal education paper often requires dozens, if not hundreds, of hours of researching and understanding a particular topic. It helps a lawyer build presentation skills. And when the paper appears online or even on your firm's website, it is an easy way to get "published" so that the author's name and expertise become more widely known.

The biggest benefit of CLE writing and speaking is to build the lawyer's reputation. Many of the most successful appellate lawyers in Texas can point the origin of their success to one CLE speech that made them known as one of the leading "experts" in the state on a particular subject. Some well-known Texas appellate practitioners cemented their reputations by giving a ground-breaking topic on such subjects as motions for summary judgment, supersedeas bonds, and petitions for review in the Texas Supreme Court.

The keys to a good CLE presentation are thorough knowledge and research, a new approach to the subject, and a well-organized, engaging presentation. The best CLE presentations not only give the audience an overview of an aspect of the law—they offer a new paradigm for seeing that aspect of the law.

To make effective use of a CLE presentation, the author should do more than simply present at a conference. The author should let potentially interested colleagues and clients know about the upcoming speech. The author may want to post the paper on the firm's website. And the author may want to mention the paper in bios and resumes. The ethical rules, for instance, may not allow a lawyer to advertise that he or she is an expert in appeals of arbitration awards. But the rules do allow a lawyer to post online her CLE paper about arbitration appeals.

18-4:2 Bar Service and Leadership

To get the full benefit of bar activities, it is often helpful to work on bar projects and seek to become a bar leader. Often our best relationships come from working with colleagues. Bar activities and service projects not only can help the community, but they help expand the range of lawyers with whom we work. They help us meet others and develop relationships.

Bar leadership is a useful way to build a reputation. For instance, when a lawyer advertises himself or herself as an appellate lawyer, he has even more credibility when he has been president of the appellate-law section of a local, state, or even national appellate law organization. Election to leadership of a substantive bar group, such as civil appellate law, is a sign that an attorney has been accepted by his or her peers as a leader in that field.

18-4:3 Board Certification

One useful tool to demonstrate appellate competency and experience is to be certified in Civil Appellate Law by the Texas Board of Legal Specialization. The numerous certification requirements for appellate law include handling a substantial part of 12 civil appeals, appearing as lead counsel in six appeals, presenting an oral argument in four appeals, obtaining references, and passing a rigorous exam.

Although board certification is a difficult process, there more than 500 Texas attorneys certified in civil appellate law. Becoming certified does not guarantee a client base. But for potential clients looking for an experienced appellate lawyer, board certification can be one additional indication of expertise.

18-4:4 Marketing and Advertising

Some lawyers have found many clients through billboards or television ads. But we are aware of no lawyers who have used advertisements alone to build a successful appellate practice.

That does not suggest that appellate lawyers should forego advertisements or marketing. Marketing alone does not build an appellate reputation. But it does expose a lawyer's name to a broader audience. For instance, an in-house counsel who has never heard of a firm may be unlikely to hire it. But if the same in-house counsel has seen a firm's name in the Dallas Business Journal, then the firm is likely to have valuable name recognition when someone recommends the firm's appellate expertise.

Marketing efforts such as email campaigns, print ads, holiday cards, and firm parties are a useful way to remind your base of potential referrals and clients of your name. When someone asks them to recommend three appellate lawyers, you want them to have your name on the tip of their tongue.

18-4:5 Popularity Contests—the "Best Lawyer" Lists

The past decade has seen an explosion of "best lawyer" lists. National, statewide, and local publications have published lists of the allegedly "best" lawyers, voted on by their peers. In turn, the publications sell advertising opportunities to the lawyers who are elected to these lists.

Being listed on these lists can be a helpful marketing tool. Some potential clients look at the lists. Others may note on a lawyer's website that she has been listed on these lists. It is a sign of recognition in the legal community. And it can be a useful part of a broader effort to build a reputation as a leader in the field.

These lists are unlikely to distinguish you from competitors, many of whom appear on the same list. But they do indicate that you are playing in the same league as others included on the list.

18-5 Finding Clients

For many appellate lawyers, it is difficult to identify their marketing target, in other words their sources of business. Insurance lawyers often target their marketing at insurance companies. Banking lawyers target banks. But for appellate lawyers, who often do not specialize in a substantive subset of appellate law, the referral sources for potential clients are more difficult to identify. These are several sources to consider.

18-5:1 Sources for Potential Clients

Your own firm. A number of appellate lawyers get most of their business from other lawyers in their firm. Large firms and litigation boutiques generate a number of appeals. And many of those firms hire an appellate lawyer or group to handle or at least assist in those appeals. To be successful at developing this sort of work, it is important to be a team player. Successful appellate lawyers in firms are often "on call" 24 hours a day to handle emergencies in trial, or for firm clients who need to seek rapid appellate relief. They become the "go to" lawyer for the firm when appeal-related issues arise.

Trial lawyers. The past few decades have seen a proliferation of litigation boutiques. Small- or midsized litigation firms often seek help outside the firm on appeals, particularly when an important verdict demands the help of an appellate specialist. For many appellate lawyers, the best source of business and potential referrals are trial lawyers in firms that do not have appellate lawyers.

Other appellate lawyers. A primary source of work for appellate lawyers is other appellate lawyers. A lawyer who receives a call from a potential client often will refer that client to other lawyers when the lawyer is too busy, has a conflict, is outside the potential client's fee range, or has too little experience or interest in the subject matter of an appeal.

In-house counsel. Most appellate clients are not repeat clients. The most likely repeat clients are corporations, particularly larger corporations with a greater volume of litigation. For this reason, in-house counsel can be a good source of repeat business. Participation with in-house bar groups and organizations also is a useful way to be introduced to in-house counsel.

The community. Sometimes it is hard to predict the source of appellate work. If an appellate lawyer is well known in the community, business can come from unexpected sources. Lawyers may be referred from their friends from former students or classmates, civil organizations, churches and synagogues, clubs, and non-profit boards. Wider participation in the community is not only good for growing business, but also for giving lawyers a broader perspective, beyond the halls of the law firm.

18-6 Generating Appellate Work Before the Appeal

Lawyers developing an appellate practice should not limit themselves to handling the appeal. For most successful appellate lawyers, appellate work on a big case begins before trial when a legal strategy is planned. It continues through trial when legal arguments are made to the trial judge, and arguments are preserved for appeal. It is often helpful to clients for appellate lawyers to be a key part of this process. And for lawyers developing an appellate practice, seeking this pre-appeal legal work is a useful way to expand work opportunities and gain experience.

18-6:1 Strategy and Planning in Complex Litigation

An appellate lawyer can play an important role in managing and planning complex litigation. To succeed in complex litigation, it is important to define the goals and strategy early. Often a key part of the strategy is shaping the legal framework of the dispute and planning for the endgame, which often is the appeal.

Early participation by appellate lawyers can help lower litigation costs, and maximize chances of success, in a number of respects:

- *Evaluation of choice-of-law, forum, jurisdiction, and party issues.* Often the key legal decisions on which an ultimate appeal will depend are made at the outset of litigation. These decisions include the choice of law, identifying a proper and advantageous forum, resolving jurisdictional issues, and making sure that the correct parties are joined. An appellate lawyer's law perspective can save clients from expensive mistakes early in litigation.

- *Early formulation of jury charge to narrow discovery.* Often appellate lawyers are in the best position to predict the ultimate jury charge that will be given at trial. By developing a draft charge early, the appellate lawyer can help the trial team focus the issues that should be discovered and tried.
- *Summary-judgment practice.* Because of their focus and experience with "as a matter of law" and "no evidence" arguments, appellate lawyers are uniquely experienced to help with the legal argument to support or respond to a motion for summary judgment. The appellate lawyer can help resolve the case early or avoid summary disposition before trial.

18-6:2 Trial Court Advocacy From the Appellate Perspective

There are some instances when the most effective advocate in the trial court is the appellate lawyer. Trial judges often appreciate the law perspective of an appellate lawyer in making summary-judgment or directed-verdict arguments, arguing the jury charge, or assisting with legal decisions that are likely to be reviewed on appeal.

Appellate lawyers bring a number of unique benefits to trial advocacy. First, they help bring an appellate perspective—focused not on just quotes from cases, but on helping the judge understand the broader perspective of the law or the development of an issue. Second, they often appear as less adversarial, and more objective, than trial lawyers whose job often requires them to focus more on attacking the other sides' credibility rather than presenting an objective view of the law. Finally, appellate lawyers focus most of their time on the type of advocacy skills that are needed to help judges make legal determinations—skills such as research and legal writing and analysis.

18-6:3 Preserving Arguments for Appeal

Appellate lawyers are also uniquely qualified to know what is required to preserve an argument for appeal. Because many appellate arguments fail because they were not properly preserved, appellate lawyers are trained to make this determination.

More frequently, litigation teams are bringing appellate lawyers to trial. They help devise legal strategies for preserving evidentiary issues for appeal, preserving legal arguments through directed verdicts and post-trial motions, and navigating the difficult preservation traps in preserving appellate arguments about the jury charge.

If you are seeking more appellate work, getting involved with a case before and at trial is a good way to secure work on the appeal of the case. Your familiarity with the case and the arguments give you an advantage over other potential appellate counsel.

Table of Cases

Table of Other Authorities

TEXAS AGRICULTURE CODE

58.036	6-2:1.2

TEXAS ALCOHOLIC BEVERAGE CODE

11.67(a)	8-1:5
11.67(b)(4)	8-1:5

TEXAS BUSINESS ORGANIZATIONS CODE

2.106(b)	5-2

TEXAS CIVIL APPELLATE PROCEDURE

44:10	2-4:2

TEXAS CIVIL PRACTICE AND REMEDIES CODE

6.001	8-3:5.1, 13-5:2.2
10.005	2-3:2.6
15.003(b)	5-2
15.003(c)(1)	2-2:2.4, 5-2
15.003(c)(2)	5-2
15.064(b)	3-3:3
15.0642	6-2:1.1, 6-2:1.2, 6-5:2
26.051(b)	5-2
27.003	5-2
27.003-.011	2-5:2
27.005(c)	2-5:2
27.008	5-2
30:20	8-4
31.002(b)(1)	8-1:7
33.004(a)	6-5:3
33.004(d)	6-5:3
34.022	8-6, 13-5:1
37.009	2-3:4.1
41.003(a)	2-4:3.1
41.003(a)(3)	2-4:3.2
41.003(b)	2-4:3.1
41.003(c)	2-4:3.1
41.003(d)	2-4:3.1
51.012	8-1:3
51.014	5-1, 5-3:1.1, 8-1:4.2
51.014(a)	5-2, 5-7:1
51.014(a)(1)	5-2
51.014(a)(2)	5-2
51.014(a)(3)	5-2, 5-5:2.1
51.014(a)(4)	5-2, 6-5:3
51.014(a)(5)	5-2, 5-5:2.1

TEXAS CODE OF CRIMINAL PROCEDURE

TEXAS CONSTITUTION

TEXAS ELECTION CODE

TEXAS FAMILY CODE

TEXAS GOVERNMENT CODE

TEXAS HEALTH AND SAFETY CODE

TEXAS RULES OF CIVIL PROCEDURE

TEXAS RULES OF EVIDENCE

TEXAS RULES OF JUDICIAL ADMINISTRATION

Index

Section numbers in bold font indicate sections with charts, illustrations, or tables.

A

B

E

K

L

N

O

P

R

S

U

V

W